LISTENING

LISTENING
FIFTH EDITION

ANDREW WOLVIN

University of Maryland—College Park & University College

CAROLYN GWYNN COAKLEY

Santa Rosa Junior College

Brown & Benchmark
PUBLISHERS

Madison   Dubuque, IA   Guilford, CT   Chicago   Toronto   London
Caracas   Mexico City   Buenos Aires   Madrid   Bogota   Sydney

Book Team

Executive Publisher *Edgar J. Laube*
Acquisitions Editor *Eric Ziegler*
Publishing Services Coordinator *Peggy Selle*
Proofreading Coordinator *Carrie Barker*
Production Manager *Beth Kundert*
Production/Costing Manager *Sherry Padden*
Visuals/Design Freelance Specialist *Mary L. Christianson*
Marketing Manager *Katie Rose*
Copywriter *M. J. Kelly*

Basal Text *10/12 Palatino*
Display Type *Helvetica Bold*
Typesetting System *Mac/QuarkXPress*
Paper Stock *50# Solutions*
Production Services *Shepherd, Inc.*

President and Chief Executive Officer *Thomas E. Doran*
Vice President of Production and Business Development *Vickie Putman*
Vice President of Sales and Marketing *Bob McLaughlin*
Director of Marketing *John Finn*

A Times Mirror Company

The credits section for this book begins on page 425 and is
considered an extension of the copyright page.

Cover design and illustration by Cunningham & Welch Design Group, Inc.,
Madison, WI

Copyedited by Shepherd, Inc.; Proofread by Kate McKay

Library of Congress Catalog Card Number: 95–75267

ISBN 0–697–24664–7

Printed in the United States of America by Times Mirror Higher Education Group, Inc.,
2460 Kerper Boulevard, Dubuque, IA 52001

10 9 8 7 6 5 4 3 2 1

CONTENTS

PART II   DEVELOPING PURPOSEFUL LISTENING SKILLS   151

---

5   Discriminative Listening   157

6   Comprehensive Listening   211

7 Therapeutic Listening 263

8 Critical Listening 309

PREFACE

The study of listening can offer you tremendous insight into what is one of the most complex of all human behaviors and one of the most enriching and rewarding of all human interactions. Indeed, improved listening can enable you to

- comprehend information more clearly and accurately
- understand verbal and nonverbal messages more precisely
- reduce misunderstandings
- make fewer mistakes
- improve your academic performance
- think more critically
- respond more meaningfully to yourself and to others
- improve the quality of your relationships with others

Listening is designed to offer you insight into improved listening. From the field of listening behavior as well as from a variety of disciplines including speech communication, reading, audiology, neurology, psychology, education, and sociology, we draw theory and research concerning the process of listening as the basis for knowing about listening behavior. We then apply that knowledge to the development of listening skills.

Organization of the Book

Part I (chapters 1 to 4) helps you understand the importance of effective listening and the complexities of listening as a communication behavior. Part II (chapters 5 to 9) focuses on the development of effective listening skills at the levels of the Wolvin-Coakley taxonomy of discriminative, comprehensive, therapeutic, critical, and appreciative listening. Part III (chapter 10) details a perspective of framing the understandings and skills of listening in the communication context—intrapersonal, interpersonal, public, and mass communication.

In each chapter of the text, we recognize that listening is a communication function that involves decision-making throughout the entire process. We hope that listeners will be convinced that they must assume equal participation in and equal responsibility for effective communication transactions.

Likewise, in each chapter we illustrate that good listening is critical to personal, academic, and professional success. Indeed, the importance of the study of listening has been with us throughout history. The ancient scholar, Plutarch, stressed that "right listening is the beginning of right living."[1] Plutarch's conclusion has a contemporary resonance. As we write this fifth edition of *Listening*, the winter season of 1994 has brought to the American landscape profound changes—economical, political, and social changes that more than ever demonstrate the need to develop a listening society.

To facilitate your understanding of listening, we offer at the beginning of each chapter *Principles You Will Encounter* to enable you to focus the material in your reading. At the end of each chapter, we offer you additional activities so that you can apply the principles of effective listening and develop solid skills as a listener. Many of these activities can be used by both individual readers and by groups in classroom settings.

New to the Fifth Edition

This fifth edition of our book builds on the strengths of the first four editions. We provide you with updates on the information and concepts offered in each of our chapters. Indeed, we are proud to note how much the study of listening has become a central part of the communication discipline, thanks to the excellent research conducted by researchers in the listening field. The advances made in understanding listening behavior serve as an integral part of the content of our chapters. Moreover, in addition to a new formatting design and a variety of chapter introductions, this fifth edition offers

- A new section on listening role models and an additional listening misconception in a restructured chapter 1
- New thoughts on the communication process in chapter 2
- A revised Wolvin-Coakley listening definition that includes visual stimuli and a condensed view of listening definitions and the listening process in chapter 3
- Additional information and variables—attitudes and listener preferences—in chapter 4
- A treatment of accents as a discriminative influence in chapter 5
- Additional material on questioning and paraphrasing in chapter 6
- New material on the need for therapeutic listening in chapter 7
- Additional material on the interaction of critical thinking and critical listening and additional examples of persuasive appeals in chapter 8

- New insights on appreciative listening in chapter 9
- A revised discussion of listening to mass media in chapter 10

The Instructor's Resource Manual

The *Instructor's Resource Manual* that accompanies this text is available free to adopters of this book. The manual includes syllabi, objectives, test questions, many additional activities designed for classroom use, as well as descriptions of recommended films, published listening tests, and the International Listening Association.

We Want to Listen to You

We are encouraged by the interest in listening behavior that we encounter both in academic institutions and the corporate world. The dedication to improved listening is a commitment that can lead to improved communication in all aspects of our personal, academic, and professional lives, for through listening, we can grow as individuals, as relationship partners, and as world citizens. As researchers and writers, we are pleased to have the opportunity to contribute to the improvement of listening in your communication life. And, we want to listen to your ideas. Please let us know: How has listening made a difference in *your* communication life?

Andrew D. Wolvin
Carolyn Gwynn Coakley
Department of Speech Communication
University of Maryland
College Park, Maryland 20742

Notes

1. Plutarch, *Plutarch's Moralia*, trans. Frank Cole Babbitt (Cambridge, MA: Harvard University Press, 1987), p. 259.

ACKNOWLEDGMENTS

Preparing a book like this requires the assistance and support of many people. We are especially grateful to Darlyn Wolvin and Tom Hickerson for their patience, understanding, and empathic listening throughout the process. We likewise are indebted to our listening students at the University of Maryland at College Park and University College and at Santa Rosa Junior College. Their ideas, interests, and responses have helped to shape our thoughts about listening and have given us the framework for these ideas. We also appreciate the support and encouragement we have received from our colleagues in the International Listening Association. Interaction in this professional association provides us with a stimulating forum of listening scholars, teachers, and practitioners.

We are grateful to all of you who have used this book throughout the world for the substantial amount of constructive feedback that you have given to us. We appreciate knowing the strengths of this book, and we have adapted those areas of the book that our readers believed should be changed. We hope that you will continue to provide us with feedback, an essential component of true communication, whether oral or written.

Additionally, we are grateful to our photographers, Bob Tocha, Tom Noonan and the Sonoma *Index-Tribune*, and Glen Moll, and our illustrators, Ted Metzger and Neal Ashby. All willingly shared with us their time and creativity.

No book can be produced without the unfailing editorial support we have received from Brown & Benchmark Publishers. Our developmental editor, Mary Rossa, our project editor, Erika Mitchell, our production coordinator at Shepherd, Inc., Pat Eichhorst, and our reviewers have played a major role in putting this book in final form. The reviewers were Melissa Beall, University of Northern Iowa; Dan Curtis, Central Missouri State University; Gregory Lampe, University of Wisconsin/Rock; Leonard Leary, Eastern New Mexico University; Roseanna Ross, St. Cloud State University; and Kent Zimmerman, Sinclair Community College.

Finally, we want to thank you, our readers, for your interest in listening and for your dedication to improving your own listening skills. We believe that effective listening should be a major communication objective for everyone, and we are pleased that you share that objective with us.

Andrew D. Wolvin
Carolyn Gwynn Coakley

PART I

Understanding the Listening Process

On 28 January 1986, the world watched in horror as television screens recorded the explosion of NASA's *Challenger* space shuttle. The subsequent investigation of the loss of the shuttle and its eight-member crew revealed that the pressure to launch had interfered with the willingness and ability of launch officials to listen to engineers concerned about the safety of the spacecraft. The investigation of this tragedy led the presidential team to recommend that NASA develop plans and policies for improved communications at all levels of the organization.[1]

The NASA tragedy dramatically illustrates the vital importance of the complex human communication process of listening. We believe that it is important for the student of listening to develop a thorough understanding of both the crucial role that listening plays in personal and professional lives and the complexities of the listening process—a process that is an integral part of the human communication system of interactions. This understanding, combined with positive attitudes toward listening's rewards and a strong desire for listening improvement, is essential before the listener embarks on a plan to develop skills and improve individual listening behaviors.

It should be recognized that much of our understanding of human communication has been shaped by a source perspective. The study of communication has centered on a study of effective messages and behaviors of the communication source—with very little research or specific understanding about the role of the listener/receiver in this complex process. Since the listener/receiver shares at least 51 percent of the responsibility for the communication, we feel strongly that understanding communication from the listener's perspective is an important step toward improving human communication throughout the world.

The first part of this book, then, provides the listener with an understanding of how important effective listening is and what effective listening is. Having developed a sensitivity to the important role that listening plays in personal and professional lives, the student of listening is then introduced to the listening process itself. Understanding the intricacies involved in the complex human behavior of listening is the foundation for the eventual development of more effective listening skills and behaviors. Therefore, it is helpful to analyze the listening process in detail to determine what the essential components of listening are and what variables influence this process as we function in communication situations. Thus, the first four chapters of the book address listening as communication.

Notes

1. National Aeronautics and Space Administration, *Report to the President: Actions to Implement the Recommendations of the Presidential Commission on the Space Shuttle Challenger Accident*, mimeographed (Washington, D.C.: NASA, 14 July 1986), p. 3.

PRINCIPLES YOU WILL ENCOUNTER

- *Meaningful oral communication is the result of both the sending and the receiving of messages.*

- *The failure to listen effectively is prevalent in American society.*

- *There are not enough personal and professional listening role models.*

- *Costly communication barriers are often the result of ineffective listening.*

- *Listening is the most basic language skill.*

- *Listening consumes most of our daily communication time.*

- *Advancements in technology and the mass media have greatly increased the significance of listening in individuals' daily lives and, thus, in personal development.*

- *Among the rewards of effective listening are increased sales; customer and employee satisfaction, productivity, and enjoyment; expanded information base; improved social ties and family relations; heightened self-esteem; and enriched lives.*

- *Misconceptions about listening are embedded in the thinking of many individuals.*

- *Instructional emphasis on the development of effective listening remains inadequate in America's schools.*

- *Recognizing the essential role listening plays in organizational success, an increasing number of corporations are providing needed listening training for their employees.*

- *The effective listener*
  - *knows the need for personal and professional listening role models, the costliness of ineffective listening, the importance of effective listening, the rewards of effective listening, and the fallacy of common listening misconceptions*
  - *has the desire to become an even more effective listener and engage in effective listening behavior*

CHAPTER 1

The Need for Effective Listening

A father is reading a newspaper when his son enters the room and says, "Hey, Pop? Can I talk to you?"
The father, never looking up from the paper, says, "Sure, what is it?"
First, the son discusses school; he says, "I'm gonna be short some credits for graduation, and I'm going to need to go to summer school."
Dad, who is obviously not listening, responds by saying, "That's good."
The son then makes a second attempt to gain his father's attention. He says, "You know, I think I'll drop out of school, Pop. I'm not going anywhere."
Dad, still reading his paper, mutters, "Well, whattaya know?"
Finally, the son says, "Say, I took my first trip today. That acid. Man. . . ."
Dad replies, "Okay. Whatever you think's best."
The son leaves, and the mother enters the room. She asks what the son had said.
Dad replies, "Oh, it wasn't important."[1]

Wasn't important? Oh, but it was to the son who needed his father to listen to him.

"Is anyone *really* listening?" is a question that too many of us ask when we are interacting with our family members, friends, instructors, classmates, bosses, co-workers, and numerous other individuals we encounter daily. Unfortunately, many people fail to realize that *meaningful* oral communication is a result of *both* the sending *and* the receiving of messages. If only our ears were as actively involved as our mouths, our failure to listen would not be of such vital concern to so many individuals.

Listening—truly listening—involves more than just hearing.

In Search of Listening Role Models

Many listening scholars believe that our failure to listen too often stems from a lack of "model" listening behavior from those whom we tend to imitate. Please join us in our search for model listeners in both our personal and professional lives.

Personal Role Models

In our personal lives, there are numerous individuals we might examine. However, we will limit our search to three of the most influential—parents, partners, and friends.

Observing our **parents**, we ask: Do they listen effectively to one another? To other family members? To us as infants . . . young children . . . teenagers . . . adults? Komaiko reminds us that children receive significant listening messages from their parents:

> A child first learns to listen by imitating others. He watches his parents, and if they listen to one another with interest and respect, he comes to sense the rightness of having a give-and-take relationship with people. Even more important to the kind of listener he will become is how his parents listen to him. If at home he finds only talkers, but no listeners, he may pack up his troubles and lug them elsewhere—or worse, seal them inside of himself.[2]

Landfried suggests that listening parents nurture listening children:

> Children imitate what they see. They will share things with people they think will hear them out and respect their opinion. Parents who embrace a

parents

"listener" role not only provide good role models for their children—they make it much more likely their children will respect them as persons worthy of being listened to. . . . Children learn how to listen—and not listen—from their parents. What they see is what we usually get. Indeed, parents who want their children to be good listeners must demonstrate a willingness to listen to their kids often.[3]

One child, finding unwilling listeners at home, left this note to his parents before he packed up his problems and ran away: "If anyone asks you where I am, tell them I've gone looking for someone with time because I've got a lot of things I want to talk about."[4]

All children need parental listening models who will give them the precious commodity of time. But how much time do parents and children spend communicating with each other? Goff-Timmer, Eccles, and O'Brien at the University of Michigan Institute for Social Research investigated the amount of quality time in which parents and children (aged 3–17) in 500 families engage. Defining *quality time* as "the time parents spend interacting with their kids—in discussion, teaching, reading with them or joint activity," the researchers obtained the following results:

	Weekday	**Weekend Day**
Working mothers	11 minutes	30 minutes
Homemaking mothers	30 minutes	36 minutes
Fathers	8 minutes	14 minutes[5]

Perhaps more revealing is another finding that the average family with teenagers spends only about fourteen minutes a day engaging in parent-child communication—with twelve of these minutes devoted to the discussion of such topics as "What's for dinner?" "Where's the *TV Guide*?" and "Who's using the car tonight?" We quickly realize that the remaining two minutes (or "quality time") spent in communicating openly and forming relationships are hardly adequate.[6]

The listening family includes our **partners** as well as our children. **partners**
Studying fifty-seven married couples, Holman and Burr substantiate that communication—covering the ability to talk out problems without defensiveness or emotional outbursts and the willingness to listen to another point of view—is the most important factor in marriage.[7] Conversely, Winokur found the opposite is likewise true: The inability or unwillingness to listen is a major detriment to relationships.[8]

It is likely that not all of us perceive our partners to be listening role models. Some of us females would join the 77 percent of Shere Hite's 4,500 female respondents who, when asked, "What does your partner do that makes you the maddest?" replied, "He doesn't listen."[9] And, some of us males might argue that our not saying "uh huh," "mm-hmmm," or "I see," which females perceive to be active signs of listening, doesn't mean we are not listening; it just means we have learned that these sounds are signs of agreement rather than listening.[10] Indeed, there is much potential for each gender to be a listening role model for the other, but to realize this potential, each must understand how the other listens—and each must combine the other's listening perspective with his/her own. But how many of us have this knowledge and skill? (See chapter 4 for additional information on gender and listening.)

friends

We will end our personal search with our **friends**. During our teenage years, the majority of us place our friends first on our list of preferred listeners. Although our adolescent peers may not possess role model listening behaviors, they are prized largely because they accept us as we are; they nurture our self-esteem at a time when we are defining who we are. Why we—as adults—continue to rank our friends at or near the top of our list of chosen listeners is a question for us to contemplate and for researchers to answer. We might hypothesize, though, that we hold them dear because we have a true listening relationship with them.

Professional Role Models

In our professional lives, there are *countless* individuals with whom we communicate . . . and in whom we seek listening role models. A few of these listening individuals are teachers, government officials, police officers, healthcare providers, business personnel, and airline pilots.

teachers

Teachers are in the position to be our first professional role models of effective listening. The importance of teachers presenting themselves as models of desirable listening attitudes, behaviors, and skills is, indeed, emphasized in John Stammer's four-step MAPP (representing Model, Assess, Prepare, and Practice) listening plan in which he places modeling as the first step that teachers should take in order to help students improve their listening effectiveness.[11]

Likewise, Radford University President Donald Dedmon recognizes the importance of teachers as model listeners. He states, "The heart of the teaching transaction is skilled oral communications. Teachers must consistently practice them and encourage the practice of them by their students. The good teacher is both a good speaker and listener. The latter may, indeed, be more important than the former."[12]

Unfortunately, not all teachers are listening models for their students to emulate. In his popular book, *Love*, Leo Buscaglia presents this poignant example of a teacher who misses an opportunity to foster effective listening habits among her students:

> I used to love the idea of "share and tell" in the classroom. I thought this was a time when people would listen. But, you see, someone told the teachers that they had to have their enrollment slips in by 9:05 so they used this time for share and tell. Little kids went up and said, "Last night my daddy hit my mommy with the rolling pin and knocked out two front teeth, and the ambulance came and took her away, and she's in the hospital." And the teacher looked up and said, "All right, who's next?" Or the little kid came up and showed teacher a rock, "I found a rock on the way to school today." She said, "Fine, Johnny, put it on the science table." I wonder what would happen if she picked up the rock and said, "Let me see the rock. Look at that.

Kids, look at the color of that rock. Feel it. Who made a rock? Where does a rock come from? What's a rock? What kind of rock is this?"[13]

We wonder, too. We wonder whether Johnny will react in the same way that his teacher did when Johnny is an adult and his child or his student or his employee shares a possession or an idea with him. Without role models of effective listening behavior, he just might react in the same way.

Or, Johnny could have become a central player in the 5 April 1993 NCAA men's title game between Michigan and North Carolina. With eleven seconds left, Michigan—trailing 73–71—had the ball when Michigan's Chris Webber signaled for a timeout. Unfortunately, Michigan had no more time-outs! The result: Michigan was assessed with a technical foul for excessive timeouts, North Carolina was awarded two free throws and the ball out of bounds, and North Carolina won the national championship game 77–71. What role did listening play here? Steve Fisher, Michigan's coach, claimed he had told his players during their last time out that the team had no additional timeouts. However, as CBS analyst James Brown noted, "But the real issue was were the players listening?"

Outside the academic community, we include **government officials** in our search for professional role models. While campaigning, many politicians—knowing voters value listening—ostensibly strive to portray themselves as effective listeners of the people. But, as we watch these self-proclaimed listeners talk, shake hands, and smile as they move among the people, we often sense that they are not really present, not really connecting with us. Columnist Molly Ivins calls attention to this questionable presence of many politicians when she notes that their "smile never reaches their eyes. . . ."[14] In contrast, Ivins views Bill Clinton as being unique among politicians: "The different thing about Clinton is that he listens to people as he moves among them—Humphrey and Yarborough were always talking. Clinton listens and remembers and repeats the stories he hears."[15]

Other public servants we might observe are **police officers**. Angela V. Woodhull, author of *Police Communication in Traffic Stops*, describes several types of listening errors that police officers may make. Three of these errors—making incorrect assumptions, assuming too quickly, and responding inappropriately—are illustrated here:

DRIVER: How much is this ticket going to cost me?
POLICE OFFICER: Listen, lady, you were speeding. I didn't tell you to speed. You earned the ticket.
DRIVER: All I did was ask how much the ticket will cost.
POLICE OFFICER: I'm not going to listen to your sob story, lady. If you're broke, go tell it to the judge.[16]

Another of Woodhull's examples illustrates serious consequences of poor listening by a police officer:

An intoxicated driver was arrested for reckless driving and DWI after his car flipped off the highway, rolled repeatedly, and crashed head-on into a tree. The driver walked away from his vehicle seemingly unharmed, but told the arresting officer he was not feeling well and would like to go to the hospital. The officer assumed the violator was simply trying to get out of going to jail. Later that evening the man was rushed to the hospital for severe internal hemorrhaging. The department was sued for negligence after his death. In court it was mentioned that the man had repeatedly requested medical attention but the officer did not listen.[17]

healthcare providers

As our search continues, we call on **healthcare providers**. Unfortunately, we may find that our physician interrupts us within the first 18 seconds of our beginning to explain what is wrong just as 51 of the 74 internists did in sociolinguist Richard Frankel's study of medical interviews.[18] Or, we may find that our physician is similar to those studied by researchers at the Presbyterian Medical Center in Denver: Many physicians do not listen carefully to their patients.[19] Or, we may find, as Coakley did, that our doctor listens with little compassion:

> Two weeks after my lumpectomy, my general surgeon removed the remaining stitches. Then, while I was still on the office cot and nude from the waist up, he told me we should begin the chemotherapy.
> After I had told him I had an appointment with an oncologist that afternoon, he yelled, "Why are you going to an oncologist? I've spent more time consulting with you than I have in ages with any other breast cancer patient, and then you go to an oncologist who is absolutely unnecessary. I can oversee your treatment!"
> I don't think I'll ever forget those intimidating moments; I felt like a naked little girl being scolded by an evil parent because I had challenged his authority.[20]

Indeed, the testimony of former Surgeon General of the United States C. Everett Koop, who is now making "the education of new doctors his priority," adds impetus to the preceding findings: "If you talk to people who receive health care, the No. 1 concern is, 'My doctor is not the kind of man or woman I want a doctor to be. He doesn't listen to me.' Or, 'When I talk to her, she doesn't understand me.'"[21]

In the view of psychiatrist Dr. Walt Menninger, many people who need someone to listen to them desperately turn to physicians, who are not always the caring listeners whom patients need:

> In my work as a psychiatrist, I sense again and again the desperate feelings of people who feel no one respects what they have to say. . . . Often, people's physical ills are a disguised message, a "ticket of admission" to see someone who will listen to a complaint. Regrettably, many doctors don't want to be bothered by anything other than a clear physical problem. Yet, a sensitive doctor realizes some time spent in careful listening will point to a hidden agenda of a patient's concern. And that act of listening can give more relief to a patient than any 10 prescriptions of a tranquilizer.[22]

business personnel

As consumers, employers, and employees, we continue our search for effective listening role models among **business personnel**. Yet, what we find is that inefficient listening is *"one of the most important* problems facing them [organizations], and that poor listening leads to ineffective performance or low productivity."[23] Corporate consultant Lyman K. Steil graphically describes some of the many problems that poor listening creates:

> With more than 100 million workers in this country, a simple $10 mistake by each of them, as a result of poor listening, would add up to a cost of a billion dollars. And most people make numerous listening mistakes every week.
>
> Because of listening mistakes, letters have to be retyped, appointments rescheduled, shipments rerouted. Productivity is affected and profits suffer.[24]

Moreover, inefficient listening in business is costly to consumers: "Poor listening is one of the most significant problems facing business today. Business relies on its communications system, and when it breaks down, mistakes can be very costly. Corporations pay for their mistakes in lower profits, while consumers pay in higher prices."[25]

Ineffective listening in business is not a new problem. In fact, Nichols reported in a 1957 issue of *Nation's Business* that the average white-collar worker demonstrates only about 25 percent listening efficiency.[26] Since then, many other researchers have documented that listening skills of organizational members are deficient. Specifically, their findings reveal the following:

Listening is

the communication competency most lacking in organizational personnel[27]

the most frequently reported communication deficiency among new employees[28]

the skill in which high school graduates entering the work force are most deficient[29]

the second most troublesome communication aspect (after motivating people) for all employees[30]

the second most critical area (after motivating people) in which additional communication education is needed for supervisors[31]

the second (after learning to learn) of thirteen areas of development essential to the "upskilling" of workers in America[32]

With Barker, Pearce, and Johnson's finding that three-fourths (74.3%) of the 129 managers they surveyed perceived themselves to be passive and detached listeners (the least effective of four types of listeners),[33] organizations cannot act too quickly on Tom Peters's suggestions:

> "Listening," like so many of these apparently simple ideas, turns out to be anything but simple. Since it must be practiced if we [organizations] are to survive, it will become a mindset and a way of life for everyone—or else.[34]

We will end our search for professional role models by examining **airline pilots**. Surely, pilots—with millions of lives in their hands—are effective listeners. Is this what the National Aeronautics and Space Administration (NASA) discovered when it studied the causes of

airline pilots

commercial-airline accidents? To NASA's surprise, it found that 60 percent of the accidents were caused by poor communication in the cockpit. Prather offers this solution:

> Cockpit tapes suggest that ["teaching captains to listen respectfully to what others in the cockpit had to say before making major decisions"] might have prevented a 1987 crash costing 10 lives when a deferential flight engineer failed to warn his autocratic captain that their circling jet was running out of fuel. And it might have saved 78 who died in the icy Potomac River in 1982 when an Air Florida co-pilot failed to forcefully inform his authoritarian skipper that the jet's engines weren't delivering enough takeoff power.[35]

Furthermore, it might have prevented many deaths in the ground collision of two Boeing 747 jumbo jets in Tenerife, the largest Canary Island. Preparing for takeoff at Tenerife's Los Rodeos Airport, the KLM pilot was told by the tower controllers to taxi eastward up the full length of the runway, make a 180 degree turn, and hold until the plane was given takeoff clearance. Meanwhile, the tower controllers told the Pan American pilot, who also was preparing for takeoff, to follow (about three minutes behind) up the same runway, to turn off at the "third intersection" (ramp C-3), and then to report when his plane had cleared the runway. Taxiing eastward, the Pan Am pilot did not count ramp C-1 because the crew considered it to be inactive since it was blocked by aircraft. Thus, the pilot headed on toward ramp C-4, which he assumed to be the "third intersection." At the same time, the KLM pilot—rather than holding after he had made his 180 degree turn at the east end of the runway and waiting for takeoff clearance as he had been told to do—rolled westward on the runway for takeoff. Just as the Pan Am plane was approaching ramp C-4, the KLM plane—at a speed of 186 miles per hour—reached ramp C-4. The two planes collided in the fog and exploded in flames; 576 lives were lost. Investigators of the accident noted what would have happened if there had not been listening errors: "If both pilots and the tower controllers had fully heard—and understood—one another, the KLM pilot would never have sent his craft hurtling toward takeoff before the Pan Am plane was off the runway."[36] We might add that if the Pan Am pilot had not assumed that he was not to count ramp C-1 as one of the intersections and had asked for clarification from the tower controllers, his plane might have been clear of the runway before the KLM plane reached the "third intersection" (ramp C-3).

Our search for personal and professional listening role models could extend to siblings, grandparents, lawyers, accountants, carpenters, insurance and real estate agents, and others. The point, however, is that in all aspects of life, it is rare to encounter truly good listeners. We do not have many role models when it comes to listening behavior.

Listening Is Important

While we encounter few listening role models, listening *is* important. Answers to the following four questions provide strong evidence of its important role in contemporary society:

1. What position does listening have in our language development?
2. How much time do we spend engaged in listening?
3. What role does listening have in our lives?
4. How does listening influence us?

Listening Is the Most Basic Language Skill

Of the four major areas of language development, listening is the most basic. Listening is the **first language skill that we develop**, and it is followed by the other language skills in this order:

1. Listening
2. Speaking
3. Reading
4. Writing[37]

first language skill developed

Thus, our ability to speak, read, write, and master complex cognitive skills is directly and indirectly dependent upon our ability to listen. This ability to listen is necessary at an early age—especially during a child's first year of life when everyday exchanges between child and caregivers "are crucial in helping babies acquire the building blocks of language."[38] Studies at the University of North Carolina reveal that children who were not provided with listening opportunities at home—whose parents talked to them less than average—were more likely to be required to repeat kindergarten.[39] Lacking proficiency in listening, then, can handicap us in the processes of learning and communicating, two activities that are necessary for us to participate productively in life.

While much of this language development occurs in early childhood, it has become clear that language development begins through listening as the fetus develops in the mother's womb. Dr. Henry T. Gruby, professor of pediatrics, linguistics, and anthropology at the University of Miami, points to evidence that reveals that the fetus hears clearly from the sixth month in utero and that the fetus moves his or her body rhythm to the mother's speech. A popular technique for pregnant mothers today is to listen to soothing classical music to help the fetus relax and respond to sound and melody.[40]

Listening Is Our Most Frequently Used Form of Verbal Communication

Throughout all levels of our educational development, listening is the **main channel of classroom instruction**. This can be seen readily from "Show and

main channel of classroom instruction

Tell" periods at the kindergarten level to two-hour lecture sessions at the graduate level. This also can be substantiated by the findings of researchers who have investigated the amount of time students are expected to listen in the classroom:

Researcher	Level of Students	Percentage of Classroom Time Students Are Expected To Listen	Percentage of Classroom Listening Time Students Are Expected to Listen To the Teacher
Wilt	Elementary	58%	54%
Markgraf	Secondary	46%	66%
Taylor	Secondary/college	90%	N/A[41]

As Wilt and Markgraf did, Goodlad explored the amount of time students are expected to listen to the teacher. He reports that observations of over 1,000 American classrooms reveal that teachers and students verbally interact approximately 53 percent of their classroom time and that teachers "out talk" students by a ratio of three to one.[42]

Other researchers examining college students' listening—*in and out of the classroom*—include Bird, Barker et al., and Perras and Weitzel. Their findings are as follows:

Researchers	Percentage of Communication Time College Students Listen
Bird	42%
Barker et al.	53%
Perras and Weitzel	42%[43]

An additional finding of Bird's is that 82 percent of his surveyed college students considered listening to be equal to or more important than reading as a factor contributing to academic success in college.[44] The results of these studies demonstrate that listening is a major vehicle for learning in the classroom.

The importance of listening in learning and communicating is also apparent in our daily lives. Not only do **we spend more time listening than we spend in any other form of verbal communication**, but thanks to modern technological advancements, we engage in considerable interpersonal communication and mass communication.

Beginning in 1926 with Rankin and his landmark study, many researchers have investigated the frequency of use of listening—as well as speaking, reading, and writing—in the lives of adults. Findings—rounded off—of five of these researchers are as follows:

most used
language skill

Researchers	Subjects	Percent of *Daily* Verbal Communication Time Spent Engaged in			
		Listening	Speaking	Reading	Writing
Rankin	Adults	42%	32%	15%	11%
Brieter	Homemakers	48%	35%	10%	7%
Weinrauch/Swanda	Business personnel	33%	26%	19%	23%
Werner	High school/college students, employees, and homemakers	55%	23%	13%	8%
Barker et al.	College students	53%	16%	17%	14%[45]

Although the percentage of time spent listening is lower in Weinrauch and Swanda's study than it is in the other cited studies, it must be noted that this study *does not include* the amount of time the business participants spend listening *beyond* their working hours. However, even when we include Weinrauch and Swanda's findings, we discover that the subjects spend a mean average of 46 percent of the verbal communication time engaged in listening and 26 percent speaking, 15 percent reading, and 13 percent writing. The late Walter Loban creatively described Rankin's and others' findings in this manner: We listen a book a day, we speak a book a week, we read a book a month, and we write a book a year.[46]

In addition to Weinrauch and Swanda, others have investigated the amount of time business personnel spend engaged in listening. For example, the U.S. Department of Labor offers the following response to the question, "Why are communication skills important in the new economy?"

> Reading and writing are essential communication tools, but it is through listening or speaking that we interact most frequently at work. The average worker spends 8.4 percent of his or her communication time at work writing, 13.3 percent reading, 23.0 percent speaking, and 55.0 percent listening.[47]

Brown maintains that most employees of major corporations in North America spend even more of their workday—about 60 percent—listening,[48] and Keefe reports that executives spend as much as 63 percent of their workday engaged in listening.[49] These numbers suggest that business personnel are being paid up to 63 percent of their salaries for listening.

Studies investigating the frequency of the function of listening, in and out of the classroom, conclude that listening consumes more of our daily communication time than does any other form of verbal communication. Hence, quantitatively, the most important form of verbal communication is listening, a skill that does not automatically improve with use.

Listening Plays a Vital Role in Our Lives

Because modern technological advances in **modes of transportation** enable us to gather in groups with greater ease, the role of listening in interpersonal, group, and public communicative situations has become more significant in the economic, political, social, mental, and spiritual phases of our lives. Whether the purpose of our coming together is to settle differences between nations (such as those between the United States and North Korea regarding the inspection of North Korea's nuclear arms), to investigate a country's affairs (such as the Congressional hearings on healthcare reform), to advance a cause (such as "speak-outs" on needed funding to combat domestic abuse), to introduce a new product (such as the robotic solar lawn mower), to search for or strengthen social ties (such as newcomers' meetings or block parties), listening plays a vital role in our efforts to attain our goals.

Moreover, technological advancements in the **miniaturization of electronic circuits** have contributed to listening's growing importance in our lives. Miniaturization has played a major role in providing many communication vehicles, such as audiocassette tapes/recorders and

modes of transportation

miniaturization of electronic circuits

teleconferences. Small, relatively inexpensive audiocassette tapes/recorders can now be easily transported (carried or worn, as the Sony Walkman is), installed in vehicles, or included in home entertainment centers. Although we primarily rely on audiocassette tapes/recorders for listening to music, we also use them for recording presentations—such as lectures, interviews, and speeches—that we want to later listen to, study, review, transcribe, analyze, and so on. A more recent use of the audiocassette tape/recorder is to listen to audio "magazines" produced by some companies for their own employees and by other companies for the general public. Geared toward the person who is interested in business but does not have time to read such magazines as *The Wall Street Journal, The Economist, U.S. News & World Report, Forbes, Fortune,* and *Investors Business Daily,* these audio tapes provide the listener with the latest business ideas and trends.

Still another innovative use of the audiocassette tape/recorder is to listen to books on tape. Recorded books include classic and current selections, such as Emily Brontë's *Wuthering Heights* and Robert James Waller's *The Bridges of Madison County,* as well as self-improvement books like Robert Bramson's *Coping with Difficult People* and Bernie Siegel's *Humor and Healing.*[50] An even more innovative use of the audiocassette tape/recorder is to listen to Cliffs Notes. Called "Cliffs Cassettes—Companions to the Classics," these audio-taped notes, like the original written Cliffs Notes, are accompaniments to such classics as *The Odyssey* and the *Canterbury Tales.* As of 1993, the audio book industry had become a 1.3 billion dollar industry.[51]

The use of the audiocassette tape/recorder has also extended to travel, or sight-seeing, cassettes. Many companies now manufacture audiocassette tapes that guide tourists as they travel by car or foot. Included on these tapes are detailed descriptions of visitation sights, locations of notable restaurants and cafes, occasional anecdotes, background music, sound effects, and/or general local lore, culture, and history.

Another means of communication that miniaturization has helped to create is teleconferencing, a communications system that allows participants who are "tied in" through the system to interact with one another. Teleconferencing is advantageous to groups of individuals who cannot afford to travel to meetings but find it necessary to communicate as a group. For example, in one of our graduate seminars we arranged for John Murphy, former Director of Training for New England Bell Telephone, to speak about his listening program to our students on the University of Maryland campus via audio teleconferencing. The students were able to ask Mr. Murphy questions and offer comments about his program. Likewise, the executive committee members of the International Listening Association conduct meetings to discuss the business of the organization through telephone teleconference hookups to all of their offices throughout the country. Videophone technology may also result in further advances. For instance, the Walt Disney EPCOT Center uses an interactive video system that allows visitors to make dining reservations by communicating through videophone with a reservation clerk in a central office. Management Recruiters

International, Inc., which arranges more than 250,000 interviews per year, offers clients a videoconferencing service for conducting long-distance interviews with job candidates.[52] According to the International Teleconferencing Association, the teleconferencing industry had total revenues of 2.3 billion dollars in 1993, an increase of 31 percent over the previous year.[53] (See chapter 10 for additional coverage of teleconferencing.)

The growing importance of listening in our lives can be noted in numerous other technological innovations. Among the many additions are the following:

video yearbooks	video encyclopedias	voice-activated telephone cards
voice mail systems	cellular and cordless phones	voice-powered VCR programmers
video resumés	sound story books	telephone speech recognition systems
sound greeting cards	pagers	talking signs, elevators, cameras, cars, etc.
interactive videotape instruction (IVI)	interactive voice-response systems	voice-recognition/speech-powered computer programs

How routine have electronics' effects on listening become? Examining only two of the above additions, we learn that sales in the voice mail systems' industry have increased from 5 million dollars in 1981 to 635 million dollars in 1989[54] and that cellular phones now account for 10 percent of all phones in use.[55] It appears, then, that electronic devices are listening to us when, for example, our VCRs respond to our asking them to zap through commercials and our telephone cards respond to our asking them to determine if we are authorized users. Likewise, we are listening to electronic devices when, for example, our PCs proofread aloud our on-screen text and read our electronic mail to us or our cameras say, "C'mon, look happy." Indeed, we are experiencing electronics' heightened effects on listening in today's world.

Despite such technological advancements, there are jobs that electronic devices will never be able to do. Even though AT&T has partially automated its directory assistance service, an AT&T operator's experience illustrates the importance of high touch in a high-tech environment:

> Two weeks ago, Diane Wardlaw, a directory assistance operator in Baltimore, spent half an hour helping a frantic woman who was having trouble breathing. She calmed the woman, took her name and address between breaths, called paramedics and called a relative to arrange care for the woman's 1-year-old son. Then she went on to her next call—finding the number of an income-tax preparer for the caller. Said Wardlaw: "I don't know if a computer could do that."[56]

The importance of listening has also been accented by advances in the **mass media** (covered in greater depth in chapter 10). With the arrival of radio, motion pictures, videocassettes/recorders, and television, we have come to rely more and more on the spoken word for information about local, state, national, and international affairs, as well as for enjoyment. The mass media advancements and the quickened pace of life have helped to effect a shift from the eye and the printed page to the ear and the word of mouth. Recognizing this new reliance, Freedman states that "we

mass media

have slowly but emphatically shifted our means of communication from the printed word to images and sounds, from books to television, movies, radio, and recordings. Instead of reading today, most of us prefer to look and listen."[57]

In this mass communication revolution, the increasing importance of the spoken word can be gauged by the amount of time that Americans spend in radio listening and television and videocassette viewing. According to 1993 statistics compiled by the Radio Advertising Bureau, there are more than 9,700 radio stations on the air today, and 96 percent of all Americans age 12 and over listen to the radio an average of 22.5 hours per week. The Radio Advertising Bureau also estimates that radio's daily audience is highest between 6 A.M. and 10 A.M. and that radio is the morning's major source of news (with 38 percent of Americans obtaining morning news from radio, 37 percent from television, 20 percent from newspapers, and 5 percent from another source or no source).[58] Data compiled by Nielsen Media Research in 1993 reveal that an estimated 93.1 million American households own at least one television set, 69 percent of these homes own more than one television set, and 98 percent own color television sets. Of these 93.1 million television-owning households, 80 percent can receive 15 channels, and the average national household can receive 39.4 channels, including those available through cable service. The most viewed half-hour prime time period is 9:00 to 9:30 P.M. and Sunday evening is the most popular night for viewing television. The report found that the average television household views an estimated 7 hours and 13 minutes of television per day. The estimated weekly viewing time of specific age groups follows:

Women ages 55 and over	44 hours and 11 minutes
Men ages 55 and over	38 hours and 47 minutes
Women ages 25 to 54	31 hours and 05 minutes
Women ages 18 to 24	28 hours and 54 minutes
Men ages 25 to 54	28 hours and 44 minutes
Men ages 18 to 24	23 hours and 31 minutes
Children ages 2 to 11	23 hours and 01 minute
Teens ages 12 to 17	21 hours and 50 minutes[59]

Additionally, 77 percent of the American television-owning population also own videocassette recorders and rent more than 50 million videos per week.[60] Assuming that those who rent videos watch them and that the average video is 2 hours in length, Americans watch rented videocassettes for an average of 1 hour and 40 minutes per week. This viewing-time figure does not include video games and purchased prerecorded videos (which, along with rented videos, created a 12-billion-dollar video industry in 1993[61]), nor does it include personally recorded videos, pay-for-view videos, and so on. According to Michael Schrage, "The video has superseded print as the culture's medium of choice."[62]

Based on these findings, we can infer that young people, from ages two to eighteen, spend more than 20,000 hours before television sets, which is over 7,000 hours more than they spend in school from kindergarten through twelfth grade. Moreover, as they advance in age, their television viewing time increases.

Listening Influences Our Personal Development and Information Management

The Commission on the English Curriculum of the National Council of Teachers of English concludes that people's "economic concepts, political ideals, and ethical standards are influenced, if not largely determined, by their listening."[63] Since much of our listening time is spent listening to the media, we should examine how the media affect both our personal development and our information management.

Personal Development

According to McLuhan and Fiore, the electric media "far surpasses any possible influence mom and dad can now bring to bear. . . . Now, all the world's a sage."[64] They further stress the impact that media have on us:

> All media work us over completely. They are so persuasive in their personal, political, economic, aesthetic, psychological, moral, ethical, and social consequences that they leave no part of us untouched, unaffected, unaltered. The medium is the massage.[65]

Also recognizing the impact that the media have on us, the Commission on the English Curriculum has emphasized that many of our attitudes, principles, understandings, and ideas are being increasingly "left to the tutelage of the radio, talking pictures, and television."[66]

Additional sources have noted the impact that one particular medium, television, has on us. Testifying before the Commission on Violence, Gerbner commented on the influence of television:

> . . . television has transformed the political life of a nation, has changed the daily habits of our people, has moulded the style of the generation, . . . redirected the flow of information and values from traditional channels into centralized networks reaching into every home . . . it has profoundly affected what we call the process of socialization, the process by which members of our species become human.[67]

Further emphasizing the effects of television, the Interim Report of the Dodd Committee as early as 1965 concluded "that television, whose impact on the public mind is equal to or greater than that of any other medium, is a factor in molding the character, attitudes, and behavior patterns of America's young people. . . ."[68] Splaine notes television's effects not only on America's youth but also on all American viewers:

> It has been posited—that our televised "education" conveys a set of values. Commercial television teaches that we should have fun, that we deserve it, and that we should get what we want in any way we can. . . .
>
> Possibly even more deleterious, television directs our perceptions, teaches us how to behave, tells us how to think and what to think about. Television programming is simple, superficial, and segmented. Its steady viewers learn to think inanely and vacuously.[69]

According to Charles D. Ferris, former chairman of the Federal Communication Commission, "television has influenced our national and international affairs—from civil rights, Vietnam, and Watergate to Afghanistan and Iran. . . . It makes viewers participants in these events, and viewer reactions add another dimension to the events themselves."[70]

Information Management

Although studies of the mass media have demonstrated that the spoken word is influential in the formation of habits and attitudes, they have also revealed that the mass media do not have as much direct influence on us as do our interpersonal contacts.[71] Results of several early experiments led Katz to hypothesize that any effect of the mass media on the general public normally operates through a **two-step flow of communication**; that is, ideas flow from the mass media to opinion leaders (such as friends, coworkers, and family members) and from them to the rest of the community. Thus, personal contact influences us more than the mass media, although many of the ideas we discuss with others originate in the mass media.[72]

two-step flow of communication

Later research findings by Rogers and Haven, working toward identifying the process by which a new idea spreads in a social system, suggest that impersonal information sources (who originate nearly always from the mass media) are most important at the awareness stage. Personal information sources (interpersonal contacts) increase in significance during the next two stages (interest and evaluation) and then decline in importance at the fourth, or trial, stage. After the fifth stage (adoption of a new idea), the adopter may again turn to the media for assurance that he or she has made the proper decision.[73]

A more recent view, presented by Schramm, is that the flow of information—rather than being a two-step flow involving the mass media, opinion leaders, and others—is a **multistep process**, with the mass media greatly influencing what information flows and with "all people, at some time or other, in some relationship or other, on some subject or other, . . . probably influenc[ing] the flow."[74] The O.J. Simpson trial illustrates Schramm's theory. On 17 June 1994, television networks influenced the information flow by providing live television coverage of the slow-speed car chase involving O.J. Simpson (with Al Cowlings) and the California Highway Patrol. An estimated 95 million Americans watched the chase. The flow of information from the media continued as the public awaited Simpson's preliminary court hearing. On 30 June 1994, as many as one in four American homes viewed the opening day of the hearing.[75] During the following week (5 July–8 July) of live coverage of the hearing, the number of viewing households—according to Nielsen Media Research figures—climbed daily and reached 26 percent above normal viewing levels on 7 July.[76] Despite the fact that networks were losing millions of dollars a day in advertising revenue from pre-exempted regularly scheduled programming, networks continued their coverage. Why? According to television columnist Bill Mann, the coverage would continue "until there's some significant evidence of mass TV tune-out." Mann further noted, "This Simpson-coverage mania is simply a matter of broadcasters doing what

multistep process

Understanding the Listening Process

they do best: . . . Giving the public what it wants."[77] Thinking it was giving its public what it wanted, ABC curtailed its coverage of the hearing for one hour on 6 July to broadcast *One Life to Live*; the results were that its ratings dropped 32 percent.[78] Indeed, the people's daily viewing response greatly influenced the flow of information.

Further emphasizing the effect that mass media have on our managing of information, media specialist Tony Schwartz, in *Media the Second God*, argues that the advances of radio, television, and telephone have taken Americans into a postliterate society in which the "shift in the communication of non-face-to-face information from the written word to the electronic media is now dominant and has a deep and fundamental significance. It is restructuring much of the world."[79] Futurist John Naisbitt concurs; he describes America as shifting from an industrial society to an information society.[80] Such a shift requires the development of new communication strategies, including effective listening skills, to cope with the vast amount of information we must process as we function as receivers of both interpersonal and mass communication messages.

How important is listening in this contemporary information society? It is the most basic skill in our language development; it is the most frequently used language skill; it plays an integral part in our everyday lives; and it appears to have a profound effect on the formation of our attitudes, skills, behavioral patterns, and understandings as well as our management of information. The importance of listening has received ample endorsement:

> Listening can make the difference between knowledge and ignorance, information and misinformation, involvement and detachment, enjoyment and boredom.[81]
>
> The art of listening holds for us the desperate hope of withstanding the spreading ravages of commercial, nationalistic, and ideological persuasion.[82]
>
> What this country needs is not a good five-cent cigar. What this country needs is more good listeners![83]

Effective Listening Is Rewarding

Effective listeners can reap *numerous* rewards, including the following:

Increased sales	Improved social ties
Increased customer satisfaction	Improved family relations
Increased employee satisfaction	Heightened self-esteem
Increased productivity	Increased enjoyment
Expanded information base	Enriched lives

One reward of effective listening in business is monetary. For example, the salesperson who first asks the customer about his or her needs and then listens to the customer's verbal and nonverbal responses is better able to determine how a product will meet the customer's needs than is the salesperson who believes that selling chiefly involves assuming the role of speaker. Through listening and meeting customer needs, the salesperson is in a position to realize **increased sales**. In a televised advertisement that was aired in 1991, Dean Witter illustrated its awareness of the value of listening in selling. (See fig. 1.1.)

increased sales

Likewise, many other businesses are acknowledging—through their advertisements—that potential customers want to be listened to before they decide to invest in a product or service. Among these businesses are Nationwide Insurance ("Nationwide listens to your goals. . . ."[84]); HL Financial Resources (". . . we take the time to analyze your goals and—more important—listen to your dreams."[85]); and First National Bank of Maryland ("An experienced banker . . . takes the time to listen and to understand your problems. . . ."[86]) These businesses, indeed, link **increased customer satisfaction** to listening to the customer.

increased customer satisfaction

Businesses with effective listeners are rewarded not only with increased sales and more satisfied customers but also with **increased employee satisfaction** and **increased productivity**, both of which often lead to increased profits. Through effective listening, we gain more information, upgrade decision making, make fewer mistakes, spend time more productively (in conducting meetings, performing job tasks that are more clearly understood, avoiding misunderstandings, etc.), share more viewpoints, and improve management/employee relations. Indeed, businesses with effective listeners are more likely to prosper. John L. DiGaetani, writing about

increased employee satisfaction

increased productivity

(MUSIC: UNDER THROUGHOUT)
1. (AVO): Dean Witter believed in listening.

2. DEAN WITTER: Listen... not only to what our clients say...

3. but what they mean.

4. Each client has a level of comfort. Endeavor to find it.

5. DEAN WITTER (VO): We measure success...

6. one investor at a time.

FIGURE 1.1.
Advertisement by Dean Witter Discover and Company.

"The Business of Listening," summarizes some of the rewards of effective listening in business:

> The effects of really good listening can be dramatic. These effects include the satisfied customer who will come back, the contented employee who will stay with the company, the manager who has the trust of his staff, and the salesman who tops his quota. Good listeners are valued highly by the people they work with. . . .[87]

Indeed, *Fortune* magazine's board of editors recognized the high value placed on good listeners when it inducted six industry leaders into the National Business Hall of Fame in 1994. Nulty described the new inductees as individuals who never stop listening:

> They are hear-aholics, ever alert, bending their ears while they work and while they play, while they eat and while they sleep. They listen to advisers, to customers, to inner voices, to enemies, to the wind. That's how they get word before anyone else of unseen problems and opportunities. . . . Each [is] blessed with as much forehearing as foresight.[88]

Effective listeners also can be rewarded by acquiring more information. Although many people prefer talking when they engage in communication situations, learning comes not from talking but rather from listening. Largely through listening, one can become more informed as a student, citizen, worker, consumer, spouse, parent, and in any of the numerous other roles in which one serves. Having an **expanded information base**, one is then better equipped to perform such activities as fulfilling assignments, making sound decisions, completing work-related tasks, purchasing items, resolving conflicts, solving problems, and engaging in conversations involving a wide variety of topics. Indeed, one of Sperry's advertisements provides an easily remembered slogan regarding the reward of obtaining new information through listening: "Nothing new ever entered the mind through an open mouth."[89]

> **expanded information base**

Furthermore, the effective listener is rewarded with **improved social ties**. In a study in which college students listened to three taped conversations between a man and a woman who varied the amount of time each talked and each listened, psychologist Chris Kleinke found that the person who talked 80 percent of the time but listened only 20 percent of the time was the least liked.[90] A friend who truly listens rather than just waits for an opening to express his or her ideas not only is sought after but also, when found, is usually retained as a friend. Psychologist Julie Rogers notes the binding effect the act of listening can have: "The most vital activity of any friend . . . interested in building good interpersonal relationships is listening, and listening and listening and listening. If you want a friend for life, listen, truly listen to each other, for nothing so permanently binds two people together."[91]

> **improved social ties**

Another reward of listening is **improved family relations**. Woelfle, quoting prominent psychologist Lee Salk, notes that "a happy home, the source of a happy child, is simply a place 'where people talk to one another,

> **improved family relations**

listen to one another, where they're important in one another's lives. . . .'"[92] Numerous books, such as Thomas Gordon's *Parent-Effectiveness Training* and Adele Faber and Elaine Mazlish's *How to Talk So Kids Will Listen and Listen So Kids Will Talk*,[93] as well as many family relations seminars conducted throughout the country, stress the values of effective listening within the family. When a family member is truly listened to, he or she has **heightened self-esteem**. He or she feels recognized, accepted, understood, valued, and—as is expressed in the following impressive public service announcement—loved:

heightened self-esteem

> **Opening song:**
> Take the time to listen—listen;
> Take the time to care.
> If I know you understand me,
> Then my mind is yours to share.
> Listen with your heart—listen;
> Listen with your mind.
> When you really listen,
> Love is what you find.

Dialogue:
OLDER SON: Hey, Dad, can you help me figure this out?
DAD: Later, I'm busy. (Here begins a telephone busy signal that continues throughout the remainder of the dialogue.)
MOM: Honey, I'm worried about Robby. Let's talk.
YOUNGER SON: Daddy, do you know what happens to bears in the winter time?

> **Announcer:**
> If all they hear is your busy signal, some very important people might stop calling; and there are messages you can't afford to miss.
> **Closing song:**
> When you really listen—really listen, love is what you find.[94]

increased enjoyment

Still another reward of listening is **increased enjoyment**. Effective listening can heighten one's enjoyment of presentations such as plays, films, lectures, television or radio programs, and songs. For example, Coakley increased her appreciation of Ronnie Milsap's song, "What a Difference You've Made in My Life," when she listened to the country musician explain what had inspired him to write the song. Learning that he had written it to let his fans know how they have changed his life has increased her understanding and appreciation of the song. Enjoyment is not limited, however, to creative presentations; any sound, such as a cat's purr or a grandson's giggles, can bring delight to a particular listener.

Any discussion of the rewards of effective listening, which are far more numerous than those mentioned here, should include the reward of knowing that you have contributed to the growth of another person, an individual who needs to understand himself or herself and to be understood. Many, many individuals are pleading to be understood. Their pleas often express or imply such questions as "Do you see where I'm coming from?" "Can you see my point of view?" "Can you relate to how I feel?"

"Will you see it my way?" and "Will you put yourself in my place?" The best way to answer their pleas is to listen as they share their fears, hurts, doubts, views, whatever their concerns may be. When they find someone who truly listens to their verbal and nonverbal messages and their thought and feeling messages and then communicates his or her understanding to them, they understand themselves better, feel understood, and perceive themselves as worthwhile individuals. Indeed, effective listeners can **enrich the lives** of others and of themselves by helping others fulfill, according to Ralph G. Nichols, their most fundamental need: *"The most basic of all human needs is to understand and to be understood."*[95]

enriched lives

Listening Is Often Misunderstood

For a number of individuals, the failure to listen may result from their misunderstanding of listening. For example, Nicole may believe that there is no difference between hearing and listening; thus, her listening consists of only engaging in the passive, physical act of receiving sound waves. Or Sunil may believe that listening means obeying; hence, he believes he is an effective listener because he does whatever others orally ask him to do. Mistaken notions about listening contribute to listening failures, to educators neglecting listening instruction, to poor listeners not seeking listening training, and to society continuing to perpetuate fallacies about listening.

Before you read this section, label each of the following eight statements as *True, False,* or *Don't Know*:

1. Listening and hearing are synonymous.
2. Listening competency develops naturally through daily practice.
3. Listening ability is largely dependent upon intelligence.
4. Listening and reading are the same process.
5. Listening is primarily a passive act.
6. Effective communication is the responsibility of the speaker.
7. Listening means agreement or obedience.
8. Actual listening is equated with perceived listening.

As you study the following eight commonly held misconceptions about listening, use your above responses to identify the misconceptions that you presently hold; then strive to replace your unsupportable notions with supportable beliefs and, thus, build a sound knowledge base about listening.

1. Listening and Hearing Are Synonymous

Listening ability depends upon hearing acuity since hearing—the physiological act of sound waves being received by the ear and transmitted to the brain—is the first step of the listening process. Hearing, then, is an integral component of the process. If one does not hear the aural message, one cannot engage in the complete process of listening, which includes two other acts—attending to and assigning meaning to the aural stimuli. While an estimated 28 million hearing-impaired Americans[96] might honestly be able to say "I didn't hear you" as their reason for not engaging in the total listening process, the remaining 230 million Americans must attribute their ineffective listening behavior to a factor other than impaired hearing. We may hear well and be efficient listeners, but we might also hear well and be inefficient listeners.

2. Listening Competency Develops Naturally; Thus, Daily Practice in Listening Eliminates the Need for Systematic Listening Training

Since many children coming to first grade appear to have acquired—without systematic training—relatively adequate oral communication skills, it is assumed that through normal classroom activities at various educational levels, students will develop listening skills sufficient to meet their needs. Testing this assumption, Nichols and Stevens conducted an informal survey in which they investigated the percentage of students who could tell what their teachers were talking about when the teachers stopped in the middle of their lectures. The investigators found that 90 percent of the first graders, 80 percent of the second graders, 43.7 percent of the junior high students, and 28 percent of the senior high students could correctly answer the question.[97] Studies by Jones and Nichols, among others, have reported that without direct listening training, college subjects correctly answer 50 percent of the items on an immediate recall test (covering the material in a 10-minute lecture) and 25 percent of the items on a delayed recall test.[98] These studies provide evidence that practice in listening does not sufficiently develop proficient listeners. Commenting on the effects of practice (that is, experience), Elbing cautions that "although we all *learn experiences*, there is no guarantee that we *learn from experiences*. In fact, it is possible to learn downright errors and second-rate methods from experience, as in playing golf without taking lessons from a professional . . . it is only training in systematic method which enables us to correctly analyze situations so that we can truly learn from experiences."[99] Regarding this misconception, we concur with Adler: "How utterly amazing is the general assumption that the ability to listen well is a natural gift for which no training is required."[100]

3. Listening Ability Is Largely Dependent upon Intelligence

This misconception appears to have gained much impetus when Kelly reported the findings of his 1965 study of listening ability. Kelly compared the first two published listening tests, the 1955 Brown-Carlsen Listening Comprehension Test and the 1957 Sequential Test of Educational Progress (STEP), with an intelligence test, the Otis Test of Mental Ability. Finding the two listening tests correlated more highly with the intelligence test than they did with each other, Kelly claimed that the two listening tests were really intelligence tests.[101]

The high correlation that Kelly found is reasonable when one considers that these two early listening tests are products of the traditional approach of measuring one's listening ability by determining one's ability to retain information presented orally. The verbal processing that is required when an individual is listening or engaging in any other cognitive act is one of the many intelligences in Gardner's theory of multiple intelligences.[102] Thus, there is an understandable relationship between intelligence and listening—as measured by listening tests that largely subscribe to the retention model of listening (a model based upon Nichols' 1948 conclusions).[103]

However, when one views listening ability as including more than the traditional lecture listening, one finds that listening and intelligence are not highly related. For example, Bostrom compared four scales of the contemporary Kentucky Comprehensive Listening Test (KCLT) with two measures of reading and four ACT subscales, which are measures "roughly corresponding to intelligence."[104] The data "show definitely that reading skill, ACT scales and our [KCLT's] scales are quite different."[105]

It is apparent that listening—as well as any other cognitive act—depends somewhat on intelligence since intelligence places limitations on all mental processes. The degree of the relationship, however, will depend on how one defines and measures listening and how one defines and measures intelligence. We agree with the observations of Bostrom and the conclusion of Nichols and Stevens:

> Almost everyone involved in the practical study of communication has had experience with persons who are obviously intelligent but could never be called "good listeners." Most of us know persons of obvious intelligence who listen poorly.[106]

> To be a good listener we must apply certain skills that have to be learned, either through experience or training. If a person hasn't acquired these listening skills, his [or her] ability to understand what he [or she] hears will be low. This can happen to people with both high and low levels of intelligence.[107]

4. Reading and Listening Are the Same Process; Therefore, through Learning To Read, One Learns To Listen

The identification by researchers of many similarities between reading and listening may have lent credence to this misconception. Among the many likenesses are the following:

> Both are receptive processes concerned with the decoding of messages.
> Both use language; both seem to consist of a complex of related skills.
> Both manifest, at the language or applied level, the same set of cognitive processes.
> Both require motivation and readiness.
> Both reach a level of comprehension through retention and recall.
> Both are affected by the message receiver's frame of reference.
> Each *seems* to be affected by the teaching and learning about the other.[108]

While the many similarities between the two processes perpetuate the misconception, the identified differences clearly reveal that listening and reading are separate processes. Among the differences are the following five:

1. **Physical acts involved**—Reading involves seeing, while listening involves hearing.
2. **Time element**—
   A. The reader controls his or her own reading pace, while the listener is controlled by the speaker's pace.
   B. The reader's material is permanent, while the listener's message is transitory. When the reader becomes tired or distracted or does not understand the material, he or she can stop reading, rest, perhaps check a word's meaning in the dictionary, and then return later to the material, re-create focus on the material, and reread, reexamine, or continue reading. In contrast, when the listener tires, loses focus due to external or internal distractions, or does not understand the message, he or she cannot go back in time unless he or she is listening to a taped message.
3. **Situational context**—Reading tends to be a private process with the writer and reader separated and with the reader having the choice of where to read. Listening tends to be a social process involving reciprocity between speaker and listener as well as a process that often does not allow the listener to choose the place in which he or she desires to listen.
4. **Signals involved**—Reading requires processing only visual signals without competing stimuli. Listening requires processing aural signals, and often accompanying visual signals, under the pressure of competing stimuli.
5. **Message structure**—The reader's messages are generally linear, tightly structured, presented in full sentences, and succinct. The listener's message is often nonlinear, loosely structured, introduced but not completed, redundant, and characterized by frequent topic shifts.[109]

While some skills developed through training in reading seem to improve listening and vice versa, many other skills—unique to each process—must also be taught if students are to become competent in both reading and listening. Separate processes demand separate instruction.

5. Listening Is Primarily a Passive Activity

Ralph G. Nichols was the first listening instructor for many students of listening. On his tape, "He Who Has Ears,"[110] and in his 1957 article published in *Nation's Business*,[111] Nichols described ten of Americans' most common ineffective listening habits, along with their positive counterparts. One poor habit he addressed was the misconception that listening is passive or easy.

Discussing this habit, Nichols noted, "Listening is hard work. It is characterized by faster heart action, quicker circulation of the blood, a small rise in bodily temperature."[112] These physical actions hardly come to mind when one thinks of the many times he or she has been asked to "sit back, relax, and listen" or has been directed to "just listen." Such references make it easy to understand how this misconception has continued despite Nichols's claims.

Coakley has found that when her listening seminar participants take the Kentucky Listening Comprehensive Test, they do not sit back, relax, and just listen; rather, they each portray Nichols's description of the physically active listener. In addition to listening to participants' reports of physical changes in the heart, blood circulation, and bodily temperature, Coakley has observed their active attempts to block out distractions by closing their eyes or lowering their heads, to stay alert by sitting up, and to concentrate intensely by stilling the body and mouth.

Listening is hard work not only for the body but also for the mind. Commenting on the mental activity needed by the listener to grasp only *one* of the speaker's thoughts, Adler notes that "the mind of the receiver . . . must somehow penetrate through the words used to the thought that lies behind them. . . .This, in effect, means discovering what the idea is regardless of how it is expressed in words."[113] When one considers the numerous thoughts and feelings often expressed by a speaker, one realizes that the only easy aspect of listening is the ease with which one who actively engages in the total listening process can dismiss this misconception.

6. Effective Communication Is the Responsibility of the Speaker

Recently, in an oral communication course taught by Coakley, a student asked, "May I be excused from class today? I'm not scheduled to speak until Tuesday." Even though the student had stated on his first chapter test that both the speaker and the listener are responsible for successful communication, his request indicated that he did not believe he had the responsibility to listen to his classmates' speeches. In fact, he did not feel that he was even responsible for being physically present during their speeches. Other students enrolled in oral communication courses often hold similar views. Bostrom addresses these students:

> When you enrolled in this course, you probably thought that your major job would be preparing and delivering speeches. While that is surely important, you can now see the importance of active, attentive listening. No speaker can do well without listeners. No one can have a significant public speaking experience without an audience, and your job as a member of the audience is vital to your classmates.
>
> Clearly your classmates need a friendly, supportive group that shows interest in the topic and the situation. Boredom, disinterest, and hostility are terrible "turnoffs," even if exhibited by only one audience member.[114]

The ancient Greek philosopher Plutarch was one of the first individuals to call attention to how the speaker should not be left fully responsible for successful communication. In "On Listening to Lectures," he gives the following advice:

> There are others who think that the speaker has a function to perform, and the hearer none. They think it only right that the speaker shall come with his discourse carefully thought out and prepared, while they, without consideration or thought of their obligations, rush in and take their seats exactly as though they had come to dinner, to have a good time while others toil. And yet even a well-bred guest at dinner has a function to perform, much more a hearer; for he is a participant in the discourse and a fellow-worker with the speaker.[115]

As Plutarch has suggested, both speaker and listener share the responsibility for successful communication since they are "fellow-worker[s]" or partners. Using a sports analogy, Plutarch further describes this partnership: "Just as in playing ball it is necessary for the catcher to adapt his movements to those of the thrower and to be actively in accord with him, so with discourses, there is a certain accord between the speaker and the hearer, if each is heedful of his obligation."[116] If both speaker and listener enter *every* communication transaction with the view that each will accept at least 51 percent of the responsibility—or "obligation"—for making the transaction successful, effective communication will much more likely be the result.

Among the many behaviors of the responsible listener are preparing (mentally, psychologically, and physically) to listen, engaging in attending behaviors, focusing attention, cognitively processing verbal and nonverbal messages, and being responsive. The responsible listener is an active, involved listener prior to and throughout communication transactions.

7. Listening Means Agreement or Obedience

Frequently, people use the term *listen* to mean agree with or obey. For example, after leaving the negotiation table, a union representative might say, "What's the use of talking? Management refuses to listen to our position." Or, after stumbling over Chad's shoes, Chad's father might say, "I've told Chad umpteen times not to leave his tennis shoes in the family room. Why won't he listen?"

Another example of this misconception can be seen in an editorial titled "Make Exxon Listen." Commenting on the "foot-dragging on the part of those in charge of the cleanup" following the running aground of the oil tanker Exxon Valdez in Alaska, the writer of the letter to the editor proposed that "there is really only one way to make Exxon listen. . . . I suggest that anyone who really cares for the environment simply avoid Exxon gas stations until the company does something about oil cargo safety."[117]

Lewis and Reinsch found this misconception to be widespread among organizational members. In a 1988 study, the researchers found that in describing effective and ineffective listening in the work environment, organizational members cited "[d]id/did not follow my directions or suggestions" as the number one listening factor and "[d]id/did not try to get the changes made or results I requested" as the twelfth factor.[118] The high rankings of both of these factors out of the 38 factors identified by the employees indicate that employees often equate listening with agreeing and/or obeying.

Weaver refutes the truth of each aspect of this misconception. Denying the claim that listening means agreement, he states, "We may listen carefully and at length to the presentation of our opponent. We may question; we may explore; we may do our best to hold our own biases in abeyance as we try to see the world through his eyes. And we may, after all this, decide that our own position is the better and cling to it still. This does not mean we did not listen."[119] Rebutting the misconception's second claim that listening means obeying, he argues, "Let us assume that the single word 'come' is a command. Whether you obey it or not does not concern the process of listening. You have 'heard' it, which means you have received and attended to the data. The listening process concerns only the selecting of such stimulus data in order to 'receive' it and the cognitive structuring of it."[120]

In summary, listening does not mean agreeing or obeying. First, one willingly, openly, and actively engages in the total listening process. Then, as a result of having listened, one agrees or disagrees, or obeys or disobeys.

8. Actual Listening Is Equated with Perceived Listening

Two years ago, Coakley attended a session on listening training trends at a communication conference. During the speaker's presentation, a man entered the room, sat next to Coakley, opened a package of sunflower seeds that he began eating, squirmed in his chair, leafed through the convention program book, and never made eye contact with the speaker. Having completed her presentation, the speaker welcomed questions. Coakley's seatmate, a college professor, quickly responded: "My colleagues complain that I don't listen to them. I'll grant that I'm usually doing something else when they're talking to me, but I'm still listening to them. I know what they are saying. Isn't it true that only I know if I am actually listening?"

Seemingly without knowing it, this college professor was calling attention to the difference between perceived listening and actual listening—a distinction made long ago by Daly: "No matter how effective, skilled, or competent an individual is in listening, unless he or she is perceived as listening by the other interactants, little may be accomplished."[121] In *You Are the Message*, Roger Ailes states Daly's position another way: " . . . the more accurate numbers [in your listening/talking ratio] are the ones reflecting how others view you. Their perception is what's real."[122]

Indeed, others base their evaluation of our listening behavior on how they perceive we listen rather than on how we actually listen. Others' perceptions can have far-reaching effects, as Emmert, Emmert, and Brandt propose: "The extent to which we are perceived as effective listeners . . . [has] an effect on our perceived credibility and our subsequent effectiveness as speakers, managers, teachers, counselors, lawyers, and any other professions that are significantly based on the listening skills of the professional."[123]

Unable to observe our actual listening (which is a nonobservable, internal, mental process), others use observable, external, physical behaviors to form their impressions about how effectively we are listening. Lewis and Reinsch present a practical view: "The concept of perceived listening may have little utility to the scholar seeking to investigate actual listening but great value to the organizational consultant attempting to improve the communication climate of an organization."[124]

Listening scholars investigating organizational listening—particularly managerial listening—frequently study perceived listening. For example, both Brownell and Husband et al. have explored how managers perceive themselves as well as how their subordinates perceive them as listeners. The results of such studies reveal that managers' and subordinates' perceptions of managers' listening differ significantly. Subordinates consider managers' listening behaviors to be less adequate than managers do.[125]

Feedback gained from such studies can benefit us as listeners. First, it can confirm that actual listening and perceived listening are *not* the same. Also, as Emmert, Emmert, and Brandt suggest, it can give us useful input for self-improvement: "Knowledge of others' perceptions of our listening abilities should provide insight into our own listening behavior so that we can improve it when necessary."[126] Such improvement can be heightened, as Brownell recommends, if we *regularly* explore others' perceptions of our listening and act on their feedback: ". . . direct and frequent feedback is necessary in order for managers [or any other personal or professional listeners] to align their self-perceptions with the impressions others have of their behavior."[127]

While there are other misconceptions about listening, these are the ones we most frequently encounter. Students of listening, with a strong knowledge base about listening, should be able to recognize these and other listening misconceptions and be equipped to dispel them.

The State of Listening Instruction

We believe that misunderstandings about listening may contribute to the insufficient number of effective listening role models and contend that a more significant contributing factor is that many individuals have never received direct, focused listening training. This contention is supported by over sixty years of research that has examined listening instruction in the academic classroom and the corporate classroom.

In spite of the importance and the rewards of effective listening, as well as considerable educational and occupational recommendations and research findings that support the need for listening training (see tables 1.1[128] and 1.2[129]), instructional emphasis on the development of effective listening remains inadequate in America's schools and businesses. In this section, we will examine listening instruction in each of these institutions.

Table 1.1. Recommendations as Support for Listening Training[128]

---

1. The incorporation of listening competencies in the "Basic Skills and Competencies for Productive Employment" in a 1983 report entitled *Action for Excellence*, developed by the Task Force on Education for Economic Growth of the Education Commission of the States (consisting of corporate executives, representatives of labor and education, and state legislators)[a]
2. The recommendation for listening skill development by college and university systems such as the Coordinating Board of the Texas College and University system (in their pamphlet entitled "Goals for College Success: A Practical Reference for College Preparation")[b]
3. A recommendation of the National Commission of Excellence in Education that high school graduates be equipped to "listen effectively"[c]
4. The inclusion of learning outcomes for listening in the College Entrance Examination Board's report entitled *Academic Preparation for College: What Students Need to Know and Be Able to Do*[d]
5. The urging of Ernest Boyer, President of the Carnegie Foundation for the Advancement of Teaching and former United States Commissioner of Education, that all high school students be required to take a one-semester course in speaking and listening[e]
6. The National Council of Teachers of English's placement of speaking and listening as part of their "Essentials to English" statement[f]
7. The National Association of Secondary School Principals' call for "greater recognition of the *need for a more realistic balance of instruction in the four communication vehicles . . . the emphasis on *listening for receiving messages and speaking for sending messages* should be increased substantially"[g]
8. The Association of American Colleges' inclusion of instruction in listening (which—along with writing, reading, and speaking—is defined as *literacy*) as an integral part of all undergraduate curricula[h]
9. The expectation that all college graduates and non-graduating adults be competent communicators (speakers and listeners) as stated in Goal 5 of the Goals 2000: Educate America Act[i]

Although an accepted principle of curriculum making is that students "ought to be taught to do well those things which current living demands of them,"[130] America's educational system has, quantitatively, placed a nearly inverted emphasis on the four major language art skills. In 1929, Rankin found that the schools' instructional emphasis on reading and writing was 52 percent and 30 percent respectively, while the schools' instructional emphasis on speaking and listening was 10 percent and 8 percent respectively.[131] Even today, the two oral language arts skills continue to receive less instructional emphasis: "For years the skills of oral communication have been neglected, or have been taught only incidentally or sporadically in most of our elementary and secondary schools."[132]

The **most neglected language art skill** at all educational levels, however, is listening. As we reflect on our own early school days, can any of us remember receiving direct, focused, structured listening training? Too frequently, the only listening *instruction* we received was requests and commands to pay

most neglected language art skill

Table 1.2. Research Findings as Support for Listening Training[129]

Researchers	Subjects	Findings
Smith	282 members of the Academy of Certified Administrative Managers	Of 20 listed competencies, subjects ranked active listening as the most critical managerial competency[a]
DiSalvo	25 studies (including Smith's) conducted between 1972 and 1980	Listening was identified as the most important communication skill necessary for entry-level positions in various organizational contexts[b]
Wasylik/Sussman/Leri	55 in-house corporate trainers who are members of the Pittsburgh chapter of the American Society for Training and Development	Of 7 communication skills, subjects ranked listening as the most important communication skill in the organization[c]
Kessler	128 corporate executives	Subjects ranked listening as the third most important skill (after writing for print and writing for oral communication/ electronic media) that people entering the corporate communication field should possess[d]
Harvard's Institute for the Management of Lifelong Education	Directors of managerial training programs in over 50 corporations	Subjects ranked the development of listening skills fourth (preceded only by the abilities to interact, to think critically about ideas received, and balance conflicting viewpoints); all of these involve abilities that relate directly to the listening process[e]
Speech Communication Association task force	194 community college Career Advisory Board members (representing a wide range of occupations)	Subjects consistently ranked listening skills as the most important communication skills for career competence[f]
Downs/Conrad	700 middle managers from private industry and government agencies	Subjects ranked listening as the fifth most important skill for effective supervisors and first for subordinates to possess; failure to listen was ranked as the second most critical problem that distinguishes ineffective from effective subordinates[g]
Staley/Shockley-Zalabak	52 organizations (such as Hewlett-Packard, Honeywell, Texas Instrument, and Ford Aerospace and Communications)	Subjects most frequently rated listening as being a very important component of organizational competency[h]
Austin/Ventura	71 personnel managers in the Buffalo, Rochester, and Syracuse, New York area	Subjects ranked the ability to train employees to improve their listening skills as the most important training variable for graduate speech communication majors, hired as trainers, to possess[i]
Painter	129 graduates of Linn Technical College in Linn, Missouri	Subjects—across all 8 majors, organizational positions, and ages—ranked "listening actively" as the most important communication skill (of 20 communication skills) on the job[j]

Researcher	Subjects	Findings
Rhodes	148 midwestern personnel managers	Although subjects perceived all 15 specified listening skills as being important to organizational communication, they rated "active" listening skills as being most important[k]
Curtis/Winsor/Stephens	428 members of the American Society for Personnel Administrators	Subjects ranked listening second (after speaking) of 17 skills deemed most valued in the job-entry market[l]
Sypher/Bostrom/Seibert	36 employees of a large insurance corporate headquarters located in the northeast	The researchers—after examining relationships between listening and communication-related abilities, employee level in the company, and upward mobility—concluded that listening is related to job success. More effective listeners held higher-level positions and were promoted more frequently than were less effective listeners[m]
Conaway	172 professional in-house trainers	Of 7 communication areas, subjects ranked listening as the second most important communication area (only after interpersonal communication) for training[n]
Bednar/Olney	100 entry-level employees in Fortune 500 corporations	Subjects ranked listening as the most serious communication problem encountered with individuals in business organizations[o]
Wilmington	126 University of Wisconsin—Oshkosh graduates from the colleges of business, nursing, administration, education, and human services	To be successful in their fields, subjects perceived effective listening to be the most important communication skill and poor listening to be the most detrimental[p]
Wilmington	44 individuals who hire or supervise graduates of the University of Wisconsin—Oshkosh	Of 37 communication behaviors considered, subjects ranked "understanding what others are saying" as the one in greatest need of improvement[q]
Hiemstra/Schmidt/Madison	269 members of the Certified Management Accountants	Of 3 areas of communication skills—speaking, writing, and listening—subjects perceived listening skills to be most important to them in both their first professional position and their current management position[r]
Brownell	Study I: 91 general managers and 153 middle managers in the hospitality industry (all alumni of the School of Hotel Administration at Cornell University). Study II: 318 general managers of 19 of the 20 largest hospitality companies listed in the 1993 *American Hotel and Motel Association Directory*	Study I: Of 8 communication skills, general managers perceived listening to be the most frequently performed skill on the job. Middle managers perceived listening as the skill in which their peers were least adept. Study II: Of 7 communication skills, general managers perceived listening as the skill most essential to their career development[s]

attention and/or a few lists of listening dos and don'ts. During our later school days (from junior high through higher education), we can recall that we continued to receive little or no training in developing our proficiency in listening, the skill we use most frequently and the skill Conaway has demonstrated to be a stronger factor than reading skills or academic aptitude in the achievement and retention of information by college students.[133]

status of the teaching of listening

The fact that listening still remains the orphan of the language arts is substantiated by the reports of several listening scholars who have investigated the **status of the teaching of listening**. In 1948, only one school in the United States, Stephens College, taught listening. In 1952, Anderson found—through correspondence with hundreds of teachers—that listening was being taught in very few schools.[134] Five years later, Letton reported that there was scarce evidence that listening was being taught in the schools.[135] In 1962, Brown and Keller noted that although there were approximately fifty thousand speech courses taught in institutions of higher learning, there was "only a handful of courses in listening." They believed that these findings demonstrated that Americans "have conceived the dual act of speaking and listening almost entirely from the speaker's point of view"[136] while neglecting the receptive aspect of the oral communication process.

Beginning with Markgraf's 1962 study, listening scholars began to use more scientific methods to explore listening training in the schools. Among the results of their studies are the following:

Researchers	Date	Subjects	Findings
Markgraf	1962	406 teacher-training institutions	3 offered listening courses 134 offered listening units in other courses 44% included units on methods of teaching listening in methods courses[137]
Wolff	1977	70 colleges/universities with whom SCA members were affiliated	10 offered listening courses[138]
Pace/Ross	1983	100 departments with the basic survey course in organizational communication	60 of 100 courses included a listening component (ranging in coverage from 25 to 155 minutes) Listening ranked 25th of the 38 course content areas[139]
Wolvin/Coakley/Disburg	1988	82 colleges/universities with whom ILA members were affiliated	44 offered a listening course 63 offered listening units in other courses[140]
Wolvin/Coakley/Disburg	1989	134 colleges/universities with whom SCA members were affiliated	19 offered a listening course 63 offered listening units in other courses[141]
Wolff	1990	126 colleges/universities with whom SCA members were affiliated	42 offered listening courses 40 offered listening units in other courses[142]
Smith/Turner	1993	682 colleges/universities with communication studies departments	52 offered a listening course[143]

While the number of schools that provide listening training is increasing, these findings support our contention that many individuals do not receive direct, focused listening instruction during their academic years. Consider, for example, that only three states that issue a secondary teaching certificate with a speech, speech communication, or speech/drama endorsement currently require listening as an area of study, and no state designates listening as an elective.[144] It is apparent that many educators do not understand what the omission of listening in the language arts instructional program means as well as one sixth-grade girl does. After listening to Brown speak about the importance of *auding* (listening), she inquired, "Then leaving out auding in language would be like leaving out home plate in baseball, huh?"[145] A portion of one of Sperry's advertisements summarizes the schools' emphasis on listening: ". . . listening is the one communication skill we're never really taught. We're taught how to read, to write, to speak—but not to listen."[146]

While listening scholars have suggested many reasons why instruction in listening has received such little emphasis in American schools,[147] a previously unmentioned possibility is the incorrect perception of the skills in which our students are, indeed, deficient. The findings of a study conducted by New York's Center for Public Resources illustrate differences between business and union officials' and school officials' perceptions of the skills possessed by persons entering the work force in the United States. Union and business officials identified mathematics and science skills as deficient, but they also noted a decline in speaking and listening skills. Likewise, these officials noted that speaking and listening skills were essential in all job categories at all job levels. Although business and union officials considered communication skills to be essential and in need of further development, school officials in this same survey assessed their graduates as being "adequately prepared" for entry-level employment.[148] It would seem that there is a gap between what skills a person needs to enter the work force, especially skills in speaking and listening, and what the schools are providing to our future workers, our students.

Also concerned with the skills needed by competent individuals in the high-performance workplace is the Secretary's Commission on Achieving Necessary Skills (SCANS). In 1991 and 1992, SCANS called on the American educational system from pre-school through post-graduate to attend to the following set of *foundation skills and competencies* that are essential to all in the modern world: (1) the basic skills—reading, writing, arithmetic and mathematics, speaking, and listening; (2) thinking skills; and (3) personal qualities.[149]

Perhaps if all states had responded more quickly to a significant federal government action in 1978, SCANS would not be asking the American educational system to attend to the responsibility of teaching listening. This federal action, the 1978 Elementary and Secondary Education Act, added listening and speaking to reading, writing, and arithmetic, as measures of literacy and as needed basic competencies. As the following 1990 findings indicate, though, the states' response time to the 1978 legislation has been slow:

Reported Actions Taken	Number of States
Identified listening skills	35
Developed curriculum materials for teaching these skills	31
Developed listening assessment procedures	12[150]

corporate listening training

Because of the educational lag in developing efficient listeners, **some leading corporations**, who recognize the cost of poor listeners and the need for effective listening from the executive suite to the shop floor, **are providing listening training** for their employees. For example, in 1979 Sperry (now a part of UNISYS) retained Lyman K. Steil as a consultant and trainer to work with Sperry's own management development specialists in developing a listening training program modeled in many respects after the pioneering work of Ralph G. Nichols. As of August 1983, twenty thousand of Sperry's ninety thousand employees (beginning with top management) had taken the six-to-eight-hour course, which was tailored to meet the professional and personal listening needs of the various participants, whether they were salespersons, receptionists, systems analysts, customer engineers, or top executives.[151]

Although many other corporations, such as Xerox, Pfizer, 3M, American Telephone and Telegraph, General Electric, Dun and Bradstreet, and Pitney Bowes, had included listening in their training programs before 1979, Sperry's well-received, in-house listening training program and advertising campaign, whose theme was "We understand how important it is to listen,"[152] generated much interest in listening among many other businesses. In fact, the results of Wolvin and Coakley's 1988 survey of training directors of the Fortune 500 industrial and the Fortune 500 service corporations revealed that 59 percent of the 248 responding corporations provide listening training for their employees.[153] Wolvin and Coakley's results are lower than those reported in *Training* magazine's 1993 Industry Report. The report finds that 69 percent of the corporations surveyed are providing training in listening skills and that training in listening skills ranks ninth of the forty-three types of training cited.[154] Indeed, listening training is now being offered by such corporations as Delta Airlines, Ford, Honeywell, Control Data, IBM, Pacific Telephone, Pillsbury Company, Bank of America, and Tektronix.[155]

These companies, recognizing that listening training improves employees' listening skills,[156] are adopting the following view:

> The most important factor for successful communication is not only the ability to use language well or to speak well or to present one's own point of view; it is rather the ability to listen well to the other person's point of view.[157]

But, of even greater significance, these companies are doing more than merely acknowledging the importance of effective listening; they are working toward eliminating the question, "Is anyone *really* listening?"

Summary

In this chapter, we have called attention to the lack of a sufficient number of listening role models in our personal and professional lives despite the importance of listening in our lives and the rewards effective listening can bring. We have shown that listening is the most basic of the four major areas of language development; that listening is the most frequently used form of verbal communication, and thus plays a significant role in our educational, personal, and professional lives; and that listening appears to have a profound effect on the formations of our attitudes, skills, behaviors, and understandings as well as our management of information. Furthermore, we have pointed out many of the benefits of effective listening, such as increased sales, productivity, customer and employee satisfaction, knowledge, and enjoyment; improved family and social relations; heightened self-esteem; and enriched personal lives. Also, we have described—and shown the falsity of—common listening misconceptions, which, when held by listeners, may contribute to the lack of listening role models. Finally, we have stressed that in spite of the importance of listening, America's schools—at all educational levels—have been negligent in providing instruction in listening. As a result of the schools' insufficient emphasis on the development of adequate listening skills, many leading corporations are recognizing the need to provide listening training for their employees so that costly communication barriers resulting from poor listening will be minimized or completely eliminated.

Suggested Activities

1. Collect articles, cartoons, lines from songs and commercials, quotes, etc. that call attention to ineffective listening and then share them orally with the class.
2. Compile a list of listening skills that you should improve or develop in order to be an effective listener in your *personal* life. Share this list orally with the class.
3. Maintain a listening log for a week. Construct daily time charts divided into fifteen-minute intervals. Using S (for speaking), W (for writing), R (for reading), L (for listening), and N (for nonverbal communication or no communication), code your communication time during each waking hour. Use the code that represents the type of communication in which you engage during the major portion of each fifteen-minute interval. Then tabulate the following:
   a. The total number of fifteen-minute intervals you were awake.
   b. The total number of fifteen-minute intervals you engaged in no (or nonverbal) communication.
   c. The total number of fifteen-minute intervals you engaged in *each* type of verbal communication: speaking, writing, reading, and listening.

     d. The total number of fifteen-minute intervals you engaged in verbal communication (a sum of the four totals calculated in c).

     e. The percentage of waking hours you spent engaged in no (or nonverbal) communication, verbal communication, writing, reading, listening, and speaking.

Finally, compare your findings with those of Rankin, which are as follows:

No (or nonverbal) communication	30	percent
Verbal communication	70	percent
Listening	42.1	percent
Speaking	31.9	percent
Reading	15	percent
Writing	11	percent[158]

4. From your listening logs, determine the percentage of time you are expected to listen in your classes.

5. From your listening logs, determine the percentage of time you are expected to listen on your jobs. Then compare your findings with those of Weinrauch and Swanda (see page 14).

6. Maintain a seven-day listening log of time you spend listening to television. Then calculate the average number of hours you listen to television per day and compare your personal television viewing habits with those reported in the *1992-1993 Report on Television* (see page 18).

7. Explore the importance of good listening in your planned or chosen profession/vocation. Interview, in person or over the telephone, at least one person working in your field of interest. Among the questions you should ask are the following:

     a. Specifically, what is your occupation?

     b. During a typical work day, what percentage of the day do you spend verbally communicating with others?

     c. Rank the four means of verbal communication in which you engage (reading, writing, listening, and speaking), ranging from the one you use most to the one you use the least.

     d. List specific situations in which you engage in listening.

     e. In your area of specialization, how important is listening?

     f. What specific listening skills does a person holding your position need to possess?

     g. Do you consider yourself to be a good listener? Why or why not?

     h. Does your company provide any direct listening training? If so, what kind of training?

After conducting the interview(s), discuss your findings on paper. Submit a copy of your findings to all other students and to the instructor.[159]

8. Begin compiling a list of personal, social, and professional rewards you will derive from effective listening; add to this list as other rewards occur to you.

9. Contact educators at the elementary, secondary, and college levels and investigate what, if any, direct listening instruction they provide and why they do or do not provide it. Then share your findings with the class.

10. Contact several local companies and find out whether any of them provide direct listening training for their employees. If they do, inquire about the type of training that is provided. Then share your findings with the class.

11. List any listening behaviors that you find irritating; then examine your own listening behavior to see whether you engage in any of these annoying behaviors.

12. Audiotape excerpts of songs that include references to listening and then share the tape with the class.

Notes

1. Franciscan Communications, Public Service Announcement, WJZ-TV, Summer, 1972. Reprinted by permission of the publisher.
2. J. R. Komaiko, "The Fine Art of Listening," *Parents*, August 1961, p. 78.
3. S. E. Landfried, *Ways to Listen Effectively to Your Kids* (Washington, D.C.: NEA, 1989), pp. 4–6.
4. D. Hooper, "Spend Time Helping Youth to Build Self-Image," *Grit*, 16 August 1981, p. 15.
5. S. Goff-Timmer, J. Eccles, and K. O'Brien, "How Children Use Time," in *Time, Goods, and Well-Being*, eds. R. T. Juster and F. P. Stafford (Ann Arbor, MI: University of Michigan, 1985), pp. 353–380.
6. S. Fornaciai, "How to Talk to Kids about Drugs," cited by J. Barbour, "Lines of Communication," *The Evening Sun,* 18 March 1981, p. B1.
7. "Communication Vital, Marriage Study Finds," *Grit* 18 April 1982, p. 2. See also E. Krupat, "A Delicate Imbalance," *Psychology Today* 20 (November 1986): 22–26.
8. S. Winokur, "What Happy Couples Do Right," *Redbook,* June 1991, pp. 65–69.
9. S. Hite, *Women in Love* (NY: Alfred Knopf, 1987), p. 31.
10. D. Borisoff and L. Merrill, "Gender Issues and Listening," in *Listening in Everyday Life*, eds. D. Borisoff and M. Purdy (Lanham, MD: University Press of America, Inc., 1991), p. 69.
11. J. D. Stammer, "MAPPing Out a Plan for Better Listening," *Teacher* 98 (March 1981): 37–38.
12. D. N. Dedmon, "Education: Confirming What We Know," *Vital Speeches* 50 (15 October 1983): 19.
13. L. Buscaglia, *Love* (NY: Fawcett Crest Books, 1972), pp. 44–45.
14. M. Ivins, "Talking, and Listening, to the People," *Santa Rosa Press Democrat,* 1 September 1992, p. B4.
15. Ibid.
16. A. V. Woodhull, *Police Communication in Traffic Stops* (Rochester, VT: Schenkman Books Inc., 1993), p. 56.
17. Ibid., p. 57.
18. D. Goleman, "All Too Often, The Doctor Isn't Listening, Studies Show," *The New York Times,* 13 November 1991, p. C15.
19. D. D. Burns, "The All-Hits, No-Misses Way to Get What You Want," *Self,* April 1981, pp. 69–70. See also D. Colburn, "Patients Often Sue over Miscommunication," *The Washington Post Health,* 12 July 1994, p. 5.
20. C. G. Coakley, "Listening Opportunities for Breast Cancer Patients and Their Supporting Cast" (Paper presented at the International Listening Association Convention, Boston, MA, 1994), p. 8.
21. M. Ryan, "We Need to Teach Doctors to Care," *Parade Magazine,* 3 July 1994, p. 8.
22. Taken from Dr. Walter Menninger's column. Copyright 1979 UNIVERSAL PRESS SYNDICATE. Reprinted with permission. All rights reserved.

23. G. T. Hunt and L. P. Cusella, "A Field Study of Listening Needs in Organizations," *Communication Education* 32 (October 1983): 399.
24. L. K. Steil, "Secrets of Being a Better Listener," *U.S. News & World Report* 88 (26 May 1980): 65.
25. S. Porter, "Poor Listening Is Big Problem for Businesses," *The Washington Star*, 14 November 1979, p. FB.
26. R. G. Nichols, "Listening Is a 10-Part Skill," *Nation's Business* 45 (1957): 56. See also, R. G. Nichols and L. A. Stevens, *Are You Listening?* (NY: McGraw-Hill Inc., 1957), pp. 5–6.
27. J. Carstens, "Listening: A Business Communication Survey," Unpublished manuscript, University of Wisconsin, River Falls, WI, 1979.
28. J. E. Meister and N. L. Reinsch, "Communication Training in Manufacturing Firms," *Journal of Business Communication* 25 (1978): 49–67.
29. J. F. Henry and S. U. Raymond, *Basic Skills in the U.S. Work Force* (NY: Center for Public Resources, 1982), pp. ii, iii, and 14.
30. M. S. Hanna, "Speech Communication Training Needs in the Business Community," *Central States Speech Journal* 34 (Fall 1978): 260–267.
31. T. E. Harris and T. D. Thomlison, "Career-Bound Communication Education: A Needs Analysis," *Central States Speech Journal* 34 (Winter 1983): 260–267.
32. A. Carnevale et al., "Workplace Basics: The Skills Employers Want," *Training and Development Journal* 42 (October 1988): 22–30.
33. R. T. Barker, C. G. Pearce, and I. W. Johnson, "An Investigation of Perceived Managerial Listening Ability," *Journal of Business and Technical Communication* 6 (October 1992): 438–457.
34. T. Peters, *Thriving on Chaos* (NY: Alfred A. Knopf Inc., 1988), p. 145.
35. S. E. Prather, "The Choice Is Yours—Communicate or Be Sued," *Medical Economics*, 17 April 1989, pp. 94–95.
36. " 'What's He Doing? He'll Kill Us All!' " *Time* 109 (11 April 1977), p. 22.
37. S. Lundsteen, *Listening: Its Impact on Reading and the Other Language Arts*, 2nd ed. (Urbana, IL: NCTE ERIC, 1979), p. xi.
38. C. Cantor, "How Babies Learn by Listening," *Working Woman*, November 1992, p. 58.
39. P. Berg, "Talking to Infants Improves School Performance," *Washington Post Health*, 9 July 1986, p. 5.
40. T. Verny and J. Kelly, *The Secret Life of the Unborn Child* (NY: Summit Books, 1981), p. 3.
41. M. E. Wilt, "A Study of Teacher Awareness of Listening as a Factor in Elementary Education," *Journal of Educational Research* 43 (April 1950): 631; B. Markgraf, "An Observational Study Determining the Amount of Time That Students in the Tenth and Twelfth Grades Are Expected to Listen in the Classroom," in *Listening: Readings*, ed. S. Duker (NY: Scarecrow Press Inc., 1966), pp. 90–94; S. E. Taylor, *What Research Says to the Teacher; Listening* (Washington, D.C.: National Education Association, 1964), p. 3.
42. J. Goodlad, "A Study of Schooling: Some Findings and Hypotheses," *Phi Delta Kappan*, March 1983, pp. 465–470.
43. D. E. Bird, "Teaching Listening Comprehension," *Journal of Communication* 3 (November 1953): 127–128; L. Barker et al., "An Investigation of Proportional Time Spent in Various Communication Activities by College Students," *Journal of Applied Communications Research* 8 (November 1980): 101–109; M. T. Perras and A. R. Weitzel, "Measuring Daily Communication Activities," *The Florida Speech Communication Journal* 9 (1981): 19–23. Perras and Weitzel's findings need further explanation. Data collected by 113 college students who maintained weekday logs of the amount of time they engaged in eight oral, written, and intrapersonal communication activities revealed the following time percentages that subjects engaged in *oral* communication activities: primarily conversation (23.8 percent), primarily listening only (15.3 percent), radio (7.4 percent), television (7.0 percent), and primarily speaking only (3.3 percent). If these subjects spent one-half of their conversational time listening (that is, 11.9 percent), the results would indicate that they spent 41.6 percent of their oral communication time engaged in listening.
44. Bird, "Teaching Listening Comprehension," pp. 127–128.
45. P. T. Rankin, "The Measurement of the Ability to Understand Spoken Language" (unpublished Ph.D. diss., University of Michigan, 1926), *Dissertation Abstracts* 12 (1952): 847–848; L. R. Brieter, "Research in Listening and Its Importance to Literature," cited by L. L. Barker, *Listening Behavior* (Englewood Cliffs, NJ: Prentice-Hall, 1971), p. 4; J. D. Weinrauch and J. R. Swanda, Jr., "Examining the Significance of Listening: An Exploratory Study of Contemporary Management," *The Journal of Business Communication*

13 (February 1975): 25–32; E. K. Werner, "A Study of Communication Time" (M.A. thesis, University of Maryland–College Park, 1975), p. 26; L. Barker et al., "An Investigation of Proportional Time Spent in Various Communication Activities by College Students," pp. 101–109.

46. W. Loban, *The Language of Elementary School Children* (Champaign, IL: NCTE, 1963).

47. U.S. Department of Labor, *Skills and New Economy* (Washington, D.C.: U.S. Government Printing Office, 1991), p. 12.

48. L. Brown, *Communicating Facts and Ideas in Business* (Englewood Cliffs, NJ: Prentice-Hall, 1982), p. 380.

49. W. F. Keefe, *Listen, Management!* (NY: McGraw-Hill, 1971), p. 10.

50. The National Library Service provides this service for older Americans: By telephoning from their homes, senior citizens may arrange to borrow—at no cost—audio books from participating regional and local libraries. For specific information, call 1-800-424-9100. From "Hear Any Good Books Lately?" *Modern Maturity*, December 1993/January 1994, p. 6.

51. Audio Publishers Association, "Audio Publishers Association 'Fact' Sheet" (Hermosa Beach, CA: APA, October 31, 1994).

52. J. Cummings, "Videoconferencing Gives Recruiter Edge," *Management World*, 1 March 1993, p. 25.

53. Press Release. International Teleconferencing Association, McLean, VA, 19 June 1994, p. 1.

54. L. Cauley, "Voice Mail a Routine Part of Electronic Landscape," *Santa Rosa Press Democrat*, 22 June 1992, p. E1.

55. M. Mills, "Cellular Phones Become Police's Best Friend," *Santa Rosa Press Democrat*, 26 June 1994, pp. A1, A14.

56. C. Skrzycki, "'Robot' Computer Operators Come Calling," *The Washington Post*, 14 April 1991, p. H5.

57. M. Freedman, "Not So; It's a Communications Revolution," *The Evening Sun*, 7 April 1982, p. A15.

58. Radio Advertising Bureau, *Radio Marketing Guide and Fact Book for Advertisers 1993–1994* (NY: Radio Advertising Bureau, Inc., 1993).

59. Nielsen Media Research, *1992–1993 Report on Television* (NY: Nielsen Media Research, 1993).

60. Ibid; B. Story, "$3 Billion in '93," *Video Store Magazine*, December 1993, p. 4.

61. Ibid.

62. M. Schrage, "The Challenge for Newspapers: Transforming Readers into Participants," *The Washington Post*, 6 April 1990, p. D3

63. Commission on the English Curriculum of the National Council of Teachers of English, *The English Language Arts* (NY: Appleton-Century-Crofts, 1952), pp. 329–330.

64. From *The Medium Is the Massage* by Marshall McLuhan and Quentin Fiore. Coordinated by Jerome Agel. Copyright 1967 by Bantam Books, Inc. Reprinted by permission of the publisher. All rights reserved.

65. Ibid.

66. Commission on the English Curriculum of the National Council of Teachers of English, *The English Language Arts*, pp. 329–330.

67. G. Gerbner, quoted in N. Johnson, *How to Talk Back to Your TV Set* (Boston: Little, Brown & Co., 1970), p. 24.

68. The Interim Report of the Dodd Committee, quoted in N. Johnson, *How to Talk Back to Your TV Set*, p. 37.

69. J. Splaine, "Veiled: Television's Effects on Learning, A Research Challenge," *The Pen*, March 1988, pp. 6–7.

70. C. D. Ferris, "The FCC Takes a Hard Look at Television," *Today's Education* 69 (September/October 1980): 66GS.

71. D. J. Bem, *Beliefs, Attitudes, and Human Affairs* (Belmont, CA: Brooks/Cole Publishing Co., 1970), pp. 75–77.

72. E. Katz, "The Two-Step Flow of Communication: An Up-to-Date Report on a Hypothesis," *Public Opinion Quarterly* 1 (1957): 61–78.

73. E. M. Rogers, *Diffusion of Innovations* (NY: The Free Press of Glencoe, 1962), pp. 99, 101.

74. W. Schramm, *Men, Messages, and Media* (NY: Harper and Row, Publishers, 1973), p. 124.

75. "TV Ratings Neared That of Gulf War," *Santa Rosa Press Democrat*, 24 June 1994, p. A16; "1 in 4 Tuned in to O.J. Coverage," *Santa Rosa Press Democrat*, 2 July 1994, p. A13.

76. "Simpson TV Coverage Cost Dearly," *Santa Rosa Press Democrat*, 9 July 1994, p. A7; P. Patsuris, "O.J. by the Numbers," *TV Guide*, 30 July 1994, p. 19.

77. B. Mann, "Networks Caught in O.J. Paradox," *Santa Rosa Press Democrat*, 8 July 1994, p. A3.

78. "Simpson TV Coverage Cost Dearly," *Santa Rosa Press Democrat*, p. A7.
79. T. Schwartz, *Media the Second God* (NY: Random House Inc., 1981), p. 14.
80. J. Naisbitt, *Megatrends* (NY: Warner Books, 1982).
81. Commission on the English Curriculum of the National Council of Teachers of English, *The English Language Arts in the Secondary School* (NY: Appleton-Century-Croft, 1956), p. 251.
82. W. Johnson, "Do We Know How to Listen?" *ETC* 7 (Autumn 1949): 3.
83. Taken from Dr. Walter Menninger's column. Copyright 1979 UNIVERSAL PRESS SYNDICATE. Reprinted with permission. All rights reserved.
84. Advertisement by Nationwide Insurance. Reprinted by permission of Nationwide Insurance.
85. Advertisement by HL Financial Resources. Reprinted by permission of HL Financial Resources.
86. Advertisement by First National Bank of Maryland. Reprinted by permission of the First National Bank of Maryland.
87. J. L. DiGaetani, "The Business of Listening," *Business Horizons* 23 (October 1980): 42.
88. P. Nulty, "The National Business Hall of Fame," *Fortune* 129 (4 April 1994): 118.
89. Advertisement by Sperry. Reprinted by permission of Sperry Corporation.
90. C. Benton, "Listen—You'll Make a Good First Impression," *National Enquirer*, 2 February 1982, p 37.
91. Taken from Dr. Walter Menninger's column. Copyright 1979 UNIVERSAL PRESS SYNDICATE. Reprinted with permission. All rights reserved.
92. G. Woelfle, "Family Man," *Texas Flyer*, April 1981.
93. T. Gordon, *Parent Effectiveness Training* (NY: Peter H. Wyden, 1970); A. Faber and E. Mazlish, *How to Talk So Kids Will Listen and Listen So Kids Will Talk* (NY: Rawson, Wade Publishers, 1980).
94. The Church of Jesus Christ of Latter-Day Saints, Public Service Announcement. Used with permission of The Church of Jesus Christ of Latter-Day Saints.
95. R. G. Nichols, "The Struggle to Be Human" (Address delivered at the First Annual International Listening Association Convention, Atlanta, GA, 17 February 1980), p. 4.
96. National Institute on Deafness and Other Communication Disorders, *Biennial Report of the Director, National Institutes of Health, 1991–1992* (Washington, DC: The National Institutes of Health, 1993), p. 84.
97. R. G. Nichols and L. A. Stevens, *Are You Listening?* pp. 12–13.
98. R. G. Nichols, "Do We Know How to Listen? Practical Helps in a Modern Age," *Speech Teacher* 10 (March 1961): 119–120.
99. A. O. Elbing, *Behavioral Decisions in Organizations* (Glenview, IL: Scott, Foresman and Co., 1970), pp. 13–14.
100. M. J. Adler, *How to Speak How to Listen* (NY: Macmillan Publishing Company, 1983), p. 5.
101. C. Kelly, "An Investigation of the Construct Validity of Two Commercially Published Listening Tests," *Speech Monographs* 32 (June 1965): 139–143.
102. H. Gardner, *Frames of Mind: The Theory of Multiple Intelligence* (NY: Basic Books, 1983).
103. R. G. Nichols, "Factors in Listening Comprehension," *Speech Monographs* 15 (April 1948): 154–163.
104. R. N. Bostrom, *Listening Behavior: Measurement and Application* (NY: The Guilford Press, 1990), p. 11.
105. Ibid., p. 23.
106. Ibid., p. 5.
107. Nichols and Stevens, *Are You Listening?* p. 11.
108. T. G. Devine, "Listening: What Do We Know after Fifty Years of Research and Theorizing?" *Journal of Reading* 21 (January 1978): 296–304; E. Erway, "What Is Listening Competence?" (Paper presented at the International Listening Association Summer Conference, St. Paul, MN, 12 July 1984); S. Lundsteen, *Listening: Its Impact on Reading and the Other Language Arts*, pp. 2–11; S. Rhodes, "Listening Assessment: Formal and Informal Methods" (Paper presented at the International Listening Association Summer Conference, St. Paul, MN, 13 July 1984); T.G. Sticht et al., *Auding and Reading: A Developmental Model* (Alexandria, VA: Human Resources Research Organization, 1974); C. G. Coakley and A. D. Wolvin, "Listening in the Native Language," in *Listening, Reading, Writing: Analysis and Application*, ed. B. H. Wing (Middlebury, VT: Northeast Conference on the Teaching of Foreign Languages, 1986), pp. 21–22.
109. R. J. Bracewell et al., "Cognitive Processes in Composing and Comprehending Discourse," *Educational Psychologist* 17 (Fall 1982): 146–164; Devine, "Listening: What Do

We Know after Fifty Years of Research and Theorizing?" pp. 296–304; Erway, "What Is Listening Competence?"; Lundsteen, *Listening: Its Impact on Reading and the Other Language Arts*, pp. 2–11; N. A. Mead, "Developing Oral Communication Skills: Implications of Theory and Research for Instruction and Training" (Paper presented at the National Basic Skills Orientation Conference, Arlington, VA, 1980); P. D. Pearson and L. Fielding, "Research Update: Listening Comprehension, *Language Arts* 59 (September 1982): 617–629; Rhodes, "Listening Assessment: Formal and Informal Methods"; F. I. Wolff and N. C. Marsnik, *Perceptive Listening*, 2d ed. (NY: Holt, Rinehart and Winston Inc., 1983), pp. 52–54; Coakley and Wolvin, "Listening in the Native Language," pp. 21–22.

110. R. G. Nichols, "He Who Has Ears" [audiotape]. (St. Paul, MN: Telstar, Inc.), n.d.
111. R. G. Nichols, "Listening Is a 10-Part Skill," pp. 56–58.
112. Ibid.
113. Adler, *How to Speak How to Listen*, p. 91.
114. R. N. Bostrom, *Communicating in Public: Speaking and Listening* (Edina, MN: Burgess Publishing, 1988), p. 49.
115. Plutarch, *Plutarch's Moralia*, trans. Frank Cole Babbitt (Cambridge, MA: Harvard University Press, 1927), p. 245.
116. Ibid.
117. J. R. Conrad, "Make Exxon Listen," *The Sun*, 22 April 1989, p. 1A.
118. M. H. Lewis and N. L. Reinsch, Jr., "Listening in Organizational Environments," *Journal of Business of Communication* 25 (Summer 1988): 49–67.
119. C. H. Weaver, *Human Listening: Processes and Behavior* (Indianapolis: Bobbs-Merrill Company, 1972), p. 22.
120. Ibid., p. 6.
121. J. Daly, "Listening and Interpersonal Evaluations" (Paper presented at the Central States Speech Convention, Kansas City, MO, 1975).
122. R. Ailes (with J. Kraushar), *You Are the Message* (NY: Doubleday Currency, 1988), p. 55.
123. P. Emmert, V. Emmert, and J. Brandt, "An Examination of the Dimensional Structure of the Listening Practices Feedback Report" (Paper presented at the International Listening Association Convention, Seattle, WA, 1992), p. 1.
124. M. H. Lewis and N. L. Reinsch, Jr., "Listening in Organizational Environments," p. 64.
125. R. L. Husband, T. Schenck, and L. O. Cooper, "A Further Look at Managerial Listening" (Paper presented at the International Listening Association Convention, Scottsdale, AZ, 1988); L. O. Cooper and R. L. Husband, "Developing a Model of Organizational Listening Competency," *Journal of the International Listening Association* 7 (1993): 6–34; J. Brownell, "Listening: The Toughest Management Skill," *Cornell Hotel and Restaurant Administrative Quarterly* 27 (1987): 64–71; J. Brownell, "Perceptions of Effective Listeners: A Management Study," *Journal of Business Communication* 27 (Fall, 1990): 401–415.
126. P. Emmert, V. Emmert, and J. Brandt, "An Examination of the Dimensional Structure of the Listening Practices Feedback Report," pp. 1–2.
127. J. Brownell, "Perceptions of Listening Behavior: A Management Study," (Paper presented at the International Listening Association Convention, Scottsdale, AZ, 1988), p. 27.
128. D. M. Boileau, ed., "Education Research Notes Development," *Spectra* 19 (September 1983): 5[a]; D. Boileau, ed., "Education Research Notes Development," *Spectra* 19 (May 1983): 9[b]; The National Commission on Excellence in Education, *A Nation at Risk* (Washington, D.C.: United States Department of Education, April 1983), p. 25[c]; D. Boileau, ed., "Education Research Notes Development," *Spectra* 19 (August 1983): 8[d]; D. Boileau, ed., "Education Research Notes Development," *Spectra* 20 (May 1984): 4[e]; Ibid[f]; National Association of Secondary School Principals, "Speaking/Listening: Much Used, Little Taught," *Curriculum Report* 14 (December 1984): 1[g]; Association of American Colleges, *Integrity in the College Curriculum* (Washington, D.C.: Association of American Colleges, 1985), pp.16–17[h]; R. Berko, ed., "How Will Goals 2000 Affect Speech Communication?" *Spectra* 30 (May 1994):1, 11.[i]
129. "The 20% Activities that Bring 80% Payoff," *Training/HRD* 15 (June 1978): 6[a]; Vincent S. DiSalvo, "A Summary of Current Research Identifying Communication Skills in Various Organizational Contexts," *Communication Education* 29 (July 1980): 283–290[b]; J. E. Wasylik, L. Sussman, and R. P. Leri, "Communication Training As Perceived by Training Personnel," *Communication Quarterly* 20 (1976): 32–38[c]; M. S. Kessler, "Communicating Within and Without: The Work of Communication Specialists in American Corporations," *Association for Communication Administration Bulletin*, 35 (January 1981): 45–50[d] A. E. Keller, "The Quest for Professionalism," *Infosystems*, February 1983, p. 94[e];

J. Muchmore and K. Galvin, "A Report of the Task Force on Career Competencies in Oral Communication Skills for Community College Students Seeking Immediate Entry into the Work Force," *Communication Education* 32 (April 1983): 207–220[f]; C. W. Downs and C. Conrad, "Effective Subordinancy," *The Journal of Business Communication* 19 (Spring 1982): 27–38[g]; C. C. Staley and P. Shockley-Zalabak, "Identifying Communication Competencies for the Undergraduate Organizational Communication Series," *Communication Education* 34 (April 1985): 156–161[h]; A. Austin and P. G. Ventura, "Employer Perceptions of Needed Communication Functions in Business Organizations" (Paper presented at the Eastern Communication Annual Convention, Providence, RI, 1985)[i]; C. M. Painter, "A Survey of Communication Skills Needed On-the-Job by Technical Students," *Journal of Studies in Technical Careers* 7 (Summer 1985): 153–160[j]; S. Rhodes, "Specific Listening Skills Important in Organizations," *Communication Research Bulletin* 7 (December 1985): 1–2[k]; D. B. Curtis, J. Winsor, and R. D. Stephens, "National Preferences in Business and Communication Education," *Communication Education* 38 (January 1989): 6–14[l]; B. D. Sypher, R. N. Bostrom, and J. H. Selbert, "Listening, Communication Abilities, and Success at Work," *Journal of Business Communication* 26 (Fall 1989): 293–301[m]; R. N. Conaway, "Who Trains the Trainers? Background and Resources of Trainers and Perceived Importance of Listening in Organizations" (Paper presented at the Speech Communication Association Convention, Atlanta, GA, 1991)[n]; A. S. Bednar and R. J. Olney, "Communication Needs of Recent Graduates," *The Bulletin,* December 1987, pp. 22–23[o]; S. C. Willmington, "Oral Communication Instruction for Careers in Business, Nursing, and Teaching" (Paper presented at the Speech Communication Association Convention, Chicago, IL, 1986)[p]; S. C. Willmington, "Oral Communications for a Career in Business," *The Bulletin,* June 1989, pp. 8–12[q]; K. M. Hiemstra, J. J. Schmidt, and R. L. Madison, "Certified Management Accountants: Perceptions of the Need for Communication Skills in Accounting," *The Bulletin,* December 1990, pp. 5–9[r]; J. Brownell, "Managerial Listening and Career Development in the Hospitality Industry," *Journal of the International Listening Association* 8 (1994): 31–49.[s]

130. H. A. Anderson, "Needed Research in Listening," *Elementary English* 29 (April 1954): 216.

131. Paul Tory Rankin, "Listening Ability: Its Improvement, Measurement, and Development," *Chicago Schools Journal* 12 (January, June 1930): 177–179, 417–420.

132. Speech Association of America, "Speech Education in the Public Schools," *Speech Teacher* 16 (January 1967): 79.

133. M. S. Conaway, "Listening: Learning Tool and Retention Agent," in *Improving Reading and Study Skills,* eds. A. S. Algier and K. W. Algier (San Francisco: Jossey-Bass, 1982), pp. 51–63.

134. Anderson, "Needed Research in Listening," p. 221.

135. M. C. Letton, "The Status of the Teaching of Listening," *Elementary School Journal* 57 (January 1957): 181.

136. C. T. Brown and P. W. Keller, "A Modest Proposal for Listening Training," *Quarterly Journal of Speech* 48 (December 1962): 395.

137. B. Markgraf, "Listening Pedagogy in Teacher-Training Institutions," *Journal of Communication* 12 (March 1962): 33–35.

138. F. I. Wolff, "A Pragmatic 'Sharing' Workshop in Listening Pedagogy: Who's Teaching Listening and How?" (Presentation delivered at the International Listening Association Convention, Atlanta, GA, 1980).

139. R. W. Pace and R. F. Ross, "The Basic Course in Organizational Communication," *Communication Education* 32 (October 1983): 402–412.

140. A. D. Wolvin, C. G. Coakley, and J. E. Disburg, "An Exploratory Study of Listening Instruction in Selected Colleges and Universities," *Journal of the International Listening Association* 5 (1991): 68–85.

141. A. D. Wolvin, C. G. Coakley, and J. E. Disburg, "Listening Instruction in Selected Colleges and Universities," *Journal of the International Listening Association* 6 (1992): 59–65.

142. F. I. Wolff, "A 1990 Study: Listening Instruction Trends in Randomly Selected Colleges and Universities" (Paper presented at the International Listening Association Convention, Jacksonville, FL, 1991), pp. 1–3.

143. J. H. Smith and P. H. Turner, "A Survey of Communication Department Curriculum in Four-Year Colleges and Universities," *JACA* 1 (1993): 34–49.

144. M. G. Most, "Certification Standards for Speech Communication Teachers: A Nationwide Survey," *Communication Education* 43 (July 1994): 195–204.

145. D. P. Brown, "What Is the Basic Language Skill?" *ETC* 14 (Winter 1956–1957): 118.
146. Advertisement by Sperry. Reprinted by permission of Sperry Corporation.
147. H. Anderson, "Teaching the Art of Listening," *School Review* 57 (February 1949): 66; R. G. Nichols, "Listening Instruction in the Secondary School," in *Listening: Readings*, ed. S. Duker, pp. 242–243; D. Spearritt, *Listening Comprehension—A Factorial Analysis* (Melbourne, Australia: G. W. Green and Sons, 1962), p. 3; Lundsteen, *Listening: Its Impact on Reading and the Other Language Arts*, p. xvi; C. H. Swanson, "Teachers As Listeners: An Exploration" (Paper presented at the International Listening Association Convention, San Diego, CA, 1986); A. W. Heilman, "Listening and the Curriculum," *Education* 75 (January 1955): 285–286; J. J. Lynch and B. Evans, *High School English Textbooks: A Critical Examination* (Boston: Little, Brown & Co., 1963), pp. 495–496; K. L. Brown, "Speech and Listening in Language Arts Textbooks," *Elementary English* 44 (April 1967): 336–341; P. J. Anderson, "Listening: What Do the Elementary Language Basals Teach?" (Paper presented at the International Listening Association Convention, Scottsdale, AZ, 1988).
148. J. F. Henry and S. U. Raymond, *Basic Skills in the U.S. Work Force*, pp. ii, iii, and 14.
149. "The SCANS Agenda," *Spectra*, March 1994, p. 5.
150. D. D. VanRheenen and M. H. Casmir, "The Status of State Practices in Speaking and Listening Skill Assessment: 1981–1990" (Paper presented at the Speech Communication Association Convention, Chicago, IL, 1990). In 1994, J. Litterst, D. D. VanRheenen, and M. H. Casmir updated this study in "Practices in Statewide Oral Communication Assessment: 1981–1994" (Paper presented at the Speech Communication Association Summer Conference, Alexandria, VA, 1994); however, the authors combined speaking and listening data, so separate data for listening practices are not available.
151. J. L. DiGaetani, "The Sperry Corporation and Listening: An Interview," *Business Horizons* 25 (March/April 1982): 35; D. Clutterbuck, "How Sperry Made People Listen," *Interpersonal Management* 36 (February 1981): 23; S. Lucas, "Skills: Listening Is a Learned Art," *Working Woman*, August 1983, p. 45; L. K. Steil et al., "The Sperry Story" (Presentation delivered at the International Listening Association Convention, Denver, CO, 1981); M. Kernan, "Listen . . . Now Hear This, You Aural Degenerates!" *The Washington Post*, 23 September 1980, pp. B1, B7.
152. Advertisement by Sperry. Reprinted by permission of Sperry Corporation.
153. A. D. Wolvin and C. G. Coakley, "A Survey of the Status of Listening Training in Some Fortune 500 Corporations," *Communication Education* 40 (April 1991): 152–164.
154. P. Froiland, "Who's Getting Trained?" *Training*, October 1993, pp. 53, 63.
155. Clutterbuck, "How Sperry Made People Listen," p. 23; Lucas, "Skills: Listening Is a Learned Art," p. 45.
156. R. A. Austin, "Power Listening: An Experimental Investigation of the Effects of Listening Instruction on the Listening Skills of White Collar Business Executives" (Unpublished M.A. thesis, University of Maryland, College Park, MD, 1989); M. J. Papa and E. C. Glenn, "Listening Ability and Performance with New Technology: A Case Study," *Journal of Business Communication* 25 (Fall 1988): 5–15; L. R. Smeltzer and K. W. Watson, "A Test of Instructional Strategies for Listening Improvement in a Simulated Business Setting," *Journal of Business Communication* 22 (1985): 33–42; J. E. Wasylik, L. Sussman, and R. P. Leri, "Communication Training As Perceived by Training Personnel," pp. 32–38.
157. J. D. Weinrauch and J. R. Swanda, Jr., "Examining the Significance of Listening: An Exploratory Study of Contemporary Management," *The Journal of Business Communication* 13 (February 1975): 26.
158. A. D. Wolvin and C. G. Coakley, *Listening Instruction* (Urbana, IL: ERIC Clearinghouse on Reading and Communication Skills, 1979), pp. 19–20.
159. Ibid., p. 20.

PRINCIPLES YOU WILL ENCOUNTER

- *Communication is an ongoing, dynamic, symbolic transaction involving a source, message, channel, receiver, feedback, noise, and environment.*

- *Communication is facilitated or diminished by communicator skills, knowledge, attitudes, and frame of reference; by message content, structure, and language code; by channel selection; and by environmental factors.*

- *Communication is a transactional process in which source and receiver simultaneously encode and decode messages.*

- *The effective listener*
  - *is actively involved in decoding and encoding messages*
  - *knows the influence of the communication components and variables*
  - *knows how to control these variables for effective communication*
  - *participates fully in the communication transaction*

CHAPTER 2

The Process of Communication

"To capture the essence of communication, and thus the essence of listening, we must try to visualize it as a process in which we are a source and at the same time a receiver—in which we are speaking and listening at the same time. We encode and send messages while we are decoding and receiving other messages. We are not sources, then receivers, then sources, then receivers. We are both participants involved in a communication event—affecting and affected by one another, functioning continuously and simultaneously."[1]

As human communicators, listeners interact with speakers. Since listening is an integral part of human communication, it is best to study listening behavior within the context of the *process* of communication. Scholars in the communication field have come to recognize the *process* nature of human communication, viewing it as an ongoing, dynamic interaction of components. Communication, as a process, is thus never ending in that one message may well influence yet another and serve as the stimulus for a continuation of the communication.

This chapter provides an overview of the process of human communication through the identification of components and variables that make up this complex behavior that enables individuals to link with and relate to each other. Within this communication context, listening can be viewed as a critical determinant of the process and its results. This contextual view of listening as communication should shape one's understanding of how listeners function as communicators in the transaction.

Components of Communication

As an ongoing human interaction, communication involves a number of components that make up this complex phenomena: source, message, channel, receiver, feedback, environment, and noise.

The first component is a communication **source**, a speaker who originates a message. The process begins with an original stimulus (an event, object, person, idea) that the source wishes to communicate. The source encodes this idea, sorting and selecting symbols to translate the idea into a **message** to communicate by way of verbal and nonverbal language symbols.

The encoded message is then transmitted via a communication **channel**. In face-to-face communication, the five senses—sight, sound, touch, smell, and taste—serve as the major channels for this transmission. As Americans, we use the auditory and visual channels as our primary media in most communication, whereas in other cultures touch and smell may be utilized. In our society we also make extensive use of electronic channels in telecommunication such as telephone, radio, and television.

The verbal and nonverbal messages transmitted via these channels are then received and decoded—filtered and translated into a person's language code to assign meaning—by the communication **receiver**. The receiver, in turn, responds to the source, message, and channel by encoding and sending **feedback**—the response/reaction of the receiver as perceived by the source. This feedback creates the ongoing, dynamic nature of the communication process. The source decodes, or interprets, the feedback and, ideally, adapts and adjusts the communication accordingly.

Throughout this process, the communication will be affected by two other important components. The **environment**—where the communication takes place—is one of these components. We communicate in specific settings or physical surroundings that will influence us as communicators. Temperatures, ventilation, lighting, and room size all affect the outcome of our communication.

We also are affected by **noise**—internal and external interference—throughout the system. This interference can be internal, within the communicators themselves. A person may be preoccupied with personal concerns (worried, fatigued, hungry, ill, troubled about a relationship with a supervisor) or may develop an emotional barrier in response to a word or idea presented in the message. This interference can also be external to the system such as a loud sound in the room, other people talking, simultaneous messages being sent, static in the channel, or a lack of coherency in the message. Such interference can cause a person to lose track of the message being sent.

The communication components can be depicted in a simple model that illustrates the interaction of the various parts that make up the process. (See fig. 2.1.)

source

message

channel

receiver

feedback

environment

noise

Understanding the Listening Process

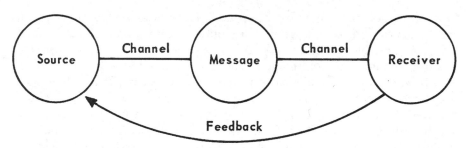

ENVIRONMENT

FIGURE 2.1.
Simple Model of Communication.

Communication Variables

Critical to the effectiveness of communication as a human process are variables in the system—factors that facilitate or diminish the outcomes of the communication.[2] Variables such as the following can affect the different components of the communication process:

Communication skills
Communication knowledge
Communication attitudes
Communication and frame of reference
Message content and structure
Language code and symbolism
Channel selection
Environment

Communication Skills

One key variable that affects the communication source and receiver is the communication **skills**—ability—that the communicators bring to the process. Skills in sending and receiving messages are learned by humans from early infancy; they include the ability to analyze and adapt to various communicators and communication situations. Abilities in encoding messages may incorporate verbal language facility, skill in structuring messages, and such nonverbal skills as vocal dynamics and physical expressiveness. Decoding skills, which will be the focus of much of this book, may include the individual's attention span, willingness to listen, vocabulary level, and listening effort.

    These elements are essential not only to the sending of messages but also to the sending of feedback, or responses to messages. Substantial training in speaking and listening skills can help communicators improve their effectiveness with these communication skills.

skills

Communication Knowledge

knowledge

Communication skills combine with communicator **knowledge**—information and understanding—to influence the entire process. Communicators, both source and receiver, should know about the subject matter under discussion, and they should share information about the verbal and nonverbal language code used to convey the messages. Communicators should know about message structure and about environmental control (how to regulate temperature, decrease noise, etc.) in order to communicate more precisely. It is also helpful for communicators to know about channel selection: how to choose the most appropriate medium to convey a message or feedback. The more extensive the knowledge about the communication itself and about the material to be communicated, the more effective the communicators should be.

Communication Attitudes

attitudes

Likewise, communicators share **attitudes**—predispositions to respond positively or negatively. These may be shared attitudes toward each other as communicators. For example, a speaker may not care for a group of union representatives he or she must address, or a listener may be too supportive of a particular political candidate to overlook major flaws in the candidate's platform.

These positive and negative attitudes affect us as communicators in our orientation toward the message as well. As listeners, we may be so opposed to foreign aid programs, for instance, that we refuse to accept the basic thesis of a message by an official from the Agency for International Development. Similarly, a manager may be asked to brief employees on a new company procedure that he or she does not believe is the most efficient method. This attitude, of course, will carry through in his or her presentation.

Attitudes can affect us as communicators as well. Considerable research in the communication field indicates that a substantial number of people suffer communication apprehension, that is, anxiety about communicating with others. Speakers who experience stage fright may have negative attitudes toward their own abilities as communicators. Moreover, these negative attitudes certainly can influence our self-concepts as listeners. Many people believe they are not effective listeners, and, consequently, they are *not* effective listeners. But this negative self-concept may stem from the negative messages we hear as listeners during our formative years: "Be quiet and listen," "You're not listening to me," "Don't you ever listen?" We seldom hear positive, reinforcing messages about our listening behavior.

Positive and negative attitudes extend to other components of the communication process. We may dislike a particular classroom and thus have difficulty paying attention to instruction in that room, or we may have negative attitudes toward certain communication channels. There are people, for instance, who cannot talk into telephone answering machines. They hang up to avoid the trauma of "At the sound of the tone, please leave your message!"

Communication and Frame of Reference

The attitudes, knowledge, and communication skills of communicators, both speakers and listeners, contribute to the **frame of reference**—personal perspective—of the communicators. This frame of reference consists of background, life experiences, social-cultural context, and everything else that makes one a unique individual. All these elements create the **perceptual filter** through which we receive stimuli, send messages, and relate to the world around us. In short, the sum total of all that makes up our being as humans becomes part of our encoding and decoding as communicators.

frame of reference

perceptual filter

The perceptual filter serves as our screen through which we process the stimulus we are receiving. Our *physical and psychological states* at any given time will affect our perceptions. A person who is depressed or who does not feel well, for example, undoubtedly perceives messages more negatively than an individual who is psychologically sound and physically well. Likewise, an individual's *sensory acuity* affects these perceptions. A person who has suffered sensory loss (such as blindness) must rely more on the other senses to perceive the world. Furthermore, our *expectations* will shape our perceptions. Those who study perception stress the old adage, "We see and hear what we want to see and hear." If we are anticipating that a message will carry a specific point of view, then we tend to perceive that message to have that viewpoint. As a result, each person's perceptual filter will lead him or her to perceive a message differently from others. McCroskey describes this influence of perception in communication: "People tend to perceive what they want to perceive or what they expect to perceive, whether or not such perceptions are in accord with what other people might consider reality."[3]

A classic Japanese movie, *Rashomon*, illustrates the principle. The film is based on the sixteenth-century Japanese folk tale in which a bandit murders a traveling nobleman and rapes the nobleman's wife. Revealed through flashbacks, each character's description of the incident places that character in the best possible light. Each interpretation is subject to the individual's frame of reference. The bandit and the nobleman describe their mortal combat in heroic terms, while the lady describes the fight as two bumbling sissies quarrelling and her husband being accidentally killed. Likewise, the lady describes her role as a loyal wife defending her husband, while the nobleman characterizes her as being flirtatious and self-absorbed. Each character, then, has his or her own view of the reality of the events.

Like these characters, listeners make interpretations constantly throughout the communication process. These perceptual interpretations, based as they are on our frame of reference, can lead to major difficulties in communicating and understanding messages.

Message Content and Structure

Just as key factors relating to the source and the receiver will affect the outcome of the communication, so, too, will variables of the message itself have an influence on the communication.

The message is composed of **content**—the ideas and the point of view that the communicator wishes to express. These very ideas, structured and presented by means of verbal and nonverbal language code, may or may not be consistent with the attitudes and the knowledge of the receiver. Consequently, it may be necessary for the source to adjust and adapt the message more satisfactorily to meet the needs of the listener. Norman Thomas, six times the Socialist candidate for the American presidency, presented in his Socialist platform messages that were not consistent with basic democratic ideals held by most Americans. As a result, Thomas's fundamental messages were never acceptable to the majority of the voters.

message structure

The **message structure**—arrangement of content—likewise influences the understanding and acceptance of the ideas. Americans, brought up with a Western philosophical orientation, are accustomed to deductive structure consisting of generalizations leading to a specific conclusion. (Good listeners pay attention to the material. You pay attention to the material. Therefore, you are a good listener.) Persons raised under the influence of Eastern philosophical thought, on the other hand, may not be so accustomed to a deductive structure of messages. Whereas American communicators are trained to develop a message with one structure, Chinese communicators may give a different structure to a message:

American Message Structure		Chinese Message Structure	
Introduction	(secure listeners' attention through a variety of means)	Ki	(introduce by offering an observation of a concrete reality)
Central Point	(state main idea)	Sho	(tell a story)
Body	(state and discuss each point used to establish the central point)	Ten	(make a shift or change in which a new topic or aspect is brought into the message)
Conclusion	(summarize points discussed)	Ketsu	(gather loose ends, a "nonconclusion")
		Yo-In	(present a last point to think about, which does not necessarily relate)

The Chinese communicator, in contrast to the communicator using the American format, allows the audience to draw its own conclusion; a central point is not presented in such a structure.

Language Code and Symbolism

language code

The message structure, stemming from the cognitive orientation of the person, extends to the **language code**—verbal and nonverbal symbols. The language code, a key variable in effective communication, is central to the entire process. Speakers encode and listeners decode messages based on their understanding of the verbal and nonverbal symbols that are available to them as communicators.

Indispensable to the comprehension of the verbal message, of course, is the sharing of common language symbols. Through the course of time and accepted usage, we have come to associate certain meanings with words. However, the words themselves are empty representations or symbols of the stimulus we have chosen to communicate.[4] Thus, the word *chair* is a collection of letters arbitrarily assigned to that piece of furniture on which we sit; the word itself represents the chair, much as a road map is used to represent the freeway on which we travel to work.

Because we use our verbal language to represent *symbolically* what we intend to communicate, communicators are well advised to remember that it *is* a process of **symbolism**—a process of representing our concepts and objects with words. It is foolish to react to a symbol, a word, as if it were the referent itself. Remembering that it is a symbolic process is particularly important for listeners responding to highly volatile messages, for instance to hate rhetoric. We need to set aside our biases and prejudices while decoding communications and to remember that speakers are using words to represent symbolically their ideas.

symbolism

The study of semantics has been concerned with the human use of language as symbols to communicate meaning. It is clear that often we cannot simply transfer our intended meaning to another person through a carefully worded message. The message must be one in which the other communicator can share some common elements to interpret the message and assign his or her own meaning to it. This principle is graphically illustrated in a Hitachi America, Ltd. ad. (See fig. 2.2.)

"The ability to use language," Condon reminds us, "means the ability to transfer something of experience into symbols and *through the symbolic medium to share experience.*"[5] The late semanticist S. I. Hayakawa cautions that "the habitual confusion of symbols with things symbolized, whether on the part of individuals or societies, is serious enough at all levels of culture to provide a perennial human problem."[6] To avoid such confusion, semanticists remind us that "words don't mean; people do." This reminder stresses the point that the effective communicator does not lose sight of the representative nature of verbal language; rather, he or she recognizes that it is the individual's interpretation of the message that gives verbal symbols their meanings.

Messages are transmitted not only by symbolic verbal codes but also by nonverbal language, which includes everything but the word itself. Communicators, then, ought to be sensitive to such nonverbal dimensions as vocal inflections and vocal quality; gestures and physical animation; eye contact; and even a person's physical appearance and dress. All these elements communicate messages about a speaker's emotional state, self-concept, and attitudes toward the communication itself.

The nonverbal and verbal messages are presented via the sensory channels: sound, sight, smell, touch, and taste. Our sensory acuity will greatly influence the effectiveness of these channels. A sensory block can, of course, eliminate the use of a particular conduit and perhaps require persons to

Hitachi's wide-ranging technologies in communication (from left to right): optical fibers, image signal processor, advanced telephone exchange system, satellite communication, and machine translation system.

FIGURE 2.2.
Advertisement by Hitachi America, Ltd.

compensate through other channels. A deaf or hearing-impaired person, for instance, must make extensive use of visual communication channels in order to lip-read, use sign language, and read the nonverbal cues of the communicator.

A recognized example of a deaf individual who compensates through the visual channel is Heather Whitestone, Miss America 1994. During her first news conference, Ms. Whitestone instructed reporters, "If you have a question, talk slowly and look at me directly, and I'll do my best." To photographers who snapped her picture while she was trying to read a

COMMUNICATION

Communication is not simply sending a message…it is creating true understanding— swiftly, clearly and precisely.

"I know he's trying to tell me something: but what does he really mean?" In our world of proliferating technologies and new terminology, this kind of question is asked a lot. Here is what we are doing about it.

Hitachi's scientists and technicians' long-term goal is to break the language barrier. They are diligently at work today on an array of projects that will vastly improve the communications of tomorrow.

For example, we've made tremendous progress on a system to translate Japanese into English.

This system can be used to translate various scientific/technical papers and machinery/equipment manuals. Special "glossaries" can be developed to adapt it for fields as diverse as medicine, electronics and aeronautics. Further development could lead to automatic telephone translation or even portable verbal translators for travelers.

In addition to the machine translation system, Hitachi's research specialists are also developing advanced transmission systems that send your phone calls or business data across great distances using hair-thin optical fibers and laser beams. They are also working on other new methods of communications, such as advanced telephone exchange systems, satellite communication systems, TV conferences, and so forth.

At the root of much of this is our highly advanced computer technology: because Hitachi is producing some of the fastest, largest-capacity systems available today.

We link technology to human needs. We believe that Hitachi's advanced technologies will result in systems and products that are functionally sophisticated but easy to use. Our goal in communications—and transportation, energy and consumer electronics as well—is to build products and systems that will improve the quality of life the world around.

@ HITACHI

Hitachi, Ltd. Tokyo, Japan

American Sign Language is a full language taking place through the visual channel.

reporter's lips, she admonished, "Hold up for a minute. You keep flashing, and it makes it hard for me to see his lips. Can you hold off for a minute?"[7]

Channel Selection

The effectiveness of a particular conduit at a particular time is influenced not only by the communicator's sensory acuity but also by the **channel selection**—choice of medium. As we have noted, a sensitive communicator will carefully consider decisions as to when to place a phone call, when to conduct face-to-face interviews, or when to send a memo. As listeners, we may respond consciously or unconsciously to these channels. Some individuals may have an aversion to the telephone, for example, as an invasion of privacy. Indeed, the telephone can be obtrusive. A person standing in line at a ticket window may have to wait while the clerk handles telephone calls, which take precedence when the callers interrupt the clerk.

As communicators, we probably are not very sophisticated when it comes to understanding the importance of channel selection. A manager should know when to send a memo, use a telephone call, conduct a person-to-person interview, or post a notice on a bulletin board, in order to reach employees most effectively. Parents should understand when the use of touch can be reinforcing to a child, when to put a note on the refrigerator door, and whether to discuss issues at the dinner table or in private. Likewise, relaying messages through another person requires special consideration.

Environment

The channels we select relate to the **environment**—physical setting—in which we communicate. Again, elements in the setting can enhance or can detract from the communication. We can exercise some control over the lighting, ventilation, seating arrangements, and even room colors, but a failure in electric power, for instance, could darken the room and end the communication.

It is clear, therefore, that communication is a complex process, made up of many interrelated factors that serve to facilitate or to impair the effectiveness of the process itself. All communicators within a particular situation should recognize what is operating within the process and should work to enhance participation. Too frequently, we tend to sit back and require the speaker to assume full responsibility for the communication. Effective communication, however, is a *shared*, meaningful, active process that imposes upon speakers and listeners alike equal responsibilities for the outcome.

environment

Communication as a Simultaneous Process

Although all of these variables have an influence—positive or negative—on the outcome of the communication, we can work to maintain some control over them to facilitate the process. Throughout our communication efforts, it is helpful to us, as listeners, to keep in perspective the fact that communication is *symbolic* and that it is a *process*. As we have noted, our language system comprises symbolic words and nonverbal dimensions that we use to *represent* the ideas we are expressing. We are constantly involved in a process of encoding and decoding messages in a fairly simultaneous sequence. We really function as source and receiver at the same time, sending messages and receiving/decoding feedback from the listener. The listener, in turn, receives/decodes the message and simultaneously encodes/sends feedback messages.[8] This **simultaneous process** suggests that, ideally, we ought to view the source and the receiver as communicators rather than separating the two roles.[9] Thus, a model of the communication process might more realistically depict this simultaneous role-taking. (See fig. 2.3.)[10]

simultaneous process

This perspective of communication as the simultaneous interaction of the roles of source and receiver has come to be known as a **transactional perspective**. This view implies that communication is more than the interaction of a source and a receiver and that we function as communicators in the process by encoding and decoding the messages. This simultaneous process implies that we do not function as just a source or a receiver but, rather, that we perform both functions within most communication transactions. Smith and Williamson offer a description of the transactional model of communication:

transactional perspective

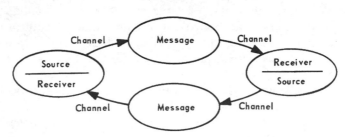

FIGURE 2.3.
Transactional Model of Communication.

> Both persons in the communication situation are participating simultaneously. They are mutually perceiving each other; and both persons (not just the sender) are making adjustments to messages exchanged within the transaction. Both parties are simultaneously listening to each other; they are simultaneously and mutually engaged in the process of creating meaning in a relationship.[11]

John Stewart, a proponent of the transactional perspective in interpersonal communication, emphasizes the meaning center of the process:

> From a transactional perspective, human communicating is a process of meaning-creating rather than idea- or message-sending. When you're communicating, you're not transmitting your ideas to others but evoking their own ideas or meanings. . . . Consequently, although the words you use are important, your communication is also significantly affected by the other person's mood, needs, goals, attitudes, assumptions, past experiences, etc.[12]

Thus, as communicators, we constantly use our communication skills, knowledge, attitudes, and frame of reference to function in the entire process of understanding verbal and nonverbal messages.

If you communicate with your professor in the classroom, for example, you may receive his or her lecture on intrapersonal communication and, at the same time, send him or her feedback through your nonverbal language that you agree with, approve of, or support what the professor is telling the class about intrapersonal communication. As the professor develops the lecture, he or she should read the feedback he or she is receiving from you and your classmates and adapt the lecture accordingly.

Although such a view of the communication process is an important perspective for understanding the complexities of our roles as communicators, it is necessary to study the communication skills involved from a more distinct source and/or receiver perspective. And it is the focus of this book to examine the listening skills involved in the receiving process.

Within most communication transactions, we simultaneously serve as sources and receivers.

Implications for the Listener

The transactional perspective of the process of communication is a useful perspective for the listener. It is helpful to remember that as a communicator, the listener is actively involved in receiving and sending (decoding and encoding) messages. While we listen to the verbal and the nonverbal messages of a speaker, we send verbal and nonverbal messages back to our communication partner. We send these messages through our perceptual filters: the frame of reference that comprises our background, experience, knowledge, attitudes, and communication skills. These variables affect our efficiency and our effectiveness in decoding and encoding the messages as we handle them simultaneously.

Rhodes describes the transaction: "As I listen, I simultaneously 'speak' to you with my nonverbal responses, and periodically provide you with verbal responses. As you speak, you simultaneously 'listen' to the nonverbal messages, periodically tune in to the verbal messages, and continuously adapt your communicative behaviors according to your assessment of the extent to which you feel you have been understood."[13] At the same time, Rhodes argues, both communicators listen to themselves. If neither communicator listens, understanding or misunderstanding or agreement or disagreement cannot be communicated. "Any single message, then," concludes Rhodes, "reflects only one perspective, not a perspective shared by both of the participants."[14] Thus, listening is a relational process in the sense that communication occurs with listeners and speakers in transactional relationships.

To be effective in this transactional relationship, the listener must develop a clear understanding of his or her frame of reference to know what perceptual filters are influencing responses to messages. Moreover, the effective listener needs to develop the necessary listening skills to decode the messages, listen to self, and encode feedback messages in the communication transaction. Effective feedback is as vital to true communication as is an effective message.

It is evident that the listener assumes the most important, involved role as a communicator in this transactional view. In the old, linear model of communication, the speaker essentially pushed buttons to get a listener response, while the interactional view provides for the use of feedback from the receiver. The transactional approach, however, describes the listener as integral to the process, participating fully *throughout* the communication, not just as one who responds to messages. It is apparent, also, that this full participation of the communicator extends to participation on an intrapersonal—that is, within the self—communication level. While engaged in communication with another, we likewise are engaged in communicating with ourselves—listening to ourselves as we communicate.

Summary

In this chapter, we have examined the components of the communication process: source, message, channel, receiver, feedback, noise, and environment. These elements are affected by variables that facilitate or distort the communication process, depending largely on how effectively the communicators are able to control them. Such variables as communicator skills, attitudes, and knowledge combine with message structure, as well as with code and channel dimensions, to complicate the communication process. Throughout, it is useful to retain the perspective that communication is symbolic (that we use verbal and nonverbal language to symbolically *represent* our ideas) and that it is an ongoing, transactional *process* in which source and receiver simultaneously encode and decode messages.

Suggested Activities

1. Design your own model of the communication process. Incorporate the components of communication and the variables that you think are essential to the process. Attempt to illustrate the simultaneous nature of the source and receiver functions within the process.
2. Illustrate the process of communication with a real-life situation involving an incident in which communication variables played a major role in the outcome of the communication.
3. Make a list of barriers to effective communication. Illustrate these obstacles with examples from your own communication experience.
4. Reflect on *your* frame of reference and attempt to identify those features (education, experience, individuals, etc.) that have had the greatest impact on shaping your frame of reference. Recall an experience in which you and another person had difficulty as communicators because your frames of reference were so different.

Notes

1. S. C. Rhodes, "Listening: A Relational Process," in *Perspectives on Listening*, eds. A. D. Wolvin and C. G. Coakley (Norwood, NJ: Ablex, 1993), p. 225.
2. For a detailed discussion of variables influencing the communication process, you might like to read D. K. Berlo, *The Process of Communication* (NY: Holt, Rinehart and Winston, 1960).
3. J. C. McCroskey, "Human Information Processing and Diffusion," in *Speech Communication Behavior*, eds. L. L. Barker and R. J. Kibler (Englewood Cliffs, NJ: Prentice-Hall, 1971), p. 172.
4. This is the perspective held by semanticists, who argue that "words don't mean; people do." See, for instance, S. I. Hayakawa, *Language in Thought and Action* (NY: Harcourt, Brace and World, 1949).
5. J. Condon, *Semantics and Communication* (NY: Macmillan Publishing Company, 1975), p. 9.

6. Hayakawa, *Language in Thought and Action*, p. 30.
7. T. Barrientos, "Miss America Wants to Be a Role Model," *Santa Rosa Press Democrat*, 25 September 1994, p. D6.
8. An early proponent of this view was W. Schramm in "How Communication Works," *The Process and Effects of Mass Communication* (Urbana, IL: University of Illinois Press, 1955), pp. 3–26.
9. For a discussion of this perspective, see R. M. Berko, A. D. Wolvin, and D. R. Wolvin, *Communicating: A Social and Career Focus*, 6th ed. (Boston: Houghton Mifflin Co., 1995), pp. 30–31.
10. One of the earliest communication scholars to develop a model of communication from a transactional perspective was W. Schramm in "How Communication Works," *The Process and Effects of Mass Communication*, pp. 4–8.
11. D. Smith and K. Williamson, *Interpersonal Communication* (Dubuque, IA: Wm. C. Brown Publishers, 1981), p. 16.
12. J. Stewart, *Bridges Not Walls* (Reading, MA: Addison-Wesley, 1973), p. 16.
13. S. C. Rhodes, "A Study of Effective and Ineffective Listening Dyads Using the Systems Theory Principle of Entropy," *Journal of the International Listening Association* 1 (Spring 1987): 32–33.
14. Ibid., p.33.

- *Listening, a distinct human behavior, is an integral part of the total communication process. Wolvin and Coakley's structural definition of listening, depicted by the sequential process model of listening, is that* listening is the process of receiving, attending to, and assigning meaning to aural and visual stimuli.

- *Aural stimuli are involved in the act of listening.*

- *Visual stimuli, when present, can assist listeners in assigning meaning to senders' messages.*

- *The structural components or processes encompassed in the listening act are receiving, attending to, and assigning meaning to aural and visual stimuli.*

- *Receiving is the physiological process of hearing aural stimuli (or, when applicable, seeing visual stimuli).*

- *Among the factors that weaken the receiving process or hearing are otitis media, tinnitus, otosclerosis, sensorineural impairment, presbycusis, sociocusis, binaural hearing, masking, and auditory fatigue.*

- *Attention is selective, energetic, and fluctuating.*

- *Assigning meaning is the process of interpreting or understanding stimuli that are received and attended to.*

- *Assigning meaning involves the listener's categorical system and cognitive schema to process and interpret the messages received.*

- *Listeners' personal frames of references and perceptual filters, limited knowledge, narrow experiences, inadequate vocabularies, rigidity in categorical assignment or cognitive schema, and emotional triggers can all cause listeners to assign incorrect meanings to messages.*

- *Responding covertly is inherent in all aspects of the listening process.*

- *The effective listener*
    - *knows what aspects are encompassed in the total listening process*
    - *takes proper care of the hearing mechanism*
    - *concentrates attention energy on one stimulus instead of many*
    - *engages frequently in elaborative rehearsal*
    - *increases concentration ability and length of attention span through self-motivation, self-discipline, and practice*
    - *strives to attach meaning as similar as possible to that intended by the message sender by recognizing that meanings reside in people rather than in words and by assigning meaning from the speaker's frame of reference rather than from his or her own frame of reference*
    - *seeks out information that is not only consistent but also inconsistent with his or her predispositions*
    - *is aware of his or her emotional triggers and endeavors to control their effect on his or her listening effectiveness*
    - *engages in numerous strategies to minimize errors in meaning assignment*
    - *responds covertly*
    - *furthers the communication process by responding overtly*

CHAPTER 3

The Process of Listening

Marty ran into her friend, Janet, at the local Safeway. Janet unloaded all sorts of problems that she had encountered at work, and then she started in on how difficult it is to deal with her significant other. "If only he'd just listen to me," she pleaded.

One of the messages that irritate us as listening scholars is the admonition, "Just listen." People use this to tell others to listen to them, and they don't realize how grating (much like a fingernail scraping a chalkboard) that can be to those of us who study the complexities of listening behavior. As we will see in this chapter, listening—one of the most complex of all human behaviors—is a process that cannot be reduced simply to "Just listen." Rather, listening is an active, involving human behavior that takes a great deal of work. After you have read through this chapter's technical descriptions of what is involved in listening, we hope that you, too, will be convinced that you cannot "Just listen."

Communication is an ongoing, transactional process involving both the sending and the receiving of messages. Although in this chapter we will focus specifically on the receptive aspect of the communication process, we must keep in mind that even though listening is, in itself, a process, it is also an integral part of the total communication process.

Listening as a Distinct Behavior

Basic to any attempt to define listening is the following question: Is listening a distinct behavior that is separate from other intellectual behaviors?

Several factor studies—including those conducted by Caffrey; Caffrey and Smith; Karlin; and Hanley—have provided evidence that listening is indeed a distinct activity.[1] However, the factor analysis that has given decisive support to the theory that there is a separate listening factor was performed by Spearritt in Australia.[2] In his research, Spearritt tested more than 400 sixth graders in ten schools in Melbourne. He used thirty-four different tests to measure the reasoning, verbal comprehension, attention, auditory resistance, memory, and listening comprehension of these students. The factor analysis of the results of all of these tests isolated a disparate listening comprehension factor, distinct from the students' performance in reasoning, verbal comprehension, attention, auditory resistance, and memory.[3]

The studies that have isolated a listening component, particularly the study by Spearritt, illustrate that "listening is a kind of human behavior in itself, separate from reading, from memory, and from other intellectual behaviors, although dependent on them as they are probably dependent on it."[4] Since listening is a distinct function, it is useful to define this activity.

A Definition of Listening

The definition of listening continues to be in the developing stages. Because listening is such a complex human behavior, because listening as a covert behavior is difficult to investigate, and because research in listening is in an exploratory state, conceptualizing the process of listening continues to occupy the attention of listening scholars throughout the world.

Meanwhile, researchers have considered a number of listening definitions and conceptualizations. One of the earliest definitions, by Tucker (1925), conceptualized listening as "an analysis of the impressions resulting from concentration where an effort of will is required."[5] Rankin (1926), who was among the first to focus on auditory listening, defined listening as "the ability to understand spoken language."[6] Later scholars became more specific regarding the elements or processes involved in listening. For example, Lewis (1958) included four elements in his definition of listening: "the process of hearing, identifying, understanding, and interpreting spoken language."[7] Likewise, more recent listening scholars have included a number of elements and have focused on auditory stimuli in their listening definitions. Floyd's conceptualization of listening is illustrative: "a process that includes hearing, attending to, understanding, evaluating, and responding to spoken messages."[8]

As listening scholars grapple with a conceptual understanding of what is involved in the process or listening, it is apparent that differences and even confusion arise when one attempts to define listening. Too frequently, it is assumed to be synonymous with hearing even though, as we observed in chapter 1, this assumption is erroneous. Listening goes beyond hearing. Attempting to be more precise, Brown proposed that the term *auding* be used to designate the comprehension of verbal messages: ". . . the gross process of listening to, recognizing, and interpreting spoken symbols."[9] While other scholars have used the term, it has not become the term of choice to describe this complex communication process.

Listening researchers in the International Listening Association[10] have made periodic attempts to define more specifically the listening process. One such attempt will be part of a 1995 research conference devoted to conceptualizing listening as a base for coordinated research efforts on the part of many scholars in the field. Meanwhile, listening scholar Lundsteen describes the problem: "Defining listening is a challenge. There are many unknowns in this problem calling for creativity and commitment. . . ."[11]

Wolvin-Coakley Definition and Model of Listening

It is apparent that *listening* is an elusive concept. However, the progress that listening scholars have made in understanding the process is reflected in their definitions. Having carefully analyzed these definitions, we have chosen to define listening as **the process of receiving, attending to, and assigning meaning to aural and visual stimuli**. This structural definition is depicted as a sequential process in the model shown in fig. 3.1.

the process of receiving, attending to, and assigning meaning to aural and visual stimuli

This model illustrates the process of listening, or the decoding of the stimulus through the auditory *and* visual senses. As you study the model, keep in mind that throughout the listening process our listening is enhanced or diminished by the efficiency of the sensory system and by the listening objectives that we set for ourselves. Indeed, many variables affect our efficiency or inefficiency as listeners; these variables are reviewed in chapter 4.

You should first note in the model that it contains two separate, conical-shaped parts: the listening cone (the upper cone) and the feedback cone (the lower cone). The listening (upper) cone is wider at the top and narrower at the bottom to indicate that a given stimulus (aural or visual) can be interpreted in as many ways as there are listeners. Since the assignment of meaning is a very personal matter, an individual will limit the meaning to fit his or her own schema or categories stored in the cortex. The feedback (lower) cone, on the other hand, is narrower at the top and wider at the bottom. This sizing illustrates that if a listener chooses to respond overtly, the listener—who thus becomes the communication source— draws on his or her personal schema or categories to encode the message and then sends a feedback stimulus that is open to varied interpretations by various receivers.

You should observe that the listening (upper) cone contains the three components that we consider integral to listening: receiving, attending, and assigning meaning. These three components, which are separate but interrelated processes, are portrayed as overlapping to stress their intricate interaction.

You should also notice that a cylinder runs through the core of the listening cone. This cylinder represents the processes of remembering and covertly responding. Listeners remember the stimulus as they run it

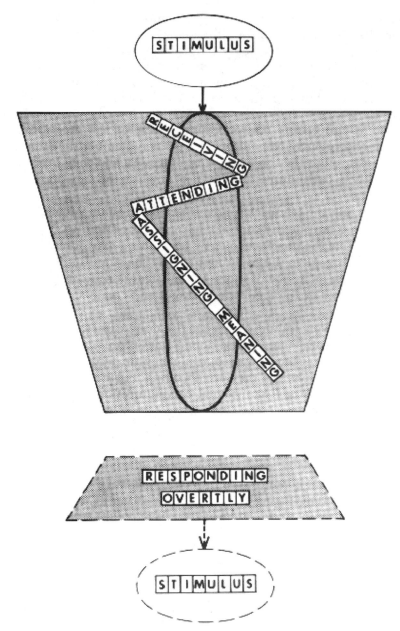

Figure 3.1.
Wolvin-Coakley Model of the Listening Process.

Understanding the Listening Process

through the three listening processes, and they probably respond covertly to the stimulus as they use it while they are decoding the stimulus.

Notice, too, that on the lower feedback (or overt response) cone, broken lines outline the cone and surround the stimulus. The broken lines show that the process of overtly responding may or may not occur when listeners engage in the listening process, whereas the solid lines in the upper listening cone illustrate three processes that must occur. The stimulus indicates that an overt response is a second message. If listeners send feedback, they then become the sources of the feedback messages and thus create a different stimulus in the process.

The last important aspect is the dotted lines that run diagonally throughout both cones. These dotted lines represent the perceptual filters through which listeners operate while they are decoding and through which sources operate while they are encoding. Furthermore, the dotted lines serve to emphasize that the total communication process is very personal and highly complex.

Stimuli Involved in Listening

Two general types of stimuli are involved in the act of listening. **Aural stimuli** consist of verbal data (phonemes, or language sounds, and words), vocal data (voice cues, such as increased volume and lowered pitch), and nonlinguistic data (such as sounds of a smoke alarm or doorbell). **Visual stimuli** could be a wink, slumping posture, or head nod. These stimuli serve as the triggers for listening.

aural stimuli

visual stimuli

While most of the definitions of listening used in the field to date focus on listening to aural stimuli, we stress that visual stimuli are also an important part of listening communication. Their importance to assigning meaning cannot be ignored when we consider Birdwhistell's findings that spoken words account for no more than 30 to 35 percent of meanings in social interactions and Mehrabian's estimates that as much as 93 percent of the total meaning of a feeling message may stem from nonverbal cues.[12] Reviewing the literature on listening and visual communication, Sewell concludes that "the visual aspect of listening has been overlooked in the majority of our research, and it is time to include it in our thinking, our models, and our research on the listening process."[13]

Components Encompassed in Listening

Three elements—**receiving, attending, and assigning meaning**—are encompassed in the listening act. These three components of listening, as depicted in our definition of listening, illustrate the intricate, complex nature of listening behavior. For the reader to better understand this human communication function, it is useful to look in detail at each of the listening components and to examine the roles of remembering and responding in the listening process. This thorough review of the elements of listening draws, of necessity, on research in many fields, including listening, communication, psychology, and physiology.[14]

receiving, attending, and assigning meaning

Component 1: Receiving

The first component—receiving—refers to the physiological process of hearing and/or seeing aural and/or visual stimuli including phonemes, words, vocal cues, nonlinguistic sounds, and nonverbal visual cues. This physiological process, often mistaken for listening itself, is the foundation for listening behavior.

vision

The Seeing Process.   The seeing process begins with light rays—reflected from an object—falling on the cornea in the front of the eye. (See fig. 3.2). The cornea is made up of tough, transparent tissue with no blood vessels. The rays then pass through the liquid aqueous humor contained in the anterior chamber directly behind the cornea. The rays proceed through the lens and the vitreous humor behind the lens. The cornea and the lens are separated by the iris, which contains the pupil, an opening that can vary in diameter from approximately 2 to 8 millimeters. The constriction of the pupil can improve the quality of the image formed and increase the depth of focus of the eye.

Once the light rays pass through the lens, they fall on the retina, which is the innermost part of the eyeball. The back of the retina, which acts as a photographic plate for the eye, contains the receptors that are sensitive to light. To reach these receptors, the rays pass back and forth across the surface of the retina, containing the optic nerve fibers.

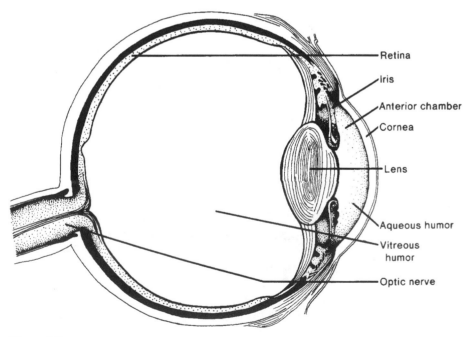

Figure 3.2.
Anatomy of the Human Eye.

The optic nerve fibers pass through the back of the eye to the optic thalamus (a station through which fibers pass) and on to the visual cortex, the visual center of the brain, where the nerve fibers are formed into images. These fibers are set into stimulation throughout the system by the light rays.[15]

Care of the Seeing Process.   Care of the eye requires regular eye checkups, especially for those who may risk such disorders as **glaucoma** (fluid pressure inside the eye) or **cataracts** (a cloudy or opaque area in the lens of the eye). The National Eye Institute estimates that as many as two million adult Americans suffer from glaucoma, a disorder that usually begins during middle age or after.[16] Cataracts frequently are the result of aging and usually occur after the age of fifty.[17] A third major cause of vision loss is **macular degeneration**, a deterioration of the retina that leads to the progressive loss of central vision. This disease is often inherited and is the leading cause of blindness in people between the ages of 45 and 74.[18] Vision specialists emphasize that adults should recognize that most people over the age of 65 need eyeglasses or contact lenses. This need results from the aging process that leads to the gradual weakening of the ability to focus on near objects—presbyopia—which can begin as early as the age of forty.[19]

While eyeglasses and contact lenses are the standard treatment for visual impairments, some individuals who suffer from a loss of central vision may get help in the future with an enhancement system that incorporates a headset with tiny video cameras. Much less expensive low-tech, hand-held magnifiers are presently available.[20]

The Hearing Process.   The process of hearing is complicated by the intricacies of the hearing mechanism. Sound waves are received by the ear and transmitted to the brain. The **outer ear** (see fig. 3.3), which consists of the pinna and the canal, serves to direct the sound waves into the hearing mechanism. In humans the pinna, or the prominent part of the outer ear, serves only this purpose, whereas in other forms of animals, the pinna—having the ability to move—can play a greater role in detecting and directing sounds. The external (auditory) canal of the human outer ear is a passage that may be a bit over one inch in length. It contains hairs and wax to protect the tympanic membrane (eardrum) from penetration by dirt and objects.

The **middle ear** connects the eardrum with the ossicular chain that contains the smallest bones in the body: the malleus (hammer), the incus (anvil), and the stapes (stirrup). These bones connect the eardrum to the opening of the inner ear, or the oval window. The middle ear also includes the Eustachian tube, which serves to equalize air pressure.

The **inner ear** serves as the sensory organ for balance and as the final organ for hearing. The balance results from the vestibular apparatus containing the utricle, saccule, and semicircular canals. The hearing part of the inner ear is the cochlea, which resembles a snail shell. The entire inner ear is filled with fluid. The cochlear duct, containing this fluid, includes the organ of Corti, which is the end organ of hearing. This organ consists of four or five rows of hair cells that connect with nerve fibers that run into the center

glaucoma

cataracts

macular degeneration

outer ear

middle ear

inner ear

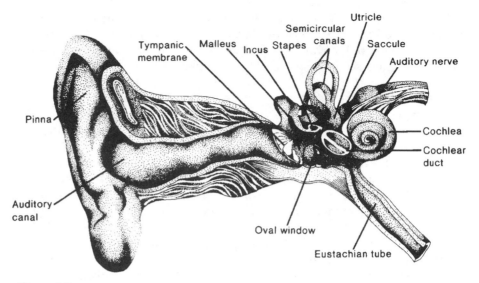

Figure 3.3.
Anatomy of the Human Ear.

of the cochlea and form the cochlear branch of the VIIIth, or auditory, nerve. This branch joins the vestibular branch, and the VIIIth nerve proceeds to the brain stem and the cerebral cortex.

Normally, we hear by air conduction because most sounds are airborne and the air conduction mechanism is more sensitive than the mechanism of bone conduction. The sound waves, channeled through the external canal, set the eardrum into vibration. The ossicular chain, connected by the hammer to the eardrum, is then set into vibration. The three tiny bones of the ossicular chain vibrate as a unit and produce a rocking motion of the stapes in the oval window, matching the sound waves of the air to that of the fluid. The fluid of the oval window, transmitted through the cochlear duct, causes the round window to bulge outward. This bulging leads to movement of the membrane, initiating nerve impulses carried to the cochlear portion of the VIIIth nerve and then to the cerebral cortex, which hears the vibrations set in motion on the eardrum.

The vibrations in the cochlea are then converted to electrical impulses that lead to a release of a chemical that "fires" the fibers within the acoustic nerve and conveys the signal to the brain. The ear responds to a band of frequencies—the number of times a sound wave vibrates in a second, measured by hertz (Hz)—and to intensity—the pressure the sound waves exert on surfaces, measured by decibels (dB). Normal conversational speech is in the range of 400 to 4000 Hz and 60 dB.[21]

Some Causes of Hearing Impairment.   The complex process of hearing, which may never be fully understood by scientists, is made even more complicated by malfunctions *in* or *of* the hearing mechanism. The National Institutes of Health estimates that more than 28 million Americans suffer hearing loss, ranging from profound deafness to a loss of particular tones.[22] These staggering statistics suggest that one out of every nine Americans is hearing-impaired. Hearing impairment results from any of a number of physical malfunctions.

The most common problem results from the blockage of the outer ear by an excessive **accumulation of wax**. The ear also may be subject to what is known as **swimmer's ear**, an infection that results when water remains in the ear canal. Respiratory infections can lead to **otitis media**, infection in the middle ear. A common malady in children, it frequently requires antibiotic drug therapy or myringotomy, a surgical process of making an incision in the eardrum and inserting a tube to drain built-up fluid.

accumulation of wax

swimmer's ear

otitis media

Still another common problem is **tinnitus**, or ringing of the ears. Some 46 million Americans may suffer some form of this condition for which there is no specific treatment.[23] Ear noise can be an unrelenting buzzing, whistling, or even roaring sound that can result from a number of causes such as high blood pressure, wax plugs, or inner ear damage from drugs or exposure to loud sounds.

tinnitus

Less common is a hereditary condition, **otosclerosis**, a progressive disease that turns the hard bone of the inner ear into spongy bone matter. For some unknown reason, the disease primarily affects Caucasian women. A new surgical technique, stapedectomy, consists of replacing the stapes with a prosthetic link between the incus and the oval window. This technique can restore hearing, at least temporarily, to within 10 dB.

otosclerosis

Almost all individuals suffer, to some extent, from sensorineural impairment, which relates, in part, to the physical deterioration of the hearing mechanism through aging. Known as **presbycusis**, the process of progressive hearing loss starts at about the age of twenty and becomes increasingly evident during each decade of an individual's life.[24] While attempts can be made to arrest further sensory loss, most hearing specialists feel that it is practically impossible to restore sensory loss once the nerve fibers in the cochlea or in the VIIIth nerve are destroyed.

presbycusis

Some Mechanical Devices Available For Restoring Auditory Acuity. Various mechanical devices are available to restore the auditory acuity of persons who suffer hearing loss. A recent but expensive new technology is a **cochlear implant**. Recommended for only about 10 percent of the two million Americans who are profoundly deaf, the implant involves the placement of a lapel microphone that picks up sound and transmits it to a receiver implanted behind the ear on the mastoid bone. The impulses are transmitted through the skin to the receiver and then sent by an electrical wire to the cochlea in the inner ear. The procedure is viewed by audiologists as a major breakthrough for dealing with profound hearing loss.[25]

cochlear implant

Another sound device that improves the quality of sounds for individuals with up to 75 percent hearing loss is the **infrared earphone**, used extensively in theaters and concert halls today. The user puts on earphones, and an infrared light beamed from emitters near the stage is changed into

infrared earphone

sound for the individual amplifier. Delivering sound directly to the ear, this system blocks out any background or surrounding noise.[26]

hearing aid

The most common sound device is the **hearing aid**, which conducts sound through amplification. A new electronic aid using digital technology has been designed with a noise blocker to monitor the low frequencies for volume and automatically dampen them to distinguish sounds from background noise.[27] This new device can provide excellent sound quality and adaptation to specific kinds of hearing losses. For years Americans perceived a stigma attached to hearing loss and viewed it as an infirmity that must be hidden away. However, in 1983, then-President Ronald Reagan put on two hearing aids to balance his hearing, which had been impaired by a film studio accident in the 1930s. His public acceptance was hailed as an important step forward in changing American attitudes about the use of hearing aids.

Noise Pollution—a Cause of Hearing Loss for Everyone. All persons are affected by **sociocusis**—hearing loss from exposure to occupational and nonoccupational noise sources such as tractors, riveting machines, rock music, and jet planes. The influence of noise pollution continues to be a major environmental problem in the United States. Some citizens, however, have taken action. For example, residents of several towns in Westchester County, New York—annoyed by the noise produced by gas-powered leaf blowers—regulated or banned the leaf blowers during the summer of 1994. Other individuals, claiming hearing loss as a result of exposure to loud sounds, have launched law suits against rock concert promoters and against airport authorities . . . and have been granted compensation. Table 3.1 shows the decibel levels of common environmental sounds. It is important to note that sound measurement is logarithmic; that is, the sound is ten times more intense with every increment of 10 (for example, 70 decibels is 10 X 10 more intense than 60 decibels).

sociocusis

Despite what we know about noise pollution, we continue to purchase noisy appliances (a noise-free vacuum introduced a few years ago did not sell), turn up head sets to a dangerous level, and attend rock concerts. The Deafness Research Foundation has determined that as many as 61 percent of first-year college students have a measurable hearing loss.[28] Pondering why so many American young people continue to listen to loud music in the face of dramatic evidence about the damage it causes, Lipscomb suggests that sound vibrations must be a factor. A Florida teenager told him: "The sounds embalm you. They numb you. You don't want to hear others talk. You don't want to talk. You don't know what to say to each other anyway."[29]

The key to controlling the effects of noise pollution must rest with each individual listener. Protective actions range from turning down our televisions, listening to Walkman-type headsets at a volume of 4, and improving home insulation to operating only one noise-producing product at a time, reducing people noise by talking rather than yelling, and wearing ear protectors while using power tools. While some federal efforts to legislate noise control have led to airport workers wearing ear protectors, for example, no

Table 3.1. 'A' weighted sound levels of some noises found in different environments

Sound Level, dBA	Industrial (and Military)	Community (or Outdoor)	Home (or Indoor)
—130—	Armored Personnel Carrier (123 dB)		
—120—			
Uncomfortably Loud	Oxygen Torch (121 dB)		
—110—	Scraper-Loader (117 dB)		
—100—	Compactor (116 dB)	Jet Flyover @ 100 ft. (103 dB)	Rock 'n' Roll Band (108–114 dB)
Very Loud	Riveting Machine (110 dB)	Power Mower (96 dB)	Inside Subway Car @35 mph (95 dB)
— 90—	Textile Loom (106 dB)	Compressor @ 20 ft. (94 dB)	
— 80—	Electric Furnace Area (100 dB)	Rock Drill @ 100 ft. (92 dB)	Cockpit-Light Aircraft (90 dB)
Moderately Loud	Farm Tractor (98 dB)	Motorcycles @ 25 ft. (90 dB)	Food Blender (88 dB)
— 70—	Newspaper Press (97 dB)		Garbage Disposal (80 dB)
— 60—	Cockpit-Prop Aircraft (88 dB)	Propeller Aircraft Flyover @ 1000 ft. (88 dBA)	Clothes Washer (78 dB)
— 50—	Milling Machine (85 dB)	Diesel Truck, 40 mph @ 50 ft. (84 dB)	Living Room Music (76 dB)
Quiet	Cotton Spinning (83 dB)	Diesel Train, 40–50 mph @ 100 ft. (83 dB)	Dishwasher (75 dB)
— 40—	Lathe (81 dB)	Passenger Car, 65 mph @ 25 ft. (77 dB)	TV-Audio (70 dB)
— 30—	Tabulating (80 dB)	Near Freeway-Auto Traffic (64 dB)	Vacuum (70 dB)
Very Quiet		Air-Conditioning Unit @ 20 ft. (60 dB)	Conversation (60 dB)
— 20—		Large Transformer @ 200 ft. (53 dB)	
— 10—		Light Traffic @ 100 ft. (50 dB)	
Just Audible			
— 0—			
Threshold of Hearing (1000–4000 Hz)			

Note: Unless otherwise specified, listed sound levels are measured at typical operator-listener distances from source. Noise readings taken from general acoustical literature and observations by PHS.

government agency can support the inspectors necessary to keep our environment relatively noise-free. Some states are erecting sound barriers next to busy highways to protect neighborhoods from undue traffic noise, but, at the same time, architects persist in designing open space office facilities in which all workers are supposed to do their work in one large room.

Three Other Factors Affecting Hearing.   Three additional factors weaken the hearing process. One of these factors results from **binaural hearing problems**—a lack of coordinated functioning of both ears and, consequently, the inability to discriminate the direction of the source of the sound. Another factor is **masking**—the existence of background noise or other

binaural hearing problems

masking

We can suffer hearing loss from exposure to occupational noise sources.

Understanding the Listening Process

types of interference (such as conflicting simultaneous messages) while the individual is attempting to hear the intended oral message. A third problem is that of **auditory fatigue**—fatigue from continuous exposure to sounds of a certain frequency, such as a ticking clock or a monotonous voice.

auditory fatigue

Clearly, listening and hearing are not synonymous. The listening receptors, auditory and visual alike, require care and control for the listener to maximize his or her listening abilities. Listening, however, goes beyond the reception of the message to the process of attending to it. Merker, in her book describing what happened to her as a listener when she lost her hearing, emphasizes this important point:

> So then, when we listen . . . when we are really listening . . . we are not just hearing. Hearing, after all, is merely receiving, the brain's recognition of sound, something that will happen without personal will, unless our hearing mechanism is defective or temporarily denied access by earplugs, by sorrow, by some acute concentration that shuts off our sensibilities. Listening happens when we are attentive, when we choose responsibility to receive and understand an earth message of some kind.[30]

Component 2: Attending To

The second component of listening—attending to—refers to focused perception on selected stimuli. This act embraces the moment before and during the reception of a potential stimulus. Many consider the elusive nature of attention to be the major trap that listeners encounter in their efforts to focus on messages.

At any moment, numerous stimuli in our immediate environment are vying for our attention. These stimuli may be external, such as a speaker's words or noise in the hall; or they may be internal, such as a headache or a distracting thought. Can you divide your attention among several stimuli? If so, how many stimuli can you attend to at any given time?

Selective Attention. There are a number of stimuli to which we can attend at any one time.[31] However, there is no limit to the number of stimuli constantly competing for our attention. If all stimuli seeking our attention at any given instant were sent to the cortex, a neural overload would result. Thus, we must constantly engage in a process of selecting only those stimuli to which we will attend. It is believed that some discriminatory mechanism assists us in selecting the wanted from the unwanted aural stimuli.

selective attention

Attention Models.   Beginning with the first formal attention model proposed by Broadbent in 1958, many explanations of how this discriminatory process operates have been proposed. Like Broadbent's model, other early attention models (such as those developed by Deutsch and Deutsch, by Treisman, and by Neisser) viewed information-processing as a series of steps, with selecting attention operating at a particular stage. A more recent attention model proposed by Kahneman also recognizes the limited capacity of attention energy; however, it treats attention as a resource that can be flexibly allocated, or distributed, to different stages—rather than to one

attention models

stage—of information-processing. As the following descriptions of the attention models illustrate, various theorists provide different views of the nature of selective attention.

Broadbent

According to **Broadbent's** 1958 model of attention, aural stimuli enter the nervous system through a number of sensory input channels. Broadbent posited that the various input lines converge onto a sensory filter that functions as a selective mechanism. The filter selects stimuli, not on the basis of analysis of meaning but rather on the basis of analysis of certain physical features (such as location in space, pitch, and intensity) toward which it is biased. It then allows the selected stimuli to penetrate consciousness through a limited-capacity channel. Unselected stimuli are held in a short-term store for a brief time, after which they are attended to or lost.[32] The filter even allows the brain to fill in the missing pieces to organize a "whole" message. When individuals are exposed to an incomplete or even scrambled musical melody ("Happy Birthday," for example), they can complete the tune.[33]

Deutsch and Deutsch

Deutsch and Deutsch found Broadbent's theory to be attractive when applied to simple and few discriminations. They questioned its application, however, to cases where numerous and complex discriminations are required. Thus, they proposed a different model:

> Another mechanism is proposed, which assumes the existence of a shifting reference standard, which takes up the level of the most important arriving signal. . . . Only the most important signals coming in will be acted on or remembered. On the other hand, more important signals than those present at an immediately preceding time will be able to break in, for these will raise the height of the level and so displace the previously most important signals as the highest.[34]

Deutsch and Deutsch also proposed that some degree of general arousal is necessary for attention to operate. When aroused, an individual will attend to any incoming stimulus, provided that it is not accompanied by a more important one. When asleep, however, an individual will respond only to very important messages, such as one's own name or the cry of an infant.[35] Experimental studies conducted by Moray and by other researchers have indicated that some selective mechanism functions when a person recognizes his or her own name (an important word) during dichotic listening, during sleep, and during normal listening under noise.[36] Treisman has suggested that such important words and, perhaps, danger signals, "have permanently lower thresholds for activation or are more readily available than others . . . others would be lowered temporarily by incoming signals on some kind of conditional probability basis. . . ."[37]

Research concerning attention centers on measuring the brain's emission of electrical impulses known as the alpha and beta waves. Inattention is indicated by fast medium-amplitude alpha waves, whereas rapid, small beta waves identify active mental engagement. Electroencephalograph research on these brain waves has enabled a University of Wisconsin researcher to identify the specific elements of television commercials that are most likely to arouse viewers.[38] Other research demonstrates the influence of such factors as the content and the segment on the fluctuating attention of television viewers.[39] Such research offers all sorts of possible implications for advertising professionals.

The third model of attention was proposed by **Treisman**. She posited that messages, having arrived at some part of the nervous system over different input channels, are first analyzed for physical characteristics such as pitch, loudness, and location in space. A filter uses the information obtained by this analysis to identify the messages that will be selected for attention. On other occasions, the filter bases its selection on more complex discriminations, such as the analysis of syllabic patterns, grammatical structure, or meaning. Treisman further postulated that the selective filter's tuning flexibility, determined by the perceived meanings in an individual's state of awareness, allows the filter to attenuate incoming information (i.e. make the information more or less perceptible) rather than completely block it out.[40]

In 1967, **Neisser** proposed the two-process theory of analysis-by-synthesis. He postulated that incoming stimuli go through preattentive processing. During this processing, stored knowledge is actively used to analyze the stimuli's sensory and semantic features for important information. Viewing such focused attention as a result of all processing, Neisser theorized that attended and unattended stimuli differ only in the amount of processing given to them. Discounting the others' view that some incoming stimuli are never attended to because they have been blocked out or attenuated, Neisser theorized that they are not attended to merely because they have not been processed as fully as attended stimuli have been.[41]

More recently, **Kahneman** proposed a capacity model that views attention as a limited-capacity resource that can be flexibly allocated to various stages of information-processing. The way one distributes his or her attentional energy is governed by (1) automatic, unconscious rules (such as focusing on a speaker who states the listener's name), (2) conscious decisions (such as choosing to focus on the boss's message rather than on a co-worker's simultaneous message), and (3) the difficulty of the mental task (with more attentional energy being required and, therefore, being allocated to complex mental tasks). According to Kahneman, an individual can change his or her attentional distribution from moment to moment in order to meet the varying attentional requirements of conscious mental tasks (which demand considerable attentional energy) and automatic mental tasks (which demand little attentional energy and so do not interfere with other ongoing information-processing tasks, such as rehearsal and elaborative mnemonic devices, which also require attentional energy).[42]

An interesting variation of Kahneman's understanding of attention as the allocation of resources is **Wickens's** multiple resource theory of attention. Wickens suggests that an individual may use attentional resources that are specific to a particular modality or to a particular processing task.[43] Attention results from activating a sensory modality (visual or auditory) through the allocation of the attention resources that the person has available. Since our

Treisman

Neisser

Kahneman

Wickens

attention resources are limited by such factors as time and energy, interference to attention is a major challenge for listeners.

The dominant view of attention presently follows Kahneman's capacity theory, which—like Shiffrin and Schneider's capacity theory[44]—emphasizes the flexible nature of attention. However, disagreements continue as to how selective attention operates, where discriminatory decisions are made, and what happens to unselected stimuli. There is, though, experimental evidence—as previously cited—that attention is selective. As listeners, we base our selection of aural stimuli upon a priority system that exists within each of us. This priority system may stem from the "tendency for people to pay close attention to information that is consistent with their attitudes, beliefs, values, and behaviors, and little attention to stimuli which are inconsistent."[45] This need for consistency has led McCroskey to conclude that "selective attention is not so much the conscious 'tuning out' of inconsistent information as it is the unconscious 'tuning in' of consistent information."[46]

This process of tuning in and tuning out on messages has critical implication for our understanding of listening behavior. Bartlett summarizes the relationship of selective attention to listener perception: "Selective listening is determined mainly by the qualitative differences in stimuli in relation to predispositions—cognitive, affective, and motor—of the listener."[47]

energetic attention

Energetic Attention.   Attention is not only selective but also energetic. It requires both effort and desire. Although we can divide our attention, we can give complete attention to only one stimulus at a time. If we expend too much energy on too many stimuli, we will no longer be attending; instead, we will be **scanning** (i.e. sweeping the perceptual field to discover what should be attended to).[48] Thus, by concentrating our attention energy on one stimulus instead of on many, we can focus more sharply on the selected stimulus.

scanning

Once we have selected a stimulus to which we will attend, it has our attention; that is, we become aware of it and we further process it. In some cases, according to Hasher and Zacks, processing the stimulus will require minimal attentional energy, and so it will not interfere with other ongoing information-processing operations. In other cases, the processing will require considerable attentional energy and will interfere with other cognitive operations. Whether the processing is automatic (as it appears to be when one is processing information such as spatial, temporal, and frequency-of-occurrence information) or effortful (as it appears to be when one is engaging in operations such as rehearsal and elaborative mnemonic devices), we must attend to the stimulus.[49] However, there is some evidence that some stimuli that never seem to be attended to (or of which the individual never seems to be aware) enter and remain in the memory system.[50] Generally, only stimuli that have been attended to enter the listener's memory system.[51]

A View of the Human Memory System.   The aforementioned memory system is the long-term memory system (LTM). While a **multistore view of human memory** prevailed in the late 1960s and early 1970s, no prevailing

multistore view of human memory

view of the structure of the human memory presently exists. However, many notions incorporated in the multistore models (such as those conceived by Atkinson, by Shiffrin and Norman, and by Rumelhart)[52] are still accepted today. Indeed, the multistore view is an important forerunner to current trends in memory research.

Adherents to the multistore view posit that the human memory consists of two, or three if the sensory register is included, functionally separate and distinct structural components or stores: sensory register, short-term memory system (STM), and long-term memory system (LTM). The **sensory register** is the least permanent memory store; it is here that the stimuli in their raw form enter the memory system through various senses. For example, the sensory register would contain a brief echo of the last auditory stimulus to which one had been exposed. Upon entering, or registering (without conscious effort on the part of the receiver), the stimulus is temporarily stored. The sensory register's capacity is large and, thus, capable of holding virtually all of the stimuli that reach one's senses. However, the length of time a given sensory stimulus can remain in the sensory register without the stimulus being lost—decaying with the passage of time or being replaced by new sensory stimuli entering the sensory register—is quite limited. Research shows that visual (iconic) sensory storage lasts only several hundred milliseconds,[53] while auditory (echoic) sensory storage lasts up to 3 or 4 seconds.[54] Thus, if the sensory stimulus is not immediately selected for attention (i.e. transferred to the short-term memory store), it is lost.

sensory register

The **short-term memory store**, or the working memory "where conscious mental processes are performed on information from both the sensory register and the long-term store,"[55] is also a temporary store. The selected incoming stimulus—having been converted through the process of pattern recognition from its raw, sensory form (for example, the separate sounds of ō' pĕn to a meaningful form *open*)—is stored only briefly because of two notable limitations on the STM. One limitation is the length of time that a stimulus may be stored in it. Research indicates that if the stimulus in the STM is not attended to, it will decay in a period ranging from 20 seconds to 1 minute.[56] However, the stimulus may be preserved as long as one desires if one gives it constant attention by engaging in the process of rehearsal (the silent or vocal repetition of the stimulus/stimuli or concentration on the stimulus/stimuli). In addition, rehearsal (especially elaborative rehearsal that involves attempting to relate the stimulus to long-term knowledge)[57] appears to increase the chances of a stimulus reaching the cortex for attention[58] and consequently being committed to the long-term memory system.[59]

short-term memory store

If, however, a person, during rehearsal, is interrupted by another person's question or request, internal noise, or some other distraction that results in a shift of attention, the disruption probably will cause the previously-rehearsed information to be lost within 60 seconds. Bostrom and Waldhart observe that the LTM is not activated until at least 60 seconds after the presentation of a stimulus.[60] In addition to this time limit, the STM has a limitation on the number of stimuli that it can hold simultaneously. Experimental evidence indicates that this limit is approximately seven units, or "the magical number seven, plus or minus two."[61] A unit, or a chunk of information, is characterized as a stimulus that has a single representation in the LTM; for example, the letters KSED constitute four chunks, but in reverse order, the letter string DESK is one chunk.

Despite its limitations, the STM is adequate in many listening situations. For example, your STM meets your needs when you retain an orally-given telephone number until you dial it or when you retain a speaker's question until you answer it. Bostrom and Waldhart postulate that the short-term retention of a stimulus may be more useful in some interactions than long-term retention, particularly in communication situations in which the relationships of the communicators (e.g., maintaining a friendship) may be more important than the details of the interactions.[62]

**long-term
memory system**Unlike the STM, which consists of the current contents of a person's awareness, the **long-term memory system** is essentially a permanent storage system consisting of all that one has previously learned. A principal difference between the two memory systems is that the STM is considered to have ". . . a fixed capacity that is subject to overload and consequently loss of elements in it . . . while LTM is, in effect, infinitely expansible."[63]

Short-Term Memory	Long-Term Memory
Consists of the current contents of a person's awareness	Consists of all that a person has previously learned
Is a temporary store	Is essentially a permanent store
Has a fixed capacity	Is, in effect, infinitely expansible

The Functioning of the STM and LTM in Listening. To understand the functions of these two systems in listening, suppose you are attending a party where you know very few of the other guests. If you are introduced, by names only, to several people in succession, your STM is presented with the names of Sheryl, Tom, Stacia, and Matt before you have learned the names of Michelle, Lenora, Eric, and John. The new names tend to push the former names out of your STM. Unless you quickly transfer each name to the LTM, you most likely will lose the name. However, the stimuli in the STM may be preserved longer and moved to the LTM if they go through rehearsal. Thus, if you concentrate while you rehearse each name as you meet each person, the chances are greater that each name will reach the LTM. The listener must engage in elaborative rehearsal of the aural stimuli in order to transfer the stimuli to the LTM for further processing and storage.

As we noted in the beginning of our discussion of memory, the multi-store view of memory no longer prevails in experimental psychology, primarily because the emerging pattern in memory research is shifting from emphasis on fixed structure (distinct and separate memory systems) to emphasis on flexible processing (with individuals actively using their cognitive skills and stored knowledge to process information).[64] This new focus has led some researchers to view the STM as an activated portion of the LTM rather than a separate store. It is clear, however, that attention in the memory system is a matter of energy.

Fluctuating Attention. Just as attention is energetic and selective, so, too, is it fluctuating. This waning of attention is particularly relevant to our understanding of the act of listening. We cannot pay attention to the selected stimulus for as long as we desire. Attention fluctuates. The fading of attention is sometimes not caused by distraction; instead, attention fades because of a succession of lapses that Haider has termed **microsleep**. Thus, periodically, our attention energy will wane because we are "asleep."[65] At other times, though, when our attention wanes, it is not due to "sleep"; instead, it is the result of our short attention spans or our lack of effort. The fluctuation of attention relates directly to the degree of effort that an individual has the capacity to exert at any given time in processing information. It becomes a process, therefore, of allocating our attention to those stimuli that we perceive to be most in need of our attention at any given time. "Different mental activities," Kahneman notes, "impose different demands on the limited capacity. An easy task demands little effort, and a difficult task demands much. When the supply of attention does not meet the demands, performance falters, or fails entirely."[66]

fluctuating attention

microsleep

Research on the attention span in advertising furthers our understanding of the role of attention in the listening process. The effectiveness of advertising messages is generally believed to be moderated by the level of audience involvement with, or attention to, the message. Reviewing the levels, Greenwald and Leavitt conclude that higher levels of involvement in advertising require greater attentional capacity but result in more durable efforts on the consumer who is being persuaded to buy, give, vote, or do.[67] Although the attention capacity has decided limits, we can increase the length of our attention span through "concentration, practice, and self-discipline."[68]

The Lack of Attention Control. A listener's attention is not always under control. Research on learning disability has identified what is known as **attention deficit hyperactivity disorder** (ADHD), typically found in younger children and characterized by restlessness, irritability, impulsiveness, and minimal attention span. An estimated two million children have been diagnosed with ADHD, a disorder that is particularly acute for elementary students. The most prevalent treatment for attention deficit hyperactivity disorder is methylphenidate (Ritalin) medication. The late Benjamin Feingold, a California allergist, proposed dietary controls—such as avoiding artificial colors and flavors, certain preservatives, many medications, and foods containing natural salicylates—as one treatment. Although nutritional research disputes the Feingold diet as being the only approach to treating hyperactivity and attention deficit, many American teachers and parents have found it to be useful.[69] As further research is conducted on attention disorder, we will likely gain a greater understanding of the many factors that influence the human attention span.

attention deficit hyperactivity disorder

The lack of attention control may extend to the listener's exposure to **subliminal messages**, or messages that are presented below the threshold of consciousness but make impressions on the mind. The classic demonstration of this technique was part of a movie shown at a theatre in F. Lee, New Jersey, in 1957. "Eat Popcorn" and "Drink Coca-Cola" were

subliminal messages

flashed—below the level of consciousness—on the screen during the Kim Novak film, *Picnic*. Patrons reportedly were subliminally induced to buy popcorn and Coke during the intermission. Such a technique has tremendous power, of course, because as listeners we cannot counter the message since we are not even aware that we are receiving it.

Wilson Bryan Key popularized the notion of subliminal perception and its threat to the public in three books titled *Media Sexploitation*, *Subliminal Seduction*, and *Clam Plate Orgy*, which describe how sex appeals at the subliminal level are used in advertising.[70] Since the publication of these controversial books, the Federal Trade Commission and the Federal Communication Commission have designated the use of subliminal techniques in advertising as being contrary to public interest. However, subliminal techniques continue to be used. For example, Hal Becker of the Behavioral Engineering Corporation has developed subliminal audiotapes that can program the Muzak system in department stores to subliminally persuade people not to shoplift. Another example is one that has become a fifty-million-dollar business: subliminal audiotapes and videotapes designed to facilitate self-help projects such as weight loss, control of smoking, and even creative thinking through subliminal messages embedded on ocean sounds, gentle breezes, classical music, or peaceful cloud formations.

While the development of subliminal techniques has progressed as computers have become more sophisticated, we should recognize that the research on the use of these techniques is far from conclusive. On one hand, researchers have found neither theoretical nor experimental evidence that supports enhanced performance by consumers who listen to purported subliminal self-improvement audiotapes. On the other hand, "recent research has led to a growing consensus that subliminal perception is a valid phenomenon that can be demonstrated under certain well-defined conditions. . . . If this latter view is correct, then, it is conceivable that subliminal auditory stimulation could have some impact upon behavior."[71]

Although the use of subliminal techniques is justified by their users as means to legitimate ends, we can understand the dangers to us as receivers if the messages should be programmed to encourage us to act against our will. A 1990 lawsuit against the British rock band Judas Priest sought damages for two young men who shot themselves on a deserted playground. The relatives of the two victims claimed that hidden messages in the group's album "Stained Class" spurred the two men to form a suicide pact.[72] Others argue that subliminal messages can only influence us if we are already predisposed to the recommended course of action. It is clear, however, that as listeners we should always have the right to be perceptually aware of the messages to which we are attending.

Listening efficiency is profoundly affected by the attention process. Limits to the attention span, a lack of motivation to concentrate, or an inadequate priority system for selecting stimuli all enter into the process. The fluctuating, selective, energetic nature of attention affects a listener's performance at any given point in the communication process.

Cognitive specialist Robert Marzano suggests that listeners be strategic in controlling their attention. He recommends four steps to attention control:

1. Become aware of your level of attention.
2. Identify the level of attention required for the task at hand.
3. Compare your level of attention with that required.
4. If necessary raise your level of attention by raising your energy through bracketing—consciously putting aside some thoughts that might be important but not relevant to the task at hand—or by looking for meaning.[73]

Just as *hearing* (e.g. "You don't hear a word I say!") and *listening* are often erroneously used as synonyms, *attending* (e.g. "Can't you pay attention to what I say?") and *listening* are often incorrectly equated. The listening process encompasses more than the two processes of receiving and attending. We can, for example, hear and attend to a foreign language, but if we cannot assign meaning to the aural stimuli, we have not engaged in the total listening process.

Component 3: Assigning Meaning

The third component of listening—assigning meaning—refers to the interpretation or understanding of the stimuli heard and/or seen and attended to. In this process, the listener's goal is to attach meaning as similar as possible to that intended by the message sender; however, we must realize that assigning meaning is a very personal process. Therefore, because of the senders' and the receivers' different past experiences, present feelings, and even future expectations, we often do not reach the desired goal.

Theories on How Meaning Is Assigned. Various theories have been posited as to how meaning is assigned. Among these are the image theory, classical conditioning, linguistic reference, meaning as an implicit response, meaning as a mediating response, meaning as a behavioral disposition, and human information-processing.[74]

meaning assignment

Lundsteen favors the **image theory**. Using evidence established by memory research and theories proposed by Anderson,[75] she suggests that listeners go through two separate processes: acoustical encoding (the translation of the aural data into internal speech) and semantic encoding (the translation of the aural data into tentative, perceptual images or internal pictures).[76] After having formed these initial images, the listener searches through images held in the memory store to find possible matches for the data. We may then compare the cues we have selected with previous knowledge and experience so that we can form further tentative images. If we have not yet found a match, we may test the cues by questioning and summarizing, or we may return to our memory store for further search. When we have matched the cues with the aural input by forming tentative images, searching, comparing, testing, and decoding, we have achieved meaning. We then, finally, decide what the aural stimuli means to us.[77]

image theory

Although Barker does not elaborate on how meaning is assigned, he notes that there are two levels of meaning. The first level, or the primary meaning assignment, is associated with the **classical conditioning** responses to the aural stimuli. After integrating past experience with this primary meaning, however, listeners arrive at a secondary meaning. This is the meaning listeners believe was intended by the message sender.[78]

Weaver supports, with slight modification, the theory of **meaning as a behavioral disposition**.[79] This theory is based on a system of categories into which the mind sorts and assigns aural stimuli. Although the system was devised by Bruner, Goodnow, and Austin in 1956,[80] Roger Brown popularized this categorical system.[81] Categories are stored in the memory. After we have selected an aural stimuli for attention—for instance, *bicuspid*—we search our memory to find the category in which this stimulus fits, that is, where memories of other stimuli with a similar pattern are stored. We cannot assign meaning until we have found a match. Having found the match (*tooth*, in our example), we then ascribe approximate meaning because of the category evoked. The stimulus then assumes the meaning of the category—in this case, a *double-pointed jaw tooth*.

More than a decade after Brown made the categorical system prominent, cognitive theorists embraced a **human information-processing** model of assigning meaning. Most commonly, this model depicts the human as analogous to a computer. Information is input from both auditory and visual signals to the sensory organs. These input messages are then processed and interpreted on the basis of previous information that has been stored in the memory.

The stages in this processing of information have been described by Loftus and Schooler.[82] The cognitive stages include the sensory memory, similar to the buffer of a computer, which briefly stores, sorts, and interprets some portion of the message. The initial message interpretation then transfers to the short-term memory, much like the working memory of a computer, where chunks of information are stored in a serial manner, usually at a limit of four to six bits of information at a time.[83] Next, the message moves to the long-term memory, which is analogous to the auxiliary memory of a computer. The short-term memory draws from this store of information to make interpretations. Tulving suggests that the information in the long-term memory constitutes both semantic memory (general facts such as words, rules, etc.) and episodic memory (personal facts in terms of the time and place).[84] Underscoring the place of cognition in listening behavior, Fitch-Hauser and Hughes' review of the research on cognitive processing led them to conclude that "listening and cognitive processing are inexorably linked."[85]

The information-processing model has encouraged cognitive psychologists to develop another perspective to describe how information is stored and how humans handle the complex task of decoding/interpreting messages. This current perspective, **schema theory**,[86] is based on the concept that we all carry schemata—mental representation of knowledge—in our brains. These organized information structures consist of nodes (concepts, events, objects) and links (relationships of the nodes). New information is first run through existing schemata, or scripts, and then interpreted.

Listeners carry scripts for every life experience. If a friend describes a trip to Disney World and you have visited the theme park, you can use your experiences to interpret your friend's descriptions of the Epcot Center, the Jungle Cruise, the Studio Tour, and the Contemporary Hotel. If you have not visited Disney World, however, you will have to call on experiences from other theme parks to build a new script to interpret your friend's message. Or, your attempt to explain the customs and traditions for celebrating Halloween in the United States can prove difficult to a new friend from a culture that does not observe the holiday. Your friend will not have a script for some of the bizarre aspects of Halloween costumes and "trick or treat." The scripts function to create the schema for interpreting messages.

Schemata, therefore, represent the generic concepts that are stored in memory and the stereotypes of these concepts.[87] These schemata relate persons or objects to attributes or relate actions to anticipated consequences. Smith suggests that schemata serve three listening purposes:

1. Schemata tell us to what we should attend.
2. Schemata serve as a framework for interpreting incoming information.
3. Schemata guide the reconstruction of messages in memory.[88]

A familiar schemata scenario is the parent who temporarily loses sight of the child in a crowded shopping center. He or she goes into a panic script while visualizing television news reports of kidnapping.[89]

Judd and Kulik demonstrate that attitudes also can function as schemata in listeners. Schemata represent expectations that individuals have concerning the structure of the information to be encountered. These researchers found that subjects who expected to encounter agreeable or disagreeable information, consistent with their own attitudes, processed the information according to their expectations more readily than they processed either positive or negative information that did not conform to their prior expectations.[90] Judd and Kulik conclude that information that is either very agreeable or disagreeable or that advocates an extreme position appears to be easier for the listener to process and to recall.

Schema theorists stress, however, that information needed to understand many messages may not be explicitly present; rather, listeners must provide information from their own schema. Recognizing this communication gap, Richards notes the significance of schema theory in understanding listening behavior: "The information needed to understand many utterances is . . . not explicitly present in the utterance but is provided by the listeners from their repertoire of scripts."[91]

The schemata or scripts that individuals hold in their long-term memory store make up their cognitive structure. How these mental representations fit together is the subject of much debate in the field of cognitive psychology. Listening researchers have discovered, however, that individuals who are more cognitively complex (that is, individuals who potentially have more schemata for perceiving than other persons), have greater listening recall than less cognitively complex persons.[92] Describing what he terms the "Good Information Processor," Pressley agrees that such individuals—whether listeners or readers—possess both extensive knowledge about important concepts and superior short-term memory capacities to strategically plan and monitor their thinking and behavior for maximum benefit.[93]

Although there are differences between any two of the theories of how individuals assign meaning to messages, it is apparent that the process is far from simple. As listeners, we assign a message to some sort of category or schema that we carry in our long-term memory. Making this assignment allows us to make some initial sense of a message. This requires a search of the categories or schemata to find a match in which the message fits. Once this interpretation is made, listeners move to a more "reflective processing" stage to "think about the message, make more extensive inferences, evaluate and judge the speaker and the message, etc."[94]

The meaning derived from this complex decoding process results from one's linguistic code, which is based on one's experience with and learning of the language system. The linguistic development of the language categories enables one to create semantic interpretations from the message, which consists of symbols selected by the speaker to represent the concepts, objects, or events being communicated.[95] Linguist Steven Pinker, describing the complexities of human language, concludes that "understanding, then, requires integrating the fragments gleaned from a sentence into a vast mental database. For that to work, speakers cannot just toss one fact after another into a listener's head."[96] Since meaning is heavily derived from individual representations and experiences in the process, and since the process is so very complex, the possibilities for assigning incorrect meanings to aural stimuli are great. Halley notes that errors in assigning meaning to stimuli will lead to considerable errors in listening: "Learning how often and under what conditions you do this process well and others where you do it poorly can greatly aid you in learning to listen effectively."[97]

Some Causes of Incorrect Assignment of Meaning.

different schema or categorical system

There are many reasons why incorrect assignment of meaning frequently occurs. The major reason is that **each person has a different schema or categorical system**; that is, because each person is unique, each develops meanings based on his or her own personal experiences. While the speaker's meanings for the words *mother* or *boss*, for example, may be those meanings that the speaker has for his or her own mother or boss, the listener's meanings may be quite different. In *Through the Looking-Glass*, Humpty Dumpty illustrates the personal quality of meaning assignment when he tells Alice "When I use a word . . . , it means just what I choose it to mean—nothing more nor less."[98]

The investigation of the fatal crash of Avianca Flight 052 on 25 January 1990, onto a Long Island hillside provides a sobering example of how the meanings of words differ among communicators. A study of the tape from the recovered black box reveals that the crew realized that they were running out of fuel: "I think we need priority" and "We're running out of fuel."

The copilot's calm vocal intonation and his failure to use the key terms "minimum fuel" or "emergency" as prescribed in the air traffic control manual led the controllers in the tower not to realize the seriousness of the situation. At a hearing on the disaster, the International Federation of Airline Pilots pointed out that the terminology is not required by their rules and that, further, the controllers should have asked the crew how many minutes of fuel they had remaining. "I'm very surprised that 'running out of fuel' means nothing to them," said an Avianca captain in his testimony.[99] Clearly, meanings reside not in the words themselves but in the individual communicators who use the words.

The individual communicator's point of view—one's **frame of reference**—consists of all that makes each person a unique individual. It consists of one's culture, life experiences, attitudes, knowledge, communication skills, background, present thoughts and feelings, expectations of self and others, values, beliefs, personality factors, interests, concerns, fears, pressures, tensions, needs, biases, prejudices, stereotypes, fantasies, morals, convictions, physical health—everything that makes up the sum total of the individual. All of these elements that govern the way one views the world create the **perceptual filter** through which the listener screens each message before assigning a personal meaning to the message. Jiddu Krishnamuriti, in *The First and Last Personal Freedom*, stresses the impact that each individual's perceptual filter has on one's listening:

frame of reference

perceptual filter

> To be able to really listen, one should abandon or put aside all prejudices, preformulations, and daily activities. When you are in a receptive state of mind, things can be easily understood; you are listening when your real attention is given to something. But unfortunately most of us listen through a screen of resistance. We are screened with prejudices, whether religious or spiritual, psychological or scientific; or with our daily worries, desires, and fears. And with these for a screen, we listen. Therefore, we really listen to our own noise, to our own sound, not to what is being said.[100]

Not only do the listener's frame of reference and perceptual filter alter the meanings of the speaker's words, but also they affect **the listener's selection of information to process**. To preserve internal balance, one tends to be selective in what one exposes oneself to, attends to, perceives, and remembers.[101] Therefore, the listener seeks information that is consistent with his or her personal beliefs and information that confirms his or her personal expectations. One perceives what one wants to perceive or is set to perceive (see, hear, and believe) so as to be able to assign meanings that conform to expected meanings. Thus, rather than seeking out information that may prove one wrong, paying attention to information with which one may disagree, checking out one's perceptions against those of others who have different views, and retaining information that is inconsistent with one's own beliefs, the listener often chooses to continue interpreting from his or her own frame of reference rather than from the speaker's frame of reference.

Furthermore, the listener's frame of reference affects assignment of meaning when his or her emotional biases are aroused. Now serving

listener's selection of information to process

primarily as an emotional sifter, the listener's perceptual filter is a powerful source for meaning distortions. Each listener has certain words, phrases, ideas, topics, and people (including some speakers) to which old emotions associated with previous emotional events still cling. Thus, these **emotional triggers** arouse immediate, unthinking, positive or negative reactions within the listener. What may create a positive reaction in one listener may lead to a negative reaction in another. Whether the emotional triggers produce within a particular listener a positive reaction such as *justice, equal opportunity*, or *nonfat* may (or may not) or a negative reaction as *severance, "please hold,"* or *Newt Gingrich* may (or may not), they have a powerful impact on the listener's assignment of meaning.

Emotional triggers result in incorrect categorization, because the listener receives little or none of the message if he or she is overreacting emotionally. If the listener dislikes a particular speaker, for instance, his or her negative reactions may prevent him or her from listening to the speaker's message, much less assigning meaning to that message. Moreover, if the listener encounters opposition to deeply-rooted views, he or she is apt to become emotionally "deaf." The listening time then is either spent reflecting on some aspect of the speaker's message or planning a strategy to refute or destroy the opponent's point of view rather than on processing the complete message. We should remember, though, that not all emotional triggers are negative. For example, a listener may admire the speaker so much or may be so positively influenced by certain of the speaker's words or phrases that he or she is willing to accept whatever is said without question.

Both positive and negative emotional triggers contribute to incorrect categorization and faulty schema. These triggers are recognized as a serious communication barrier. Teachers and parents alike are admonished to be aware of the emotional impact that words can have on their listening children.[102] Indeed, the National Council on Child Abuse uses a "Words Hit As Hard As A Fist" theme in their parent-awareness campaign. (See fig. 3.4). Continuing the council's theme, Ossie Davis speaks of the brute force that words reflecting racism have:

> Those words are attacks upon your physical and emotional well being; your pulse rate is possibly higher, your breath quicker; there is perhaps a tremor along the nerves of your hands and your legs; sweat begins in the palms of your hands, perhaps. With these few words I have assaulted you. I have damaged you, . . .[103]

So, how does the listener deal with emotional triggers? To begin with, it is helpful to be aware of how the listener's frame of reference and perceptual filter affect his or her assignment of meaning. As Howell stresses, however, awareness is not a solution in itself: "Recognizing differences in perception among interacting people helps us understand the gap of misunderstanding but does little to reduce it."[104] To reduce misunderstanding, the listener must develop the desire and the ability to enter another's frame of reference—to attempt to see the message from the speaker's point of view—especially when the speaker's point of view differs greatly from that

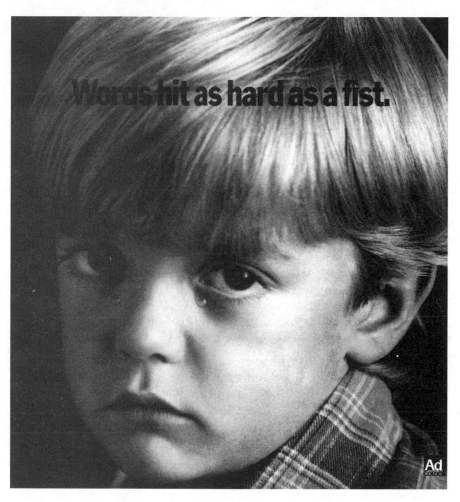

"You're pathetic. You can't do anything right!"

"You disgust me! Just shut up!"

"Hey stupid! Don't you know how to listen."

"Get outta here! I'm sick of looking at your face."

"You're more trouble than you're worth."

"Why don't you go find some other place to live!"

"I wish you were never born."

Children believe what their parents tell them. Next time, stop and listen to what you're saying. You might not believe your ears.

Take time out. Don't take it out on your kid.

 Write: National Committee for Prevention of Child Abuse, Box 2866E, Chicago, Illinois 60690

Figure 3.4.
Advertisement by the National Committee for Prevention of Child Abuse. Reprinted by permission of the National Committee for Prevention of Child Abuse.

of the listener. For one to enter into another's world, another's frame of reference, Hugh Fellows recommends the following mental activity:

> You are walking alongside a stream of water and you hear a tiny voice say, 'I am a fish. I have never seen a man, but I have heard men talk. Tell me, please: What are shoes?' Try to put into words what you would say to the fish to make him understand what shoes are. (You cannot say simply, 'They are covering for one's feet,' for if he has never seen a man, he would not know what feet are.)[105]

To reduce misunderstanding, the listener must also recognize his or her emotional triggers and endeavor to minimize their effect on meaning assignment. The first step is to identify one's own emotional biases. Although one can never be *completely* free of emotional biases, one can become aware of them and, thus, recognize when they are working against his or her accuracy of meaning assignment. The second step is to control one's emotional reactions. Although the listener often may not be able to regulate the outer environment, it is possible to control the inner environment. Rather than exposing one's emotional biases to others for their control, the listener should curb his or her emotional reactions to maintain self-control. Perhaps each listener would do well to go through the same kind of emotional de-sensitivity training that many in law enforcement positions must undergo:

> Military and civilian law enforcement personnel are trained to recognize the words that tend to trigger a personal emotional response so that they maintain control of themselves should an occasion arise when they are subjected to verbal abuse wherein these trigger words are directed at them. . . . [T]o effectively do their jobs and assist in crisis intervention situations, they must remain detached and objective. If they are triggered into losing their objectivity and become emotionally involved, they are no longer an objective third party mediator who can help solve the problem, but instead become part of the problem.[106]

Although listeners may never be in positions in which they must assist in a crisis intervention situation, they will likely be involved in several personal crises in which emotional triggers will be directed at them. Thus, in order to avoid becoming a part of the problem in these crisis situations, listeners, like law enforcement personnel, must maintain emotional control. Borisoff and Purdy urge listeners to develop emotional control by first listening to and acknowledging one's feelings—to "take a short break to listen to how we are feeling"—before responding at an emotional level.[107] However irritating a speaker may be or however offensive his or her ideas may be to the listener, the listener who has emotional control is in a better position to detect the speaker's illogical thinking on issues with which he or she strongly disagrees as well as to detect the speaker's errors on issues with which the listener agrees. In addition, the listener who seeks out ideas that might prove him or her wrong as well as those that might prove him or her right may prevent self-enslavement by emotional biases that may, in fact, be held on irrational grounds. Moreover, the listener who, while maintaining emotional control, has learned to listen to others' views can, according to Lynch, author of *The Language of the Heart,* lower his or her blood pressure and, thus, be healthier.[108]

Gaining control of one's **linguistic** environment, like the rest of the listening process, takes work. Buchminster Fuller is reputed to have spent two years, mostly by himself, studying what words meant to him: "Only after a two-year period did he feel sufficiently free from language traps to use language as an agent for bringing things closer rather than pushing them away, for making language his tool."[109] While we may not all wish to spend two years on the process, the goal is admirable. By knowing our emotional triggers, by employing self-discipline to curb our emotional reactions, by listening to speakers with whom we disagree as well as those with whom we agree, by delaying judgment until we have listened to the complete message, by remaining open to views different from our own, by searching for evidence that might prove speakers or ourselves wrong or right, by conserving emotional energy directed toward attending to what speakers mean when using words or phrases, and by accepting the uniqueness of each individual, we can minimize the impact that emotional triggers may have.

linguistic control

Other common causes of inadequate meaning assignment arise from the listener's limited knowledge, narrow experiences, inadequate vocabularies, and rigidity in category or schema assignment. Fortunately, as listeners increase their knowledge, broaden their experiences, enlarge their vocabularies, and temper their stubbornness, errors in meaning assignment can be minimized. Each listener, however, must demonstrate flexibility in recategorizing or reconceptualizing stimuli through his or her schema if he or she truly desires to achieve more reliable meanings. Levin describes the heights one can reach in achieving meaning as a listening communicator:

other common causes of inadequate meaning assignment

> When listening really echoes and resonates, when it allows the communication to reverberate between the communicants, and to constitute, there, a space free of pressure and constraint, it actively contributes, quite apart from the speaking, to the intersubjectivity constellation of new meanings, meanings actually born within this intercorporeality; and it promises, because of this, the achievement of mutual understanding—if not also consensus.[110]

Control of the listening process, then, is a matter of dealing with the three listening components in our definition of listening: *receiving, attending to,* and *assigning meaning.* We have not, however, included in our definition two components found in others' conceptualizations of listening: remembering and responding. We agree with Lundsteen's view regarding where the process of listening actually ends: "The term listening is appropriate when the person reaches the part in the series of steps where his experience brings meaning to verbal symbols."[111]

Remembering and Responding

It is our position that **remembering**—the process of storing stimuli in the mind for the purpose of recalling them later—is probably involved in all

remembering

aspects of listening and is, thus, inherent in the listening process when a listener actively engages in the total process. The importance of remembering can be seen as it relates to holding accumulated sound while we are initially receiving and attending to a message.[112] Also, it is relevant to the act of attending to, since, in general, only those stimuli to which we attend reach the LTM. Moreover, as we categorize or conceptualize input data, we must search our memory bank for a "fit" in order to assign meaning.

Since remembering as it relates to listening has been discussed under the listening components of receiving, attending to, and assigning meaning, it is not necessary to include a discussion of memory as a separate component of the listening process. It is sobering, however, to reflect on how much information that we receive probably is not stored in the LTM in a way that facilitates recall. Indeed, most cognitive psychologists believe that "a substantial part of what we learn on one exposure may be forgotten until the next exposure provides a relearning opportunity."[113] Research on television viewing, again, reveals how much listeners depend on repetition for LTM recall.[114]

responding

In analyzing **responding**, we think that it is important to determine whether covert (internal response perceivable only to the listener) or overt (external response perceivable to others) response is intended. If covert response is meant, the response could be a part of (1) the receiving process as our auditory and sensory mechanisms respond to the original stimulus, (2) the attention process, since the very act of attending to the stimulus is a response by the system, or (3) the assignment of meaning process when we respond by categorizing the stimulus through our schema so that it matches the intended meaning of the source. However, if overt response is indicated, we do not consider responding to be a part of the listening process. When listeners respond overtly, they are no longer listeners; rather, they become the senders—that is, the encoders of new messages—in the communication process. Although we do not consider overt responding to be a part of the listening process, we fully acknowledge its primacy in communication transactions. It is only through feedback that a speaker can judge whether a listener has or has not engaged in the listening process. Indeed, our perceptions of others as good or bad listeners are based largely on how others display their listening through the feedback that they communicate.

Summary

In this chapter, we have presented a detailed description of contemporary views and conclusions about the complex process of listening. We have noted research that provides empirical evidence that listening is indeed a distinct activity. We have looked at definitions of listening. And we have presented our structural definition—and a sequential process model—of listening: *Listening is the process of receiving, attending to, and assigning meaning to aural and visual stimuli.* We hope that you, too, are now convinced that listening is a highly complex human behavior and that it is impossible to "just" listen.

Suggested Activities

1. Now that you have read about the process of listening, how would you define or describe listening? Write out your definition of listening.
2. List ten sounds you hear in a normal day. Then, rank the sounds according to the amount of auditory fatigue each sound causes you.
3. Identify five words you have acquired through unique personal experiences and for which, as a result of these experiences, you have specialized meanings. Some of these words can be shared with the class.[115]
4. Identify five words that evoke highly emotional feelings in you and analyze what personal experiences have influenced these reactions. Some of these words can be shared with the class.
5. List three words whose once-empty categories have become meaningfully filled since this course began. Some of these words can be shared with the class.
6. Create your own model of the listening act. All models should be photocopied, shared with the class, and then carefully analyzed and evaluated by the students and instructor.
7. Go to a public place, such as a shopping mall, department store, health club, sporting event, playground, amusement park, golf course, beach, library, or cafeteria. For several minutes, close your eyes and listen to all of the sounds that are present; then, list the sounds you heard. Repeat the listening experience, but this time focus your attention on listening only to nonhuman sounds; list the nonhuman sounds you heard. Next, focus your attention on listening only to human sounds, such as paralanguage, words, phrases, sentences, and so on; list the human sounds you heard. This exercise will demonstrate how you use selective attention.
8. List at least five specific beliefs, views, attitudes, and/or biases that you presently have regarding general subjects such as government, family, marriage, religion, economics, health, death, success, freedom, and/or entertainment. Trace each belief, and so on, back to its origin. Share a few of these and their origins with the class to determine in what ways you and other students have similar/dissimilar frames of reference. How did these likenesses/differences affect your listening to other students as they shared their beliefs, views, attitudes, and/or biases?
9. Listen to and view a televised episode of *People's Court*, and point out examples of ineffective listening. Also, identify possible causes (emotional "deafness," selective listening, concentration on defending self rather than on listening to the speaker's complete message, etc.) of ineffective listening.
10. Draw cartoons of your listening experiences, and then share the cartoons with the class.
11. Schemata represent expectations that listeners have concerning the structure of the information to be encountered in a message. Reflect on

a listening situation in which your schemata have shaped your response to the message. What expectations, positive and negative, did you have about the message? Did your expectations, then, assist with or interfere with your processing of the message?

12. Throughout the semester, keep a journal of your listening experiences. Each day, record one or more listening experiences in "diary" fashion. The following format may be most helpful:

Date:
Type of Listening (Appreciative, Discriminative, etc.):
(We recognize that you will not fully appreciate these categories until you have covered chapters 5 through 9. For the time being, leave this section blank and plan to go back, at a later date, to designate the types of listening you have done.)

Description of the Listening Event:
Your Response As a Listener:
What You Learned about Your Listening:
Try to provide a variety of experiences in the various types of listening. Avoid recording just experiences you have at work, and so on, but rather go to some events you might not otherwise attend so that you can broaden your listening skills as you prepare this journal. At the end of the semester, submit your journal to your instructor.

The following are examples of possible journal entries:

September 18
Therapeutic Listening
Today I listened as a friend described the options available to her family about her mother's illness. Her mother has terminal brain cancer and recently underwent an unsuccessful operation and radiation therapy. The decision must be made as to whether to have her undergo another operation or to leave things as they are and let the woman die in peace.

I served as a sounding board, offering no advice, but trying to give comfort and support. She finally decided to leave things as they are. I'm sure that her opportunity to talk through the situation with me was helpful.

I know people can solve their own problems, but I certainly realize how important it is to have that other person as a "sounding board" to articulate your thoughts and come up with a solution. If only more people would listen to others. . . .

October 10
Appreciative Listening
Tonight I went to the Convention Center to hear Al Jarreau. The man's voice is an instrument in itself. I had never fully realized that parts of his album that I thought were instrumental were actually his voice. The drummer would beat, and he would copy the sound to the exact pitch.

Jarreau's band was great. While much of the concert was his pop music, I thought his jazz pieces, "Take Five" and "All Blues," were his best. Jarreau is terrific on albums, but he's superb on the concert stage.

It was a very sensual experience. I wonder why certain music has such power. I love music and have finally learned to avoid picking it apart. I now just let it "happen" to me at a concert such as this one. It's a wonderful way to appreciate an artist's work.

November 18
Comprehensive and Critical Listening

This evening I watched a PBS presentation, *Keepers of the Wild*. One segment dealt with the preservation of bats. I've always been afraid of bats. I don't like them, and my first impulse was to turn to something else. However, I decided to stay with the show. The Bat Conservation International (BCI) organization educates the public on the importance of bats in our ecosystem. The group gives public demonstrations as well as rescues orphaned or injured bats. It even relocates bats from unwanted areas in order to save their lives. Volunteers from all over the country are affiliated with BCI, setting up rehabilitation centers for the care of bats. They go into the schools with educational programs to teach children the importance of bat conservation.

I can now see that we do need bats in our environment. By consuming vast numbers of insects, they help to control many crop pests and other insects that spread disease to humans or livestock. The announcer noted that a single little brown bat is capable of capturing 600 mosquitoes in 1 hour. He gave an example of a central Texas colony of some 20 million free-tailed bats that can eat nearly a half million pounds of insects in a single night.

Bats are also crucial to the survival of the world's tropics because fruit- and nectar-eating bats are vital for pollination. The announcer used the example of West African bats carrying 90 to 98 percent of the seeds of pioneer plants that begin the cycle of forest regrowth on cleared land. Additionally, he revealed a BCI study that documented more than 300 plant species in the Old World tropics alone that need bats for pollination or seed dispersal. Since I am interested in saving our rain forests, I feel enlightened to know that more than 450 commercial products come from these plants, all of which are crucial to the economies of those developing countries. I did not know, for example, that many of our cultivated crop plants—including bananas, breadfruit, dates, figs, peaches, mangoes, cloves, cashew nuts, and even tequila—rely on bats for their survival. A sobering fact is that other plants that yield essential medicines (and many that have not yet been discovered) are vulnerable to the endangerment of bats.

During the show, I jotted down a few notes, mainly statistics that were given. Most of the time, though, I concentrated on gathering information—listening for main ideas and the significant details to help me understand the overall message. From the show, I was then able to evaluate the message and to understand the problem of the dwindling bat population. It was quite moving. From now on, I'll be more aware of the fine qualities of our little winged night creatures.

November 28
Discriminative Listening

I talked to my brother yesterday, and he said that he thought my mother (who is a manic depressive personality) was going into a manic phase. He wanted me to call her in Ft. Lauderdale and see if I could tell. She has had this illness for at least five years, so by just listening to her talk, we can usually pick up on the warning signs. I called her this morning to check it out. I was listening for an increased pace in her speech, higher pitch in her voice, disjointed thoughts, and irrational thinking. After listening to her, I decided that she hadn't gone into this phase yet, but I could tell it was coming on. It's very important to detect it immediately so that adjustments can be made in her medication.

I am pleased that I've been able to sharpen my discriminative listening skills and deal with what could be an important medical situation. I wish more physicians and nurses could have this training!

Notes

1. J. Caffrey, "Auding Ability at the Secondary Level," *Education* 75 (January 1955): 303–310; J. Caffrey and T. W. Smith, "Preliminary Identification of Some Factors in the Davis-Bells Games," cited by Donald Spearritt, *Listening Comprehension—A Factorial Analysis* (Melbourne, Australia: Australian Council for Educational Research 1962), pp. 14–15; J. E. Karlin, "A Factorial Study of Auditory Function," *Psychometrika* 7 (December 1942): 251–279; C. N. Hanley, "Factorial Analysis of Speech Perception," *Journal of Speech and Hearing Disorders* 21 (March 1956): 78–87.
2. Spearritt, *Listening Comprehension—A Factorial Analysis*, pp. 14–15.
3. Ibid., pp. 21–22.
4. C. H. Weaver, *Human Listening: Processes and Behavior* (Indianapolis: Bobbs-Merrill, 1972), p. 132.
5. W. Tucker, "Science of Listening," *19th Century* 97 (April 1925): 548.
6. P. T. Rankin, "The Measurement of the Ability to Understand Spoken Language" (Ph.D. diss.,University of Michigan, 1926), *Dissertation Abstracts* 12 (1952): 847.
7. T. R. Lewis, "Listening," *Review of Educational Research* 28 (April 1958): 89.
8. J. J. Floyd, *Listening: A Practical Approach* (Glenview, IL: National Textbook, 1985), p. 4.
9. D. P. Brown, "Teaching Aural English," *English Journal* 39 (March 1950): 128.
10. Established in 1979, the purpose of the International Listening Association (ILA) is to promote the study, development, and teaching of effective listening in all settings. For additional information on the association, contact Kathy Thompson, ILA Executive Director, at 1–800–ILA–4505.
11. S. W. Lundsteen, *Listening: Its Impact on Reading and the Other Language Arts* (Urbana, IL: NCTE/ERIC, 1971), p. 9. See also, N. J. McKenzie and A. J. Clark, "The All-in-One Concept: How Much Must Listening Research Include?" (Paper presented at the International Listening Association Convention, 1994, Boston, MA) and P. Emmert and V. J. Emmert, "The Multivariate Nature of Listening" (Paper presented at the Speech Communication Association Convention, 1993, Miami, FL). For an analysis of listening definitions, see E. C. Glenn, "A Content Analysis of Fifty Definitions of Listening," *Journal of the International Listening Association* 3 (1989): 21–31.
12. R. L. Birdwhistell, as cited in M. L. Knapp and J. A. Hall, *Nonverbal Communication in Human Interaction*, 3d ed. (NY: Holt, Rinehart and Winston, 1992), p. 29; A. Mehrabian, *Silent Messages* (Belmont, CA: Wadsworth, 1971), pp. 43–44. An interesting discussion of the functions of nonverbal cues is offered in D. G. Leathers, *Nonverbal Communication Systems* (Boston: Allyn and Bacon, 1976).

13. E. H. Sewell, Jr., "Visual Communication in the Listening Process" (Paper presented at the International Listening Association Convention, 1989, Atlanta, GA).

14. The reader should note that our statement of the listening process is very much a description derived from a human information-processing model of the cognitive psychologists. This information-processing model is not without its critics among psychologists, critics who argue that the information process is not so simple as the model would suggest and that the information stimulus is not merely transferred from one stage to another to ultimate storage in the long-term memory. We certainly agree that any view of listening should not be perceived as a simple serial progression of stages, because the process is highly dynamic and interrelated at any given time. For reviews of the research on information-processing and listening, see B. R. Witkin, "Constructs in Information Processing" (Paper presented at the International Listening Association Convention, 1986, San Diego, CA) and R. Edwards, "Cognitive Issues for Listening Theory: Schemas, Memory and Stages" (Paper presented at the International Listening Association Convention, 1989, Atlanta, GA). See, too, B. Goss, *The Psychology of Human Communication* (Prospect Heights, IL: Waveland Press, 1989).

15. For readings on the intricacies of visual discrimination, see C. H. Graham, ed., *Vision and Visual Perception* (New York: Wiley, 1965).

16. National Eye Institute, *Glaucoma* (Bethesda, MD: National Eye Institute, 1986).

17. National Eye Institute, *Cataracts* (Bethesda, MD: National Eye Institute, 1989).

18. National Eye Institute, *Age-Related Macular Degeneration* (Bethesda, MD: National Eye Institute, 1986).

19. Better Vision Institute, *Visual Problems of the Aging* (NY: Better Vision Institute, n.d.)

20. T. Friend, "Treating Low Vision," *The Ithaca Journal*, 12 May 1994, pp. 11B, 12B.

21. For a complete discussion of the physiology of hearing, see H. A. Newby and G. R. Popelka, *Audiology* (Englewood Cliffs, NJ: Prentice-Hall, 1992). See, too, S. Handel, *Listening* (Cambridge, MA: The MIT Press, 1989), ch. 2 and J. B. Nadel, "Hearing Loss," *New England Journal of Medicine* 329 (7 October 1993): 1092–1102.

22. National Institute on Deafness and Other Communication Disorders, *Biennial Report of the Director, National Institutes of Health, 1991–1992,* (Washington, DC: The National Institutes of Health, 1993), p. 84.

23. S. Shane, "Tinnitus: Constant, Inescapable Noise from Within," *The Sun*, 7 September 1986, pp. B-1, B-3.

24. Newby and Popelka, *Audiology*.

25. J. A. Smith, "Ear Implant Gives Man Limited Hearing—and a Whole New Life," *The Sun*, 8 December 1985, pp. B-1, B-10 and T. Balkany, "A Brief Perspective on Cochlear Implants," *New England Journal of Medicine* 328 (1 October 1993): 281–282.

26. S. Miller, "Infrared Earphones Bring Opera to the Hearing-Impaired," *The Evening Sun*, 30 November 1984, pp. D-1, D-5.

27. D. Holzman, "Noises in the Ear May Begin to Fade," 3 *Insight* (31 August 1987), 62.

28. M. Dickey, "Sounds That Silence," *The Washingtonian*, 1988, p. 57.

29. D. Lipscomb, *Noise: The Unwanted Sounds* (Chicago: Nelson-Hall, 1974), pp. 59–65.

30. H. Merker, *Listening* (NY: Harper Collins, 1994), p. 28.

31. N. Moray, "Attention in Dichotic Listening: Affective Cues and the Influence of Instructions," *Quarterly Journal of Experimental Psychology* 11 (February 1959): 56–60; A. T. Welford, "Evidence of a Single-Channel Decision Mechanism Limiting Performance in a Serial Reaction Task," *Quarterly Journal of Experimental Psychology* 11 (November 1959): 193–210; A. M. Treisman and G. Geffen, "Selective Attention and Cerebral Dominance in Perceiving and Responding to Speech Messages," *Quarterly Journal of Experimental Psychology* 20 (May 1968): 139–150; N. Moray, *Listening and Attention* (Baltimore, MD: Penguin Books, 1969).

32. D. E. Broadbent, *Perception and Communication* (London: Pergamon Press, 1958); N. Moray, *Attention: Selective Processes in Vision and Hearing* (London: Hutchinson Educational LTD, 1969), pp. 28–30.

33. "The Musical Brain," *U.S. News and World Report* 108 (11 June 1990): 56–62.

34. J. A. Deutsch and D. Deutsch, "Attention: Some Theoretical Considerations," *Psychological Review* 70 (1968): 80, 84.

35. Ibid., p. 84.

36. Moray, "Attention in Dichotic Listening: Affective Cues and the Influence of Instructions," pp. 56–60; I. Oswald, A. Taylor, and M. Treisman, "Discrimination Responses to Stimulation During Human Sleep," *Brain* 83 (1960); 440–453; C. E. Howarth and K. Ellis," The Relative Intelligibility Threshold for One's Own Name Compared with Other Names," *Quarterly Journal of Experimental Psychology* 13 (November 1969): 236–239.

37. A. M. Treisman, "Contextual Cues in Selective Listening," *Quarterly Journal of Experimental Psychology* 12 (November 1960): 246.
38. H. Bering-Jensen, "Switched-On Brains Screening Ads," *Insight* 5 (13 February 1989): 236–239.
39. M. D. Basil, "Multiple Resource Theory I: Applications to Television Viewing," *Communication Research* 21 (April 1994): 177–207; M. D. Basil, "Multiple Resource Theory II: Empirical Examination of Modality-Specific Attention to Television Scenes," *Communication Research* 21 (April 1994): 208–231.
40. Treisman, "Contextual Cues in Selective Listening," pp. 242–248; Moray, *Attention: Selective Processes in Vision and Hearing*, pp. 30–32; Moray, *Listening and Attention*.
41. U. Neisser, *Cognitive Psychology* (NY: Appleton-Century-Crofts, 1967), pp. 79–107.
42. D. Kahneman, *Attention and Effort* (Englewood Cliffs, NJ: Prentice-Hall, 1973).
43. C. D. Wickens, "The Structure of Attentional Resources" in R. Nickerson, ed. *Attention and Performance VIII* (Hillsdale, NJ: Lawrence Erlbaum, 1980): 239–257; C. D. Wickens, "Processing Resources in Attention," in R. Parasuraman and D. R. Davies, eds. *Varieties of Attention* (Orlando, FL: Academic Press, 1984): 63–102.
44. R. M. Shiffrin and W. Schneider, "Controlled and Automatic Human Information Processing: II. Perceptual Learning, Automatic Attending, and a General Theory," *Psychological Review* 84 (1977): 127–190.
45. J. C. McCroskey, "Human Information Processing and Diffusion," in *Speech Communication Behavior*, eds. L. L. Barker and R. J. Kibler (Englewood Cliffs, NJ: Prentice-Hall, 1971): p. 172.
46. Ibid.
47. Sir F. C. Bartlett, *Remembering* (Cambridge: Cambridge University Press, 1932), p. 190.
48. Weaver, *Human Listening: Processes and Behavior*, pp. 33, 37.
49. L. Haser and R. T. Zacks, "Automatic and Effortful Processes in Memory," *Journal of Experimental Psychology: General* 108 (1979): 356–388.
50. M. D. Vernon, "Perception, Attention, and Consciousness," in *Attention*, ed. Paul Bakan (Princeton, NJ: D. Van Nostrand Company, 1966), pp. 37–57.
51. For reviews of the history of memory theory and current perspectives on memory development, see: A. F. Collins, S. E. Gathercole, M. A. Conway, and P. E. Morris (eds.), *Theories of Memory* (Hillsdale, NJ: Lawrence Erlbaum, 1993); D. J. Herrmann, H. Weingartner, A. Searleman, and C. McEvoy, *Memory Improvement* (NY: Springer-Verlag, 1992); A. J. Parkin, *Memory: Phenomena, Experiment and Theory* (Cambridge: Blackwell, 1993); and L. T. Thomas, "Separating Verbal Memory from Listening: Which Are We Measuring?" (Paper presented at the International Listening Association Convention, Memphis, TN, 1993).
52. R. C. Atkinson and R. M. Shiffrin, "Human Memory: A Proposed System and Its Control Processes," in *The Psychology of Learning and Motivation: Research and Theory*, Vol. 2, eds. K. W. Spence and J. T. Spence (New York: Academic Press, 1968), pp. 89–195; D. A. Norman and D. E. Rumelhart, "A System for Perception and Memory," in *Models of Human Memory*, ed. D.A. Norman (NY: Academic Press, 1970), pp. 19–64.
53. G. Sperling, "The Information Available in Brief Visual Presentations," *Psychological Monographs* 74 (1960): 1–29; R. N. Haber and L. G. Standing, "Direct Measures of Short-Term Visual Storage," *Quarterly Journal of Experimental Psychology* 21 (February 1969): 43–54; E. Averbach and A. S. Coriell, "Short-Term Memory in Vision," *Bell System Technical Journal* 40 (January 1961): 309–328.
54. C. J. Darwin, M. T. Turvey, and R. G. Crowder, "An Auditory Analogue of the Sperling Partial Report Procedure: Evidence for Brief Auditory Storage," *Cognitive Psychology* 3 (April 1972): 255–267; A. D. Baddeley, *The Psychology of Memory* (NY: Basic Books, 1976); R. Efron, "The Minimum Duration of a Perception," *Neuropsychologia* 8 (January 1970): 57–63; D. W. Massaro, *Experimental Psychology and Information Processing* (Chicago: Rand McNally, 1975).
55. R. Lachman, J. L. Lachman, and E. C. Butterfield, *Cognitive Psychology and Information Processing: An Introduction* (Hillsdale, NJ: Lawrence Erlbaum Associates, 1979), p. 211.
56. D. A. Norman, "Memory While Shadowing," *Quarterly Journal of Experimental Psychology* 21 (February 1969): 85–93; M. I. Posner, "Short Term Memory Systems in Human Information Processing," in *Attention and Performance*, ed. A. F. Sanders (Amsterdam: North-Holland Publishing Company, 1967), pp. 267–284; R. M. Shiffrin and R. C. Atkinson, "Storage and Retrieval Processes in Long-Term Memory," *Psychological Review* 76 (March 1969): 179–193; L. R. Peterson and M. J. Peterson, "Short-Term Retention of Individual Verbal Items," *Journal of Experimental Psychology* 58 (1959): 193–198.

57. F. I. M. Craik and R. S. Lockhart, "Levels of Processing: A Framework for Memory Research," *Journal of Verbal Learning and Verbal Behavior* 11 (December 1972): 671–684.
58. Posner, "Short-Term Memory Systems in Human Information Processing," p. 276.
59. D. Rundus, "Analysis of Rehearsal Processes in Free Recall," *Journal of Experimental Psychology* 89 (July 1971): 63–77.
60. R. N. Bostrom and E. S. Waldhart, "Memory Models and the Measurement of Listening," *Communication Education* 37 (January 1988): 1–18.
61. G. A. Miller, "The Magical Number Seven, Plus or Minus Two: Some Limits on Our Capacity for Processing Information," *Psychological Review* 63 (1956): 81–97.
62. R. N. Bostrom and E. S. Waldhart, "Components in Listening Behavior: The Role of Short-Term Memory," *Human Communication Research* 6 (Spring 1980): 123.
63. A. W. Melton, "Implications of Short-term Memory for a General Theory of Memory," *Journal of Verbal Learning and Verbal Behavior* 2 (July 1963): 5.
64. Lachman, Lachman, and Butterfield, *Cognitive Psychology and Information Processing: An Introduction*, p. 273.
65. M. Haider, "Neuropsychology of Attention, Expectation, and Vigilance," cited by Weaver, *Human Listening: Processes and Behavior*, p. 42.
66. Kahneman, *Attention and Effort*, p. 9.
67. A. G. Greenwald and C. Leavitt, "Audience Involvement in Advertising: Four Levels," *Journal of Consumer Research* 11 (June 1984): 581–592.
68. L. L. Barker, *Listening Behavior* (Englewood Cliffs, NJ: Prentice-Hall, 1971), p. 32.
69. B. Henker and C. K. Whalen, "Hyperactivity and Attention Deficits," *American Psychologist* 44 (February 1989): 216–218; and A. Kurzius, "Attention Deficit Disorder: Does the Feingold Diet Really Help?" *NEA Today* 5 (June 1989): 12.
70. W. B. Key, *Media Sexploitation* (NY: New American Library, 1977); W. B. Key, *Subliminal Seduction* (NY: American Library, 1974); W. B. Key, *Clam Plate Orgy* (NY: New American Library, 1981).
71. P. M. Merikle, "Subliminal Auditory Messages: An Evaluation," *Psychology & Marketing* 5 (Winter 1988): 357. See a summary of past research in W. C. Fotheringham, *Perspectives on Persuasion* (Boston: Allyn and Bacon, 1966), pp. 97, 150. Current work with the technique is described by Merikle, "Subliminal Auditory Messages: An Evaluation"; T. M. Moore, "The Case Against Subliminal Manipulation," *Psychology & Marketing* 5 (Winter 1988): 297–316; D. Oldenburg, "Hidden Messages," *The Washington Post*, 3 April 1990, p. C–5; and P. Recer, "It's All in Your Mind," *San Francisco Chronicle*, 25 September 1991, p. D3.
72. "Album Blamed in Suicide Pact," *The Washington Post*, 17 July 1990, p. B3.
73. R. J. Marzano and D. E. Arredondo, *TACTICS A Program for Teaching Thinking* (n.d.), p. 2.
74. R. Brown, *Words and Things* (NY: Free Press of Glencoe, 1958), pp. 82–109.
75. R. C. Anderson, "Control of Student Mediating Processes During Verbal Learning and Instruction," *Review of Educational Research* 40 (June 1970): 349–369.
76. Lundsteen, *Listening: Its Impact on Reading and the Other Language Arts*, p. 37.
77. Ibid., pp. 37–41.
78. Barker, *Listening Behavior*, p. 33.
79. Weaver, *Human Listening: Processes and Behavior*, pp. 42–59.
80. J. S. Bruner, J. J. Goodnow, and G. A. Austin, *A Study of Thinking* (NY: Wiley, 1956).
81. Roger Brown, *Words and Things*, pp. 82–109.
82. E. F. Loftus and J. W. Schooler, "Information-Processing Conceptualizations of Human Cognition: Past, Present, and Future," in *Information and Behavior*, Vol. 1, ed. B. D. Ruben (New Brunswick, NJ: Transaction Press, 1987), pp. 225–250.
83. The notion of seven bits of information was postulated by G. A. Miller, "The Magical Number Seven, Plus or Minus Two: Some Limits on Our Capacity to Process Information." Other cognitive psychologists dispute the notion that the short-term memory can handle this many. See G. Mandler, "Organization and Memory," in *The Psychology of Learning and Motivation*, Vol. 1, eds. K. W. Spence and J. T. Spence (NY: Academic Press, 1967), pp. 328–372.
84. E. Tulving, "Episodic and Semantic Memory," in *Organization of Memory*, eds. E. Tulving and W. Donaldson (NY: Academic Press, 1972), pp. 382–403.
85. M. Fitch-Hauser and M. A. Hughes, "Defining the Cognitive Process of Listening: A Dream or a Reality?" *The Journal of the International Listening Association* 2 (1988): 76.
86. For a review of schema theory and listening, see R. Edwards and J. L. McDonald, "Schema Theory and Listening," in *Perspectives on Listening*, eds. A. D. Wolvin and C. G. Coakley (Norwood, NJ: Ablex, 1993), pp. 60–77.

87. D. E. Rumelhart, "Schemata: The Building Blocks of Cognition," in *Theoretical Issues in Reading Comprehension*, eds. R. J. Spiro, B. C. Bruce, and W. F. Brewer (Hillsdale, NJ: Lawrence Erlbaum Associates, 1980), pp. 33–58.

88. M. J. Smith, "Cognitive Schemata and Persuasive Communication: Toward a Contingency Rules Theory," in *Communication Yearbook 6*, ed. M. Burgoon (Beverly Hills, CA: Sage, 1982), pp. 330–362.

89. R. C. Schank and R. P. Abelson, "Scripts Plans and Knowledge," in *Thinking: Readings in Cognitive Science*, eds. P. N. Johnson-Laird and P. C. Watson (Cambridge: Cambridge University Press, 1977) pp. 421–432. See also M. J. Smith, "Cognitive Schemata and Persuasive Communication: Toward a Contingency Rules Theory," pp. 330–362.

90. C. M. Judd and J. A. Kulik, "Schematic Effects of Social Attitudes on Information Processing and Recall," *Journal of Personality and Social Psychology* 38 (1980): 549–578.

91. J. C. Richards, "Listening Comprehension: Approach, Design, Procedures," *TESOL Quarterly* 17 (June 1983): 219–240.

92. M. J. Beatty and S. K. Payne, "Listening Comprehension As a Function of Cognitive Complexity: A Research Note," *Communication Monographs* 51 (March 1984): 85–89.

93. M. Pressley, J. G. Borkowski, and W. Schneider, "Good Information Processing: What It Is and How Education Can Promote It," *International Journal of Educational Research* 13 (1989): 857–867.

94. B. Goss, "Listening As Information Processing," *Communication Quarterly* 30 (Fall 1982): 306.

95. For a review of language theory in communication, see S. W. Littlejohn, *Theories of Human Communication* (Belmont CA: Wadsworth, 1992), pp. 63–84.

96. S. Pinker, *The Language Instinct* (NY: William Morrow, 1994), p. 227.

97. R. D. Halley, "Processing Data for Listening: Using a Cognitive Processing Model to Improve Your Listening" (Paper presented at the International Listening Association Convention, 1989, Atlanta, GA), p. 6.

98. L. Carroll, *Through the Looking-Glass* (NY: International Collectors Library, n.d.), p. 230.

99. D. Phillips, "Avianca Crash: A Fatal Misunderstanding," *The Washington Post*, 25 June 1990, p. A5.

100. J. Krishnamuriti, *The First and Last Personal Freedom* (NY: Harper and Row, 1975), quoted in R. B. Adler, L. B. Rosenfeld, and N. Towne, *Interplay*, 2d ed. (NY: Holt, Rinehart and Winston, Inc., 1980), p. 153.

101. J. C. McCroskey, "Human Information Processing and Diffusion," pp. 170–173.

102. See, for instance, M. Faber, "Sticks and Stones Can Break My Bones," *NEA Today* 8 (November 1989): 6.

103. O. Davis, "The English Language Is My Enemy," *IRCD Bulletin* 5 (Summer 1969): 13.

104. W. S. Howell, *The Empathic Communicator* (Belmont, CA: Wadsworth, 1982), p. 48.

105. H. P. Fellows, *The Art and Skill of Talking With People* (Englewood Cliffs, NJ: Prentice-Hall, 1964), pp. 38–39.

106. R. W. Lucas, "Trigger Words" (Unpublished paper, College Park, MD: University of Maryland, 1983). Used with permission.

107. D. Borisoff and M. Purdy, *Listening in Everyday Life* (Lanham, MD: University Press of America, 1991), pp. 23–42.

108. J. J. Lynch, "Listen and Live," *American Health* 4 (April 1985): 39–43.

109. L. Buscaglia, *Love* (NY: Fawcett Crest Books, 1972), pp. 150–151.

110. D. M. Levin, *The Listening Self* (London: Routledge, 1989), p. 181.

111. Lundsteen, *Listening: Its Impact on Reading and the Other Language Arts*, p. 41.

112. Ibid., p. 26.

113. M. J. Farr, *The Long-Term Retention of Knowledge and Skills* (NY: Springer-Verlag, 1987), p. 30.

114. B. Gunter, *Poor Reception: Misunderstanding and Forgetting Broadcast News* (Hillsdale, NJ: Lawrence Erlbaum, 1987).

115. R. O. Hirsch, *Listening: A Way To Process Information Aurally* (Dubuque, IA: Gorsuch Scarisbrick, Publishers, 1979), p. 17.

- *Effective communication is influenced by the homophily (sharing) between the listener and the speaker.*

- *Communication is the result of careful, responsible decision making by speaker and listener.*

- *The listener is affected by key variables: culture, gender, age, hemispheric specialization, physical and psychological states, attitudes, self-concept, receiver apprehension, time, and listener preferences.*

- *The effective listener*

  - *assumes, with the speaker, at least equal responsibility for the success of the communication transaction*

  - *understands the listening self*

  - *motivates the listening self*

  - *listens actively*

  - *sends effective feedback*

  - *knows the influence of the key variables at any given point in his or her listening*

CHAPTER 4

Listening as a Communication Function

Having called a staff meeting, Project Manager Seniorina Chavez begins by stating the purpose of the meeting: "Our client wants us to develop a more personal approach for meeting customer needs. His major concerns are . . . ."

While Seniorina continues to speak, various listening choices, strategies, and variables—revealed to us through staff members' thoughts and actions—are operating.

Some of their thoughts are these:

I'm not listening to this.

I wish she would use visuals to support her comments.

I need this information; I've not dealt with customer needs before.

So far I don't agree, but I'll reserve final judgment until she has completed her message.

I need to move closer to Seniorina so I can hear her better.

Why can't she be more specific?

Please don't let her ask me a question.

My, Seniorina certainly seems to be distressed about that issue.

I surely hope this meeting will be over before my business luncheon.

And, some of their actions are these:

One noisily rummages through her brief case.

Another interrupts Seniorina to give his perspective.

Still another nods her head.

These are only a few of the numerous listening choices, strategies, and variables that affect the way listeners function during communication transactions.

Listening—as the process of receiving, attending to, and assigning meaning to aural and visual stimuli—is very much a communication function. As we have seen in chapter 2, communication is a transactional process in which the source and the receiver *share* the communication experience as they simultaneously send and receive messages. Thus, the ongoing nature of the communication transaction requires that we—as receivers/sources—participate actively as decoders of the source's messages and as encoders of our own feedback messages. Active participation includes making responsible listening decisions, applying key listening strategies, and recognizing key listening variables.

Listening as Sharing

homophily

Much of the communication effectiveness of both listeners and speakers results from a principle termed "**homophily**." Homophily represents the degree to which interacting individuals have significant similarities in such attributes as background, education, social status, beliefs, and values. In contrast is "heterophily" in which interacting individuals have significant differences. When the source and the receiver have common characteristics that enable them to share the message, communication undoubtedly becomes more effective. Furthermore, Rogers and Bhowmik emphasize that "effective communication between source and receiver leads to greater homophily in knowledge, beliefs, and overt behavior."[1]

The principle of homophily is particularly important to communicators who must interact with persons from other cultures. Business executives and diplomats, for example, must understand that the individuals with whom they are communicating in international settings may not necessarily share their frames of reference or even their language code. Consequently, they must be trained in the communication patterns of different cultures so that they will be able to adapt to differing communication conventions and to understand the impact of these differences on the communication transaction.

Listening as Decision Making

decision making

Just as communication results from the homophilous sharing of messages by source and receiver, so, too, is communication the result of careful, responsible **decision making** throughout the system. The source must select the original stimulus and translate that stimulus into a message. The development of the message requires decision making: deciding which code (verbal and/or nonverbal) will best express the message, through which channel(s) to present the message, in what context, when, and to whom. Although all of these decisions may occur instantaneously as they often do, for example, in conversation, the skillful communicator is at all times aware of what he or she is doing while making these communication decisions.

Communication as responsible decision making should not be viewed, however, as the sole function of the source. For centuries, communication scholars have focused on the source of the communication by formulating the strategies for developing and structuring speeches, for understanding audiences, and for presenting ideas through effective delivery. Until recent times, little if any attention has been focused on the listener. As communication scholars have come to understand the psychology of processing human communication, they have also recognized the central role that the listener must assume in the communication process. This central role assumes at least equal participation by the listener. But equal participation can result only from careful, responsible decision making throughout the process.

Viewing listening as a communication act implies that the listening communicator must have understanding and skills about the listening process to function effectively. First of all, the listener must make decisions about the reception of and attention given to the stimulus. It is possible to decide to hear or not to hear the sound of a radio, for example, just by the simple control of the radio's on-off knob. We make these receiving decisions on the basis of whether we have the time and/or energy to listen, whether we perceive we have anything to gain from the listening experience, whether we desire to listen to the particular source of the communication, whether we feel satisfied with the communication channel, and a host of other influences that can affect this initial decision.

Once the listener has decided to receive and to attend to the message, it is necessary to make choices about assigning meaning to the stimulus. Assignment of meaning requires decisions about the categorization or conceptualization of the stimulus within the category or schemata, decisions about the interpretations of the terms used by the speaker, decisions about the degree of emotional involvement the listener can allow in these interpretations, and numerous other decisions that provide for the linguistic and semantic processing of the stimulus within the individual's language system. Recognizing the semantic principle that meanings reside in people— not directly in the symbols that we use to communicate—leads to the realization that decisions about the verbal message also extend to the nonverbal message. It is essential for the listener to distinguish the nonverbal messages and to interpret these messages as they can complement, contradict, replace, accent, or repeat the verbal messages.

Although the actual listening process stops with the assignment of meaning, the listening communicator also has a responsibility to provide some form of feedback in the system. Consequently, the listener must make choices about the form and the function of the feedback he or she intends to send to the source. At this stage in the communication process, however, the listener becomes the sender of the feedback message.

Thus, to participate in a communication transaction in which the listener has the responsibility of decoding the messages of others and also of encoding feedback messages, the listener must make choices. A listener must decide the following:

> not to listen
>
> to listen
>
> to listen for a purpose
>
> to set aside biases and attitudes in order to understand the message
>
> to concentrate on the message, not the speaker
>
> to overcome emotional barriers to listening
>
> to know why he/she is listening at a given time
>
> to know how she/he is listening at a given time
>
> to understand the process of listening—and the process of communication—to know what he/she is (or should be) doing as a listening communicator throughout this process

It may interest the reader to note that we have included as one choice to decide "not to listen." A listener has a responsibility to oneself and to the other person to make this choice if it is appropriate. You may choose not to listen, for example, if you do not have the time to listen. If you have a pressing deadline for a project at work, it would be appropriate to attend to the project and not break your concentration to try to listen to another person. It would be likely that the listening in such a situation would not be particularly satisfying for either party. You would feel frustrated because you needed to get on with the project, and the other person would feel frustrated because you were not truly "tuned in" as a listener.

You may need to decide not to listen, also, if you are suffering from what might be termed "information overload." There are times when we all receive too much information at one time, so that it becomes difficult to process it meaningfully. It is projected that we double the amount of information that we have to process every two to five years, so it is no wonder that, as listeners, we sometimes feel overwhelmed by messages.

The listener's decision-making process is not an easy one. The lifetime of experiences, attitudes, knowledge, and skills that make up our frame of reference—our very self—influences the way we deal with these choices. How we react to situations and how we process them through our own perceptions is a dominant force in our decision making. A listener might decide to listen with careful comprehension, for example, if he or she perceived the outcome to be rewarding. Listening so as to thoroughly comprehend a lecture in order to do well on a test on the material may be a familiar choice.

Many decisions we make as listeners relate to others as well as to ourselves. We may listen with empathy to someone we would like to have as a friend, but we may listen more comprehensively if the other person is a stranger who wants to discuss a faulty product. Each listener must make choices based on the relationship that he or she has, or wants to have, or does not want to have with the other person.

Whether the decisions affect the listener, the other person, or both, every listening choice creates its own problems, generates its own difficulties, and pays its own rewards. As human beings, listeners make their choices and then must live with the positive or negative consequences of those decisions. It would seem, therefore, that the responsible listener must be aware of the choices that he or she faces, make those choices within some sort of valid framework for the listener and the other person, and then be prepared to live with or to change the results of the choices he or she makes.

As a listening communicator, an individual has responsibilities both to self and to others. A listener likewise shares responsibility for the listening process itself. To be an effective communicator, a listener should assume at least *51 percent* of the burden of the communication. Such a responsibility requires that the listener be committed to active, involved, dynamic listening and engage constantly in the communication. The prevalent notion of listening as a passive, simple act is not consistent with our view of listening as *communication,* a process that requires involvement and responsibility for the outcome of the communication. Thus, the listening communicator is a responsible communicator. To function as a responsible listening communicator, one must understand and acquire certain key listening strategies as a necessary part of any communication transaction.

Four Listening Strategies

Once you understand what is involved in the complex process of listening, you can monitor how you are functioning as a listener at any given point in the listening process. Understanding and self-monitoring can be enhanced by adapting four strategies to your own listening behavior: understanding your self, motivating your listening self, listening actively, and sending feedback.

Strategy #1: Understanding the Self

The first strategy for effective listeners is to understand ourselves as communicators. Just as the sources of the communication messages should be trained in self (intrapersonal) communication, so too should listeners know themselves. Brooks states the case eloquently:

understanding self

> To see one's self accurately; to understand and know one's self clearly and honestly; to have acquired those abilities and characteristics associated with a strong, wholesome, self-concept—these objectives are directly related to liking one's self, being confident in one's self, and in relating and living effectively and satisfyingly with others.[2]

Learning about yourself is a major focus of popular workshops and self-help books such as Marriage Encounter, Covey's *The 7 Habits of Highly Effective People*, etc. A useful technique for beginning this self-analysis is through the Johari Window.[3]

Dimensions of the Self

The Johari Window accounts for the dimensions of the self. (See fig. 4.1) As the diagram indicates, there are four basic areas of the self: free, blind, hidden, and unknown. Area I is the **free area**—the open, public self. Area III, the **hidden area**, could systematically be diminished through communicating information about yourself to others—a process of self-disclosure.

Area II, the **blind area**, consists of all the information other persons know about you but that you do not know about yourself. This may be information that individuals are reluctant to reveal to you. Some enterprising individuals have formed companies in metropolitan areas to handle the communication of such messages. One firm in Washington, D.C., for instance, provided a message service to send bad news anonymously—so you could tell your boss that he or she has bad breath—for a fee!

The **unknown area** (Area IV) represents all aspects of a person that really are not known to the individual or to others. Some persons may argue that the more you communicate about yourself and create an "open" window, the more you diminish your unknown area. Others may contend that we can never specify the unknown and, thus, never narrow our unknown area. (The more you know, the more you don't know.)

Through self-disclosure, a communicator can design his or her own window so that the configurations may change. Each individual's window, of course, will have different proportions. An open individual may have a window that resembles that in figure 4.2.

free area

hidden area

blind area

unknown area

	Known to Self	Not Known to Self
Known to Others	I Free Area	II Blind Area
Not Known to Others	III Hidden Area	IV Unknown Area

Figure 4.1.
The Johari Window.

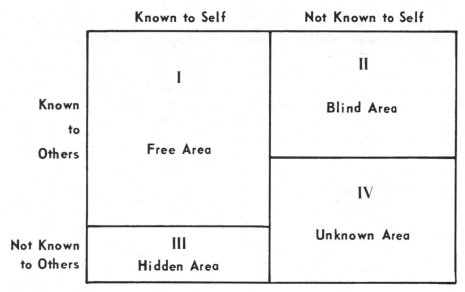

	Known to Self	Not Known to Self
Known to Others	I Free Area	II Blind Area
Not Known to Others	III Hidden Area	IV Unknown Area

Figure 4.2.
The Johari Window as Modified Through Self-disclosure.

The value of self-disclosure for improved mental health has been documented by the pioneer of this technique, Sidney Jourard:

> . . . no man can come to know himself except as an outcome of disclosing himself to another person. . . . When a person has been able to disclose himself utterly to another person, he learns how to increase his contact with his real self, and he may then be better able to direct his destiny on the basis of knowledge of his real self.[4]

Risks of Self-Disclosure

Although there are great benefits to the process of self-disclosure, it should be recognized that the process also carries with it considerable risk. As one discloses the dimensions of one's self to another person, the other individual must be able to accept the information that is disclosed. Consequently, a great deal of trust in the relationship is necessary for self-disclosure to be meaningful, and this trust results from continuous negotiation of the relationship. Most readers probably can recall a situation when they disclosed some confidential aspect about themselves to a friend or classmate who, in turn, communicated that information to the entire circle of friends or fellow students. As in all relationships, it then became necessary to reconsider the relationship with this individual. The risks involved in the disclosing process, however, are well worth the sacrifices we all make in developing and maintaining human relationships and in defining our own self-concept through the process.

Self-Understanding of Attitudes toward Listening

attitudes

This process of understanding yourself can help you as a listener to know something about your self-concept, your attitudes, and your values and how they affect your listening behavior. Understanding your self-concept can lead to a better self-understanding of your attitudes, not only toward messages you receive but also toward the receiving process itself. Just as a negative attitude about one's listening behavior may be fostered, one may develop apprehension about listening or come to have a distorted attitude about the process as simply a passive act. Through social conditioning at home and school it is possible that listeners have come to view listening communication as a very passive phenomenon: Sit back and let the speaker (for example, the teacher) talk.

Channel Preferences of the Listening Self

channel preferences

Not only are we conditioned to view listening as a rather passive process, but also most listeners may be conditioned to prefer to rely on visual stimuli for information. Some research has been conducted on visual discrimination as it relates to receiver preferences for stimuli. Researchers have concluded that three factors may account for our visual preferences: the potential for discriminability, the informative value, and the saliency of the stimulus itself.[5]

While listeners in general may prefer visual stimuli, our channel preferences may switch when it comes to processing advertising. Ries and Trout point out that advertisers spend 55 percent of their advertising dollars on visual media and only 45 percent on audio messages. Yet research in advertising suggests that consumers spend 85 percent of their time with ear-oriented media (radio and television) and only 15 percent of their time with print (visual) media. Ries and Trout stress that television can be considered an audio medium in that "sound plays a far more important role in the communication effectiveness of television than most advertisers or their agencies are willing to admit."[6]

Channel preference may depend upon the content of the message as well. Schnapp has determined that listeners may process positive and negative messages differently: "The verbal channel may be a more effective channel for negative statements, while the visual channel is appropriate for affirmative messages."[7]

Our channel preferences probably are tied up in the educational process. Research in reading indicates that most young learners prefer to learn through listening in the early years. At about the age of twelve, however, the learner begins to prefer to learn information through reading rather than listening.[8] Acknowledging such differences, educators strive to identify the individual learner's preferred style—visual, auditory, or haptic (moving and doing)—and then develop strategies for processing information most effectively within that style.[9]

Understanding visual discrimination as it relates to auditory discrimination can be of assistance in becoming more discerning in the reception of stimuli. McLuhan and Fiore noted listeners' tendency not to trust the auditory input:

> Most people find it difficult to understand purely verbal concepts. They *suspect* the ear; they don't trust it. In general we feel more secure when things are *visible*, when we can 'see for ourselves.' We admonish children, for instance, to 'believe only half of what they *see*, and nothing of what they *hear*.' All kinds of 'shorthand' systems of notation have been developed to help us *see* what we *hear*.
>
> We employ visual and spatial metaphors for a great many everyday expressions. . . . We are so visually biased that we call our wisest men *vision*aries, or *seers*![10]

This distrust of auditory input may have an effect on our discrimination of auditory stimuli. If, indeed, we prefer to receive information visually, that preference could lead us to more careful attention to and discrimination of visual communication codes. Reviewing the research on tonal, verbal, and visual channels, Corley concludes that there is little agreement among researchers as to just what the influence of the channels on receiver attitudes and comprehension is.[11] Despite one's preference, however, the listener certainly must not disregard auditory communication codes. And, clearly, listeners who are not comfortable with a particular channel—the telephone, for instance—will not be as efficient when that channel is in use.

Value System of the Listening Self

Just as understanding one's attitudes toward channel preferences aids in knowing the listening self, so does knowing one's value system. How you process the information that you receive through the category system depends to a great extent on how consistent your categories are with what you value. Thus, as a receiver, you run the risk of stereotyping nonverbal and verbal messages and drawing false conclusions from them.[12] Clearly, nonverbal, physical characteristics make up the first impressions that individuals have of others, and "despite people's best intentions, their initial impressions of others are shaped by their assumptions about such characteristics."[13]

values

These assumptions are **stereotypes** that individuals hold. Snyder points out that "these assumptions are not merely beliefs or attitudes that exist in a vacuum; they are reinforced by the behavior of both prejudiced people and the targets of their prejudice."[14] Walter Lippmann once explained the concept of stereotype:

stereotypes

> . . . an ordered, more or less consistent picture of the world, to which our habits, our tastes, our capacities, our comforts, and our hopes have adjusted themselves. They may not be a complete picture of the world, but they are a picture of a possible world to which we are adapted. In that world, people and things have their well-known places, and do certain expected things. We feel at home there. . . .[15]

Psychologist Daniel Katz views stereotyping as necessary to the linguistic process in that stereotyping is the only way that one can quickly, efficiently assimilate and thus interpret a new stimulus. Yet Katz warns that stereotyping emotionally limits the intellectual process. Because an individual has very narrow experiences, a person must assimilate information to his or her own frame of reference. This limitation of experience, thus, is essentially formed by a person's tendency to assign all of a group or classification to one simple cognitive category. One who has had little or no interaction with persons of a particular ethnic group will tend to stereotype (or to assimilate to his or her own frame of reference) messages about persons of that ethnic group. "The mere fact we lack the experience or the imagination to understand another point of view," cautions Katz, "does not mean that we realize our inadequacy and remain open-minded about it."[16] Rather than recognize the limitation of stereotyping, most individuals will process the stereotype to handle the information that is being communicated and, consequently, make it meaningful to their own frame of reference.

Although it is apparent that stereotyping is part of the verbal, linguistic process of assigning meaning to a stimulus, it should be recognized that listeners can run risks with stereotyping nonverbal stimuli as well. Your authors caution that many of the principles offered by popular writers on the subject of "body language" can perpetuate stereotypes. Though increasing awareness of nonverbal communication, some of the popular treatments of the subject tend to overgeneralize and almost encourage listeners to stereotype the nonverbal message being sent, whether it is how to recognize the sexually available person or how to identify the status-seeking individual.

Despite the oversimplification inherent in attempting to interpret nonverbal codes, research indicates that there are some nonverbal acts or events that can serve as perceivable stimuli for a listener. These stimuli can only carry meaning to the listener if, as in verbal communication, the intent of the stimuli and the code are *shared* by the two communicators.

It is desirable, therefore, for the listener to know when he or she is stereotyping verbal and nonverbal messages and to recognize the limitations that these "short cuts" bring to the communication. Coming to terms with your own stereotyping behavior can be a significant part of knowing the listening self.

Understanding your own listening behavior, then, involves discovering your self-concept, attitudes, and values as they relate to your listening responses. We owe it to ourselves to know how we are responding and sincerely attempt to avoid any of the pitfalls in the listening process.

Strategy #2: Motivating the Listening Self

motivating self

As a second listening strategy, the listener should strive for individual motivation in the process.[17] As we have defined listening as an active process involving the complex interaction of our sensory channels, responsible listeners should recognize that they cannot remain passive partners in the communication.

Weaver notes that developing a desire to listen is basic to effective listening. Unfortunately, developing this desire is not a simple behavioral act, because, as Weaver states, "most people do not really want to listen, but to talk."[18] He concludes that the desire to listen requires that the listener suppress the desire to talk and develop a desire to learn. We have a capacity to listen, composed of all the dimensions treated in this book; but this capacity to listen is not meaningful unless we combine it with a willingness to listen.[19]

The motivation to listen is closely tied to the concept of the listener's **willingness to listen**. Researchers in the field have begun to study this concept.[20] Listening reluctance, the unwillingness to receive and/or decode messages, has been found to influence the effectiveness of the communication.[21] It should be recognized that some research efforts have not successfully identified willingness to listen as a specific communication variable.[22] On the other hand, Vinson and Roberts have developed a "Willingness-to-Listen Scale" designed to account for the influence of the familiarity of the speaker, the importance of content, and the effect of the communication environment on the listener. Empirical testing of this scale has led Vinson and Roberts to conclude that willingness to listen is a unique communication variable that may be used to predict an individual's listening success in different contexts (educational, social, and/or professional).[23]

The impact of motivation on listening comprehension was demonstrated in a study in which subjects were asked to comprehend and to recall information presented by means of compressed speech tapes. Subjects in one of the groups were promised extra credit points commensurate with their comprehension scores as an added incentive to performing well as listeners. The results of this experiment indicate that the motivated group actually scored higher, leading researchers to conclude that the capacity to listen combined with willingness to listen affects listening performance.[24]

Since listening requires active behaviors, good listeners will assume the responsibility for their own motivation to listen and will not passively wait for the speaker to provide such motivation. An overreliance on the speaker to carry the burden in the communication process results in serious barriers to effective communication transactions. Such passive behavior on the part of most of us as listeners almost represents a cultural conditioning: We have come to rely on the speaker for motivation. The speaker who fails to provide such motivation frequently is tuned out. Such an attitude toward the motivation to listen is irresponsible, because it represents a renunciation of the equal responsibility to make a communication work.

Building intrinsic motivation to listen is not easy. There is no specific drive to listen. Rather, a combination of factors enters into our listening motivation: drives, habits, predispositions, cognitive states. If the listening experience can fulfill basic needs, then motivation can be maintained at a high level. This maintenance can be strengthened by efforts on the part of the listener to establish goals and identify specific purposes for listening before entering into the listening situation.

Likewise, the listener can enhance intrinsic motivation to listen by establishing his or her own **rewards system**.[25] Rather than relying on external rewards (the familiar gold stars from teachers), we can motivate ourselves by providing our own satisfactions for effective listening. Often this

willingness to listen

rewards system

reward system can result from establishing and then achieving a goal in a listening situation. For instance, you may set as your goal acquiring new information from a technical briefing in a field with which you are not familiar. Your internal reward can come from the satisfaction of knowing that you did listen well and that you did gain new information.

We ought to consider the effect of social conditioning on our listening motivation as well. We tend to emphasize the passive nature of listening in American society. School children are expected to "Be quiet and listen." Adults are advised to "Just sit back and listen" by emcees, personnel trainers, and even ministers. We should reorient our communication to the advice, "Sit *up* and listen."

To overcome the unwillingness to listen and to establish internal motivators require that the listener place greater premium on effective listening behavior. It would seem, therefore, that we have a serious responsibility to ourselves as listeners to place a high priority on listening motivation.

Strategy #3: Listening Actively

listening actively

A third strategy for effective listening is **listening actively**, by consistently participating responsibly and willingly in the communication process. Since communication is a transactional process, it is necessary, as we have seen, that listeners assume at least 51 percent of the burden in that communication. The motivated listener will be a communication partner, participating actively with the source throughout the transaction. Indeed, empowering the listener to be an active participant in the communication process may very well change the dynamics of power in the speaker-listener relationship; instead of allowing the speaker to be the controlling force in the communication, the active listener could shift that locus of control to him- or herself.

Although it may seem simplistic to advise someone to listen, it is unfortunate that many people do not assume the responsibility for active listening. Because we are so conditioned to view listening as a passive act in our society, many listeners do not assume an active role as listening communicators. The passive listener is more likely to sit back and let the speaker assume the sole burden for making the communication work. Listeners too frequently dismiss their own poor listening with "Oh, he's a boring speaker" or "What a worthless subject." Such responses serve as convenient excuses for not assuming responsibility to participate actively in the communication.

right to free listening

Active listening throughout the communication transaction should be regarded as a parallel to our right to free speech. Just as speakers have the right to speak out in our democratic society, no matter how unpopular their message may be, listeners also have the **right to free listening**. As we have seen, we can make choices to listen or not to listen. However, once we have made the decision to listen, that decision should be accompanied by a commitment to listen with responsibility. The active listener is willing to meet this obligation and to listen to an entire message before passing judgment.

The importance of this willingness to listen has been demonstrated by the violent reactions that the aide to activist Louis Farrakhan, Khallid Abdul

The motivated listener actively participates with the source throughout the communication transaction.

Muhammad, has received on college campuses. Muhammad allegedly has made some anti-Semitic statements that have angered Jewish people and Muhammad's African American audiences alike. While colleges and universities have been called to task for providing Muhammad with a forum, the alternative censoring of what messages that audiences can receive certainly runs counter to our First Amendment rights of free expression. A coalition of organizations in higher education articulated the point best: "Unless there is freedom to speak and to teach, even for those with whom we differ on fundamentals . . . and unless there is freedom for all to listen and to learn, there can be no true college or university. . . ."[26]

It is clear that, as listening communicators, we should be willing to participate equally in the process. Such participation extends to our responsibility to hear the speaker out before we decide to accept or to reject that person's message. People who *share* the communication transaction and allow speakers the opportunity to present their messages serve as active listeners throughout the process.

Strategy #4: Sending Feedback

A fourth strategy that characterizes the listener as an effective communicator is the strategy of **sending feedback**. Feedback—the response or reaction of the listener as perceived by the source in the communication transaction—plays a very valuable role in the entire process. Ranging from questions and paraphrases to head nods and postural shifts, the verbal

sending feedback

and nonverbal feedback we send to individuals can have a significant effect on them. First, it can affect greatly the development of their self-concept.[27] As we have seen, self-concept results primarily from our perceptions of how others perceive us. A person who receives positive feedback gains self-confidence. On the other hand, negative feedback can be disruptive and discouraging to a speaker and thus diminish the self-confidence the speaker may have as a communicator.[28]

Feedback from listeners can also regulate speaker's actions, such as how they organize their remarks as they are communicating to listeners. The denial of feedback has been found to be disruptive to speakers and to result in speeches that are less coherent, less accurate, and more wordy.[29] The listener who intends to participate actively in the communication transaction, then, must decide to send feedback that will be supportive to the speaker's efforts to further the communication process.

Supportive feedback can be valuable not only to individuals but also to organizations. In an informative study that demonstrates the impact of feedback on an organization, Tubbs and Widgery trained managers and supervisors in a large automotive factory to send feedback to workers about their job performance. As a result of the training in feedback skills, managers and supervisors improved their communications with their workers. The factory workers, in turn, were found to improve their job performance and to be more satisfied with their work.[30]

Many organizations have come to recognize the benefits of feedback in conducting the business of the organization. Dreyfack urges executives to use feedback techniques by questioning the speaker and/or repeating what the individual has said as "a virtual guarantee of efficiency."[31] "In communicating," he stresses, "it is as important to make good feedback—or checkback—habitual as it is important from a health standpoint to make deep breathing habitual."[32] The payoff for effective feedback ultimately is increased productivity for the organization and more supportive interpersonal relationships for individuals.

A classic study on the use of feedback illustrates the impressive potential for strengthening the communication transaction for both the speaker and the listener. In this study, Leavitt and Mueller asked a speaker to describe a diagram to another person. In different treatments, the level of feedback was shifted so that, in some situations, the speaker received no direct verbal or nonverbal response whatsoever, while in other situations the speaker could look at the listener, ask questions, or enter into a complete conversation about the diagram with the listener. The research demonstrated that the more feedback there was between the listener and the speaker, the more accurate was the listener's interpretation of the message. Likewise, with increased feedback, both listener and speaker became confident that the message was communicated with accuracy, and, as feedback increased, both received greater satisfaction from the communication. Not surprisingly, introducing feedback into the communication system did increase the amount of time required for the communication transaction.[33]

Despite the time required, it should be recognized that the role of feedback enhances the communication because the listener's feedback creates the **perception of listening**. As Daly observes, "No matter how effective, skilled, or competent an individual is in listening, unless he or she is perceived as listening by the other interactants, little may be accomplished."[34] Urging managers to demonstrate listening skills, Brownell discovered that the "appropriateness and timeliness of the response" are measures by which employees form judgments of their managers' listening ability.[35] Listening competency has even been defined as the perception created through feedback behaviors that "show an *accurate* understanding of the message as well as demonstrate *support* for the relationship between the communication participants. . . ."[36]

perception of listening

In our professional organizations and in our personal lives, feedback can strengthen the communication and create a true transaction for the communicators. To be effective, however, the listener's feedback should be open, direct, constructive, and meaningful to the speaker. Barker offers **ten helpful guidelines for sending feedback effectively**:

guidelines for sending feedback

1. Send feedback that is appropriate to the speaker, message, and context (e.g., say "Amen" rather than applaud after a prayer has been said).
2. Be certain the speaker perceived the feedback (e.g., let the speaker see a quizzical look).
3. Make certain the feedback is clear in meaning (e.g., send complementary messages such as saying "No" while shaking the head from side to side).
4. Send the feedback quickly (e.g., consider the confusing effect delayed laughter at a speaker's humorous comment would have on a speaker who is now discussing a serious issue).
5. Beware of overloading the system (e.g., temper smiling and head nodding to prevent these acts from being excessive and appearing insincere).
6. Delay in performing any activity that might create an unintentional effect (e.g., recognize that a stretching movement could be perceived as a sign of the desire to speak).
7. Keep feedback to the message separate from personal evaluation (e.g., realize that frowning to indicate dislike of a speaker's tie could be perceived by the speaker as an indication of disapproval of his or her message).
8. Use nondirective feedback ["an attempt by the listener to replicate the message"] until the speaker invites evaluation of his message (e.g., ask, "What actions by Tom make you think he's inflexible?").
9. Be certain that you understand the message before you send directive feedback [feedback that "involves a value judgment"] (e.g., say, "I understand your concern about not making many

sales this quarter. My observations of your interactions with prospective clients suggest to me that you need to listen more and talk less.").

10. Realize that early attempts at giving more effective feedback may seem unnatural but will improve with practice.[37]

As basic guidelines for sending feedback, Barker's suggestions can prove useful. Listeners need to sharpen their feedback skills and to recognize that they are sending verbal and nonverbal messages through the feedback channel. Since sending feedback is a continuous process while we are communicating with someone, it is essential that the feedback clearly express what it is we want to communicate to the other person.

A good listener will avoid sending distracting, unintentional feedback through responses that may not be appropriate to the situation. A good listener will recognize that open, honest feedback certainly is the best form of communication. We realize, however, that honest feedback may sometimes have a negative effect on a speaker and lead to the termination of the communication. Consequently, the listener should assess carefully the possible effects of his or her response and act accordingly.

attending behaviors

Essential to effective listening is a special kind of feedback—**attending behaviors**. Attending behaviors not only demonstrate the listener's interest in the speaker and the speaker's message but also enhance the listener's comprehension of information.[38] By demonstrating attending behaviors, the listener conveys a message that represents an open invitation to the sender to talk:

> I'm interested in you as a person, and I think that what you feel is important. I respect your thoughts, and even if I don't agree with them, I know they are valid for you . . . I . . . want to understand you. I think you're worth listening to, and I want you to know that I'm the kind of person you can talk to.[39]

eye contact

One important attending behavior is **eye contact**. The effective listener must be careful not to shift his or her gaze, look around the room, stare, or maintain an out-of-focus (or "zoned out") look. Rather, the listener should maintain an appropriate and comfortable gaze and look directly at the speaker. A comfortable gaze includes blinking, for the listener who does not blink at an average rate of fifteen to twenty blinks per minute may be off on a mental tangent. With increased blinking, the listener may be experiencing physical or psychological stress—anxiety, anger, excitement, boredom—while with decreased blinking, the listener may be acquiring information or engaging in visual activity that requires concentration.[40]

bodily positioning

Attending behaviors also include the listener's **bodily positioning**. Three bodily behaviors that communicate a positive attitude are (1) direct—face-to-face—body orientation, (2) forward trunk leans, and (3) close, but not uncomfortably close, interactional distances.[41] Another attending behavior of the body is an open, receptive posture—a posture free of body crosses that convey that the listener has little desire to interact with the sender. These open, natural, and relaxed bodily behaviors reflect listener interest and involvement. The listener should avoid, then, such bodily behaviors as noninclusive body orientation, excessive postural shifts, fidgeting, greater interactional distance, and closed bodily posture, for these can suggest restlessness, uneasiness, or unresponsiveness to the other communicator.

Additional attending behaviors include **nodding the head, maintaining responsive facial expressions, verbalizing brief and encouraging expressives**, and **speaking in a warm and pleasant voice tone**. Research shows a significant positive relationship between perceived helping effectiveness and frequency of positive head nodding and smiling.[42] Besides smiling at the appropriate times, the listener should convey other facial expressions that indicate involvement. To signify a lack of understanding, for example, the listener may knit one's brow or drop one's jaw. Above all, the concerned listener should avoid displaying an "expressionless" face, for a lack of facial responsiveness can quickly destroy a communication interaction.

nodding the head, maintaining responsive facial expressions, verbalizing brief and encouraging expressives, speaking in a warm and pleasant voict tone

Research also shows that the listener's verbalization of expressiveness indicates to the sender that the listener is attending to the sender's message.[43] Examples of these signal cues are vocal segregates such as "mm-hmm," "uh huh," "ah," "umm," and brief comments such as "oh," "I see," "yes," and "right." By verbalizing these expressives, the listener demonstrates an important attending behavior and encourages the sender to continue speaking. Likewise, research indicates that another positive attending behavior is the listener's use of a generally warm, quiet, and pleasant vocal tone—a tone that communicates caring and involvement.[44]

To develop skill in the use of caring, attentive feedback, we, as listeners, "should not only be providing some kind of feedback, but we should be aware of the other person's response to that feedback."[45] Perceptions of the other person's response to feedback require total involvement in the communication transaction. The listener must be aware not only of the feedback he or she is sending but also of how that feedback is being received. Should you find, for instance, that the speaker is being antagonized by the responses you are giving, then you ought to consider adjusting the feedback messages so as not to create a defensive communication climate.

One of the most dramatic examples of the need for developing sensitive feedback skills is in the classroom. Students should learn how to send teachers useful and supportive feedback that can facilitate the learning process. Students who read their notes or campus newspapers in class often fail to realize what their "silent messages" communicate to a teacher who is presenting a lecture. Or the student who responds to a teacher's questioning look with "I'm sorry that I've missed the last two weeks. Have we done anything important?" clearly needs to analyze the impact of the message that he or she is sending. Attention to the feedback that a student sends to a teacher—as well as the feedback that a teacher sends to a student—can serve to create a positive, supportive communication bond that ought to enhance the learning process.

Developing useful, supportive feedback skills can be a major task for all sensitive listeners. Feedback skill results from conscious effort; you must know what you are doing as a communicator. Practice and experience can enable one to develop and perfect these skills. As Barker points out in his tenth recommendation, concentration on feedback skills may seem unnatural at first. However, listeners may find that using feedback skills over a period of time leads to a comfortable level for communicating messages to speakers.

Indeed, sending feedback is an important listening strategy, just as knowing one's self, developing self-motivation to listen, and listening actively serve as devices to enhance the communication transaction between listeners and speakers in conversations, in the classroom, on the job, and in all aspects of life. It is evident, then, that the listener is a communicator, maintaining at least equal responsibility for the communication process as it is being transacted. As a communicator, the listener must make use of these key communication strategies in order to fulfill his or her responsibilities.

Ten Factors Influencing the Listening Process

Just as there are strategies that affect the listener's participation in the communication process, so, too, are there key influences that will affect our listening performance. Clearly, as listeners we are affected by the many aspects of the entire communication process: the source of the message, the message itself, the channel(s) through which the message is transmitted, the communication environment, and the noise surrounding the communication. All of these factors were described in chapter 2.

As listeners, we are also affected by other key factors that influence the way we function at any given time in the listening process. Research in listening behavior stresses the significance of these influencing factors that we carry with us into each communication encounter. Erway concludes that competency in listening "can only be defined by examination of the interaction of the variables of both the message and the listener."[46] The major interrelated variables that affect us as listeners include culture, gender, age, hemispheric specialization, physical and psychological state, attitudes, self-concept, receiver apprehension, time, and listener preferences.

Factor #1: Culture

culture

Culture is understood as the set of customs, behaviors, beliefs, and language that distinguish a particular group of people and make up the background, experience, and perceptual filters of those individuals within that group. Communication scholars have come to recognize that culture is a primary determinant of all communication behaviors—including listening—because one's culture essentially serves to define who one is and how one will communicate through one's perceptual filter.

The influence of culture is especially prominent when one attempts to communicate across cultures. The American traveling to Japan, for instance, finds many different communication conventions, both verbal and nonverbal, which are part of the Japanese culture and which require understanding and adaptation. Likewise, subcultures within the United States illustrate differences that require adaptation for the listener to understand and to respond appropriately. Communication scholars recognize, for example, that communication between blacks and whites is shaped by cultural influences. The profound impact of culture on our listening behavior has been described by intercultural communication scholars Samovar and Porter: "The ways in which we communicate, the circumstances of our communication, the language and language style we use, and our nonverbal behaviors are primarily all a response to and a function of our culture. And, as cultures differ from one another, the communication practices and behaviors of individuals reared in those cultures will also be different."[47]

Thomlison observes that "the ultimate goal of the crosscultural listener is to reduce uncertainty in the communication process."[48] Further, he argues that listening is a critical aspect of communicating across cultures and that we must recognize that what is considered "effective listening" in one culture may be totally inappropriate or misunderstood in another culture.[49] Tannen agrees that the means by which people communicate that they are listening differs across cultures, including male and female cultures.[50] As a result, "intercultural listening," concludes Ostermeier, "is a challenging arena for the participants to enter. Factors other than language such as cultural values and nonverbal cues take on significant importance."[51]

What international students think of Americans as listeners illustrates the significance of cultural differences. A study of perceptions of listening behavior revealed that international students perceived Americans to be less willing and less patient as listeners than they perceived listeners in African, Asian, South American, or European cultures to be. But the respondents in the study also indicated that good listeners in any culture are those who *care* about their relationships with others.[52]

Anthropologist Edward Hall has identified cultures as low context and high context and has described how different cultures manage time and information in different ways. In **low context cultures**, such as the United States and Canada, communicators expect to give and to receive a considerable amount of information since their perception is that most message information is explicitly contained in words. Thus, in general, their messages are longer, more specific, and more elaborate. On the other hand, the perspective of communicators in **high context cultures**, such as Japan and Saudi Arabia, is that much more information is contained in the communication setting (external context) and in the communicators themselves (internal context) than is contained in the words transmitted. Thus, in general, their messages are faster, shorter, and less specific. As a result, speakers and listeners in high context cultures rely on a common understanding of cultural values and rules, including those pertinent to communication and communication behaviors.[53] The implications of Hall's model for intercultural listening are significant: "In high context cultures, it is the responsibility of the listener to understand; in low context, it is the speaker who is responsible for making sure the listener comprehends all. Hence, an Arab

low context cultures

high context cultures

may take offense when an American seemingly patronizes him by overexplaining, while a German may feel left out when a Japanese speaker begins his talk with the assumption that everyone already knows about a topic."[54] International marketer and author of *Communicating with Customers around the World*, K.C. Chan-Herur, recommends the following approach when Americans are conducting business abroad: "1. Observe. 2. Listen. 3. Speak. In America, we tend to do it in reverse order. For instance, while Americans value quickness, in many other countries, waiting to respond to a comment or proposal is a sign of respect."[55]

organizational cultures

Intercultural listening extends beyond international boundaries to **organizational cultures** as well. Every organization has its own culture; indeed, within an organization, each unit or even office group may have a culture. It can be a challenge to adapt one's communication style to listen and respond appropriately in these differing cultures. One office may be more laid back, for instance, while a group on the floor above you may operate with more rules and rigidity. Organizational culture may be manifested in the linguistic symbols (stories, sagas, legends, myths) or the physical symbols (layout, furnishings, building architecture) as well as the shared experiences of the group members.[56]

Moreover, cultural differences extend to listening in personal settings. Linguist Deborah Tannen describes the "tendency of people from similar cultural backgrounds to have habitual ways of speaking that are similar to each other's and different from those of people from other cultural backgrounds." Her finding stems from her observations of conversational styles when she lived in New York as contrasted to the styles she observed when she lived in California.[57] These cultural backgrounds apply to the different linguistic cultures of men and women as well.

Factor #2: Gender

Research points out that men and women have different attention styles and perhaps even different cognitive processing styles. Also, some neurologists are discovering that female and male brain structures are different; this difference may influence the way individuals process information.[58] These factors can affect the way men and women, even at a very early age, respond in different ways to the same stimuli. Although some early researchers concluded that men were superior to women as listeners, careful study of the literature does not substantiate such generalizations.[59] Rather, men and women have been found to "learn to listen for different purposes and have different listening goals. The primary contrast appears in task versus interpersonal understanding: Males tend to hear facts while females are more aware of the mood of the communication."[60]

female/male

Some researchers point to **female/male differences** that impact on listening styles. Psychologist Diane McGuinness has determined that males and females do have different attention styles: Females tend to be more attracted to people whereas males tend to prefer objects, and males have shorter attention spans.[61] Gender differences in brain development and

Understanding the Listening Process

hemispheric organization also are reflected in female/male listening behaviors. Pearson suggests that females hear more of a message because they reject less of it by accepting the pattern of the message as it is. Males, on the other hand, tend to restructure messages in terms of their own goals and to be less responsive to emotions.[62] Moreover, there is evidence for the widely held view that females tend to be more accurate at perceiving emotions.[63]

It is clear, however, that the sex roles of females and males are so dominant in American culture that it is likely that individuals are conditioned while young to respond according to those ascribed sex roles.[64] Such conditioning has been found to affect conversation patterns between males and females. West and Zimmerman's research supports the point that males control conversations, so much so that females are likely to ask 70 percent of the questions while males are likely to interrupt as much as 96 percent of the time.[65] Later research by Dindia, however, reveals that each gender is just as likely to interrupt the other in same-sex dyads.[66]

Efforts to explain these differences center on cultural conditioning. Studying the differences in male-female communication, Tannen has observed that females and males are conditioned to different communication styles at a very young age. Little girls share secrets with a best friend, while little boys play and compete in groups where what they do is more important than what they say.[67] Education specialists Myra and David Sadker observe that much of this conditioning is unwittingly transmitted by teachers in our nation's classrooms. Active, loud little boys get the teacher's attention, while the little girls are expected to be docile and quiet students.[68]

When adult men and women protest "He/she's not listening to me," argues Tannen, the issue probably is more in "displaying listenership."[69] Females have been shown to display more overt signs of listening (head nods, "uhum," facial expressions), so "women see men who listen quietly and attentively as not really listening at all . . . [while] a man who expects a woman to show she's listening simply by fixing her eyes on his face, feels she is overreacting when she keeps up a steady stream of 'mhms' and 'uhuhs.'"[70]

Anthropologists Maltz and Borker explain that these assumptions about the use of language may develop in close relationships with childhood friends. They observe that males tend to equate such sounds as "uh huh," "mmhmm," or "I see" with agreement, whereas females interpret such responses as "I am listening."[71] Some research does indicate that females have the advantage in some listening abilities: Females may be more effective than males at verbal memory and at decoding nonverbal behaviors (particularly when both auditory and visual stimuli are present) as well as more accurate than males in perceiving gender-related traits.[72]

It is interesting to consider how the differences in male and female listening styles may not be as consistent as we have been led to believe. The research may lead one to conclude that "men dominate workplace conversations just as they controlled classroom discussions."[73] However, studies of supervisory communication styles suggest that subordinates' perceptions of male and female supervisors' attentiveness vary according to the situation and the culture of the organization.[74] Clearly, our impressions of female and male listening styles result from each individual's experience in interpersonal communication situations in school, in family and social settings, and in the workplace.

Expectations of such female and male responses continue to shape the communication differences in American society, despite the changes in sex roles that are advocated by those involved in the feminist movement. Indeed, these communication differences reflect women's and men's different styles of communication, differences that may create "formidable barriers" to communication.[75]

Warren Farrell, founder of the National Organization for Changing Men, urges males and females to come to a better understanding of each other's perspectives through listening: "I'm asking women and men before they blame the other sex, to listen to the other sex's experience of the world—both their power experiences and powerless experiences."[76] "By fostering greater understanding about each other's communication styles, communication needs, and communication goals," conclude Borisoff and Merrill, "women and men can learn to become better listeners—to themselves and to each other."[77]

Factor #3: Age

age

Like gender, **age** is a given in human life. A listener may very well "grow" with age and gain greater experience and sensitivity so as to achieve effective listening. However, an individual's sensory mechanisms—particularly hearing affected by presbycusis and vision affected by presbyopia—will deteriorate with age and thus increase one's difficulty in receiving messages.[78] Such sensory deterioration may lead to a loss of confidence in one's communicative competence as well.[79] While research has led us to infer that young people may have shorter attention spans but have greater memory capacity, such conclusions may not be warranted as more contemporary studies demonstrate few, if any, enduring distinctions between younger and older subjects.[80]

The aging process, of necessity, is bound to the listening process, for it is through communication that aging transpires in human interactions. Research on communication and aging suggests that as men grow older, they tend to become less dominant and competitive, while women tend to be more dominant and competitive.[81] At the same time, elderly men *and* women become increasingly dependent on others. This increasing dependence, frequently resulting from a loss of mobility, often affords older individuals with fewer opportunities for interaction with others. Upon retirement, older people also find that they have more time available. Such behavioral changes can create very different listening needs, attitudes, and behaviors.

Benjamin believes that "older adults effectively adapt messages and interact with others while adjusting to and compensating for changes in sensory acuity, reaction time, and central processing."[82] Villaume and colleagues have analyzed participation in conversations across various age groups to determine what effect, if any, a decline in hearing and listening abilities may have on communicators. Some of their research would suggest that as hearing acuity begins to decline in middle age, communicators heighten their attention in conversations.[83] Other research notes that declining visual acuity as a result of aging reduces visual discrimination skills in decoding nonverbal messages.[84]

Factor #4: Hemispheric Specialization

In recent decades, clinical and experimental research on the brain has led to the formation of the dual-brain theory. The brain is seen to consist of two halves or cerebral hemispheres (the left and right hemispheres) that are connected by the corpus callosum (a thick bundle of nerve fibers), which mediates "a constant flow of information from one hemisphere to the other."[85] Three claims of this dual-brain theory are the following:

dual-brain theory

1. Each hemisphere governs the actions of the opposite side of the body, with the left hemisphere controlling the right side and the right hemisphere controlling the left side.
2. Each hemisphere specializes in a different mode of processing information, with the left hemisphere processing highly structured information logically and analytically by thinking in words, numbers, and symbols and the right hemisphere processing patterns of information spatially, holistically, nonverbally, and perceptually by mainly thinking in pictures and images.[86] (See fig. 4.3)
3. Each hemisphere has *dominance* (i.e., "the *tendency* . . . to process a particular type of information and to control response behavior based on that information")[87] over various functions.

Exploring the differences in hemispheric functions by studying subjects with intact brains as well as subjects with brain damage, researchers have found that some of the major **hemispheric functions** appear to be as follows:

hemispheric functions

Left Hemisphere	Right Hemisphere
verbal—reading, writing, speaking, and listening to verbal messages; thinking in word symbols	*nonverbal*—projecting and perceiving nonverbal cues
linguistic—being competent in the grammar, syntax, and semantics of language	*nonlinguistic*—seeing objects, events, etc., as they are without names/words connected to them; lacking the linguistic elements of grammar syntax, and semantic
analytical—reducing the whole to its parts	*holistic*—seeing in wholes

logical/rational—reasoning

mathematical/digital—computing, measuring, and timing

linear—perceiving objects, events, etc., in their true relation to one another

syntactical—arranging information in an orderly / systematic manner

objective—being independent of mind

articulate—expressing oneself clearly / distinctly

ordered—organizing; categorizing information

aesthetic—enjoying stimuli

emotional—responding to / with feeling

intuitive—having insight; responding with "ah ha" premonitions

creative—exhibiting inventiveness / imagination

spatial/relational—recognizing patterns, configurations, shapes, forms, etc., even though part of the data may be missing

perceptual—seeing in three dimensions; having depth perception

visual—thinking in images / pictures

artistic—having skill in such activities as art, music, dance

novel—responding to new / unknown stimuli; being innovative.[88]

Moreover, Hogen has noted these possible differences: The left hemisphere may be superior in detecting sameness and may cause one to use "I think . . ." more often, to be efficient at name identification and concept identification tasks, and to possess "right-ear advantage for auditory perception of spoken sounds, words, digits, consonants, words in music, and recognition of speakers' voices"; the right hemisphere may be superior in detecting differences and may cause one to use "I feel . . ." more often and to be efficient at physical identification and fact recognition.[89]

During given tasks, both hemispheres may work together (hemispheric enhancement), or they may interfere with each other (hemispheric conflict). Ideally, there should be internal cooperation between the hemispheres; however, the left hemisphere seems to dominate within most individuals (especially right-handed persons). George Prince, author of *Mindspring,* suggests a reason for this left dominance: "Because we operate in such a sequential-seeming world and because the logical thought of the left hemisphere is so honored in our culture, we gradually damp out, devalue and disregard the input of our right hemispheres. It is not that we stop using it altogether; it just becomes less and less available to us because of established habit patterns."[90] Fincher furthers our understanding of this dominance in his summary of the view of Roger Sperry and his followers:

> Our society . . . especially in the fields of science and education, is inherently prejudiced against the intellect of the right, or nonlanguage, hemisphere. It is the linguistic, the abstract side of ourselves we test and educate and

reward—and by such powerful social stratagem catapult to an overarching prominence in the human scheme of things.[91]

Many researchers who have studied creativity claim that "the educational process concentrates on the functions of the logical brain while neglecting the creative brain."[92] Edwards, author of *Drawing on the Right Side of the Brain*, conjectures that "long and exclusive emphasis on the verbal mode in education may have the effect of diminishing an individual's ability to make cognitive shifts in information process mode as required for specific tasks."[93] Whatever the reason(s) may be for left hemispheric dominance, the left hemisphere appears to be quite proficient in restricting the actions of the right hemisphere and even assuming control of the tasks at which the right hemisphere excels. Thus, interference between the hemispheres prevents maximum performance as well as maximum understanding.[94]

Research also indicates that gender may be related to hemispheric specialization.[95] The female brain tends to be less specialized than the male brain is; for example, adult females appear to have verbal and spatial abilities on both sides of the brain.[96] Another gender difference is that the left hemisphere generally develops first in the female whereas the right hemisphere generally develops first in the male; thus, many little girls read and write better than many little boys.[97]

Further, each gender seems to excel in certain abilities. For instance, males appear to excel in certain types of spatial perceptions, mathematics, mechanical tasks, responsiveness to verbal cues, and detection of simple pitch patterns, melodies, and environmental sounds. Females appear to be superior in verbal skills, to process information faster, to respond more readily to facial cues, to be more empathic, to be less distracted by visual images while listening, and to be better able to remember names and faces of former classmates.[98] Moreover, females appear to be more perceptive about people; that is, they are more skilled at "listening between the lines" (sensing the difference between what people say and what they mean and detecting nuances that reveal the true feelings of others).[99]

The **influence of hemispheric dominance on listening** has been analyzed by Stacks and Sellers, researchers who have drawn several important conclusions about this influence. This research suggests that two different kinds of language styles exist; these styles differ in logical formulation, function, intensity, and *receiver perception*. They also have determined that message acceptability is influenced by the hemispheric processing of the message and that the intensity of the language utilized in the message will alter that processing. Additionally, the perceptions of a message source differ according to which hemisphere is activated and the degree of threat perceived in a message.[100]

influence of hemispheric dominance on listening

The dual-brain theory has many implications relevant to the listening process and listening behavior. The major implication of this theory is that we may listen differently as a result of being left- or right-hemisphere oriented. As we have noted, there are hemispheric differences in the types of information attended to, modes of information-processing employed,

A CAR FOR THE LEFT SIDE OF YOUR BRAIN.

The left side of your brain, recent investigations tell us, is the logical side.

It figures out that $1+1=2$. And, in a few cases, that $E = mc^2$.

On a more mundane level, it chooses the socks you wear, the cereal you eat, and the car you drive. All by means of rigorous Aristotelian logic.

However, and a big however it is, for real satisfaction, you must achieve harmony with the other side of your brain.

The right side, the poetic side, that says, "Yeah, Car X has a reputation for lasting a long time but it's so dull, who'd want to drive it that long anyway?"

The Saab Turbo looked at from all sides.

To the left side of your brain, Saab turbocharging is a technological feat that retains good gas mileage while also increasing performance.

To the right side of your brain, Saab turbocharging is what makes a Saab go like a bat out of hell.

The left side sees the safety in high performance. (Passing on a two-lane highway. Entering a freeway in the midst of high-speed traffic.)

The right side lives only for the thrills.

The left side considers that *Road & Track* magazine just named Saab "The Sports Sedan for the Eighties." By unanimous choice of its editors.

The right side eschews informed endorsements by editors who have spent a lifetime comparing cars. The right side doesn't know much about cars, but knows what it likes.

The left side scans this chart.

Wheelbase	99.1 inches
Length	187.6 inches
Width	66.5 inches
Height	55.9 inches
Fuel-tank capacity	16.6 gallons
EPA City	19 mpg *
EPA Highway	31 mpg *

The right side looks at the picture on the opposite page.

The left side compares a Saab's comfort with that of a Mercedes. Its performance with that of a BMW. Its braking with that of an Audi.

The right side looks at the picture.

The left side looks ahead to the winter when a Saab's front-wheel drive will keep a Saab in front of traffic.

The right side looks at the picture.

The left side also considers the other seasons of the year when a Saab's front-wheel drive gives it the cornering ability of a sports car.

The right side looks again at the picture.

Getting what you need vs. getting what you want.

Needs are boring; desires are what make life worth living.

The left side of your brain is your mother telling you that a Saab is good for you. "Eat your vegetables." (In today's world, you need a car engineered like a Saab.) "Put on your raincoat." (The Saab is economical. Look at the price-value relationship.) "Do your homework." (The passive safety of the construction. The active safety of the handling.)

1982 SAAB PRICE ** LIST		
900 3-Door	5-Speed	$10,400
	Automatic	10,750
900 4-Door	5-Speed	$10,700
	Automatic	11,050
900S 3-Door	5-Speed	$12,100
	Automatic	12,450
900S 4-Door	5-Speed	$12,700
	Automatic	13,050
900 Turbo 3-Door	5-Speed	$15,600
	Automatic	15,950
900 Turbo 4-Door	5-Speed	$16,260
	Automatic	16,610

All turbo models include a Sony XR70, 4-Speaker Stereo Sound System as standard equipment. The stereo can be, of course, perfectly balanced: left and right.

The right side of your brain guides your foot to the clutch, your hand to the gears, and listens for the "zzzooommm."

Together, they see the 1982 Saab Turbo as the responsible car the times demand you get. And the performance car you've always, deep down, wanted with half your mind.

*Saab 900 Turbo. Remember, use estimated mpg for comparison only. Mileage varies with speed, trip length, and weather. Actual highway mileage will probably be less. **Manufacturer's suggested retail price. Not including taxes, license, freight, dealer charges or options desired by either side of your brain.

Figure 4.3.
Advertisement by SAAB-SCANIA of America, Inc.

A CAR FOR THE RIGHT SIDE OF YOUR BRAIN.

SAAB
The most intelligent car ever built.

communication codes used, and functions performed. In addition, there is experimental evidence that memory may be related to hemispheric differences. Paivio has found that the right hemisphere has an advantage for visual memory because it is easier to remember pictures than words; yet he has also found that "naming enhances memory for pictorial items and image coding increases memory for words."[101] These findings seem to indicate that hemispheric cooperation should contribute to memory improvement.

Likewise, hemispheric cooperation may contribute to improvement in prolonging attention. Neurobiologist Jerre Levy asserts that attention is sustained longer when the two hemispheres work together to handle complex tasks than when one hemisphere handles simple tasks alone.[102] Unfortunately, there frequently is hemispheric interference rather than cooperation when one is processing messages consisting of both verbal and visual (nonverbal) components.[103] This observation is only one example of the many findings that illustrate how hemispheric conflict prevents maximum performance in processing, including remembering, information as well as in listening. However, by establishing internal cooperation between the hemispheres and by developing the ability to switch from one hemisphere to the other (e.g. by activating and venting the hemispheres through internal brainstorming, daydreaming—when appropriate—and using memory aids to increase memory capacity),[104] individuals may significantly improve their efficiency in both information-processing and listening.

Factor #5: Physical and Psychological States

physical state

As we have seen, a listener's **physical state** has profound influence on his or her auditory and/or visual acuity. The effects of presbycusis and presbyopia (sensory loss due to aging) is a reality that we all must face and the need for hearing and visual hygiene in order to maintain the sensory organs at the highest possible level of efficiency should be apparent to all serious listeners.

psychological state

The Clinton administration's efforts for health care reform have had a profound effect on Americans' consciousness of the role of both physical state and **psychological state**. As the costs of health care continue to escalate, the need for physical and psychological wellness has become apparent. The continuing AIDS crisis, the persistence of cancer, the return of tuberculosis, and the rise in depression and eating disorders all dramatize the critical nature of health issues and how much they affect the way we deal with ourselves and with others. Indeed, Maryland oncologist Daniel Rosenblum observes that "good listening enables us to appreciate the significance which illness has for people. . . ."[105]

stress

Perhaps the greatest physical/psychological condition that affects listeners today is **stress**. Stress is recognized as a major factor in heart disease, gastrointestinal disorders, and mental disorders. Techniques for stress management center on many elements of control: deep breathing, diet and sleep, exercise, goal setting, biofeedback, realistic approach to personal and work problems, strategies for dealing with difficult people, and finding enjoyable outlets.[106] James Lynch of the University of Maryland School of Medicine has studied the link between physical health and interpersonal communication. He has discovered that, physiologically, a listener's blood pressure drops below baseline when concentrating on a conversation partner.[107]

Factor #6: Attitudes

A listening variable closely related to psychological states is attitudes. Indeed, positive **listening attitudes**, along with pertinent listening knowledge and appropriate listening skills, are a critical ingredient of effective listening. Positive attitudes give the listener the willingness—the desire—to listen.[108] Six of the most essential positive listening attitudes are interested, responsible, other-oriented, patient, equal, and openminded.

listening attitudes

Interested (not Disinterested)

Many listeners quickly label a speaker or a speaker's subject as uninteresting, dull, or boring. They approach each listening situation in this manner: "Well, speaker, here I am. Keep me interested or I'll tune out and think about something that *is* interesting." All too often, such passive listeners are basically uninterested people: They are not interested in many subjects—or in many people. Lacking self-motivation or desire to learn about a wide variety of subjects from a wide variety of people and having limited interests, they frequently are unwilling to listen.

In contrast, effective listeners are basically **interested** people. They are interested in many subjects and many people. But, their basic concern is not whether the speaker or the speaker's message is interesting; rather, they are concerned with value. They approach each listening situation with this question: "What is in this for me?" They are selfish, opportunistic listeners who actively listen for information that is or will be useful to them. They also know that they can't see into the future to know when the speaker will provide useful information or when the information provided today will be useful tomorrow. So, they constantly seek out—actively listen for—information that might be useful to them now or in the future.

interested

Responsible (not Irresponsible)

As we noted earlier in this chapter in our discussion of the second listening strategy, listeners have been culturally conditioned to depend upon the speaker to motivate them to listen. As a result, the speaker who fails to motivate them is frequently tuned out, and the speaker who provides such motivation is tuned in.

On the other hand, effective listeners approach each listening situation with a sense of being **responsible**. They know that communication is a partnership and that they share in the responsibility for successful communication. They enter each communication situation with this view: "I will accept at least 51 percent of the responsibility for making this communication transaction successful." Their displays of responsibility range from

responsible

preparing mentally and physically to listen to being responsive. (See chapter 1, the sixth misconception about listening, for further discussion of this attitude.)

Other-Oriented (not Self-Centered)

Self-centered listeners are more concerned about themselves than they are about others. They really don't want to listen; they would rather talk—talk about anything, but mainly about themselves (their accomplishments, their views, their feelings, their needs, their goals, and so on). Their favorite words are *I*, *me*, *my*, and *mine*, and their favorite voices are their own.

If you observe any informal conversation, you will probably notice that most people do not really listen to others—except for an opening for their own comments. The typical conversation can be called "swapping fish stories." Each person is more interested in telling his or her own story than in listening to the other person's story. Often, we engage in trying to outdo the other by telling a "bigger and better" story than was just told.

other-oriented

The counterpart of self-centered is being **other-oriented**. The other-oriented listener has a genuine interest in others and an inquisitive attitude toward others. Being other-oriented does not mean that we should not talk about ourselves. But, it does mean that first we should fully acknowledge the other person's comments. We can acknowledge another's comments by asking open-ended questions. Open-ended questions begin with who, what, when, where, and how and request more background information, more description, more supporting evidence, more personal points of view, more expression of feelings, and more reactions.

Other-oriented listeners suppress their desire to talk. When they find themselves talking more than half of the time during a normal conversation, they force themselves to talk less. They realize that they already know what they think, so they focus on learning as much as they can from others. Other-oriented listeners *care* about the other communicator(s). Indeed, caring about others may be a distinguishing characteristic of truly effective listeners.

Patient (not Impatient)

Ineffective listeners display numerous verbal and nonverbal signals of impatience. For example, they ask "When is this meeting scheduled to end?" or "Anything else?" and they check their watches, move toward the door, fidget with objects, drum their fingers, and so on. Their reasons for becoming impatient are as varied as their signs of impatience; their reasons range from thinking they already know what the speaker is going to say to having somewhere else to go to finding the speaker's rate too slow.

patient

In contrast, **patient** listeners are ones who care—care about themselves as listeners, care about others as human beings, and care about how their listening behaviors affect others' self-esteem. They know that exploring friendships, checking out hunches, tuning in to feelings, and developing better working relationships often take patience and time, and they are willing to invest that time.

Equal (not Superior)

Some listeners consider themselves superior to some speakers in position, wealth, talent, intellect, power, appearance, or some other area. Having a "better-than-the speaker" attitude, listeners often nonverbally—and, at times, verbally—convey this message to speakers: "You have little or nothing of importance or value to say to me." The expressing of this "prima donna" attitude often raises feelings of inadequacy in speakers and creates defensiveness and hostility.

A markedly different attitude is that of equality. Possessing an attitude of equality does not mean that we should view all speakers as being our **equal** in position, wealth, talent, etc. Rather, it means that effective listeners **equal** attach little importance to these distinctions. And, it means holding the view that all speakers have the equal right to communicate openly and freely. Recognizing the worth of all individuals, effective listeners willingly and respectfully listen to others, because they believe that both they and others can learn from each other.

In the book *In Search for Excellence*, Peters and Waterman stress that excellent companies treat their people as adults, as partners, as people with dignity and worth. They quote former IBM chair Thomas J. Watson, Jr.: "IBM's philosophy is largely contained in three simple beliefs. I want to begin with what I think is the most important: Our respect for the individual."[109] The authors conclude that there is "hardly a more pervasive theme in the excellent companies than respect for the individual" and that it "lives in these companies. . . ."[110] Indeed, a major way of showing respect is by listening.

Openminded (not Closeminded)

Closeminded individuals seldom listen—except to those who agree with them and, thus, reinforce what they already "know" is true or right. They have preconceived ideas of what is, what should be, and what will be. They have all the answers, they need no additional information, they see their ideas as truths to be defended, and they are unwilling to change. Rather than work cooperatively on problem-solving, these dogmatic individuals have to be right. They have low tolerance for those who are "wrong"—that is, those who do not see the world as they do. Thus, they refuse to expose themselves to ideas, opinions, positions that are different from their own.

The opposite of the **closeminded** listening attitude is being open- **closeminded** minded. These listeners are open to others' ideas. They are willing to investigate issues, share in problem-solving, and reconsider their own behavior, ideas, views, values, and attitudes. In fact, they encourage others to share their knowledge and views with them, for they know that the more information they have and the more points of view they have listened to and soundly evaluated, the more informed decisions they will make. They also realize that even people whom they do not particularly like may have useful ideas; thus, they do not let their feelings toward a speaker interfere with their listening to that speaker's ideas.

Openminded listeners are both confident and humble and, as a result, seldom defensive. They can accept opposing views, be challenged, admit errors, and "back down" without fear of "losing face" or without feeling threatened. For example, if they disagree with someone, they do not respond with a defensive statement such as "You're crazy to think that way." Rather, they say "I don't agree with you" and explain why they disagree. Then they listen to their conversational partner's response, and they learn even more.

Factor #7: Self-Concept

listener's self-concept

Psychologically, a significant influence on the communication process is the **listener's self-concept**. The effect of the self-concept on listening behavior has not been researched to any great extent. Research in reading, however, supports the idea that better self-concepts can improve reception: "Sufficient evidence has been found . . . and enough support from authorities in education and psychology has been accumulated to suggest that many disabled readers can be helped by improving their self-concepts."[111]

negative listening self-concept

For most of us, the **listening self-concept is too negative**. Throughout our lives, we probably have experienced few rewards for good listening. Instead, we have been subjected to negative reinforcement: "You're not listening to me." "Sit down and listen to me." "You don't listen." "Why don't you ever listen to me?"

Such messages have to have a significant impact on one's ability to function as a listener. If you are told often enough that you are not a good listener, you will start to believe that you are a poor listener and will behave accordingly. Anastasi points out that "once you label yourself a poor listener, you probably won't use the skill you have."[112] Research in psychology supports the idea that an individual will behave in accordance with his or her self-concept and "live up to the label" through a self-fulfilling prophecy.[113] The negative messages that impact on the self-concept of listeners finally must influence one's willingness to listen. A person who holds a **positive listening self-concept** probably is willing to listen without fear of losing self while feeling secure with the ultimate choice of accepting or rejecting the message.

positive listening self-concept

The influence of the significant others who shape the self-concept can be profound. In a study of the listener's self-concept, Wolvin discovered that students reported that parents, friends, and other family members were most instrumental in shaping their perceptions about themselves as listeners. As hypothesized, all too frequently these significant others were reported to be instrumental in shaping negative perceptions of these students' listening behaviors.[114] Gallwey best sums up the important role that self-concept plays in our listening lives: "I know of no single factor that more greatly affects our ability to learn and perform than the image we have of ourselves. Who we think we are influences everything we do, every thought we have, every feeling we allow."[115]

Understanding the Listening Process

Factor #8: Receiver Apprehension

Our psychological state and/or negative self-concept can further affect us as listeners by inducing **receiver apprehension**. Although to date most of the research on this construct has centered on the communication apprehension of the source, Wheeless has pioneered some study of the listener's apprehension, which he conceptualizes as "the fear of misinterpreting, inadequately processing, and/or not being able to adjust psychologically to messages sent by others."[116] The small amount of research focused on receiver apprehension suggests that "the anxiety or fear stemming from the listening situation may in turn result in inefficient listening."[117]

receiver apprehension

Though current research reveals little correlation between receiver apprehension and listening ability, receiver apprehension has been found to be a problem at all levels of education.[118] McDowell and McDowell, for example, discovered that receiver apprehension was higher in primary and secondary schools than on college campuses.[119] Clark suggests that receiver apprehension may couple with willingness to communicate as factors in listening comprehension. The person who feels more confident in a communication setting may listen more effectively to message content.[120]

The apprehension that a listener may experience can stem from any of a number of sources. It is possible, for example, that one is worried about the outcome of the communication and approaches listening with a high level of anxiety. A medical patient listening to a physician report results of a recent test may well experience this type of apprehension. The **anxiety** a listener feels could stem from inexperience and unfamiliarity with the speaker, the subject, or the communication situation itself. The marketing manager who faces that first meeting with a Chinese industrial executive feels anxiety as a listener as he or she enters a new communication environment with a communicator who has a very different frame of reference. The apprehension could also result from the speaker's power and status. Communicating with the chief executive of an organization, for instance, can evoke nervousness and tension in almost any listener. Barnlund points out that stressful situations in which one's self-esteem is threatened can interfere with effective listening so that messages become distorted and misunderstandings result.[121]

anxiety

Additionally, there is evidence that receiver apprehension can result from **inadequate information-processing**. McReynolds hypothesizes that the processing of material that is difficult to assimilate tends to accumulate (resulting in "cognitive backlog") and to produce anxiety.[122] Beatty has used correlations of Wheeless's Receiver Apprehension Test and McReynolds's anxiety assimilation scale to determine that receiver apprehension is a function of unassimilated information that results from processing difficulties because of the cognitive backlog.[123] Preiss's research on receiver apprehension leads him to conclude that those with high apprehension use low order communication logics (interpretive schemes for message interpretation).[124] As researchers gather more data on the interrelationship of information-processing and anxiety levels, it will be possible to understand better the influence of receiver apprehension on listening behavior.

inadequate information-processing

Factor #9: Time

time

The influence of **time** on all communicators is significant. Time has become such a precious commodity to Americans today that we even try to practice principles for success such as *The One Minute Manager* and *The Sixty Second Employee*. Tubbs and Moss point out that "the pressures of too much to do in too little time would appear to be influencing both the quantity and the quality of modern-day communication."[125] The Americans' Use of Time Project, using research from individuals' time diaries, reveals that Americans have more free time at their disposal than they did twenty years ago, but an increasing proportion of Americans indicate that they always feel rushed, that there just is not enough time to get everything done.[126] Time can affect the intensity of the communication relationship (e.g., a group that meets for only 1 hour each week for an extended period of time would have less intensity than a group that meets for a marathon weekend); time can change the channel of communication (a parent and a child move from non-verbal to verbal communication as the child develops verbal language skills); and time can alter the style of the communication (a couple who have been together for a long period of time probably uses fewer words because each is able to anticipate the other's thoughts and feelings).

Listening communicators are influenced continuously by various dimensions of time. The time that is manifested in the aging process itself can affect one's listening efficiency. The physical deterioration of the hearing mechanism over a lifetime can reduce the listener's auditory acuity. Likewise, the time it takes to actually listen is a significant factor. Research illustrates that listeners can listen (and think) about four times faster than the normal conversation rate, so we have a great deal of "lag time" in the system for attention to wander and to lose focus.[127]

Time also becomes a factor in the listening process in that the time in which the communication occurs, such as the time of day, can affect one's attentiveness and overall motivation to listen. Speakers often cite differences in audiences for luncheon speeches as contrasted with after-dinner speeches or even breakfast presentations. Research reveals that people deal with information differently at different times of the day. We are more likely to retain verbal information presented in the afternoon than in the morning (so that memorization of facts or the use of previously-memorized factors in math and science, for instance, are best handled in the morning).[128]

The amount of time that one has available to listen has a profound effect on the process as well. If the listener is rushed or unable to devote much time to the process, then the listening may well be short-circuited. Most of us probably have experienced a conference with a busy adviser, salesperson, or manager who really did not have time to listen and nonverbally communicated a desire to end the conversation. It can be a very frustrating experience for both speaker and listener if, indeed, there is not enough time to listen. Time certainly plays a significant role in the listening communication process.

Factor #10: Listener Preferences

Just as listeners are influenced by any of a number of internal and external factors, so, too, are listening differences the result of **listening preferences**—differences in the ways people choose to listen. These preferences result from a listening style of habitual responses developed over the course of one's listening lifetime. Listening preferences also emerge from the type of information with which listeners feel most comfortable. In developing their Listening Preference Profile, Watson, Barker, and Weaver discovered that a female person-oriented listening preference most closely matched with a relational rather than a task orientation. Male preferences for content-oriented or action-oriented listening were more closely aligned with a task orientation.[129] As a result, individuals with a people-oriented listening style focus on the emotional and relational aspects of a communication, while content-oriented listeners deal with complex information. Action-oriented listeners prefer clear, efficient information, while time-oriented listeners have a preference for short-limited messages.[130]

listening preferences

Researchers have done some preliminary exploration of the relationship of listener preferences to **personality** traits[131] and to the **"listenability"** of the speaker and the message.[132] While the results of such research are not yet definitive, it certainly makes sense that some types of personalities (extroverted or introverted, for instance) may very well lead listeners to prefer types of information (stories or statistics), message structures (inductive or deductive), styles of speakers (dynamic or laid back), and even the communication channels (live or television).

personality and listenability

The listener as communicator, then, is influenced by a number of factors that can affect his or her behavior as a listener at any given time throughout the communication transaction. These key factors—culture, gender, age, hemispheric specialization, physical and psychological states, self-concept, receiver apprehension, time, and preferences—can deter or facilitate listening efficiency, depending on the nature of the influence at the time. It should be clear, however, that a listener can overcome any negative, deterring influence by systematically employing the listening strategies in the communication. The listener who strives to know and to motivate himself or herself, to listen actively, and to send appropriate feedback can become a more effective listening communicator.

The improvement of listening behavior requires effort. Understanding your own listening behavior is a first step, but building the additional strategies to improve your listening must follow. Lundsteen has noted that "superior performance in listening skill probably not only requires possession of a wide range of basic competencies, but also the ability to *mobilize* them for a particular communicative situation and then to apply them beyond the listening moment."[133] Building competency with these strategies takes practice. Once you understand how you function as a listener and how effective listeners *should* function, you must practice using the listening strategies for your own improvement.

Summary

In this chapter, we have stressed that listening is a communication function. Throughout the process, the listener and the speaker communicate with each other, and the more homophilous the communicators are (the more they share common attributes), the more effective that communication can be. The listener, as a communicator, must make decisions throughout the listening process to receive and to attend to that message, to assign meaning to that message, and to utilize appropriate listening strategies to participate effectively in the communication transaction. These strategies include developing an understanding of the self as a listener, motivating the listening self, listening actively throughout the process, and sending appropriate feedback to the speaker.

Just as these strategies, if carefully chosen and applied throughout the communication process, can influence the outcome of the communication transaction, so, too, can certain key factors affect the listener during the process. The listener's culture, gender, age, hemispheric specialization, physical and psychological states, attitudes, self-concept, apprehension, time, and listening preferences all can combine to affect the way a listener will function at any point in the transaction.

As listening communicators, then, individuals must know themselves and must be sensitive to others as they assume equal participation in the communication transaction. It is clear that the speaker alone should not be forced to carry the burden for successful communication. The listener shares that responsibility and makes his or her decisions accordingly.

Suggested Activities

1. Interview two people who are especially effective as listeners (perhaps professional counselors or friends/family members who are noted for listening). Ask them to reflect on their techniques and on their sense of responsibility to themselves and to other communicators.
2. Interview a politician who has recently conducted an election/reelection campaign. Ask the person about the general responsiveness of his or her audiences and his or her impression of how seriously the listeners took their responsibilities as listeners. What do you perceive to be the general state of listening responsibility in the United States?
3. Participate in a self-disclosure conversation with another person on some topics that you have not discussed before. After the discussion, draw your Johari Window and discuss it with your partner. Does it reflect the extent to which you did self-disclose? What did you learn, then, about your self-concept through the Johari Window?
4. Create a list or a chart of those ideas and beliefs that are important (of value) to you. Then, prepare another list or chart of objects that you value. What do these lists or charts tell you about yourself? What do

they tell you about your listening behavior? Do these values influence the perceptions through which you listen? How?

5. Practice the skill of sending feedback to speakers in interviews, group discussions, and public speeches. Make a conscious effort to apply the principles described in this chapter. Ask the speakers to whom you send feedback what their impressions are. Does your feedback communicate the messages you intend? Are you effective in sending feedback?

6. Design your plan for listening improvement. Make a list of those aspects that you wish to improve and detail what strategies you plan to implement in order to improve. Arrange a conference with your instructor to discuss the strategies to ensure that your plans will lead to improvement of your listening behavior.

7. Go to your library and locate current literature on the key factors that influence listening behavior: culture, gender, age, hemispheric specialization, physical/psychological states, attitudes, self-concept, apprehension, time, and listener preferences. Summarize the literature in a paper, which can then provide the subject matter for a class discussion on these salient listening factors.

8. Make an effort to identify your stereotypes. List those that you can recognize, and consider how you came to develop these particular stereotypes. What are some of the more "universal" stereotypes that characterize American values?

9. Identify those factors that seem to have the greatest impact on how you function as a listener. Do these factors facilitate or interfere with your listening abilities? How do, or can, you compensate for their influence?

10. Reread the opening scenario, and determine—from the staff members' thoughts and actions—what listening choices, strategies, and variables are operating.

Notes

1. E. M. Rogers and D. K. Bhowmik, "Homophily-Heterophily: Relational Concepts for Communication Research," in *Speech Communication Behavior*, eds. L. L. Barker and R. J. Kibler (Englewood Cliffs, NJ: Prentice-Hall, 1971), p. 214.
2. W. D. Brooks, *Speech Communication*, 3d ed. (Dubuque, IA: Wm. C. Brown, 1978), p. 56.
3. J. Luft, *Group Process: An Introduction to Group Dynamics*, 3d ed (Mountain View, CA: Mayfield Publications, 1984).
4. S. M. Jourard, *The Transparent Self* (NY: Van Nostrand Reinhold, 1964), p. 5.
5. C. R. Gilner, et al., "A Developmental Investigation of Visual and Haptic Preferences for Shape and Texture," *Monographs of the Society for Research in Child Development* 24 (September 1969): 36.
6. A. Ries and J. Trout, "The Eye Vs. the Ear," *Advertising Age* 54 (14 March 1983): M30.
7. D. C. Schnapp, "The Effects of Channel on Assigning Meaning in the Listening Process," *Journal of the International Listening Association* 5 (1991): 105.
8. See, for example, D. D. Durrell, "Listening Comprehension Versus Reading Comprehension," *Journal of Reading* 12 (March 1969): 455–460.
9. L. O'Brien, "Learning Styles: Make the Students Aware," *National Association of Secondary School Principals' Bulletin* 73 (October 1989): 85–89.

10. From *The Medium Is the Massage* by Marshall McLuhan and Quentin Fiore. Coordinated by Jermone Agel. Copyright 1967 by Bantam Books, Inc. Reprinted by permission of the publisher. All rights reserved.

11. D. Corley, "The Relationship of Channel to Meaning" (Ph.D. diss., University of Maryland, 1986).

12. For a dated but interesting review of research on stereotyping, see W. L. Brembeck and W. S. Howell, *Persuasion* (Englewood Cliffs, NJ: Prentice-Hall, 1952), pp. 108–119.

13. M. Snyder, "Self-Fulfilling Stereotypes," *Psychology Today* 16 (July 1982): 60.

14. Ibid.

15. W. Lippmann, *Public Opinion* (NY: Macmillan, 1922), p. 95.

16. D. Katz, "Psychological Barriers to Communication," in *Messages*, ed. J. M. Civikly (NY: Random House, 1974), p. 326.

17. For a look at communication motivation, see R. B. Rubin and A. M. Rubin, "Antecedents of Interpersonal Communication Motivation," *Communication Quarterly* 40 (Summer 1992): 305–317.

18. C. Weaver, *Human Listening: Process and Behavior* (Indianapolis: Bobbs-Merrill, 1972), p. 82.

19. Weaver notes this distinction and emphasizes the importance of the willingness to listen, Ibid., pp. 7–8.

20. Willingness to *Communicate* is a line of research explored by V. Richmond and J. C. McCroskey. See J. C. McCroskey, "Reliability and Validity of the Willingness to Communicate Scale, " *Communication Quarterly* 40 (Winter 1992): 16–25.

21. J. A. Overton and D. G. Bock, "A Study of the Development, Validation, and Application of the Construct of Listening Reluctance," *Journal of the Illinois Speech Teachers Association* 38 (1986): 31–41.

22. A. J. Clark, "Communication Confidence and Listening Competence: An Investigation of the Relationships of Willingness to Communicate, Communication Apprehension, and Receiver Apprehension to Comprehension of Content and Emotional Meaning in Spoken Messages," *Communication Education* 38 (July 1989): 236–248.

23. L. Vinson and C. V. Roberts, "A Refinement and Validation of the Willingness to Listen Scale" (Paper presented at the Speech Communication Association Convention, Chicago, IL, 1990).

24. M. J. Beatty, R. R. Behnke, and D. L. Froelich, "Effects of Achievement Incentive and Presentation Rate on Listening Comprehension," *Quarterly Journal of Speech* 66 (April 1980): 193–200.

25. Motivation researchers have come to regard motivation as equivalent to reinforcement. See, for example, R. C. Bolles, *Theory of Motivation* (NY: Harper and Row, 1967), chapter 15.

26. Press Release, American Council on Education, Washington, DC, 29 March 1983.

27. R. Edwards, "Sensitivity to Feedback and the Development of Self," *Communication Quarterly* 38 (Spring 1990): 101–111.

28. Gardiner surveyed over fifty studies of feedback and drew similar conclusions as to the effect of feedback. See J. C. Gardiner, "A Synthesis of Experimental Studies of Speech Communication Feedback," *Journal of Communication* 21 (March 1971): 17–35. See also W. B. Bishop, "The Functions of Feedback in Listening" (Paper presented at the International Listening Association Convention, San Diego, CA, 1986).

29. This research is summarized in R. E. Kraut, S. H. Lewis, and L. W. Swezey, "Listener Responsiveness and the Coordination of Conversation," *Journal of Personality and Social Psychology* 43 (October 1982): 718–731.

30. S. L. Tubbs and R. N. Widgery, "When Productivity Lags, Check at the Top: Are Key Managers Really Communicating?" *Management Review* 67 (January 1978): 20–25.

31. R. Dreyfack, *What An Executive Should Know About Listening More Effectively* (Chicago: The Dartnell Corporation, 1983), p. 12.

32. Ibid., p. 13.

33. H. J. Leavitt and R. A. H. Mueller, "Some Effects of Feedback on Communication," in *Interpersonal Communication: Survey and Studies*, ed. Dean Barnlund (Boston: Houghton Mifflin, 1968), pp. 251–259.

34. J. Daly, "Listening and Interpersonal Evaluations" (Paper presented at the Central States Speech Convention, Kansas City, Missouri, 1975), pp. 1–2.

35. J. Brownell, "Listening Environment: A Perspective," in *Perspectives on Listening*, eds. A. D. Wolvin and C. G. Coakley (Norwood, NJ: Ablex, 1993), p. 245. For further work on perceptions of listening, see J. Brownell, "Perceptions of Effective Listeners: A

Management Study," *The Journal of Business Communication* 27 (Fall 1990): 401–416 and M. Gilbert, "Perceptions of Listening Behaviors of School Principals" (Paper presented at the International Listening Association Convention, Atlanta, GA, 1989); and R. L. Husband, L. O. Cooper, and W. M. Monsour, "Factors Underlying Supervisor's Perceptions of Their Own Listening Behavior," *Journal of the International Listening Association* 2 (1988): 97–112.

36. L. O. Cooper and R. L. Husband, "Developing a Model of Organizational Listening Competency," *Journal of the International Listening Association* 7 (1993), p. 13.

37. L. L. Barker, *Listening Behavior* (Englewood Cliffs, NJ: Prentice-Hall, 1971), pp. 118–124.

38. L. O'Heren and W. E. Arnold, "Nonverbal Attentive Behavior and Listening Comprehension," *Journal of the International Listening Association* 5 (1991): 86–92. For research results on the relationship between listening and head nods, eye gaze, and verbal expressives, see L. T. Thomas and T. R. Levine, "Disentangling Listening and Verbal Recall—Related but Separate Constructs?" *Human Communication Research* 21 (September 1994): 103–127.

39. C. R. Rogers and R. E. Farson, "Active Listening," in *Readings in Interpersonal and Organizational Communication* 2d ed, eds. R. Huseman, C. M. Logue, and D. I. Freshley (Boston: Holbrooks, 1973), p. 548.

40. S. Chollar, "In the Blink of an Eye," *Psychology Today* 22 (March 1988): 8, 10.

41. J. P. Stokes, "Model Competencies for Attending Behavior," *Counselor Education and Supervision* 32 (September 1977): 23–27; F. D. Kelly, "Communication Significance of Therapist Proxemic Cues, *Journal of Consulting and Clinical Psychology* 39 (October 1972): 345; R. F. Haase and D. T. Tepper, Jr., "Nonverbal Components of Empathic Communication," *Journal of Counseling Psychology* 19 (September 1972): 417–424; F. F. Haase, "The Relationship of Sex and Instructional Set to the Regulation of Interpersonal Interaction Distance in a Counseling Analogue," *Journal of Counseling Psychology* 17 (May 1970): 233–236; P. K. Hamilton and W. A. Glasgow, "An Experimental Study of the Effect of Listening Behavior on Self-Disclosure and Interpersonal Trust" (Paper delivered at the Central States Speech Communication Association Convention, Lincoln, NE, 1983).

42. A. R. D'Augelli, "Nonverbal Behavior of Helpers in Initial Helping Interactions," *Journal of Counseling Psychology* 21 (September 1974): 360–363; Hamilton and Glasgow, "An Experimental Study of the Effect of Listening Behavior on Self-Disclosure and Interpersonal Trust"; E. W. L. Smith, "Postural and Gestural Communication of A and B 'Therapist Types' during Dyadic Interviews," *Journal of Consulting and Clinical Psychology* 39 (August 1972): 29–36; H. Hackney, "Facial Gestures and Subject Expression of Feelings," *Journal of Counseling Psychology* 21 (May 1974): 173–178.

43. S. D. Duncan, Jr., "On the Structure of Speaker-Auditor Interaction during Speaking Turns," *Language in Society* 2 (October 1974): 161–180; Hamilton and Glasgow, "An Experimental Study of the Effect of Listening Behavior on Self-Disclosure and Interpersonal Trust."

44. Stokes, "Model Competencies for Attending Behavior," pp. 23–27.

45. S. L. Tubbs and S. Moss, *Human Communication* (NY: Random House, 1987), p. 43.

46. E. Erway, " Listening As a Communication Competency" (Paper presented at the Speech Communication Association Convention, Denver, CO, 1985), p. 10.

47. L. A. Samovar and R. E. Porter, *Intercultural Communication: A Reader* (Belmont, CA: Wadsworth, 1994), p. 19.

48. T. D. Thomlison, "Intercultural Listening," in *Listening in Everyday Life*, eds. D. Borisoff and M. Purdy (Lanham, MD: University Press of America Inc., 1991), p. 130.

49. Ibid, pp. 87–137.

50. D. Tannen, "That's Not What I Meant: Foreign Language Learning As Cross-Cultural Communication" (Keynote Address to the Northeast Conference, New York City, 1990).

51. T. H. Ostermeier, "Learning Intercultural Listening Concepts through Participation in Intercultural Communication Exercises/Simulations" (Paper presented at the International Listening Association Summer Conference, Toronto, Canada, 1987), p. 7.

52. A. D. Wolvin, "Culture As a Listening Variable" (Paper presented at the International Listening Association Summer Conference, Toronto, Canada, 1987).

53. E. T. Hall and M. R. Hall, *Understanding Cultural Differences* (Yarmouth, ME: Intercultural Press, 1989).

54. R. Reisner, "How Different Cultures Learn," *Meeting News* 17 (June 1993), p. 31.

55. J. Applegate, "Translation Shows Commitment," *Santa Rosa Press Democrat*, 3 October 1994, p. E2.

56. M. R. Louis, "An Investigator's Guide to Workplace Culture," in *Organizational Culture*, eds P. J. Frost, L. F. Moore, M. R. Louis, C. C. Lundberg, and J. Martin (Beverly Hills: Sage, 1985), pp. 73–93.

57. D. Tannen, *You Just Don't Understand* (NY: Ballantine Books, 1990), p. 206.

58. See Weaver, *Human Listening: Process and Behavior*, pp. 70–78, for a review of the research on sex differences.

59. This research is reviewed in K. W. Watson and S. C. Rhodes, "A Preliminary Study of the Effects of Gender and a Video Tape Instructional Strategy on Listening Effectiveness as Measured by the Watson-Barker Listening Test," (Paper presented at the International Listening Association Convention, Scottsdale, AZ, 1988).

60. M. Booth-Butterfield, "She Hears . . . He Hears. What They Hear and Why." *Personnel Journal*, May, 1984, p. 39.

61. "Men Vs. Women," *U.S. News & World Report* 105 (8 August 1988): 55.

62. J. C. Pearson, *Gender and Communication* (Dubuque, IA: Wm. C. Brown, 1985). See, too, L. J. Shedletsky, "Listening As A Sex-Related Cognitive Behavior" (Paper presented at the International Listening Association Convention, Atlanta, GA, 1989); C. V. Roberts and J. C. Pearson, "Listening, Gender, and Grades" (Paper presented at the International Listening Association Convention, Scottsdale, AZ, 1988).

63. K. W. Watson and S. C . Rhodes, "Gender Roles, Biological Sex, and Differences in Listening Comprehension and Emotional Perceptivity" (Paper presented at the International Listening Association Convention, Jacksonville, FL, 1991).

64. See B. W. Eakins and R. G. Eakins, *Sex Differences in Human Communication* (Boston: Houghton Mifflin, 1978). A thorough review of sex roles is found in J. A. Doyle, *Sex and Gender* (Dubuque, IA: Wm. C. Brown, 1985).

65. J. Pfeiffer, "Girl Talk-Boy Talk," *Science* 6 (January/February 1985): 58–63.

66. Reviewed in V. Bozzi, "Interruptions: An Equal-Opportunity Disturber," *Psychology Today* 21 (September 1987): 201.

67. Tannen, *You Just Don't Understand*, p. 206.

68. M. Sadker and D. Sadker, *Failing at Fairness* (NY: Charles Scribner's Sons, 1994).

69. D. Tannen, "Did You Say What I Just Heard?" *The Washington Post*, 12 October 1986, p. D3; D.Tannen, "Sex, Lies, and Conversation," *The Washington Post*, 24 June 1990, p. C3.

70. Tannen, "Did You Say What I Just Heard?" p. D3.

71. D. N. Maltz and R. A. Borker, "A Cultural Approach to Male-Female Miscommunication," in *Language and Social Identity*, ed. J. J. Gumper (Cambridge: Cambridge University Press, 1982).

72. This research is reviewed in Watson and Rhodes, "A Preliminary Study of the Effects of Gender and a Video Tape Instructional Strategy on Listening Effectiveness as Measured by the Watson-Barker Listening Test."

73. Sadker and Sadker, *Failing at Fairness*, p. 195.

74. J. L. Allen, E. J. Rybczyk, and B. Judd, Jr., "Subordinates' Perceptions of Male and Female Supervisors' Communication Style and Effectiveness" (Paper presented at the Eastern Communication Association Convention, Washington, DC, 1994).

75. D. Borisoff and D. F. Hahn, "Dimensions of Intimacy: The Interrelationships Between Gender and Listening," *Journal of the International Listening Association* 6 (1992): 28.

76. W. Farrell cited in D. Oldenburg, "The New Male, Phase 2," *The Washington Post*, 17 October 1986, p. B5.

77. D. Borisoff and L. Merrill, "Gender Issues and Listening," in *Listening in Everyday Life*, eds. Borisoff and Purdy, p. 78.

78. For summaries of some of this research, see Barker, *Listening Behavior*, pp. 45–46; and Weaver, *Human Listening: Processes and Behavior*, pp. 13–14.

79. See W. A. Villaume, M. H. Brown, R. Darling, D. Richardson, D. M. Henry, T. Reid, and R. Hawk, "An Investigation of Listening, Aging, and Conversational Behavior" (Paper presented at the International Listening Association Convention, Jacksonville, FL, 1991) for results on the effects of presbycusis on interpersonal communication.

80. For a review of this research, see A. Wingfield and D. L. Byrnes, *The Psychology of Human Memory* (NY: Academic Press, 1981), pp. 365–368. See also A. C. Wilkinson and R. Koestler, "Repeated Recall: A New Model and Tests of Its Generality from Childhood to Old Age," *Journal of Experimental Psychology* 112 (September 1983): 423–451.

81. J. F. Nussbaum, T. Thompson, and J. D. Robinson, *Communication and Aging* (NY: Harper and Row, 1989). See pp. 32–33 for a review of research on the communication characteristics of the elderly.

82. B. J. Benjamin, "Changes in Speech Production and Linguistic Behaviors with Aging," in *Communication Behavior and Aging: A Sourcebook for Clinicians*, ed. B. B. Shadden (Baltimore: Williams and Wilkins, 1988), p. 173.

83. W. A. Villaume and T. Reid, "An Investigation of the Relationships Among Listening Ability, Aging, and the Use of Aligning Actions in Conversation" (Paper presented at the International Listening Association Convention, Atlanta, GA, 1989); and R. Hawk and W. A. Villaume, "Listening and Patterns of Verbal Immediacy in Conversation: How Adults Cope With an Aging Auditory System" (Paper presented at the Southern States Communication Association Convention, Louisville, KY, 1989).

84. This research is summarized in J. Allman, "The Effects of Aging on Nonverbal Decoding Abilities: An Exploratory Study" (Paper presented at the Speech Communication Association Convention, Miami, FL, 1993).

85. J. Fincher, *Human Intelligence* (NY: G. P. Putnam, 1976), p. 55.

86. M. Ferguson, *The Aquarian Conspiracy* (Los Angeles: J. P. Tarcher, 1980), pp. 298–300; B. A. Edwards, "The Effect of Verbal/Visual Interactions on Drawing Ability," in *Nonverbal Communication Today*, ed. M. R. Key (Berlin: Mouton Publishers, 1982), pp. 35–37.

87. E. Perecman, "Introduction: Discovering Buried Treasure—A Look at the Cognitive Potential of the Right Hemisphere," in *Cognitive Processing in the Right Hemisphere*, ed. E. Perecman (NY: Academic Press, 1983), p. 2.

88. R. W. Sperry, "Hemisphere Disconnection and Unity in Conscious Awareness," *American Psychologist* 23 (October 1968): 723–733; Ferguson, *The Aquarian Conspiracy*, pp. 78–79, 297–300; Edwards, "The Effect of Verbal/Visual Interactions on Drawing Ability," pp. 33–53; G. Prince, "Putting the Other Half of the Brain to Work," *Training HRD* 15 (November 1978): 57–60; M. C. Kirkland, "What Are the Choices?" *Future* 20 (May/June 1982): 24– 27; L. J. Shedletsky, "Can We Use Our Brains to Define Communication?" *The Encoder*, (Fall 1980): 30–40; D. Goleman, "Special Abilities of the Sexes: Do They Begin in the Brain?" *Psychology Today* 12 (November 1978): 48–59, 120; J. Brothers, "Men and Women—The Differences," *Woman's Day*, 9 February 1982, pp. 58, 60, 138, 140, 142; H. A. Sackheim, R. C. Gur, and M. C. Saucy, "Emotions Are Expressed More Intensely on Left Side of Face," *Science* 202 (October 1978): 434–436; J. Mann, "What Is TV Doing to America?" *U.S. News & World Report* 93 (2 August 1982): 27–30; H. Gardner, "The Music of the Hemispheres," *Psychology Today*, June 1982, pp. 91–92; J. Sonnenfeld, "The Communication of Environmental Meaning: Hemispheres in Conflict" in *Nonverbal Communication Today*, M. R. Key, ed., pp. 17–29; O. M. Hogen, "An Introduction to Bilateral Communication," cited by R. O. Hirsch, *Listening: A Way to Process Information Aurally* (Dubuque, IA: Gorsuch Scarisbrick Publishers, 1979), pp. 28–30; P. Andersen, J. Garrison, and J. Andersen, "Implications of a Neurophysiologial Approach for the Study of a Nonverbal Communication," *Human Communication Research* 6 (Fall 1979): 74–89.

89. Hogen, "An Introduction to Bilateral Communication," pp. 29–30.

90. Prince, "Putting the Other Half of the Brain to Work," p. 58.

91. Fincher, *Human Intelligence*, p. 73.

92. Kirkland, "What Are the Choices?" p. 24.

93. Edwards, "The Effect of Verbal/Visual Interactions on Drawing Ability," p. 34.

94. Ibid., p . 36; Prince, "Putting the Other Half of the Brain to Work," p. 58.

95. C. Johmann, "Mind: Sex and the Split Brain," *Omni* 5 (August 1983): 26, 113.

96. Shedletsky, "Can We Use Our Brains to Define Communication?" p. 33; Goleman, "Special Abilities of the Sexes: Do They Begin in the Brain?" pp. 48–59, 120; Brothers, "Men and Women—The Differences," p. 142.

97. Brothers, " Men and Women—The Differences," p. 140; Goleman, "Special Abilities of the Sexes: Do They Begin in the Brain?" pp. 48–59, 120.

98. Brothers, "Men and Women—The Differences," p. 142; Goleman, "Special Abilities of the Sexes: Do They Begin in the Brain?" pp. 48–59; Ferguson, *The Aquarian Conspiracy*, p. 299; Hogen, "An Introduction to Bilateral Communication," p. 29.

99. Brothers, "Men and Women—The Differences," p. 142.

100. D. W. Stacks and D. E. Sellers, "Toward a Holistic Approach to Communication: The Effect of 'Pure' Hemispheric Reception on Message Acceptance," *Communication Quarterly* 34 (Summer 1986): 266–285.

101. A. Paivio, "On Exploring Visual Knowledge," in *Visual Learning, Thinking and Communication*, eds. B. S. Randhawa and W. E. Coffman (NY: Academic Press, 1978), p. 116.

102. J. Power, "The Mind: How Does It Work?" *NEA Today* 2 (June 1984): 5.
103. Sonnenfeld, "The Communication of Environmental Meaning: Hemispheres in Conflict," p. 28.
104. J. Wonder and P. Donovan, *Whole-Brain Thinking: Working from Both Sides of the Brain to Achieve Peak Job Performance* (NY: Morrow, 1984).
105. D. Rosenblum, *A Time to Hear, A Time to Help* (NY: The Free Press, 1993), p. 283.
106. L. Jones, "Managing Stress," *Baltimore Sun*, 7 March 1989, pp. 4–6.
107. J. J. Lynch, *The Language of the Heart: The Body's Response to Human Dialogue* (NY: Basic Books, 1985).
108. C. G. Coakley, *Teaching Effective Listening* (New Orleans: Spectra Incorporated, Publishers, 1993), pp. 82–85; C. G. Coakley and A. D. Wolvin, eds. *Experiential Listening: Tools for Teachers and Trainers* (New Orleans: Spectra Incorporated, Publishers, 1989), pp. 1–3.
109. T. Peters and R. H. Waterman, *In Search of Excellence* (NY: Harper & Row, 1982), p. 238.
110. Ibid.
111. I. Quandt, *Self-Concept and Reading* (Newark, DE: International Reading Association, no date), p. 31.
112. T. E. Anastasi, Jr., *Listen! Techniques for Improving Communication Skills* (Boston: CBI Publishing Company, 1982), p. 34.
113. For an interesting review of some of the research on the self-fulfilling prophecy, see R. Rosenthal, "Self-Fulfilling Prophecy," *Readings in Psychology Today* (Del Mar, CA: CRM Books, 1967), pp. 466–471.
114. A. D. Wolvin, unpublished manuscript, "The Listener's Self-Concept."
115. W. T. Gallwey, *Inner Tennis: Playing the Game* (NY: Random House, 1976), p. 111.
116. L. R. Wheeless, "An Investigation of Receiver Apprehension and Social Context Dimensions of Communication Apprehension," *Speech Teacher* 24 (September 1975): 263.
117. K. Paschall and A. J. Clark, "An Investigation of the Effects of Receiver Apprehension and Source Apprehension on Listening Comprehension" (Paper presented at the International Listening Association Convention, Scottsdale, AZ, 1984), p. 12. See also M. J. Beatty, R. R. Behnke, and L. S. Henderson, "An Empirical Validation of the Receiver Apprehension Test As a Measure of Trait Listening Anxiety," *Western Journal of Speech Communication* 44 (Spring 1980): 132–136. For an updated review of receiver apprehension, see R. W. Preiss and L. R. Wheeless, "Affective Responses in Listening: A Meta-Analysis of Receiver Apprehension Outcomes" in *Listening Behavior: Measurement and Application*, ed. R. N. Bostrom (NY: The Guilford Press, 1990), pp. 91–118.
118. M. Fitch-Hauser, D. A. Barker, and A. Hughes, "Receiver Apprehension and Listening Comprehension: A Linear or Curvilinear Relationship?" *The Southern Communication Journal* 56 (Fall 1990):62–71.
119. E. E. McDowell and C. E. McDowell, "An Investigation of Source and Receiver Apprehension at the Junior High, Senior High, and College Levels," *Central States Speech Journal* 29 (Spring 1978): 11–19.
120. A. J. Clark, "Communication Confidence and Listening Competence: An Investigation of the Relationships of Willingness to Communicate, Communication Apprehension, and Receiver Apprehension to Comprehension of Content and Emotional Meaning in Spoken Messages," pp. 236–248.
121. D. Barnlund, *Interpersonal Communication: Survey and Studies* (Boston: Houghton Mifflin, 1968), pp. 364–368.
122. P. McReynolds, "Assimilation and Anxiety," in *Emotions and Anxiety: New Concepts, Methods, and Applications*, eds. M. Zuckerman and C. D. Spielberger (NY: John Wiley, 1976), pp. 35–86.
123. M. J. Beatty, "Receiver Apprehension As a Function of Cognitive Backlog," *The Western Journal of Speech Communication* 45 (Summer 1981): 277–281.
124. R. W. Preiss, "Cognitive Consequences of Receiver Apprehension: Evidence of Reasoning about Communication and Self-Persuasion" (Paper presented at the Western Speech Communication Association Convention, Salt Lake City, UT, 1987).
125. Tubbs and Moss, *Human Communication*, p. 15.
126. J. P. Robinson, "The Time Squeeze," *American Demographics*, February 1990, pp. 30–32.
127. See R. G. Nichols and L. A. Stevens, *Are You Listening?* (NY: McGraw-Hill, 1957), pp. 77–88.
128. C. Graeber, "When to Teach What to Whom," *Today's Education* 71 (1982–1983 Annual): 35–37. See also M. Simonson, "Tick-Tock-Tick Listening to the Tempo of Internal Clock Keeps You Humming Along," *The Sun*, 28 March 1989, pp. 12–13.

129. K. W. Watson, L. L. Barker, and J. B. Weaver III, "Development and Validation of the Listener Preference Profile" (Paper presented at the International Listening Association Convention, Seattle, WA, 1992). See also K. W. Watson and L. L. Barker, *Guide to Using Listener Preference Profile: Tips for Trainers and Facilitators* (New Orleans, LA: Spectra, 1993).

130. Ibid.

131. T. Wirkus, "Personality and Listening Preferences: Do You Hear What I Hear?" (Paper presented at International Listening Association Convention, Memphis, TN, 1993).

132. D. L. Rubin, "Listenability = Oral – Based Discourse + Considerateness," in *Perspectives on Listening*, eds. Wolvin and Coakley, pp. 261–281; E. Glenn, V. Emmert, and P. Emmert, "A Scale for Measuring Listenability Phase III—The Factors that Determine Listening Ease and Difficulty" (Paper presented at International Listening Association Convention, Boston, MA, 1994).

133. S. W. Lundsteen, *Listening: Its Impact at All Levels on Reading and the Other Language Arts* (Urbana, IL: ERIC Clearinghouse on Reading and Communication Skills, 1979), p. 75.

PART II

Developing Purposeful Listening Skills

As one serves as a listening communicator in various communication transactions, one must understand not only what is involved in the listening process itself but also what listening behaviors are appropriate in each transaction. While the listening process in each transaction always remains the same—with the listener engaging in the behaviors of receiving, attending to, and assigning meaning to the aural and/or visual messages of the sender(s)—the listener also engages in additional behaviors as the purposes for which he or she listens change. To provide the student of listening with a better understanding of these additional behaviors, we have developed a taxonomy of listening that describes how listeners function at various listening purposes or levels.

While Part I of this book deals with understanding the listening process, Part II explores the skills necessary to listen effectively at the various levels described by our taxonomy. The Wolvin-Coakley Listening Taxonomy provides a framework for dealing with specific skills so that students can reinforce, improve, or change their listening behaviors as they discover how to function effectively within this taxonomy. Inherent in our view of listening skills, which will be detailed in the next five chapters, is the concept that listening can be considered in a hierarchy *and* that specific skills are involved.

Through our experiences as listening educators, we have learned that effective listening behaviors can be developed in a systematic program. The skilled listener must learn what he or she is doing as a listener, to what extent a particular behavior is effective or ineffective to his or her purposes, and how ineffective listening behaviors can be replaced by effective listening behaviors. Then, through *repeated* practice and reinforcement, the newly acquired, effective listening behaviors can become a natural part of the listener's repertoire.

Practice with each newly developed listening skill ought to be spread out over a time frame that will enable the listener to experiment with each new approach until he or she feels comfortable and proficient with this skill. As the listener practices with any new listening skill, it is important that he or she practice *the correct skill*. Learning specialists stress the need for this distributed practice to develop proficiency, but it is crucial that the listener, when practicing, also remembers Duffin's argument: "[Since] 'practice makes perfect' only if it is correct practice, practicing existing listening habits probably serves to reinforce ineffective listening behaviors and attitudes."[1]

Following the lead of Nichols, whose early work established a listening skills foundation for the field, many listening educators have worked to identify just what these listening skills ought to include. Lundsteen, one of the first to analyze these listening skills as a hierarchy, offered an instructional taxonomy of general listening skills and of critical listening skills in particular.

Further extending the previous work on the hierarchical nature of listening skills, we utilize five basic purposes of listening as the framework for our taxonomy. Just as there are specific listening skills important to each of these listening purposes, we believe that the skills that listeners develop and use operate in a hierarchical sequence—depending on what each listener's intended objective or objectives for listening might be at any particular time.

discriminative listening

At the first level, a listener listens for **discrimination**—to distinguish the auditory and visual stimuli. Discriminative listening is at the base of all listening that we do; we must differentiate the auditory and visual messages and identify their distinguishing features before we can process the messages at any other level. However, we may not wish to listen at a higher level; our sole objective may be to listen for discrimination, for example, to determine why an infant is crying, to assess the facial cues of a conversational partner, or to tune up an automotive engine.

comprehensive listening

At the next level, we listen for **comprehension**. The comprehensive listener strives to understand the message in order to retain, recall, and—possibly—use that information at a later time. We listen for comprehension to lectures, directions, briefings, conversations—any message we want to understand. We suggest that listening with understanding requires that we first function as discriminative listeners, for it is necessary to distinguish the auditory and visual cues in a message before we can further process that message. Please recognize that, for the sake of consistency in labeling the listening objectives, we have chosen "comprehensive listening" as the descriptor. We do not intend to suggest that this is the overall, broad, comprehensive category of listening, though we realize that the phrasing can be confusing if taken out of the context of chapter 6.

Just as discriminative listening forms the base for the Wolvin-Coakley Listening Taxonomy, so, too, does listening comprehension serve as a foundation for the third level, which incorporates other special purposes for which we listen. This taxonomy could be viewed graphically as a tree, with discrimination as the root of the listening hierarchy and comprehension as

Developing Purposeful Listening Skills

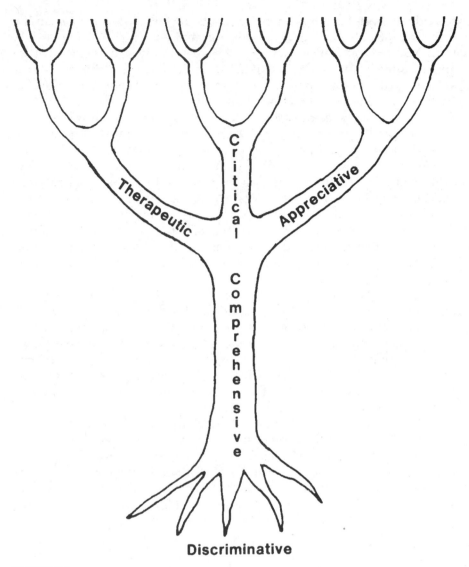

FIGURE II.1.
The Wolvin-Coakley Listening Taxonomy.

the trunk, supporting the other listening purposes that shape our behaviors as listeners. (See fig. II.1.)

At the first of the three higher levels of listening, we can listen for a **therapeutic** purpose—to provide help to a person who needs to talk through a concern. We do not intend to suggest with the "therapeutic" label that listeners should play amateur psychiatrists. Clearly, serious problems must be handled by professional therapists. However, we find that the listening approaches of professional therapists best describe this category, that listening therapeutically is the all-encompassing category of listening to

therapeutic listening

provide support, help, and empathy. The therapeutic listener is a sounding board for a troubled friend, colleague, or family member who can benefit from talking through the issues he or she is confronting. To be effective therapeutic listeners, we must first discriminate the verbal and nonverbal messages sent and then comprehend those messages so that our communicating partners have listeners who truly do understand.

critical listening

The second of the three higher levels of listening is **critical** listening—listening to evaluate the merits of the message. Individuals who listen to evaluate persuasive ads, speeches, or sales talks, for instance, are required first to use the repertoire of discriminative and comprehensive listening skills. Only after carefully detecting senders' auditory and visual messages and fully comprehending the messages will effective critical listeners assess the messages or make judgments about them. On the other hand, effective therapeutic listeners—to develop empathic bonds with their communication partners—must suspend all judgments; that is, while serving as sounding boards, their listening purpose should not be to evaluate senders' messages.

appreciative listening

The last of the higher levels of listening is **appreciative** listening. Listening to appreciate a message requires the listener to distinguish the auditory and visual cues in the message, comprehend the message at some basic level, and then process the message with some type of appreciative response. The appreciative listener may also engage in critical listening; however, he or she must develop the skill of suspending critical judgment until after the appropriate comprehension of the piece—whether that piece be music, a story, or pleasant sounds.

Thus, listening skills can be established for five basic purposes that form our hierarchy of listening behaviors. Through the systematic development and practice of these skills, the listener should develop behaviors that will become a natural part of his or her listening repertoire and enable him or her to function more effectively at each listening level. Our next five chapters, then, detail what is involved and what skills are required to listen discriminatively, comprehensively, therapeutically, critically, and appreciatively.

Notes

1. John Duffin, "DLA's: Teaching Listening Skills with Videotape," *Teacher Talk* 2 (Fall, 1982): 5–6.

- *Discriminative listening is listening to distinguish auditory and/or visual stimuli.*

- *Discriminative listening, which is basic to all listening purposes, forms the foundation for listening comprehensively, critically, therapeutically, and appreciatively.*

- *Auditory discrimination is important for detecting and recognizing verbal and nonverbal sounds, for recognizing the sound structure of the language, for detecting and isolating vocal cues, for understanding dialectal and accentual differences, and for recognizing environmental sounds.*

- *Visual discrimination is important for recognizing nonverbal cues through posture, bodily action, gestures, facial expressions, eye behavior, appearance, artifacts, space/distance, time, touch, and environmental factors.*

- *Auditory and visual discrimination are important for detecting deception and regulatory cues.*

- *The effective discriminative listener*

  - *strives to distinguish auditory and/or visual stimuli*

  - *is sensitive to the verbal and nonverbal cues offered by the communicator source*

  - *recognizes the importance of careful discrimination in the listening process*

CHAPTER 5

Discriminative Listening

As you read the following letter-coded, abridged excerpt of a scenario (which appears in its entirety in the Instructor's Manual *accompanying the fifth edition of* Listening*), attempt to determine what is occurring nonverbally at any given (coded) point in the situation.*

At 6:45, fifteen minutes before his first University of Maryland listening class is scheduled to begin,[a] Bob enters Room 4205. Surveying the room already occupied by several students and the instructor, who meets him with a smile and a warm hello,[b] Bob selects the seat at the head of the middle table.[c]

As Bob waits for class to begin, he makes several observations. He observes the other students who are quietly rummaging through papers, leafing through the textbook, and observing the surroundings as he is.[d] He also observes the room where he'll spend the next six weeks on Monday and Wednesday evenings; he immediately finds relief in the fact that the room is comfortably air-conditioned and not sticky-hot as the Maryland summer weather is outside.[e]

Before long, the classroom contains nearly twenty students. Mark, who seats himself two chairs to Bob's right,[f] introduces himself to Bob, and the two begin conversing about their course expectations. Janice enters the room, places her notepad and textbook on the table space to Bob's left,[g] and exits to the ladies' room. A few moments later, Janice returns and seats herself to Bob's immediate left.

At 7:00, the instructor begins her introduction to the course. Then, she introduces a taped listening test which the students are to take. . . . During the last part of the test, consisting of a ten-minute lecture, she

*observes various students' behavior: Kay "checks out" the room and other
students; Pat lets her eyelids slowly droop; Gordon repeatedly checks his
watch; Deanna has a blank, out-of-focus look; Mike drums his fingers on
the table; Irene props her head up with the palm of her hand; Sherry
makes excessive postural shifts and jiggles a foot;[h] and Bob frequently
blinks.[i] At the end of the test many students emit deep sighs[j]. . . .*

*A Descriptive Commentary of what is occurring nonverbally in this
scenario is on pages 200–201 immediately following Suggested
Activities for this chapter.*

**discriminative
listening: listening to
distinguish aural, and
sometimes visual,
stimuli**

One purpose for listening is **discriminative listening** to distinguish the
aural stimuli. Depending on the communication context, however, the stimuli
may also be visual, such as a smile, a clenched fist, or a shrug of the shoulder.

Discriminative listening is placed first among the five purposes of listening because it is basic to the other four purposes. As the following examples illustrate, the listener who has developed effective discriminative
listening skills is more efficient when engaging in each of the other four purposes of listening. For example, the comprehensive listener who can detect
changes in the sender's pitch, volume, and/or rate is better equipped to
determine when the sender is moving from one main idea to another. Also,
if the comprehensive listener is sensitive to dialectal differences, he or she
can more quickly recognize the sender's intended meaning. Likewise, the
therapeutic listener who recognizes the structure of the language and vocal
cues is better able to determine the degree of the sender's distress by noting
his or her use of vocal characterizers (such as speaking at a barely audible
volume), vocal segregates (such as frequently pausing and/or vocalizing
pauses with sounds such as *uh* and *umm*), and speech nonfluencies (such as
starting the same sentence twice and/or beginning with one thought and
then jumping to another thought without completing the first).
Furthermore, the critical listener skilled in detecting and accurately interpreting nonverbal cues can more readily determine from the sender's leg,
foot, and hand movements as well as facial expressions whether or not the
sender is "speaking" the truth. Finally, the appreciative listener who can
detect the sounds of the individual instruments in an orchestra can increase
enjoyment of the total artistic expression while the appreciative listener who
recognizes the distinct as well as subtle differences in sounds' intensity,
pitch, and duration can heighten appreciation of the voices of singers like
Beverly Sills and Luciano Pavarotti.

Uses of Auditory Discrimination

Throughout our lives, we rely heavily on our auditory discrimination
ability. We begin the development of discriminative listening as we learn to

perceive and identify the sounds in our environment and then to use these sounds to adapt to that environment. During our first few months of life, we recognize the human voice and respond to it. Later, we turn our heads in search of the direction from which sounds are coming, and shortly thereafter we move toward the sources of the sounds. During our lulling stage, we listen to our own sounds and repeat them. Then, we begin to imitate the sounds that make up our world—the sounds of family members, pets, and our environment. We are learning a language, which at this stage consists of coos, cries, happy tones, angry tones, loud noises, soft noises, close sounds, distant sounds, vowel sounds, consonant sounds, chirping sounds, perking sounds, continuous sounds, sporadic sounds, nonsensical sounds, sensible

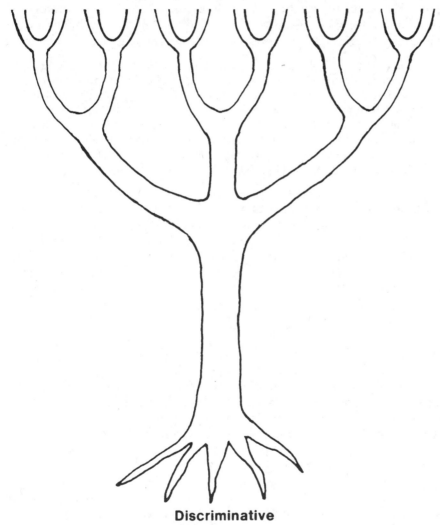

Discriminative

Discriminative branch of the Wolvin-Coakley Listening Taxonomy.

sounds, nasal tones, throaty tones, high-pitched sounds, low-pitched sounds, twangy sounds, and drawling sounds. As we grow older, we continue to enlarge our inventory of sounds and to test our ability to discriminate among varied sounds. Indeed, listening discriminatively—whether it be to detect the arrival of a rainstorm, a pet's desire to go outside, or the sincerity in a sender's voice—is essential to acquiring information that enables us to adapt more effectively to our environment.

The Importance of Auditory Discrimination

Research on the language acquisition of children documents the importance of auditory discrimination. It is generally agreed that the effective development of both oral and reading vocabularies depends upon our auditory discrimination. One specialist in language development, Perkins, notes the role of auditory discrimination in the process of our oral language development:

> Long before his first true word is spoken, the infant has been working on his system for deciphering the mysterious stream of jabber he hears when people talk. The fact that he can recognize the meaning of what is spoken before he himself can speak reveals the ability to recognize at least gross differences in sounds on which meaning hinges before he can produce these differences. This ability is often called *auditory discrimination*. Less is known about how this capacity to recognize differences develops than about development of capacity to produce speech sounds.[1]

Ebel, summarizing the research on the development of reading skills, concludes that "the strength of many developmental reading programs appears to lie in their success in improving auditory discrimination of language sounds."[2] Neuman also surveyed the literature and noted that the research consistently supports one major conclusion: "The child who is unable to hear and distinguish sounds will most likely have difficulty in learning to read."[3] Thus, auditory discrimination ability has played, and continues to play, an important role in the development of our listening, speaking, and reading effectiveness.

As adults, it is essential that we possess highly developed auditory discrimination skills so that we can help others develop their discriminative ability. Those of us who are teachers, speech therapists, or parents especially need to develop our discriminative ability, for we are responsible for guiding a child's language acquisition. Only through careful auditory perception can we discriminate the child's language development (e.g., *wabbit* and *yights* to *rabbit* and *lights*) and provide the necessary guidance.

It is clear, then, that as adults, we need to develop our discriminative ability so that we can help ourselves become more efficient listeners. (See fig. 5.1). According to Fessenden, the first level of listening involves the isolation of the individual aspects of a message. This level does not include evaluation or analysis; it involves only "the recognition of the presence of specific, independent items."[4] Our proficiency in recognizing specific items

One of the most sensitive instruments aboard our flight.

At British Airways, listening to and anticipating a passenger's needs go far beyond an extra pillow or refilling a glass of mineral water. Which is why our Club World™ seats have been redesigned to include their very own seatback videos as well as new headrests, footrests and lumbar supports. *It's the way we make you feel* that makes us the world's favourite.

BRITISH AIRWAYS
The world's favourite airline

FIGURE 5.1.
Advertisement by British Airways.

depends especially on our auditory discrimination ability, and without highly developed auditory discrimination skills, we cannot achieve our goal of becoming complete listeners.

Skills Involved in Auditory Discrimination

Developing the auditory discrimination skills is an ongoing process. When we are quite young, we begin to develop many of the essential auditory skills. This imitative development of sound is not just speech but also music: "Children are not raised in an acoustic vacuum. The tunes they sing no less than the words they repeat will reflect the sounds they hear in their society rather than some universal, preordained pattern."[5] As we grow older, we often need to refine those discriminative skills that are underdeveloped. Also, we need to acquire and cultivate additional discriminative skills to master discriminative listening.

Refining Skills Included in Weaver and Rutherford's Hierarchy

refining auditory discrimination skills generally developed early

After surveying the literature dealing with the development of discriminative and other listening skills, Weaver and Rutherford developed a hierarchy of auditory skills grouped according to the estimated time periods at which the various skills are generally developed. Although the authors of the hierarchy have distinguished between environmental skills (pertaining to sounds other than verbal) and discrimination skills (pertaining to verbal sounds), both sections are relevant to the development of auditory discrimination:

Environmental Skills

> *Prenatal*
> Fetal movement in response to sound
> *Infancy*
> Responds reflexively to sudden loud noises
> Responds to loud noises by crying
> Listens to the human voice
> Is quieted by sound
> Changes activity in response to the human voice
> Turns head in search of sound (VH*)[6]
> Learns that people and objects make sound
> Learns that objects make sound with manipulation
> Localizes sound sources and moves toward them (VH*)
> *Preschool*
> Associates a sound with an object
> Repeats a sequence of sounds
> Learns that unseen objects make sounds

Learns that sound sources can be labeled or named

Given three noisemakers, can find the one that sounds different

Can identify people and animals by sound

Kindergarten–Grade 3

Learns that sounds differ in intensity (VH*)

Learns that sounds differ in pitch (VH*)

Learns that sounds differ in pattern

Learns that sounds differ in duration (the length of time they can be heard)

Learns the concept distance in relation to sound localization and movement (VH)

Grade 4–Grade 6

Identifies sounds in the environment at certain times of day and evaluates them in terms of orientation and mobility (VH)

Promotes growth of echo perception and spatial orientation (VH)

Discrimination Skills

Infancy

Responds differentially to sounds

Responds to his or her name

Begins imitating speech sounds

Preschool

Separates certain sounds from background sounds

Identifies like sounds and different sounds

Can match verbal sounds

Kindergarten–Grade 3

Learns that sounds differ in intensity (VH*)

Learns that sounds differ in pitch (VH*)

Learns that sounds differ in pattern

Learns that sounds differ in duration

Recognizes differences in word sounds

Recognizes differences in initial consonants (cat-mat) auditorily

Recognizes differences in final consonants (mat-map) auditorily

Recognizes differences in medial sounds (map-mop) auditorily

Recognizes discrete words within a sentence

Recognizes sequence of words within a sentence

Identifies accented words within a sentence

Identifies number of syllables within a word

Identifies accented syllable within a word

Changes accent from one syllable to another

Recognizes initial and final consonant sounds

Recognizes short vowel sounds

Recognizes long vowel sounds

Recognizes rhyming words

Recognizes and discriminates word endings (-s, -ing, -er)

Discriminates temporal order of sounds within words[7]

Recognizing that responding to sound during the prenatal and early infancy stages is the first auditory skill developed, several specialists advocate behavioral communication between parent and child. They encourage the pregnant mother to use soothing words, sing lullabies, and listen to calming music to help the unborn child begin to experience life with emotional and intellectual stimulation.[8] Mozart's music, for example, has been found to calm six-month-old fetuses, whereas rock music stimulates intense kicking in the mothers' wombs.[9] Likewise, newborn babies prefer such auditory stimulation as classical music, their parents' voices, and the sound of the mother's heartbeat. Advocates of infant stimulation point to studies that illustrate that infants who have been stimulated (primarily by auditory means) develop faster, have longer attention spans, and are generally more curious.[10]

To help children develop other skills listed in the hierarchy of auditory skills, we can devise numerous exercises. Children, with their eyes closed, can be asked to (a) focus on sounds outside the room, inside the room, and within their bodies; (b) distinguish changes in cadence when they listen to the tapping of a pencil; and (c) determine differences in intensity of the clapping of hands. These exercises can develop the auditory skills of (a) spatial location—locating from where the sound is coming; (b) frequency spectra—determining how often sounds occur; and (c) loudness—determining the intensity of the sound that reaches the ear.[11] Exercises devised to assist children in developing other auditory skills listed in Weaver and Rutherford's hierarchy can likewise be beneficial.

Although the skills listed by Weaver and Rutherford are concentrated at the lower educational levels, many of these skills can be further developed throughout a person's life. Again, developing our auditory discrimination skills is an ongoing process.

Recognizing the Sound Structure of Our Language

recognizing sound structure of language

A skill that we cultivate after our primary grade years is that of **recognizing the sound structure of our language**. If, for example, we are proficient in the previously cited skill of recognizing the various vowel and consonant sounds in the initial, medial, and final positions (a skill that we generally develop early in our schooling) and we know that English words do not begin with *sr*, we will not mishear *this rip* as *this srip*. Likewise, if we are trying to identify words at the beginning of a sentence, where they are quite unpredictable, and we know that *mg* cannot start a word in English, we will not perceive a sentence beginning with *I'm g* . . . as anything but *I'm* plus the start of a new word. However, we could perceive a sentence beginning with *I'm a* as *I may* or the start of *I'm making*).[12] Research indicates that when we are categorizing stimuli, our initial decisions are made on a phonetic basis.[13] Goss, in his information-processing listening model, directs attention to the listener's need to make phonetic decisions in the initial phase of listening. During this phase, which Goss refers to as the signal processing (SP) stage, the listener must segment and structure the speech signal into potentially meaningful units.[14] For example, the listener who recognizes the sound structure of the language would know that a rapidly spoken *Idrankitfirst* could be segmented and structured in two ways: *I drank it first* or *I'd rank it first*. The examples in this section illustrate that if we wish to improve our discriminative listening and, thus, our assigning of meaning, we must increase our understanding of *phonology* (the structure of sound).

Detecting and Isolating Vocal Cues

Effective discriminative listeners must develop the skill of **isolating vocal cues**—not only noting how a message is vocalized but also interpreting what message is vocalized. Knapp cautions that listeners "should be quick to challenge the cliché that vocal cues only concern *how* something is said—frequently they are *what* is said. *What* is said might be an attitude ('I like you' or 'I'm superior to you'), it might be an emotion, it might be the coordination and management of conversation, or it might be the presentation of some aspect of your personality, background, or physical features."[15] Becoming efficient in this skill involves developing a sensory awareness to and increasing an understanding of vocal cues, recognizing the influence that vocal cues have on interpretations of messages and perceptions of speakers, and increasing a knowledge base by examining research findings relevant to vocal cues.

> **detecting and isolating vocal cues**

Isolating vocal cues involves first recognizing various **types of cues**—such as the following four types—to which one responds when making interpretive judgments.

> **types of vocal cues**

1. Paralanguage or vocal cues that accompany one's spoken language, such as pitch, inflection, tension, volume, intensity, rate, quality, tone, and dynamics of the speaking voice
2. Vocal characterizers such as laughing, sighing, and yawning
3. Speech disturbances or nonfluencies, such as repetitions, omissions, slips of the tongue, sentence corrections or changes, false starts, sentence incompletions, stutters, etc.
4. Filled pauses, which are pauses filled with nonverbal vocalizations—also known as vocal segregates—such as *ah*, *uh*, and *um*[16]

Furthermore, one may isolate aspects relating to speech time and pause time—such as latency of response, duration of utterance, duration of silence or unfilled pauses, and interaction rates.

influence of vocal
cues on message
interpretation

Knowing the types of vocal cues to isolate, one then must become aware of the **influence that vocal cues have on one's interpretations of speakers' messages**. For example, effective discriminative listeners recognize what the speaker considers to be important by the vocal stress he or she places on certain words or when the speaker is asking a question or making a statement by the rise or fall of his or her pitch. Moreover, listeners distinguish whether the speaker's vocal cues contradict or reinforce the verbal message. When the vocal cues are contradictory and listeners are making judgments about the speaker's emotional state, research shows that listeners more heavily rely on the vocal expression to infer the sender's feelings.[17] Mehrabian believes that a reasonably safe generalization regarding the impact of nonverbal communication, including vocal expression, can be made:

> When any nonverbal behavior contradicts speech, it is more likely to determine the total impact of the message . . . touching, positions (distance, forward lean, or eye contact), postures, gestures, as well as facial and vocal expressions, can all outweigh words and determine the feelings conveyed by a message.[18]

Mehrabian illustrates how this generalization may apply to a recorded message or a telephone conversation; if the vocal expression contradicts the verbal message, the vocal expression will determine the total impact. The impact will be negative if the words are positive and the vocal expression is negative, or the impact will be positive if the words are negative and the vocal expression is positive.[19] In contrast, other researchers have studied vocal cues that reinforce verbal messages, and they have identified specific emotions that are conveyed through particular vocal cues. Scherer has found, for example, that pleasantness, boredom, and sadness are revealed through low pitch while activity, potency, fear, and surprise are revealed through high pitch.[20] Among Davitz's many findings are that affection and sadness are conveyed through slow rate while anger and joy are expressed through fast rate.[21] Examining the findings of Scherer, Davitz, and many others who have conducted similar research, Knapp and Hall conclude, "Generally speaking, tempo and pitch variation seem to be very influential factors for a wide range of judgments about emotional expressions."[22]

To become more accurate interpreters of others' vocally expressed emotions, discriminative listeners might engage in self-monitoring—that is, becoming more conscious of and having more control over their own expressive behavior, for high self-monitors tend to be better at interpreting others' expressed emotions.[23] Still another way that vocal cues influence listeners' judgments is that they help clarify a speaker's intentions in respect to turn-taking in communication interactions. For instance, when a listener interrupts a speaker who desires to maintain a speaking role, the speaker's volume may increase and/or pitch rise. When the speaker wants to yield the floor, he or she may end an utterance with a falling pitch, a softer volume, and a drawling out of the last stressed syllable.

Additionally, one must become aware of the **influence that vocal cues may have on one's perceptions** of various aspects of speakers—such as their personalities, backgrounds, and physical features. For example, listeners perceive speakers who have variety in their pitch as having more positive personalities[24] and speakers who have low pitches as being more dominant.[25] Listeners also use vocal cues to make judgments about speakers' backgrounds; for instance, Harms found that listeners could very accurately determine, by voice only, a speaker's social class and status and that listeners perceived high-status speakers as being most credible.[26] Physical features—such as age, sex, and height—are additionally judged from speakers' voices.[27]

influence of vocal cues on listener perception

Finally, discriminative listeners can improve their sensitivity to vocal cues by increasing their knowledge base of research findings relevant to vocal cues. From the many reported findings, the following are some that are most pertinent to students of auditory discrimination:

- Females' voices are higher in pitch and tend to be more expressive in pitch than males' voices.
- Females are more likely to raise their pitch at the ends of sentences (even when they are not questions) than males are.
- Males speak louder and are more loudly spoken to than females.
- Males speak slightly faster than females speak.
- Speakers who speak faster are more persuasive than are those who speak slower.
- Speakers' use of vocal variety increases listener comprehension and retention of speakers' messages.
- Voice qualities of breathiness and nasality have a negative effect on listener comprehension.
- Females' voices are judged to be more positive, pleasant, honest, personal, admiring, respectful, anxious, and enthusiastic and less confident and dominant than males' voices.
- Females' speech is more fluent than males' speech.
- Males have more filled pauses than females do.
- Increased use of nonfluencies tends to impair speaker credibility.
- Speakers who are in a state of anxiety tend to use speech disturbances or nonfluencies and have filled pauses.
- Speakers who use more intonation and volume, faster rate, and less halting speech increase their persuasiveness.
- Males tend to talk slightly more and are more often talked to than females.
- In same-sex dyads, females tend to talk more than males.
- In mixed-sex dyads, males tend to talk more than females.
- Females engage in more interruptive questions than males do.
- Males take the initiative when there is a pause more frequently than females.
- Females engage in more back-channel behaviors (listener feedback responses exhibited while another is speaking) than males do.

- Individuals who engage in back-channel behaviors—including vocalizing *mm-hmm*—are perceived to be warmer than those who do not, and they are more effective in increasing other interactants' verbal output[28]

Becoming more sensitive to and knowledgeable about vocal cues, recognizing the effects that vocal cues have on interpretive judgments, and learning to distinguish both obvious and subtle differences in vocal characteristics will assist discriminative listeners in understanding the messages of others, whether the speakers are political candidates, job supervisors, or family members. Additionally, the more exposure listeners have to a wide range of emotional expressions conveyed by the voice, the more accurate their interpretive judgments should be.

Understanding Dialectal and Accentual Differences

understanding dialectal differences

On a less involved level, auditory discrimination can enhance listeners' sensitivity, particularly in their understanding of and their reactions to the speech of others. As listeners, we tend to stereotype a speech pattern as a southern drawl, a midwestern twang, New York Brooklynese, "Havahd." In 1970, Dubin conducted a study that illustrates listeners' stereotyped reactions. He asked personnel interviewers in the Washington, D.C., area to react to tapes of speakers demonstrating the following dialects: general American white, general American black, light black, southern American white, and strong black. Predictably, the interviewers (who were not told what dialects they were listening to) more frequently selected the speaker with the standard white dialect for upper-level managerial positions and the speakers with the nonstandard dialects for lower-level positions.[29]

In a more recent study conducted by Terrell and Terrell, six black college women—using equivalent bogus letters of recommendation and job experience—were randomly sent to be interviewed by one hundred southwestern personnel managers. During the interviews, half of the women spoke black English dialect while half spoke standard English. The secretly made tapes of the interviews revealed that interviewees speaking black English " 'were given shorter interviews and fewer job offers' " than those speaking standard English. [30] Furthermore, of those offered jobs, the black-English speakers " 'were offered positions paying significantly less money than standard English speakers.' "[31]

understanding accentual differences

Accents, too, appear to have adverse influence on North American listeners' perceptions of speakers. For example, Gill and Badzinski's study on the impact of accent on perception formation revealed results similar to those of other researchers: "American listeners ascribe more favorable ratings to accents similar to their own, and make more negative assessments of non-American accented speakers."[32] Being aware of various regional and local dialects, as well as accents, and understanding their differing characteristics through auditory discrimination can not only diminish the frequency with which we misunderstand words pronounced differently than

Developing Purposeful Listening Skills

we pronounce them but also diminish our stereotyped reactions, which can greatly interfere with human relations.

Recognizing Environmental Sounds

Likewise, **sensitivity to environmental sounds** through more careful discriminative listening can enhance our listening efficiency. One of the most phenomenal examples of auditory discrimination in the environment has to be the capabilities of the mockingbird to imitate sounds it hears; "it takes the most sophisticated electronic analysis to tell the copy from the original."[33] Stories about the discriminative listening sensitivity that mothers develop to listen to their infants exemplify this level. Additionally, comedians such as Rich Little develop extraordinary discriminative listening sensitivity to incorporate into their routines the mimicking of others' voices. Owners of automobiles also must develop discriminative listening skills. Most of us, as commuters, depend on our cars to transport us to where we want to go, and our cars tell us their general state of health. Describing the many ways racing experts such as A. J. Foyt and local auto mechanics tune in to their cars, Robert Ross says that "you will learn by listening whether to take your car home to fix it yourself, or to a service station for minor repairs, or to a more expensive garage for major surgery."[34] Rarely is a person ordered to listen to his or her car, but at least one man has been. A Detroit man was convicted of drunken driving and plowing into a car driven by a woman whose two young children were passengers playing with a tape recorder. As part of his sentence, Ingham County (Michigan) Judge Claude Thomas ordered the man to listen to the automobile accident, which had been recorded on the children's tape recorder. Judge Thomas believed that listening to the sounds of the accident should heighten the convicted man's understanding of the harm he had caused.[35]

Those in business also must listen with discrimination. For example, one of Wolvin's students manages an ice cream shop. He must carefully listen to the sounds of the freezers, for any malfunction of the machines could ruin the ice cream products and be quite costly. Another business owner who listens discriminatively is the prominent poultry producer on Maryland's Eastern Shore, Frank Perdue. He points out in one of his television commercials that he has learned to listen to his chickens! Indeed, in a listening program designed by one of our former students, the firm had installed sound monitors in the various poultry buildings to enable the staff to listen to the chickens. They communicate a great deal about their general state of health through the sounds they emit.

While Frank Perdue listens to his chickens, Larry Smith of Kingsport, Tennessee, listens to his basketball players' footsteps and dribbles. Blind as a result of diabetes, Smith relies solely on the sounds of the game for his coaching of three teams, which win consistently. Indeed, as Smith notes, he has mastered the sounds of basketball: "I know the players' footsteps and how they dribble. I know whenever they're doing the jobs they're supposed to—I can almost tell you who shoots and who makes bad passes. I know where they're supposed to be on the floor. I guess I know where they're supposed to be better than they do."[36] A more serious discriminative listening sensitivity that many American soldiers developed during World War II was the recognition of the sound of mechanical, hand-held crickets, which often served to alert American soldiers that German soldiers were near. Clearly, listening to sounds in the environment can be an important part of coping with the demands of control in that environment.

Unfortunately, the results of a study conducted by two of our students reveal that many listeners do not adequately listen with discrimination to environmental sounds. The instrument used in this study was a tape recording of fifty sounds ranging from a pen clicking and coffee perking to an elephant bellowing in a zoo. Students at different grade levels in various urban, suburban, and rural schools were asked to identify the sounds. The results illustrated how nondiscriminative we can be. The researchers concluded that the problem is not so much that we are not exposed to a variety of sounds but that we do not attend consciously to the sounds.[37] Thus, by expending more attention energy in perceiving the sounds of our environment, we can improve our recognition of these sounds.

Visual Discrimination

Detecting and Isolating Nonverbal Cues

detecting and isolating nonverbal cues

Just as effective listeners must distinguish auditory stimuli, so, too, must listeners discriminate the visual stimuli whenever the sender is visually present. Like our development of the auditory capabilities of discriminating sounds, our visual discrimination capacities are developed through imitation. Research by Andrew Meltzoff, for example, has illustrated that 12- to 21-day-old babies can imitate facial expressions, even when their response is delayed until after the demonstration has ended.[38] The capacity to discriminate visual cues is an important function in the listening process. Analysis of messages in human interactions indicates that the greatest **impact of the meaning of a message may well stem from what is communicated through the visual channel** (as those hearing-impaired persons who are primarily visual listeners well know). Ray Birdwhistell, for instance, has determined that in a normal, two-person conversation, 35 percent of the meaning of the message is carried verbally, while as much as 65 percent is conveyed nonverbally.[39] Albert Mehrabian's formula for determining the impact of the various channels in communicating inconsistent or contradictory feeling messages attributes even more importance to the nonverbal channels. He shows 38 percent of the message's meaning coming from the vocal, 55 percent coming from the facial, and only 7 percent coming from the verbal.[40]

impact of visual channel on message meaning

Two newsworthy examples illustrate how listeners detect and isolate nonverbal cues. Citing "Negative facial expressions, i.e., scowling, glaring and frowning," the prosecutor in the 1991 William Kennedy Smith rape case

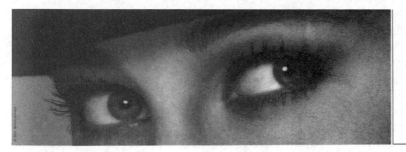

FIGURE 5.2.
Advertisement by British Airways.

asked the judge to disqualify herself because of "obvious prejudice."[41] In another court case, observers—noticing that a juror in the 1993 Rodney King case "leaned back in his chair and rigidly folded his arms" during the closing argument of prosecutor Steven Clymer—had this interpretation of the juror's movements: "The juror simply wasn't buying Clymer's pitch for conviction of the four police officers accused of violating King's civil rights."[42]

The prominence of the visual channel as a conveyor of meaning enables us, as listeners, to understand better the messages of others. (See fig. 5.2). Research suggests that the visual system especially conveys more affective (emotional) information than do the verbal or vocal systems and that this affective information is highly reliable.[43] The face, for example, reveals much of how the sender feels at any given time, while the body reveals the intensity of a particular feeling. A major reason why nonverbal messages are so reliable is that they are less well-controlled and, thus, are more likely to be genuine.[44]

Six Principles of Nonverbal Communication

While using the visual channel system to interpret others' nonverbal messages, discriminative listeners should keep nonverbal communication in perspective by remembering six principles.

principles of nonverbal communication

1. Any nonverbal act can have many possible meanings and, thus, should be viewed not as a fact but rather as an indicator—a clue—that should be checked out. The meaning of any nonverbal message, as Knapp notes, "will vary according to a multitude of factors—for example, cultural and environmental context, the relationship between the communicators, the intensity and duration of the message, whether it was perceived as intentional or unintentional, and so on."[45]
2. Every individual has his or her own nonverbal behavior. Thus, the more knowledge communicators have of one another, the more accurately they should interpret each other's nonverbal behavior. For example, if the listener knows that Derrick—when seated—

finds it comfortable to fold his arms across his rotund stomach, the listener will not quickly interpret Derrick's crossed arms as a commonly decoded signal of defensiveness or resistance.

3. Every culture has its own nonverbal behavior. Here again, possessing knowledge of others' cultures assists listeners in assigning more accurate meanings to senders' messages. Following are a few of the numerous cultural differences that some researchers have identified. Arabs are more likely to interact at closer distances, touch more, orient bodies more directly, and speak louder than Americans do.[46] Compared with Americans, the Japanese have stricter rules regarding the public display of certain negative emotions (such as anger and sadness) and, therefore, suppress or mask such emotions by maintaining neutral expressions or by resorting to smiling and laughter.[47] Although North Americans prefer to maintain direct eye contact, Asians (especially the Japanese) consider direct eye contact to be rude and intrusive.[48] Russians consider it impolite for one to sit on anything other than a chair.[49] Although punctuality for business appointments is the rule for North Americans and Europeans, Latin Americans and Asians often arrive late.[50] Differences within cultures, too, may exist. For instance, an individual from New York generally expects a shorter pause time than does a Californian.[51]

4. A cluster (or group) of nonverbal behaviors carries more meaning than a single nonverbal signal. The relationship between an individual nonverbal behavior and a cluster can be compared to the relationship between an individual word and a sentence; the full meaning of an individual unit is normally derived only after one has examined the overall context in which the unit appears. One example is a cluster of social behaviors that Mehrabian has labeled ingratiating behaviors: "frequent questioning, smiling and other pleasant vocal and facial expressions, frequent verbal agreement such [as] 'Uh-huh,' 'Yes,' or 'Same here,' and the complete exclusion of unpleasant remarks"—interpreted as being false/insincere as well as dependent/submissive.[52] Another cluster of behaviors includes leaning backward, casting one's eyes "toward the heavens" while heaving a great sigh, and closing one's eyes—interpreted as indicating negativity, annoyance, and closemindedness.[53]

5. Nonverbal behaviors should be kept in a contextual perspective. For example, if the last described cluster of nonverbal behaviors were exhibited by someone who opposed another's decision, the interpretation given would be more accurate than if the cues were exhibited by someone who had just completed a difficult long-term project; in this second context, the cues would likely mean relief and thankfulness. Knapp further exemplifies this principle: "While a given configuration of nonverbal cues seems to convey the feeling of interpersonal warmth, the same configuration may

take on a completely different meaning in a context in which the warmth behaviors are neutralized, added to, or canceled out by other factors."[54]

6. Males and females seem to be modality specialists. Males tend to be better than females at expressing and interpreting vocal cues, and females tend to better than males at expressing and interpreting facial and body cues.[55]

Uses of Nonverbal Communication

Not only should discriminative listeners understand some of the principles of nonverbal communication, but also they should know the five principal ways that senders use nonverbal messages. One way is to **complement** verbal messages. They shake their heads affirmatively, for example, to accompany a "yes" response. Or they firmly grasp others' hands as they say, "It's so good to see you." As listeners, we generally believe these senders, for "the people we trust are usually those people whose nonverbal behavior consistently confirms and reinforces the content of their verbal communication."[56]

Nonverbal messages also can **contradict** verbal messages. For instance, communicators respond with "Yes, I'm listening" while they continue to attend to a newspaper or a television program, or a father does not succeed at suppressing a smile while he is reprimanding his son. When these nonverbal messages do contradict the verbal messages, we tend to trust what we derive from the nonverbal messages. The old adage, "Actions speak louder than words," certainly holds true in our visual interpretations.

At other times, nonverbal messages can **replace** verbal messages. Americans who travel in foreign countries, for example, often must communicate by gestures and other nonverbal means when they do not know the native verbal code. Because each culture has its own nonverbal language, replacing the verbal language can be difficult. To illustrate, suppose you are an American in Greece, and you want the elevator operator to take you to the fifth floor. Making this request requires that you hold up your hand to show all five fingers while the palm of your hand is directed toward you. If you are unaware of the significance of the direction of your palm, you may turn your palm toward the elevator operator and find yourself the receiver of an unexpected insult. Why? In Greece, the palm turned toward the operator would be interpreted as an obscene gesture! Indeed, awareness of cultural differences can prevent misunderstandings between senders and receivers who do not share the same nonverbal language code.

While being held a prisoner of war by the North Vietnamese, Jeremiah Denton, Jr., realized the value of replacing a verbal code with a nonverbal code. When featured in a North Vietnamese propaganda film, Denton and other American POWs stated that they were being treated in compliance with the requirements of the Geneva Convention. An alert intelligence man who viewed the film, however, noted that Denton was blinking. The intelligence staff carefully scrutinized the film and discovered that Denton was blinking "torture" in Morse code. Denton's knowledge of the Morse code enabled him to communicate an important nonverbal message to America.

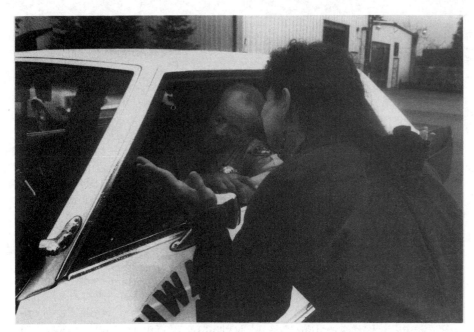

Our understanding of a sender's message often depends on our ability to "listen" with our eyes.

However, "his knowledge would have been in vain had there not been someone who was able to listen with his eyes."[57] Indeed, the listener who "listens" with visual discrimination can receive significant messages.

accent

Moreover, nonverbal messages can **accent** or stress parts of verbal messages. For instance, a teacher's glaring eyes may accent the word *dare* as he or she says to a student, "I dare you to say one more word." Or, to insist that an unresponsive child answer a question immediately, a parent may say "I want an answer now!" and accompany the word *now* with a squeeze of the child's leg just above the kneecap.

repeat

A final way that speakers use nonverbal messages is to **repeat** verbal messages. A hair stylist, for instance, might verbally recommend a particular hairstyle for a customer and then follow the recommendation with hand gestures describing the style. Or, a person may verbally describe the habitual walk of another individual and then bodily imitate the walk.

Forms of Nonverbal Communication

forms of nonverbal communication

In addition to using nonverbal messages in these five principal ways, speakers—as well as listeners—use nonverbal language in many forms, including kinesics, appearance, artifacts, proxemics, chronemics, touch, and environment.

kinesics

Kinesics. Perhaps the most revealing visual form is **kinesics**, or the language of the face and body. Through posture, bodily actions (movements of the feet, legs, trunk, shoulders, head, etc.), gestures (movements of the hands and arms), facial expressions, and eye behavior, communicators convey numerous messages ranging from "I have some exciting news to share with you" to "I don't have time to listen now." Though some scholars are attempting to equate body language to verbal language and develop nonlinguistic categories, Knapp maintains that kinesics probably does not have the same structure as spoken language. Rather, he notes, various bodily movements can communicate "liking or dislike for another, status, affective states or moods, intended and perceived persuasiveness, approval seeking, quasi-courtship behavior, need or desire for inclusion, leakage and deception clues, interpersonal warmth, and various interaction 'markers' to accompany certain spoken behaviors."[58] Polygraph expert William Majeski has found that his professional success depends heavily on his ability to "listen" to the silent messages of kinesics during pre-test interviews. He has discovered that "people almost always unconsciously reveal their guilt through the silent language [which he describes as natural and/or intentional movements, gestures, and nuances of reaction]—but this can only be seen by those who watch."[59]

Effective discriminative listeners watch the facial and bodily behavior of message senders, and they are also sensitive to the listener responses they send through kinesic cues. Knowledge of these behavioral cues assists listeners in assigning more accurate meanings to others' messages as well as in sending more accurate nonverbal messages of their own.

One way to begin learning about kinesic cues is by examining Ekman and Friesen's classification system of **nonverbal acts**. This system consists of five categories: emblems, illustrators, affect displays, adaptors, and regulators.[60]

categories of nonverbal acts

1. **Emblems** are nonverbal behaviors that have direct verbal translations well known to other interactants. They are performed with awareness and intent and are most frequently—but not exclusively—produced by the hands. For example, holding up the palm of the hand and wagging just the index finger or all the fingers is an emblem signaling "Come here." Placing the palm of one's hand on an empty area beside one and gently patting the area with four fingers is an emblem signaling "Sit down beside me."

   emblems

2. **Illustrators** are nonverbal behaviors directly tied to verbal content that serve to accentuate, punctuate, index, signal, specify, clarify, amplify, and underscore accompanying speech.[61] An individual might, for instance, direct a chin nod toward someone to indicate that that is the person about whom he or she is speaking, or one might shift one's posture to signal a change in point of view.

   illustrators

3. **Affect displays** are nonverbal behaviors that express emotions; they are most frequently—but not exclusively—produced by the face. To illustrate, fear can be conveyed by the raising of the eyebrows and the widening of the eyes, and boredom can be communicated by foot tapping, fidgeting, finger drumming, or shifting postures frequently.

   affect displays

4. **Adaptors**, which are seldom intentional, are nonverbal "behaviors which once served a useful purpose [such as satisfying physical and psychological needs, managing emotions, performing actions, etc.—all learned in one's early life], but which now are part of the individual's habit repertoire."[62] The two most common types of adaptors are self-adaptors (touching of self) and object-adaptors (touching of objects or artifacts). Indicators of the user's inner state, especially the inner state of anxiety and discomfort, self-adaptors may include rubbing the back of one's neck and tugging one's ears to signal tenseness. Object-adaptors may include tearing a paper napkin into pieces or wadding a tissue into a small, compact ball to signal nervousness.

5. **Regulators** are nonverbal behaviors that maintain and regulate communication interactions. For example, avoiding eye contact at pauses may signal that the speaker desires to continue talking, and putting on one's coat may signal a desire to end the communication interaction. (Regulators will be discussed in more depth in a later section of this chapter.)

A second way to learn about kinesic cues is by studying research findings relevant to each of the bodily and facial behavioral components included in the study of kinesics. A careful examination of each of these components should assist the student of visual discrimination in understanding the importance of each component as a message conveyor.

Bodily Actions and Postures.   This component consists of behaviors relating to the total body—such as bodily orientation, bodily positions, trunk leans, postural positions, gestures, and head movements. The following research findings are among those that are most pertinent to discriminative listeners.

1. **Bodily orientation** (the degree to which one interactant's shoulders and legs are turned toward, rather than away from, the other interactant):
   - In same-sex interactions, females have more direct body orientation than males do.
   - Individuals have more direct body orientation with interactants they like than they do with those they dislike.
   - Individuals with more direct bodily orientation are perceived to be more empathic.
   - Individuals interact with more direct bodily orientation with those of equal status.
   - Standing individuals interact with more direct orientation with those of higher status than with those of lower status.
   - Females interact with more direct body orientation than males do.
   - Males use a less direct body orientation with a liked partner.[63]

2. **Open and closed bodily positions**[64] (with open positions consisting of knees apart, legs stretched out, elbows away from body, hands not touching, legs uncrossed, etc., and closed positions consisting of legs crossed at either knees or ankles, hands folded on lap, arms crossed, etc.):

open and closed
bodily positions

   - Individuals are more open with interactants they like than they are with those they dislike.
   - Individuals with open body positions are perceived more positively than those with closed body positions.
   - Individuals with open body positions are more persuasive than those with closed body positions.
   - Males are more expansive than females.
   - Individuals in opposite-sex dyads engage in more full extensions of their arms and legs than do those in same-sex dyads.
   - Females' movements are less open than males are.[65]

3. **Trunk lean** (the direction in which one interactant positions his or her trunk, forward/toward or backward/away from, in relation to the other interactant):

trunk lean

   - Individuals engage in more forward trunk leans with interactants they like than they do with those they dislike.
   - Individuals who engage in forward trunk leans are perceived to possess more warmth.
   - Individuals who engage in forward trunk leans increase the verbal output of their interactional partner more than those who do not.
   - Sideways-leans, when interactants are seated at an angle to each other and when the lean is toward the interactional partner, may indicate liking.
   - Individuals who engage in forward leans are perceived to be more empathic.
   - Individuals in opposite-sex dyads engage in more forward leans than do those in same-sex dyads.
   - Males tend to be more relaxed than females during interactions and, thus, engage in more backward leans.
   - Individuals tend to engage in more sideways-leans when interacting with lower-status than with higher-status individuals.[66]

4. **Postural positions:**

postural positions

   - Individuals engage in more postural relaxation (such as reclining, feet on table, and sideways-leaning angles) with interactants they like than they do with those they dislike.
   - Males engage in more postural relaxation than females do.
   - Standing individuals engage in more leg and hand relaxation when interacting with those of lower status.

- Higher-status individuals engage in more postural relaxation when interacting with lower-status individuals.
- Same-sex, intimate interactants engage in postural relaxation when they are of equal status.
- Extreme postural tension and extreme postural relaxation during interactions are perceived more negatively by interacting partners than is a moderate level of postural relaxation.
- Men engage in more restless behaviors (such as lower body movements, fidgeting, manipulating objects, body shifts, leg shifts, etc.) than women do.
- The adoption (or imitation) of common bodily postures (identified as posture matching) by interactants in pairs or groups tends to enhance rapport between/among the interactants, because it signals that the interactants are open to and with one another. The adoption of noncongruent postures tends to indicate attitudinal and perceptual differences or relationship distance.[67]

5. **Gestures** (hand and arm movements):
   - Women are more likely to engage in self-conscious behaviors (which are primarily self-touching behaviors such as "manicuring" their nails, fidgeting with their clothes, touching hair, biting nails) than are men.
   - Individuals in opposite-sex dyads manipulate objects more than do those in same-sex dyads.
   - Individuals in opposite-sex dyads engage in more hand gesturing than do those in same-sex dyads.
   - In female-female interactions, a high level of gestural activity is characteristic of approval-seeking behavior.
   - Females tend to gesture more rapidly than males do.
   - Greater warmth is conveyed through the use of the index and middle fingers pointing together.
   - While speaking, males gesture as frequently as females do.
   - Elaborate gestures precede longer and less familiar words.
   - Speakers engage in more manipulative gestures (such as touching self or surroundings) when they are responding to intimate questions and when they are interacting at a close interpersonal distance.
   - Individuals whose hands are still are perceived to be warm, whereas individuals who drum their fingers are perceived to be cold.
   - Individuals' hand movements—especially vertical ones—can indicate a positive interpersonal relationship.

- Frequent hand gestures have been identified as affiliative behavior that shows liking, preference, or exchange of pleasant feelings.
- Greater liking is conveyed through the use of outreaching gestures during greetings.
- Gesturing increases as individuals age.
- Individuals increase their amount of self-touching as their levels of anxiety and discomfort increase (until they reach an anxiety level that is so high that they may "freeze" and engage in very little movement).[68]

6. **Head movements:**
    - In female-female interactions, frequent head nodding is characteristic of approval-seeking behavior.
    - Listeners who engage in head nodding increase the speech duration of speakers.
    - Listeners who engage in head nodding provide positive reinforcement for speakers.
    - Individuals who engage in affirmative head nodding convey liking of their interacting partners.
    - Individuals with increased frequency of head nods are perceived to have more empathic understanding, warmth, and open-mindedness.[69]

head movements

Facial Expressions.   This component—through rapid changes of the forehead, eyebrows, eyelids, eyes, nose, lips, mouth, tongue, cheeks, and chin—is the primary site for communicating feelings (affects) and attitudes. According to Ekman and his colleagues, six facially conveyed feelings (referred to as the primary affects)—happiness, sadness, anger, disgust, surprise, and fear—are universally expressed and recognized.[70] For example, disgust is shown by a wrinkled nose, raised cheeks, raised (or lowered and protruded) lower lip, raised upper lip, pushed-up lower eyelid, and lowered eyebrows.

facial expressions

In communication interactions, facial expressions convey not only emotions but also other dimensions of meanings:

1. The extent to which the interactants find the interaction pleasurable or unpleasurable
2. The level of interest of the interactants
3. The level of involvement of the interactants
4. The extent to which the interactants understand one another
5. The spontaneity (naturalness or control) of the interactants' responses to one another[71]

This last dimension calls attention to an aspect that makes interpreting facial expressions difficult: The face is the most controllable part of the body.[72]

As listeners, we often convey—through our facial expressions—our responses to the sender's message.

With practice and effort, individuals can voluntarily control their facial muscles in order to (1) de-intensify an affect (make a strong feeling appear milder), (2) overintensify an affect (make a mild feeling appear stronger), (3) neutralize an affect (inhibit or suppress an actual feeling), and (4) mask an affect (cover a true feeling with a false one or show an emotion when none is felt).[73] Such control is found especially in Western males who, through socialization, have been trained to be internalizers (low facial response/high physiological response); Western females, on the other hand, have been trained to be externalizers (high facial response/low physiological response).[74] Another major difficulty in interpreting facial expressions is that the face often shows multiple emotions known as "affect blends," such as the simultaneous showing of anger or fear in the eyebrows and happiness in a smile or a rapid sequence of two primary affects.

Although it is often difficult to interpret facial cues, the following research findings are among those that can help listeners understand interactants' facial expressions:

- Females have more expressive faces.
- Females engage in more facial behavior of all sorts (including the positive smile and the negative form, such as grimace, scowl, wary brow, etc.) than do males.
- Negative facial expressions such as frowns and sneers convey disliking.

- Liking is revealed through more positive facial expressions.
- Smiling may reflect (a) habit acquired by observation or reinforcement and thus no particular meaning, (b) warmth, friendliness, or pleasure, (c) appeasement (an attempt to placate someone, reduce threat, obtain approval, or signal submission), or (d) social unease or nervousness.
- The smile is the best indicator of interpersonal warmth.
- Those who smile are perceived to be warmer than those who do not smile.
- Females laugh and smile more than males do.
- Same-sex interactants tend to smile more than opposite-sex interactants.
- In same-sex interactions, females tend to smile more than males do.
- Females are smiled at more than males are.
- Within opposite-sex pairs, adult females smile more at adult males than vice versa.
- Females engage in more smiles while trying to seek approval of other females.[75]

Eye Behavior.   According to Knapp and Hall, individuals convey and receive many messages through eye behavior:

> Downward glances are associated with modesty; wide eyes . . . with frankness, wonder, naivete, or terror; raised upper eyelids . . . may mean displeasure; generally immobile facial muscles with a rather constant stare . . . with coldness; eyes rolled upward . . . with fatigue or a suggestion that another's behavior is a bit weird.[76]

In interpreting these and other messages of the eyes, discriminative listeners should consider the type of eye behavior used: **gaze** (one individual's looking behavior—at or not at another individual), **mutual gaze** (two individuals looking at each other—usually in the region of the face), and **eye contact** (two individuals looking directly in each other's eyes).[77] Additionally, they should consider the frequency of looks, instances of gaze aversion, and duration of gaze. And, they should consider factors that affect eye behavior. Among these factors are the emotions, attitudes, personalities, sex, status, and culture of the communication interactants; the distance between the interactants; the topic of discussion; and the communication function of each interactant.

The following research findings relevant to these factors are among those that may be most pertinent to discriminative listeners:

- Interacting partners who like each other engage in more mutual gaze than those who do not like each other.
- Individuals tend to gaze at interaction partners with whom they are interpersonally involved (whether the involvement is motivated by affection or hostility).

eye behavior

gaze

mutual gaze

eye contact

- Individuals who engage in more gazing behavior with interactional partners project more attentiveness and interest, warmth, empathy, intimacy, and positive attitudes than those who do not engage in gazing behaviors.
- Individuals who engage in low gazing behavior are perceived to be cold, pessimistic, cautious, defensive, immature, evasive, submissive, indifferent, and sensitive, while individuals who engage in high gazing behavior are perceived to be friendly, self-confident, natural, mature, and sincere.
- Speakers who engage in more gazing behavior are perceived to be more persuasive, truthful, sincere, and credible than those who engage in less gazing behavior.
- Individuals who are extroverts tend to gaze more at others than do those who are introverts.
- Individuals who are embarrassed, ashamed, sad, submissive, or trying to hide something (such as guilt or deception) tend to engage in less gazing behavior.
- Adult females are gazed at more than males are.
- Females tend to gaze at others—regardless of the sex of the others—more than males do.
- Individuals in opposite-sex dyads engage in less gazing behavior than do individuals in same-sex dyads.
- Individuals gaze more at same-sex interactional partners than they do at opposite-sex partners.
- Female-female interactional partners gaze more at each other than do male-male interactional partners.
- Females who have high affiliative or inclusion needs engage in more gazing behavior than do females who have low affiliative or inclusion needs.
- Females gaze more than males in terms of duration, while males gaze more than females in terms of frequency.
- Females tend to avert their eyes more than males do.
- Individuals who are more dominant or of higher ranking receive more gaze than do individuals who are less dominant or of lower ranking.
- Individuals who are more dominant or of higher ranking engage in more gazing while speaking and less while listening, whereas individuals who are less dominant or of lower ranking engage in less gazing while speaking and more gazing while listening.
- Individuals gaze less at lower-status interactional partners than they do at higher-status interactional partners.
- Natives of traditionally known "contact cultures" tend to engage in more gazing behavior during interactions than do those of "noncontact cultures."
- Communication interactants tend to increase gazing behavior as the distance between them increases.

- Individuals tend to engage in less gazing behavior when they are discussing intimate topics than they do when they are discussing impersonal topics.
- Individuals tend to engage in at least twice as much gazing behavior when listening than when speaking.
- When interacting with same-sex individuals, females engage in more overall gazing, more gazing while listening, more gazing while speaking, and more mutual gazing than males do.
- Females tend to engage in more gazing behavior while listening, and males tend to engage in more gazing behavior while speaking.
- Individuals who are dependent on their interactional partners and who have unresponsive partners tend to engage in more gazing behavior than do those who are not dependent on their interactional partners and those who have responsive partners.[78]

Due to the large number of components comprising kinesics, it is an extremely revealing visual form. From their heads to their toes, senders convey numerous messages, which are only received by knowledgeable, skilled, and observant discriminative listeners who also sensitively monitor their own kinesic behavior.

Appearance and Artifacts. Two other nonverbal visual forms are appearance and artifacts. **Appearance**—which includes aspects such as body shape, body or breath odor, height, weight, hair, and skin color or tone—tends to be most influential when we first meet others. During an initial communication transaction, a listener may stereotypically perceive his or her communication partner and respond accordingly; that is, the listener may associate a thin person with nervousness and stubbornness,[79] a tall person with power,[80] a long-haired male with undesirability,[81] or a tanned person with healthiness.[82] Effective listeners, then, must recognize the stereotypes they hold and strive to prevent these stereotypes from interfering with their listening efficiency. Discriminative listeners may, however, find it difficult to prevent their communication partners' odors from interfering with their listening efficiency. An individual's odor—which may communicate a general message of being aware or unaware of the importance of personal hygiene or a specific message of having engaged in an activity such as exercising, drinking, smoking, or eating—can either foster or inhibit communication interactions.[83]

Likewise, **artifacts** (such as clothing, makeup, jewelry, eyeglasses, insignia, plaques, art objects, vehicles, equipment, furniture, offices, and homes) can influence listeners' perceptions of their communication partners. From other people's use of artifacts, observant listeners can detect messages of status, style, and self-esteem. For example, one's clothing can indicate such aspects as one's knowledge of appropriate attire, occupation, sexual availability, group affiliation, or organizational culture (such as IBM's

appearance

artifacts

white shirt and tie culture or Apple Computer's blue jeans, sweatshirt, and tennis shoes culture). Moreover, one's makeup can reveal, or conceal, such features as one's innocence or worldliness or one's youthfulness or maturity. The importance of some of these artifacts (especially clothing, makeup, and jewelry) as message-senders is attested by the growing enterprise of "wardrobe engineering," in which consultants assist individuals (usually those who desire to advance socially, economically, and/or professionally) in selecting the proper colors and styles to communicate the desired image. For example, CNN News reported on 28 September 1994, that during the first day of the jury selection for the O.J. Simpson trial, Simpson wore a white sweater—rather than a dark suit—so he would appear to be a warmer, more approachable person. John Molloy initiated much of this image interest in his popular book, *Dress for Success*,[84] and now wardrobe engineering has become so specialized that color consultants are available to determine the proper shades of colors for individual skin tones, eyes, and hair.

While discriminative listeners should be observant of messages sent by speakers' appearance and artifacts, they should guard against responding to stereotypes, being distracted by a woman's jangling bracelets or a man's earring, or becoming preoccupied with their own perceptions of attractiveness such as a woman's wispy hair and full lips or a man's large eyes and strong jaw. Rather, they should determine whether the speakers' verbal messages complement or contradict the observed nonverbal messages.

proxemics

Proxemics. Furthermore, listeners can use the visual channel to interpret messages conveyed through the nonverbal form of **proxemics**, or the language of space and distance. The spatial distance that communicators keep between themselves is significant, especially in North America where individuals tend to keep a considerable amount of space between themselves and those who, they feel, are invading their personal space. Indeed, one of the first observations visitors to the United States make is this distance. In contrast, Latin Americans, for example, communicate at a much closer distance. Anthropologist Edward Hall describes how this cultural difference can create misunderstandings: "When they [Latin Americans] move close, we [North Americans] withdraw and back away. As a consequence, they think we are distant or cold, withdrawn and unfriendly. We, on the other hand, are constantly accusing them of breathing down our necks, crowding us, and spraying our faces."[85] To avoid such misinterpretations, discriminative listeners of proxemics should learn about social norms and factors of interpersonal distance and personal space as well as become sensitive to their own and others' use of space and distance and reactions to spatial violations.

Hall has identified four main distances in which most middle-class North Americans interact with one another:

intimate distance

1. The **intimate distance**, ranging from actual physical contact to eighteen inches, is reserved for private exchanges such as sharing intimate thoughts and feelings. To prevent intruders from entering

this intimate zone, Americans typically carry with them an invisible, two-foot (arm's length) "bubble of personal space," which may expand or contract, depending on the given situation. Each communicator's two-foot bubble (which is not necessarily spherical) allows interactional partners to maintain the second distance within which individuals usually feel most comfortable.

2. The **personal distance**, ranging from eighteen inches to four feet, is used for less intense exchanges such as family members or friends conversing.

3. The **social distance**, ranging from four to twelve feet, is used for more formal exchanges such as impersonal business transactions.

4. The **public distance**, covering from twelve feet to the limits of visibility or hearing, is used for casual exchanges such as calling to a friend across a street or formal exchanges between a speaker and an audience.[86]

personal distance

social distance

public distance

When distance expectations are violated (i.e., when one interactant perceives that another interactant has approached too closely and has, thus, invaded his or her personal space), defensive reactions will likely result.[87] Argyle and Dean's **affiliative conflict theory of intimacy** posits that any change in one of the intimacy indicators (which include physical proximity as well as eye contact, touch, bodily orientation, intimacy of topic, amount of smiling, etc.) on the part of one individual will result in compensatory change in one or more of the intimacy cues exhibited by the other individual. For example, if one person moves too close to the other, anxiety will be created in the other person. The anxious one will attempt to restore the appropriate distance by backing away, angling the body less directly, reducing eye contact, changing the topic to a more impersonal one, smiling less, placing a barrier such as a chair between them, and so on—all of which are behaviors that lower involvement.[88] On the other hand, when communication interactants perceive that they are too far from one another (for instance, seated far apart at a long, rectangular table in a restaurant), they will attempt to compensate for the lack of physical proximity by leaning toward each other, angling bodies more directly, increasing eye contact, and/or engaging in some other nonverbal behavior indicating involvement. The observant listener should also note abrupt or uncharacteristic changes in interactional distances and attempt to detect their meaning; whereas nonverbal changes such as a warm smile or a gentle touch indicate more desired involvement, turning away or adopting an angry expression indicates less desired involvement. Additionally, the discriminating listener should recognize and assign meaning to intentional violations of personal space or territory; an individual may, for example, stand too close to another with the intent of intimidating the other or sit on or at another's desk to challenge territorial control.

affiliative conflict theory of intimacy

There are many factors that modify the distances that interactants choose. Among these factors are the gender, age, culture, physical characteristics, status, and personality traits of the interactants, the nature of the relationship of the interactants, and the setting for the interaction. The following research findings relevant to these factors are among the most pertinent to discriminative listeners:

Gender

- Males and females alike tend to approach females more closely than they approach males.
- Females tend to approach others more closely than males do.
- Adult opposite-sex pairs tend to interact at closer distances than same-sex pairs.
- Female-female pairs tend to interact at closer distances than do male-male pairs.
- Males tend to establish farther interactional distances than females do—in all cultures studied.
- Males tend to engage in more intimate self-disclosure as interactional distance increases whereas females tend to engage in more intimate self-disclosure as distance decreases.[89]

Age

- The personal space of individuals tends to increase as individuals become older.[90]

Culture

- Natives of traditionally known "contact cultures" (such as Latin Americans, Italians, Spaniards, Israelis, Middle Easterners, French, and Russians) tend to interact at closer distances than do those of "noncontact cultures" (such as Germans, English, North Americans, Scandinavians, and Chinese).[91]

Physical Characteristics

- Smaller same-sex individuals tend to interact at closer distances than do larger same-sex individuals.[92]

Status

- Individuals tend to approach equals more closely than they approach people of either higher or lower status.
- North Americans of higher status are generally allotted more space.[93]

Personality Traits

- Introverted and socially uncomfortable individuals tend to prefer greater interactional distances whereas extroverted and socially comfortable individuals tend to prefer closer interactional distances.
- Individuals who interact at closer distances are often perceived as being warmer, friendlier, and more empathic and understanding as well as liking one another more.

- Individuals experiencing negative emotional states, such as depression or fatigue, tend to prefer increased interactional distances whereas individuals experiencing positive emotional states, such as extreme joy or excitement, tend to prefer decreased interactional distances.[94]

Nature of the Relationship

- Individuals who perceive that they share similar attitudes try to reduce the distance between them.
- Individuals tend to develop positive attitudes with those who are in close proximity to them.
- Individuals interact at significantly closer distances with friends than with acquaintances and least closely with strangers.
- Individuals interact at closer distances with persons they like than with persons they dislike.
- Married couples who are happy and low in conflict tend to interact at closer distances than do those who are unhappy and high in unresolved conflicts.[95]

Environment

- Lighting, temperature, noise, available space, furniture arrangement, and seating arrangement are among the environmental aspects that affect interactional distance.[96]

In sum, the language of space and distance—when sensitively discerned by discriminative listeners—can strongly impact the meanings they assign to others' messages. Knowledge of spatial norms and expectations along with spatial tendencies should better prepare students of listening to apply these understandings to their daily communication interactions.

Chronemics.   The visual channel also assists listeners in discriminating **chronemics**, or the language of time. Discriminative listeners observe how their communication partners perceive, structure, and use time, and the listeners act according to the meanings they assign to their observations. For instance, discriminative listeners recognize their communication partners' nonverbal cues that convey such messages as the following:

chronemics

- Their perception of the importance of or respect for the event (and other communication interactants) as well as their sense of responsibility to be punctual (in most Western societies)[97]
- Their cultural orientation to time
- Their psychological orientation to the past, present, and future
- Their expectations of the proper and improper length of events
- The regularity/irregularity comprising their behavior and routines[98]
- The desire to avoid confrontation
- The lack of time to interact at the moment
- The urgency of the need to communicate (such as at 4:30 in the morning)

- The need to reflect before reacting to an order or request
- The desire to conclude an interaction

Additionally, discriminative listeners are sensitively aware of how their own use of and perception of time affects their listening behavior. For example, they know at what times of the day (or night) they listen most effectively. They also know how they must control their emotions when they have had to wait for what they perceive to be "too long" for their communication partners to arrive or when their communication partners do not allow adequate time for understanding their concerns. Moreover, discriminating listeners know that much time is needed to develop coded silent messages between close dialogue partners; such silent messages range from "They're interested" to "I think you've said enough" to "It's time to leave."

touch

Touch. **Touch**, too, is a powerful conveyor of messages that listeners both receive and send. Acquiring discriminative proficiency in nonverbal behaviors of touch requires listeners to develop the abilities to do the following: (1) detect meanings of touches they observe or receive; (2) discern meaning assignment as well as appropriateness of touches they send as feedback; and (3) become sensitive to others' responses to their feedback touches.

Developing these discriminative abilities necessitates that listeners understand various considerations relevant to whether one should or should not engage in touching behavior. Among considerations regarding the touch itself are the type of touch, the part of the body touched, the duration of the touch, the intensity of the touch, the nature of the touch, and the frequency of the touch. Four of these considerations are self-explanatory, but two—type of touch and nature of touch—may not be. Heslin has classified **touch types** based on the nature of the interactants' roles and relationships:

types of touch

- Functional/professional—such as a hairstylist holding a customer's head
- Social/polite—such as acquaintances shaking hands
- Friendship/warmth—such as a ball player patting a teammate's back or buttocks
- Love/intimacy—such as a child embracing a parent's neck
- Sexual arousal—such as a person stroking his or her mate[99]

While these types of touch appear to be easily understood, Heslin cautions that the interpretation of the meanings of the various touches can lead to feelings of confusion and threat. Although, as he suggests, "the most appreciation of the other as an individual occurs in the Friendship/Warmth relationship,"[100] this type of touching behavior is often the most difficult for persons to interpret because it might be misinterpreted as love or sexual attraction. It is especially threatening when it occurs between same-sex pairs in privacy; thus, when two friends are alone, friendship/warmth touching will generally decrease as a result of privacy being associated with love and sex.

touching behaviors

Perhaps the best-known research on the nature of touch is Argyle's. He has identified the following **touching behaviors** as being the most

Developing Purposeful Listening Skills

common in Western culture: patting, slapping, punching, pinching, stroking, shaking, kissing, licking, holding, guiding, embracing, linking, laying-on, kicking, grooming, and tickling.[101] While interpreting the meanings of the nature of touches can be difficult for discriminative listeners, Nguyen and others have found some agreement between males and females regarding the pat and the stroke: Both sexes perceived the pat as being the most friendly and playful and the stroke as being the most loving, sexual, and pleasant.[102]

In addition to considering aspects of the touch itself, the discriminative listener should consider other factors such as the gender, status, culture, and personality traits of communication partners as well as the interpersonal relationship of the interactants, the environment, and the communication purpose of the interactants. Among the many reported research findings relevant to these factors, the following are some that may be most pertinent to students of visual discrimination:

Gender

- Females respond more favorably to touch than do males.
- Opposite-sex touch is more frequent than same-sex touch.
- Males touch females more than vice versa.[103]

Status

- Higher-status individuals initiate touches more frequently than do lower-status individuals.[104]

Culture

- Natives of traditionally known "contact cultures" tend to engage in more touching than do those of "noncontact cultures" (as specified in the previous discussion of proxemics).

Personality Traits

- Individuals who are less fearful and suspicious of others' motives and intentions, have less daily anxiety and tension, and are more pleased with their bodies and physical appearance are more comfortable with touch than those who are apprehensive about communicating, have lower self-esteem, and are more authoritarian and rigid.[105]

Nature of the Relationship

- Touched strangers have more positive feelings toward the senders of the touches than do untouched strangers.
- Pats, holds, teasing touches, embraces, and kisses are indicative of closeness between family members and friends.[106]

Environment

- Individuals are more likely to touch at a party than at work.

- Individuals are more likely to touch during "deep rather than casual" conversation.[107]

Communication Purpose

- Individuals are more likely to touch when they are trying to persuade others and are giving information, advice, or an order than when they are being persuaded, asking for information or advice, or responding to an order.[108]

A better understanding of touching behavior should assist the listener in being a more discriminating observer, receiver, and sender of touches in beginning, managing or developing, and ending communication interactions. The listener is often the sender and receiver of **touch when greeting** another at the opening of an interaction. Whereas men in Latin America and Italy may greet each other with an embrace and men in India with a palm-to-palm touch, the initial greeting of men and women in North America is customarily the handshake (verbally translated as "Good to meet you," "Hello," etc.). The way in which one shakes another's hand communicates feelings and attitudes. Mehrabian has identified three styles of handshakes and how they tend to be interpreted: firm handshake—greater liking and warmth; loose handshake—aloofness and unwillingness to become involved; and limp handshake—lack of affection and friendliness.[109] Other common greetings of touch in North America are the pat, hug, kiss, and spot touch (which involves contact with hand movement or holding).[110] During the interaction, touches—performed by either the sender or the receiver (as sender of feedback)—may be used to indicate such functions as the following:

- Support for one experiencing distress (e.g., by the receiver "reaching out" his or her hand to the body of the sender as if to say, "I'm here")[111]
- Appreciation (by one interactant touching the arm or shoulder of the other as if to say, "I'm thankful for your support")[112]
- Direction of behavior without interrupting (such as a receiver spot touching, holding, or patting a sender to say, "Move over")[113]
- Attention (such as a sender spot touching a receiver by tapping his or her hand, arm, or shoulder to indicate, "I want you to listen to me")[114]
- Emphasis (such as a sender tapping the receiver's arm to say, "I'm very serious about this")
- Reinforcement (such as a sender patting or softly punching the shoulder of the receiver to strengthen the accompanying verbal message)
- Strong affect (such as the sender engaging in extended touches, which may be caresses or holds, or spot touches to emphasize a feeling state translated as "I'm so excited," "I'm shocked," etc.)[115]

Henley's research findings suggest two additional functions of touch during communication interactions: Interactants are more likely to touch when asking a favor (sender) rather than agreeing to do one (receiver) and

greeting touches

functions of touch during communication interactions

when expressing excitement (sender) rather than receiving it from another (receiver).[116] At the interaction's termination, the listener is often the sender and receiver of touch. While many parting touches are similar to greeting touches (the handshake, pat, hug, kiss, and spot touch), **parting touches** tend to be more intimate and affectionate with caresses, holds, and squeezes (verbally translated as "I love you," "I'll miss you," etc.) also being common.[117]

parting touches

Throughout the communication interaction, the discriminative listener should also observe the sender's—as well as his or her own—self-adaptors. Self-adaptors involve **self-touch** and may emerge unconsciously as an indication of the user's inner state (especially the inner state of anxiety). For example, covering one's eyes or placing one's fingers at one's lips may indicate shame;[118] and grooming one's self may show concern for one's self-preservation.[119] The observant listener can learn much about the feeling state of the sender (as well as him- or herself) from noting acts of self-touching.

self-touch

Additionally, from the beginning to the ending of a communication interaction, the listener should be sensitive to **responses to his or her touching behavior**. According to Jones and Yarbrough, "a touch virtually demands a response, and even a seeming lack of any reaction may carry the implications of rejection."[120] Among the nonverbal rejecting responses these researchers have identified are moving away, grimacing, tensing the body, and remaining immobile.[121] Berko and others stress the importance of the need to recognize responses to touch:

responses to touch

> Many people don't like to be touched but don't really know why. This dislike may well stem not from something unique to themselves but from their cultural training. When someone who does not like to be fondled is confronted by a "toucher," the situation can be quite uncomfortable. If the toucher places a hand on the arm of the nontoucher and the second person jerks away, the first person may well get the idea that a rejection has taken place when in fact it is the touch, not the person, that has been scorned.[122]

To complement the nonverbal message of jerking away, the nontoucher might verbally express his or her discomfort by saying, "I would prefer that you not put your hand on my arm; I'm not comfortable with touching."

Indeed, touch, which has been referred to as "the most powerful of all the communication channels,"[123] can send numerous messages to listeners if they are sensitive to the touches—or lack of touches—that occur in communication interactions. As discriminating receivers of touch, they can derive meanings ranging from attention to dominance; as discriminating observers of touch, they can derive meanings ranging from tension to shame; and as discriminating feedback senders of touch, they can derive meanings ranging from thankfulness to rejection.

Environment. The last form of nonverbal communication is **environment**, consisting of such factors as sound, lighting, temperature, furniture, size, and colors. Communicators' perceptions of factors such as these can influence communicative interactions. Knapp and Hall believe, for example, that the "types of **sounds** and their intensity . . . seem to affect interpersonal behavior."[124] Sharing Knapp and Hall's view, Newman acted to prevent

environment

sounds

clients from hearing the sounds of her children, the television, and other items in her home from where she operated her business; to project a more professional image, she created a tape of office sounds to play in the background as she engaged in telephone conversations with clients.[125] Although the image that sounds project should be of some concern to interactants, of more concern should be the minimizing of distracting and unpleasant sounds.

lighting and temperature

Lighting and temperature, too, should be of concern, for they stimulate or deter communication. For instance, a dimly lit room provides a feeling of warmth and tends to be more conducive to intimate conversations,[126] but rooms that are not well lit also tend to make interactants drowsy.[127] Regarding the effects of temperature, Griffitt and Veitch have found that room temperature affects one's psychological disposition as well as one's social behavior with others. High room temperatures produce more negative feelings than do lower, more moderate and comfortable room temperatures.[128] Brownell adds that high room temperatures also tend to produce drowsy interactants.[129]

furnishings and room size

Additionally, the **furnishings and the size of the room** in which interactions occur may have an influence on the interaction. According to Mehrabian, "the ideal environment would be one that provides opportunities for immediacy as well as privacy, so that immediate contacts are a matter of choice and are readily available."[130] Communication interactions are facilitated when comfortable chairs and/or sofas are placed about four feet apart and are oriented from a face-to-face position to a ninety-degree angle[131] and when barriers such as desks do not separate the interactants.[132]

color

Finally, **color** can affect communication behavior. Wexner has found that various colors are often associated with various moods: blue—security, comfort, tenderness, and calm; red—excitement, stimulation, defiance, hostility, and protection; yellow—cheerfulness, joviality, and joyfulness; black—power and strength; black and brown—despondency, dejection, unhappiness, and melancholy; orange—distress; and purple—dignity.[133] Communicators react emotionally to these as well as other environmental factors and, thus, perceive the interaction environment in such terms as being warm or cold, private or public, free or constrained, close or distant, relaxed or tense, alert or sluggish, and important or insignificant.

Auditory and Visual Discrimination

Having separately examined each visual form of nonverbal behavior and the auditory form of voice, discriminative listeners should be better prepared to detect, interpret, and/or engage in clusters (or groups) of nonverbal behaviors. Two relevant clusters are deception cues and regulatory cues.

Detecting Deception Cues

detecting deception cues

In a well-known study on deception, Ekman and Friesen found that the best sources of **deception cues** (which reveal that a deception is occurring but

Developing Purposeful Listening Skills

provide no specific information) and **nonverbal leakage cues** (which reveal specific hidden information) are (1) legs/feet, (2) hands, and (3) face, with the legs/feet being the most revealing and the face least revealing. Although, as the researchers suggest, the face is the best nonverbal sender of feeling messages (followed by the hands and legs/feet), the face is also the part of the human anatomy over which a person can exercise the most control (followed again by the hands and legs/feet). Thus, the face is the best "liar" while the hands and legs/feet are better at "telling the truth." Being over-attentive to the face, as many people are when they are attempting to detect deception, can hinder individuals from detecting the cues of the more revealing sources—the legs/feet and hands. Unfortunately, one's hands, legs, and feet are often obscured from view, and the listener cannot observe them.[134]

best sources of deception cues and nonverbal leakage cues

Studies indicate that the **nonverbal leakage cues** signaling deception are complex. Cues of the legs and feet include tense (unnaturally still) leg positions, less body orientation toward the listener(s), frequent postural shifts, abortive flight movements, aggressive footkicks, and restless and repetitive foot and leg activity. Among deception signals of the hands are suppressed hand movements (achieved by sitting on hands, putting them in pockets, clasping one hand with the other in order to allow them to hold each other down, holding knees with hands, etc.) normally used as illustrators, frequent hand-to-hand actions (such as the chin stroke, lip press, cheek rub or dig, eyebrow scratch, ear-lobe pull, fingernail tear, hair groom, and—especially—the mouth cover and nose rub), the one-shoulder shrug, and frequent use of the hand shrug. Nonverbal cues of the face consist of increased smiling (with less activity of the outer muscle that circles the eye), unnatural simulations (such as a smile that is drawn out too long or a frown that is too severe), crooked or asymmetrical facial expressions, decreased nodding, and tiny, fleeting, and truth-leaking facial expressions that most people never perceive.[135] One additional speculation regarding hand movement is that left-handed gestures may be more truthful in revealing feelings, since the right hemisphere is believed to house emotions.[136] Although these cues have been found to be signals of deception, it should also be noted that many of these same cues appear when one is experiencing an inner/outer conflict (such as when one has been asked a complicated question).

nonverbal leakage cues

Vocal cues, too, may serve as deception cues. For example, a person trying to deceive someone tends to use a higher pitch, make more speech errors (which may be in the form of a grammar error such as "He don't. . . ." or a false start such as "When I . . . after we. . . ."), use more meaningless expressions (such as "you know," "stuff like that," etc.), and have more silent or vocalized (filled with *ah, er, um,* etc.) pauses—especially after questions.[137]

vocal deception cues

Detecting Regulatory Cues

A second cluster of nonverbal behaviors are **regulatory cues**, which are non-verbal acts that control and direct (or serve as traffic signals for) the back

detecting regulatory cues

and forth flow of speaking and listening between/among communication interactants. From the initiation to the termination of face-to-face conversations, the interactants' hands, bodies, voices, and—primarily—eyes[138] all serve as regulators to open communication channels, to exchange speaking and listening turns, and to close communication channels.

Individuals begin an interaction with the establishment of mutual eye contact, which is a regulating cue that signals that communication channels are open and that there is an obligation to communicate. This cue may occur when two people simultaneously look at each other or after one individual has made a prompting remark such as "Pardon me." Other behaviors accompanying mutual gaze may be a vertical sideways motion of the head, a brief raising of the eyebrows, a smile, an oval shape of the mouth (suggesting a readiness to begin speaking), and hand movements such as those used in saluting, handshaking, handslapping, embracing, hitting another on the arm, forming emblematic gestures (thumbs up, raised fist, etc.), and grooming.[139]

Both visual and vocal regulatory cues are prominently found in turn-taking signals—signals by which interactants manage the smooth exchange of speaking and listening turns in conversations. Noting the importance of developing effective turn-taking skills, Knapp and Hall state the following:

> We seem to base important judgments about others on how the turns are allocated and how smoothly exchanges are accomplished. Effective turn-taking may elicit the perception that you and your partner "really hit it off well" or that your partner is a very competent communicator; ineffective turn-taking may prompt evaluations of "rude" (too many interruptions) or "dominating" (not enough turn-yielding) or "frustrating" (unable to make an important point).[140]

There are four turn-taking behaviors: Speakers engage in turn-yielding and turn-maintaining, and listeners engage in turn-requesting and turn-denying. Each of these behaviors will be discussed separately.

Turn-Yielding

turn-yielding behaviors

A speaker engages in **turn-yielding behaviors** to signal that he or she is giving up his or her speaking turn and is expecting his or her interactional partner to begin speaking. A speaker who does not know turn-yielding regulators (and, thus, does not use them or signals them when he or she does not desire to give up a speaking turn) is likely to create more awkward interactions and be interrupted more frequently. On the other hand, the speaker who does know turn-yielding regulators and uses them effectively is apt to create smoother interactions and increase the turn-taking behavior of the listener.

Among the numerous turn-yielding regulators are the following: The speaker terminates hand gestures accompanying speech; the speaker relaxes hand or body tenseness; the speaker ends on a prolonged rising (for asking a question) or falling (for completing a statement) pitch; the speaker ends by trailing off in volume or by adding a "trailer" such as "you know," "or something like that," and so on; the speaker places a drawl on the final stressed syllable; the speaker pauses silently; and the speaker returns his or her gaze to the listener(s) and gives the listener(s) a prolonged look at the end of his or her utterance. When the listener fails to perceive these cues as turn-yielding signals and gives no turn-denying signals, the speaker may touch the listener, raise the eyebrows, or make a remark such as "So?"[141]

Turn-Maintaining

A speaker engages in **turn-maintaining behaviors** to signal that he or she intends to continue speaking (even though turn-yielding and/or turn-requesting signals may be being displayed simultaneously). Turn-maintaining signals, when detected, decrease the turn-taking of listeners, who almost always respond to them by remaining silent. Among the numerous turn-maintaining regulators are the following: The speaker raises his or her volume when another interrupts and speaks louder than the other if the other continues to speak; the speaker speaks faster; the speaker keeps a hand or hands in mid-gesture at the ends of utterances; the speaker combines a change in inflection with a pause but also includes upward eye movement to decrease eye contact; the speaker slightly raises a hand or finger as if to say "Wait a minute"; the speaker reduces the number of silent pauses; and the speaker avoids eye contact at pauses (often filled with segregates—*uh, um, ah*, etc.) when he or she is reflecting, processing feedback, collecting thoughts, concentrating, selecting words, preparing for another utterance (and when he or she is avoiding the display of turn-requesting signals). If a listener ignores these turn-maintaining signals and attempts to gain a speaking turn, the speaker may extend his or her hand out with palm toward the listener or lightly pat the listener as if to say "I still have more to say; just be patient for a few more seconds and then you can speak."[142]

turn-maintaining behaviors

Turn-Requesting

A listener engages in **turn-requesting behaviors** to signal that he or she wants a speaking turn. Among the turn-requesting regulators that a listener may exhibit are the following: The listener raises an index finger; the listener audibly inhales; the listener moves from a slumped-shoulder posture to an upright, straight-back position or from a straight-back position to a leaning forward position; the listener initiates gestures; the listener engages in rapid head nods often accompanied by repeated verbalizations such as *yes, yes, yes* and *uh-huh, uh-huh, uh-huh* or single words such as *but, well,* and so on (to hurry the speaker); the listener engages in stutter starts (such as "She . . . She . . . She nev . . . "); the listener shifts his or her head direction away from direct orientation toward the speaker; the listener speaks simultaneously with and louder than the speaker and looks away as if he or she now has the speaking turn; and the listener holds his or her mouth open.[143]

turn-requesting behaviors

Some speakers refuse to yield the floor despite the turn-requesting signals being sent by a listener. Marsh suggests that if you are a listener interacting with a speaker who continues on and on and avoids looking at you when you want to request a speaking turn, you should "switch off some of the support that you give by looking directly at the speaker. Look to one side, but in such a way that you can tell when you are looked at. Receiving less feedback, the speaker will eventually be drawn to look at you. . . . At this point, meet the speaker's gaze and initiate your turn."[144]

Turn-Denying

**turn-denying
behaviors**

A listener engages in **turn-denying behaviors** to signal that he or she does not desire to speak after a speaker has given turn-yielding signals. With the addition of silence, turn-denying regulators are the same (though displayed more slowly) as the positive back-channel behaviors that a listener displays; that is, they consist of the back-channel behaviors that show the listener's continuing involvement in the speaker's message.

**back-channel
behaviors**

In addition to engaging in turn-taking signals during communication interactions, each interactant—while serving as listener—engages in **back-channel behaviors**. Back-channel behaviors are listener responses (or feedback), either positive or negative, that acknowledge or accompany a speaker's utterances. They are not turn-requesting signals nor are they interrupting behaviors; rather, they provide the listener with a way in which to participate, actively and overtly, in the communication interaction by acknowledging "the receipt and understanding—or lack thereof—of the speaker's message."[145] Additionally, they are used to encourage—or discourage—speaker continuation, to show attention or lack of attention to the speaker and his or her message, and to convey positive and negative reaction(s) to the speaker's message. Positive back-channel behaviors can also be used to deny a speaking turn when the speaker has given one or more turn-yielding signals. Among the back-channel behaviors that a listener may display are the following: slow, deliberate, and thoughtful head-nodding (continued even after the speaker has given a turn-yielding signal); head nodding in rapid succession (as if to say, "Hurry up and finish speaking"); facial expressions (such as smiles of warmth, frowns of puzzlement, or wide eyes and raised brows of surprise); attentive eye contact; gaze aversion (to indicate, e.g., boredom or disinterest); brief verbalizations (such as "Yes," "No," "Uh-huh," "That's true," etc.); yawning (with the intent to persuade the speaker to stop talking); brief requests for clarification of the speaker's remarks; and brief restatement of the speaker's preceding statement. These behaviors are distributed evenly throughout the speaker's utterances, and they serve as valuable indicators for the speaker who monitors them and then makes the adjustments necessary for a successful communication interaction.[146] Unfortunately, 901 teachers in one study perceive that only about 50 percent of their students from kindergarten through grade twelve provide speakers with these essential back-channel behaviors.[147]

Leave-Taking

Finally, individuals engage in regulating cues to signal the closing of communication channels—the ending of an interaction. These cues, known as

leave-taking signals, become more frequent during the last minute of an interaction and become most prevalent during the last fifteen seconds prior to the standing of the interactants.[148] Seated interactants engage in leave-taking signals such as breaking eye contact more frequently and for longer periods of time, nodding the head rapidly, looking at one's watch, organizing items on one's desk, leaning forward or moving forward to a more upright and less relaxed position, turning out from each other, edging forward in chair, pushing chair back, stretching legs, placing hands on thighs (to gain leverage in standing), rising, making nonlinguistic sounds (such as slapping thighs as one rises, tapping a desk or wall with knuckles or palms, etc.), stepping back, positioning one's body toward the nearest exit, placing hand on doorknob, opening door or ushering one through door, and engaging in a final terminating behavior (such as shaking hands, embracing, smiling, etc.).[149] In addition to engaging in many of the same acts as a seated interactant does, a standing interactant may turn away and make small circles away from and back to the other person and look away from that person.[150] Knapp and Hall humorously note that partings are not "fail-safe" and can cause much frustration "when our partner calls us back with 'Oh, just one more thing. . . .' It means we have to go through the entire process of leave-taking again!"[151]

This chapter reveals that there are many nonverbal messages being sent to the discriminatory listener who listens with more than his or her ears. Indeed, the effective listener, as Gerald Egan notes, must "listen" to all of the perceivable cues that the sender emits:

> One does not listen with just his ears; he listens with his eyes and with his sense of touch . . . he listens with his mind, his heart, and his imagination. He listens to the words of others, but he also listens to the messages that are buried in the words or encoded in the cues that surround the words. . . . He listens to the voice, the demeanor, . . . and the bodily movements of the other. He listens to the sounds and to the silences. He listens not only to the message itself but also to the context, or in Gestalt terms, he listens to both the figure and the ground and to the way these two interact.[152]

Effective discriminatory listening, then, requires careful concentration, keen observation, and conscious recognition of the auditory and/or visual stimuli. Visual and auditory acuity—developed through an understanding of the dimensions involved, motivation, sensory awareness, receptiveness to others' feedback regarding the accuracy of our interpretations of their nonverbal behaviors, concentration, experiential learning, practice, and care of the hearing and seeing mechanisms—can help us to listen with discrimination. There is so much in the world around us that we may be missing because we only see and hear it; we are not listening to it with any level of discrimination.

Summary

In this chapter, we have discussed discriminative listening—listening to distinguish the aural stimuli. First, we have noted the role that auditory discrimination plays in our listening effectiveness, language acquisition, and reading development. Also, we have presented a hierarchy of auditory discrimination skills that are developed during a child's early years, from infancy through grade six, and are strengthened throughout a person's life. Knowing this developmental sequence of discrimination skills and becoming adept in these skills can provide the adult with the tools necessary to assist a child in developing proficient auditory discrimination skills. Too, we have discussed additional discriminative skills that adults·should possess. Among these are recognizing the sound structure of our language, detecting and isolating vocal cues, becoming more sensitive to and understanding dialectal and accentual differences, and being more sensitive to environmental sounds. Finally, we have stressed the importance of applying visual discrimination in communication settings where an awareness and understanding of nonverbal communication can enhance the listener's understanding of the message conveyed by a sender whom the listener has the opportunity to observe. By developing and strengthening our discriminative listening skills, we can broaden our world of sound and sight as well as improve our understanding of the messages of others.

Suggested Activities

1. Prepare a list of twenty words; each list will consist of some words that are similar in sounds (such as yes, yet, gold, cold, low, blow, jaw, flaw, etc.). Participants will be paired and will sit back to back. One participant (the sender), stating each word only once, will clearly read his or her list while the partner (the listener) writes down what he or she hears. Then, the participants will exchange roles. There will be no feedback between partners. Participants may change partners as often as time permits. Before changing partners, each participant should score him- or herself by checking the sender's list. This practice helps listeners discriminate sounds and words.

2. In current communication texts, study the differences among the three major regional dialects (Eastern, Southern, and General American). Then, attempt to pronounce the following words as a native from Boston, Georgia, and Cleveland would pronounce them: there, laugh, court, car, better, board, Alaska, after, years, past, ask, path, answer, hot, four, house, high, class, and Florida. This practice helps you become more aware of and more sensitive to differing dialectal characteristics.

3. Participants will sit in a circle and close their eyes. Each individual will vocalize "oh" in such a way as to express a different emotion. Participants will interpret the meaning of each "oh." This practice helps listeners become more sensitive to emotions expressed in vocal cues.

4. Each student is to bring to class five sound-producing objects (such as a whistle or a pair of dice that can be rolled or shaken). Students are to conceal their items until the exercise has been completed. One at a

time, each student—while being out of view of the other students—should produce a sound with each of his or her objects while the other students listen to identify each sound and list each sound-producing object. Students will check their answers and discuss why the sounds were easy or difficult to identify.

5. To test your ability to discriminate among the sounds of various musical instruments, listen to an orchestra performance, and then focus your attention on the sounds of individual instruments such as the harp, saxophone, oboe, cello, clarinet, and violin.

6. Turn the sound off and watch a dramatic or comic television program. Take notes on what you believe is occurring in the program. Have a friend watch the same program (with the sound on) on another set. At the conclusion of the program, discuss your interpretations with your friend. How well did you "listen" to the nonverbal messages that the actors/actresses communicated?

7. Interview someone from another culture to determine the differences that exist between his or her culture and yours with respect to nonverbal communication aspects such as spatial distance, eye contact, voice patterns, touching behavior, regard for time, clothing, gestures, bodily movements, and regulatory cues. Which of these aspects are potential sources of communication barriers between communicators from the interviewee's culture and your culture? Discuss your findings with the class.

8. Each student is to describe, in one sentence, a situation that might produce a distinct emotional reaction. Students are then to exchange cards. Each card holder will portray an emotion that the situation suggests, and students will interpret the emotions being portrayed.

9. Recall your first memory of touching and being touched. What were your feelings? What are your present feelings about touching and being touched? Are you satisfied with these feelings? During what communication situations would you like to be touched more/less? During what communication situations would you like to touch more/less? Experiment with your touch behavior. Discover what happens when you touch more/touch less.

10. Experiment with eye contact by violating "civil inattention" behavior. Rather than glancing at an approaching stranger (in an uncrowded space on neutral ground) and then looking away until the two of you have passed one another, keep looking at the stranger until he or she has passed. Observe the stranger's reactions and report them to the class.

11. Experiment with head nods by reinforcing the speaker with appropriate head nods and then not moving your head. How did the speaker react? Report your findings to the class.

12. Experiment with spatial distance. Violate the personal space of one person and/or maintain an inappropriately far away distance from someone else with whom you are conversing. Note your dialogue partner's reactions and report them to the class.

13. Occupy a seat where someone has left a "territorial marker" (a personal possession such as a book, umbrella, coat, etc.). Note the reactions of the person who had "reserved" his or her space when he or she returns. Report the person's reactions to the class.

14. List various ways that a speaker *nonverbally* indicates (or attempts to indicate) his or her status to listeners. How do you react to these status signals? Share your reactions with the class.

15. The next time you converse with someone, attempt to mirror his or her posture. Determine if mirroring assists you in identifying the other's feelings.

16. Collect comic strips or cartoons that show characters smiling, block out the captions/messages, and bring the comic strips/cartoons to class. Share them with the class, and have students give their interpretations of the meanings of the differently depicted smiles.

17. Make a deliberate effort to change your nonverbal behavior when you communicate with someone whom you dislike. Notice whether your behavioral changes result in the other person altering his or her behavior or whether there are changes in your feelings toward the other person.

18. Identify a nonverbal behavior that is unique to a specific culture and describe it to the class.

19. Refuse several speakers' turn-taking offers by remaining silent and motionless. Note speakers' verbal and nonverbal reactions and share them with the class.

20. Discuss how the following quote by Andre Kostelanetz applies to you: "We listen too much to the telephone and we listen too little to nature. The wind is one of my sounds. A lonely sound, perhaps, but soothing. Everybody should have his personal sounds to listen for—sounds that will make him feel exhilarated and alive, or quiet and calm. . . . As a matter of fact, one of the greatest sounds of them all— and to me it is a sound—is utter, complete silence."[153]

Descriptive Commentary

The following is a commentary that describes what is occurring nonverbally at any given (coded) point in the abbreviated scenario that introduces this chapter.

a. Time communicates. Formal time, labeled by Hall and measured by a calendar or clock, suggests that one be prompt. One's punctuality may indicate one's perception of the importance of or respect for the event (and the other participants) as well as one's sense of responsibility.[154]

b. In a study in which Bayes examined ratings of interpersonal warmth, she found that "smiling is the best single indicator of warmth."[155] Morris refers to the smile (one of the many affect displays, which are behaviors that reflect emotional states) as "the most important social bonding signal in the human gestural repertoire."[156]

c. Where one chooses to sit in a room containing fixed furniture can foster or inhibit communicative interaction. In a regular classroom, students sitting up the middle as well as in the central front rows tend to participate more.[157]

d. Displacement signals, such as repeatedly opening and closing the clasp of a bracelet, repeatedly checking a ticket prior to an airplane flight, tapping a cigarette that has no ash, dusting dust-free furniture, etc., are small behaviors in which one may engage when he or she is in a tense situation.[158] Rummaging through papers and leafing through the textbook may be displacement signals in which students who are together for the first time may engage.

e. Griffitt and Veitch have found that room temperature affects one's psychological disposition as well as one's social behavior with others; high room temperatures produce more negative feelings than do lower, more moderate and comfortable room temperatures.[159]

f. Liebman suggests that prevailing social norms promote closer interpersonal distances between females than between males.[160]

g. "Territorial markers" (personal possessions such as books, umbrellas, coats, open notebooks, etc.) are used to reserve space when the owner of the item(s) temporarily vacates the spatial area (such as in a library, cafeteria, or classroom).[161]

h. The actions displayed by the students are signs of inattention, disinterest, boredom, and preoccupation with something other than the test lecture.[162]

i. One sign of attentive listening may be blinking; the blink rate is typically every three to ten seconds.[163]

j. Sighing, which is a vocal adaptor (one of many "behaviors which once served a useful purpose, but which now are part of the individual's habit repetoire"[164]), here indicates relief.[165]

Notes

1. W. H. Perkins, *Speech Pathology* (St. Louis: Mosby, 1971), p. 115.
2. R. L. Ebel, ed., *Encyclopedia of Educational Research* (NY: Macmillan, 1969), p. 1083.
3. S. B. Neuman, "Effect of Teaching Auditory Perceptual Skills in Reading Achievement in First Grade," *Reading Teacher* 34 (January 1981): 422.
4. S. Fessenden, "Levels of Listening—a Theory," *Education* 75 (January 1955): 34–35.
5. H. Gardner, "Do Babies Sing a Universal Song?" *Psychology Today* 14 (December 1981): 70–76.
6. Discrepancies in the time when some skills are said to develop in sighted and visually handicapped persons are indicated by (VH*), and skills that apply only to the visually handicapped are indicated by (VH).
7. Susan W. Weaver and William L. Rutherford, "A Hierarchy of Listening Skills," *Elementary English* 51 (November/December 1974): 1148–1149. Reprinted with permission of the publisher.

8. S. B. Breathnach, "The World According to the Unborn . . . and After," *The Washington Post*, 10 January 1983, p. B5.

9. C. Atwater, "It Can Get Pretty Lively in the Womb," *USA Today*, 2 August 1983, pp. 1–2.

10. Breathnach, "The World According to the Unborn . . . and After," p. B5.

11. D. Tutolo, "Attention: Necessary Aspect of Listening," *Language Arts* 56 (January 1979): 34–35.

12. R. A. Cole, "Navigating the Slippery Stream of Speech," *Psychology Today* 12 (April 1979): 78–79.

13. Ibid., p. 80; G. Mandler, "Words, Tests and Categories: An Experimental View of Organized Memory," in *Studies in Thought and Language*, ed. J. L. Cowan (Tucson, AZ: University of Arizona Press, 1970), pp. 128–129.

14. B. Goss, "Listening As Information Processing," *Communication Quarterly* 30 (Fall 1982): 304–307.

15. M. Knapp, *Nonverbal Communication in Human Interaction*, 2d ed. (NY: Holt, Rinehart & Winston, 1978), p. 361.

16. J. A. Hall, *Nonverbal Sex Differences* (Baltimore: The Johns Hopkins University Press, 1984), p. 130.

17. A. Mehrabian, *Silent Messages* (Belmont, CA: Wadsworth, 1971), p. 56.

18. Ibid., p. 45.

19. Ibid., p. 43.

20. K. R. Scherer, "Acoustic Concomitants of Emotional Dimensions: Judging Affect from Synthesized Tone Sequences," in *Nonverbal Communication: Readings with Commentary*, ed. S. Weitz (NY: Oxford University Press, 1974), pp. 105–111.

21. J. R. Davitz, *The Communication of Emotional Meaning* (NY: McGraw-Hill, 1964), p. 63.

22. M. L. Knapp and J. A. Hall, *Nonverbal Communication in Human Interaction*, 3d ed. (NY: Holt, Rinehart and Winston, 1992), p. 349.

23. Ibid., p. 469, citing M. Snyder, "Self-Monitoring of Expressive Behavior," *Journal of Personality and Social Psychology* 30 (October 1974): 526–537.

24. D. W. Addington, "The Relationship of Selected Vocal Characteristics to Personality Perception," *Speech Monographs* 35 (November 1968): 492–503.

25. J. C. Weaver and R. J. Anderson, "Voice and Personality Interrelationships," *Southern Speech Communication Journal* 38 (Spring 1973): 262–278.

26. L. S. Harms, "Listener Judgments of Status Cues in Speech," *Quarterly Journal of Speech* 47 (April 1967): 164–168.

27. See Knapp and Hall, *Nonverbal Communication in Human Interaction*, 3d ed., pp. 339–344 for a review of research investigating the interrelationships of vocal characteristics and speakers' physical features.

28. Hall, *Nonverbal Sex Differences*, pp. 130–140; N. Miller et al., "Speed of Speech and Persuasion," *Journal of Personality and Social Psychology* 34 (October 1976): 615–624; Knapp and Hall, *Nonverbal Communication in Human Interaction*, 3d ed., pp. 351, 353, 361; C. F. Diehl and E. T. McDonald, "Effect of Voice Quality on Communication," *Journal of Speech and Hearing Disorders* 21 (June 1956): 233–237; R. P. Harrison, *Beyond Words* (Englewood Cliffs, NJ: Prentice-Hall, 1974), p. 108; A. Mehrabian and M. Williams, "Nonverbal Concomitants of Perceived and Intended Persuasiveness," *Journal of Personality and Social Psychology* 13 (September 1969): 37–58; M. LaFrance and B. Carmen, "The Nonverbal Display of Psychological Androgyny," *Journal of Personality and Social Psychology* 38 (January 1980): 36–49; M. M. Reece and R. N. Whitman, "Expressive Movements, Warmth, and Verbal Reinforcement," *Journal of Abnormal and Social Psychology* 64 (March 1962): 234–236.

29. H. L. Dubin, "Standard and Non-Standard Phonological Patterns as Related to Employability" (Master's thesis, University of Maryland—College Park, 1970), p. 51.

30. J. Raloff, "Language," *Science News* 122 (4 December 1982): 360.

31. Ibid.

32. M. M. Gill and D. M. Badzinski, "The Impact of Accent and Status on Information Recall and Perception Formation," *Communication Reports* 5 (Summer 1992): 99–106.

33. M. Fichtner, "Listen!" Columbia, S.C.: *The State Magazine*, 7 August 1983, p. 10.

34. R. O. Ross, *Listen to Your Car* (NY: Walker Publishing Company, 1981), p. 16.

35. S. Goode, "Driver Must Listen to Sounds of Accident," *Insight* 3 (31 August 1987): 53.

36. "The Coach's Secret Is to Listen Carefully," *The Washington Post*, 8 July 1984, p. F6.

37. L. Dobres and C. Gaffney, Discriminative Listening Project (University of Maryland—College Park, 1972).

38. S. Rovner, "Baby See, Baby Do," *The Washington Post Health*, 25 December 1985, p. 9.

39. R. L. Birdwhistell, as cited in Knapp and Hall, *Nonverbal Communication in Human Interaction*, 3d ed., p. 29.
40. Mehrabian, *Silent Messages*, p. 44.
41. "Disqualification of Smith Judge Sought," *The Washington Post*, 21 August 1991, p. A4.
42. P. Lieberman, "Reading Jurors' Minds: It's Risky Business," *Santa Rosa Press Democrat*, 12 April 1993, p. A8.
43. D. Leathers, *Nonverbal Communication Systems* (Boston: Allyn and Bacon, 1976), p. 236; G. E. Myers and M. T. Myers, *The Dynamics of Human Communication* (NY: McGraw-Hill, 1973), p. 180.
44. M. Argyle, *Bodily Communication* (NY: International Universities Press, 1975), pp. 362–363.
45. Knapp, *Nonverbal Communication in Human Interaction*, 2d ed., p. 254.
46. Mehrabian, *Silent Messages*, p. 71.
47. P. Marsh, "Reading Facial Expressions," in *Eye to Eye*, ed. P. Marsh (Topsfield, MA: Salem House Publishers, 1988), p. 83.
48. S. Thiederman, "Planners Beware: Meeting Planners Vary by Country," *Meeting News*, April 1990, p. 48.
49. D. Manning, "Understanding Foreign Protocol," *Meeting News*, October 1990.
50. K. Passer, "Learn Protocol to Sidestep Faux Pas," *Corporate Travel*, September 1990, p. 61.
51. C. Douglis, "The Beat Goes On," *Psychology Today* 21 (November 1987): 39.
52. Mehrabian, *Silent Messages*, pp. 59–65.
53. Ibid., p. 22; G. I. Nierenberg and H. H. Calero, *How to Read a Person like a Book* (NY: Pocket Books, 1973), pp. 68, 84, 91–92.
54. Knapp, *Nonverbal Communication in Human Interaction*, 2d ed., p. 232.
55. Hall, *Nonverbal Sex Differences*, p. 140; G. H. Graham, J. Unruh, and P. Jennings, "The Impact of Nonverbal Communication in Organizations: A Survey of Perceptions," *Journal of Business Communication* 28 (Winter 1991): 45–62.
56. Myers and Myers, *The Dynamics of Human Communication*, p. 180.
57. J. W. Drakeford, "From Tuning Out: The Most Debilitating Social Disease," *New Woman*, July 1983, p. 67.
58. M. L. Knapp, *Nonverbal Communication in Human Interaction* (NY: Holt, Rinehart and Winston, 1972), p. 113.
59. W. J. Majeski, "Can You Tell When Someone Is Lying?" *Parade*, 6 July 1986, p. 8.
60. P. Ekman and W. V. Friesen, "The Repertoire of Nonverbal Behavior: Categories, Origins, Usage, and Coding," *Semiotica* 1 (1969): 49–98.
61. Harrison, *Beyond Words*, p. 134.
62. Ibid., p. 137.
63. J. R. Aiello and R. E. Cooper, "Use of Personal Space as a Function of Social Affect," *Proceedings of the 1972 80th Annual Convention of the American Psychological Association* 7 (1972): 207–208; A. Mehrabian, "Significance of Posture and Position in the Communication of Attitude and Status Relationships," *Psychological Bulletin* 71 (May 1969): 359–372; R. F. Haase and D. T. Tepper, "Nonverbal Components of Empathic Communication," *Journal of Counseling Psychology* 19 (September 1972): 417–424; Hall, *Nonverbal Sex Differences*, pp. 100, 102; Knapp, *Nonverbal Communication in Human Interaction*, 2d ed., p. 228.
64. The general interpretation is that an open body indicates a positive attitude toward those with whom one is interacting and a closed body indicates a negative attitude. However, Mehrabian has suggested that "an open arm position of seated communicators may more appropriately be considered an index of relaxation [than an index of positive attitude/liking/inclusion], with relatively more open positions indicating greater relaxation. In contrast, for standing communicators, a folded arm position may be more relaxed than one with the arms hanging." A. Mehrabian, "Significance of Posture and Position in the Communication of Attitude and Status Relationships," p. 368.
65. Ibid., pp. 359–372; H. McGinley, R. LeFevre, and P. McGinley, "The Influence of a Communicator's Body Position on Opinion Change of Others," *Journal of Personality and Social Psychology* 31 (April 1974): 686–690; Hall, *Nonverbal Sex Differences*, pp. 121–123, 126.
66. Mehrabian, "Significance of Posture and Position in the Communication of Attitude and Status Relationships," pp. 359–372; F. D. Kelly, "Communicational Significance of Therapist Proxemic Clues," *Journal of Consulting and Clinical Psychology* 39 (October 1972): 345; M. M. Reece and R. N. Whitman, "Expressive Movements, Warmth, and

Verbal Reinforcement," pp. 234–236; A. Mehrabian, *Nonverbal Communication* (Chicago: Aldine-Atherton, 1972); Haase and Tepper, "Nonverbal Components of Empathic Communication," pp. 417–424; Hall, *Nonverbal Sex Differences*, pp. 121–123, 126; Knapp, *Nonverbal Communication in Human Interaction*, 2d ed., p. 228.

67. Mehrabian, "Significance of Posture and Position in the Communication of Attitude and Status Relationships," pp. 359–372; Hall, *Nonverbal Sex Differences*, pp. 121–123; Knapp, *Nonverbal Communication in Human Interaction*, 2d ed., p. 228; E. Goffman, *Encounters* (Indianapolis: Bobbs-Merrill, 1961); N. M. Henley, *Body Politics: Power, Sex, and Nonverbal Communication* (Englewood Cliffs, N.J.: Prentice-Hall, 1977); A. Mehrabian, *Nonverbal Communication*; A. Kendon, "Movement Coordination in Social Interaction: Some Examples Described," *Acta Psychologica* 32 (April 1970): 101–125; S. Dellinger and B. Deane, "People-Watching for Hidden Emotions," *Self* 3 (April 1981): 76–79; W. S. Condon and W. D. Ogston, "Sound Film Analysis of Normal and Pathological Behavior Patterns," *Journal of Nervous and Mental Disease* 143 (October 1966): 338–347.

68. Hall, *Nonverbal Sex Differences*, pp. 121–124, 126; H. Rosenfeld, "Instrumental Affiliative Functions of Facial and Gestural Expressions," *Journal of Personality and Social Psychology* 4 (July 1966): 65–72; R. Friedman, "Hand Jive," *Psychology Today* 22 (June 1988): 10; N. K. Austin, "The Subtle Signals of Success," *Working Woman*, April, 1991, p. 106; R. Schulz and J. Barefoot, "Nonverbal Responses and Affiliative Conflict Theory," *British Journal of Social and Clinical Psychology* 13 (September 1974): 237–243; Reece and Whitman, "Expressive Movements, Warmth, and Verbal Reinforcement," pp. 234–236; B. R. Fretz, "Postural Movements in a Counseling Dyad," *Journal of Counseling Psychology* 13 (Fall 1966): 335–347; Mehrabian, *Silent Messages*, pp. 22, 75; A. Kendon, "Gesture and Speech," in J. M. Wiemann and R. P. Harrison, eds. *Nonverbal Interaction* (Beverly Hills: Sage Publications, 1983), pp. 13–45; P. Ekman and W. V. Friesen, "Hand Movements," *Journal of Communication* 22 (December 1972): 353–374.

69. Rosenfeld, "Instrumental Affiliative Functions of Facial and Gestural Expressions," pp. 65–72; J. D. Matarazzo, et al., "Interviewer Head Nodding and Interviewee Speech Duration," *Psychotherapy: Theory and Practice* 1 (January 1964): 54–63; H. Hackney, "Facial Gestures and Subject Expression of Feelings," *Journal of Counseling Psychology* 21 (May 1974): 173–178; S. Duncan, "On the Structure of Speaker-Auditor Interaction during Speaking Turns," *Language in Society* 3 (October 1974): 161–180; G. L. Clore, N. H. Wiggins, and S. Itkin, "Judging Attraction from Nonverbal Behavior: The Gain Phenomenon," *Journal of Consulting and Clinical Psychology* 43 (August 1975): 491–497; G. L. Clore, N. H. Wiggins, and S. Itkin, "Gain and Loss in Attraction: Attributions from Nonverbal Behavior," *Journal of Personality and Social Psychology* 31 (April 1975): 706–712; A. R. D'Augelli, "Nonverbal Behavior of Helpers in Initial Helping Interactions," *Journal of Counseling Psychology* 1 (September 1974): 360–363.

70. P. Ekman, W. V. Friesen, and P. Ellsworth, *Emotion in the Human Face: Guidelines for Research and an Integration of the Findings* (NY: Pergamon Press, 1972).

71. L. Rosenfeld and R. M. Berko, *Communicating with Competency* (Glenview, IL: Scott, Foresman, 1990), p. 56.

72. Ekman, Friesen, and Ellsworth, *Emotion in the Human Face: Guidelines for Research and an Integration of the Findings*.

73. Knapp and Hall, *Nonverbal Communication in Human Interaction*, 3d ed., pp. 265–266.

74. Hall, *Nonverbal Sex Differences*, p. 59; V. L. Emmert and P. Andersen, "What Is the Role of Nonverbal Communication in Listening?" (Presentation delivered at the International Listening Association Convention, Scottsdale, AZ, 1988).

75. Clore, Wiggins, and Itkin, "Judging Attraction from Nonverbal Behavior: The Gain Phenomenon," pp. 491–497; Mehrabian, "Significance of Posture and Position in the Communication of Attitude and Status Relationships," p. 368; P. Noller, "Channel Consistency and Inconsistency in the Communications of Married Couples," *Journal of Personality and Social Psychology* 43 (October 1982): 732–741; Hall, *Nonverbal Sex Differences*, p. 60; M. S. Bayes, "Behavioral Cues of Interpersonal Warmth," *Journal of Consulting and Clinical Psychology* 39 (October 1972): 337; Reece and Whitman, "Expressive Movements, Warmth, and Verbal Reinforcement," pp. 234–236; Hall, *Nonverbal Sex Differences*, pp. 59, 61–63, 69–71; Rosenfeld, "Instrumental Affiliative Functions of Facial and Gestural Expressions," pp. 65–72.

76. Knapp and Hall, *Nonverbal Communication in Human Interaction*, 3d ed., p. 295.

77. Ibid., p. 297.

78. R. V. Exline and L. C. Winters, "Affective Relations and Mutual Glances in Dyads," in *Affect, Cognition, and Personality*, ed. S. S. Tomkins and C. E. Izard (NY: Springer

Publishing Company, 1965), pp. 319–350; Mehrabian, "Significance of Posture and Position in the Communication of Attitude and Status Relationships," pp. 359–372; Knapp and Hall, *Nonverbal Communication in Human Interaction*, 3d ed., pp. 305, 314, 315; Knapp, *Nonverbal Communication in Human Interaction*, 2d ed., p. 313; Reece and Whitman, "Expressive Movements, Warmth, and Verbal Reinforcement," pp. 234–236; Haase and Tepper, "Nonverbal Components of Empathic Communication," pp. 417–424; S. E. Scherer and M. R. Schiff, "Perceived Intimacy, Physical Distance, and Eye Contact," *Perceptual and Motor Skills* 36 (June 1973): 835–842; Kelly, "Communicational Significance of Therapist Proxemic Cues," p. 345; R. E. Kleck and W. Nuessle, "Congruence between the Indicative and Communicative Functions of Eye-Contact in Interpersonal Relations," *British Journal of Social and Clinical Psychology* 7 (December 1968): 241–246; Mehrabian and Williams, "Nonverbal Concomitants of Perceived and Intended Persuasiveness," pp. 37–58; S. A. Beebe, "Eye-Contact: A Nonverbal Determinant of Speaker Credibility," *Speech Teacher* 23 (January 1974): 21–25; J. Wills, "An Empirical Study of the Behavioral Characteristics of Sincere and Insincere Speakers," Ph.D. diss., University of Southern California, Los Angeles, 1961; J. Licht, "Eye Contact and Attitudes," *The Washington Post Health*, 9 July 1991, p. 9; P. Marsh, "Making Eye Contact," in *Eye to Eye*, p. 76; N. Mobbs, "Eye Contact in Relation to Social Introversion/Extroversion," *British Journal of Social and Clinical Psychology* 6 (December 1967): 256–266; Hall, *Nonverbal Sex Differences*, pp. 73–78, 80, 82–83, 126; Henley, *Body Politics: Power, Sex, and Nonverbal Communication*; J. S. Efran, "Looking for Approval: Effects on Visual Behavior of Approbation from Persons Differing in Importance," *Journal of Personality and Social Psychology* 10 (September 1968): 21–25; R. V. Exline, "Visual Interaction: The Glances of Power and Preference," in *Nebraska Symposium on Motivation, 1971*, ed. J. K. Cole (Lincoln, NE: University of Nebraska Press, 1972), pp. 163–206; S. S. Fugita, "Effects of Anxiety and Approval on Visual Interaction," *Journal of Personality and Social Psychology* 29 (April 1974): 586–592; S. Weitz, "Sex Differences in Nonverbal Communication," *Sex Roles* 2 (March 1976): 175–184; S. L. Ellyson, J. F. Dovidio, and B. J. Fehr, "Visual Behavior and Dominance in Women and Men," in *Gender and Nonverbal Behavior*, eds. C. Mayo and N. M. Henley (NY: Springer-Verlag, 1981), pp. 63–79; R. V. Exline, S. L. Ellyson, and B. Long, "Visual Behavior as an Aspect of Power Role Relationships," in *Nonverbal Communication of Aggression*, eds. P. Pliner, L. Krames, and T. Alloway (NY: Plenum, 1975); J. S. Effran and A. Broughton, "Effect of Expectancies for Social Approval on Visual Behavior," *Journal of Personality and Social Psychology* 4 (July 1966): 103–107; J. S. Efran, "Looking for Approval: Effects on Visual Behavior of Approbation from Persons Differing in Importance," *Journal of Personality and Social Psychology* 10 (September 1968): 21–25; R. M. Berko, A. D. Wolvin, and D. R. Wolvin, *Communicating: A Social and Career Focus*, 6th ed. (Boston: Houghton Mifflin, 1995), pp. 168–169; Schulz and Barefoot, "Nonverbal Responses and Affiliative Conflict Theory," pp. 237–243; M. Argyle and R. Ingham, "Gaze, Mutual Gaze, and Proximity," *Semiotica* 6 (1972): 32–49; M. Argyle and J. Dean, "Eye Contact, Distance and Affiliation," *Sociometry* 28 (Summer 1965): 289–304; M. L. Goldberg and A. R. Wellens, "A Comparison of Nonverbal Compensatory Behaviors within Direct Face-to-Face and Television-Mediated Interviews," *Journal of Applied Social Psychology* 9 (May/June 1979): 250–260; R. V. Exline, D. Gray, and D. Schuette, "Visual Behavior in a Dyad as Affected by Interview Content and Sex of Respondent," *Journal of Personality and Social Psychology* 1 (March 1965): 201–209; Argyle, *Bodily Communication*, p. 229; R. V. Exline, "Explorations in the Process of Person Perception: Visual Interaction in Relation to Competition, Sex, and Need for Affiliation," *Journal of Personality* 31 (March 1963): 1–20.

79. W. Wells and B. Siegel, "Stereotyped Somatypes," *Psychological Reports* 8 (February 1961): 77–78; K. T. Strongman and C. J. Hart, "Stereotyped Reactions to Body Build," *Psychological Reports* 23 (December 1968): 1175–1178.

80. Knapp and Hall, *Nonverbal Communication in Human Interaction*, 3d ed., p. 112.

81. Ibid., p. 118.

82. Ibid., p. 115.

83. R. W. Moncrieff, *Odour Preferences* (NY: Wiley, 1966).

84. J. T. Molloy, *Dress for Success* (NY: Warner Books, 1976).

85. E. T. Hall, *The Silent Language* (Greenwich, CT: Fawcett Publications, 1959), p. 185.

86. E. Hall and M. Hall, "Body Talk," in *Communicating Interpersonally*, ed. R. W. Pace, B. D. Peterson, and T. R. Radcliffe (Columbus, OH: Merrill, 1973), pp. 129–130.

87. E. T. Hall, "The Anthropology of Manners," *Scientific American* 192 (1955): 84–90.

88. M. Argyle and J. Dean, "Eye-Contact, Distance and Affiliation," *Sociometry* 28 (Summer 1965): 289–304; P. Marsh, "Keeping a Distance," in *Eye to Eye*, p. 42.

89. Hall, *Nonverbal Sex Differences*, pp. 93, 94, 101, 104, 105, 143; F. N. Willis, "Initial Speaking Distance as a Function of the Speaker's Relationship," *Psychonomic Science* 5 (June 1966): 221–222; Knapp and Hall, *Nonverbal Communication in Human Interaction*, 3d ed., p. 161; M. Leibman, "The Effects of Sex and Race Norms on Personal Space," *Environment and Behavior* 2 (September 1970): 208–246; V. P. Skotko and D. Langmeyer, "The Effects of Interaction Distance and Gender on Self-Disclosure in the Dyad," *Sociometry* 40 (June 1977): 178–182.

90. L. A. Hayduk, "Personal Space: An Evaluative and Orienting Overview," *Psychological Bulletin* 85 (January 1978): 117–134.

91. Berko, Wolvin, and Wolvin, *Communicating: A Social and Career Focus*, pp. 168–169; Knapp and Hall, *Nonverbal Communication in Human Interaction*, 3d ed., pp. 162–163.

92. M. E. Caplan and M. Goldman, "Personal Space Violations as a Function of Height," *Journal of Social Psychology* 114 (August 1981): 167–171; R. M. Learner, "The Development of Personal Space Schemata toward Body Build," *Journal of Psychology* 84 (March 1973): 229–235.

93. B. S. Lott and R. Sommer, "Seating Arrangements and Status," *Journal of Personality and Social Psychology* 7 (September 1967): 90–95; Knapp and Hall, *Nonverbal Communication in Human Interaction*, 3d ed., pp. 162, 381.

94. M. Cook, "Experiments on Orientation and Proxemics," *Human Relations* 23 (February 1970): 61–76; Marsh, "Keeping a Distance," in *Eye to Eye*, p. 42; R. Kleck, "Physical Stigma and Task Oriented Interaction," *Human Relations* 22 (February 1969): 51–60; M. Patterson, "Spatial Factors in Social Interaction," *Human Relations* 21 (November 1968): 351–361; Knapp, *Nonverbal Communication in Human Interaction*, 2d ed., p. 129.

95. Knapp, *Nonverbal Communication in Human Interaction*, 2d ed., p. 138; K. B. Little, "Personal Space," *Journal of Experimental Social Psychology* 1 (August 1965): 237–247; Mehrabian, *Silent Messages*, p. 1; J. R. Aiello and R. E. Cooper, "Use of Personal Space as a Function of Social Affect," *Proceedings of the 1972 80th Annual Convention of the American Psychological Association* 7 (1972): 207–208; A. H. Rosenfeld, "So Near and Yet So Far," *Psychology Today* 22 (March 1988): 14.

96. P. Marsh, "Marking Territory," in *Eye to Eye*, p. 35; Knapp and Hall, *Nonverbal Communication in Human Interaction*, 3d ed., pp. 164, 167–176.

97. Hall, *The Silent Language*, pp. 15–30; R. McGarvey, "Beat the Clock," *USAir Magazine*, October 1993, pp. 102, 104, 107, 109–110, 112.

98. Knapp and Hall, *Nonverbal Communication in Human Interaction*, 3d ed., pp. 59–61.

99. R. Heslin, "Steps toward a Taxonomy of Touching" (Paper presented at the Midwestern Psychological Association, Chicago, IL, May 1974).

100. Ibid., pp. 3–4.

101. Argyle, *Bodily Communication*, p. 287.

102. T. Nguyen, R. Heslin, and M. L. Nguyen, "The Meanings of Touch: Sex Differences," *Journal of Communication* 25 (Spring 1975): 92–103.

103. Hall, *Nonverbal Sex Differences*, pp. 114–115.

104. Henley, *Body Politics: Power, Sex, and Nonverbal Communication*; C. Radecki and J. (Walstedt) Jennings, "Sex as a Status Variable in Work Settings: Female and Male Reports of Dominance Behavior," *Journal of Applied Social Psychology* 10 (January/February 1980): 71–85.

105. S. Thayer, "Close Encounters," *Psychology Today* 22 (March 1988): 33–34.

106. Ibid., p. 34; J. D. Fisher, M. Rytting, and R. Heslin, "Hands Touching Hands: Affective and Evaluative Effects of Interpersonal Touch," *Sociometry* 39 (December 1976): 416–421; S. Thayer, "The Language of Touch," in *Eye to Eye*, p. 95.

107. Henley, *Body Politics: Power, Sex, and Nonverbal Communication*, p. 105.

108. Ibid.

109. Mehrabian, *Silent Messages*, p. 7. For a discussion of women and handshakes, see N. K. Austin, "The Subtle Signals of Success," p. 106.

110. S. E. Jones and A. E. Yarbrough, "A Contextual Analysis Study of the Meanings of Interpersonal Touch" (Paper presented at the Speech Communication Association Convention, Washington, D.C., November 1983), pp. 32, 34.

111. Henley, *Body Politics: Power, Sex, and Nonverbal Communication*, p. 105.

112. Thayer, "The Language of Touch," p. 90.

113. Jones and Yarbrough, "A Contextual Analysis Study of the Meanings of Interpersonal Touch," p. 29.

114. Ibid.

115. Ibid., p. 30.
116. Henley, *Body Politics: Power, Sex, and Nonverbal Communication*, p. 105.
117. Jones and Yarbrough, "A Contextual Analysis Study of the Meanings of Interpersonal Touch," pp. 32–33, 35–36.
118. Knapp and Hall, *Nonverbal Communication in Human Interaction*, 3d ed., p. 244.
119. Ibid.
120. Jones and Yarbrough, "A Contextual Analysis Study of the Meanings of Interpersonal Touch," p. 2.
121. Ibid., p. 7.
122. Berko, Wolvin, and Wolvin, *Communicating: A Social and Career Focus*, p. 169.
123. Thayer, "Close Encounters," p. 31.
124. Knapp and Hall, *Nonverbal Communication in Human Interaction*, 3d ed., p. 71.
125. "Best Image News," *Parade*, 1 January 1989, p. 10.
126. Knapp and Hall, *Nonverbal Communication in Human Interaction*, 3d ed., p. 72.
127. J. Brownell, "Listening Environment: A Perspective," in *Perspectives on Listening*, eds. A. D. Wolvin and C. G. Coakley (Norwood, N.J.: Ablex Publishing Corporation, 1991), pp. 250–252.
128. W. Griffitt and R. Veitch, "Hot and Crowded: Influences of Population Density and Temperature on Interpersonal Affective Behavior," *Journal of Personality and Social Psychology* 17 (January 1971): 92–98.
129. Brownell, "Listening Environment: A Perspective," p. 251.
130. Mehrabian, *Silent Messages*, p. 79.
131. Ibid., pp. 84–85.
132. Knapp and Hall, *Nonverbal Communication in Human Interaction*, 3d ed, pp. 73–74.
133. L. B. Wexner, "The Degree to Which Colors (Hues) Are Associated with Mood-Tones," *Journal of Applied Psychology* 38 (December 1954): 432–435.
134. P. Ekman and W. V. Friesen, "Nonverbal Leakage and Clues to Deception," *Psychiatry* 32 (February 1969): 88–106; for a quantitative review of deception research, see P. J. Kalbfleisch, "Listening for Deception: The Effects of Medium on Accuracy of Deception," in R. N. Bostrom, *Listening Behavior: Measurement and Application* (NY: The Guilford Press, 1990), pp. 155–176.
135. Ekman and Friesen, "Nonverbal Leakage and Clues to Deception" pp. 88–106; A. Mehrabian, "Nonverbal Betrayal of Feeling," *Journal of Experimental Research in Personality* 5 (March 1971): 64–73; D. Morris, *Manwatching* (NY: Abrams, 1977), pp. 106–111; "Anatomy of a Lying Smile," *Science News*, 19 March 1988, p. 187; J. Leo, "The Fine Art of Catching Liars," *Time*, 22 April 1985, p. 59; Knapp and Hall, *Nonverbal Communication in Human Interaction*, 3d ed., pp. 390–393.
136. Harrison, *Beyond Words*, p. 138.
137. D. Goleman, "Can You Tell When Someone Is Lying to You?" *Psychology Today* 16 (August 1982): 14–23; W. Buchert, "Fibbers often Betrayed by their Body Language," *USA Today*, 14 November 1989, p. 11A; P. Ekman, W. V. Friesen, and K. R. Scherer, "Body Movement and Voice Pitch in Deceptive Interaction," *Semiotica* 16 (1976): 23–27; M. Zuckerman, M. Amidon, S. Bishop, and S. Pomerantz, "Face and Tone of Voice in the Communication of Deception," *Journal of Personality and Social Psychology* 43 (1982): 347–357.
138. S. Dellinger and B. Deane, "People-Watching for Hidden Emotions," *Self* 3 (April 1981): 76–79.
139. Knapp and Hall, *Nonverbal Communication in Human Interaction*, 3d ed., p. 383.
140. Ibid.
141. Ibid., p. 384; Argyle, *Bodily Communication*, p. 166; Harrison, *Beyond Words*, p. 126; R. G. Harper, A. N. Wiens, and J. D. Matarazzo, *Nonverbal Communication: The State of the Art* (NY: Wiley, 1978), pp. 185–186; S. Duncan, "Some Signals and Rules for Taking Speaking Turns in Conversations," *Journal of Personality and Social Psychology* 23 (August 1972): 283–292.
142. Knapp and Hall, *Nonverbal Communication in Human Interaction*, 3d ed., p. 385; Argyle, *Bodily Communication*, p. 166; Harrison, *Beyond Words*, pp. 111, 126; Harper, Wiens, and Matarazzo, *Nonverbal Communication: The State of the Art*, pp. 185–186.
143. J. A. Harrigan, "Listeners' Body Movements and Speaking Turns," *Communication Research*, 12 (April 1985): 233–250; Harper, Wiens, and Matarazzo, *Nonverbal Communication: The State of the Art*, pp. 147–149, 185–186; Knapp and Hall, *Nonverbal Communication in Human Interaction*, 3d ed., p. 385.

144. P. Marsh, "Making Eye Contact," in *Eye to Eye*, p. 73.
145. S. Duncan, "On the Structure of Speaker-Auditor Interaction during Speaking Turns," *Language in Society* 3 (October 1974): 177
146. Knapp and Hall, *Nonverbal Communication in Human Interaction*, 3d ed., p. 386; Harper, Wiens, and Matarazzo, *Nonverbal Communication: The State of the Art*, pp. 147–149, 185–186; P. Marsh, "How People Interact," in *Eye to Eye*, p. 85.
147. P. A. Andersen, J. F. Andersen, and S. M. Mayton, "The Development of Nonverbal Communication in the Classroom: Teachers' Perceptions of Students in Grades K–12," *The Western Journal of Speech Communication* 49 (Summer 1985): 188–203.
148. Knapp and Hall, *Nonverbal Communication in Human Interaction*, 3d ed., pp. 386–387.
149. Ibid., p. 387; Mehrabian, *Silent Messages*, pp. 1–3.
150. Mehrabian, *Silent Messages*, p. 3.
151. Knapp and Hall, *Nonverbal Communication in Human Interaction*, 3d ed., p. 387.
152. G. Egan, "Listening As Empathic Support" in *Bridges Not Walls*, 2d ed., ed. J. Stewart (Reading, MA: Addison-Wesley, 1977), p. 228.
153. *The International Dictionary of Thoughts*, s.v. "Silence."
154. Hall, *The Silent Language*, p. 185.
155. Bayes, "Behavioral Cues of Interpersonal Warmth," p. 337.
156. Morris, *Manwatching*, p. 259.
157. Harrison, *Beyond Words*, p. 153.
158. Morris, *Manwatching*, pp. 179–181.
159. W. Griffitt and R. Veitch, "Hot and Crowded: Influences of Population Density and Temperature on Interpersonal Affective Behavior," pp. 92–98.
160. M. Liebman, "The Effects of Sex and Race Norms on Personal Space," *Environment and Behavior* 2 (September 1970): 208–246.
161. F. D. Becker, "Study of Spatial Matters," *Journal of Personality and Social Psychology* 26 (June 1973): 439–445.
162. Morris, *Manwatching*, pp. 186–187; Nierenberg and Calero, *How to Read a Person like a Book*, pp. 121–124.
163. Argyle, *Bodily Communication*, p. 230.
164. Harrison, *Beyond Words*, p. 137.
165. Ibid., p. 111.

PRINCIPLES YOU WILL ENCOUNTER

- *Comprehensive listening is listening to understand the message.*
- *Three of the most significant variables to effectiveness in comprehensive listening are memory, concentration, and vocabulary.*
- *The use of memory techniques—such as the loci, link, peg-word, and phonetic systems, rhyming, mnemonic devices, categorical clustering, and chunking—facilitates recall.*
- *Concentration on senders' messages may well be listeners' most difficult task.*
- *The effective comprehensive listener*
  - *knows when to listen for understanding*
  - *knows what variables are directly related to comprehensive listening*
  - *has a strong desire for memory improvement, concentrates on memory improvement, and practices memory improvement techniques*
  - *develops self-discipline to control distractions, is self-motivated to listen, and accepts responsibility for the success of each communication interaction in which he or she is a participant*
  - *internalizes and practices behaviors that improve concentration*
  - *desires to improve both general and listening vocabularies*
  - *possesses vocabulary acquisition skills such as the ability to analyze the structure and context of words*
  - *strives continually toward vocabulary improvement*
  - *engages in active listening behaviors during the time differential between speech speed and thought speed*
  - *is adept at identifying key concepts and significant details of messages*
  - *is skilled in drawing justifiable inferences*
  - *is an effective and flexible notetaker who utilizes a variety of notetaking methods*
  - *is proficient in recalling items in a sequence*
  - *is accurate in following oral directions*
  - *formulates and asks meaningful questions*
  - *paraphrases to check understanding of senders' messages*

CHAPTER 6

Comprehensive Listening

In You Are the Message, *Roger Ailes tells the following story about a man who has just moved to a new town:*

He goes down to the courthouse to try to make some new friends. He sees an old fellow sitting on the curb with a dog beside him. The new man in town walks over and asks, "Does your dog bite?" The old guy looks up at him and says, "Nope." So the fellow reaches down to pet the dog, and the dog nearly rips his arm off. He jumps back quickly and says, "I thought you said your dog doesn't bite." The old guy looks up and says, "Ain't my dog." [1]

Not until the end of the story do the two communicators reach understanding. What could each man have done to co-create understanding earlier in their communication transaction?

The second purpose for listening goes beyond the discrimination of aural, and sometimes visual, stimuli to the understanding of the message. This listening for understanding we prefer to term **comprehensive listening**—listening for the comprehension of the message. We recognize that the phrase comprehensive listening suggests an overall category that might include all dimensions of listening behavior, but we have selected this phrase to be consistent with the terminology of the other listening purposes: discriminative listening, therapeutic listening, critical listening, and appreciative listening. The comprehensive listener is successful if the message that he or she receives, attends to, and assigns meaning to is as close as possible to that which the sender intended. Remembering plays a major role in comprehensive listening when the listener's purpose is not only to understand the message being presented but also to retain it for future use.

comprehensive listening: listening for understanding of the message

Uses of Comprehensive Listening

In all phases of our lives, we listen to understand. Much of the educational process is based on comprehensive listening. We must carefully listen to lectures and class discussions to understand and retain an extensive amount of information. At work, we are often expected to learn new skills and procedures through training programs that use lecture and discussion methods to impart knowledge. In our professional lives we also listen to briefings, reports, seminars, conferences, oral papers, and other oral messages. In our personal lives, too, we listen to understand. We listen to insurance agents

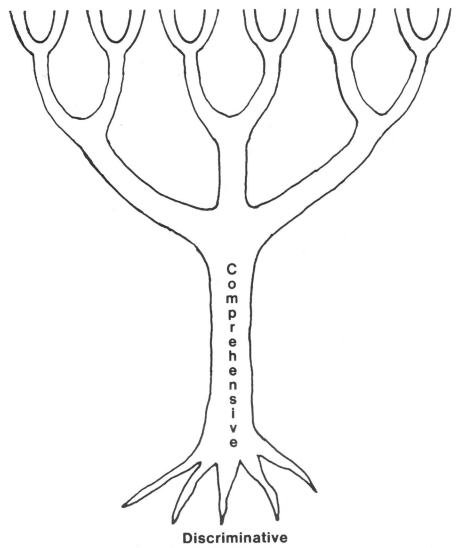

Comprehensive branch of the Wolvin-Coakley Listening Taxonomy.

explain various policies, auto mechanics explain why the car is not operating properly, accountants inform us of items that are now tax deductible, our children describe how their soccer game ended, physicians explain a diagnosis, media personalities share their views on current issues, and countless other people with informative messages. To be effective comprehensive listeners in each of these phases of our lives, we must concentrate on the message strictly to understand, not to make a critical judgment of it.

Variables Related to Comprehensive Listening

Of the five purposes for listening, comprehensive listening has received the most attention. A major reason why it has been studied so frequently is that it is the most testable. A study that provides a pre-test of information, a presentation of the information, and then a post-test covering the presented information can yield results from which we can make some generalizations about the listening comprehension of the persons in the study. Although test results provide some clues about the listening efficiency of the comprehensive listener, such data also illustrate some of the many variables that tend to influence the listener's comprehensive ability.

Memory

One of the variables directly related to comprehensive listening is **memory**. In fact, according to proponents of the schema theory, we cannot process information (which we must do as we listen at any level) without bringing the memory into play throughout the system. They further suggest that we draw up schemata or "scripts" that "represent relationships among concepts rather than among words"[2] and that perform three important functions:

1. They establish expectations of what we are going to encounter in our activities.
2. They serve to structure our comprehension of activities when described by others.
3. They guide recall of our experiences and/or information.[3]

Thus, since comprehensive listening involves information-processing and since we often measure comprehensive listening by a person's ability to remember information that has been presented, memory is a significant variable.

Theories of and Reasons for Forgetting

Extensive research on human memory provides us with valuable information that can greatly aid us in improving our memory. Before we examine some of this information, however, it is useful to consider some theories on

memory

why we forget or why we cannot retrieve information that we have stored in our memory system. Among the **theories of forgetting** are the following:

- **Fading theory:** Information that is not used frequently enough tends to fade from memory.
- **Distortion theory:** Information is often distorted due to its becoming similar to and eventually indistinguishable from other stored information.
- **Suppression theory:** Information that may have unpleasant associations or may be emotionally painful to recall tends to be consciously (though perhaps not subconsciously) forgotten.
- **Interference theory:** Previously learned information interferes with presently learned information while subsequently learned information interferes with previously learned information.
- **Processing break-down theory:** No part, or only a portion, of the information sought (as in the tip-of-the-tongue phenomenon) can be recalled due to an individual's poor retrieval cues, loss of nerve cells in the brain and a slowing of connectivity between the cells as one ages, or a weak or ambiguous coding system in the long term memory (LTM).[4]

This last theory is critical because "successful memory performances depend on a compatibility between the strategies of retrieval and the strategies of the original encoding."[5]

reasons for forgetting

Memory specialists—such as Lorayne, Cermak, Montgomery, and Mendels—postulate a number of **reasons why we do not remember**. One major reason that we may "forget" (as many of us would say) information is that we do not pay attention to it; thus, we do not remember it in the first place. We frequently observe this type of "forgetting" when we are introduced to several people in succession. Later, when conversing with one of these individuals, we may say, "I'm sorry; I've forgotten your name," when we actually never learned (remembered) the name initially. As we have noted in chapter 3, usually only information that has been attended to reaches the LTM. Memory specialists cite additional reasons for our forgetting; among these are poor organizational methods of storing information, distractibility, a lack of caring for people, and a lack of motivation to improve our ability to remember.[6]

Types of Information More Easily Remembered

Besides knowing some of the theories of and reasons for forgetting, knowing *what* is more easily remembered can assist us in impeding the forgetting process. What **information is more easily remembered**? Research shows that we remember more easily information that is meaningful, useful, and of interest to us; particularly striking/out of the ordinary; organized; and visual.[7] In addition, we remember best that information that we learned well during our first exposure to it, with which we associate pleasant feelings, with which we associate (by relating in some way such as comparing and/or contrasting) previously learned, familiar information, and with which we associate great emotional intensity.[8] Many of these same features are characteristic of the **flashbulb memory theory**. This theory posits that shocking and consequential events (such as the assassination of John F. Kennedy and the explosion of the space shuttle Challenger) are indestructible memories and, thus, are remembered more vividly, accurately, and completely than ordinary events are remembered.[9]

flashbulb memory theory

Ausubel, for example, has incorporated several of these principles of learning and remembering in his concept of **advance organizers** and has found that they facilitate the learning and remembering of new information—especially when they are presented in the aural mode and at the college level.[10] Specifically, an *advance organizer* is material introduced to the learner prior to the presentation of the material to be learned. The content of an advance organizer is carefully selected on the basis of its relevance, inclusiveness, and appropriateness for explaining, interpreting, and interrelating the material it precedes. Although it is presented at a higher level of abstraction and generality than the material to be learned, it is stated in familiar terms. The advance organizer delineates the principal similarities and differences between the ideas to be learned and the ideas already established in the learner's LTM. Thus, it provides key anchoring ideas for the learner to both learn (with fewer ambiguities, competing messages, and misconceptions) and retain the more detailed and differentiated material that follows it. Briefly, then, *"the principal function of the organizer is to bridge the gap between what the learner already knows and what he needs to know before he can successfully learn the task at hand."*[11]

advance organizers

Prerequisites for Memory Improvement

Knowing how information is more easily remembered is also critical to **memory improvement**. According to Montgomery, a memory training specialist, there are prerequisites we must meet to improve our memory. We must have a strong desire to improve our memory, concentrate on improving our memory, and care about people. Once we have met these initial requirements, Montgomery recommends that we then practice improving our memory.[12] In a 1980 experimental study of the LTM, Ericsson, Chase, and Faloon found that "there is seemingly no limit to improvement in memory skill with practice."[13] The effects of motivation and practice on retention and recall are vividly illustrated by Michael Barber, a former waiter at the Iron Gate House Restaurant in Virginia Beach, Virginia. Barber has the capacity to elaborate the entire menu of this gourmet restaurant. No menus are issued to diners, so the entire gourmet offering, which changes nightly, must be explained by the waiter. Moreover, Michael takes the orders without writing down any of the details (and diners are offered a vast array of appetizers, entrees, desserts, wines, etc.) and delivers, without error, these orders to the correct individuals. When we asked Michael how he had developed his tremendous memory capacity, he stressed that it was necessary for him, just like a professional actor or singer, to (a) want to work from

prerequisites for memory improvement

memory, that is, have *motivation*, and (b) *practice* with the information until he felt satisfied with the explanation of the evening's menu.

Memory Techniques

memory techniques

Through studying the processes of information storage and retrieval, researchers and practitioners have discovered many **techniques** we can practice to improve our memory. All of these procedures depend extensively on our intention to remember and our ability to attend to incoming information, organize/structure the information, form associations, and rehearse. Many other techniques also rely on our ability to create vivid mental images—images that are visual and striking in color, action, exaggeration, and absurdity. Researchers and memory training specialists have determined that by using these skills, we will remember more effectively, whether we are remembering issues in a speech, items in a list, numbers in a series, rules, or names.

loci system

One of the oldest memory techniques is the **loci system**, which involves learning a sequence of familiar, yet uncrowded, locations (loci) and matching the to-be-remembered items with the locations. The ancient Roman orator Cicero told the story of a man, Simonides, who had perfected this system. After Simonides had been called outside a banquet hall, the roof of the hall collapsed and killed all the revelers inside. By visually recalling where each person had been seated prior to the tragic event, Simonides was able to identify each of the mangled bodies. Physical locations can serve as meaningful loci. To remember the five purposes of listening that are described in a lecture, for example, you might mentally travel around your family room and associate, by creating unbelievable, ridiculous, and comical images, a different area with each purpose. You might clearly visualize the stereo as appreciative listening, the crackling fire as discriminative listening, the sofa as therapeutic listening, the desk where you usually read the newspaper as comprehensive listening, and the draperies that you intensely dislike as critical listening. To recall the purposes, you would visualize in turn each of the previously assigned sequence of areas where the room items are located and, thereby, discover each purpose. The same set of loci can be used over and over for remembering new items. This system has been found to facilitate the learning of ordinarily difficult material.[14]

link system

A second memory technique is the **link system**, which involves vividly and imaginatively linking (or associating) the first to-be-remembered item to the second item, the second to the third, and so on through the use of ridiculous images that you must clearly visualize in your mind. For instance, if you wanted to remember a shopping list consisting of carrots, cigars, milk, and an all-purpose cleaner, you might mentally picture a blue carrot smoking a footlong cigar and wiping up an ocean of spilled milk with a tiny container of all-purpose cleaner. To prevent your forgetting the first item (to which all other items are linked), you should also associate the first item with a location that will remind you of the item. Thus, for your grocery list, you might visualize a carrot bending over a grocery cart. Both imagery and linking have been found to increase recall ability.[15]

Another complex yet highly effective technique with endless possibilities for aiding in learning and recalling is the **phonetic system**. This consists of associating or connecting numbers, phonetic sounds, and words representing these numbers and sounds with the items to be remembered. This system involves four steps:

phonetic system

1. Learning the association between numbers and a ten-sound phonetic alphabet consisting only of consonants
2. Forming and learning words that correspond to the numbers
3. Forming a strong visual image of each word that corresponds to each number
4. Forming a strong visual association between each item to be remembered in sequence with each word formed and visualized (in steps two and three).

In this system, the first three steps, which must be known very well, are permanent; only the to-be-remembered items in step four change.

To use this system, one must first learn the associations between numbers and a phonetic alphabet. Since memory training specialists vary their versions of the phonetic alphabet slightly, we will not present a standard alphabet. Montgomery's version is descriptive of this system:

$$1 = t, d, th$$
$$2 = n$$
$$3 = m$$
$$4 = r$$
$$5 = l$$
$$6 = j, ch, sh, tch, dg, soft\ g$$
$$7 = k, ng, q, hard\ c, hard\ g$$
$$8 = f, v, ph$$
$$9 = p, b$$
$$0 = z, s, soft\ c^{16}$$

To help one in remembering this alphabet, cues can be used. For example, 1 is represented by t (which has a single downstroke), 2 is represented by n (which has two downstrokes), . . . 9 is represented by p (which resembles 9), 0 is represented by z (which is the last alphabet letter as well as the first letter of the word *zero*, the name of 0). Moreover, one who is familiar with voiced and voiceless sounds will recognize that these sounds (such as t and d, j and ch, k and hard g, f and v, p and b, and z and s) are paired. Having learned and associated the numbers and sounds, you then form a concrete word to represent each number; for example, 1, which is represented by t, d, th, might be *tie*; 2, represented by n, might be *Noah*; . . . 14, represented by t, d, th and r, might be *tree* (or it could be *tar, tear, tier, trio,* etc.). Remember, vowel sounds and y, h, and w do not count in this system. Thus, in the example of each word that could possibly be the learned word for 14, only t and r, which represent 1 and 4 = 14, remain when the vowel sounds are omitted. After having learned the number and the phonetic sounds, as well as each word you will associate with each number/phonetic sound, you next associate a strong visual image of each word that corresponds to each number. For example, a mental picture of *tea* will always represent the number *1*.

Having learned (really learned) the three permanent steps of the phonetic system, you are equipped to utilize the system as an aid in remembering items in and out of sequence as well as backward, by twos, by threes, and so on. To remember lists of words, such as supplies that you must obtain from the supply room, you mentally link—in a strong visual image—each learned word with the supply item occupying that numbered position; if the fourteenth supply item were scissors, you might picture a gigantic tree (remember, 14 = t + r = tree) with thousands of silver scissors as branches. This system is also useful for remembering numbers. For instance, to remember the telephone number, 996-8043, you would use what you learned in step one and convert the numbers to their corresponding letters: p p j f z r m. Then you would create a word, phrase, or sentence that includes these letters (as well as vowels and y, h, and w, which do not count when you are decoding); your phrase might be one similar to this one: *Papa Joy of zoo room*. To recall the telephone number, you would recall the phrase and then decode it.

rhyming

Rhyming, too, can facilitate learning and recall. How many of us recall a rhyme in order to determine, for example, the number of days in March ("Thirty days hath September. . . .") or the spelling of *receive* and *freight* ("Use *i* before *e*, except after *c*, or when sounded like *a* as in *neighbor* and *weigh*; the exceptions are the *weird foreigner seizes neither leisure* nor sport at its *height*.")? A more complex rhyming device is the **peg-word system**. This system involves three steps:

peg-word system

1. Learning a number-word rhyme
2. Associating vivid mental images with each number-word combination
3. Using vivid association to interact (link) each to-be-remembered item in its sequence with the corresponding item in the peg-word sequence

The first two steps, which must be learned well (forward and backward), are permanent; only the to-be-remembered items change. The rhyme, though it differs slightly among memory training specialists, may be as follows: "One is bun, two is glue, three is key, four is store, five is drive, six is mix, seven is heaven, eight is ape, nine is dine, and ten is pen."[17] Having learned the complete rhyme, you then associate a mental picture with each number-word combination in the rhyme; for example, for "one is bun," you might visualize a gigantic red hamburger bun sun-tanning atop McDonald's golden arches. After creating your own images for the complete rhyme and becoming familiar with both rhyme and images, you associate each item to be learned with its corresponding number-word/image in the peg-word sequence. To illustrate, suppose you use the peg-word system to remember

Developing Purposeful Listening Skills

the tasks you have been told to accomplish during the day. For the first task—to type a letter of complaint to the Consumer Protection Agency—you might visualize yourself angrily typing as you are sitting in a leaking swimming pool being held up by the suntanned, red hamburger bun that is atop McDonald's golden arches. The remaining tasks would also be visually associated, in order of priority, with the peg-word rhyme. This system has been proven to result in high levels of recall.[18]

Mnemonic devices—or memory tricks such as acronyms, acrostics, and key word—also are commonly used to improve the memory. Two closely related mnemonic devices are acronyms and acrostics. **Acronyms** are letter cues such as NATO (North Atlantic Treaty Organization), EPA (Environmental Protection Agency), AIDS (Acquired Immune Deficiency Syndrome), PUSH (People United to Serve Humanity), RAM (Random Access Memory), and DOS (Disk Operating System). Similar to acronyms are acrostics. In **acrostics** the letters of a word or the first letter of each word in a sentence represents an item of information to be remembered. Coakley remembers from her elementary school days an acrostic that her teacher taught to help the students learn to spell the word *geography*: George's eldest oldest girl rode a pig home yesterday. Other examples of acrostic sentences are (1) *Every good boy does fine* (representing the lines on the treble clef: EGBDF); (2) *Bless my dear aunt Sally* (presenting the correct order for algebraic operations: brackets, multiply, divide, add, and subtract); (3) *Do men ever visit Boston?* (relating the ranking of English titles: duke, marquis, earl, viscount, and baron); and (4) *Mother visits every Monday, just stays until noon period* (presenting the sequential order of the planets: Mercury, Venus, Earth, Mars, Jupiter, Saturn, Uranus, Neptune, and Pluto). These four examples assist one in remembering items in sequential order.

To remember items that are not sequential, you might list the first letter of each item to be remembered, then rearrange the letters until you create a word, phrase, or sentence. To illustrate this technique, you might remember the cabinet posts by creating the sentence, *Hail the D.C. jets* (representing secretaries of health, agriculture, interior, labor, transportation, housing and urban development, energy, defense, commerce, justice, education, treasury, and state). Examples of acrostic words are HOMES (representing the Great Lakes: Huron, Ontario, Michigan, Erie, and Superior); PAIL (representing the four types of skin cuts: puncture, abrasion, incision, and laceration); STAB (representing four members of a quartet: soprano, tenor, alto, and bass); and ROY G. BIV (representing the ordered colors of the visible spectrum: red, orange, yellow, green, blue, indigo, and violet). A third type of mnemonic device is the **key word**, which involves creating a story around key words that sound like the names of the to-be-remembered items or words. For example, to remember the ordering of the twelve cranial nerves, you might create the following story: "At the *oil factory* (olfactory nerve) the *optician* (optic) looked for the *occupant* (oculomotor) of the *truck* (trochlear). He was searching because *three gems* (trigeminal) had been

mnemonic devices

acronyms

acrostics

key word

abducted (abducents) by a man who was hiding his *face* (facial) and *ears* (acoustic). A *glossy photograph* (glossopharyngeal) had been taken of him, but it was too *vague* (vagus) to use. He appeared to be *spineless* (spinal accessory) and *hypocritical* (hypoglossal)."[19]

categorical clustering

Still another memory technique is **categorical clustering**, an organizational technique that one uses systematically to modify incoming information by imposing structure on unstructured information. This technique, although not helpful in recalling items in a sequence, will assist one in free recall. For example, if you were given a list of words, such as rose, dog, apple, mouse, daisy, lemon, and so on, to recall, you would cluster the items categorically (rose / daisy, apple / lemon, dog / mouse, etc.) and thus remember them more easily. There is substantial evidence that this technique facilitates recall.[20]

chunking

Finally, a memory technique described as **chunking** involves combining single elements into larger units. Although this technique can be useful in transferring information to the LTM (as it is, for example, for those who learn the English alphabet by dividing the twenty-six letters into three chunks with each chunk containing two elements, each element containing two units, and each unit containing one to four letters: "[(ab-cd) (ef-g)] [(hi-jk) (lmno-p)] [(qrs-tuv) (w-xyz)]"[21]), it is frequently used to retain items in the STM (e.g., while one is taking the first two parts of the *Brown-Carlsen Listening Comprehension Test*[22] or the first two parts of the *Kentucky Comprehensive Listening Skills Test*).[23] As you may recall from chapter 3, Miller determined that the STM can hold only about seven units.[24] The letters *r, o, s, e, p, a,* and *n* would make up seven units; however, if you were to utilize chunking, combining the seven single units into larger units (forming the words, *rose* and *pan*), you would then have two units, and your STM would still have the capacity to hold five additional units. To illustrate further the chunking technique, suppose you are asked to recall these seven words: *sacrifice, fly, run, and, hit, drag,* and *bunt*. A person unfamiliar with baseball terminology would probably use seven units (the seven words) to retain this information, whereas a baseball fan would likely use only three units by chunking, or combining, these seven units into three: *sacrifice fly, run and hit,* and *drag bunt*. Thus, we see that chunking allows us to retain more information in the STM.

Another way to use chunking is to create one word to represent several letters in sequence; for instance, to retain the letters *t, n, i,* and *o,* you might use one unit, the word *attention*—a word that contains in sequence the four letters / four units. One must be aware, however, that the use of chunking in this way will be effective in retaining information only if one can correctly decode the chunk and recall its components. In other words, remembering *attention* will not be useful if you do not recall the correct sequential letters that the word represents (*t, n, i,* and *o,* not *a, e, t,* and *n*). Still another way that chunking can be used is to recall numbers. For instance, to remember a long number, such as 8153219, you might break up the number into a series of two- or three-digit numbers (81-532-19, 815-32-19, etc.). Experts at remembering through chunking use fewer words per chunk, focus more on beginnings of sentences, and select specific vocal intonation and cadence during rehearsal.[25]

Although the previously described memory techniques have been proven to facilitate recall, some memory experts do not use many of these techniques in their day-to-day lives. Psychologists Cavanaugh, Park, and Smith, who surveyed sixty-eight colleagues actively involved in memory research, found that their respondents' least favorite techniques included the loci system, link method, phonetic system, and peg-word method. Rather, these memory experts most often used and recommended the following: making written notes and lists; clustering items categorically; using placement (such as placing an umbrella near the door after rain had been forecast); engaging in rehearsal; and telling others to remind them of something.[26] Memory specialist Robin West has suggested that the main reason the responding experts had not favored some of the formal memory devices may have been that not enough research has been done on their practical application in day-to-day tasks.[27] Nevertheless, we agree with West that the possible benefits of such methods should not be discounted unless future experiential evidence proves that they have little practical value.

Strategies for Remembering Names

American listeners' number one memory complaint is not how to improve their memory of dictionary terms or multiple-digit numbers; rather, it is how to remember people's names.[28] Although there is no specific technique for remembering names, there are several steps to take and a number of strategies to use to remember names more effectively. You will observe that many of these steps/strategies, such as attending to, rehearsing, associating, and visualizing images, are based on what we have already learned about memory improvement. Lorayne and Lucas describe remembering names in a series of three steps: learning the name, learning the face, and linking the name and the face.[29]

Step 1: Learn the name. To remember the name, you must first hear the name correctly and attend to it; that is, you must really listen to it. If you did not clearly hear it, ask the person to repeat it until you do clearly hear it. Second, discuss the person's name with him or her; ask for its spelling, its pronunciation, and/or its origin. Ask whether the name has a special meaning, and/or ask whether the person knows of a special way to help you remember the name. Third, consider whether you know anyone with a similar name; if you do, tell the person. Also, rehearse the name silently to help transfer the name to the LTM. Additionally, state the person's name several times during the conversation—when you are introduced, while you are conversing, and when you are leaving. Later, repeat the name to yourself and write it down. Last, associate the name with some ridiculous image. If the person's name is Cal Ripkin, for example, visualize a monstrous cow and its kin—miniature purple cows—ripping down a fence, piece by piece, so that they can graze in a more fertile field.

remembering names

learn the name

Step 2: Learn the face. Look, really look, at the person; concentrate on his or her face. Then select *one* outstanding feature (or any feature if none is outstanding) that will help you remember the face. Let us say, for example, that Cal Ripkin's outstanding facial feature is his receding hairline.

Step 3: Link the name and face. To link the name and face, add another image to the mental picture that you have already created. For our example, we might visualize the monstrous cow stacking each ripped-down fence piece on its horns (across its forehead). With this mental addition, you have linked the name to the face. It is essential that you remember the purpose of creating the absurd mental pictures. You are forcing yourself to be aware—to concentrate; you are attending to the name and face and, thus, increasing the chances that you will transfer the information to the LTM. Two additional memory strategies that do not involve creating ridiculous images but can facilitate learning and recalling names are composing a rhyme about a person's name (such as, Steady Eddie Murray is never in a hurry) and associating the person's name with his or her work (such as, Jim Palmer throws a palm ball in the gym).

The effectiveness of the memory techniques presented in this section is supported by experimental findings in the laboratory as well as by experiential findings outside of the laboratory. Unfortunately, unless a person is trained or given specific instructions in the use of these techniques, he or she does not spontaneously utilize many of them. Since memory is so closely related to comprehensive listening, one way that a listener can improve such comprehensive listening is to improve the ability to remember. An effective way to begin this improvement is to use these as well as other memory techniques, which are limited only to one's own creativity.

Concentration

Another significant variable to effectiveness in comprehensive listening (as well as in any type of listening) is the listener's ability to concentrate or pay attention. **Concentration** on the sender's message, in fact, may be the listener's most difficult task. Quite frequently, we hear senders complaining about their intended listeners' lack of concentration or poor attention, and almost as frequently, we hear listeners bemoaning their own lack of concentration or poor attention. Indeed, lack of concentration is a pervasive problem that existed long before television, the medium commonly mentioned as a major cause of listeners' poor attention spans. Approximately twenty years before television became a household item in most American homes, former president Franklin Delano Roosevelt suspected that those who passed through receiving lines did not really pay attention to what he said to them. His suspicions were confirmed when he reportedly said to one dignitary, as they shook hands, "I shot my grandmother this morning," and the dignitary replied, "How lovely! What a splendid celebration."

Unfortunately, recent studies and testimonials indicate that the attention of listeners apparently has not improved since Roosevelt's time. For example, psychophysiologist Thomas Mulholland tested the attention spans of forty young television viewers by attaching to each an instrument that shut off the television set whenever each youngster's brain produced many alpha waves (which are normally associated with daydreaming or falling asleep). Mulholland found that even though the children were told to concentrate, only a few could keep the television set on for more than thirty seconds.[30] To our knowledge, no similar experiment has been conducted in the classroom; however, those in education are well aware of the frequent complaints of teachers regarding students' poor attention spans.

Although children may have difficulty concentrating, they are often quick to recognize that adults do not always pay attention either. Two third-grade students, for instance, made these comments about their parents: "They don't look at me, or they just walk away" and "Sometimes you think they're listening to you, and maybe they're walking around or talking to someone else."[31] Adults' lack of concentration extends to television viewing, according to William F. Buckley. Commenting on a 1983 Public Broadcasting Service series highlighting great orators in American history, Buckley notes one of the problems that the series' directors had to confront: "The television audience . . . is not trained to listen—unstroked, no peanuts or candy bars, no fireworks or bullets or one-liners—to 15 uninterrupted minutes."[32] Viewers' short attention spans may even be encouraged by television news programs whose objectives, according to Robert MacNeil (of the MacNeil-Lehrer news hour), "is to keep everything brief, not to strain the attention of anyone but instead to provide constant stimulation through variety, novelty, action, and movement. You are required . . . to pay attention to no concept, no character, and no problem for more than a few seconds at a time."[33] Concentration also is a problem adults have at work. Watson and Smeltzer found that while business students ranked internal distractions and business practitioners ranked environmental distractions as the most serious barrier to effective listening at work, both groups ranked inattentiveness as the third most serious barrier.[34]

Some Reasons for Lack of Concentration

Though few research studies have investigated *why* listeners do not concentrate and why they have poor attention spans, many reasons, such as the following, have been adduced:

reasons for lack of concentration

1. Listeners may feel that time constraints require them to divide their attention energy between/among various stimuli rather than to give their undivided attention to any one stimulus. At home, they do family and household tasks, operate appliances, read, watch television, eat, do homework, and so on, *while* they engage in conversations. At school, they prepare yesterday's unfinished assignments, plan today's events, prearrange tomorrow's activities, and so on, *while* they participate in classroom lecture-discussions. At work, they study schedules, perform job tasks, operate equipment, design future projects, and so on, *while* they take part in telephone and face-to-face communication

interactions. After dividing their attention energy by day, however, they still frequently do not get sufficient rest at night, and, thus, their lack of alertness the following day further adds to their inability to concentrate on senders' messages. Being so time-oriented in a fast-paced society, listeners often become selfish and impatient. They think they cannot afford to give their time to only one stimulus, and they are too impatient to attend to senders who, for example, provide detailed accounts of events, are repetitious, have poor communication skills, discuss subjects with which the listeners think they are familiar enough, and so on. Hence, many listeners attend to only portions of senders' messages, assign incomplete meanings, and then direct their attention energy to other pressing concerns.

2. Listeners misdirect their attention energy, due to causes other than time constraints. According to Erving Goffman, standard forms of misinvolvement include the following:

    a. **External preoccupation**—being easily distracted by external stimuli and, thus, concentrating on unrelated stimuli such as the hot room, the sound of an airplane, a person walking down the hall, or the senders' appearance

    b. **Self-consciousness**—focusing on how well or how poorly they are doing as interactants in communication situations

    c. **Interaction-consciousness**—focusing on how the interactions are going as, for instance, hosts and hostesses would during dinner parties

    d. **Other-consciousness**—focusing on other participants (their positive or negative communication skills, personal qualities, viewpoints, etc.)[35]

These four forms of misdirected attention energy, coupled with listeners expending energy on rehearsing what they are going to say during their turns to speak rather than on listening to others' verbal and nonverbal messages, all contribute to listeners' poor concentration.

3. Listeners may be too ego-involved. They may focus on internal distractions such as physical pains, hunger, inappropriate clothing, injured feelings resulting from senders' use of emotional triggers, personal concerns, and so on, rather than concentrating on senders' messages. Also, listeners may be so "sure" that they "know" what the senders are going to say or so resent the senders' opposing viewpoints that they focus on planning their responses rather than on listening to the senders' complete messages.

4. Listeners may lack curiosity or drive. Rather than attending to what they do not know or what they do not understand, they avoid that which demands concentration. Such listeners prefer comfort and laziness to challenge and exertion.

5. Listeners have become conditioned not to pay attention to various stimuli. For instance, many messages are repeated so often that listeners have become used to attending to different portions of the same message each time it is repeated; our world is so noisy that listeners have learned to tune out many stimuli; and there is so much information presented daily that listeners have mastered ways to avoid information overload.

Underlying the five reasons for lack of concentration are three **additional factors**: lack of self-discipline, lack of self-motivation, and lack of responsibility. There is no doubt that listeners must be disciplined, motivated, and responsible if they are to concentrate on and be attentive to senders' messages. Just as mountain climbers and car racers must discipline themselves to direct their undivided attention to their tasks, so must listeners develop mental discipline to control distractions.

additional underlying factors

Self-discipline is much more easily practiced when listeners are personally motivated to listen. If each listener were as motivated to listen in all other listening situations as he or she is when being told he or she had been awarded a scholarship, been promoted, or won the grand prize in a contest, concentration would seldom be a listening problem. Unfortunately, listeners do not have this same motivation in all other listening situations. However, they can develop a high degree of motivation if they approach each listening experience as opportunists looking for what will bring them personal rewards—enjoyment/pleasure, friendship/love from those important to them, respect from those whom they admire, praise from those who "count," fulfillment of basic needs, monetary gains, job advancements, and/or information they can use in some way that will be beneficial to them. Listeners are not prophets and, thus, do not know when these rewards will come or when the results will prove to be beneficial. Therefore, they must concentrate on each sender's complete message so that they will not prevent themselves from gaining rewards that may be useful to them (now or in the future)—in their personal lives, schooling, and/or jobs—or to individuals important to them. Listening for "what is in the message for me or for someone important to me" will provide each listener with intrinsic motivation to concentrate.

Having an opportunistic attitude not only helps listeners to provide their own motivation to listen (rather than depending on senders to provide this incentive) but also helps them to accept responsibility for the success of each communication interaction. Accepting responsibility entails single-minded involvement in each sender's message, not ruling out a message as "uninteresting" or useless until the entire message has been searched for some personal value, searching through an anticipated "I've-heard-it-all-before" message for information that was not relevant earlier but may be relevant now, being responsive, and caring how their listening behavior affects the senders. In addition, each listener assumes more responsibility and improves concentration if he or she internalizes the following behaviors.

Behaviors Leading to Improved Concentration

**behaviors leading
to improved
concentration**

To improve his or her concentration when listening, an effective listener engages in the following thirteen behaviors:

1. Is honest with the sender when he or she is having difficulty focusing on the sender's message due to being too tired, too busy, or too pressured by other concerns and then establishes another time to continue the interaction.

2. Eats foods that stimulate an active, energetic mind. While high-fat foods slow down the mental process, high-protein foods (such as skim milk, low-fat yogurt, beans, chicken, very lean beef, and fish) serve as mind nutrients that increase one's mental acuity.[36]

3. Takes measures (such as exercise, meditation, and deep breathing) to reduce stress, because stress causes the listener to expend so much energy on anxiety that he or she has little remaining energy to expend on the sender's message. Cole-Hamilton suggests one way to relieve stress: Recognize which brain hemisphere is stressed and then switch to the other hemisphere. For example, if you are depressed or overwrought (right hemisphere stress), do math, write factual prose, or organize (left hemisphere activities). Or, if you feel time-stressed or overburdened (left hemisphere stress), sing or play a sport (right hemisphere activities).[37]

4. Self-questions in order to be more attentive: Am I giving my single-minded attention to the sender? Why or why not? Am I inwardly listening to myself and outwardly listening to the sender? What am I considering more important than the sender's message? Can these concerns be set aside until a later, more appropriate time? Am I paying attention to paying attention, or am I paying attention to the sender's message?

5. Deals effectively with external distractions (such as the soft volume or extreme attractiveness of the speaker, the whispering or fidgeting of other receivers, or the operating of the television or unusual wall decorations in the communication environment) by (a) eliminating the distractions (e.g., moving closer to the speaker or asking him or her to speak louder, politely asking others to stop talking or moving to another area, or turning off the television) or (b) ignoring the distractions by practicing self-discipline and giving full attention to the speaker's message.

6. Deals effectively with internal distractions (e.g., physical conditions such as feeling the pressure of new shoes or the pain of a headache, external conditions such as not liking the speaker or having an overloaded agenda, or psychological conditions such as being concerned about the health of a friend or the status of one's marriage) by engaging in the following:
   a. Practicing self-discipline to control the directions of his or her thoughts

b. Freeing the mind of unrelated concerns to permit the speaker's ideas to enter the mind

c. Recognizing the presence of internal distractions as quickly as possible to control their impact

d. Acknowledging that while personal concerns can be dealt with at a more appropriate time, most speakers' messages are temporary in nature and, thus, must be attended to at the time they are presented, or they will be lost

e. Developing the habit of writing down any unrelated, internal concern that appears while he or she is listening and then dealing with the concern after, rather than during, the listening experience

7. Schedules a time each day to deal with concerns written down earlier that day and also to engage in daydreaming, an activity that is deemed beneficial to one's psychological health.

8. Develops the desire to learn as much as he or she can by realizing that the curious listener is a concentrative listener as he or she explores, discovers, and grows.

9. Does not fake attention, for he or she knows that attempting to deceive speakers only results in denying him- or herself of opportunities to learn.

10. Listens with the intent to ask the sender the most penetrating question he or she can devise.

11. Listens with the intent to share each sender's message with another person and then actually shares the message (i.e., reviews the details, reports the conversation, retells the story, recounts the event, etc.) with someone within the next few hours.

12. Listens—at the group, public, and mass levels of communication—as if the sender were speaking to him or her individually.

13. Practices the appropriate listening skills, as they are presented in this book, in each communication situation in which he or she is an active participant.

Vocabulary

Another variable that appears to influence the listener's comprehensive ability is size of **vocabulary**. Although the precise relationship between listening and vocabulary has not been determined, "it can be concluded tentatively that size of listening vocabulary is probably an important variable in listening comprehension"[38] just as it is an important factor in reading. Since the assignment of meaning is an integral part of the listening process, we must have a sufficiently developed vocabulary to expand our categorical system or schema and minimize our categorical or conceptual errors. Only then can we assign more reliable meanings to the stimuli to which we attend.

vocabulary

Four Functional Vocabularies

four functional vocabularies

As communicators, we have **four functional vocabularies** that vary in size. Until we reach approximately age twelve, our largest functional vocabulary is our listening vocabulary (followed, in order, by our speaking, reading, and writing vocabularies). After age twelve, our listening vocabulary is generally surpassed by our reading vocabulary (and followed, in order, by our writing and speaking vocabularies).[39] Although our listening vocabulary generally ranks, throughout our lives, as either our largest or second largest functional vocabulary, it is still quite limited when we consider that the average adult's personal vocabulary consists of only about forty thousand words (which is a small fraction of the estimated one million words in the English language).[40] After noting how the average adult communicator's functional vocabularies vary in size, one may initially conclude that if the speaking vocabulary (estimated to be about ten thousand words)[41] of the average adult speaker is smaller than the listening vocabulary of the average adult listener, a listener should encounter few problems in assigning meaning. However, individuals' general vocabularies are as unique as are individuals themselves. While two communicators may share many words, the same two communicators may not share many others. Thus, to improve our listening effectiveness, we must continually work toward improving our listening vocabularies to narrow the vocabulary gap (as well as the understanding gap) that exists between us as listeners and others as speakers.

Steps toward Improving General and Listening Vocabularies

There are several steps we can take to improve our general as well as our listening vocabularies.

Step 1: Develop a genuine interest in words.[42] Fortunately, some of us have already developed this interest. It may have been instilled by another individual, perhaps an instructor, a writer, or a parent, who was enthralled with words and shared his or her fascination with us. It may have arisen within us, perhaps by chance, as we completed our first crossword puzzle, consulted our first dictionary or thesaurus, or composed our first composition. If, on the other hand, we have yet to develop a genuine interest in words, we should strive to remedy this deficiency by taking courses (such as courses in vocabulary building, word study, dialects, or language history) or by establishing our own self-study programs (such as studying vocabulary books, thesauri, and general, specialized, and unabridged dictionaries; developing a program built around the material in this section; or completing the vocabulary exercises listed at the end of this chapter). Regardless of how our interest in words—their origins, meanings, functions, structures, subtle differences, and beauty—begins, this interest will provide the impetus we need to continue building our vocabularies.

Step 2: Develop vocabulary acquisition skills. Two basic skills, which can assist us in learning new words and their meanings, are the abilities to

structural analysis

analyze the structure and the contexts of words. The first skill, **structural analysis**, requires that we initially learn key root words as well as common prefixes and suffixes. Then, when we encounter unfamiliar words, we can break them down, if possible, into their component parts (i.e., their prefixes, root words, and suffixes) and apply our previously learned knowledge of structure to the unfamiliar words to determine their meanings. To illustrate the word power that structural analysis can give us, we shall consider the following fourteen words that, according to James I. Brown, "contain prefix and root elements found in over 14,000 relatively common words or close to an estimated 100,000 of unabridged dictionary size":[43]

Word	Prefix	Common Meaning	Root	Common Meaning
precept	pre-	before	capere	take, seize
detain	de-	away, down	tenere	hold, have
intermittent	inter-	between, among	mittere	send
offer	ob-	against	ferre	bear, carry
insist	in-	into	stare	stand
monograph	mono-	alone, one	graphein	write
epilogue	epi-	upon	legein	say, study of
aspect	ad-	to, toward	specere	see
uncomplicated	un-	not	plicare	
	com-	together, with		
nonextended	non-	not	tendere	stretch
	ex-	out, beyond		
reproduction	re-	back, again	ducere	lead
	pro-	forward, for		
indisposed	in-	not	ponere	put, place
	dis-	apart, not		
oversufficient	over-	above	facere	make, do
	sub-	under		
mistranscribe	mis-	wrong	scribere	write
	trans-	across, beyond[44]		

Having learned these twenty prefixes and fourteen root words, along with eight common suffixes (-*able*—capable of; -*ate*—to make; -*ed*—indicating the past participle verb form or an adjective; -*ence*—act or quality of; -*er* or -*or*— one who; -*ous*—characterized by; and -*tion*—act or state of), we can deter-mine—through structural analysis—the meanings, for example, of the following words:

adscript	epigraph	monologue	remise
complice	explicate	nondeferrable	scrivener
defect	inductile	obstinate	subtend
deference	inexplicit	oversubscribe	tenacious
desist	intercessor	prescript	transposition
distend	misinferred	prospectus	untenable

The second skill, learning the meanings of unfamiliar words from their contexts, requires that we initially learn **contextual clues** that speakers

contextual clues

frequently use. Then, when we as listeners encounter unfamiliar words, we apply our knowledge of contextual clues by noting the meanings of familiar words that surround the unfamiliar words and determining whether or not they provide us with clues to the meanings of the unfamiliar words. There are two main types of contextual clues with which we should be familiar: semantic (word meaning) and syntactic (sentence structure) clues. Among

semantic clues

the **semantic clues** are the following:

- **Synonym clues** (often signaled by *and*): Jim's dull, *lethargic*, and sluggish manner made us question the success of his recovery.
- **Contrasting clues** (often signaled by *but, not, although, however, nevertheless, instead,* and *rather*): Janet's spaghetti sauce has always been quite flavorful, but the sauce she made today is *insipid*.
- **Description clues:** Some animals are *herbivorous*. They feed chiefly on grasses, plants, and seeds.
- **Example clues** (often signaled by *for example, like, such as, in the way that,* and the pronouns *this, that, these,* and *those*): At their daughter's graduation party, the Chobots *regaled* the guests with a rock band, a fortune teller, and a delicious meal.
- **Summary clues:** At home, Susan willingly helps her younger siblings. At school, she actively participates in class discussions and activities. At work, she eagerly completes her tasks. Indeed, Susan's display of *alacrity* makes others envious of her.
- **Explanation clues** (often signaled by *that is, by, I mean, or, is, in other words,* and *in short*): The romance was *ephemeral*—that is, short-lived.
- **Experience clues** (relating one's own experiences to the context): His mouth was *agape* as he, standing within the Roman Colosseum, was filled with awe and wonder. (The listener has experienced this facial expression when he or she has been filled with awe and wonder.)
- **Mood, intent, tone, or situation clues:** Lisa's arguing, pleading, and threatening had no impact on changing her father's original decision; he remained *adamant* regarding his refusal to allow Lisa to work at the beach during the summer.

syntactic or sentence structure clues

The second type of contextual clues is **syntactic or sentence structure clues**. Among these clues are those found in *sentence patterns* (such as in "Psoriasis is one example. . . .", *psoriasis* is a noun, *is* is a verb, *one* is an adjective, *example* is a noun); *inflectional endings* (such as in "He deferred. . . .", defer*red* signals a verb); *markers* (such as in "A heliotrope is. . . .", *a* signals a noun; in "After the neolithic period. . . .", *after* signals an adverb phrase or clause; in "She has retained. . . .", *has* signals a verb; and in "Between the cold photosphere and. . . .", *between* signals a prepositional phrase); and, possibly in oral sentences, *pauses* (such as in "An example of a predator—an animal that hunts and kills other animals for food—is a lion," the dashes of the written sentence represent pauses in an oral statement).

Step 3: Get firsthand experiences with words. Although using contextual clues is generally recognized as being "the best single way of developing word power,"[45] we cannot doubt the effectiveness of a final way of improving our vocabularies: learning new words by having firsthand experiences that are associated with the words. For example, when we take a computer course, attend a computer exhibit, or operate a computer, we learn terms such as *interface, modem, icons, gigabyte,* and *expansion slot.* Thus, by broadening our personal experiences and subjecting ourselves to a wide variety of listening experiences—especially experiences involving complex material that is more challenging than that to which we are generally accustomed—we can broaden our word power and therefore improve our comprehensive listening.

Additional Variables

Relationships between listening and many other variables have been investigated by listening scholars; however, many factors have contributed to the delay of precise conclusions regarding the variables that influence listening comprehension. Among the contributing factors are these: (1) there has been a lack of scientifically controlled experiments; (2) not enough is known about the validity and reliability of the listening tests used in the studies; thus, many of the "listening" tests may be measuring abilities other than listening, while many of the variables may involve measurement of the same general abilities; and (3) much of the research has not been coordinated and collated. Although these factors have prevented conclusive results, the following **additional variables**—as measured by statistical correlations[46]— **additional variables** currently appear to be slightly to moderately related to listening comprehension: *age* (with students gradually improving as they advance through school);[47] *intelligence* (with the estimated correlation being .46);[48] *motivation* (with subjects—who had been forewarned that recall tests would follow the presentation of material, promised monetary rewards for listening and recalling, and mentally prepared by the anticipatory sets created by the experimenter—scoring significantly higher on listening tests than those subjects who had not been forewarned, promised rewards, or mentally prepared);[49] *scholastic achievement* (with correlations ranging from .24 to .82);[50] *speaking ability* (with correlations ranging from .36 to .79);[51] *reading comprehension* (with the average correlation estimated at being about .53 by Erickson and .59 by Duker);[52] *verbal ability* (with correlations ranging from .37 to .76);[53] *language and study skills* (with correlations ranging from .25 to .67);[54] *organizational ability* (with correlations ranging from .36 to .53);[55] *rate of presentation* (to be discussed later in this chapter); and *cultural status* (with correlations ranging from .33 to .48).[56] The relationships between listening and the following variables are presently less conclusive than the variables previously cited: *sex, personality characteristics, interest in the subject matter discussed, auditory acuity, experience in listening, speech training, notetaking ability, visibility of the speaker, the speaker's use of gestures, speaker effectiveness, source* *credibility, difficulty of material, time of day, room temperature and ventilation, seating, position in family,* and *size of family.* As we can see, additional and more controlled research investigating the relationships between listening and these variables, as well as other variables, is greatly needed for us to better understand the variables involved in listening comprehension.

Skills Involved in Comprehensive Listening

Although at present we do not know all of the variables or all of the sub-skills involved in listening comprehension, scholars in the field of communication and related areas of study have provided us with several findings that, when put into practice, can enhance our listening comprehension.

Capitalizing on the Differential between Speech Speed and Thought Speed

capitalizing on the differential between speech speed and thought speed

Ralph G. Nichols, whose research in comprehensive listening pioneered the field, cautions that the efficient comprehensive listener should be careful not to waste the **differential between speech speed and thought speed**. As listeners, we can think (or process) about 500 words per minute while the normal speaking rate is about 125 to 150 words per minute. Thus, we may have close to 400 words of thinking time available to us each minute we are listening.

Because we can think so much faster than speakers can speak, we tend to "tune in" and "tune out" during the message; while we are "tuning out," we are attending to other stimuli. We can imagine the danger here when some other stimulus attracts more attention than the message; we then cease concentrating on the message. The efficient comprehensive listener will be certain to "tune in" with regularity; instead of attending to external and/or internal stimuli, he or she will actively use the **spare thinking time** by engaging in the following mental acts:

efficient use of spare thinking time

- Identifying the speaker's purpose(s)
- Paraphrasing what has been presented
- Relating the message content to what he or she already knows and/or has experienced
- Reviewing and summarizing what has been presented
- Identifying and determining the relationship between/among main ideas
- Recognizing verbal and nonverbal transitional cues and determining their meanings
- Weighing the evidence used
- Applying points of support to his or her own life
- Predicting the speaker's next point and then confirming or negating the prediction
- Formulating questions
- Noting and assigning meaning to nonverbal messages being presented

- Listening for what is not said by searching for deeper—and possibly hidden—meanings in the speaker's verbal and nonverbal messages

Nichols emphasizes the importance of using our spare thinking time efficiently:

> Not capitalizing on thought speed is our greatest single handicap. The differential between thought speed and speech speed breeds false feelings of security and mental tangents. Yet, through listening training, this same differential can be readily converted into our greatest asset.[57]

A relatively new research technique may help the comprehensive listener reduce the time differential between speech speed and thought speed. Communication scholars have been studying the effects of **compressed speech**—speech that consists of increasing the word rate of a previously recorded message without essential alteration. The process was first applied by having the speaker speak more rapidly. It was then accomplished by speeding up the recorder. Next, a cut-and-splice method was employed. Now, material can be compressed electronically. Until 1950, most scholars believed that "increasing rate led to a decrease in listening efficiency."[58]

compressed speech

Recently, however, researchers have demonstrated that (1) speed of speech can be effectively doubled without impairing intelligibility[59] and that (2) speaking rates can be increased with 50 percent compression without loss of comprehension.[60] The optimal speaking rate for comprehension appears to be between 275 and 300 words per minute.[61]

Since we think much more rapidly than the normal conversational speech rate, it is evident that we can handle auditory input at a much faster rate. Many studies have supported this view. Foulke, and others, studying the effect of compressed speech on the comprehension ability of 291 blind children, found that there was no significant loss of comprehension of messages recorded at up to 275 words per minute.[62] It has also been found that sighted students benefit from using time-compressed speech. In 1974, Short, using a Syracuse University population of 90 students, found that subjects who used variable speed compressors saved significant amounts of time (an average time savings of 32%) and scored significantly higher on post-tests than those subjects who learned the same material at normal speed. In addition, 70 percent of those who used variable speech adapted to it quickly and liked listening at faster than normal rates.[63]

Currently, compressed speech is being used in many segments of society, including business, education, and public services. In industry, it has been found to be a cost-effective tool. In addition to providing its users with a time-saving means to review recorded dictation, check recorded meetings/reports/and telephone answering tapes, and compile taped inventory records, it has been found to improve the concentration and comprehension of new employees when it has been used in training programs. In the field of education, it has led to substantial savings in time. Instructors can preview auditory material faster, media specialists can review media seminar tapes in less time, and students—as they listen to taped lecture material—can decrease their review time while they increase their comprehension ability. Still another educational application of compressed speech is its instructional use in foreign languages, English as a second language, reading comprehension, and tutorial programs. Rome, who originated the use of speech compressors in the autotutorial program at Western Connecticut State College, believes speech compressors have a promising future:

> We can finally provide something effective for those students who do not learn best through the visual modality. With the introduction of lower cost rate-controlled recorders, we have a viable alternative for learning which may rival the printing press as a way of disseminating information.[64]

Law enforcement officers and hospital personnel also have found compressed speech useful. It can assist them in providing professional training, reviewing and previewing auditory data, checking logged calls and interviews, rapidly transferring information between shifts, and providing professional updating. The current use of compressed speech indicates that it offers widespread potential for application in improving the listening and learning of those involved in these as well as many other segments of society.

The use of compressed speech has extended beyond business, education, and public services to television, radio, and videotapes. Both television commercials and television programs are presently being time-compressed. An estimated one out of ten commercials is compressed,[65] generally by a subtle, barely perceptible 15 percent. Although 15-percent compression may not seem very significant to us, to advertisers it means cutting costs. For instance, a 35-second commercial aired during the 1994 Super Bowl would have cost over one-million dollars. The same commercial, run in 30 seconds, would have saved the advertiser over $150,000.[66] Likewise, advertisers running a 35-second commercial in 30 seconds on ABC's regularly scheduled series, "Home Improvement," during the 1994 season would have saved over $83,000.[67] Not only do advertisers save money by compressing the rate of their commercials, but it appears that they also increase the attention and retention of their listeners. LaBarbera, Shoaf, and MacLachlan found that subjects who listened to (and viewed) commercials increased in speed by 25 percent had higher levels of attentional effort and greater recall two days later than did subjects who listened to (and viewed) commercials played at their regular speed.[68] Perhaps this comparison by Michael Klasco, director of research and development at Integrated Sound Systems, Incorporated, a New York time-compressor manufacturer, best explains the higher levels of attention energy: "If you're driving 30 m.p.h., you tend to daydream, but at 90 m.p.h. you pay attention."[69] Moreover, advertisers using compressed commercials may find that their listening viewers perceive rapid speakers as being more credible and more persuasive.[70] Furthermore, television stations throughout the country are compressing programs,[71] radio stations that play Top 40 songs often time-compress them, and videotape production houses are compressing movies to fit onto 90-minute cassettes (rather than the more expensive 120-minute cassettes) for home use.[72]

Speech compressors or rate-controlled recorders are now readily available (for example, at Radio Shack) and are fairly inexpensive. They could offer interesting demonstrations as to the possibilities of reducing time and improving listening comprehension. We should note, though, that despite the technological advances in compressed speech, its usefulness to the general listener remains limited. Just as speed readers have difficulty applying the speed-reading techniques to difficult technical material, "speed listeners" report little carryover to complex listening situations.

Listening for Main Ideas

One important skill, which can help to enhance our efficiency in using the speech speed thought speed differential, is knowing for what we should listen. Several scholars suggest that the efficient listener listens to acquire the main ideas from the message; he or she should concentrate primarily on the main points rather than on the supporting data. If you consider that we tend to be able to recall no more than 25 percent of what we listen to today, it is evident that we should strive to concentrate on understanding the key concepts of a message rather than the details that exemplify the concepts.

listening for main ideas

There are several ways we can become more adept at identifying the main idea(s) of an oral message, provided that the speaker clearly knows his or her purpose and direction. We must strive to identify the main idea of the entire message as well as the main concepts presented within the message. To help us identify the principal idea of the entire message (known also as the central idea or thesis statement), we must learn where most senders place the main idea. It may be stated in the title, stated shortly after the introduction has been presented, repeated throughout the speech (since senders often repeat important concepts), stated in the summary of the speech, or subtly implied (suggested) in the speech as a whole and recognized only after we have listened to the complete message. If the main idea is stated, we must learn to identify **transitions** that speakers use when they are introducing or discussing the main idea. Some of these transitions are the following:

transitional cues

"I want to make one impression on you, and that is. . . ."   "Today, we are going to discuss. . . ."

"Simply stated, the issue is. . . ."   "Let us today examine why. . . ."

"Today, we will be covering. . . ."   "There are three methods that we. . . ."

"Our subject this evening is. . . ."   "And so we can conclude that. . . ."

"In conclusion, then, I want you to understand that. . . ."   "To summarize, ..."

"In summing up, we must remember that. . . ."   "As can be seen, ..."

Efficient listeners must also know what **nonverbal behavioral changes** speakers often use when they are stating a main idea. For example, when terminating one idea and introducing a new one, speakers often change

nonverbal cues

their positioning by making body shifts (such as drawing back the legs or raising a foot when they are seated), pointing with or raising a hand, joining hands by placing one palm over the back of the other or by interlocking fingers, and so on.[73] If we become skilled in listening to and watching for these changes in rate, volume, pitch, bodily movements, gestures, eye contact, and other nonverbal cues, we will be able to identify more readily the main idea of a message. Moreover, when we are identifying the main idea, we must exercise caution that we not make it too broad (by including more than is in the message) or too narrow (by including only some concepts); we must be specific, yet comprehensive enough to include all of the relevant concepts that have been presented.

When identifying the principal concepts within a message (those concepts that are used to establish the main idea of a speech), we must have knowledge of many general **organizational patterns**. Among these patterns are the following:

organizational patterns

unfolding

Unfolding
Introduction
Statement of thesis sentence
Statement of first point
Discussion of first point
Statement of second point
Discussion of second point
Statement of third point
Discussion of third point, etc.
Conclusion

one-point

One-point
Introduction
Statement of thesis sentence
Example
Example
Example, etc.
Conclusion

partitioning

Partitioning
Introduction
Statement of thesis sentence
Restatement of thesis and division
Statement of first point
Discussion of first point
Restatement of first point
Statement of second point
Discussion of second point
Restatement of second point
Statement of third point
Discussion of third point

Developing Purposeful Listening Skills

Restatement of third point, etc.
Conclusion—Summary[74]

Furthermore, we must be aware of the previously mentioned nonverbal cues and numerous **other transitions**, such as "first," "along with," "not only . . . but also," "finally," "next in importance," "in addition to this," "on the other hand," "also," "following this step is," "a somewhat similar method is," "above all," "of even more importance," "in connection with this," "equally important," and "together with this." If we train ourselves to listen primarily for main ideas or concepts, we will not become so preoccupied with facts and details that we overlook the main ideas; we must be first idea listeners and then fact and detail listeners.

other transitional cues

Listening for Significant Details

After we have become proficient in listening for main ideas, we should then develop the skill of listening for significant details that the speaker uses to support his or her main ideas. These details may be in the form of facts, examples, statistics, restatements, anecdotes, personal incidents, analogies, descriptions, contrasts, definitions, or references to reliable sources. As we listen for essential details, we must again be aware of **transitions** that indicate that details are following. Some of these transitions are listed below:

listening for significant details

transitional cues

"for example"	"to illustrate this point"	"this can be seen by"
"for instance"	"to describe"	"that is"
"to explain"	"in other words"	"comparable to"
"the fact is"	"on the contrary"	"according to"
"namely"	"to be more specific"	"a case in point is"

By recognizing these transitional words, we can more readily identify supporting details. We must, however, distinguish between those details that are relevant and those that are irrelevant to the main ideas that the speaker is presenting. We must also separate what we have learned in the past from what we are listening to now if we hope to be accurate in our listening. Identifying the main ideas and supporting details and understanding the interrelationships between the ideas and details will aid us in assigning more reliable meanings to the sender's message.

Drawing Justifiable Inferences

Another skill the comprehensive listener should develop is the ability to **draw justifiable inferences**. Inferences (implications) are data that are not stated but are implied. Efficient listeners will not only listen to what is explicitly stated but also listen for what is implicitly suggested. Because each listener draws his or her own inferences, they are very personal and subject to error. Weaver stresses the importance of making inferences and

drawing justifiable inferences

the difficulty of separating personal meanings or interpretations from the speaker's meanings: "It is likely that the most important part of our communication is the part we infer. And yet we do this through our screen of personal biases, our needs, and our affective states."[75] The more we know about ourselves and our personal biases, needs, and emotions, the less likely we are to make errors in drawing inferences. The following steps will help us in drawing justifiable inferences:

1. Fully understand the stated ideas
2. Reason by logical thinking to the inferred idea
3. Determine the fairness or justice of the inferred idea
4. Base reasoning on the idea stated by the sender; do not be misled by your personal opinions, feelings, biases, or "what seems reasonable" but is not stated by the communicator

understand fully the stated idea

These four steps can be applied as we listen. Suppose we hear a woman who is running for county executive make this statement about her opponent: "How can you think of voting for him? He didn't even attend his own mother's funeral!" Our first step is to **understand fully the stated idea**, which—in our example—is in the form of a question and a statement. The question is why or for what reason(s) are we thinking of voting for her opponent; the statement is that her opponent was not present at his mother's funeral. Once we fully understand the stated idea, we should then apply the second step: **reason by logical thinking to the inferred idea**. In our example, the woman running for office wants us to vote for her; she does not want us to vote for her opponent. She wants to give us a reason for not voting for him. She *hopes* that we will infer, from her stated idea, that if her opponent did not care enough about his mother to attend her funeral, he certainly would not be responsive to the needs and concerns of us, most of whom are strangers. She *hopes* that if we draw the inference she wants us to draw, we will not want him to be our representative and, therefore, will not vote for him.

reason by logical thinking to the inferred idea

determine fairness or justice of inferred idea

Our third step is to **determine whether the inference we have drawn is justifiable or fair**. We have drawn the inference that she had hoped we would, but we do not have to accept what she silently said. Is the critical issue regarding her opponent's qualifications for county executive whether or not he attended his mother's funeral? Regardless of our personal feelings concerning the manner in which a person should cope with the death of a family member, a person's presence or absence at the funeral of a family member should not be the critical issue upon which we base our voting preference. We do not know, in fact, that he did not attend his mother's funeral; nor do we know why he was not present at the funeral, if he were not present. He could have been someplace where he could not be reached, he could have been a prisoner of war or a hostage, or he could be a person who prefers remembering a loved one as she or he was in life rather than in death. If we carefully analyze the justification of each

Developing Purposeful Listening Skills

inference we draw, as we have carefully analyzed this one, we will become more efficient listeners.

Let us now illustrate how listeners can apply the fourth step: **Base our reasoning on the stated idea rather than on personal views**. Suppose that we later hear the woman's opponent speak. In his speech he makes the following statement: "I spent the first fifteen years of my life in the slums and on welfare, and now I'm running for county executive." He *hopes* that we will infer from this statement that because he is a man who has overcome his poor beginnings and has become a strong, determined leader despite his early hardships, he can help us overcome our problems. However, this time we are misled by our personal views, and our personal meanings lead us to draw these inferences: Here is a man who, having been on welfare himself, will raise our taxes to provide more revenue for welfare assistance programs; then, he will provide more handouts to all the lazy, no-good people in our country. Because we often allow our personal views to be the basis of our reasoning, as we did in this illustration, we frequently make errors when drawing inferences.

base reasoning on the stated idea, not on personal views

Being aware of these four steps and practicing them should assist us in drawing justifiable inferences when the speaker does not explicitly state his or her position, specific details, or relationships. Such steps, then, can enhance our comprehension of the overall message.

Being an Effective Notetaker

Though few studies have correlated notetaking and efficient listening behavior, notetaking, when done properly, can be valuable to listener comprehension in many ways:

being an effective notetaker

values of notetaking

1. Notetaking can **improve our ability to concentrate** in lecture settings as well as in public listening situations. Experiments indicate that the behavioral involvement required for notetaking increases our attention to the message and increases the probability of retrieval of the message content later.[76]
2. Notetaking can **motivate us to take the initiative in putting the message content into our long-term memory system**. To facilitate this storing process, we must make the message content meaningful by rehearsing it and linking it to our existing store of information.
3. Notetaking tends to **make us more aware of various communication aspects**, such as organizational patterns (or lack of them), transitions, main ideas, supporting details, relevant (as well as irrelevant) content, and so on.
4. Notetaking can **"lock in print" information that we may need to refer to at a later time**. Research supports the point that, after a delayed period of time, notetakers are better able to recall information than those who do not take notes.[77]

Recommended Follow-Ups to Notetaking

To use notes effectively, we should—shortly after having taken notes—review them, clarify them, add to them, note any points about which we need additional information and obtain that information (from the sender or other sources) as soon as possible, and briefly summarize the notes (by noting the speaker's premises and assumptions, special meanings for terms, support, and conclusions). Moreover, we should list any ideas that may have come to us after we had listened to the presentation, reacted to the message (by noting points that we do not understand and points with which we agree and/or disagree), and restructured them so that they will be more meaningful to us now as well as at a later time. Adler strongly recommends that notetakers make a second set of notes that are more orderly, comprehensive, and critical than the original or "running" notes; he believes that "these concluding notes constitute the completion of the task of active listening."[78] Reviewing (rehearsing) our concluding notes will also aid us in retaining the information more permanently.[79]

Cornell System of reviewing notes

One recommended method of reviewing notes is the **Cornell System**. This system requires that listeners take notes on main ideas in a right-hand "Record" column, and then after the speaker completes the message, they summarize the recorded data by jotting down only key words and phrases in the left-hand "Recall" column. Shortly thereafter, users of this notetaking method cover the right-hand column, and then, using only the key words and phrases, they attempt to reconstruct the right-hand column as they recite the message content in their own words. Later reviews are conducted in the same manner.[80] This system of reviewing can assist users in retaining message content.

Considerations When Taking Notes

There are several points we should consider when we take notes. The first is to determine whether or not we need to take notes. Are we going to use the material presented immediately? Can we retain the information without taking notes? Do we have high concentration abilities? If the answer is *yes* to these questions, we probably do not need to take notes. If, however, we must retain the information for future reference, we should take notes in a manner that will enhance rather than detract from our listening. Second, we should be physically, mentally, and psychologically prepared to take notes. Physically, we should have pen and paper ready, we should have a firm surface on which to write, we should be sitting upright, and we should be giving our attention to the speaker. Mentally, we should, prior to the listening situation, obtain background information about the topic and the speaker. Psychologically, we should have a positive, open-minded attitude toward the communicative situation. Also, we should not begin taking notes too soon after the speaker has begun his or her presentation. However, if the speaker names (or lists on the board) the main ideas to be discussed under the principal topic and mentions the order in which they will be presented, taking brief introductory notes may be useful as a check to see whether our

Developing Purposeful Listening Skills

main ideas correspond with those initially designated by the speaker. Further, we can use the introductory notes to determine the relationships between/among the main ideas as well as the relationship between the main topic and the main ideas. On the other hand, if the speaker does not introduce the main ideas at the beginning of the presentation, we should wait several minutes until we have determined the speaker's organizational pattern, or his or her lack of an organizational pattern, and then we must adjust our notetaking style to the speaker's style of presentation.

If we are to be good listeners, we must be flexible notetakers. When we do take notes, we must not take them in a mechanical fashion for the sole purpose of external storage; our task is not accomplished unless internal rehearsal of the message accompanies the act of notetaking. In addition, we should make the notes as brief as possible so that they will not interfere with our listening; phonetically record unfamiliar words; and note any points we missed and—rather than distracting another listener—wait until the speaker has finished before we inquire about the point we missed. We should also set aside a section to list any word, phrase, idea, and so on, that evokes an emotional reaction so that we can dismiss it until we have completed the listening experience, and jot down any question(s) that we may have as we are listening. Finally, we must determine what method of notetaking we should use, for there are several methods.

Notetaking Methods

Probably the most commonly used method of notetaking is the **outlining method**. The strengths of this system are that notes are neat, organized, easily filed, useful for review, and helpful in developing our ability to coordinate items of equal rank and subordinate items of less importance. There are, however, two major weaknesses to this system: The system is impractical if the speech does not follow some definite plan of organization (and less than one half of the speeches we hear are carefully organized), and listeners often become so preoccupied with the symmetry and the mechanics (indentations, capitalizations, I, A, i, a, etc.) that they become confused and lose important concepts and supporting details of the message. Before we begin to outline our notes, we must listen for several minutes so that we can detect the structure. If the speaker's material is organized, then we may choose this method for our notetaking. However, if the speaker's material is not organized, we must choose another method. Remember Nichols's advice: "There are few things more frustrating than to try to outline an unoutlinable speech."[81] When we do choose to outline our notes, we must be skilled in identifying the central ideas, noting the significant details, understanding interrelationships between ideas and details, recognizing which ideas are important and which ones are of little concern, noting transitional devices, and knowing well the mechanics of outlining. (See fig. 6.1 for a sample of the outlining method of notetaking.)

Another method of notetaking is the **précis method**. When we use this system, we listen for several minutes, we mentally summarize what is being

outlining method

précis method

Notetaking Methods

I. Outlining—perhaps most common
  A. Strengths
    1. Neat
    2. Organized
    3. Fileable
    4. Reviewable
    5. Helpful in skill development
      a. Of coordinating items
      b. Of subordinating items
  B. Weaknesses
    1. Impractical for disorganized speaker
    2. Distractible for notetaker preoccupied with format
  C. Preparation
    1. Listening to detect speaker's structure
    2. Choosing appropriate notetaking style
  D. Skills needed
    1. Identifying central ideas
    2. Noting significant details
    3. Understanding interrelationships between / among ideas and details
    4. Distinguishing between / among important and unimportant items
    5. Recognizing transitional devices
    6. Knowing mechanics of outlining
II. Précis method
III. Fact versus principle method
V. Mapping method

FIGURE 6.1.
The Outlining Method of Notetaking.

said, and then—at widely spaced time intervals—we record a summary of what we have heard by writing a short paragraph or a one- or two-sentence abstract. We repeat these three steps until the message has been completed. The strengths of this system are that our notes are brief, easily filed, and useful for review; also, this method can be used for both organized and disorganized messages. One major weakness is that this system requires too much writing at one time. During the periods of writing, the speaker goes on, and the listener loses portions of the message. A second weakness is that significant details are often slighted or omitted. Still another weakness is that often we may not have time to write a complete précis; if we only have enough time to write down a key word or phrase, we should—as soon as possible after the speech—expand our notes so that they will be more meaningful to us when we review them later. If we use this method of notetaking, we must be skilled in recognizing the common structure of most concepts (with the speaker going from the main idea to supporting details—the deductive approach—or going from supporting details to the main idea—the inductive approach); recognizing transitional devices, which are signals that a main point follows ("More important than . . . is . . .," "Now that we have considered . . ., let's look at a second consideration," "Another main

Steps include listening, mentally processing input, and periodically recording brief summaries / abstracts (précis) of input.

Strengths include brief, fileable, and reviewable notes and useability for all message structures.

Weaknesses include losing incoming data while writing, slighting significant details, and lacking time to complete précis.

Skills needed include recognizing inductive and deductive structures and transitional devices; knowing when to complete the three steps; and knowing what to include in précis.

FIGURE 6.2.
The Précis Method of Notetaking.

point is . . .," etc.); knowing when to listen, when to mentally summarize, and when to write the abstract (at the end of spoken units of thought); and knowing what to include in our précis (the thesis sentence, generalizations or main concepts, and the final appeal that the speaker makes). (See fig. 6.2 for a sample of the précis method of notetaking.)

A third method of notetaking is the **fact versus principle method**. When using this system, we divide our paper vertically in half. In the right-hand column, we list the important principles (main ideas) and number them in Roman numerals; in the left-hand column, we list the important facts (verifiable supporting data) that we may need to recall later and number them in Arabic numbers. If a question arises as we listen, we write it at the bottom of the appropriate column. The strengths of this system are that the notes are brief and easily filed; also, this system is especially workable for disorganized messages. It flows naturally as the speaker develops the message, and it provides a clear means for recalling key concepts as they were developed. The system also has weaknesses; often our understanding of the basic structure of the message is lost, and it is often difficult to distinguish between facts and principles. If we use this method of notetaking, we must be skilled in distinguishing between supporting data and main ideas, differentiating between relevant and irrelevant data, understanding interrelationships between main ideas and details, recognizing transitional devices, and noting a possible interrelationship among the principles. Finally, it is crucial that soon after the message has been completed, we structure our notes so that we can give order to the speaker's message if it was disorganized. (See fig. 6.3 for a sample of the fact versus principle method of notetaking.)

fact versus principle method

A fourth method of notetaking is the **mapping method**, which is organizing our notes in a visual manner resembling a map. Using this method requires that we list each main idea, as it is presented, in the center of our paper, or, depending on the number of main ideas presented, we may list the main idea to the far left or right of the center and to the immediate left or right of center. We then circle each listed main idea and, as significant details are presented, we write them on lines that we connect to the main idea that they support. Finally, we place minor details on lines that we connect to the significant details that the minor details further amplify. The strengths of this system are many. The notes are brief, easily filed, useful for review, and helpful in our ability to coordinate items of equal rank

mapping method

Facts

1. Divide paper into two vertical columns.
2. Label left-hand column *facts*.
3. Label right-hand column *principles*.
4. List important to-be-remembered facts (verifiable supporting data) in left-hand column.
5. Number facts in Arabic numbers.
6. List important to-be-remembered principles (key ideas) in right-hand column.
7. Number principles in Roman numerals.
8. List any question that arises at the bottom of the appropriate column.
9. Notes are brief.
10. Notes are fileable.
11. Method is quite suitable for disorganized messages.
12. Method flows naturally as speaker develops message.
13. Method aids user in recalling key concepts as speaker developed them.
14. Basic structure of message may be lost.
15. Distinguishing between facts and principles may be difficult.
16. User must distinguish between supporting details and main ideas.
17. User must differentiate between relevant and irrelevant data.
18. User must understand interrelationships between main ideas and details.
19. User must recognize transitional devices.
20. User must note possible interrelationships between / among principles.
21. If necessary, user should give structure / order to notes after message has been completed.

Are my notes brief enough?
Should I restructure my notes in outlining form?
Should I indicate the interrelationship between facts and principles by placing the number of each fact under the principle that the fact supports? (Yes, I have done so.)

Principles

I. This notetaking method follows a specific format.
(1, 2, 3)
II. Users of this notetaking method follow specific procedures.
(4, 5, 6, 7, 8)

III. This notetaking method has recognized strengths.
(9, 10, 11, 12, 13)

IV. This notetaking method has recognized weaknesses.
(14, 15)

V. The user of this notetaking method must possess specific listening skills.
(16, 17, 18, 19, 20)

VI. There is a follow-up step to this notetaking method.
(21)

FIGURE 6.3.
The Fact Versus Principle Method of Notetaking.

with subordinate items of less importance. The system is useful for both organized and disorganized messages but is especially workable for disorganized messages or messages whose organizational structures do not emerge early in the speakers' presentations. It is a particularly effective system for the visually oriented notetaker and it allows the notetaker to use both his or her left and right hemispheres because it involves analytical, verbal, visual, and creative processes. Finally, its visual images aid in the notetaker's retention of the information recorded. Although notetakers who are proficient in mapping find few disadvantages to the system, two possible weaknesses should be noted. Listeners may become too preoccupied with the creative process of drawing the map and omit important concepts and supporting details, or listeners may spend too much time adjusting their papers to list the supporting and minor details. If we use this method of notetaking, we must be skilled in distinguishing between supporting data and main ideas, understanding the interrelationships between main ideas and details, and recognizing transitional devices.[82] (See fig. 6.4 for a sample of the mapping method of notetaking.)

Recalling Items in a Sequence

Another skill that listening scholars frequently recommend for proficiency in comprehensive listening is the ability to **recall items in a sequence**. As listeners, we often need to recall simple sequences when we are orally given phone numbers, route directions, shopping lists, names of new acquaintances, lists of tasks, dates of upcoming events, addresses, and numerous other data. A typical example of a situation in which listeners need to use this ability can be found in the *Watson-Barker High School Listening Test*. The following is an excerpt of a test item from Form A: "You must have a cover page. The cover page should have the following information in the lower right-hand corner: your name, group number, date, and my name." After listening to the entire test item, listeners are asked four questions, one of which is, "In what order should the information on the cover page appear?"[83] As we look at this example and recall similar examples from our daily lives, we become aware of the importance of being able to recall items in a sequence. In addition to attending carefully to the sequential stimuli, we can utilize appropriate memory techniques as well as notetaking to aid us in developing this skill.

recalling items in a sequence

Following Oral Directions

A skill closely related to sequential ordering and considered necessary for comprehensive listeners to develop is the ability to **follow oral directions**. Our need to develop this skill can readily be seen when we consider how frequently we are required to follow oral directions. We often need to apply this skill when we perform job tasks, order items introduced on the radio or television, perform household maintenance tasks, exercise, play a game unfamiliar to us, apply a medical treatment, or engage in numerous other activities.

following oral directions

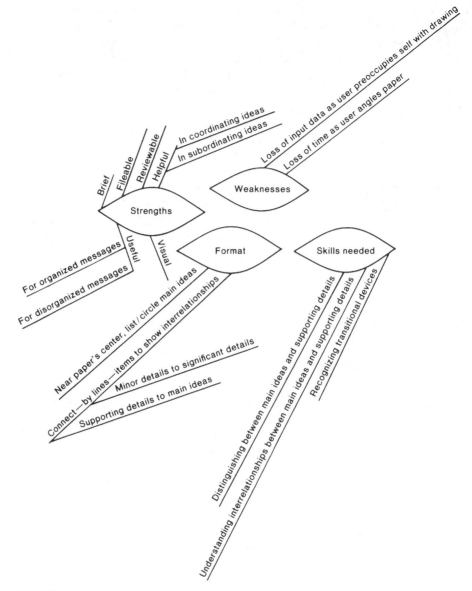

FIGURE 6.4.
The Mapping Method of Notetaking.

Not following oral directions in these and other areas can be costly to us and to others. For example, a friend of ours asked his wife to videotape *The Fugitive* one evening. Having given her directions on how to record the televised movie without recording the commercials, he went to his business meeting. Two days later when he sat down to view the movie, he found that she had only recorded the commercials. This example is minor compared to what another friend who is the owner of an industrial insulation company encountered. *Not wanting* a particular job that was estimated to cost $1,500,000, the owner decided that the best way to be on record for bidding the job but not being awarded the contract was to overprice the company's bid. Thus, he told one of his estimators to bid $1,800,000. Rather than bidding $1,800,000, the estimator bid $1,080,000. Consequently, the job was given to our friend's company, and the company lost an estimated $420,000. Whether the listener is an airline pilot, a medical surgeon, or—in our examples—a spouse or employee, the problem is still the same: We often make costly errors because we do not listen carefully to oral directions.

To learn to follow oral directions, we must apply much of what we have learned about recalling items in a sequence. However, this new skill—which also can be developed through our use of memory aids—often requires us to recall sentences and longer phrases rather than short phrases and words. We must carefully attend to the oral stimuli; by concentrating intensely, we can ensure that the oral directions will be stored in our LTM. Moreover, we can become more efficient in the skill through practice in improving our concentration and notetaking abilities as we listen to oral directions. Additionally, we can become more willing to check our understanding of the sender's directions—by asking clarifying questions, requesting elaboration, and repeating, summarizing, and/or paraphrasing directions.

Asking Meaningful Questions

Still another skill useful to the comprehensive listener is that of **asking questions**. When we consider that the goal of comprehensive listening is to understand the sender's message, we realize that if we ask a sender to clarify a point that we find confusing, that we find inconsistent with what we already know, or that we believe can be interpreted differently, we demonstrate that we are sharing the responsibility for accurate communication; thus, we are increasing the chance of reaching our goal of understanding.

asking meaningful questions

Willingness to Ask Questions

But how often do we ask questions when we wish to have a point clarified, we need additional information, or we are curious? Patterson and Cosgrove, investigating the frequency with which children ranging from preschoolers to fourth graders asked questions when they needed more information, found that only fourth graders spontaneously asked questions. The researchers have suggested that "although active, effective listening may often require students to ask questions, teachers may inadvertently foster the belief that good listening requires listeners to remain silent."[84]

Pearson and West, as well as Patterson, have discovered that the failure to ask questions is not limited to elementary students. Investigating the frequency with which 331 college students asked questions and the types of questions they asked, Pearson and West found that students asked an average of 3.3 questions per instructional hour. And, they found that college students most frequently asked relatively low-level, clarification-type questions such as "Could you please repeat that one more time?" and "What do you mean by that?"[85] Patterson, too, found that few students ask questions in the courses she teaches at the University of Virginia. When she surveyed the students in her Introductory Child Psychology course, she found that although 94 percent of the students admitted not having understood something presented in class at least once or twice, 70 percent said they had never asked a question in class. Among their reasons for not asking questions were "fear of looking stupid and a desire not to make themselves conspicuous."[86]

The fear of looking stupid or appearing ignorant is frequently a listener's rationale for not asking a question. This fear is particularly strong when the listener is greatly influenced by peer pressure and/or when the listener perceives the speaker's respect and liking for him or her as being important. However, if the listener would realize that question-asking indicates interest and a desire to learn and that the only "dumb" question is the one never asked, he or she would probably dispel the fear of appearing ignorant as a reason for not asking questions. Two other reasons that listeners frequently give for not asking questions are that they are too proud or too confused to know what question to ask. Pride should be discarded for the same reasons that fear should be dispelled. Confusion, however, should be confronted honestly; the listener should admit confusion by stating, "I'm confused about the last point you made (or how the example relates to the main idea or what the second main idea has to do with the topic of discussion, etc.)." A fourth reason may be related to class format and class size. Kendrick and Darling found that while 12 percent of college students in large classes with a lecture format did not ask questions or use other tactics to clarify problems of understanding, only 4 percent in small classes with a discussion format failed to ask for clarification.[87] Still another reason why listeners may not ask questions is that the sender does not provide a climate conducive to questioning.[88] Many teachers, parents, bosses, and so on create a feeling of unapproachability when they respond to listeners' questions in the following ways: Teacher to student—"Can't you understand plain English?"; parent to child—"No, I don't know why the dish ran away with the spoon! Now go out and play and quit asking such stupid questions!"; boss to employees at the end of a staff meeting—"None of you have any questions, do you?" Such responses definitely affect our willingness to ask these persons questions. Nevertheless, if we have a sincere desire to become more effective comprehensive listeners, we must put aside our pride or discomfort and ask questions when we do not understand.

Timing and Frequency of Questioning

Once we have developed the willingness to ask questions, we must learn when, how often, for what purposes, and how to ask them. We should wait until the sender (whether it is a speaker, a boss, or a close friend) has completed his or her message before we ask questions. Often, we interrupt (or wish to interrupt) someone so that we can ask a question prematurely,

When we ask a question, we must be willing to listen to the answer.

whereas, if we had waited for the sender to finish, he or she would have answered our question in the course of his or her message. Additionally, we should not ask questions when they are irrelevant or distracting. Does it really matter whether we saw a furniture truck in front of our friend's house on Tuesday or Wednesday when our friend is describing his or her newly acquired chairs and sofa?

The frequency with which we should ask questions lies somewhere between a car going 75 miles per hour and a car that is out of gas. Most of us know someone who interrupts to question much too often (and probably perceives questioning as a substitute for listening rather than questioning as a follow-up to listening), and most of us know someone who questions so rarely that we wonder whether he or she is even interested in what we are saying.

Purposes and Types of Questions

Our purpose/s for asking questions should determine the types of questions we ask. Among the many purposes for asking questions are to gain information, to clarify points of possible misunderstanding, to involve another in dialogue, to seek agreement, and to direct the conversation along desired lines. If, for example, we wanted to learn about the values, opinions, feelings, or thoughts of the speaker, we would ask **open-ended questions**, frequently beginning with *what, why,* or *how.* Thus, an employment interviewer might ask, "What have you done to show initiative and willingness to work?" or "Why do you think you want to work for our company?" or

open-ended questions

"How did you become interested in this field?" Or, the same interviewer might word his or her open-ended question as a statement such as "Tell me a little about yourself" or "Describe the best boss you ever had." Open-ended questions generate free thinking and allow free latitude in answering. They do what their name suggests: They encourage the speaker to open up.

If, on the other hand, we wanted to obtain specific information, we would ask **close-ended questions**, commonly beginning with *who, when,* or *where.* For instance, a student might ask, "Who is considered the 'father of listening'?" or "When is this assignment due?" or "Where do we cite our sources?" Close-ended questions, also useful in confirming understanding ("Are you saying that. . . ?") and seeking agreement ("Do you agree that. . . ?"), request a single, direct answer ("Ralph G. Nichols," "Friday," "On the final page"). They, too, do what their name suggests: They close communication, especially with a speaker who is not talkative.

close-ended questions

Manner of Questioning

The manner in which we ask questions is also important. The late S. I. Hayakawa believed that good listeners ask questions that "avoid all implications (whether in tone of voice or wording) of skepticism or challenge or hostility. They must clearly be motivated by curiosity about the speaker's view."[89] Using a condescending or angry tone, asking a question that is "loaded" or is embarrassing to the speaker, asking a series of questions without waiting for a response, and answering our own questions should not be a part of an effective listener's communication behavior. Hayakawa further stated that the most useful kind of question for clarification may be one phrased in this manner: " 'I am going to restate in my words what I think you mean. Then would you mind telling me if I've understood you correctly?' "[90]

Finally, when we ask a question, we must be willing to listen to the answer, even if we disagree with it or if the answer takes much longer than we had hoped it would. Not listening to the answer prevents us from realizing the many benefits of questioning: Expressing interest in/concern for the speaker, demonstrating a desire to understand the speaker/speaker's message, gaining accurate understanding of the speaker/speaker's message, maintaining focus on the speaker's message, affirming our listening, and earning a listener in return.

Paraphrasing

A final comprehensive listening skill that will help us check our understanding of a sender's message is **paraphrasing**, also termed reflective listening. Paraphrasing, which consists of the listener reflecting—in summary form and in his/her own words—the essence of the speaker's thoughts and the emotions behind them, greatly enhances our ability to perceive the expressed message from the sender's frame of reference[91] and to achieve our goal of understanding the sender's message.

paraphrasing

Importance of Checking for Understanding

The late psychotherapist Carl Rogers believed that the major barrier to understanding in interpersonal communication is the tendency to evaluate another's statement from our own frame of reference.[92] Most of us, while engaging in interactions with another individual, have experienced misunderstandings resulting from this tendency. The following dialogue is illustrative:

FERNANDO: I think we can complete this project by Tuesday. Let's see . . . we have to get approval from the instructor, decide where we're going to tape, schedule the equipment, do the filming, transcribe the audio portion, compile our findings, and rehearse our presentation. But, I think we can get it all done. What do you think?
SHARON: There's no way that I can do all of that in such a short time span. I have a life outside of college, you know!
FERNANDO: So do I! I'm going to school full-time and working twenty hours a week! But, we have to do this project.
SHARON: Well, so do I go to school and work! And, unlike you, I have a social life, too! I don't devote all my weekends to school work.
FERNANDO: I think we each need another project partner.
SHARON: That's your only idea that I agree with!

Thus, amid misunderstandings, the "partnership" terminated. The original misunderstanding that then led to further misunderstandings was due to Fernando's failure to specify that the Tuesday he meant was a week from the following Tuesday and Sharon's failure to check her understanding that his "Tuesday" was the following Tuesday. Sharon, knowing that it was then Thursday, that she was having a twenty-fifth anniversary party for her parents in two days, and that she had little time over the weekend to devote to the assigned project, responded to Fernando's message from her own frame of reference. Fernando, not knowing Sharon's thoughts but believing that more than a week and a half to complete the project was not an unreasonable suggestion, viewed Sharon as one who was not willing to share responsibility for completing the assigned project. The misunderstanding of "Tuesday" may seem to be minor, but communicators frequently fail to achieve understanding due to misunderstandings over trivialities.

Such misunderstandings occur not only in interpersonal interactions and small groups but also in meetings. The late S. I. Hayakawa, stressing that understanding should be our goal when we attend a conference, pointed out that "too often, the fact that misunderstanding exists is not apparent until deeper misunderstandings have already occurred because of the original one."[93] He further suggested that we can avoid such misconceptions by "entering actively and imaginatively into the other fellow's situation and trying to understand a frame of reference different from your own."[94] Another proponent of seeking understanding is Stephen Covey, best-selling author of *The Seven Habits of Highly Effective People*. "Seek first to understand, then to be understood" is one of his seven must-be-practiced habits. To help people avoid "collective monologues" by listening "with the intent to understand" rather than "with the intent to reply," Covey requires meeting participants to restate accurately the previous participant's comment before they can make their own comment.[95]

Numerous other specialists recognize the importance of checking our understanding. Among these specialists are Edelson and Venema, who help couples ease their communication problems. Edelson, a University of Wisconsin social scientist, believes that accuracy is the one communication ingredient that is truly important. When recommending basic steps toward improved communication, he cautions, "Make sure everything you said was accurate and it was understood . . . it's okay to ask questions if they [sic] understood what you were saying."[96] He further stresses that being accurate is the responsibility of both the speaker and the listener, who has to ask, "Am I hearing that right?"[97] Venema, a clinical psychologist, suggests the following approach for developing better understanding:

> An active, involved listener does a lot of talking. He uses words to "mirror back" what he thinks the other is communicating. This approach permits correction of errors. It also sends a message back to the speaker: "This person is really trying to hear what I'm saying."[98]

Tannenbaum—who conducts reflective communication workshops for couples as well as business associates, partners, singles, and family members—urges the listener not only to reflect the speaker's thoughts and feelings but also to engage in another step after the speaker has confirmed the listener's understanding: Encourage the speaker to continue by asking if he or she has more to say.[99]

Process of Paraphrasing

We can trace the origin of what we now refer to as paraphrasing or reflective listening to the late Carl Rogers, who introduced his one-rule approach over forty years ago: "Each person can speak up for himself only *after* he has first restated the ideas and feelings of the previous speaker accurately and to that speaker's satisfaction."[100] Simply stated, this approach involves two people engaging in a dialogue; as the two converse, the listener must restate what he or she thinks the speaker has expressed to the speaker's satisfaction before the listener (who then becomes the speaker) can contribute a further idea to the discussion. The key element is "to the speaker's satisfaction." After the listener has reflected his or her understanding of the speaker's message, the speaker either confirms that understanding or denies the listener's accuracy of understanding and again expresses his or her thoughts and feelings. Then, both communicators keep readjusting their messages until they achieve mutual understanding.

When and how do listeners paraphrase? Normally, listeners paraphrase at natural breaks in the transactions. However, if the speaker's message is so extensive that the listener becomes confused or suffers from information overload, he or she might politely signal nonverbally the need to paraphrase before the speaker proceeds. While there are many **ways to paraphrase**, the most common ways are these:

ways to paraphrase

1. With entry words and in a questioning tone
   "Do I understand you to say that. . . ?"
   "So, it's your opinion that. . . ?"
2. Without entry words and with a questioning tone
   "You think we should. . . ?"
   "You want us to. . . ?"
3. Without entry words and with a tag question at the end
   "You believe. . ., right?"
   "You feel we should. . . . Correct?"

As you might recognize by now, paraphrasing is a slow process, but it is an excellent skill for improving understanding of others, whether their messages are viewpoints, feelings, procedures, directions, explanations, or other informative messages requiring comprehensive listeners. Although we also discuss paraphrasing in the chapter on therapeutic listening, we do not believe that its use is limited to therapeutic situations. Certainly, it is a comprehensive listening skill as well, since understanding is the goal of the comprehensive listener.

Summary

In this chapter, we have examined comprehensive listening—listening for understanding. We have illustrated that comprehensive listening plays a significant role in all phases of our lives and that many variables—including memory, concentration, size of vocabulary, age, intelligence, motivation, scholastic achievement, speaking ability, reading comprehension, verbal ability, language and study skills, rate of presentation, and cultural status—appear to be slightly to moderately related to listening comprehension. However, we have stressed that additional research investigating these variables, as well as others, must be conducted to determine the specific variables most directly related to listening comprehension. Additionally, we have listed, discussed, and suggested ways to improve nine skills that appear to be involved in comprehensive listening: capitalizing on the differential between speech speed and thought speed; listening for main ideas; listening for significant details; drawing justifiable inferences; being an effective notetaker; recalling items in a sequence; following oral directions; asking meaningful questions; and paraphrasing. All of these skills help us improve our understanding and reach our goal as comprehensive listeners.

Suggested Activities

1. Try deliberately to improve your concentration ability in the classes that are giving you the most difficulty. Keep a log of your concentration habits. List the times you started listening and the times

you found yourself "tuning out." Also, record why you stopped listening and what you found yourself thinking about when you realized you were not concentrating on the class discussion or lecture. Keep this log for a certain period of time; then turn it in to the instructor.[101]

2. Prepare a statement that includes at least one word with which many college students would be unfamiliar. Read your statement to the class only once; the listeners are to identify the unfamiliar word(s) and guess at its/their meaning(s). When a student guesses correctly, that student is to explain what contextual clues led him or her to make the proper guess. When a student guesses incorrectly, another student should be given the opportunity to define the word. Students then discuss how the size of one's vocabulary affects listening comprehension.[102]

3. Five or six class members, assuming fictitious names and backgrounds, will form a receiving line. Other class members, designated as guests, will go through the receiving line. Each member of the receiving line will introduce each guest to the person standing next to him or her by stating the name of the guest, together with the name of and some background information on the person next in line. Each guest will state that person's name and comment on the given background information.

4. Class members will role-play a situation involving three participants. One will be assigned the role of boss while two will be assigned the role of new employees. The boss will teach a set of new procedures to the first new employee. That employee will then teach the procedures to the second new employee. All other students will note the problems involved in following (and perhaps giving) oral directions.

5. Several class members will be designated as senders. They will prepare specific, step-by-step directions for completing some simple task such as putting staples into a stapler, opening a window, opening a bottle. Each sender will be paired with a receiver. One at a time, each listener will follow, in front of the class, the sender's directions. The sender may not add directions that he or she does not have written down, and the receiver may not do anything that she or he has not been told to do. The receiver may not communicate with the sender. Participants will then discuss how this exercise has helped them to discover the difficulty of giving and following oral directions accurately.[103]

6. Conduct a survey to determine the memory techniques that others use to remember information. Share your findings with the class.

7. Discuss how the following quotation from Walter Kolesnik can be applied to improved listening and remembering: "The intensity of our interest in an activity as well as the amount of effort that we expend on it depends on our feeling of personal involvement in that activity."[104]

8. A member of the class will speak for two or three minutes about an activity, trip, sporting event, course, or such that he or she has experienced. While the speaker is making his or her presentation, you are to list any of the speaker's words/phrases that lead you to focus

on your own experience(s). Besides these words, list one or two words that you associate with the speaker's expressions. This exercise will show you how listeners freely associate the speaker's thoughts with their own experiences, and at times, tune out the speaker and become preoccupied with their own thoughts.[105]

9. Learn the meanings of the following suffixes, then collect, from your listening experiences, examples of words containing these suffixes. Attempt to define the words and share the words with the class: *-ancy, -ard, -ate, -ent, -esque, -ism, -ory, -ster*.

10. Learn the meanings of the following prefixes, then collect, from your listening experiences, examples of words containing these prefixes. Attempt to define the words and share the words with the class: *astro-, contra-, dyna-, epi-, neo-, pseudo-, retro-, ortho-*.

11. View a half-hour educational program on television and listen for three or four words with which you are not familiar. Attempt to write down the sentence in which each word is used. Share your words with the class to determine whether they, as listeners, can determine the meaning of each word from its context.

12. Keep a list of all new words that you, as a listener, encounter; also, write down the sentences in which the words are used. Using the dictionary, define these words, and then share them with the class.

13. To improve your vocabulary, consider using Hugh Fellows's plan: Each day, read an article from a magazine that contains short articles on a wide variety of subjects. Note with a check each word whose meaning is unfamiliar to you. After having read the article, look up the meaning(s) of each word checked. If you believe the word will be useful to you, write it—*just the word*—down. Then, go back to the article and observe how the word is used. The next day, review the words you have listed. Look a word up again if you have forgotten its meaning. Continue reviewing your list of words, reading a new article, and adding words to your list daily.[106]

14. Each student will prepare a set of written directions (consisting of four to six steps) on how to perform some simple task, such as how to remove ink stain from a piece of clothing. One student will then present his or her set of instructions to the class. After he or she has finished presenting, he or she will randomly select a class member to repeat orally the instructions. Discuss possible reasons why the class member could or could not repeat the instructions; consider the speaker's clarity, accuracy, organization, and word choice, the environmental influences, the listener's attention, and so on. Repeat the assignment two or three more times. Do the communicators improve in their ability to send and receive messages? Why or why not?

15. Compose three open-ended and three close-ended questions that an interviewer might ask a job applicant. Then, compose three open-ended and three close-ended questions that a job applicant might ask an interviewer.

16. On paper, describe listening situations in which you listen most effectively, and describe the methods that you use to sustain attention.
17. For a day, maintain a log of all the ways you distract others who are trying to listen.
18. Select a particular listening situation (such as a class lecture, conversation, sales pitch, sermon, etc.), and describe—in writing—the ways in which you block out the messages of the speaker(s). Also, describe strategies you could use to sustain greater attention to the messages of the speaker(s).
19. Attend to some stimulus (such as a spot on the chalkboard or a light switch) for a short period of time. Identify the physical characteristics that you associate with raising your attention energy (e.g., sitting up straight, raising your head, etc.). Share your characteristics with the class.[107]

Notes

1. R. Ailes with J. Kraushar, *You Are the Message* (NY: Doubleday Currency, 1988), p. 142.
2. A. Wingfield and D. L. Byrnes, *The Psychology of Human Memory* (NY: Academic Press, 1981), p. 130.
3. R. Schank and R. Abelson, *Scripts, Plans, Goals and Understanding* (Hillsdale, NJ: Lawrence Erlbaum Associates, 1976).
4. G. R. Lafrancois, *Psychology for Teaching*, 3d ed. (Belmont, CA: Wadsworth, 1979), pp. 169–170; T. G. Devine, *Teaching Study Skills* (Boston: Allyn and Bacon, 1981), pp. 282–285; M. Freedman, "Some Forgetfulness Normal in Later Years," *Santa Rosa Press Democrat*, 25 January 1990, p. D2.
5. Wingfield and Byrnes, *The Psychology of Human Memory*, p. 8.
6. H. Lorayne and J. Lucas, *The Memory Book* (NY: Ballantine Books, 1974); V. J. Rex, "Memory Massage," *Future*, September/October 1980, pp. 32–35; R. L. Montgomery, "How to Improve Your Memory," *U.S. News & World Report* 87 (27 August 1979): 55; R. L. Montgomery, "Executive Memory" (Paper presented at the International Listening Association Convention, Denver, CO, 1981), p. 2; C. Suplee, "Memory," *The Washington Post Good Health Magazine* (7 October 1990): 11, 25, 34.
7. Lafrancois, *Psychology for Teaching*, pp. 168–169.
8. M. Hunter, *Retention* (El Segundo, CA: TIP Publications, 1967); B. L. Benderly, "Flashbulb Memory," *Psychology Today* 15 (June 1981): 71–74; R. S. Zimmerman and K. Wibecon, "Why Is My Memory Selective?" *Modern Maturity*, July/August 1994, p. 70.
9. M. Roberts, "Flashbulb Memories: Fade to Black," *Psychology Today* 22 (June 1988): 10. It should also be noted that Roberts cites findings (from a study conducted by McCloskey et al.) that reveal that gaps and inconsistencies appear in flashbulb memory just as they do in ordinary memory. See also Suplee, "Memory," p. 25.
10. J. Luiten, W. Ames, and G. Ackerson, "A Meta-Analysis of the Effects of Advance Organizers on Learning and Retention," *American Educational Research* 17 (Summer 1980): 211–218.
11. D. P. Ausubel, *Educational Psychology* (NY: Holt, Rinehart & Winston, 1968), p. 148.
12. Montgomery, "How to Improve Your Memory," p. 55.
13. K. A. Ericsson, W. G. Chase, and S. Faloon, "Acquisition of a Memory Skill," *Science* 208 (6 June 1980): 1182.
14. G. H. Bower and J. S. Reitman, "Mnemonic Elaboration in Multilist Learning," *Journal of Verbal Learning and Verbal Behavior* 11 (August 1972): 478–485.
15. A. Paivio, *Imagery and Verbal Processes* (NY: Holt, Rinehart & Winston, 1971), p. 332; F. L. Prestianni and R. T. Zacks, "The Effects of Learning Instructions and Cueing on Free-Recall," *Memory and Cognition* 2 (January 1974): 194–200; W. D. Rohwer, Jr., "Elaboration and Learning in Childhood and Adolescence," *Advances in Child Development and Behavior* 8 (1973): 1–57; M. Pressley et al., "Short-Term Memory, Verbal

Competence, and Age As Predictors of Imagery Instructional Effectiveness," *Journal of Experimental Child Psychology* 43 (April 1987): 194–211.

16. Montgomery, "Executive Memory," p. 10.

17. Ibid., p. 7.

18. B. R. Bugelski, E. Kidd, and J. Segman, "Image As a Mediator in One-Trial Paired-Associate Learning," *Journal of Experimental Psychology* 76 (January 1968): 69–73.

19. G. H. Bower, "How to . . . Uh . . . Remember," *Psychology Today* 7 (October 1973): 63.

20. E. Tulving and Z. Pearlstone, "Availability Versus Accessibility of Information in Memory of Words," *Journal of Verbal Learning and Verbal Behavior* 5 (August 1966): 381–391.

21. D. A. Norman, *Memory and Attention* (NY: Wiley, 1969), p. 119.

22. J. I. Brown and G. R. Carlsen, *Brown-Carlsen Listening Comprehension Test* (NY: Harcourt, Brace and World, 1955). Revised in 1995, this test is now *The Brown, Carlsen, Carstens Listening Test* (River Falls, WI: Jerald Carstens).

23. R. N. Bostrom and E. S. Waldhart, *Kentucky Comprehensive Listening Skills Test* (Lexington, KY: The Kentucky Listening Research Center, 1983 rev. ed.).

24. G. A. Miller, "The Magical Number Seven, Plus or Minus Two: Some Limits on Our Capacity for Processing Information," *Psychological Review* 63 (1956): 81–97.

25. C. Simon, "Memory, Chunk-Style," *Psychology Today* 22 (March 1988): 17.

26. R. L. Jacobson, "Memory Experts' Advice: Forget about that String around Your Finger," *The Chronicle of Higher Education* 33 (3 September 1986): 49.

27. Ibid.

28. Suplee, "Memory," p. 34.

29. Lorayne and Lucas, *The Memory Book*, pp. 50–72. See also T. Crook and C. Allison, *How to Remember Names* (NY: Harper Collins, 1992).

30. J. Mann, "What Is TV Doing to America?" *U.S. News & World Report* 93 (2 August 1982): 27–30.

31. L. Ubell, "How To Listen to a Child," *Parade*, 31 July 1983, p. 16.

32. W. F. Buckley, Jr., "Has TV Killed Off Great Oratory?" *TV Guide*, 12 February 1983, p. 38.

33. R. MacNeil, "Is Television Shortening Our Attention Span?" *New York University Education Quarterly* 14 (Winter 1983): 2–5.

34. K. W. Watson and L. R. Smeltzer, "Barriers to Listening: Comparison between Business Students and Business Practitioners" (Paper presented at the International Listening Association Convention, St. Paul, MN, 1983).

35. E. Goffman, "Alienation from Interaction," in *Communicating Interpersonally*, eds. R. W. Pace, B. D. Peterson, and T. R. Radcliffe (Columbus, OH: Charles E. Merrill, 1973), pp. 144–153.

36. A. Kahn, "Brain Food: Studies Show Your Mind Is What You Eat," *York Daily Record*, 19 August 1987, p. 3E.

37. J. Cole-Hamilton, "Use Your Brain to Cut Stress," *Communication Briefings*, April 1994, p. 3.

38. C. R. Petrie, Jr., "The Listener," in *Listening: Readings*, ed. S. Duker (NY: Scarecrow Press, 1966), p. 337.

39. Devine, *Teaching Study Skills*, pp. 124–125; G. F. Tuttle and J. I. Murdock, "A Competency-Based Model for Teaching Listening within Organizational Environments" (Presentation made at the Speech Communication Association Convention, Washington, D.C., 1983).

40. Devine, *Teaching Study Skills*, p. 128; K. Baron, "The Meaning of It All," *The Washington Post*, 6 February 1989, p. C5.

41. Ibid.

42. W. Pauk, *How to Study in College*, 2d ed. (Boston: Houghton Mifflin Company, 1974), p. 86.

43. J. I. Brown, *Programmed Vocabulary* (NY: Appleton-CenturyCrofts, 1964), p. v.

44. Ibid., p. vi.

45. Devine, *Teaching Study Skills*, p. 135.

46. A correlation coefficient is a commonly used numerical measure of the degree of relationship between two or more variables. The correlation coefficient ranges in value from 1.00 for perfect negative correlation through .00 for no correlation to +1.00 for complete positive correlation. Thus, a low correlation coefficient indicates a weak relationship between variables, and a high correlation coefficient indicates a strong relationship between variables.

47. E. L. Wright, "The Construction of a Test of Listening Comprehension for the Second,

Third, and Fourth Grades" (Ph.D. diss., Washington University, 1957), *Dissertation Abstracts* 17 (1957): 2226–2227; R. Hampleman, "Comparison of Listening and Reading Comprehension Ability of Fourth and Sixth Grade Pupils," *Elementary English* 35 (January 1958): 49–53; V. L. Farrow, "An Experimental Study of Listening Attention at the Fourth, Fifth, and Sixth Grade" (Ph.D. diss., University of Oregon, 1963), *Dissertation Abstracts* 24 (1964): 3146; J. I. Brown and G. R. Carlsen, *Brown-Carlsen Listening Comprehension Test* p. 15; J. Caffrey, "Auding Ability at the Secondary Level," *Education* 75 (January 1955): 308; E. F. Condon, "An Analysis of the Difference between Good and Poor Listeners in Grades Nine, Eleven, and Thirteen" (Ph.D. diss., University of Kansas, 1965), *Dissertation Abstracts* 26 (1965): 3106; A. G. Erickson, "Can Listening Efficiency Be Improved?" *Journal of Communication* 4 (Winter 1954): 128–132; A. Beery et al., *Sequential Tests of Educational Progress: Listening Comprehension* (Princeton, NJ: Educational Testing Service, 1957).

48. Erickson, "Can Listening Efficiency Be Improved?" p. 131.
49. C. M. Kelly, "Listening: Complexity of Activities—and a Unitary Skill?" *Speech Monographs* 34 (November 1967): 456; H. T. Moore, "The Attention Value of Lecturing without Notes," *Journal of Educational Psychology* 10 (1919): 467–469; F. H. Knower, D. Phillips, and F. Keoppel, "Studies in Listening to Informative Speaking," *Journal of Abnormal and Social Psychology* 40 (January 1945): 82–88; D. W. Mullin, "An Experimental Study of Retention in Educational Television," *Speech Monographs* 24 (March 1957): 31–38; R. G. Nichols, "Factors in Listening Comprehension," *Speech Monographs* 15 (1948): 161; D. G. Ryans, "Motivation in Learning," in *Growth, Teaching, and Learning*, ed. H. H. Remers et al. (NY: Harper and Brothers, 1957), p. 125; C. T. Brown, "Studies in Listening Comprehension," *Speech Monographs* 26 (November 1959): 288–294.
50. J. A. Haberland, "A Comparison of Listening Tests with Standardized Tests," *Journal of Educational Research* 52 (April 1959): 301; R. J. Baldauf, "A Study of a Measure of Listening Comprehension and Its Relation to the School Achievement of Fifth Grade Pupils" (Ph.D. diss., University of Colorado, 1960), *Dissertation Abstracts* 21 (1960): 2979.
51. J. Stark, "An Investigation of the Relationship of the Vocal and Communicative Aspects of Speech Competency with Listening Comprehension" (Ph.D. diss., New York University, 1956), *Dissertation Abstracts* 17 (1957): 696; A. V. Evans, "Listening Related to Speaking in the First Grade" (Master's thesis, Atlanta University, 1960).
52. Erickson, "Can Listening Efficiency Be Improved?" p. 131; S. Duker, "Listening and Reading," *Elementary School Journal* 65 (March 1965): 322.
53. E. J. J. Kramer, "The Relationships of the Wechsler-Bellevue and A.C.E. Intelligence Tests with Performance Scores in Speaking and the Brown-Carlsen Listening Comprehension Test" (Ph.D. diss., Florida State University, 1955), *Dissertation Abstracts* 15 (1955): 2599; R. Ross, "A Look at Listeners," *Elementary School Journal* 64 (April 1964): 370; N. Mead, "Assessing Listening Ability: Relationships with Verbal Ability and Racial/Ethnic Bias" (Paper delivered at the Speech Communication Association Convention, Minneapolis, MN, 1978), p. 9.
54. Brown and Carlsen, *Brown-Carlsen Listening Comprehension Test*, p. 18.
55. C. R. Petrie, Jr., "Listening and Organization," *Central States Speech Journal* 15 (February 1964): 8–9; C. Spicer and R. E. Bassett, "The Effect of Organization on Learning from an Informative Message," *Southern Speech Communication Journal* 40 (Spring 1976): 290–299.
56. T. W. Smith, "Cultural Bias and Listening," in *Listening: Readings*, ed. S. Duker, p. 128; R. Ross, "A Look at Listeners," p. 370.
57. R. G. Nichols, "Listening Is a 10-Part Skill," *Nation's Business* 45 (July 1957): 4.
58. P. W. Keller, "Major Findings in Listening in the Past Ten Years," *Journal of Communication* 10 (March 1960): 34.
59. S. E. Gerber, "Dichotic and Diotic Presentations of Speeded Speech," *Journal of Communication* 18 (September 1968): 272–282.
60. G. Fairbanks, N. Guttman, and M. S. Miron, "Auditory Comprehension of Repeated High-Speed Messages," *Journal of Speech and Hearing Disorders* 22 (March 1957): 20–22.
61. D. B. Orr, "Time Compressed Speech—A Perspective," *Journal of Communication* 18 (September 1968): 288–292.
62. E. Foulke et al., "The Compression of Rapid Speech by the Blind," *Exceptional Children* 29 (November 1962): 134–141.
63. E. Foulke, ed., *Proceedings: Third Louisville Conference on Rate Controlled Speech* (NY: American Foundation for the Blind, 1975).
64. L. Olsen, "Technology Humanized: The Rate-Controlled Tape Recorder," *Media and Methods* 15 (January 1979): 67.

65. J. H. Kirk, "Time Compression Speeds the Gift of Gab," *USA Today*, 12 October 1982, p. 3B.
66. S. Wollenberg, "Ads Strive for Super Payoff," *Santa Rosa Press Democrat*, 28 January 1994, pp. E1, E6.
67. B. Sharkey, "The Secret Rules of Ratings," *New York Times*, 28 August 1994, p. H29.
68. J. MacLachlan, "What People Really Think of Fast Talkers," *Psychology Today* 13 (November 1979): 113–117.
69. J. Leo and N. P. Williamson, "As Time Goes Bye-Bye," *Time*, 19 July 1982, p. 78.
70. N. Miller, et al., "Speed of Speech and Persuasion," *Journal of Personality and Social Psychology* 34 (1976): 615–624; J. MacLachlan, "Time-Compressed Commercials," *Video Systems*, July 1980, pp.20–23; W. Apple, L. Streeter, and R. Krauss, "Effects of Pitch and Speech Rate on Personal Attributions," *Journal of Personality and Social Psychology* 37 (May 1979): 715–727. For a review of the effects of time-compressed commercials on listening viewers, see T. H. Ostermeier, "Electronically-Produced 'Fast Talkers' in TV/Radio Commercials: What Happens to the 'Speeding Listener'?" (Paper presented at the International Listening Association Convention, Indianapolis, IN, 1990).
71. T. Shales, "The Incredible Shrinking Shows," *The Washington Post*, 18 January 1983, p. D1.
72. Leo and Williamson, "As Times Goes Bye-Bye," p. 78; Lexicon's Model 1200 brochure, entitled "Case Histories in Manipulating Time," 1983.
73. P. Marsh, "Using Body Language," in *Eye to Eye*, ed. P. Marsh (Topsfield, MA: Salem House Publishers, 1988), pp. 50–53.
74. R. M. Berko, A. D. Wolvin, and D. R. Wolvin, *Communicating: A Social and Career Focus*, 6th ed. (Boston: Houghton Mifflin, 1995), pp. 447–456.
75. C. H. Weaver, *Human Listening: Processes and Behavior* (Indianapolis: Bobbs-Merrill, 1972), p. 70.
76. D. E. McHenry, "The Effects of Certain Learner, Task, and Response Variables on Immediate and Delayed Aural Comprehension of Meaningful Verbal Material" (Ph.D. diss., University of Denver, 1974), cited in P. G. Friedman, *Listening Processes: Attention, Understanding, Evaluation* (Washington, D.C.: National Education Association, 1983), p. 11; F. J. DiVesta and G. S. Gray, "Listening and Note Taking," *Journal of Educational Psychology* 63 (February 1972): 8–14.
77. F. J. DiVesta and G. S. Gray, "Listening and Notetaking: II. Immediate and Delayed Recall as Functions of Variations in Thematic Continuity, Note Taking, and Length of Listening-Review Intervals," *Journal of Educational Psychology* 64 (1973): 278–287. For a review of the effects of notetaking on listening and retention, see R. N. Bostrom, *Listening Behavior: Measurement and Application* (NY: The Guilford Press, 1990), pp. 28–30.
78. M. J. Adler, *How to Speak How to Listen* (NY: Macmillan, 1983), p. 100.
79. K. A. Kiewra, "The Process of Review: A Level of Processing Approach," *Contemporary Educational Psychology* 8 (October 1983): 366–374; K. A. Kiewra et al., "A More Equitable Account of the Note-Taking Functions in Learning from Lecture and from Text," *Instructional Science* 18 (September 1989): 217–232.
80. Pauk, *How to Study in College*, pp. 126–133.
81. R. G. Nichols, "Do We Know How to Listen? Practical Helps in a Modern Age," *Speech Teacher* 10 (March 1961): 122.
82. For a further explanation of the mapping notetaking method, see T. Buzan, *Use Both Sides of Your Brain* (NY: Dutton, 1976), pp. 83–106, and for graphic examples of mapping, see J. L. Miccinati, "Mapping the Terrain: Connecting Reading with Academic Writing," *Journal of Reading* 31 (March 1988): 542–552.
83. K. W. Watson, L. L. Barker, and C.V. Roberts, *Watson-Barker High School Listening Test — Facilitator's Guide* (New Orleans: Spectra Incorporated, Publishers, 1989), p. 28.
84. C. J. Patterson, "Teaching Children to Listen," *Today's Education* 67 (April/May 1978): 53.
85. J.C. Pearson and R. West, "An Initial Investigation of the Effects of Gender on Student Questions in the Classroom: Developing a Descriptive Base," *Communication Education* 40 (January 1991): 22–32.
86. Patterson, "Teaching Children to Listen," p. 53.
87. W. L. Kendrick and A. L. Darling, "Problems of Understanding in Classrooms: Students' Use of Clarifying Tactics," *Communication Education* 39 (January 1990): 15–29.
88. J. A. Daly, P. O. Kreiser, and L. A. Roghaar, "Question-Asking Comfort: Explorations of the Demography of Communication in the Eighth Grade Classroom," *Communication Education* 44 (January 1994): 27–41.

89. S. I. Hayakawa, "How to Attend a Conference," *ETC* 3 (Autumn 1955): 5–9.
90. Ibid.
91. C. R. Rogers and F. J. Roethlisberger, "Barriers and Gateways to Communication," *Harvard Business Review* 30 (July 1952): 46–52.
92. Ibid.
93. S. I. Hayakawa, "How to Attend a Conference," pp. 5–9.
94. Ibid.
95. S. R. Covey, *The Seven Habits of Highly Effective People* (NY: Simon & Schuster, 1989), pp. 235–260; B. Bollinger, "Three Hours and 'Seven Habits,'" *Santa Rosa Press Democrat*, 8 May 1994, p. E1.
96. "To Ease Marital Strife, Try Really Listening," *The Evening Sun*, 15 November 1976, p. A3.
97. Ibid.
98. M. Wells, "Listening Says You Really Care," *Grit*, 15 January 1978, p. 16.
99. J. Tannenbaum, "Reflective Communication and The Reflective Agreement Process" (Paper presented at the International Listening Association Convention, Boston, MA, 1994).
100. Rogers and Roethlisberger, "Barriers and Gateways to Communication," p. 48.
101. A. D. Wolvin and C. G. Coakley, *Listening Instruction* (Urbana, IL: ERIC Clearinghouse on Reading and Communication Skills, 1979), p. 16.
102. Ibid., pp. 16–17.
103. Ibid., pp. 25–26.
104. W. B. Kolesnik, *Motivation: Understanding and Influencing Human Behavior* (Boston: Allyn and Bacon, 1978), p. 105.
105. D. D. Cary, "Listening As a Discipline," *ILA Listening Post*, September 1982, pp. 18–19.
106. H. P. Fellows, *The Art and Skill of Talking with People* (Englewood Cliffs, NJ: Prentice-Hall, 1964), pp. 72–73.
107. R. J. Marzano and D. E. Arredondo, *Tactics: A Program for Teaching Thinking—Teacher's Manual* (Washington, D.C.: Association for Supervision and Curriculum Development, 1986), p. 4.

- *Therapeutic listening is listening to provide a troubled sender with the opportunity to talk through a problem.*

- *The need for an effective therapeutic listener exists in nearly everyone.*

- *The need for effective therapeutic listeners has become pervasive in American society.*

- *The effective therapeutic listener*

  - *focuses full attention on the troubled sender*

  - *utilizes every part of his or her body to engage in appropriate attending behaviors*

  - *provides a supportive communication climate in which the troubled sender feels free to express him- or herself*

  - *listens with empathy*

  - *serves as a sounding board*

  - *possesses discretion, honesty, patience, and faith*

  - *listens for thoughts and feelings*

  - *responds in ways that are helpful to the troubled sender*

CHAPTER 7

Therapeutic Listening

Consider and record on paper what you would say in response to the following hypothetical messages if these messages were conveyed to you by three of your friends. If you record your own responses, you can then analyze and assess your present therapeutic listening responses as you read this chapter and discover how an effective therapeutic listener should respond to a troubled sender. While both inappropriate and appropriate responses to Message 3 are detailed in the discussion of the fifth therapeutic listening skill, *responding appropriately*, only appropriate responses to Message 1 and Message 2 are given on pages 293 and 299.

Message 1 sent by a forty-five-year-old female friend:

I don't know what to do. I'm just. . . . Tony and I just don't seem to have anything. . . . I mean, we just don't share anything special anymore. He's always too busy for me with work and consulting and . . . playing poker with the guys. . . . He never seems to have time for us . . . for us to talk about us—about our marriage and how empty it is. I don't feel that. . . . He seems to think of me only as the kids' mother, the house's keeper, and the family's social planner . . . I'm no longer his special lady, and I want to be . . . I desperately want to. . . . We used to be content just holding each other and sharing a special smile and. . . . Now, we hardly ever touch . . . except when we pass each other in the bathroom or. . . . And we don't even look at each other . . . I mean, really look at each other. There just doesn't seem to be anything left to hold us together . . . except the kids . . . and they'll be going out on their own soon.

Your response:

Message 2 sent by a seventeen-year-old nephew:

My parents are impossible! They really are! I don't even know why they had me. . . . Yea, I know: They wanted someone to mold in their own image. I'm serious. They certainly don't think I can think for myself. According to them, there's only one way to think, and that's their way. They know what friends I should have, what activities I should participate in, what schools I should attend, what courses I should take, what career I should pursue, what. . . . They know everything that's "best for me." I only wish they knew me, but they won't give me a chance to let them know who I am.

Your response:

Message 3 sent by a co-worker who has just been told that his promotion application has been denied:

I can't believe it! I just can't believe it! After all the work I've done to make that Jones look good, that hypocrite passed me over again! I didn't get my promotion.

For this example, you are to check each of the following responses that you might tend to give.

1. *I would interrupt him before he had finished his message.*
2. *"Hey, what time are we scheduled to play racquetball this afternoon?"*
3. *"Promotions are a pain! I was in grade twelve for what seemed like years! I didn't think I'd ever get my thirteen."*
4. *"Forget it. It's water over the dam now."*
5. *"Hey, cheer up. You'll get your promotion soon."*
6. *"Your problem is that you still think diligence pays off. Maybe it did in high school where you received a college scholarship. But, buddy, the reward system is different here. Those in power here are people-users, people-abusers, people-bruisers, and people-choosers, and you've just been used, abused, and bruised. But, you haven't been 'choosed' because you don't know how to play the game. The game of organizational politics consists of doing what you have to do to become the boss's chosen one."*
7. *"Well, I told you you'd better learn how to take constructive criticism without getting so defensive and hostile."*
8. *"You probably haven't demonstrated enough initiative on the job."*
9. *"Why don't you discuss the issue with the inspector general?"*
10. *"Well, I'll tell you what you should do. Transfer over to D-4, the new section that's being formed. Rumor has it that Collins, the woman who'll be the branch chief, really takes care of her own and is not afraid to speak up for her people in front of the promotion board. I realize that your experience is in system maintenance rather than in system design, but, heck, you could take a short course or two and pick up the needed knowledge quickly. Then, you'd fit right in and get your promotion faster. Plus, you'd be rid of Jones."*

11. *"What explanation did Jones give you for turning down your application for promotion?"*
12. *"You sound as if you really feel betrayed."*
13. *"You think Jones let you down, huh?"*
14. *"Am I correct in understanding that you feel betrayed because you think Jones has let you down?"*

The third purpose of listening, **therapeutic listening**, is to provide a troubled sender with the opportunity to talk through a problem. The effective therapeutic listener uses not only many of the discriminative and comprehensive listening skills presented in chapters 5 and 6 but also five additional skills that are essential to this unique type of listening.

therapeutic listening: listening to provide a troubled sender with the opportunity to talk through a problem

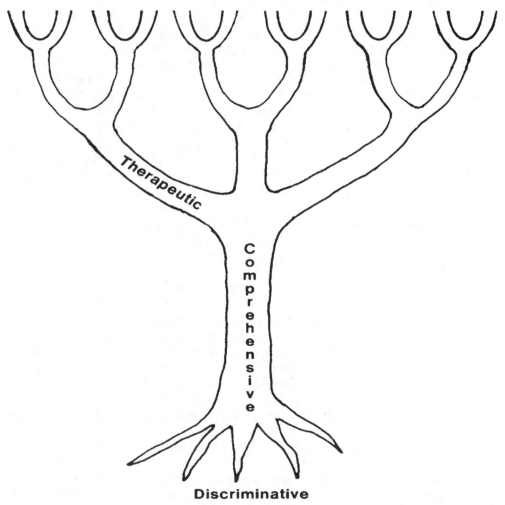

Therapeutic branch of the Wolvin-Coakley Listening Taxonomy.

The Need for Therapeutic Listening

need for therapeutic listening

The need for an empathic listener exists in nearly everyone. Indeed, this need has become pervasive in American society. For instance, "Dial-a-Shrink" enables people to call 900 numbers and talk to phone counselors for three to four dollars per minute. San Francisco's Summit Solutions Network, the largest phone therapy line, reportedly received nearly 2,000 calls during its first three months in operation. Dr. Lenard J. Lexier, medical director of another phone therapy line—Mental Help Line, run by First Home Care of Norfolk, Virginia—predicted that phone therapy may soon become video phone therapy: "The leap from the phone to the video is maybe 12 to 18 months away."[1] Busy New Yorkers now have another type of therapy available: "Therapy on the run." Mobile Psychological Services offers therapy in a van while clients are going, for example, to and from work, the airport, and business appointments.[2]

The growth of the telephone "hot line" operations in most major American cities also demonstrates the need for therapeutic listeners. These hot lines, designed to provide support to troubled persons, are serviced by individuals who are trained in therapeutic listening techniques—techniques that enable them to help troubled callers disclose their problems. Many of these hot lines, usually staffed by volunteers, have become specialized so that they offer services to particular groups of people, such as students on college campuses, rape victims, abused persons, employees of specific organizations, latchkey children, and so on. Harriett Guttenberg, director of the Montgomery County (Maryland) Hot Line program, notes that hot lines "are kind of a barometer of what's happening in a community," whether the problems center on drugs, child abuse, or economic ills.[3] Guttenberg's view is supported by the number of hot line calls received by Sonoma County, California's MEN (Men Evolving Non-Violently) during the month after O. J. Simpson's arrest in June, 1994, when domestic violence became a headline story: Calls increased from an average of 80 to 90 per month to 150.[4]

Coupled with hot lines is the development of crisis intervention centers that also provide therapeutic listening support (as well as professional help) to persons in need: battered wives, abused children, drug abusers, rape victims, homeless individuals, distressed parents, suicidal individuals, AIDS victims, and many others. Furthermore, many schools are implementing peer counselor programs. For instance, Baltimore County, Maryland, had peer helper programs in place in twenty of its twenty-four high schools in 1989. In one of these schools, Perry Hall, fifty-one student helpers were "trained by school officials to stop, look at and listen to troubled classmates, whose problems range from dating to drugs."[5] Likewise, peer mediation is practiced at Lockeland Middle School in Nashville, Tennessee, where students have biweekly "Heart to Heart" group sessions during which they talk out their feelings and share problems such as drug abuse, prostitution, and homelessness.[6] Additionally, there is a great need for therapeutic listeners in rehabilitation centers such as Straight, Incorporated, a center for drug treatment in Florida, and the House of Ruth, a center for battered women in Washington, D.C.

The need for effective therapeutic listening has been recognized by many experts. Dr. Robert Wicks, a psychologist and author, states that he "would like to see people not quickly sending everyone to a professional."[7] Instead, Wicks urges people to resist the impulse to give advice and instead spend time listening to other people's problems. After all, observes Ray Jones, "When you need someone to turn to in time of trouble or crisis, you turn to someone who . . . will listen. . . ."[8] Beier and Valens, in their interesting work on *People Reading*, stress the importance of listening to your children:

> Listening to a young person can easily be an act of love. Listening with concern but without judging is an art, and it helps the child explore his motivations, his style, and the compromises he has so far achieved. . . . It means giving him a safe place where he can speak at his own speed and explore new options, however unrealistic they may appear to us.[9]

Psychologists recognize that the importance of listening to children extends to the adolescent years and the years beyond. Psychologist/author Manford Sonstegard has developed a series of workshops on "Listening to Teens." In his work, Sonstegard advises parents to be willing to listen to their teens "without always making value judgments. And be willing to concede that parents don't always know the right answer."[10] Indeed, as the following example illustrates, parents who are effective therapeutic listeners are not expected to have the "right answers" for their children's problems. After a troubled married daughter had called her, Colleen Onnen of Cherokee, Iowa, was worried that she had not helped her daughter with her problem. But the mother was wrong, for shortly after the first call had been completed, the daughter called her back and thanked her for having been such a good listener: "Mom, it was so good to be able to dump it all on you and know that you'd understand. I didn't expect you to fix anything; I just needed to talk."[11] Clearly, one of the most valuable skills of parenthood is developing the ability to listen empathically to their children. A lifetime of family communication can be sustained through listening with empathy to family members in need of people who will listen. Perhaps if more therapeutic listeners existed in families, fewer troubled individuals would have to unburden themselves on popular television talk shows. Then again, listening to talk show guests describe their horrible lives can be therapeutic for those whose own problems may then seem less disturbing.

Just as workshops on family communication have become popular, so, too, have workshops on couple communication. These workshops are designed to facilitate the development of communication skills such as empathic listening in couple relationships. In one such workshop, Dr. Jeffrey Moss, a social worker, conducts a seminar on "Communication Skill Building and Problem Solving in the Couple Relationship." Moss contends that listening with empathy is important because being a couple "is never easy. Feelings become hurt, angers mount, disagreements grow, and as a result there is a need to give vent to these feelings."[12] Moss stresses that effective listening does not require that you take on your partner's problems. "Rather, to be a good listener is to be a sounding board for your mate's thoughts and feelings. You help the other person clarify feelings which have plagued him/her."[13]

The need for listening with empathy extends to the workplace. B. D. Sorrell notes that the effective manager must "convey the idea that he understands and appreciates what the speaker said. This requires listening with empathy."[14] The effective manager or supervisor must also recognize the need to listen with empathy to employees troubled by personal problems. Meyer and Meyer observe that "it has long been recognized that personal problems affect workers' productivity," but only recently "have corporations begun to examine closely the link between personal problems and productivity."[15] Indeed, the supervisor skilled in therapeutic listening may greatly contribute to workers' increased productivity. Glen Morgan, a training and development specialist, urges organizations to develop training programs that would "expose managerial personnel to therapeutic listening training to improve the ability of managers to concentrate actively on and react positively to an employee."[16] Therapeutic listening in organizations also applies to the advances in labor relations. Unionized workers today increasingly have turned to negotiations for renewing contracts and for setting forth salary and employment conditions in their agreements with their employers. When negotiations concerning salary and working conditions take place, both management and labor are encouraged to listen with understanding to the positions advanced by each side. Such efforts to achieve careful, empathic listening can advance the needs and understandings of both management and workers and can lead to successful, continuing labor relationships.

Therapeutic listening plays an essential role in educational organizations as well. Teachers are encouraged to listen with empathy to help their students grow as persons. To develop an atmosphere in which student self-exploration is possible, teachers should demonstrate "understanding of and skill at communicating these concepts of empathy, respect, and genuineness."[17] Such skill helps teachers communicate with their students as well as with other school personnel and with parents. Some school systems place such a premium on effective teacher communication (including therapeutic listening) that they offer workshops to assist teachers in developing their skills.

The development of therapeutic listening skills is important to yet another professional group—those individuals who must deal directly with terrorists. Throughout the world, political figures, corporate officials, diplomats, and military officers have become targets of terrorists. Attacks of terrorism range from bombing military installations, hijacking airplanes, and kidnapping ambassadors to threatening destruction of the White House and Washington Monument in Washington, D.C. One of the major strategies on which terrorism experts have come to rely is that of therapeutic listening. Experts attempt to understand the terrorist's point of view and provide a willing listener while negotiating the release of the victim(s) and/or negotiating an end to the threatened attack. United States Department of State officials and Department of Defense security officers have come to understand the value of therapeutic listening as one means of dealing with terrorism, both for the attackers and for the victims of these vicious attacks.

The need for therapeutic listening is also dramatically evident in the field of medicine. The ravages of cancer have created a tremendous need for a support system of listeners in health care organizations, hospice affiliations, chaplaincy services, and support groups. Studying the problem of "shutdown," described as the stopping of the listening process when bad news is being communicated, Victor Cohn notes that cancer patients report that no one seems ready to listen to them and that cancer physicians are often "too impersonal, too detached, too busy to listen."[18] Physicians and psychologists are also recognizing that ineffective listening is a contributing cause to the rising suicide rate. Indeed, there is some concern that teenage suicide may be reaching epidemic proportions, with suicide now ranking as the third leading cause of death in the adolescent population.[19] The pressures of our intense society are felt by many adolescents—and the need for supportive listeners at school and in the home are profound. After her own seventeen-year-old son tragically committed suicide, Susan White-Bowden, a Baltimore television newscaster, articulated this need:

> What parents and friends need to learn is to listen. I remember one day when I got home from work and was rushing around the house watering my plants and Jody was trailing along behind me, trying to talk to me. I was too busy. He looked at me and said, "Mom, can't you stand still and listen a minute?" I would sit and listen to Jody for a lifetime now if I could. But it's too late.[20]

Although it is evident that there is a great need for therapeutic listeners in our society, it may not be so evident that we are able to function as therapeutic listeners when others come to us with problems—provided that these problems are not of a serious psychological nature. A study by two psychologists compared the results of two groups of patients who suffered neurotic depression or anxiety reactions. One group was treated by psychotherapists, and the other group was treated by college professors who demonstrated the ability to form understanding relationships. The results of the study indicated that the patients treated by the professors showed, on the average, as much improvement as patients treated by the professional therapists.[21] It is possible for people to serve a therapeutic function as listeners.

Skills Involved in Therapeutic Listening

Following are five essential therapeutic listening skills:

1. Focusing attention
2. Demonstrating attending behaviors
3. Developing a supportive communication climate
4. Listening with empathy
5. Responding appropriately

Focusing Attention

focusing attention

Having accepted a troubled person's invitation ("Do you have some time? I need to talk.") or having had an invitation to a troubled person accepted ("You seem to be preoccupied lately. Is there something I can do to help?"), the effective therapeutic listener gives full attention to the sender. In other words, he or she focuses completely on the sender rather than dividing his or her attention energy between/among the sender and some other concern(s). The attentive listener does not become preoccupied with personal concerns such as lint or a loose thread on his or her clothing, an annoying hangnail, the time, or his or her own unrelated thoughts. Nor does he or she engage in such energy-consuming activities as reading the newspaper, watching television, operating equipment, fiddling with items on his or her desk, or looking at each person who passes in the hall.

Rather than creating or tolerating distractions that compete for his or her attention, the effective therapeutic listener attempts to establish a receptive listening environment that is quiet and has an atmosphere of privacy. The listener can close the door of the room or the office in which the interaction is occurring; turn away from open windows; hold phone calls; discourage interruptions; turn off the radio, stereo, or television; and engage in any other act that will keep the communication interaction as free as possible of external distractions. Another consideration, though, should be the sender's particular style; for instance, while a rather sedate sender may find a quiet, private, distraction-free room most conducive to unburdening, a more active sender may prefer disclosing during a long walk outdoors. Regardless of where the interaction occurs, the effective therapeutic listener makes a conscious effort to free him- or herself of personal concerns or internal distractions by directing all of his or her attention energy to the sender and the sender's concern.

Demonstrating Attending Behaviors

demonstrating attending behaviors

eye contact

To indicate that he or she is focusing attention on the sender, the listener—using every part of his or her body—engages in appropriate attending behaviors. The most frequently cited and highly expected attending behavior is **eye contact**, a nonverbal behavior proven to indicate a positive therapeutic attitude and judged as an important nonverbal behavior for showing empathy.[22] The effective therapeutic listener maintains an appropriate and comfortable gaze (an individual gaze when the listener looks directly at the sender even though the sender may be looking elsewhere as he or she is speaking and a mutual gaze when the listener and sender look directly at one another).[23]

The following example illustrates how important eye contact is as an attending behavior:

> While a mother is washing dishes, her five-year-old daughter, Kenzie, enters the kitchen and says, "Mama."
> "Yes, Kenzie?" the mother responds sweetly.

Ten seconds of silence elapse.

"Ma-ma," Kenzie repeats.

"What, dear?" the mother asks (still in a sweet tone).

Ten seconds of silence elapse.

"M-a-a-ma!" Kenzie again repeats.

"What?" the mother asks less sweetly.

Ten seconds elapse.

"Ma-a-a-ama!" Kenzie yells.

"What do you want?" the mother yells back.

Then, Kenzie says something such as, "I have two blue dresses," "I saw a bird in the back yard," or "What are you doing?"

This type of dialogue and behavior continues until one day the mother finally shouts at Kenzie, "I'm listening!"

"But you're not looking at me," replies Kenzie.

The mother suddenly realizes that she, in fact, hadn't been looking at her daughter—at least not until she had become angry with her. With this realization, she now understood why Kenzie had tried to make her angry: to get her to look at Kenzie.

From that day on, the mother consciously tried to make eye contact with Kenzie whenever they communicated. Her five-year-old had taught her what giving eye contact can mean to a child: "Looking at a child eye to eye gives her assurance. She knows you are really paying attention, knows that you really care."[24]

This example depicts a troubled child who, despite her young age, understood long before her mother did how essential eye contact is as an attending behavior. Unfortunately, there are many individuals who never learn what Kenzie's mother learned from her daughter. In addition to comfortable eye contact, attending behaviors also include receptive **bodily positioning**, encouraging **head nods**, responsive **facial expressions**, brief and encouraging **verbal expressives**, and caring and involved **voice tone** (all of which are described in depth in chapter 4).

Showing thoughtful **consideration for the sender's comfort** is another type of attending behavior in which the therapeutic listener should engage. This type of behavior may entail offering the sender a chair, a tissue, a drink of water, time to gain self-composure, and—depending on the listening situation—a host of other nonverbal comforting acts, such as softening a light or lowering a window blind to block out the glaring sun.

Closely related to comforting behavior is **touching**, a potent therapeutic attending behavior. Although non-Anglo-Saxon and non-Germanic Americans tend to be physically expressive, Americans in general are viewed as low-contact or, quite often, noncontact individuals. Thus, by not touching, many American listeners are missing numerous opportunities to assist troubled senders. According to research findings, touching results in greater self-exploration by senders; touching facilitates openness, honesty, and trust; touching reduces stress and tension; and touching, "used lovingly as a therapeutic tool, can get through to troubled people who are otherwise

bodily positioning

head nods

facial expressions

verbal expressives

voice tone

consideration for the sender's comfort

touching

unreachable, and can go a long way toward healing their emotional wounds."[25] The effective therapeutic listener, therefore, should consider touching (hugging, holding a hand, etc.) to be a part of his or her attending behavior.

A final attending behavior is **silence**. Attentive and active silence, like touching, can carry a powerful message: "I have interest in and concern for you; your thoughts and feelings are of worth because you are of worth." In the field of psychotherapy, the value of silence has long been recognized. Psychoanalyst and author Theodor Reik, in *Listening with the Third Ear*, discusses the powerful effects that the therapeutic listener's silence can have on the sender:

> Silence has a calming, beneficial effect. The patient interprets it preconsciously as a sign of quiet attention. . . . This silence seems to ask him to speak freely. . . . The active power of silence . . . has a force that pulls the patient forward, driving him into deeper layers than he intended. . . . The silence of the analyst works upon the patient encouragingly, and works even more strongly than words could.[26]

Though many listeners become anxious when there is silence and thus cut off the silence prematurely, the therapeutic listener must recognize that a troubled speaker often needs silent times to gain self-composure, to reflect on what he or she has just said, to recall thoughts and feelings, and to organize these thoughts and feelings. Likewise, the therapeutic listener must recognize that he or she needs to be silent during these times. Perhaps it is not coincidental that the word *listen* is made up of the same letters that make up the word *silent*, for silence can be a powerful attending behavior. However, the listener also must recognize that a prolonged silence may be an open invitation for the listener to ask the sender to share his or her present thoughts and feelings with the listener.

The nine attending behaviors presented in this section help to communicate the listener's concern and involvement. Moreover, they make the sender feel valued and worthwhile. Effective therapeutic listening behavior, however, involves more than outward, visible signs of attention. Unlike the little boy who, after his father had gently pushed him into a sitting position in the moving car, said, "I may be sitting down on the outside, but I'm standing up on the inside," effective therapeutic listeners must engage in appropriate external *and* internal listening behaviors.

Developing a Supportive Communication Climate

Suppose a woman sends the following message to Karl, her co-worker: "I've taken just about all that I'm going to take from Betty. If she makes one more 'put down' remark about me in front of the boss, I'm going to have it out with her."

Karl's responding message will likely set the communication climate for the continuation (or, possibly, termination) of this interpersonal dialogue. If he chooses to respond by rolling his eyes, emitting a deep breath, and saying, "Oh, Susan, you're just too sensitive," he is apt to be creating a defensive communication climate. On the other hand, if he chooses to respond by looking directly at Susan, showing concern in his eyes, and saying, "Sounds as if you're quite disgusted with Betty's belittling you in Mrs. Walker's presence," he is apt to be creating a supportive communication climate.

The effective therapeutic listener provides a supportive communication climate—a climate in which the sender feels free, safe, and comfortable to express him- or herself. By providing a supportive atmosphere, the listener communicates a message that says, "I'm here; I care. Although I may not agree with you, I accept you, and I'm interested in you, your thoughts, and your feelings." The sender then knows that the listener has interest in and unconditional regard for him or her and feels secure and free to let down his or her guard, to self-disclose without the fear or threat of being personally attacked, and to explore—at his or her own pace—various options without feeling anxious that the listener may regard some (or even all) of them as being totally unrealistic and/or foolish. Truly, the creation of a supportive communication climate promotes self-exploration and facilitates problem-solving for the sender.

Just as the sender benefits from a supportive communication climate, so do both the listener and the sender-listener relationship benefit. Perhaps the greatest benefit to the listener is a fuller understanding of the sender's thoughts and feelings—from the sender's frame of reference rather than from the listener's own frame of reference. Perhaps the greatest benefit to the dialogue partners' relationship is the open communication resulting from mutual trust and acceptance, which are essential to developing and maintaining positive interpersonal relationships.

As the introductory example in this section illustrates, the listener plays a major role in creating a communication climate by the way he or she nonverbally and verbally responds to the troubled sender. Rather than responding with acceptance, many listeners offer responses that communicate nonacceptance and create a defensive communication climate. Such a response usually results in the sender becoming defensive (and, therefore, bringing the action-reaction principle into play with both communicators becoming defensive) or silent (and, therefore, terminating the communication interaction).

To avoid communicating nonacceptance, the listener should be aware of responses that senders perceive as indicating disapproval. According to Dr. Thomas Gordon, author of the popular *Parent Effectiveness Training* and *Leader Effectiveness Training*, the twelve most commonly expressed, **nonaccepting responses** are the following:

"typical twelve" nonaccepting responses

1. Ordering, directing, commanding ("You have to. . . .")
2. Warning, admonishing, threatening ("You'd better not. . . .")
3. Moralizing, preaching, exhorting, imploring ("It's your duty to. . . .")
4. Advising, giving suggestions or solutions ("What you should do is. . . .")

5. Persuading with logic, lecturing, arguing, teaching ("Experience says that. . . .")
6. Judging, criticizing, disagreeing, blaming ("You'd be foolish to. . . .")
7. Praising, agreeing, evaluating positively, buttering up ("You're such a good. . . . ")
8. Name-calling, ridiculing, shaming ("How naive can you be?")
9. Interpreting, analyzing, diagnosing ("Your problem is that. . . .")
10. Reassuring, sympathizing, consoling, supporting ("Tomorrow will be better.")
11. Probing, questioning, interrogating ("Why did you? . . .")
12. Distracting, diverting, kidding, avoiding, withdrawing, humoring ("Hey, have I told you? . . .")

Gordon notes that these "typical twelve" responses are highly inappropriate as therapeutic responses. They are the very kinds of responses that professional therapists and counselors try to avoid when they are establishing a supportive communication climate.[27]

verbal behaviors producing defensive and supportive communication climates

To understand further how to avoid developing a **defensive communication climate** while developing a **supportive communication climate**, the listener should note the classic study conducted by Jack R. Gibb. Gibb identified six types of characteristics that can arouse defensiveness and six contrasting characteristics that can create supportive communication climates.[28] These contrasting characteristics—exemplified by responses that the parents of a recent high school graduate might give after their son has remarked, *"I don't know if I want to go to school, join the military, or get a job; I'm having a tough time deciding"*—are as follows:

Defensive Climates	Supportive Climates
1. Evaluation—judging others from one's own frame of reference; accusing; blaming	1. Description—imposing no judgments on others; describing thought and feeling perceptions; questioning to gain information
"You never have been any good at making decisions."	*"We sense that you are confused about what direction to take in your immediate future."*
2. Control—directly attempting to change others (whom the sender views as inadequate) so that they will do what the sender wants them to do/see as the sender does; attempting to restrict others' options	2. Problem-Orientation—expressing a desire to share in the defining of a mutual concern and the seeking of a solution or allowing others to work through their own problems.
"If you want our support, you'll go on to school and prepare yourself for a good-paying job."	*"Is there any way we can help you with this difficult decision?"*

Defensive Climates	Supportive Climates
3. Strategy—manipulating others through dishonesty/trickery	3. Spontaneity—being honest and direct; being free of deception/hidden motives
"We have several friends in high places; they're just waiting for an educated young man with a degree in electrical engineering."	*"These three options do give you a great deal to consider, don't they?"*
4. Neutrality—expressing an attitude of cold detachment/uncaring indifference	4. Empathy—identifying with another's problems, accepting and sharing feelings, and expressing understanding
"We don't care what you choose to do. Do what you want."	*"We understand the anxiety and confusion that you're feeling as you're making this decision."*
5. Superiority—expressing an attitude of being better than others; raising feelings of inadequacy in others	5. Equality—recognizing and respecting the individual worth of others; recognizing others' ability to explore their own problems and reach their own tentative solutions; being willing to share in participative planning/problem-solving
"You're not old enough or experienced enough to make this decision that will affect the rest of your life. We'll decide; we know the 'real world.' "	*"We respect your judgment, son, and we will willingly listen as you work through your options."*
6. Certainty—having preconceived notions about how something should be, what ideas are "true"/ "right"—without considering anyone else's ideas; being unwilling to change; appearing dogmatic	6. Provisionalism—being open to and willing to investigate information/ideas; being willing to reconsider one's own behavior, ideas, attitudes; being willing to share in problem-solving
"You will go on to college, and we don't want to hear another word about it."	*"Shall we explore what you see as the pluses and minuses of each option?"*

In this example, what the son needs is understanding, caring, and accepting listeners—not critics, controllers, manipulators, nonparticipants, superiors, or authorities.

A supportive communication climate provided by a listener can, indeed, assist a troubled sender in exploring a problem that does not directly involve the listener. However, there are many occasions when the sender believes that the listener or the listener's behavior is the problem. On such occasions, defensiveness may again appear—with the listener displaying the defensive behavior. As a result, listening effectiveness may greatly suffer. To illustrate, let us begin with the listener's spouse making this statement: "I am fed up with doing all the work around this house while all you do is sit around and watch television. I've never in my life seen anyone as lazy as you!" (This sender undoubtedly does not know how to express his or her feelings without creating a defensive communication climate; sadly, neither do many, many other people so this illustration is not atypical.) Listening to this message—like listening to most hostile messages that come from a spouse, friend, boss, child, sibling, or anyone significant to the listener—often is quite difficult. Having received this message, the listener—whose self-esteem has been threatened and diminished by the sender's name-calling, accusing, and evaluating—will most likely become defensive if he or she does not totally withdraw from the communication interaction. Feeling defensive here seems quite natural; however, one should realize that it interferes with listening effectiveness. When a person becomes defensive, he or she frequently becomes controlled by emotions and stops listening. Rather than expending energy on solving the problem at hand, he or she focuses attention energy on the aroused and festering feelings or on rehearsing what to say and how to say it in order to protect/defend his or her self-image, win the battle by destroying the opponent's viewpoint, make a verbal counterattack, and so on.

The effective therapeutic listener faces a strong challenge in situations like this one. It would be so easy to reply, "And who does all of the lawn work, maintains the car and pool, does the garden work, buys the groceries, . . . while you play bridge, ride your bike, lounge around the pool, . . . If you want to see someone who's lazy, go look in the mirror!" Indeed, it would be easy to respond in this manner, but it would hardly be productive. With the action-reaction principle in effect, much that could be gained may never come to be. The feelings of one's partner may never be explored; the problem-solving process may never be undertaken; knowledge about one's self may never be known; further dialogue may never be encouraged; and potential hostility and a damaged relationship may never be prevented.

When the listener considers the potentially negative effects of defensive behavior, he or she may realize that although it may be much more difficult to (1) control one's emotions (or to acknowledge and express one's emotional tensions to the sender in order to release them and be free to listen), (2) focus on understanding the sender's message rather than defending one's self, and (3) make a response such as, "Sounds as if you're feeling overwhelmed with the amount of housework you have to do and you'd like my help," any of these three behaviors would be more productive. Moreover, these supportive listening behaviors are likely to create the more positive effect of the action-reaction principle, as the late Carl Rogers, in *On Becoming a Person*, maintains: With one party's dropping of defensiveness comes the other party's dropping of defensiveness.[29] Furthermore, creating a supportive communication climate should be the goal of the effective therapeutic listener.

The two listener responses made to the sender's message in the example introducing this section call attention to still another component that strongly affects the communication climate: the nonverbal message that the

Developing Purposeful Listening Skills

listener conveys. Just as effective therapeutic listeners should provide supportive verbal feedback, they should also provide supportive nonverbal feedback to develop a supportive communication climate. Frequently, one's verbal message indicates acceptance while one's nonverbal message may indicate nonacceptance. For example, if one responds by saying, "I really enjoy working with you," but does not look at his or her dialogue partner and turns his or her body away, the response is likely to create defensiveness.

To create a **supportive, rather than a defensive, communication climate**, the listener should first become aware of what **nonverbal behaviors** tend to produce each climate and then should consciously engage in the behaviors that are more likely to produce an atmosphere of acceptance. Some of the many nonverbal behaviors that tend to create each communication climate are the following:

nonverbal behaviors producing defensive and supportive communication climates

Defensive Climates	Supportive Climates
leaning back (possibly with both hands supporting the head) or away	leaning forward
positioning body to exclude partner, pointing feet or entire body toward the exit	positioning body to include partner
turning face away from partner	turning face toward partner
shaking head horizontally (negatively)	nodding head vertically (affirmatively)
assuming incongruent (dissimilar) body posture	assuming congruent (similar) body posture
making excessive postural shifts, fidgeting, tapping or jiggling a foot, maintaining a fixed or rigid body posture	maintaining a relaxed/involved body posture
elevating one's self, "standing tall"	maintaining same elevation as partner
holding head and/or body erect, tilting head back	tilting head slightly to the side
increasing distance between self and partner or invading partner's personal space	maintaining a close and comfortable distance from the partner
maintaining a closed body posture (crossing or locking arms/legs or camouflaging body crosses)	maintaining an open body posture
crossing legs away from partner	crossing legs toward partner
avoiding tactile contact with partner	touching partner
engaging in highly expansive gestures	engaging in natural gestures

Defensive Climates	Supportive Climates
shifting gaze, staring, looking around, casting eyes down, not blinking, peering over glasses, looking down one's nose, directing one's eyes "toward the heavens"	maintaining an appropriate eye gaze with partner
flickering flat hand(s), clenching fists, steepling fingers, rubbing nose or eyes, tapping or drumming fingers, propping head up with hand, pointing or shaking index finger at partner, rubbing hands together, covering face with hands, hitting head with fist, placing palm on back of neck, holding chin in palm of hand while extending index finger along cheek with remaining fingers positioned below the mouth	having open hands, showing relaxed hands, touching one's heart with hand(s)
extending palms out, holding palms down	holding palms up
having a harsh and/or firm voice tone, accentuating vocal emphasis	having a warm and pleasant voice tone (soft volume, low pitch, slow speed)
frowning	smiling
demonstrating judgmental facial expressions (narrowing or closing eyes, drooping eyelids, squinting eyes, raising eyebrows, wrinkling or knitting eyebrows, tilting eyebrows downward, tightening jaw muscle, thrusting out chin, pursing lips, jutting jaw forward, turning up nose)	demonstrating facial expressions that indicate concern/acceptance/interest/involvement/responsiveness
using vocal characteristics and vocal segregates that indicate nonacceptance and/or disapproval (such as clicking the tongue/tsking, sighing deeply, gasping, emitting a deep breath/shhhing and harumphing, sneering and/or laughing at partner)	using vocal segregates that indicate support and concern (such as "uhhh" and "uh huh")[30]

Clearly, the way a listener responds verbally and nonverbally has a major impact on the success or failure of the therapeutic interaction. Paul Friedman summarizes well the difference between a therapeutic listening response conveying acceptance and one that conveys nonacceptance:

> An acceptant response imposes no judgment on the speaker. It is descriptive of what has been heard, not critical. Its intention is to comprehend or understand. It is problem-oriented rather than control-oriented, expressing a desire to collaborate in defining a mutual concern and seeking its solution, rather than trying to get the other person to see something the way we do. It is receptive, indicating a need for additional data and seeking clarification of a situation as the speaker views it, rather than having all the answers. It indicates respect for and supports the use of the speaker's own ability to think through and respond appropriately to what is bothering him or her.[31]

The listener who employs a verbal and nonverbal response of acceptance will be developing a supportive communication climate—a climate essential to effective therapeutic listening.

Listening with Empathy

Frequent references to therapeutic listening as empathic listening accentuate the importance of the listener developing empathy when he or she is listening to a troubled individual.[32] In fact, empathy may be, as Robert Carkhuff believes, the basic dimension of helping: "Without an empathic understanding of the helpee's world and his difficulties as he sees them there is no basis for helping."[33] Indeed research by Raskin supports Carkhuff's view. After surveying practicing therapists to determine what qualities they thought the ideal therapist must possess, he found that they ranked empathy as the most important quality.[34]

listening with empathy

To develop empathy, the listener must first understand what empathy is. Empathy is not apathy, which is an unfeeling attitude, nor is empathy sympathy, which is feeling for or about another person; rather, **empathy is feeling and thinking with another person**. To feel and think with another, the listener must recreate the other person's world by sensing that world as if it were his or her own world ("without ever losing the 'as if' quality"[35]); identify with the other's feelings and thoughts by entering the other's frame of reference (without losing his or her own identity); and replicate the other's feelings and thoughts by becoming a rational and emotional mirror (without foregoing his or her own convictions and sentiments). Covey describes the power of feeling and thinking with another:

empathy: feeling and thinking with another person

> Empathic listening is so powerful because it gives you accurate data to work with. Instead of protecting your own autobiography and assuming thoughts, feelings, motives and interpretation, you're dealing with the reality inside another person's head and heart. . . .
>
> It's deeply therapeutic and healing because it gives a person "psychological air."[36]

According to Milton Mayeroff, author of *On Caring*, the caring, empathic listener does not merely look at the sender "in a detached way from outside, as if he were a specimen," but rather the listener is "able to be with him in his world, 'going' into his world in order to sense from 'inside' what life is like for him, what he is striving to be, and what he requires to grow."[37] As an unknown writer has described, being empathic is being able "to see with the eyes of another, to hear with the ears of another, [and] to feel with the heart of another."[38] Seeing, hearing, and feeling with another, however, does not mean that two separate people seek to be one entity; rather, they are, as Floyd describes, "separate people seeking to come together without denying their separateness."[39]

the personal factor in developing empathy

A major problem in **developing empathy is the personal factor**. First, because of the many personal differences existing between the sender and listener, their shared perceptions and experiences are limited. For example, the listener may never have experienced the world of being handicapped, unemployed, divorced, a minority, a single parent, a prisoner-of-war, a widower, on welfare, in debt, on strike, and so on, whereas the sender may have been a participant in such a world. Thus, separate worlds create separate perceptions, experiences, feelings, and thoughts and prevent two people from ever sharing complete empathy. Second, there is considerable personal risk involved in entering another's world and sensing the way life appears to that person from his or her frame of reference. By truly identifying with and understanding the other person in his or her world, the listener risks being changed by this new understanding. Most listeners perceive being changed as a threat to be feared, for they are accustomed to and comfortable with their own selective way of seeing, hearing, and feeling. Indeed, most listeners are afraid to take the risk of empathically entering another's world, and as a result of this fear, feeling and thinking with another is rarely achieved.[40] With an interesting reference to the Japanese symbol for *listen*, Edgar Wycoff stresses that the listener must possess inner security to develop empathy with the sender:

> The Japanese character for "listen" is made up of the character for "ear" placed within the character for "gate." In effect, we enter into the other person's gate or world and we might sacrifice a bit of self to do so. A good deal of inner security is necessary to truly listen and to understand another person.[41]

Finally, the personal factor affects the listener's ability to empathize when he or she must hear what he or she does not want to hear. For example, when the sender discusses information that may be offensive to the listener or when the sender verbally attacks the listener, the listener is likely to allow emotions to interfere with his or her entering the sender's frame of reference and listening with understanding. Instead, the listener will tend to listen to what his or her own emotions are saying, such as, "Defend yourself; retaliate." Rather than listening to his or her emotions during these times when empathy is most needed, the listener should, as Rogers and Farson suggest, listen to himself or herself and share his or her feelings with the sender:

To listen to oneself is a prerequisite to listening to others. . . . The ability to recognize and understand the meaning which a particular episode has for you, with all the feelings which it stimulates in you, and the ability to express this meaning when you find it getting in the way of active listening, will clear the air and enable you once again to be free to listen. That is, if some person or situation touches off feelings within you which tend to block your attempts to listen with understanding, begin listening to yourself. . . . A person's listening ability is limited by his ability to listen to himself.[42]

Rogers and Farson suggest that it may be difficult to listen not only to these negative expressions but also to positive feelings. Emotional outbursts of praise and joy can be difficult for some persons to handle. Much of this problem, particularly in management, may stem from our social conditioning. As listeners, we may well hear negative complaints and criticism much more frequently than positive reinforcement. Indeed, persons of authority—managers, teachers—probably do not pay enough attention to communicating praise and reinforcement. Instead, many of us hear only negative messages from superiors.

Despite the personal factor, the listener can **develop empathy**. Essential to such development is learning about the other person. The more the listener knows about the sender's background and how this background affects his or her present perceptions, feelings, thoughts, and reactions, the better equipped is the listener to understand the sender's frame of reference. For the listener to gain this understanding, the sender must self-disclose. Realizing that self-disclosing makes one vulnerable and involves risk-taking—risking evaluation, ridicule, or rejection from the listener—the sender will more likely self-disclose if the listener self-discloses and is open. Kogler Hill suggests that the following may be the result of listener self-disclosure: "Perhaps as we [listeners] self-disclose to others they reciprocate and disclose to us in return. In so doing, we have made ourselves vulnerable and so our receivers are less defensive and less vulnerable as well. With their guard down they will provide us with more accurate information as to who they are and how they feel."[43] Additionally, the sender will more likely self-disclose if he or she feels safe from personal harm. To provide a safe world for the sender, the listener must develop a supportive communication climate and establish trust in the relationship. The listener's key to establishing a trusting rapport with the sender is to be trustworthy—to communicate to the sender that he or she will not take advantage of the sender's vulnerability in self-disclosing. David Johnson describes the communication of this trust:

> The expression of warmth towards the other person in a relationship builds a high level of interpersonal trust because it increases the other person's expectations that you will respond with acceptance and support when he self-discloses. In addition, the congruence of your verbal statements, nonverbal cues such as facial expression and tone of voice, and your behavior will affect the other person's perception of your trustworthiness.[44]

Thus, through providing an atmosphere of acceptance and establishing trust in the relationship, the listener encourages the sender to self-disclose; and as

development of empathy

the sender discloses, the listener learns more about him or her and becomes better equipped to enter the sender's world.

shared feelings

The development of empathy also is facilitated when the sender and listener have **shared similar feelings**. If the two have been in a similar situation or if they have been in two completely different situations but have experienced similar feelings, they can often achieve a high degree of empathy. For example, when members of groups such as Mothers Against Drunk Drivers and Parents Without Partners meet, there is frequently a high degree of empathy achieved because many members have shared or do share similar experiences and feelings. Thus, each experience or feeling that someone has had increases that person's capability of later being an empathic listener for someone else. However, as we have noted, all too often the listener and sender have not shared similar experiences.

Still, not having shared similar experiences does not prevent the development of empathy if those who are interacting in the communication have shared similar feelings. To illustrate, suppose Gina, who has recently—and unexpectedly—been terminated from her job, needs a therapeutic listener and seeks out Bob. Now suppose that Bob has never been unemployed since he has been old enough to work. Although it might appear that Bob could easily feel sympathy for Gina by imagining how he would feel if he were fired, it might not appear that Bob could easily feel empathy with Gina, since he has never shared a similar experience. However, Bob has, indeed, shared similar feelings. He experienced feelings of rejection, abandonment, exclusion, confusion, frustration, and hurt when his wife suddenly left him. Although the experiences that led to Bob's feelings and to Gina's feelings are quite dissimilar, many of the feelings that Bob once experienced and Gina is now experiencing are quite similar; therefore, Bob can develop empathy with Gina. Just as Bob can develop empathy with his sender, most listeners can develop empathy by first understanding how the sender is feeling and then recalling a situation in which they experienced similar feelings.

Yet another way in which one can achieve empathy is by actually entering into the world of another. In preparing for various roles, actors sometimes attempt to live the lives of those whom they are to portray on the screen or on the stage. Musicians, too, sometimes attempt to experience the type of life of those about whom they write, sing, and play. Perhaps the most poignant example of one who attempted to enter the world of others is John Howard Griffin, the white author of *Black Like Me*. During 1959 and 1960, Griffin had his skin temporarily darkened by medical treatments and his hair shaved; then he traveled as a black man through the Deep South in order to truly understand the world of the American black in the southern states. Although it is rare for people to go to the extremes that Griffin did to achieve empathy, unfortunately it is also rare to find listeners who are truly empathic.[45]

desire to understand

Empathic listeners may be rare, but they do exist, and each sender may recognize them by the way they manifest their **desire to understand** the sender. To convey this desire to understand the sender from the sender's frame of reference, each listener should develop this desire from within. In

Listening As a Way of Becoming, Earl Koile states that the listener can determine if he or she has this desire by checking his or her reactions to the sender's message:

> Are you saying to yourself: "Yes, I understand or I'm trying to understand your idea or how you feel." If your intent is to understand, if you want to hear, that attitude is likely to be conveyed. . . . As you listen, are you . . . saying to yourself in one form or another: "I agree." "I disagree." "You are right." "You are wrong." "You feel like I do." "You are different from me." If you are judgmental and listening critically, that attitude is likely to be conveyed.[46]

It should be noted here that the desire to understand (as well as the desire to judge) is conveyed not only verbally but also—and possibly even more urgently—nonverbally. Research indicates that the "nonverbal systems of communication seem to be far more effective than the verbal in building empathy, respect, and a sense that the communicator is genuine."[47] Additionally, there is rather conclusive evidence that if the listener can convey an attitude of wanting to understand the sender, the intent to understand is likely to be perceived by the sender as meaning that the sender's thoughts and feelings are worth understanding. Thus, conveying intent is of great importance in establishing perceived empathy.[48]

Having the desire to understand the sender, the effective empathic listener must then strive to turn this desire into actual understanding. Nonverbally, the effective therapeutic listener increases his or her understanding of the speaker by replicating the sender's nonverbal behavior (i.e., becoming nonverbally synchronized with the sender by assuming similar posture, vocal tone, facial expression, etc.). In discussing empathy as a form of imitation, Bruneau notes that "as interactants become more and more mutually identified and congruent, they come to share similar personal tempos, especially nonverbally. This . . . results in 'mirrored reciprocity'. . . . Mirrored reciprocity can be viewed as a kind of imitation and can be called 'interactive empathy' or 'mutual empathy.' "[49] Verbally, although covertly, asking the following questions can assist the listener in achieving this understanding:

> What is the sender trying to tell me?
> What does this mean to him or her?
> How does the sender see this situation?[50]
> What is the sender feeling right now?
> How does the sender view this problem?
> What does the sender see in his or her world?[51]

Answering these questions accurately—that is, truly understanding the sender—requires the therapeutic listener to enter the sender's world, "listen" with all sensory equipment, and convey this understanding by means of appropriate verbal and nonverbal responses. Only when the sender can confirm the accuracy of the listener's responses will the sender feel understood . . . and will empathy be achieved. Without empathy, as Charles Kelly notes, the listener cannot truly understand: "Listening, by its very nature, has to be empathic; a person understands what he has heard, only to the extent that he can share in the meaning, spirit, or feeling of what the communicator has said."[52]

Responding Appropriately

responding appropriately

Appropriate listener responses are crucial to effective therapeutic listening. Unfortunately, the listener's good intentions do not always result in helpful responses. In fact, many responses may have an adverse effect on the troubled sender. Rather than encouraging the sender to continue exploring his or her problem, inappropriate responses may inhibit further self-exploration as well as inhibit further sender-listener interaction.

Responding appropriately is a skill that the listener can learn first by understanding which responses are and which are not conducive to further self-exploration by the sender. Then, the listener should practice these furthering responses. As fourteen of the most common responses are discussed in this section, the reader should analyze and assess the responses that he or she has made to the three hypothetical messages presented in the beginning of this chapter. Although all of the responses to Message 3 will be discussed, only appropriate responses will be offered for Message 1 and Message 2. The reader should use the information presented to analyze and assess his or her responses to all three messages.

Inappropriate Responses

inappropriate responses

The first ten responses, described as follows, are **inappropriate responses** that are not conducive to further self-exploration by the sender.

interrupting response

1. *I would interrupt him before he had finished his message.* Although this way of responding, at first glance, may appear atypical and very few readers may have checked that they would respond in this manner, an **interrupting response** by listeners is quite common. Among the many reasons that a listener might interrupt a sender are the following:

- The listener may have been thinking of something he or she wanted to say to the sender prior to the sender's comment, and rather than attending to the sender's message, the listener states what he or she had been planning to say.
- The listener thinks he or she knows what the sender is going to say.
- The listener does not want to listen to what he or she thinks the sender is going to say.
- The listener cannot wait to make his or her point.
- The listener wants to assist the sender by filling in information or by correcting the sender.
- The listener wants to prevent the sender from saying too much.
- The listener may arbitrarily dismiss the sender's opinion prematurely.

- The listener wants to control the communication transaction.
- The listener desires to be the focus of attention.

In a revealing study conducted by West and Zimmerman, the researchers found that in conversations between males and females, men accounted for 96 percent of the interruptions, and in conversations between parents and children, parents accounted for 89 percent of the interruptions.[53] However, in a later study, Dindia found that in opposite-sex dyads, females were just as likely to interrupt males as males were to interrupt females; participants interrupted each other approximately twenty-one times per half-hour conversation.[54] Regardless of what the reason is for the interruption or who the initiator of the interruption is, the act of interrupting is rude and goal-blocking, it conveys implicit disregard for and rejection of the sender and/or what the sender has to say, and it evokes interpersonal resentment.[55]

2. *"Hey, what time are we scheduled to play racquetball this afternoon?"* This is an **unrelated response** that the listener may give for many of the same reasons that are listed in the preceding paragraph. The first reason, which appears to be the only one that is not the result of intentional rudeness, may be prevented if the sender is certain that he or she has the listener's full attention before the sender conveys the message. Despite the listener's intention for giving the unrelated response, this kind of response—like the interruption—conveys rejection of and disregard for the sender and/or the sender's message.

unrelated response

3. *"Promotions are a pain! I was in grade twelve for what seemed like years! I didn't think I'd ever get my thirteen."* This is a **focusing-on-self response** in which the listener singles out a word or thought contained in the sender's message and then directs the conversation away from the sender's concern and toward the listener's concern to focus attention on him- or herself. Often the listener attempts to share a larger and more serious problem that he or she has; for example, the listener may respond, "You think you have a problem? Why, I've been trying to get my grade thirteen for seven years now. I. . . ." The effective therapeutic listener must expend much effort to resist a temptation to share a similar problem, relate the sender's thoughts and feelings to his or her own life, and/or use the original sender as a captive audience to listen to his or her problem(s). The listener's attention and thoughts should be focused on the sender—not on self.

focusing-on-self response

4/5. *"Forget it. It's water over the dam now." "Hey, cheer up. You'll get your promotion soon."* Both of these responses discount the sender's feelings. A **discounting response** communicates that the listener does not accept the sender's feelings as being valid, justified, or important. Although the listener does not have to approve of the sender's feelings, he or she should acknowledge that the sender does, indeed, have certain feelings—expressed through tears as well as smiles—and should encourage the sender to verbalize and explore them.

discounting response

Instead of acknowledging the sender's feelings, however, many listeners discount them. Some listeners *ignore the sender's feelings* by making responses such as, "That's life," "You can't win them all," "That's the way it is," "That's the way the cookie crumbles," and so on. Such clichés show triteness and a lack of sensitivity. Other listeners *attempt to encourage the sender to repress emotions* by responding in some variation of "Don't feel that way; instead, feel another way," "Cheer up," "Don't worry about it," "Don't cry; think of something pleasant," "Calm down. Getting angry isn't going to help; try to be reasonable," "You'd better not get too excited; you haven't been asked yet," and so on. Still other listeners respond in ways that *deny the sender's feelings or encourage the sender to deny his or her feelings:* "You know you don't hate your boss," "You shouldn't feel unsure," "There's no reason for you to feel anxious about his visit," "Oh, you don't mean that," and so on.

However unpleasant the expressed feeling may be for the listener, however uncomfortable the listener may feel as the sender discusses these feelings, or however helpful the listener may think a discounting response may be, the listener should not ignore or deny the sender's feelings and/or encourage the sender to repress or deny those feelings. Discounting the sender's feelings will not minimize or change them, nor will it help the sender to identify them and deal with them in a constructive way. Rather, discounting the other person's feelings likely will inhibit further sender-listener interaction, lead to the sender suppressing feelings, and/or have negative effects (such as headaches, ulcers, and depression) on the sender's physical and psychological health. Truly, a troubled sender needs to express feelings in order to explore, clarify, and solve his or her problems. Therefore, an effective therapeutic listener should provide the sender with a supportive communication climate that encourages the sender's expression rather than suppression of feelings.

6. *"Your problem is that you still think diligence pays off. Maybe it did in high school where you received a college scholarship. But, buddy, the reward system is different here. Those in power here are people-users, people-abusers, people-bruisers, and people-choosers, and you've just been used, abused, and bruised. But, you haven't been 'choosed' because you don't know how to play the game. The game of organizational politics consists of doing what you have to do to become the boss's chosen one."* This **philosophical response** is illustrative of the numerous listener responses that attempt to provide the sender with a lesson in psychology or philosophy. Such responses imply superiority (since the listener suggests that his or her "worldly wisdom" enables him or her to understand the sender's problem better than the sender understands his or her own problem). Such responses often create confusion, inaccuracies regarding the problem and the solution(s), and/or defensiveness in the sender.

7. *"Well, I told you you'd better learn how to take constructive criticism without getting so defensive and hostile."* The sender is likely to perceive this—the **blaming response** or "I-told-you-so"—as a personal attack or threat; thus, this response often leads to defensive behavior as the sender feels compelled to protect his or her self-image. To avoid further blaming responses, the sender also is apt to avoid sharing future problems with the accusing listener.

8. *"You probably haven't demonstrated enough initiative on the job."* This is an **evaluative response** that implies that the listener believes he or she is qualified to pass judgment on the sender's thoughts and/or behaviors. Carl

Rogers identified this natural tendency of the listener to evaluate the sender's message according to the listener's frame of reference—which is based on the listener's personal value system—as the greatest of all interpersonal listening barriers.[56] Indeed, it is an obstacle to effective therapeutic listening, and it becomes a greater impediment when the listener is emotionally involved in the communication situation since the more deeply the listener is emotionally involved, the stronger the tendency to form evaluations from his or her own point of view.[57] These evaluations, phrased not only in *statement form* (such as "You shouldn't have gone to the beach for the weekend" or "You are just being inconsiderate of my feelings") but also in *question form* (such as "How could you possibly believe something as ridiculous as that?" or "Why do you always have to be so defensive?"), pose a threat to the sender's perception of self-worth. Feeling threatened, the sender tends to become defensive, suppress self-expression, and/or resist further interaction with the listener. Perhaps the following quotation by Samuel Johnson best explains why the evaluative retort is an inappropriate therapeutic response: "God himself, Sir, doesn't propose to judge a man until his life is over. Why should you and I?"[58]

9. *"Why don't you discuss the issue with the inspector general?"* With this response, the listener also uses questioning—not to evaluate but rather to direct the sender's thoughts toward a particular point of view, one that is held by the listener. This reply tends to be a controlling response, which implies that the listener already knows how the sender should solve his or her problem. The inappropriateness of this type of response—an **advisory response** in the form of a **question**—is discussed in the next paragraph.

> **advisory response—question**

10. *"Well, I'll tell you what you should do. Transfer over to D-4, the new section that's being formed. Rumor has it that Collins, the woman who'll be the branch chief, really takes care of her own and is not afraid to speak up for her people in front of the promotion board. I realize that your experience is in system maintenance rather than in system design, but, heck, you could take a short course or two and pick up the needed knowledge quickly. Then, you'd fit right in and get your promotion fast. Plus, you'd be rid of Jones."* In this response as well as in the previous response, the listener is offering the sender advice on how to deal with his or her problem. Although some may view the previous reply as being merely a question of interest, it is advisory—just as this **advisory response** in the form of a **statement** is. Both advisory responses illustrate a natural tendency in most listeners—the tendency to tell the sender how the listener would deal with the problem. The listener attempts to try to change the sender's way of viewing the problem situation—to get the sender to view the situation through the listener's eyes—and to induce the sender to go in the direction the listener wants him or her to travel.[59] Indeed, as the reader may note when analyzing his or her responses to the three hypothetical senders' messages presented in the beginning of the chapter, listeners tend to give advice all too freely.

> **advisory response—statement**

Although advisory responses are freely given, generally with the intention to be helpful, they are often inappropriate. There are many reasons why they are unsuitable.

1. Often the listener is in no position to give advice; that is, he or she does not have all of the information needed, is not a qualified/trained counselor or an expert in the area of the sender's concern (such as law, medicine, or education), and has only limited personal experiences upon which to base this advice.

2. A listener tends to ignore the individuality of the sender. He or she disregards the fact that everyone is different and that a solution appropriate for one person may not be suitable for another. The listener suggests that the sender deal with the problem in the way the listener (or even a friend or an acquaintance) has dealt with a similar problem or in the manner in which the listener would deal with the problem.

3. Offering advice implies that the listener is not viewing the sender as an equal; rather, it indicates a superior-subordinate (such as parent-child, employer-employee, therapist-client, etc.) relationship. For women, this relational view may result from cultural conditioning. Barbara Sher, psychotherapist and founder of Women's Success Teams, notes that women—much more than men—tend to feel that listening to a troubled speaker is not enough; women feel as if they have to do something to help:

   > Women are *fixers*. We [women] aren't the only ones, but culturally and biologically, we're geared to take responsibility for another person's life. After all, when you're a mother and your baby is hungry and crying, you don't just listen sympathetically, you come up with some milk. And the baby learns that mothers fix things. So you develop this sense of responsibility for another's life, and you have a feeling that if all you do is listen and sympathize, you're cheating somebody because you're not giving everything you could give."[60]

   Borisoff and Hahn, however, report that men are more likely to be advice-givers: "When women discuss problems and share experiences, the *process* of the discussion conveys empathic communication. In contrast, men may offer *solutions* to show they are listening empathically."[61]

4. Advising can result in the listener losing a friend if the listener's advice, adopted by the sender, proves to be harmful rather than helpful to the sender.

5. Offering advice is an obstacle to the sender's self-expression; the troubled sender needs to talk and listen to him- or herself rather than to the dialogue partner.

6. Offering advice communicates a lack of trust in the sender's capacity to solve his or her own problems and can decrease the sender's feelings of adequacy/self-worth.

7. Offering advice reduces the sender's responsibility for clarifying the problem and exploring possible solutions. Indeed, some senders seek advice so they can avoid responsibility for their own decisions; then, if the listener's suggested solution does not resolve the problem, the sender can always blame the listener for

the failure. According to Mayeroff, the listener who denies the sender's "need to take responsibility for his own life" is "denying him as a person."[62]

8. Frequently, offering advice is proffering something that the sender does not want. For instance, in the three hypothetical messages presented in the beginning of this chapter, not one sender asks for advice. Yet how many readers offered advice? Even when the listener realizes that the sender has not asked for advice, this realization often does not prevent the listener from telling the sender what to do: "I know you haven't asked, but I'd like to give you a piece of advice. What you should do is. . . ." Giving advice to someone who does not ask for it is giving someone something that he or she does not want. Many of those who are trained in counseling corroborate the inappropriateness of advice-giving. For example, clinical social worker, Jeffrey Moss, who conducts seminars on the unique challenge of two-career couples, cautions the partners not to give advice:

> There is a strong tendency to give advice, even when it is not asked for, and one of the things we have learned is that partners tend to resent advice on how to handle job-related issues. People prefer to direct their concerns to a good listener, an individual who will help him or her think through a problem rather than talk to a partner who will cloud the issue with a lot of advice.[63]

Additionally, the author of *Parent Effectiveness Training*, Thomas Gordon (a clinical psychologist), notes the potentially negative results of parental advisory responses:

> Such messages are often felt by the child as evidence that the parent does not have confidence in the child's judgment or ability to find his own solution. They may influence a child to become dependent on the parent and stop thinking for himself.[64]

Finally, psychologist Carl Rogers testifies how good one feels when the listener resists the desire to provide direction for the troubled sender: "I can testify that when you are in psychological distress and someone really hears you without passing judgment on you, without trying to take responsibility for you, without trying to mold you, it feels damn good."[65]

9. Offering advice to a sender, even when he or she asks for advice, is not giving the sender what he or she needs. This final reason is explained in the following discussion of appropriate therapeutic listener responses.

Needed: A Sounding Board

Rather than needing a listener who responds by interrupting, sending an unrelated message, focusing on him- or herself, discounting the sender's feelings, philosophizing, blaming, evaluating, or advising, the troubled sender needs a listener who will serve as a **sounding board**. This sounding board must be someone who truly listens and appropriately responds while

sounding board

providing the sender with the opportunity to unburden—to talk through his or her problem or concern to reach his or her own solution or decision. One who truly listens is one who, knowing the power of silence, listens much more than he or she talks; that is, he or she is a true "sounding board" rather than a "resounding board." Research findings in clinical psychology support the view that listening is more helpful to the troubled sender than is talking. Patient improvement relates positively to patient talk time while it relates negatively to therapist talk time.[66]

Essential Personal Traits of an Effective Sounding Board

An effective sounding board is one who, through his or her nonverbal attending behaviors and verbal responses, communicates to the sender the following message: "I genuinely care about your well-being and about you as you are rather than as I might want you to be, I sincerely desire to understand your feelings and thoughts, and I honestly believe that, as Ralph G. Nichols has said, 'The best way to understand people is to listen to them.' "[67] Receiving a message such as this one, the troubled sender will probably experience what John Powell has experienced:

> There . . . have been . . . moments when someone heard my secret and accepted my confidence in gentle hands. I . . . remember what he said to assure me, the compassion in his voice, the understanding look in his eyes. I remember what those eyes looked like. I remember how his hand took mine. I remember the gentle pressure that told me that I was understood. It was a great and liberating experience, and, in its wake, I felt so much more alive. An immense need had been answered in me to be really listened to, to be taken seriously, and to be understood.[68]

willingness to listen

capacity to care

desire to understand

discretion

honesty

Indeed, for effective therapeutic listening to occur, the listener must possess the **willingness to listen**, the **capacity to care**, and the **desire to understand**.

An effective therapeutic listener must also possess four other personal traits. One of these is **discretion**. Rather than playing amateur psychiatrist with a sender whose problem is of a serious psychological nature, the listener should refer the troubled sender to a professional therapist.

Another trait is **honesty**. If the listener does not have a sincere interest in the sender, he or she should not try to pretend interest; instead, the listener should be honest with the sender and say, "I'm not the 'sounding board' you're looking for." Likewise, if the listener does not have time at the particular moment when therapeutic listening is required, he or she should honestly explain this lack of time to the sender and not enter into a rushed session. The task of talking through a problem cannot be hurried; it takes time for the sender to arrive at his or her own solution, and a sender may never arrive at a solution if he or she does not have ample time to analyze his or her problem. Thus, rather than rushing through a session, which would be neither productive to the sender nor satisfying for the listener, the listener should schedule a time—as soon as possible—to meet with the troubled sender. The listener should also be honest when he or she cannot listen effectively because of preoccupation with his or her own personal concerns. On such occasions, the listener has no room in his or her mind for the sender to enter, and the listener should share with the sender the reason for being unable to listen at that particular time.

A third trait, which is also time-related, is **patience**, a trait that the listener must possess in order to provide the sender with the time he or she needs to express him- or herself adequately. Even though the listener may have a strong desire to say, "Please, get to the point," the listener must allow the sender "to digress and expand and elaborate and repeat . . . [for] there are times when listening well means listening long, means listening very . . . very . . . patiently."[69] In addition, it means doing what the Japanese do: Listening a little longer when you think you are through listening; this extra silent time—wait time—will give the sender a sense of not being rushed. Commenting on this last point some two thousand years ago, Greek historian Plutarch advised: "In all cases, then, silence is a safe adornment . . . and especially so, when in listening to another he . . . waits for the speaker to pause, and, when the pause comes, . . . allows an interval to elapse, in case the speaker may desire to add something to what he has said, or to alter or unsay anything."[70]

patience

The last trait is **faith**—faith in the sender's ability to solve his or her own problem. That the sender can solve his or her own problem is a basic assumption, which underlies the entire premise of therapeutic listening. Essentially, it is a valid assumption. Most people can solve their own problems if only they have the opportunity to talk them through. By verbalizing one's problem to a therapeutic listener, one is able to listen more clearly to one's self, see the problem in a better perspective, reduce the problem to a manageable size, and deal with his or her problem in a more psychologically healthy manner. However, should the problem be great enough to require clinical, professional assistance, the therapeutic listener, as we noted earlier, should not attempt to deal with it. A problem that requires psychological attention must be referred to the properly trained therapist.

faith

Appropriate Responses

The preceding seven personal traits are essential characteristics that the effective therapeutic listener must possess to respond in a way that will be helpful and productive to a troubled sender. Understanding these traits as well as understanding inappropriate responses will provide the reader with a greater understanding of the **responses that are appropriate** when one is serving as a therapeutic listener. Again, as these appropriate responses are discussed, the reader should analyze and assess the responses he or she has made to the hypothetical messages presented in the beginning of this chapter.

appropriate responses

"What explanation did Jones give you for turning down your application for promotion?" "You sound as if you really feel betrayed." "You think Jones let you down, huh?" "Am I correct in understanding that you feel betrayed because you think Jones has let you down?" These four responses are types of responses that the effective therapeutic listener should use. They are appropriate because they are furthering responses. Rather than inhibiting the sender's

self-exploration, they encourage the sender to explore freely his or her feelings and thoughts on the problem and reach his or her own solution (by maintaining the focus of attention on the sender, conveying acceptance of the sender's feelings and thoughts, and expressing continued interest in the sender and the desire to understand the sender's feelings and thoughts).

Unlike an inappropriate advisory retort, these responses also enhance the sender's skills in dealing with future problems. Heun and Heun illustrate this notion of enhancement well by relating it to the following adage: "If you give a man a fish, you feed him for a day; if you teach a man how to fish, he can feed himself for a lifetime."[71] Indeed, by advising the sender on how to solve his or her problem (giving a man a fish), the listener may possibly help the troubled sender with his or her current problem (feed him for a day). However, if the listener—serving as a sounding board and responding appropriately—provides the sender with an opportunity to talk through the problem and reach his or her own solution (teaching a man how to fish for himself), the sender will learn how to cope effectively and independently with problems that he or she may encounter throughout his or her life (feeding him for a lifetime). Truly, what the sender needs, rather than advice, is the opportunity to develop those skills that will enable him or her to solve his or her own problems. As we examine closely each of these appropriate responses, we will see how each one provides the sender with this opportunity for further skill-development.

11. *"What explanation did Jones give you for turning down your application for promotion?"* This **probing response** is a furthering response that encourages the sender to continue. The listener's intent—in using the probing response—may be to seek additional information to learn more about the sender's feelings and thoughts, to assist the sender in expanding on a certain line of thought in order for the sender to gain a clearer perspective of that thought, to clarify a vague aspect of the sender's message in order for the listener to gain a better understanding of the sender's feelings and thoughts, to induce the sender to go beyond superficial statements, and/or to elicit further discussion between the dialogue partners. A probing response shows listener interest in the sender and the sender's message. It also demonstrates the listener's desire to understand. Furthermore, a probe can effectively temper or soften the "adult" image of the listener in certain interactions, such as encounters between parent-child, employer-employee, older sibling-younger sibling, and so on.

To achieve the desired results, the listener must carefully phrase the probing response. There are two especially effective ways to phrase it. First, it may be as an open-ended question—"Who exactly is saying this to you?" "How do they display their feelings?" "What do you mean by that word?" (rather than one that has an evaluative or advisory tone as "why" questions tend to have—"Why don't you? . . ."). Second, it could be a restatement in the form of a question or as a portion of the sender's message—"You really believe that the boss is after you?" "You're not going back to school?" "You don't want to see your parents again?" (rather than one that is, in reality, merely a statement of the listener's view).

probing response

Developing Purposeful Listening Skills

One last point regarding questioning responses is that the listener should avoid bombarding the sender with questions such as (in responding to Message 2 presented at the beginning of this chapter), "What makes you think your parents are impossible? What do you actually mean by impossible? What do they do to suggest this idea? Do you have any specific examples that show them being impossible? What similarities and differences are there in your mother's and father's behaviors? When do they? . . ." One questioning response at a time is generally enough! Thus, one might ask the sender of hypothetical Message 1 (also presented at the beginning of this chapter) any *one* of the following questions: "What would make you feel special again?" "When did you last feel that you and your husband had something special?" "How do you and Tony spend the time you do have together?" "What makes you think he views you 'only as' a mother, housekeeper, or social planner?"

Although the probing response is a furthering response, it does not show as much understanding as do the remaining three furthering responses. They show that the listener is truly striving to feel and/or think with—rather than about—the troubled sender.

12. *"You sound as if you really feel betrayed."* This is a **feeling response** that indicates the listener's sensitivity to the sender's feelings and the listener's desire to feel with the sender. To confirm that he or she is, indeed, feeling with the sender, the listener employs the **perception-checking** approach. This approach consists of the listener listening to the sender's total message to identify the sender's inner feeling(s) and then verbally reflecting (in a tentatively phrased manner) his or her interpretation to the sender for confirmation, modification, clarification, and/or correction. In short, the listener asks the sender to verify the listener's perception of the sender's feelings. An effective perception check does not convey listener approval or disapproval of the sender's feelings, nor does it imply mind-reading by the listener (e.g., "Why are you so discouraged [or frustrated, demoralized, fearful, etc.]?"); rather, it conveys this message: "I want to understand your feelings—is this the way you feel?"[72] To convey this message, the listener might provide feeling responses such as the following to the senders of the first two hypothetical messages presented at the beginning of this chapter: to the sender of Message 1—"You seem to be feeling lonely (or alone, neglected, sad, hurt, used, depressed, insecure). Am I right?"; and to the sender of Message 2—"I sense that you feel frustrated (or unaccepted, controlled, dominated, repressed, hurt), do you?"

Halley agrees that a tentatively phrased feeling response—such as, "Are you feeling (feeling word)?" or "It seems to me you are feeling (feeling word)"—is appropriate if the speaker is experiencing a significant emotion with moderate or high emotional intensity. A significant emotion is one that a speaker experiences when his or her feeling for the moment is more important than any other stimuli or situation with which the speaker is trying to deal.[73] However, he recommends that the listener make "a simple assertion with no expression of uncertainty"—such as "You are feeling

feeling response

perception-checking

(feeling word)"—when the speaker is experiencing a significant emotion of very high emotional intensity. He explains his recommendation as follows:

> When emotional intensity is very high the person being observed will tend to believe that what s/he is feeling is obvious. Thus a simple assertion with no expression of uncertainty is necessary. If the listener sounds unsure or asks a question, the likely response of the speaker will be that the listener isn't very sensitive to feelings and thus is not a very "safe" person to talk to. To test this idea try thinking about a person that you know very well. You walk into the room and the person is throwing things around . . . and generally ranting about. What do you think would happen if you were to say, "Are you angry?" Most readers will likely agree that the speaker would react by in some way turning his/her anger onto the listener. The speaker thinks his/her emotion is obvious, thus a simple acknowledgement [sic] of the feeling is appropriate.[74]

Halley also believes that when a speaker is experiencing a significant emotion, the listener should continue to use feeling responses appropriate to each level of intensity until the intensity of the emotion has been reduced to a nonsignificant level where the speaker can think clearly. Only then should the listener use thought responses.[75]

reasons for the difficulty of uncovering feelings

Although uncovering feelings is important both to the sender for self-exploration of the problem and to the listener for understanding the sender/sender's problem, it often is a formidable task. One reason for the difficulty is that the sender quite frequently does not verbalize his or her feelings explicitly and specifically. Perhaps others have so often discounted the sender's feelings in the past that he or she has not learned to identify feelings clearly or has learned to hide feelings by sealing them inside and, thus, has never had the practice needed to articulate feelings. Or, perhaps the sender is a male, and the listener is a male to whom the sender prefers not to disclose his emotions. Experimental research by Shimanoff, for example, indicates that males express their emotions significantly more often to females than to males. This finding has led Shimanoff to suggest that there may be supportive behavioral differences between male and female listeners or that males may "feel safer in expressing their emotions to females, who are perceived to be more nurturing and supportive of disclosures of affect."[76] Also, if the sender is a male, he may be less expressive of his emotions nonverbally than a female is, for males generally have been conditioned to believe that it is not manly to display their emotions.[77] And, as Shere Hite reports in the controversial 1987 *Hite Report*, perhaps men have been conditioned not to express their feelings verbally: "Some women say men believe not talking about 'feelings' is part of being male: Real men do not talk about 'soap opera' topics (which are for women)—real men are supposed to be only 'rational,' 'logical,' 'scientific,' and 'objective'. . . ."[78]

Still another possible reason for the difficulty of uncovering feelings is that the sender has an inadequate feeling vocabulary that prevents him or her from describing his or her feelings. Indeed, most people have deficient feeling vocabularies; too many people rely on general and vague terms, such as *good, bad, fine, okay, terrible, up, down,* and so on, to describe their feelings rather than describing them by using some of the more specific feeling words listed below:[79]

Feelings of Anger

aggravated	enervated	mean
angry	enraged	peeved
annoyed	furious	perturbed
belligerent	hateful	resentful
bitter	hostile	spiteful
bugged	intolerant	vengeful
cool	irritated	vindictive
cruel	mad	

Feelings of Sadness

abandoned	disappointed	low
alienated	down	neglected
alone	forlorn	rejected
ashamed	forsaken	sad
awful	grief	small
blue	hopeless	sorrow
crushed	humiliated	unhappy
defeated	hurt	unloved(able)
depressed	lonely	worthless
despondent		

Feelings of Fear

afraid	horrified	scared
alarmed	insecure	shy
anxious	intimidated	tense
apprehensive	nervous	threatened
desperation	overwhelmed	timid
embarrassed	panic	uneasy
fearful	restless	worried
frightened		

Feelings of Inadequacy

broken	helpless	paralyzed
cowardly	impotent	powerless
crippled	inadequate	small
deficient	incompetent	useless
demoralized	ineffective	vulnerable
disabled	inferior	weak
feeble		

Feelings of Stress

ambivalent	baffled	bothered
anxious	bewildered	caught

confused	frustrated	puzzled
conflicted	futile	skeptical
disgusted	helpless	trapped
dissatisfied	hopeless	uncomfortable
distressed	nervous	unsure
disturbed	overwhelmed	upset
doubtful	perplexed	vulnerable

Feelings of Happiness

aglow	gay	overjoyed
calm	glad	pleased
content	good	proud
elated	great	satisfied
enthused	happy	thrilled
excited	joyous	wonderful
fantastic		

Feelings of Love, Caring

affable	devoted	kind
affectionate	empathic	love(able)
altruistic	forgiving	peaceful
amiable	friendly	sensitive
caring	fulfilled	sympathy
close	genuine	tender
concerned	giving	warm(th)
considerate	humane	whole
cooperative	intimate	

Feelings of Adequacy

able	effective	powerful
adequate	fearless	robust
bold	healthy	secure
brave	important	self-assured
capable	nervy	stable
competent	peerless	strong
confident		

Another reason why uncovering feelings may be challenging is that the listener may not be skilled in listening for feelings. This lack of competence may be the result of previous interactions with senders who do not explicitly and specifically express that they are confused, depressed, anxious, and so on. Or perhaps the listener has interacted with senders who—not knowing how to express their feelings constructively—have expressed their feelings in a way that has created defensiveness in the listener (e.g., "You make me so angry when you act so stupid!") and has led the listener to stop listening rather than attempt to understand the sender's feelings. Also, it could result from the listener's inadequate feeling vocabulary; deficiency in feeling words limits the listener's ability to recognize and verbally reflect specific feelings. It is our contention, however, that the listener's difficulty in discerning feelings results, to a large extent, from the listener's inattention to and inexperience with "listening with the third ear." That is, the listener fails to listen to what is not spoken, or he or she fails to detect the contradiction(s) between what is spoken and what is unspoken. As an example, Shelia Pearce, a protective social worker for the elderly, frequently confronts contradictory messages:

> In a crisis case an elderly patient may say he agrees and is willing to go to a nursing home, thus leading me to believe that he feels there is no problem with this decision. At the same time as he rubs his face and twists his hands or a tear appears in his eye, the client is nonverbally saying the opposite.[80]

Research documents the importance of nonverbal communication in the conveying of feelings.[81] Yet, although the listener may note such obvious contradictory messages as exhibited in the situation cited above, he or she often does not attend to the more subtle messages such as the nervous fingers, strained vocal tone, downcast eyes, scarcely heard sigh, tense body, penetrating silence, and the thousands of other unspoken messages that the sender conveys.

Fortunately, by using perception-checking feeling responses, as well as by demonstrating appropriate attending behaviors, developing a supportive communication climate, and listening with empathy, the listener can assist the sender in expressing his or her feelings. Moreover, the listener can develop the skill of listening for feelings by engaging in therapeutic listening sessions in which he or she can practice helping the sender express his or her emotions, by learning how to prevent being controlled by emotions when confronted with a sender who creates a defensive communication climate, by enlarging his or her feeling vocabulary, and by becoming more attentive to and adept at decoding the sender's nonverbal messages. Developing skills to assist the sender in expressing his or her feelings clearly and improving personal skills in listening for feelings will enable the listener to make effective feeling responses. Both the sender and the listener can benefit. Feeling responses will aid the sender in exploring further his or her feelings, recognizing previously denied or buried feelings, clarifying these feelings, and dealing with a problem more effectively. Likewise, it will aid the listener in acknowledging the sender's feelings, viewing them from the sender's frame of reference, and understanding the sender/sender's problem more accurately.

13. *"You think Jones let you down, huh?"* This is a **thought response** that indicates the listener's desire to understand the sender's thoughts and to think with the sender. To test his or her understanding, the listener uses the approach of paraphrasing, which was first noted in chapter 6 as a means of increasing understanding during comprehensive listening. Equally useful for increasing understanding during therapeutic listening, this approach is discussed in detail in the following paragraph.

thought response

14. *"Am I correct in understanding that you feel betrayed because you think Jones has let you down?"* This response is both a **feeling and thought**

feeling and thought response

response. It indicates that the listener, having used all of his or her sensory equipment to listen to the sender's total message (which usually consists of both feelings and thoughts), desires to verify this understanding by using a paraphrase. In paraphrasing, the listener's goal is not to approve or disapprove, agree or disagree, praise or condemn; rather, it is to understand empathically the sender's feelings and thoughts from the sender's frame of reference. In essence, **paraphrasing** enables the listener to convey this message to the sender: "This is my understanding of how you are feeling and what you are thinking. Am I understanding you correctly?" Unfortunately, many listeners fail to test their understanding, and as a result of individual differences in assigning meaning to verbal and nonverbal expressions, true understanding never develops. Too often, listeners respond by saying, "I understand what you mean" or "I understand how you feel," and senders accept such responses as indicators of understanding when, in fact, there has been no real understanding expressed. Rogers and Farson stress the importance of testing for understanding by encouraging communicators to practice this rule of thumb: "Assume that one never really understands until he can communicate this understanding to the other's satisfaction."[82]

paraphrasing

To develop the skill of paraphrasing, the listener must recognize and practice proper phrasing and timing. Proper phrasing consists of the listener reflecting—in one's *own* words—his or her understanding of how the sender is feeling and what the sender is thinking. In selecting the appropriate words, the listener should strive to be *accurate* (by not adding new feelings/thoughts or deleting important feelings/thoughts), *concise* (by generally using fewer words than the sender has used to prevent redundancy), and *perceptive* (by showing an understanding of what is felt and said rather than just repeating word for word). In addition, the listener should develop an adequate vocabulary of entry phrases such as the following:

"If I understand you correctly, you're saying. . . ."

"Do you mean that? . . ."

"Let me tell you what I'm sensing. You. . . ."

"What I'm understanding you to say is. . . ."

"Let me repeat what I think you're saying. You. . . ."

"Are you saying that? . . ."

"Let's make sure I'm clear. You feel. . . ."

"What I'm hearing is. . . ."

An entry phrase that the listener should avoid is the commonly used "Are you trying to say? . . ." The word *trying* may be insulting to the sender, and it implies that the listener intends to supply thoughts that the sender may not be thinking. In other words, it conveys the notion that the listener is viewing the sender's thoughts from the listener's—rather than with the sender's—frame of reference.

It should also be noted that an entry phrase is not always necessary, as the thought response—*"You think Jones let you down, huh?"*—shows. To further illustrate, if the sender were to say, "I don't know what to do. I want to continue working, but then again, I would just love to be free to do what I want to do," the listener could—without an entry phrase—paraphrase by saying, "You're unsure about retiring, huh?"

When responding with feeling and thought responses to the first two hypothetical messages presented at the beginning of this chapter, the effective therapeutic listener might consider using paraphrases. For example, in response to the sender of Message 1, the listener might say, "Let me tell you what I'm sensing. You're lonely because the verbal, emotional, and physical intimacy that once existed between you and Tony now seems to be lacking," "Sounds as if you're sad because you think the romance is gone from your marriage," or "You're feeling neglected because your family members' needs are changing and you don't think you're needed much anymore, right?" Possible responses to the sender of Message 2 might be as follows: "What I'm understanding you to say is that you feel frustrated because you think your parents won't let you be yourself (or want you to remain a stranger to them)," "Sounds as if you're feeling unaccepted because you think your parents would not be satisfied with the real you, huh?" or "Are you saying that you're feeling controlled because your parents won't let you make your own decisions?"

Knowing *how* to paraphrase, the listener should also know *when* to paraphrase. The listener does not interrupt the sender to add his or her paraphrase; rather, he or she, recognizing the sender's regulatory cues, paraphrases at natural breaks in the interaction. Furthermore, he or she paraphrases when there is a meaningful purpose such as each of the following:

- To eliminate guesswork/speculation
- To admit confusion
- To ask for clarification
- To encourage the sender to continue talking so as to clarify, modify, expand, repeat, and so on, his or her feelings and thoughts
- To initiate the exploration of important feelings and thoughts that are still unexplored
- To assist the sender in listening to him- or herself with more clarity and accuracy
- To help the sender uncover layers of hidden thoughts and feelings so that he or she can then move beyond these formerly impeding thoughts and feelings
- To provide a supportive climate in which the sender feels safe, comfortable, and free of evaluation
- To develop empathy
- To establish rapport (and develop or maintain a positive relationship with the sender)
- To indicate recognition of, interest in, and concern for the sender
- To implement any other intent that will increase the listener's accurate understanding of the sender's feelings and thoughts from the sender's frame of reference and that will enhance the sender's self-exploration of his or her problem and, thus, help the sender reach his or her own solution.

Paraphrasing speakers' messages enables us to communicate that we are listening with understanding.

As we have just noted, paraphrasing is a very useful therapeutic listening skill; however, it is not without what some consider to be negative aspects. Paraphrasing is both energy-consuming and time-consuming. A great deal of time and effort is required for the listener to travel with the sender beneath the sender's surface feelings to uncover layers of hidden feelings and to identify the sender's thoughts—many of which are often disjointed and unclear—and then reflect understanding of the sender's feelings and thoughts for confirmation. Without doubt, using this skill can be exhausting and lengthy, but listening to understand—truly understand—often is such a task.

Another negative aspect is that paraphrasing can be redundant and annoying *if* the listener does no more than exchange or trade words with the sender. For example, if a sender says, "I'm depressed because you're leaving," and the listener responds, "Are you saying you're depressed because I'm leaving?" the listener is going to ridiculous extremes in using the paraphrasing approach. Such extremes often lead individuals who are first learning the paraphrasing approach to view paraphrasing as "useless parroting." In the following dialogue, Lange—a consultant—illustrates how he used paraphrasing to understand better one of his client's reservations about the effectiveness of using the paraphrasing approach during her workday as a supervisor.

CONSULTANT: You mean that you think people will find it repetitive?
CLIENT: No, not really, I just mean that it doesn't seem to get anywhere.

CONSULTANT: It doesn't?

CLIENT: No, and if my employees come to me with something to talk about, I like to be able to tell them what to do.

CONSULTANT: You prefer to give advice to your employees.

CLIENT: I just don't want to appear silly.

CONSULTANT: You think you'll appear silly if you try these skills?

CLIENT: Well, what if they come to me with a problem?

CONSULTANT: A problem?

CLIENT: Yeah, like with another {employee}.

CONSULTANT: You mean a personal conflict?

Lange continued paraphrasing in this manner until a specific employee problem had been identified. Using this approach, he convinced his client that rather than being useless parroting, paraphrasing can be a useful means of understanding another's feelings and thoughts.[83] The usefulness of paraphrasing, however, largely depends on the listener's discretion in determining when paraphrasing is and is not necessary to ensure understanding.

Yet another disadvantage is that the listener often finds the paraphrasing approach to be extremely artificial and mechanical when he or she first begins to use it. However, learning this skill is just like learning any other new skill (such as driving, skiing, or typing); the more one properly practices the skill, the more skillful one becomes and the more automatic is one's behaviors. By understanding the need for expending energy and time to achieve true understanding, by using discretion in applying paraphrasing, and by practicing properly the skill of paraphrasing, the effective therapeutic listener should find paraphrasing to be a very useful therapeutic listening approach.

Serving as an effective therapeutic listener by focusing attention, demonstrating attending behaviors, developing a supportive communication climate, listening with empathy, and responding appropriately, the listener is investing a part of his or her life in the life of a troubled sender—one who needs a sounding board to talk through a problem and reach his or her own solution. Helping a distressed person establish communication with him- or herself contributes to that person's individual strength and satisfaction; this is the real advantage of therapeutic listening. Although what we have described sounds clinical, and indeed the term "therapeutic" is clinical, we are really urging empathic, helpful listening practices. A desire to serve in such a capacity and the ability to be a true sounding board for the speaker can enable an individual listener to function effectively as a therapeutic listener.

> *We listen with our hearts.*
> When I listen with the heart
> I stop playing the game of non-listening.
> In other words,
> I step inside the other's skin;
> I walk in his shoes;
> I attempt to see things from his point-of-view;
> I establish eye contact; I give him conscious attention;

I reflect my understanding of his words;
I question;
I attempt to clarify.
Gently,
I draw the other out
as his lips stumble over words,
as his face becomes flushed,
as he turns his face aside.
I make the other feel that
I understand that he is important,
that I am grateful that he trusts me enough
to share deep, personal feelings with me.
I grant him worth.[84]

Summary

In this chapter, we have described five skills that the listener should practice when he or she is engaging in therapeutic listening—listening to provide a sounding board to allow a troubled sender to talk through a problem to his or her own solution. These five skills are focusing attention, demonstrating attending behaviors, developing a supportive communication climate, listening with empathy, and responding appropriately. Additionally, we have provided the reader with a means (1) to analyze and assess his or her present therapeutic listening responses by comparing them with those responses recognized as inhibiting or furthering self-exploration by the sender and (2) to develop, if necessary, more appropriate personal responses.

While we recognize the great need for therapeutic listeners today, particularly as people need someone to talk to, we have stressed the difficulty of this type of listening. The successful therapeutic listener must have the willingness to listen, the capacity to care, the desire to understand, honesty, and the patience to assume the role of sounding board; he or she also needs faith that the sender is, indeed, able to come to grips with his or her problem and derive his or her own solution to it. Finally, it is important for the listener to use discretion in determining when and when not to serve as a sounding board. The therapeutic listener should not play amateur psychiatrist; rather, he or she should deal only with those problems that do not have serious psychological ramifications. The rewards for listening with empathy, however, can be great, especially as you contribute to the well-being and growth of another human being.

Suggested Activities

1. If you have a hot line telephone counseling referral service in your community, arrange to attend one of the training sessions where volunteers are trained in the principles of listening with empathy.

What principles are stressed? What are the differences in listening with empathy over the telephone and listening with empathy to a person face-to-face?

2. Practice techniques of therapeutic listening. Permit a friend to talk with you about a problem (nothing of a serious psychological nature) related to his or her family, his or her school work, a friend, and so on. Listen to the problem therapeutically, providing a sounding board for your friend's problem. Employ only appropriate responses. Provide time for your friend to develop his or her own solution. After the listening experience, ask your friend how he or she felt about your role as a therapeutic listener. Have him or her react before you disclose the techniques you attempted to use. How do you feel about the experience? Were you an effective therapeutic listener? Why or why not? What will you do differently the next time you attempt to function as a therapeutic listener?

3. Arrange to interview a professional counselor. Ask him or her about his or her therapeutic listening techniques. What types of responses does he or she most frequently use? How does he or she listen with empathy and yet maintain a professional "doctor-patient" detachment? Does he or she find that the development of therapeutic listening skills improves with time?

4. Practice listening with understanding to develop skill in empathic listening. As someone talks with you about a problem, listen for both feelings and thoughts. Reflect your understanding by applying the approaches of perception-checking and paraphrasing.

5. Turn to the list of feeling words in the chapter. Expand the list with as many words as you can add. Why is it so difficult to handle such words?

6. From the list of feeling words, select five feelings that you have experienced. Recall and describe (in writing) the situation in which you experienced each feeling; also, describe other feelings that you felt in each situation.

7. Role-play communication problems that you have personally encountered recently. During the role-playing, practice therapeutic listening. Following the role-playing, discuss the important aspects and skills surrounding therapeutic listening.

8. To gain experience/practice in listening for feelings, ask a friend to discuss some event that happened to him or her in the distant or immediate past. As your friend discusses this event, listen—with all of your sensory equipment—for his or her present feelings. Reflect your understanding of his or her present feelings for confirmation or correction. How successful were you in identifying the other person's feelings?

9. Monitor your therapeutic listening experiences during the next week. Select one of your experiences and answer the following questions: In what therapeutic listening skills did you engage? How successful were

you in applying each skill in which you engaged? Which skill in which you engaged did you have the most difficulty applying? Why? What might you do—prior to or during your next therapeutic listening experience—to improve in the skill you found most difficult to apply? How helpful were you to the sender in the therapeutic listening experience?

10. What would you say to reflect the feelings and thoughts of a troubled sender who said, "I really don't know what to say"?

Notes

1. L. W. Foderaro, "Got a Problem? Dial a Shrink," *New York Times*, 6 March 1994, p. 4.
2. L. Genasci, "Therapy Hits the Road," *San Francisco Chronicle*, 19 August 1994, p. E2.
3. K. Barker, "Tending the Hot Lines," *The Washington Post*, 12 February 1984, p. C1.
4. C. Coursey, "Men Evolving Non-Violently," *Santa Rosa Press Democrat*, 21 August 1994, pp. D1, D6.
5. M. Klingaman, "Trained Students Are a Big Help to Their Troubled Peers," *The Evening Sun*, 20 January 1989, p. B1.
6. S. Adler, "Searching for Answers," *NEA Today* 11 (April 1993): 23.
7. R. Wicks, television interview with The Christophers, New York City, quoted in "Listening: First Aid for the Troubled Mind," *Grit*, 25 May 1980, p. 27.
8. R. Jones, "The Art of Listening," *Virginia Magazine*, 24 July 1983, p. 14.
9. E. G. Beier and E. G. Valens, *People Reading* (NY: Stein and Day, 1975), p. 154.
10. C. Krucoff, "Families: Listening to Teens," *The Washington Post*, 17 June 1980, p. B5.
11. C. Onnen, "Don't Try to Fix It . . . Just Listen," *Family Circle* 96 (12 July 1983): 6.
12. J. Novak, "In Touch," *The Evening Sun*, 6 October 1980, p. C2.
13. Ibid.
14. B. D. Sorrell, "Is Anybody Listening?" *Data Management* 13 (December 1975): 34.
15. J. H. Meyer and T. C. Meyer, "The Supervisor As Counselor—How to Help the Distressed Employee," *Management Review*, April 1982, p. 44.
16. G. M. Morgan, "Therapeutic Listening—A Communication Tool," *Training and Development Journal*, August 1983, p. 44.
17. L. Long, *Listening/Responding* (Monterey, CA: Brooks/Cole, 1978), p. 2.
18. V. Cohn, "Cancer and the Need to Talk," *Washington Post Health*, 20 August 1986, p. 8.
19. Statistics reported in National Center for Disease Control, "Perspective in Disease Prevention and Health Promotion," *Morbidity and Mortality Weekly Report* 34 (21 June 1985): 366.
20. L. DeNike, "Talk and Listen, A Suicide's Mother Pleads," *The Evening Sun*, 6 November 1984, p. C4.
21. H. D. Strupp and S. W. Hadley, "Specific vs. Nonspecific Factors in Psychotherapy," *Archives of General Psychiatry* 36 (September 1979): 1125.
22. F. D. Kelly, "Communicational Significance of Therapist Proxemic Cues, *Journal of Consulting and Clinical Psychology* 39 (October 1972): 345; J. P. Stokes, "Model Competencies for Attending Behavior," *Counselor Education and Supervision* 32 (September 1977): 23–27; R. F. Haase and D. T. Tepper, Jr., "Nonverbal Components of Empathic Communication," *Journal of Counseling Psychology* 19 (September 1972): 417–424.
23. Research shows that in a communication interaction between two Caucasians at a distance of six feet, the average amount of eye contact in which the communicators engage is as follows:

Individual gaze	60 percent
while listening	75 percent
while speaking	40 percent
length of gaze	3 seconds
Eye contact (mutual gaze)	30 percent
length of mutual gaze	1½ seconds

See M. Argyle, *Bodily Communication* (NY: International Universities Press, 1975), p. 229.

This nearly 2:1 ratio of looking while listening to looking while speaking may differ with black communicators. LaFrance and Mayo have found that in black-black interactions, black speakers tend to engage in more looking time at the listener while black listeners tend to engage in more looking away while attending to the speaker.

See M. LaFrance and C. Mayo, "Racial Differences in Gaze Behavior during Conversations: Two Systematic Observational Studies," *Journal of Personality and Social Psychology* 33 (May 1976): 547–552.

24. C. Broughton, "When Mother's Intuition Isn't Enough," *Redbook* 159 (May 1982): 56.

25. S. M. Jourard, *Disclosing Man to Himself* (Princeton, NJ: Van Nostrand Reinhold, 1968), p. 65; J. E. Pattison, "Effects of Touch on Self-Exploration and the Therapeutic Relationship," *Journal of Consulting and Clinical Psychology* 40 (April 1973): 170–175; A. Gottlieb, "Touching and Being Touched," *Mademoiselle* 83 (January 1982): 80–81, 167, 174.

26. T. Reik, *Listening with the Third Ear* (NY: Pyramid Books, 1948), pp. 124, 126.

27. T. Gordon, *Parent Effectiveness Training* (NY: Peter H. Wyden, 1970), pp. 41–45; T. Gordon, *Leader Effectiveness Training* (NY: Peter H. Wyden, 1977), pp. 60–62.

28. The authors' descriptions of characteristics are adapted from J. R. Gibb, "Defensive Communication," *Journal of Communication* 11 (September 1961): 142.

29. C. R. Rogers, *On Becoming a Person* (Boston: Houghton Mifflin, 1961), p. 336.

30. Stokes, "Model Competencies for Attending Behavior" pp. 23–27; D. Morris, *Manwatching* (NY: Abrams, 1977), pp. 133–135, 186–190; A. Mehrabian, *Silent Messages* (Belmont, CA: Wadsworth, 1971); S. M. Jourard, *Disclosing Man to Himself*; A. E. Scheflen, *Body Language and the Social Order* (Englewood Cliffs, NJ: Prentice-Hall, 1972); A. E. Scheflen, "The Significance of Posture in Communication Systems," *Psychiatry* 27 (November 1964): 326–329; M. Wiener et al., "Nonverbal Behavior and Nonverbal Communication," *Psychological Review* 79 (May 1972): 210–211; G. I. Nierenberg and H. H. Calero, *How to Read a Person like a Book* (NY: Pocket Books, 1973); P. F. Ostwald, *Soundmaking: The Acoustic Communication of Emotion* (Springfield, IL: Charles C Thomas, 1963), p. 25.

31. P. G. Friedman, *Listening Processes: Attention, Understanding, Evaluation*, 2d ed. (Washington, D.C.: National Education Association, 1983), p. 18.

32. While empathy is a crucial therapeutic listening skill, Rowan notes that "it [psychotherapy] is never a question of empathy alone." See J. Rowan, "Holistic Listening," *Journal of Humanistic Psychology* 26 (Winter 1986): 86. For differentiating descriptions and characteristics of empathic and therapeutic listeners, see A. J. Clark and T. M. Gudaitis, "A Synthesis of Research on Empathic Listening: Assumptions about a Paradigm" (Paper presented at the International Listening Association Preconvention Research Conference, Jacksonville, FL, 1991).

33. R. G. Carkhuff, *Helping and Human Relations*, Volume I (NY: Holt, Rinehart & Winston, 1969), p. 173.

34. N. Raskin, "Studies on Psychotherapeutic Orientation: Ideology in Practice" cited by C. R. Rogers, "Empathic: An Unappreciated Way of Being," *The Counseling Psychologist* 5 (1975): 5.

35. C. R. Rogers, "The Therapeutic Relationship: Recent Theory and Research," in *The Human Dialogue*, ed. F. W. Matson and A. Montague (NY: The Free Press, 1967), p. 250.

36. S. R. Covey, *The Seven Habits of Highly Effective People* (NY: Simon & Schuster, 1989), p. 241.

37. M. Mayeroff, *On Caring* (NY: Harper & Row, 1971), p. 30.

38. R. B. Adler, L. B. Rosenfeld, and N. Towne, *Interplay* (NY: Holt, Rinehart & Winston, 1980), p. 161.

39. J. J. Floyd, "Dialogic Listening" (Paper presented at the International Listening Association Convention, Scottsdale, Arizona, 1984), p. 6.

40. Rogers, *On Becoming a Person*, pp. 18, 333.

41. E. B. Wycoff, "Canons of Communication," *Personnel Journal* 60 (March 1981): 211–212.

42. C. R. Rogers and R. E. Farson, "Active Listening," in *Readings in Interpersonal and Organizational Communication*, 2d ed., eds. R. Huseman, C. M. Logue, and D. I. Freshley (Boston: Holbrooks Publishing Company, 1973), p. 553.

43. S. E. Kogler Hill, "The Multistage Process of Interpersonal Empathy," in *Improving Interpersonal Competence: A Laboratory Approach*, ed. S. E. Kogler Hill (Dubuque, IA: Kendall/Hunt Publishing Company, 1982), p. 86.

44. D. Johnson, *Reaching Out* (Englewood Cliffs, NJ: Prentice-Hall, 1972), p. 47.

45. Rogers, *On Becoming a Person*, p. 18.

46. E. Koile, *Listening As a Way of Becoming* (Waco, TX: Calibre Books, 1977), p. 91.
47. D. G. Leathers, *Nonverbal Communication Systems* (Boston: Allyn and Bacon, 1976), p. 236.
48. R. D. Quinn, "Psychotherapists' Expressions as an Index to the Quality of Early Therapeutic Relationships" (Ph.D. diss., University of Chicago, 1955).
49. T. Bruneau, "Empathy and Listening: A Conceptual Review and Theoretical Directions," *Journal of the International Listening Association* 3 (1989): 6; in this 20-page article, Bruneau provides a thorough review of listening and empathy.
50. Rogers and Farson, "Active Listening," p. 547.
51. L. M. Brammer, *The Helping Relationship* (Englewood Cliffs, NJ: Prentice-Hall, 1979), pp. 36–38.
52. C. M. Kelly, "Empathic Listening," in *Bridges not Walls*, 2d ed., ed. J. Stewart (Reading, MA: Addison-Wesley, 1977), p. 224.
53. C. L. Mithers, "When You Talk, Does He Listen?" *Mademoiselle* 86 (March 1980): 201.
54. V. Bozzi, "Interruptions: An Equal-Opportunity Disturber," *Psychology Today* 21 (September 1987): 201. See also S. Geiger and B. Reeves, "We Interrupt This Program . . . Attention for Television Sequences," *Human Communication Research* 19 (March 1993): 368–387.
55. E. Sundstrom, "An Experimental Study of Crowding: Effect of Room Size, Intrusion, and Goal Blocking on Nonverbal Behavior, Self-Disclosure, and Self-Reported Stress," *Journal of Personality and Social Psychology* 32 (October 1975): 645–654.
56. Rogers, *On Becoming a Person*, pp. 330–331.
57. Ibid., p. 331.
58. A. L. McGinnis, *The Friendship Factor* (Minneapolis: Augsburg Publishing House, 1979), p. 71.
59. Rogers and Farson, "Active Listening," p. 545.
60. B. L. Stern, "You and Your Friends: Keep Good Will without Good Advice," *Vogue* 170 (July 1980): 56.
61. D. Borisoff and D. F. Hahn, "Dimensions of Intimacy: The Interrelationships between Gender and Listening," *Journal of the International Listening Association* 6 (1992): 34.
62. Mayeroff, *On Caring*, p. 34.
63. J. Novak, "Separating Fantasy and Reality in Two-Career Households," *The Evening Sun*, 16 May 1983, p. B2.
64. Gordon, *Parent Effectiveness Training*, p. 322.
65. C. R. Rogers, *A Way of Being* (Boston: Houghton Mifflin, 1980), p. 12.
66. F. R. Staples and R. B. Sloane, "Truax Variables, Speech Characteristics, and Therapeutic Outcome," *Journal of Nervous and Mental Disease* 163 (August 1976): 135–140.
67. R. G. Nichols, "The Struggle to Be Human" (Paper delivered at the International Listening Association Convention, Atlanta, GA, 1980), p. 7.
68. J. Powell, "Reflections on 'Estrangement' and 'Encounter'" in *Bridges Not Walls*, ed. John Stewart (Reading, MA: Addison-Wesley, 1973), p. 178.
69. J. Voist, "May I Have Your Attention, Please?" *Redbook* 153 (September 1979): 52.
70. Plutarch, *Plutarch's Moralia*, trans. F. C. Babbitt (Cambridge, MA: Harvard University Press, 1927), pp. 213–215.
71. L. R. Heun and R. E. Heun, *Developing Skills for Human Interaction*, 2d ed. (Columbus, OH: Merrill, 1978), p. 119.
72. J. L. Wallen, "Developing Effective Interpersonal Communication" in *Communicating Interpersonally*, eds. R. W. Pace, B. D. Peterson, and T. R. Radcliffe (Columbus, OH: Merrill, 1973), p. 231.
73. R. D. Halley, "Listener Responses to Significant Emotion: A Procedural Model" (Paper presented at the International Listening Association Convention, Atlanta, GA, 1989), pp. 2, 8.
74. Ibid., p. 8
75. Ibid., pp. 1–12.
76. S. B. Shimanoff, "The Role of Gender in Linguistic References to Emotive States," *Communication Quarterly* 30 (Spring 1983): 178.
77. Ibid.
78. S. Hite, "Women's Message to Men: 'Open Up,'" *The Sun*, 18 October 1987, p. 7F.
79. From *Active Listening Skills for Staff Development: A Cognitive Viewpoint* (St. Paul: Minnesota Department of Education), pp. 8–9.
80. Sharon L. DuBose, "Interview with Shelia F. Pearce." Unpublished paper, College Park, MD: University of Maryland, 1983. Used by permission.

81. R. L. Birdwhistell, as cited in M. L. Knapp, *Nonverbal Communication in Human Interaction*, 2d ed. (NY: Holt, Rinehart & Winston, 1978), p. 30; Mehrabian, *Silent Messages*, pp. 43–44.
82. Rogers and Farson, "Active Listening," p. 549.
83. J. I. Lange, "Seeking Client Resistance: Rhetorical Strategy in Communication Consulting," *Journal of Applied Communication Research* 12 (Spring 1984): 58–59.
84. Loretta Girzaitis, *Listening a Response Ability* (Winona, MN: St. Mary's Press, 1972), p. 42. Reprinted with permission.

- *Critical listening is listening to comprehend and then evaluate the message.*

- *Critical listening is important when the intent of the message is to influence one to change an attitude and/or behavior.*

- *The effective critical listener*

  - *recognizes the dimensions of source credibility and the influence of that credibility in the process of influence*

  - *examines the arguments and evidence presented in the message in order to ascertain the truth and the validity of the message*

  - *understands the effects of the psychological appeals in responding to the message*

  - *assumes responsibility for being aware of one's own responses to messages of influence in order to develop critical listening criteria for responding appropriately*

CHAPTER 8

Critical Listening

Read the following account of the 1993 disappearance of Polly Klaas, and then follow further directions.

At approximately 10:40 P.M. on October 1, 1993, a man appeared at Polly Hannah Klaas's Petaluma, California, bedroom door where 12-year-old Polly and two friends, Kate and Gillian, were having a slumber party. Threatening the three girls with a knife, the man ordered them to the floor. With torn white cloth, he tied and gagged them before putting pillowcases over their heads. He then left with Polly. After struggling for about twenty minutes to free themselves, the unbound Kate and Gillian awakened Polly's mother, Eve Nichol, who was asleep in the adjoining room, and told her that Polly had been kidnapped. At 11:03, Mrs. Nichol called 911.

Within hours after Polly's abduction, family, friends, and the community set up the Polly Klaas Search Center. During the next 64 days, Petaluma sustained *a community outpouring that ranked with the attention given to the Lindbergh kidnapping. Thousands of volunteers raised more than $300,000 in contributions, stuffed envelopes, and circulated over 8 million missing-child fliers bearing both a photo of the curly-haired Polly with the broad, dimpled smile and a composite of the suspect (done first by the police and later by forensic artist Jean Boylan). Thousands of other friends and strangers searched ranch lands, creeks, and fields in the Petaluma area of Sonoma County. Ribbons of lavender (Polly's favorite color) adorned Petaluma's trees while a single candle—to light Polly's way home— burned in the front window of Polly's house.*

Soon, news of the abduction and efforts to bring Polly home spread across the nation and beyond. On 3 October, Polly's father, Marc

Klaas, appealed to President Clinton for help during a televised California Town Hall Meeting. Two days later, America's Most Wanted aired the story. With the fliers circulating and the national media covering the kidnapping, Polly soon became "America's Child" — "a symbol of children victimized by a culture of violence, . . . where [children] are not safe in their own bedrooms."[1] With her smiling image in airports as distant as Africa and in newspapers in Europe, Polly "became simply Everyone's Child, a symbol not just of missing kids, but of children abused, neglected, thrown away and victimized by a social violence that has become chillingly commonplace."[2] Indeed, the people of Petaluma, whose "mission became a statement about what they could not tolerate in their community,"[3] won international admiration for "their undaunted effort to get out the publicity they were determined would bring the child back."[4]

Then, after two months of coast-to-coast leads but no firm suspect, Dana Jaffe triggered a series of events that led to the arrest of Polly's kidnapper six days later. On 28 November, Jaffe called Sonoma County Sheriff Deputy Mike McManus and told him she had found some suspicious items, including clothing and white cloth, on her property off Pythian Road (about a 40-minute drive from Polly's Petaluma home). She also reminded McManus that deputies—responding to her 11:42 P.M. 911 call on 1 October—had checked out a trespasser at the same spot. After gathering the items from Jaffe, McManus then researched the earlier trespassing incident. He learned that two deputies (who were unaware of Polly's abduction because the radio frequency they were using did not carry the all-points bulletin on a kidnapping suspect) had found a man near Pythian Road at 12:08 A.M. They had questioned him, searched his car (but found nothing unusual) and conducted a routine check to see if he were wanted on an arrest warrant and found that Davis was "clean." Finally the deputies had given him a field sobriety test, helped him get his car out of a ditch, released him 38 minutes later, and escorted him off of Jaffe's property.

Having discovered that the man who had claimed to be "sightseeing" on the Pythian Road property was 39-year-old Richard Allen Davis, McManus checked Davis's background and found an eleven-page criminal record, including two previous convictions for kidnapping and others for assault, burglary, and robbery. Having spent the past twenty years in and out of jail, Davis had last been released from prison on 27 June 1993, after serving 8 years of a 16-year sentence. McManus immediately met with Petaluma police investigating Polly's abduction. FBI agents on the case sent the items

Jaffe had found to forensic experts in Washington, D.C.; FBI analysis revealed that the evidence found (including several white cloth strips matching those used to bind Kate and Gillian during the abduction) was related to Polly's kidnapping.

On 30 November, investigators tracked Davis to his sister's house on the Coyote Valley Indian Reservation in Mendocino County, California, and arrested him for violating the terms of his parole by leaving San Mateo County, California, without permission. At the scene of Davis's arrest, investigators also discovered at least 16 grams of methamphetamine. Davis was held in the Mendocino County Jail. That same day, investigators learned that Davis, who had been arrested by a California Highway Patrol officer for drunken driving on 19 October, had been jailed in that same jail for less than 24 hours and then released after computer checks had revealed once again that Davis was "clean."

During the next three days, evidence against Davis mounted. On the morning of 1 December, Petaluma police and FBI officials announced that Davis was the "prime suspect" in Polly's abduction. That afternoon, Kate and Gillian picked Davis out of a group of photos and a lineup of men and identified him as possibly being the kidnapper. On 2 December, investigators linked Davis to Petaluma when they learned that his estranged mother lived in the town. The following day, investigators announced that a palm print found in Polly's bedroom matched Davis's hand.

On 4 December, more than 50 police and FBI agents and more than 1000 volunteers searched the fields and woods off Pythian Road. Bloodhounds, helicopters with specialized equipment, and over 300 trained search-and-rescue personnel combed the rural, hilly area near the spot where Davis had been reported trespassing on 1 October. Investigators also searched the residence of Davis's sister, where Davis had been arrested three days earlier. They found no trace of Polly.

On that same day, officials transferred Davis from the jail in Mendocino County to the jail in Sonoma County where Davis confessed that he had abducted and killed Polly. He then gave investigators information that led them to her body. Late that afternoon, investigators found Polly's body—under lumber scraps— near an abandoned saw mill in a wooded area about 30 yards from Highway 101 south of Cloverdale, Sonoma County's smallest town (about a 30-minute drive from Pythian Road). At a 9:00 P.M. press conference in Petaluma, Petaluma Police Chief Dennis DeWitt announced, "Polly is dead."

Two days later, on 7 December, Davis was arraigned on kidnapping and murder charges in Sonoma County Municipal Court, and his trial was scheduled for 14 February 1995.[5]

Using the preceding information as your knowledge base, critically "listen" to each of the following speakers' thoughts and feelings and then further apply your critical listening skills as you answer the question(s) asked about each message.

To what American values do Clinton's actions appeal?

In early September of 1994, "when President Clinton signed a sweeping national crime bill with a federal three strikes law, he dedicated it to Polly and handed the pen to her father in the White House rose garden."[6]

To what needs does the mother appeal?

On 9 December 1993, towns throughout Sonoma County held memorial services for Polly. Coakley was among the 700 people who attended the memorial in Sonoma, where one mother, when asked why she had come, looked at her four young children gathered around her and responded, "They're the reason I came."[7]

What type of psychological appeal does each of the following three speakers use to gain an emotional response from you as a listener?

"The small candle flame—the one that flickered in Eve Nichol's front window every night since her daughter Polly Klaas disappeared—went out last night [4 December]."[8]

California Senator Dianne Feinstein: "To the nation, Polly is the symbol of every family's nightmare. It tells us something about the awful brutality of the world."[9]

Polly's parents, Marc Klaas and Eve Nichol: "You promised you wouldn't give up until we found Polly and you've kept your word. . . . [Y]ou held our sweet Polly in your hearts and created a community effort so compassionate, so resolute and so giving you've inspired an entire nation."[10]

1. **What kind of reasoning does Davis use in the following statement?**
2. **What questions would you as a listener ask and answer to critically evaluate Davis's reasoning?**

Claiming that the sexual assault allegation leveled against him is untrue, Davis said, "It's just all this other stuff that they're trying to stick me with. Like one guy said to me, it's like cooking spaghetti. You throw it at the wall and see what sticks."[11]

Having cited the following statistics, the speaker might make what valid claims?

Prior to kidnapping and murdering Polly Klaas, Davis had two convictions for kidnapping (in 1985 in San Mateo County and in

1977 in Alameda County), three convictions for burglary (in 1985 and 1975 in San Mateo County), two convictions for assault with a deadly weapon (in 1976 in Napa County) and another for assault (in 1985 in San Mateo County), one conviction for robbery (in 1985 in San Mateo County) and another for attempted robbery (in 1985 in Stanislaus County), and one conviction for dealing in stolen property (in 1977 in San Mateo County).[12]

Using a scale of 1 (least reliable) to 5 (most reliable), evaluate the reliability/credibility of each of the following three cited sources.

Ben Ermini, a spokesperson for the National Center for Missing and Exploited Children, stated, "The case has had a dramatic impact on raising public awareness across the country, and when you raise public awareness you raise the awareness of federal, state and local legislators. It also has caused law enforcement administration to re-evaluate the way they handle these cases."[13]

Phil Grosse, Polly Klaas Search Center volunteer, said his "most vibrant memory was working the phones the day after Davis led police to Polly's body. . . . From 8 A.M. to 11 P.M. at night he could not take his hand off the phone. A purple dot was placed under each part of the country where a call came through. By day's end it was covered."[14]

After an FBI agent (who had investigated the case from the beginning) had examined the body and the surrounding scene, he "couldn't just walk away. So he placed a poinsettia plant where the body had lain as his good-bye." Speaking of this incident, an FBI spokesperson, noted: "He has kids of his own, and he felt he should do something. It was a symbol, a gesture."[15]

Label each of the following three statements as fact, opinion, or inference.

"The day after police found her body, . . . it became clear that her kidnapper took more than the life of a 12-year-old girl. He stole a piece of every person who saw the smiling face on 8 million posters; he killed something in each heart that held on to the hope that Polly Klaas would come home alive."[16]

On 14 December and 15 December 1993, Marc Klaas appeared on five television programs: "Today," "Good Morning, America," "Donahue," "Larry King Live," and "Geraldo"; on 21 and 23 December 1993, Eve Nichol was a guest on two television programs: "Today Show" and "Prime Time Live."[17]

"Polly's death will be used often by politicians in the coming weeks and months. . . . It will be cited whenever people talk about crimes against children."[18]

Identify and analyze the propaganda techniques used in the following three messages.

"Many expressed shock that such a crime should be committed in Sonoma County, which has long prided itself as being the sort of folksy, semi-rural place where residents could sample the cosmopolitan atmosphere of San Francisco, but raise children in relative safety."[19]

"Sgt. Kevin Broin of Mendocino County said, 'It's just as well [that Davis was transferred from the jail in Mendocino to the jail in Sonoma County on December 4] because we've received a lot of calls from people saying, "Kill the bastard."'"[20]

Surprised by the political reaction to the Polly Klaas kidnapping and murder, Davis said, "All this hoopla. Even the president. Everybody jumped on this. It helps them out. I was very surprised but, hey, politicians are politicians."[21]

1. **What kind of reasoning do the following speakers use?**
2. **What is each speaker's alleged cause and alleged effect?**
3. **What questions would you ask and answer to critically evaluate each speaker's reasoning?**

"Asked why he did it, Davis blamed a potent marijuana cigarette. 'I was messed up. They don't want to believe that. I bought a joint off a dude and got more than I bargained for. There was no premeditation, no intent. . . . I made a mistake of buying a quart of beer. As I was walking back to the 7-Eleven I met the homeless dudes. I bought the weed.'"[22]

"Davis . . . is being held without bail in a special unit of the Sonoma County Jail to keep him away from other prisoners. Assistant Sheriff John Sully said isolation of prisoners jailed for offenses against children is standard practice because 'there is a code among inmates that harming children is not acceptable behavior.'"[23] Journalist John W. Sweeney elaborates on this code: "In the culture of prison, inmates who sexually abused children are looked down on and can be targets of violence."[24]

1. **What possible thoughts and/or feelings of those spreading the rumor does the following rumor reflect?**
2. **As a critical listener, what actions would you take to avoid being a part of this rumor mill?**

"The rumor took on a life of its own: A Santa Rosa cop heard it and mentioned it to a booking clerk at Sonoma County Jail, who passed it on to the sergeant, who alerted the lieutenant in charge.

A call then went to the assistant sheriff at home: A member of Polly Klaas' family [Polly's stepfather] had been arrested in connection with her abduction and was about to be booked into the same jail as Richard Allen Davis, the man who confessed to kidnapping and killing her."[25]

To evaluate the remaining messages, you may need the following background information on the "Three Strikes, You're Out" initiative (Proposition 184 on the 8 November 1994, California ballot): This initiative would (1) impose sentences of 25 years to life in prison for repeat offenders convicted of a third felony (of any kind) after having previously been convicted of two violent or serious felonies and (2) reduce from 50 percent to 20 percent the maximum amount of time off a prisoner can be credited for work-time or good behavior.[26]

1. **What kind of argument does Owens use in the following statement?**
2. **What does Owens overlook in his argument?**

Shortly after Polly's body was discovered, radio talk show host Ronn Owens urged listeners to sign the petitions for the "Three Strikes, You're Out" initiative. . . . Owens appealed to his listeners: "Polly is a symbol and Davis is a symbol. Either you sit at home and cry about Polly or you do something about it."[27]

1. **What kind of argument are Lungren and Ihde using?**
2. **Create a syllogism of Lungren and Ihde's complete argument including the missing premise.**

Both Lungren [California Attorney General] and Ihde [Sonoma County Sheriff] said "they felt confident that had such a law [the "Three Strikes" initiative] been in effect previously, Davis would have been in prison and not released on parole in San Mateo County."[28]

1. **What reasoning fallacy does Turer suggest supporters of the "Three Strikes" initiative are making?**
2. **What support does Turer give for his arguments?**

Commenting on the "Three Strikes" initiative, Sonoma County defense attorney Stephen Turer said, "To take this one case [Polly's] and use it to lock everybody up will flood our already overcrowded prisons. The reaction is very emotional and lacks common sense. This is using a bad case to make bad law."[29]

Critically evaluate the following evidence used to support the investigators' charge of sexual assault against Davis.[30]

Despite reports by sources that items found off Pythian Road "included an adult-sized sweatshirt, a used condom, a pair of girl's tights and pieces of cloth," Davis has "vigorously denied molesting" Polly Klaas.[31]

Create a syllogism of the Klaas family's complete argument for opposing the "Three Strikes" initiative.

"The Klaas Family, whose little girl's violent death spurred on 'three strikes,' opposes Proposition 184 as the wrong approach to violent crime. . . . [What is needed instead is] a repeat offender law that targets violent criminals—not one that sweeps hundreds of thousands of non-violent offenders into life prison terms."[32]

After you have studied this chapter, you may want to re-evaluate your answers to the preceding questions.

critical listening: listening to evaluate the message

The fourth purpose for listening goes beyond comprehensive listening and adds the dimension of judgment, for **critical listening is listening to comprehend and then evaluate the message**. The critical listener makes a decision to accept or reject a message on the basis of sound criteria. Listening should be critical especially when the listener is exposed to a persuasive message—a message designed to influence a change in the listener.

The Need for Critical Listeners

Now, as never before, we are confronted by speakers who want to change our attitudes and our behavior. Daily, we are flooded with persuasive messages—ranging from family members' pleas to buy that beach condominium or to vacation in Hawaii, candidates' campaign speeches, radio and television commercials and editorials (and newscasts), artists' songs, sponsors' public service announcements, recruiters' appeals, doctors' recommendations, employers' suggestions, classroom lectures, salespersons' pitches, and telephone solicitations to problem-solving discussions, conversations, lobbyists' views, briefings advocating new procedures, and leaders' pleas. The late S. I. Hayakawa described the unparalleled position in which we live:

> The citizen of today, Christian or Jew, . . . financier or farmhand, stockbroker or stockboy, has to interpret more words a day than the citizen of any earlier time in world history. Literate or semi-literate, we are assailed by words all day long: news commentators, soap operas, campaign speeches, newspapers, the propaganda of pressure groups or governments—all of these trying to tell us something, to manipulate our beliefs, whether about the kind of toothpaste to use or the kind of economic system to support.[33]

Since freedom of speech ensures equal rights to both the honest and dishonest speaker,[34] we must be effective critical listeners if we are to protect and control ourselves rather than allowing others to control us. Wendell Johnson has stressed the importance of our being critical listeners:

> As speakers, men have become schooled in the arts of persuasion, and without the counter-art of listening a man can be persuaded—even by his own words—to eat foods that ruin his liver, to abstain from killing flies, to vote away his right to vote, and to murder his fellows in the name of righteousness. The art of listening holds for us the desperate hope of withstanding the spreading ravages of commercial, nationalistic, and ideological persuasion.[35]

Developing Purposeful Listening Skills

Daly and others offer suggestions on what listeners can do to protect themselves from being controlled by skilled persuaders:

> The listener can best fortify her- or himself against the process of control through skillful persuasion . . . [with] awareness of . . . psychological appeals. Separating the message from the speaker will immediately blunt the force of much persuasion, allowing the listener to like a speaker but yet to disagree. Skill lies in exposing oneself to information as much as possible, while reducing the risk of being unduly swayed. Good listeners are conscious of the line of argument, the supporting evidence, the relevance of one to the other, facts and influence, and the appeals being employed. Values and self awareness have much to do with resisting the appeal of others. To fully open one's mind and then to resist the appeal of another is a significant transaction, not a failure to communicate.[36]

Our becoming schooled in the art of listening critically, then, as Gunn noted, "may mean not just being realistic and alert to the times in which we are alive, but quite literally it may mean being and staying alive."[37] Indeed, history is replete with examples of individuals whose lives might have been saved if they had been schooled in the art of critical listening. The men, women, and older children who obeyed the Reverend Jim Jones's command to commit suicide in a Guyana jungle compound in 1978 are nearly 1,000 tragic examples of such individuals. Other tragic examples of cult members include eighty-six followers of David Koresh in Texas in 1993 and fifty-three followers of Luc Journet in Switzerland and Canada in 1994.[38]

Interaction of Critical Thinking and Critical Listening

Many educators, observing college students' inability to critically examine their own and others' ideas, believe that direct instruction in thinking strategies (the key of which is **critical thinking** skills) can help students to better understand their own approaches to analyzing information and solving problems. Implementing educators' concern, over 800 colleges and universities now offer courses in critical thinking.[39]

critical thinking

Although definitions of critical thinking inside and outside these classrooms vary greatly, some commonalities exist. One common aspect researchers have found is that attitude is essential to effective critical thinking. This attitude, which Siegel refers to as a "critical spirit,"[40] belongs to a person who has "a certain character, . . which seeks reason and avoids arbitrary judgment. . . . There must also be a love or passion for ideas even when what is discovered is in contradiction to one's most deeply held convictions."[41] Thus, as Jones notes, "although a student may possess the cognitive abilities to think critically, the individual may not be disposed or inclined to use them. Consequently, researchers maintain that critical thinking also includes an affective dimension, called dispositions or traits of mind, that characterizes a critical thinker's way of behaving."[42]

Another commonality relates to the skills involved. Ninety-five percent of the forty-six national experts Facione surveyed agreed that **analysis** (examining ideas/identifying and analyzing arguments), **evaluation**

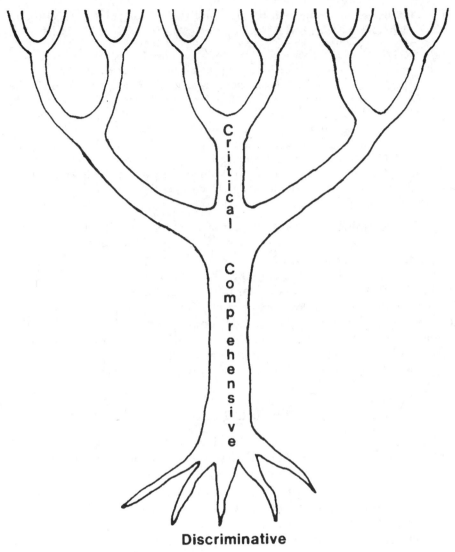

Critical

Comprehensive

Discriminative

Critical branch of the Wolvin-Coakley Listening Taxonomy.

(assessing claims and arguments), and **inference** (querying evidence, conjecturing alternatives, and drawing conclusions) are central to critical thinking.[43] Halpern discovered that the most commonly stated skills in critical thinking definitions are **application, analysis, synthesis,** and **evaluation** of information.[44] Ruminski, Hanks, and Spicer, surveying eighty-eight college communication instructors, found that 90 percent offered instruction in critical thinking and most conceptualized critical thinking as **analysis** and **evaluation.**[45] Ruminski et al. obtained other findings such as this commentary by one respondent: "They [students] complain and say they wish they could just memorize . . . because evaluation of . . . ideas is too hard."[46]

Jones cites still another area of agreement among critical thinking scholars: Metacognitive or self-monitoring skills should be included in critical thinking. She defines metacognition as "being aware of one's thinking as one performs specific tasks and then using this awareness to control what one is doing."[47]

A fourth shared aspect is the inclusion of another group of skills—communication skills, including listening—as being central to critical thinking. This aspect, as well as the previously discussed commonalities, is included in Paul and Nosich's definition of critical thinking:

> Critical thinking is the intellectually disciplined process of actively and skillfully conceptualizing, applying, analyzing, synthesizing or evaluating information gathered from, or generated by observation, experience, reflections, reasoning, or communication, as a guide to belief and action. . . . It is based on universal values . . . clarity, accuracy, precision, consistency, relevance, good reasons, depth, breadth and fairness. . . . It entails examination of purpose; questions at issues; assumptions; concepts; facts; inferences; implications and consequences; objections from alternative viewpoints, and frame of reference. . . . It entails traits of mind . . . independence of thought . . . and critical reading, writing, speaking and listening skills.[48]

Other critical thinking specialists, such as Glaser, also recognize the important interaction of critical thinking and critical listening abilities:

> One must be disposed to *listen* to another's presentation of opinion or argument, no matter whether he/she agrees with you or not. To *understand* the other person's point of view broadens one's ability to deal both with the differences in perception or values between one's self and others and with the emotional surcharge which is being represented by the other's assertions.[49]

Thus, as listeners in mass and public situations involving persuasive messages, in problem-solving groups, in interpersonal dialogues characterized by differing points of view, in reflective intrapersonal communication, and so on, we should function as both critical thinkers and critical listeners.

The development of such critical thinking and critical listening abilities is probably the result of incremental skills that grow more mature and sophisticated as an individual matures. While educators are calling for the development of curricula in schools to provide even young children with some understanding of how to deal with persuasive media, it must be recognized that the level of sophistication progresses in some way as the thinking listener gains experience and training. McQuillen, for example, discovered that fourth and fifth graders have greater capability to develop compliance-resisting strategies than do first graders, just as the ability to edit and adapt persuasive strategies to the needs of a listener increases with cognitive and social maturity.[50]

Process of Persuasion

As we have previously stated, the critical listener's decision to accept or reject a message must be based on sound criteria. Understanding the **process**

of persuasion as it applies to listeners will help listeners establish these criteria and make careful judgments whether they are listening to so-called "informative" messages that are mere rumors or to persuasive messages.

The concept of influence may be viewed as a continuum of influences. On the one end is **persuasion**, which has been defined by Goyer as "the process by means of which one party purposefully secures a voluntary change of behavior, mental and/or physical, on the part of another party by employing appeals to both feeling and intellect."[51] On the other end, we have **coercion** in which the receiver is given no choice or a choice between highly undesirable alternatives.

If you are told to vote for Raymond Ryan for city mayor because he can accomplish his campaign promises, you are given a *persuasive* choice to accept or reject the speaker's thesis. If you are told to stop smoking because you will die of lung cancer, you are presented with a more *coercive* message. The extreme of coercive influence is the use of force. A robber's message of "Hand over your money" at gunpoint is a graphic example of when you, the receiver, would be left with no choice or with a choice between highly undesirable alternatives. Likewise, on 18 September 1994, chief U.S. negotiator Jimmy Carter warned that an invasion of Haiti was imminent if Haitian military leaders did not agree to resign and accept the restoration to power of exiled President Aristide while 2000 U.S. paratroopers were flying toward Haiti and 1000 special forces were aboard a U.S. aircraft carrier off the shore. This scenario graphically illustrates the use of force. Cedras, leader of the military junta, did not agree to step down until his deputy entered the negotiation room and convinced him that the U.S. invasion was in progress. Observers noted that the agreement "wouldn't have happened if it weren't for all those troops on the carriers and the planes in the air. It wasn't just Jimmy Carter's persuasive powers that got this [the agreement] done."[52]

Most messages do not fit neatly into the persuasive or coercive category but, instead, fall somewhere along the continuum between the two extremes. Thus, advertising, propaganda, political campaigns, religion, education, and most means of social influence will share elements of persuasion and coercion. It is to be hoped, however, that these messages will ultimately be persuasive and, thus, leave listeners with a choice. The receivers' not being presented with a choice is inconsistent with a basic tenet of American democracy, that of freedom of choice.

The process of influence usually takes the form of a psychological sequence. This sequence was identified by Monroe and has been labeled the **"motivated sequence."** According to Monroe, to persuade or to be persuaded, the message must include five steps:

1. Attention—getting the attention of the listener
2. Need—demonstrating the problem or the need for the proposal
3. Satisfaction—presenting the proposal to satisfy the need
4. Visualization—illustrating what will happen if the proposal is accepted or what will happen if it is rejected
5. Action—issuing a challenge or an appeal to the listener[53]

These steps describe what occurs as communicators attempt to influence. It is a system, but it should be viewed as more of a process than the listing might suggest. Actually, some of the steps may transpire simultaneously. The results may be visualized, for instance, while the solution/satisfaction step is presented. Any persuasive message, however, whether it is an ad, a speech, or a sale's pitch, can be seen to conform to this psychological sequence.

Effective persuasion usually does not result in a behavioral change in the receiver on the basis of one persuasive message. A sequence of messages is required to accomplish the task. Thus, most persuasive efforts take the form of a campaign—television commercials, political campaigns, repeated telephone calls, a series of speeches on an issue. Contemplate, for example, the relentless campaigns of MCI and AT&T for our long distance telephone business; in a 1994 MCI televised ad, MCI acknowledges that it will take the company years to attract all of AT&T's customers. When you consider the amount of stimuli bombarding us as receivers, it is understandable why a concerted effort over an extended time is necessary for meaningful change to result.

Skills Involved in Critical Listening

Because the persuasive sequence takes time and leaves the receiver with a voluntary choice, it is useful to consider the components of an effective persuasive effort. The classical Greek rhetorician, Aristotle, first described our system of persuasion in *The Rhetoric*.[54] He determined that a persuasive message required three components: **ethos**—speaker credibility; **logos**—logical arguments; and **pathos**—psychological appeals. These three components must interact to be maximally effective in securing a voluntary change in the listener. As critical listeners, we need to be aware of how these components function to persuade us.

ethos

logos

pathos

Though we can analyze a persuasive message according to these three components, listeners often are unable to distinguish the emotional from the logical components of a particular persuasive message. Some individuals may respond on an emotional level to a logical argument, while others may be more responsive on the cognitive level.[55] Individual listeners will respond differently to the same persuasive message.

Research on speaker credibility has been helpful in identifying some of the factors and dimensions of the concept. The three most frequently cited **dimensions of source credibility** are the following:

dimensions of source credibility

- **Trustworthiness**—Is the speaker honest, reliable, fair-minded, and sincere? What is the speaker's intent? Whose interest—the listener's or his or her own—does the speaker have in mind?

trustworthiness

- **Expertise**—Is the speaker competent in, an authority on, and/or experienced in the subject about which he or she is speaking?

expertise

- **Dynamism**—Does the speaker have personal magnetism, forcefulness, enthusiasm?[56]

dynamism

Most senders are perceived by listeners as possessing these dimensions in varying degrees; however, it certainly is possible for a sender to be perceived as having a high degree of all three of these relatively independent dimensions. The independent nature of these dimensions can be illustrated by the person who, while listening to a speaker, says to her friend, "He definitely doesn't know what he's talking about, nor does he look very honest, but he surely has charisma." Although there are probably additional factors that influence a listener's perception of a sender's credibility, current research indicates that trustworthiness, expertise, and dynamism are the three dimensions that are the most influential.

Skills Related to Ethos

Identifying the Dimensions of Source Credibility

ethos

identifying dimensions of source credibility

It is difficult at this point to draw any hard and fast conclusions as to the extent to which a speaker's credibility can influence us persuasively. Each listener will respond differently to the message source—before, during, and after the message presentation. The research does support the idea that there is some impact from credibility. Andersen and Clevenger analyzed the data and drew these conclusions:

> The finding is almost universal that the ethos of the source is related in some way to the impact of the message. This generalization applies not only to political, social, religious, and economic issues but also to matters of aesthetic judgment and personal taste. Some evidence even shows that "prestige-suggestion" can affect the appetite for certain foods and can influence performance and psychomotor tasks. On the other hand, there is not enough evidence to suggest that the amount of information gained from exposure to a message is related to the ethos of the source—at least this lack of relationship seems to be true of college populations. . . .
>
> Some auditors appear to be more susceptible to ethical appeal than others; some may be contra-suggestible. However, there is no evidence to show that suggestibility to prestige correlates well with intelligence, education, speech training, subject-matter competence, age, or sex. The only variable which seems clearly related to differences in suggestibility to prestige is the initial attitude toward the topic or the purpose: consistently, those who are neutral initially shift more often than do those who are at one extreme or the other.[57]

Recognizing the Influence of Source Credibility

recognizing the influence of source credibility

initial ethos

The ethos of the source, since it does have some impact on the listener, operates even before the message is presented. Speaker credibility can influence the listener initially if the speaker has prestige, authority, and reputation with the listener. The persuasiveness of **initial credibility** once was demonstrated by a professional actor who was introduced to three sophisticated audiences (composed of psychiatrists, psychologists, psychiatric social workers, educators, and administrators) as "Dr. Fox," the possessor of several impressive (though fictitious) degrees and author of several impressive (though fictitious) books. With the introduction of the speaker, the listeners were conditioned or influenced to perceive the speaker as a highly credible source of information. With each audience, the actor presented a lecture on "Mathematical Game Theory As Applied to Physician Education" and then conducted a question and answer period. Both the lecture and discussion consisted of meaningless, irrelevant, and conflicting content. Not one of the listeners detected the hoax.[58] A highly reputed or well-known authority in his or her field, therefore, will have considerable weight with the listeners even before the speaker begins to present his or her message. As listeners, we need to be aware of how we can be influenced by a person's past reputation or even by the person's reputation itself.

As listeners, we also are influenced by the profession of a speaker, so much so, that the initial credibility of a person may well be determined by what the individual represents professionally. In a 1994 Gallup poll, interviewers found that Americans viewed those in two professions as having very high honesty and ethical standards: druggists/pharmacists and clergy. Dentists, college teachers, engineers, medical doctors, and police officers ranked next in honesty and ethical standards, while U.S. Senators, insurance salespersons, members of Congress, and car salespersons received the lowest rankings.[59] Skillful speakers who recognize the unpopularity of what they represent will make efforts to counter these negative perceptions of listeners before they present substantive issues. Public utility officials, for instance, before they deal with messages about conservation, will make an effort to counter public perceptions that utility rates are skyrocketing.

The speaker's credibility can be developed during the speech by what McCroskey has defined as **derived ethos**. This credibility is enhanced through techniques the speaker uses to demonstrate his or her character, knowledge, and goodwill. Politicians citing biblical quotations or praising the power of a Supreme Being, for example, illustrate the effort to demonstrate character. One such politician is Marion Barry, who—in his successful 1994 bid to reclaim the Washington, D.C., mayoral office he lost in 1990 after the FBI had videotaped him smoking crack cocaine—implored, "They [the voters] see that if Marion Barry can find the God force within him, so can they."[60] The speaker who discusses his or her own research and experiences with the topic will demonstrate the expertise of a credible speaker. When teenagers were asked to determine—from among eight types of individuals—who they thought "would be very effective in warning students against the harmful effects of drugs," 71 percent named former drug addicts (followed in order by sports figures, rock stars, physicians, police officers, clergy, scientists, members of congress, and teachers).[61] The goodwill of a listener can be developed by the speaker demonstrating that he or she actually has the best interests of the listener in mind as the speaker advances his or her proposal.

derived ethos

A good speaker will attempt to incorporate these techniques subtly rather than directly asserting that he or she is a credible speaker. The principle that operates in the listening process, essentially, is one of trustworthiness and belief. If we, as listeners, believe in the speaker, then it is easier for us to accept the speaker's message.

John F. Kennedy (and his presidential speechwriter, Theodore Sorenson) understood the power of credibility in developing a responsive bond with listeners. Kennedy projected a young, vigorous, dynamic image, an image that was well set in the perceptions of the American public through the televised Nixon-Kennedy debates of the 1960 campaign. As president, Kennedy was skillful in communicating with the media through press conferences and speeches. He demonstrated a solid grasp of the issues and communicated considerable authority and competence in his presentations. Further, Kennedy tried to demonstrate trustworthiness by suggesting that he shared common interests with his audience. Thus, the press was presented with opportunities to photograph his young children and beautiful wife, and the President would make references to his listeners in his speeches. One famous example of his expressing commonality with his audience occurred in a speech he presented on 26 June 1963, at the Berlin Wall. Kennedy journeyed to West Berlin and told his listeners that "Today, in the world of freedom, the proudest boast is 'Ich bin ein Berliner.' "[62] Throughout the world, people responded favorably to his effort to associate himself with his besieged Berlin audience. (Yet it is interesting to note that "Ich bin ein Berliner"—due to the inclusion of the indefinite article *ein*—translates literally as "I am a pastry," rather than "I am a Berliner," a point that Berliners still chuckle about today!) Throughout the world, speakers attempt to enhance their credibility by demonstrating their expertise and trustworthiness to their listeners.

The extensive credibility crisis suffered by former president Richard M. Nixon—as a result of the Watergate investigation—represents the power of this component of persuasion. Ultimately, the American public, as receivers, was unable to accept any of his messages, so he found it necessary to step down from office. Jimmy Carter, campaigning for re-election as president in 1980, encountered similar credibility problems as Americans lost faith in his ability to control inflation or to deal effectively with the release of American hostages in Iran. Ronald Reagan experienced what was coined a "gender gap" when he was perceived to be not very sensitive to the needs of women. While the credibility judgment is still incomplete on President Bill Clinton after serving only two years in office, 1994 Gallup polls reveal that the American public "has serious doubts about the President's effectiveness [at getting things done]. . . . Americans still believe that Clinton has good ideas and wants to do the right thing. They're just not convinced that he can do it."[63]

influence of image

As listeners, we can run the danger of being too persuaded by the credibility components. Political communicators, concerned with the **image** developed and projected by candidates, recognize that often the image is what sells the candidate to the voting public. As a result, political consultants, serving as image advisers to candidates during election campaigns, make a fortune as they develop media strategies for selling the candidates to voters. The importance of a political candidate's television image was first realized, according to Splaine, during the following historical event:

. . . all the rules changed on September 26, 1960, at the WBBM studio in Chicago where one candidate appeared in a gray suit against a gray background and this candidate "disappeared" into that background. The other candidate appeared in a navy blue suit which was strikingly elegant against the gray background. One candidate "looked" tired, pale, and had a "5 o'clock shadow" while the other candidate looked rested, tanned, and was clean shaven. Abraham Ribicoff, a supporter of the youthful Senator from Massachusetts, John Fitzgerald Kennedy, heard the debate over his car radio while traveling from Sacramento to San Francisco and believed his candidate had lost the debate and probably the election. When Ribicoff arrived in San Francisco, he saw a videotape of the debate and knew that his man had not lost, but actually won. His man looked better on television!

The rest is history. . . .[64]

Joe McGinniss's *The Selling of the President 1968* details the efforts to "package" Nixon for the voters. McGinniss cites a memo from one of Nixon's image makers, Raymond K. Price:

. . . we take the time and the money to experiment, in a controlled manner, with film and television techniques, with particular emphasis on pinpointing those *controlled* uses of the television medium that can *best* convey the *image* we want to get across. . . .[65]

Close to twenty years later, presidential candidate George Bush hired Roger Ailes as his media consultant. Prior to Bush's interview by CBS News anchor Dan Rather on 25 January 1988, Ailes offered this advice to his client:

. . . Ailes persuaded the vice president not to go along with CBS's request for a 60-minute interview from which the network would choose its clips. Better to go live, he argued, since it would put Bush on a level playing field with the network.

The day before the event, Ailes had been tipped off . . . that Rather was prepared to go after Bush on his role in the Iran-Contra scandal. Ailes, who worked with Bush for about an hour before the interview, suggested that, if the interview got ugly, the vice president should mention the time in 1987 when Rather left the set in protest of U.S. Open tennis tournament coverage cutting into the news.

. . .when Rather started pushing the vice president on Iran-Contra, Bush responded: "How would you like it if I judged your career by those seven minutes when you walked off the set?"

"It was an extraordinary nine or 10 minutes on national television," says Ailes. "I think more people should realize that you don't have to be a patsy, you don't have to sit there and allow people to kick you and then edit your remarks so that you look like an idiot."[66]

Indeed, as Splaine has concluded, "The major networks now need candidates who look good and make 'good' television."[67]

The influence of the "image" extends beyond such effects in the political arena. For example, it extends to television anchors; Splaine notes that "anchor men and women are chosen because they are attractive and will draw viewers. They are 'stars' first and journalists second."[68] In research on a simulated newscast, respondents viewing the broadcast tapes gave more positive ratings to the anchors who were dressed in conservative clothing than those in casual or "trendy" fashions.[69] Listener expectations of what a person should wear in a particular role (candidate, news anchor, executive, salesperson, teacher) can affect the perceptions of the individual's trustworthiness and/or competence. As critical listeners, we should be aware of the influence of the image and not make our decisions solely on this basis.

Skills Related to Logos

logos

The critical listener also must carefully examine the second persuasive component, **logos**: the thought content or logical arguments of the speaker.[70] The 1995 O.J. Simpson trial heightened the nation's consciousness of lines of argument. Each network news organization used a resident legal expert to provide analysis on the courtroom proceedings and arguments each day. Arguments generally consist of the following elements:

premises

> **Premises** (also referred to as claims, propositions, generalizations)— statements about issues, people, ideas, events, etc., that the speaker advances and wants the listener to accept

evidence

> **Evidence**—supporting information (data) or backing that the speaker uses to prove his or her premise(s), to lead to his or her conclusion, and to make the premise(s) acceptable to the listener

reasoning

> **Reasoning**—the thought process that the speaker goes through in order to connect the evidence to the premise(s)

conclusion

> **Conclusion**—a statement that is based on premises, is a re-expression of premises, is mere consequences of premises, and/or is supported by evidence

Although some research indicates that the listener may not be able to recall specific lines of argument from a presentation, logical arguments are prevalent in everyday discourse, serve as the foundation for technical briefings, and certainly appear in persuasive messages of all types.[71] Because the arguments are so inherent in these messages, the critical listener should be familiar with not only argument elements but also argument structures in order to identify the communicator's persuasive strategies. Basically, there are two argument structures: the inductive argument and the deductive argument.

truth

validity

Well-supported arguments of either structure have both **truth** (believability of premises and evidence) and **validity** (acceptability of the relationships between all the premises and evidence presented and all the conclusions reached). We know, then, that when a conclusion is derived from premises and evidence that are true, the argument has truth, and we know that if the conclusion *must* follow from the premises and evidence, the argument has validity.

Evaluating Inductive Arguments

evaluating inductive arguments

The inductive argument is reasoning by which one arrives at a conclusion or generalization through examining specific, factual data of the same kind

Developing Purposeful Listening Skills

or class; it is **reasoning from the specific to the general**. In this type of reasoning, the speaker compares a number of instances to conclude that all other instances are the same.

reasoning from the specific to the general

For example, a teacher, citing past and present students who have studied and done well, may conclude that students who study receive high grades. From this observation, the teacher may reason inductively that all students who want to pass must study.

To determine the truth of an inductive argument, critical listeners should ask and answer the following questions:

1. Are the validating data true?
2. Are enough cases cited?
3. Are the cited instances representative of the whole being considered? Are they typical or atypical?
4. Is the class of persons, events, or instances about which the induction is made reasonably comparable in all relevant aspects?
5. Are there exceptions that do not lead to the expected conclusions? Are these exceptions accounted for?

Using these questions to evaluate the previously cited inductive argument, we see that the conclusion drawn by the teacher is not true. We all know students who do well in courses and yet do not study. In this case, other variables may not be accounted for in the argument: intelligence, aptitude, prior training, vocabulary, personality. We realize, too, that the number of specific examples supporting the conclusion must be sufficiently large to offset the probability of chance or coincidence; the critical listener demands many representative, specific instances before he or she will grant a general rule.

Evaluating Deductive Arguments

The second argument structure, the deductive (or syllogistic) structure, is reasoning from a systematic arrangement of arguments consisting of a proposition stating a generalization (referred to as the major premise), a proposition stating a specific instance related to the generalization (the minor premise), and a conclusion that necessarily must follow from the premises. Deductive reasoning is **reasoning from the general to the specific**, and it implies that what is *presumed* true of all members of a kind or class is true of some members of that kind or class. The teacher might want to present his or her same argument deductively:

evaluating deductive arguments

reasoning from the general to the specific

> All students who want to pass must study.
> You are a student who wants to pass.
> Therefore, you must study.

To determine the truth of a deductive argument, the critical listener must ask and answer the following questions:

1. Is the generalization (major premise) universally true?
2. Does the specific item really belong to the general class?

3. Or, does the specific item represent an exception to the cited general class?

Fortunately, most people do not talk in direct syllogisms. As listeners, we are confronted with truncated deductive arguments that Aristotle identified as **enthymemes**.[72] Enthymemes are actually modified forms of rhetorical syllogisms that have one or more of their premises or conclusions omitted. They can operate effectively only if speaker and listener can share, mentally, the premise(s) or conclusion that the speaker does not state. If we are alert to their utilization, we can better analyze the speaker's argument for its validity.

The teacher, for example, who *assumes* that those in the class want to pass most likely would use an enthymeme rather than a direct syllogism. The teacher might say, "You'd better study for the exam." If the students (the listeners) mentally share with the teacher (the speaker) the omitted premises that all students who want to pass must study and that they are students who want to pass, the enthymeme can operate effectively.

In addition to the deductive enthymeme, the listener is likely to encounter the **disjunctive argument**, an argument structured by the speaker with either-or alternatives. The parent can argue with a child, "Either you do your homework, or you won't get a passing grade in this course." Implicit in this argument, extended to its unstated premises, is that "you will not get a passing grade in this course, so you will do your homework."

Deductively, the listener also may be exposed to the **conditional argument**, based on an if-then proposition. In this structure, two alternatives, following from each other, are set up. The scientist who establishes "if water reaches 220 degrees Fahrenheit, then it will boil, and since the water has reached 220 degrees, it is boiling" is developing a conditional argument—the conclusion follows from the if-then condition.

In any of these deductive argument structures, the listener should do a mental check to see what is the common premise from which the speaker is operating. Since speakers do not spell out their deductive arguments in strict syllogistic form, one of the premises for the argument undoubtedly assumes that listener and speaker share the unstated, common premise. However, this may not always be the case. Former president Jimmy Carter, for example, urged Americans to use less oil during the 1979 oil crisis by installing heat pumps, driving less, forming car pools, and so on. These messages were based on the common premise that Americans were concerned about the energy crisis and wanted to do their share in conserving oil reserves. Unfortunately, Carter and his speechwriters were operating from a faulty assumption. Opinion polls during this time indicated that Americans really did not believe in the oil crisis; rather, they perceived it as an effort by oil companies to raise prices. As a result, President Carter's appeals to the American public probably had little effect because of the misuse of the deductive argument form.

Ideally, the critical listener can evaluate the truth and validity of the speaker's deductive arguments by converting them to syllogisms and

enthymemes

disjunctive argument

conditional argument

analyzing the propositions from that framework. It is difficult, however, to work with formal syllogisms while the speaker continues to speak. In addition to looking at the deductive (or inductive) structure of an argument, the listener can find another method of assessment in a model of argument developed by Stephen Toulmin.

Analyzing Arguments by Applying the Toulmin Model of Reasoning

The analysis of argument structure through the Aristotelian model of inductive and deductive means helps the critical listener to become more aware of how any particular message is set up and to determine its logical truth and validity. Another model of the reasoning process has also been found to be valuable to listeners who must analyze arguments. This model was developed by the British mathematical philosopher, Stephen Toulmin.[73]

Toulmin's model of argument (see fig. 8.1) may consist of six parts: The **data** represent all the evidence used by the speaker, while the **claim** is the conclusion, the assertion drawn by the communicator. The **warrant** functions as the link between the evidence and the claim and is the basic premise upon which the claim is based. The **backing for the warrant** (support) is any evidence or reasoning used to make the warrant acceptable to you, the

analyzing arguments by using the Toulmin Model

data

claim

warrant

backing for the warrant

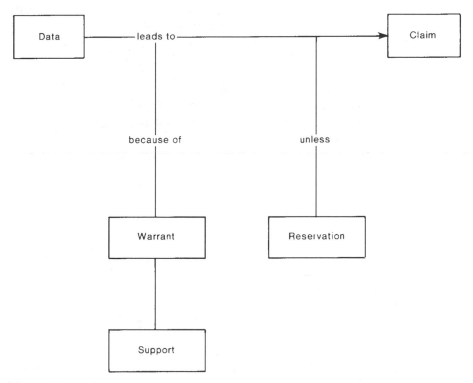

Figure 8.1.
The Toulmin Model.

listener. The argument may also have a **qualifier** to express the degree of certainty inherent in the claim, and the **reservation** would be any dimensions that reduce the certainty of the claim.

An example of an argument charted through the use of the Toulmin model can illustrate the value of this rhetorical-logical method for analyzing arguments.

> Data: Research demonstrates that training in listening skills enables one to improve as a listener.
>
> Warrant: It is important to develop effective listening skills.
>
> Claim: Listening skills should be part of a school curriculum.
>
> Backing for Warrant: Evidence from business and from education reveals that listening skills are a key to success.
>
> Qualifier: The listening curriculum should be based on sound educational objectives.
>
> Reservation: Unless such skills are already in place.

This model of argument accounts for the role of the listener through the warrant, designed to link the data and the claim so that the conclusion will be acceptable to the listener. As a result, such a model of the argument process can enable the listener to understand all of the ramifications of the speaker's argument and provide a solid framework for deciding, finally, whether the argument has sufficient merit to act upon it according to the persuasive objectives of the speaker.

We admit that applying the argument structures and/or the Toulmin model will be difficult to perform as you begin to develop greater critical powers to assess arguments. The key, however, is to understand how to analyze logical arguments by using the method that best suits your cognitive style and then practice it. Analysis, combined with intense concentration, physical and mental energy, and effective use of the difference between speech speed and thought speed, can help you in this complex process. The effective listener should also ask questions to clarify any points of an argument that might not be clear. Michael Scriven offers some helpful guidance in his seven steps of argument analysis; he recommends that the listener analyze arguments by doing the following:

1. Clarifying the meaning of the terms and the other elements of the argument
2. Identifying the stated and unstated conclusion
3. Portraying the structure (the relationships between the conclusions and the premises) of the argument
4. Formulating the unstated assumptions of the argument
5. Criticizing the stated and unstated premises and inference
6. Introducing other relevant arguments
7. Evaluating the overall argument as a result of the first[74]

Detecting and Evaluating Reasoning Fallacies

As listeners, we cannot assume that all speakers present sound arguments. Too frequently, the speaker may use faulty reasoning that allows a listener to draw from evidence a claim that is not justified. Yet sound arguments should be the only arguments acceptable to us as listeners. "The most basic demand that receivers should make of argumentation," stresses Richard Crable, "is the demand to be presented with good reasons for claims."[75] We must be able to recognize fallacies in reasoning so that we can reject the false claims advanced by some speakers.

detecting and evaluating reasoning fallacies

Hasty Generalizations. We may be exposed more to the **hasty generalization** than to any other fallacy in oral discourse. This fallacy consists of the speaker drawing unwarranted, general conclusions from an insufficient number of cases (instances). A principal whose school has been vandalized by *some* long-haired youths might fall prey to the hasty generalization. At the next PTA meeting, the principal may then condemn *all* long-haired youths as vandals and urge parents to restore law and order in the home. Such a hasty generalization, or stereotyping, is based on too few instances and does not account for many of the other variables that could be involved. To evaluate the hasty generalization, the critical listener should use the following questions:

hasty generalization

1. Is there a sufficient number of cases cited to warrant the conclusion?
2. Is the generalization consistent with all known facts?
3. Is there an exception to the generalization?
4. Have negative instances been accounted for?
5. Are qualifiers (*some, few,* etc.) used?
6. Are the instances cited representative of the entire class?
7. Have the instances been selected entirely at random?

Carefully evaluating the hasty generalizations will prevent the critical listener from falling prey to the speakers who use them.

Faulty Causal Reasoning. Another fallacy involving generalizing is the **faulty causal generalization**. Some speakers, recognizing that other factors do contribute to the effect, speak of one event being *the cause* of another because it is the important difference. They mean that there is a high degree of probability that it is the cause. Unfortunately, other speakers do not recognize that there are other contributing factors, and they argue that what *usually* (or *sometimes* or even *often*) happens *always* happens. Instead of indicating that they recognize other contributing factors by saying "a common cause," "a frequent cause," "a prominent cause," "one cause," or "a probable cause," they use "the cause" without qualification, and, as a result, they make a faulty causal generalization. For instance, Betty may say, "My allergy disappeared the day after I took Clogless. I certainly recommend the use of that medicine!" The speaker is alleging that Clogless was the *cause* of

faulty causal generalization

the disappearance of her allergy (effect). In contrast, there may be many causes for an effect. For example, in the aftermath of Susan Smith's confession that she had murdered her two young children on 25 October 1994, in Union, South Carolina, psychologists and other authorities offered several possible reasons why women might kill their children: severe depression, unbearable pileup of stresses, emotional or mental illness, inability to cope, low self-esteem, and relationship issues revolving around a man who does not want the responsibility of children.[76]

post hoc, ergo propter hoc

Another type of faulty causal reasoning is **post hoc, ergo propter hoc** ("after this, therefore, because of this") reasoning. *Post hoc* reasoning is used by the speaker, who—without proof—supposes that because one event follows another event, the first is the cause of the second. Granted, an effect must follow a cause, but a prior event does not necessarily cause the event that follows. A baseball player, for instance, would be using *post hoc* reasoning if he were to claim, "I didn't get any hits in tonight's game because I didn't eat my favorite cereal this morning." Likewise, Rossalyn is using *post hoc* reasoning when she states, "Chico bought a car; consequently, he broke up with me."

The critical listener, when listening to such faulty causal reasoning, should use the following questions to evaluate the reasoning:

1. What is the alleged cause?
2. What is the alleged effect?
3. Is the cause really capable of producing the effect?
4. Is the effect the result of a sequence of events or a coincidence of events?
5. Are there possibly other intervening causes?
6. Was the cause really operating? Have the alleged facts been verified?
7. When past experience is involved, has the alleged effect *always* followed the observed cause?
8. Does the alleged cause precede the alleged effect?

These questions—asked mentally or orally—can greatly assist the critical listener in uncovering faulty causal reasoning.

faulty analogical reasoning

Faulty Analogical Reasoning. In addition to using faulty causal reasoning, speakers frequently use **faulty analogical reasoning**. An analogy is the assertion that cases that resemble each other in some respects will resemble each other in some other respects. Every analogy must break down at some point because no cases are identical. Speakers use faulty analogies when they assume (1) that shared properties will continue indefinitely and/or (2) that shared properties are similar in all aspects relevant to the issue being discussed, when in truth they are not. For example, Mary Beth tells her friend, "Leving Motors fixed my Chevy really well; it hasn't needed any additional repair work for three years. I bet Leving mechanics can correct the problems with your Mercedes just as well." Here the speaker is assuming that the shared properties (two cars and each—at one time—in need of repair) will continue indefinitely and that the shared properties are similar in all relevant aspects. The critical listener should immediately ask several questions. Does Leving Motors still exist? Does Leving Motors specialize only in repairing Chevrolets? Does Leving Motors also repair Mercedes Benzes? Is the repair work at Leving as good now as it was three years ago? Are the mechanics who repaired the Chevy still working at Leving Motors? Are the present mechanics equally qualified to repair both Chevrolets and Mercedes Benzes? Are parts as easily accessible for the Mercedes as for the Chevy? Is the type of repair work that the Mercedes needs the same as that which the Chevy once needed? The answers to these questions may indeed illustrate that the compared cases are not alike in all essential aspects. Similarly, the student who argues, "Professor Hickerson gave an excellent course in American literature last semester. I know his course in British literature will also be one of high quality," may be overlooking fundamental differences between the compared cases.

To detect the faulty analogical reasoning of examples such as this one, the critical listener should ask and answer the following questions:

1. Are there significant points of similarity?
2. Are there enough resemblances to warrant a comparison?
3. Are the compared cases alike in all essential aspects?
4. Does the comparison overlook fundamental differences? Are the points of difference critical? Are they noncritical?
5. Is the analogous situation representative?
6. Do the points brought out really exist?
7. Are only literal analogies used as logical proof?

By using these questions when confronted with analogical reasoning, the critical listener will have one more means of controlling his or her own decision making.

Three of the many other common types of reasoning fallacies are non sequitur, arguing in a circle, and ducking or ignoring the issue. These, too, can be deceiving to the listener.

Non Sequitur.   Translated literally, **non sequitur** means "it does not necessarily follow," and it is a general name for all irrelevancies. The term is generally used to refer to the widely irrelevant conclusion although it is involved in all invalid syllogisms, since they claim that a conclusion follows when it does not.

non sequitur

A graphic example of the non sequitur is the argument critics advanced against the National Aeronautics and Space Administration's Apollo moon missions. Opponents of the program argued that the money spent on the missions should be spent on earth for domestic needs. Such an argument did not follow because it assumed that the small NASA budget would be reallocated to meaningful "earthly" causes while it overlooked the spin-off benefits of the space program to technology, medicine, and science throughout the world. This non sequitur persists today as people complain about the costs of the space program in light of the Challenger disaster.

Arguing in a Circle.   Another common fallacy is **arguing in a circle**. When using this fallacy, the speaker tries to prove a given statement with another statement that depends for its proof upon the first statement. The speaker who argues that the promises of Iraq's President Saddam Hussein cannot be trusted because Hussein does not keep his word is arguing in a circle. The "reason" that follows the word *because* is the same assertion that precedes *because*. Arguing in a circle can be seen in its height of absurdity in the following example: Living together without benefit of marriage is justified because living together without benefit of marriage is justified. Fearnside and Holther present a humorous example of arguing in a circle:

> In a picture by the famous French comedian Sacha Guitry three thieves are arguing over division of seven pearls worth a king's ransom. One of them hands two to the man on his right, then two to the man on his left. "I," he says, "will keep three." The man on his right says, "How come you keep three?" "Because I am the leader." "Oh. But how come you are the leader?" "Because I have more pearls."[77]

Ignoring the Issue.   The third common reasoning fallacy is ducking or **ignoring the issue**. The speaker who uses this type of fallacy uses irrelevant arguments to cloud the real issue or argument. One of these irrelevant arguments is the **ad hominem argument**—attacking the personal character of the source of the statement rather than focusing on the content of the issue itself.

Two of the closest Senatorial races in 1994 illustrate the use of this fallacy. In a high-profile race in Virginia, Republican challenger Oliver North—using a television "attack ad"—accused Democratic incumbent Charles Robb of cheating on his wife and partying with cocaine users. Robb's counterattack ad declared that North, a key figure in the Iran-Contra scandal, is lying—lying about former President Ronald Reagan, lying about Chuck Robb, and even lying to school children.[78] In California, Republican Michael Huffington and Democrat Dianne Feinstein waged the costliest congressional race in national history and one of the nastiest campaigns in 1994 as evidenced by their barrage of televised "attack ads." In his bid to unseat Feinstein in the Senate, Huffington charged Feinstein with serving "special interests . . . and her own," being a "tax-and-spend Democrat," and being "a career politician who will say or do anything to stay in office."[79] In her ads, Feinstein countercharged that Huffington was a liar, "a spoiled rich kid . . . trying to buy a Senate seat," and a "Texas oil millionaire Californians just can't trust."[80] During a political year when illegal immigration was the subject of a controversial California initiative, each candidate also contended that the other was a former private employer of undocumented immigrants. These charges led each candidate to accuse the other of being guilty of "telling lies" and "hypocrisy."[81] While some political strategists and media critics note that these kinds of negative commercials can work well in a campaign, others decry the extensive use of such attacks, in which character replaces the issues and innuendos replace the reasoned discourse of speeches, white papers, and interpersonal contacts.[82]

A second irrelevant argument is the **ad populum argument**—appealing to the people in terms of their prejudices and passions rather than focusing on the issues at hand. An example of this argument is the following: A woman is running for mayor of Laurel, Maryland; her opponent has been a resident of the city for only five years. In one of her campaign speeches, she states, "I was born in Laurel, and I have been a Laurelite all my life. I attended Laurel Elementary School, Laurel Junior High School, and Laurel Senior High School. Many of you were there when I missed that final desperation shot and our girls' basketball team lost that heartbreaking final game at the state tournament. And, many of you were there to share my happiness when I was crowned Laurel's Junior Miss. . . ." Appealing to the passions of a national voting public in 1988, then-presidential candidate George Bush used the *ad populum* argument when he proclaimed, "The soldiers I was shot down with in World War II didn't think I was a wimp."[83]

The final form of ignoring the issue is the **ad ignoratiam argument**. The speaker who uses this argument attempts to prove that a statement is true (or false) because it cannot be disproved (or proved). Not being able to disprove a point is not the same as proving it; only concrete evidence can prove or disprove a statement. An example of this fallacy is the following: Since the opponents of the discipline policy cannot prove that detention has *not* improved discipline in the school, it follows that detention is an effective disciplinary measure.

These are just a few of the numerous fallacies that speakers intentionally and unintentionally use. It is vital that critical listeners be aware of these fallacies as well as others if they wish to become more adept in evaluating speaker's arguments.

Evaluating Evidence

The effective critical listener will analyze the soundness of not only the speaker's argument but also the speaker's support, or evidence.[84] A speaker can support his or her assertions with any of a variety of types of evidence, including testimonies, facts, opinions, inferences, and statistics.

Regardless of the type of evidence the speaker uses, the listener can apply some tests to the evidence to assess its soundness. The listener should seek to determine the **clarity** of the evidence (how clear and intelligible it is), the **accuracy** of the evidence (how true, precise, and correct it is), and the **reliability** of the evidence (how dependable, trustworthy, and credible it is).

This determination may be made by asking some basic questions about the evidence:

1. Is the evidence clear?
2. Is the evidence consistent with other known evidence?
3. Is the evidence consistent with the speaker?
4. Is the evidence timely?
5. Is the evidence applicable to the argument?
6. Is the evidence pertinent to the argument?
7. Is the source of the evidence reliable?

8. Is the source of the evidence competent in the area in which he or she is being quoted?
9. Is the source of the evidence free to report all of his or her findings?
10. Is the source of the evidence suppressing or distorting facts to prove his or her point?
11. Is the source of the evidence sincere?

Detecting Fallacious Testimonies and Unreliable Sources.   Many of us are quite aware of the **fallacious testimonies** with which the advertising industry bombards us. In television advertising, we see Hall of Fame pitcher Jim Palmer recommending The Money Store, television comedian Candice Bergen touting Sprint, former vice-president Dan Quayle praising Lay's potato chips, and model Cindy Crawford desperately needing a Pepsi. And in television infomercials, we see Dionne Warwick inviting viewers to consult psychics, Cher heralding her cosmetics, and Jay Kordich hawking the Juiceman. Testimonies from famous models, movie stars, rock stars, television stars, and sports stars endorsing products appeal to our sense of imitation, even though experts in the field would be in a better position to offer sound support. Thus, a carpet manufacturer will call on a glamorous model rather than a Ph.D. in textiles to sell the company's product, and most of us are familiar with retired quarterback Joe Montana who has endorsed items from L.A. Gear footwear to Hanes active wear to Sega Genesis games. Unfortunately, many listeners pay no more attention to evaluating the credibility of the source when they are listening to messages of grave concern than they do when they are listening to commercials.

To detect fallacious testimonies or unreliable sources, the critical listener should ask this question: Is the source who is making the testimony, or who is being cited, an expert on the subject about which he or she is speaking or being quoted? To answer this question, the listener must know the following:

1. The **name** of the source (rather than "a top government official," "a famous author," "a person close to the singer," and so on—who cannot be identified and, thus, whose statement cannot be verified)
2. The **credentials** (qualifications) of the source (which, if not given, cannot be evaluated, and which, if given, should be evaluated for possible biases, for possible affiliations with pressure groups, for conditions under which he or she is speaking—such as the "gag rule" preventing free reporting, secrecy shield regarding classified information, political pressures, payment for the statement being made, etc.)
3. The source's **experiences** (ranging from having first-hand, second-hand, to nth-hand observation or experience with the subject being discussed)

Distinguishing among Facts, Opinions, and Inferences.   In addition to evaluating testimonies, the critical listener must distinguish between

---

fallacious testimonies

name

credentials

experiences

Developing Purposeful Listening Skills

statements of fact and statements of opinion. Many of us believe that a fact is a fact and that there is nothing else to say about facts. Too frequently, however, speakers pass opinions off as facts—often introduced by words and phrases such as the following:

"It is said that. . . ."	"They say that. . . ."	"I heard that. . . ."
"It is a fact that. . . ."	"We all know that. . . ."	"Obviously, . . ."
"It is reported that. . . ."	"An unidentified source noted that. . . ."	"Of course, . . ."
"As a matter of fact, . . ."	"There can be no doubt that. . . ."	"Allegedly. . . ."
"Apparently. . . ."	"A close source has said that. . . ."	"Reportedly. . . ."

It is apparent that often listeners do not challenge the accuracy and reliability of the speakers' so-called facts. Whether or not speakers use facts or opinions to "prove" their assertions should be a crucial question for the critical listener, or he or she may become, as Windes and Hastings believe, what the American audience has become:

> . . . the American audience has become so accustomed to hidden persuasion, so victimized by the engineers of consent that it will accept the truth of assertions with virtually no proof except the authority of the advocate, whether . . . a news commentator, politician, or public figure, or . . . a commercial announcer.[85]

Facts are truths known to exist. They can be determined by direct observation and/or they can be verified by a reliable source. When we cannot directly observe facts, we can investigate through reliable sources "as to what the facts probably were, are, and will be."[86] Facts are open to anyone who wishes to investigate them, and they can stand independent of the sources who report them. However, since few of us—as listeners—can actually investigate the majority of the facts we listen to, it is essential that we consider the credibility of the speakers who present them.

facts

Opinions, on the other hand, are statements of personal judgments and preferences. Sometimes, speakers preface their opinions with comments such as "I think, . . ." "As far as I'm concerned, . . ." "It seems to me that, . . ." "I sense, . . ." "It's my opinion that, . . ." "To me, . . ." "I believe, . . ." "I get the feeling that, . . ." and so on. These statements are easy to recognize as opinions. However, when speakers state opinions without prefatory comments, the critical listener must draw upon his or her knowledge to determine if the statements are opinions. It is important to know that opinions are open to dispute and that they cannot be positively and objectively proved or disproved because they are expressions of their possessors' own perceptions. Although opinions cannot be tested for proof, they can be evaluated. The critical listener should carefully examine whether the opinions are stated by reliable sources who are speaking in their areas of competency and whether the sources have any factual data upon which to base their opinions.

opinions

In assessing the factual basis of speakers' message content, the critical listener must not accept inferential statements as statements of facts. **Inferences** are statements of interpretation, which, limited only by the speaker's imagination, can be made by anyone (including the incompetent speaker) anytime. Sometimes directly stated and at other times merely implied, inferences are speakers' guesses or conclusions about what is not known, made on the basis of what is known. The "known" may be an observation or series of observations or an inference or series of inferences. Frequently, a speaker's inferences are in the form of predictions, as is the one that follows: "If the school year were lengthened, students' SAT scores would improve." To improve the ability to detect inferential statements formulated as predictions, the critical listener should note whether the speaker uses qualifying words, such as *if* (as in the previous example), *perhaps, possibly, may, might,* and *could*. Such terms indicate conditional—rather than factual—statements. Speakers may not, knowingly or unknowingly, identify their material, so what is presented from their inferences may appear to be facts. William V. Haney's famous uncritical inference test illustrates the inability of most of us to distinguish among what is presented to us as fact, inference, or judgment (opinion). Haney states that we have difficulty but that ". . . one can learn to make this distinction habitually and thus markedly increase his 'inference-awareness.' "[87]

Diplomats become adept at recognizing facts, opinions, and inferences. A political officer assigned to an embassy overseas, for example, spends a great deal of time interviewing officials in the host country to obtain a fair assessment of the country's conditions to report back to the United States Department of State. It is necessary for this officer to recognize what is being reported by the sources as factual and what actually represents the sources' editorial interpretation of the country's conditions. Like diplomats, we as critical listeners must learn these distinctions and then base our acceptance or rejection of inferences on the evidence used to support them as well as on the credibility of the source. We recommend that the critical listener use the following questions as guides in evaluating inferences:

1. Is the inference based on observations? How many observations? How many individuals made the observations?
2. Is the inference based on another inference or a series of inferences? What is/are the other inference(s)?
3. Do past experiences support/dispute the inference being made?
4. Is the source of the inference competent/incompetent? Honest/deceitful? Biased/objective? Trustworthy/not trustworthy?

Detecting Rumors. Another type of biased communication that can be especially troublesome to the uncritical listener is the rumor. In the classic study of rumor, Allport and Postman defined rumor as "a specific (or topical) proposition for belief, passed along from person to person, usually by word of mouth, without secure standards of evidence being presented."[88]

The rumor frequently represents a magnified inference that becomes more distorted as it is transmitted from person to person. It may not be based on any factual data at all.

North American businesses have experienced several costly rumors in the 1990s. Three examples are that the Snapple Beverage Company financially supported the Ku Klux Klan (as evidenced by the company's label bearing a small letter K, which actually means the drink adheres to kosher dietary standards); that the Domino Pizza chain sold pizza contaminated with the AIDS virus; and that Liz Claiborne stated on the *Oprah Winfrey* show (a show on which Claiborne has never appeared) that she does not design her clothes to be worn by African Americans.[89]

Another rumor, which has persisted since 1980, is that Procter & Gamble's moon and stars logo is a satanic symbol and that the corporation is a tool of Satan. The grapevine charges that the 103-year-old trademark, showing a bearded man in the moon with 13 stars, is a sign of the devil. Circulators of the rumor also charge that the man's bearded curls form three sixes and the number 666 is linked with the devil in the Bible's book of Revelation. The Procter & Gamble rumor first reached prominence in June of 1982, when the company received fifteen thousand telephone calls asking if the rumor were true. It peaked in 1985, when more than twenty-two thousand rumor-related letters and calls flooded company headquarters. Even though Procter & Gamble removed its famous logo from product packages in 1985, the rumor resurfaced again in 1990 when the company operators daily handled about 350 calls regarding the rumor. One year later, Procter & Gamble redesigned its logo by eliminating the man's beard curls. However, despite spending over fourteen years trying to convince the public that the company is not tied to the devil, Procter & Gamble still daily receives 10 to 20 calls about the rumor.[90]

Because rumors can be so disruptive, not only to the economy but also to the general welfare of the American public (as in the case of the Tylenol scare concerning tampering with pharmaceutical products), some businesses and institutions have set up rumor control centers to help individuals separate factual information from gossip and exaggeration. For instance, Procter & Gamble established a toll-free hot line to field calls regarding the rumor that on 1 March 1991, the president of Procter & Gamble appeared on the *Donahue* show and stated that a large portion of the company's profits goes to support the Church of Satan. Likewise, staffers at Donahue's headquarters in New York established a voice-mail answering system to advise the flood of callers that "the president of Procter & Gamble has never appeared on the *Donahue* show. If your family and friends say they've seen it, they are quite mistaken."[91] Other businesses and institutions, such as Shelby Memorial Hospital in Illinois, strive for rumor control by having a suggestion box into which an employee can place the rumor he or she has heard. The employee then receives a personal response or a public answer if the employee wants to remain anonymous.[92]

One rumor specialist, Ralph Rosnow, asserts that persistent rumors, such as the recurring sightings of UFO's, fulfill a very human need to "understand the human condition and a hunger for the supernatural."[93] Rosnow also believes that "rumors persist because they touch on the real anxieties and uncertainties of the times."[94] During times of unemployment, for example, anxiety and uncertainty are at a high level. Social psychologist Frederick Koenig, who has served as a consultant to McDonald's and several other rumor-plagued corporations, notes that this is a time when rumors often flourish:

> A man who is unemployed and just scraping by might well be inclined to believe a rumor—even a false one—about a company's product being contaminated. It somehow makes him feel better to see the corporate giant in trouble. He reasons that his best efforts are getting him nowhere, so the firm must be cutting corners to be successful. By striking out at a big company and clouding its reputation, he works off some of his aggression.[95]

Recognizing that rumors reflect individuals' anxieties and uncertainties as well as their hopes, prejudices, suspicions, fears, obsessions, hostilities, and cherished assumptions, the critical listener should work to avoid being part of the rumor mill, which can perpetuate costly, injurious misinformation. So that rumors are not allowed to continue, the critical listener should engage in the following:

1. Identify the message as a possible rumor.
2. Check the source; if the statement is about another person, go directly to that person—if possible and if appropriate—and ask the person to confirm or deny the rumor.
3. Check with the transmitter of the rumor to determine the source of the rumor's content; determine if the report is based upon first-hand observation or second-hand . . . nth-hand reports.
4. Consider possible consequences of the rumor for you and other people concerned if the rumor is true or if it is false; if the consequences could be harmful, continue searching for the factual basis of the rumor.
5. Try to determine what motives might have contributed to the rumor.
6. Attempt to conduct systematic research (through interviews, "undercover" investigations, direct observation, etc.) to uncover the evidence that will prove or disprove the rumor.[96]

Detecting Propaganda. Still another type of biased communication that the critical listener must be able to recognize is **propaganda**. According to Miller, propaganda is an "expression of opinion, or fact or alleged fact, or it is action—calculated to influence the opinions and actions of groups and individuals, with reference to some predetermined end."[97] If you are thinking that this definition is a definition of persuasion, you are correct, since, simply speaking, propaganda is persuasion. As a form of persuasion, it involves conflict or "sides," and it is consciously designed to influence the listener(s) to accept or reject some cause, view, action, person, or such. Although we usually view the word *propaganda* as a negative term describing an undesirable

propaganda

persuasive attempt, propaganda can be positive or desirable when, for example, the propagandist (or *persuader*) attacks racial discrimination, unequal housing standards, unfair labor practices, or air and water pollution.

If propaganda can be positive, then, why does it have such a derogatory or pejorative connotation? The blame lies with both the unscrupulous sender of propaganda and the uncritical listener of propaganda. However, we believe that the uncritical listener bears a greater share of the blame. Why? There undoubtedly will be speakers who use propaganda as long as there are listeners who are *not* skilled in *detecting* (1) emotional appeals (upon which the propagandist relies almost exclusively), (2) the speaker's purpose (which, for the propagandist, is primarily to benefit personally), (3) the speaker's evidence (which may consist only of the propagandist's biases and opinions as well as distorted or alleged "facts"), (4) propaganda techniques (which the propagandist regularly uses), and (5) the speaker's underlying and/or hidden motives/intent (which, for the propagandist, may not be readily apparent but can be held suspect if he or she heavily uses the propagandistic characteristics enumerated in this sentence). Likewise, there undoubtedly will be speakers who use propaganda as long as there are listeners who are *not* skilled in *rationally evaluating* the propagandistic characteristics that they do detect. In other words, critical listeners, skilled in detecting and analyzing propaganda, can escape from the control of unscrupulous senders of propaganda.

Again, according to Miller, the capacity to analyze propaganda "depends upon one's familiarity with relevant facts, together with one's capacity for testing the propaganda in the light of the facts. That capacity, in turn, depends upon one's education, upon the conditioning of his mind, upon what he has been trained to consider 'good' or 'bad.' "[98] To help you develop the capacity to analyze propaganda, we encourage you to (1) familiarize yourself with the facts relevant to any issue with which you are involved; (2) use the suggested guidelines for evaluating reasoning and evidence; and (3) recognize how your own emotions and frames of reference affect your listening behavior and your attempt to control their influences when you listen to propagandistic messages. In addition, you should understand the propaganda techniques that are commonly used so that you can detect them and then analyze them.

Among a number of devices recognized as propaganda techniques by The Institute for Propaganda Analysis are the following:

1. **Name-calling**—attaching an objectionable/unfavorable/ undesirable label to a person, object, event, or cause to encourage disapproval/rejection/condemnation of a person, and so on (e.g., *radical, traitor, the establishment, wimp, extremist, loser*)   **name-calling**
2. **Glittering generality**—attaching a vague but virtuous-sounding label to a person, object, event, or cause to encourage automatic approval/acceptance of a person, and so on (e.g., *dedicated to equality, strong proponent of justice, upwardly mobile, state-of-the-art, earmarked for success*)   **glittering generality**

transfer	3. **Transfer**—associating positive qualities of a respected/revered person, group, party, object, or cause with the person, object, event, or cause expounded by the propagandist (e.g., *"We Democrats, the party of FDR,"* the American flag, Puritan work ethic, *"as American as baseball and hot dogs"*)
plain folks appeal	4. **Plain folks appeal**—attempting to identify with the audience (whom the propagandist hopes to persuade) by adopting the language, dress, or behavior of the listeners (such as Virginia Senate candidate Oliver North dressing in a blue flannel shirt and using a folksy style to appeal to voters or the country group, Alabama, dedicating its music to the heart of America—the working class)
card-stacking	5. **Card-stacking**—manipulating (by withholding, ignoring, adding, over- or underemphasizing) evidence and giving only the evidence that supports the propagandist's cause, proposition, and so on (such as presenting the positive aspects of developing an amusement park—the creation of jobs, the strengthening of the local economy, the provision of entertainment—but not mentioning any problems that the park might create—sewage, traffic, noise)
half-truths	6. **Half-truths**—deliberately suppressing basic elements of the argument/story, of which the propagandist has knowledge, and telling only one part—the part he or she favors—of the argument/story (e.g., "Merit pay for teachers will improve the quality and motivation of teachers and the learning of students." Are there other sides to the issue?)
bandwagon	7. **Bandwagon**—using phrases and sentences to create the impression of universal approval and ignoring individuality (e.g., "All my friends are, . . ." "Millions can't be wrong," "Vote a straight Republican ticket," "Your friends and neighbors have signed this petition," "Don't be left out")

<table>
<tr><td>hasty generalizations

testimonials</td><td>Two other commonly used propaganda devices are **hasty generalizations** (discussed under "Detecting and Evaluating Reasoning Fallacies" in this chapter) and **testimonials** (discussed previously in this section). Knowing the characteristics of propaganda, being able to detect common propaganda devices, and developing your capacity to analyze propaganda will enable you to escape from the control of propagandists as well as to contribute to the elimination of unscrupulous communicators of propaganda.</td></tr>
<tr><td>biases</td><td>***Detecting Biases of Chief Information Sources.*** A revealing discussion of **biases** of our chief sources of information—the press, the government, pressure groups, and professional scholars—is found in Newman and Newman's book, *Evidence.*[99] Newman and Newman stress that all sources of information have limits and that these limitations affect the evidence we draw from our sources. It is essential to remember that since individuals have differing perceptual capacities to observe and transmit information,</td></tr>
</table>

distortion of evidence results: "Ideology, national or other group interest, individual self-interest, career involvement, unconscious partisanship, exile mentality, reaction against one's past, and desire for power are some of the biases which distort perception."[100]

One of the many alleged examples of source bias in the media occurred in November 1992, when an NBC news magazine segment on the safety of General Motors' pickup trucks showed a fiery crash test. Although NBC later admitted to placing sparking devices on the truck, the broadcasting company denied that the devices caused the fire.[101] Scientists in research and development for a tobacco firm called to testify in suits against the firm for contributing to an individual's death by cancer could also be an example of source bias. Despite impressive credentials, such witnesses still represent their positions on the payroll of the firm and, as such, should be understood by judge and jury alike to be not necessarily objective in testimony.[102] The critical listener would do well to assess the biases of the sources of information to determine the acceptability of the evidence from those sources.

Analyzing Statistical Data. The discerning listener also should read Huff's delightful *How to Lie with Statistics*, an eye-opening exposé of the misuses of **statistical data**.[103] Huff, a statistician, illustrates many distortions from statistical evidence and recommends that individuals ask five questions to test statistical evidence: Who says so? How does he know? What's missing? Did somebody change the subject? Does it make sense?[104] For instance, "What's missing?" is a question critical listeners should ask when AT&T displays its "true math" showing 20 percent savings with AT&T and 13 percent savings with MCI. What's missing is "20 percent" of what amount and "13 percent" of what amount. Suppose, for example, that AT&T charges 30 cents per minute per call and MCI charges 25 cents per minute per call. Which long-distance carrier—with the stated percentages of savings—would be less expensive?

statistical data

We suggest that the critical listener also use the following questions as guides in evaluating statistical evidence:

1. Who wants to prove what?
2. Do the statistics come from reliable and objective sources?
3. How were the statistics gathered?
4. Are the statistics based on an adequate and representative sample?
5. Do the statistics cover a sufficient period of time?
6. Are the units being compared actually comparable?
7. Are the statistics the most current available?
8. How were the data treated statistically?
9. What conclusion do the statistics support?
10. How relevant to the issue are the statistics?
11. Can the results be verified?
12. Are the statistics supported by other findings and other sources?

quantitative terms

relative terms

Another question that the critical listener should ask is this: Does the speaker use **quantitative terms** or **relative terms**? For example, does the speaker specifically quantify values such as, "Ten students—that is, 25 percent of the class—disagreed with the new drug-testing policy," or does the speaker use relative values such as, "Some (or few, several, many, most, etc.) of the students disagreed with the new drug-testing policy"? Suppose, for instance, that during a television appearance, author Deborah Tannen reports that 73 percent of American men and 64 percent of American women in her sample interpreted the statement "John's having a party. Wanna go?" as a direct signal. When analyzing this finding, the critical listener should ask how many men and women were included in Tannen's survey.[105] While the meanings of quantitative terms are absolute, the meanings of relative terms are highly personal and determined by each communicator's relative experiences.

average

mean average

mode average

median average

Still another question the critical listener should ask is this one: What type of **average** (mean, mode, or median) does the speaker use? Suppose, for example, that a major-league baseball player—making $109,000—was renegotiating his salary and was on a team with one player making $5 million, five players making $2 million, four players making $700,000, three players making $200,000, and eleven players making $109,000 (for a total of $19,599,000 shared by twenty-four players). The renegotiating player's agent—who wants to get his or her client a higher salary—would cite the **mean average** (the arithmetical average determined by adding all numbers and dividing by the number of figures included, which is $816,625). The owner—believing his or her player is already making an adequate salary or too high a salary—would cite the **mode average** (the figure that occurs most frequently, which is $109,000) or the **median average** (the middle figure—with half of the figures being more and half being less, which is $200,000). If, however, the salary statistics were different, either the agent or the owner (or both) might use another type of average to his or her advantage. Obtaining the answers to these and other questions relevant to assessing statistical evidence will help the critical listener, as Huff suggests, "avoid learning a remarkable lot that isn't so."[106]

Skills Related to Pathos

Recognizing Need Levels

pathos

recognizing need levels

In addition to ethos and logos, the third key component of persuasion is **pathos**, the psychological appeals used by the speaker to gain emotional response from the listener. As humans, we respond at various **need levels**. Maslow proposes that we have five such levels.[107] At the first, most basic level are physiological needs—food, sleep, sex, drink, shelter. These needs must be satisfied before an individual can be motivated at a second level—the safety needs. Safety needs such as security, stability, protection, and strength are important motivators when any sort of threat to these needs might be present. The third level consists of the need to belong and to be loved, our social motivators. Americans are highly motivated by this need to belong, as evidenced by our affiliations with many groups. The fourth need level is identified by Maslow as the esteem needs. These needs represent both self-esteem, our desire for achievement and mastery, and esteem of others, our desire for reputation and prestige. These spring from our need to belong and represent a further stage in accomplishing our goals. Finally, at the fifth level in the hierarchy, Maslow identifies the need for self-actualization, our desire for self-fulfillment and for realizing our potential. Maslow suggests that we may be striving for this if other needs have been met, but the self-actualized person probably does not exist.

The need levels are reflected in the American value system, or what people in the United States want most in their lives. In a revealing survey, William Watts identified Americans' **hopes and fears**—hopes and fears that illustrate those values that most powerfully motivate us to respond. Watt's survey identified the following major values.

hopes and fears

Personal Hopes	**Personal Fears**
Better or decent standard of living	Lower standard of living
Good health for self	Ill health for self
Economic stability in general	War
Happy family life	Economic instability in general
Peace of mind; emotional maturity	Unemployment

Hopes for the Nation	**Fears for the Nation**
Economic stability; no inflation	War
Peace	Economic instability
Employment	Unemployment
Improved standard of living in general	Lack of law and order
Law and order[108]	

The hopes and fears revealed in this 1981 survey represent some of the major motivators that we as Americans carry with us.

Although Watts's studies have revealed Americans' **conscious needs**, depth studies by social scientists have revealed Americans' **unconscious needs**. In *The Hidden Persuaders*, Vince Packard describes eight of these hidden needs: emotional security, reassurance of worth, ego-gratification, creative outlets, love objects, sense of power, sense of roots, and immortality.[109] The promise of fulfilling such needs can be found in numerous persuasive appeals. These appeals can range from the salesperson's appeal that buying a home freezer will ensure always having food in the house to the agent's appeal that life insurance "assures the buyer of 'the prospect of immortality through the perpetuation of his influence.' "[110]

conscious needs

unconscious needs

Communicators on Madison Avenue as well as in the political arena understand these need levels and motivators; thus, they target message appeals to best fill our needs as listeners. Skillful persuaders who want to change our mental or physical behavior regarding some person, belief, product, act, policy, or philosophy can—by appealing to our needs—motivate us to respond to our feelings rather than to our reasoning. Such feeling responses are often engendered through visual images as well as verbal messages. Pictures in advertisements are important because "the human mind seems to integrate the information in the message (what is being asserted) with the information in any pictures that might be presented along with that message."[111] Thus, products are depicted in luxurious surroundings to evoke a sense that the subject and the setting are inextricably interwoven. "Few consumers can isolate the subject from the setting," concludes Loftus, "and make purchase decisions on the merit of the product itself."[112]

Feeling responses also are engendered through music. In political commercials, for instance, "music is added to accentuate the negative with music suggesting evil, whereas happy sounds are used when the favored candidate is shown."[113] In a 1994 political attack ad aired in Virginia and targeted at Democrat incumbent Charles Robb, Republican Senate hopeful Oliver North used "suggestive, tabloid-style music" to remind voters of Robb's alleged marital infidelity and drug parties.[114] In product and service commercials, music ranging from classical, '50s, and rhythm and blues to rock, country, and rap is used to get listening viewers to identify the music with the product or service. For example, many individuals associate "Wipeout" with the Interplak electric toothbrush and "Like a Rock" with Chevrolet automobiles. And individuals hum original tunes, such as those accompanying "Nobody does it like you" and "We bring good things to life" long after they have listened to the commercials on radio, television, and video. Promoters of these jingles hope that such jingles—made easier to remember by music—will influence us to buy what advertisers are selling.

Politicians and Madison Avenue communicators are not the only skillful persuaders. Salespeople learn to present the most expensive item to a customer first to contrast a less expensive item. Sales motivation specialists stress that "even when a man enters a clothing store with the express purpose of purchasing a suit, he will almost always pay more for whatever accessories he buys if he buys them after the suit purchase than before."[115]

The critical listener, then, must recognize what his or her need levels are as well as when the speaker is appealing to these need levels. This recognition will help the listener to evaluate the merits of persuasive messages on appeals to reasoning rather than to feelings.

Identifying Emotional Appeals

identifying emotional appeals

If we, as critical listeners, know the appeals that are commonly used and can identify them as emotional appeals, we will be able to communicate more rationally. One method that can help us maintain our rationality and objectivity is the following visual technique. As a speaker presents a persuasive message, we can visually place his or her emotional and logical content in two continua (E-E for emotional and L-L for logical) that *intersect* at some

Developing Purposeful Listening Skills

point between the two extremes. Thus, we will have a visual means to assist us in determining whether the message content is balanced, high in emotional content, or high in logical content. (See fig. 8.2.) When we conclude that there is an excess of emotional appeal, we will become more aware of how we are being persuaded. Furthermore, to assist us in maintaining our rationality and objectivity, we should ask ourselves these questions when we are confronted with emotional appeals:

1. What is the speaker's intent?
2. Is the speaker attempting to manipulate me?
3. Does the speaker have honest motives?
4. Is the speaker making promises that he or she cannot fulfill?
5. Who will benefit if the speaker's intent is achieved?
6. Does the speaker combine emotional appeal with reasoning (evidence)?
7. How am I responding?
8. Am I responding on a purely emotional level?
9. Am I allowing my emotional weaknesses to be exploited?

Using these questions will help us understand our responses to the numerous psychological appeals we receive. Among the emotional appeals that speakers employ are the following nineteen that Monroe has identified.[116]

1. Acquisition and Savings. The speaker might appeal to our need for **acquisition and saving** by stressing how the proposal can save us money. Generally, everyone likes a bargain, especially in inflationary times, so a considerable amount of product advertising is based on this appeal.[117] The Army's promise of $30,000 (through the Army College Fund) for a qualifying employee's continuing education is an example of appealing to one's desire to obtain money. Likewise, each outlet mall's claim of "factory discount prices" is an example of appealing to one's desire to save money; indeed, as one California outlet mall advertises, "Everyone needs an outlet."

acquisition and savings

2. Adventure. A second appeal is the appeal to **adventure**. The listener's desire to explore new worlds, experience exciting occurrences, and participate

adventure

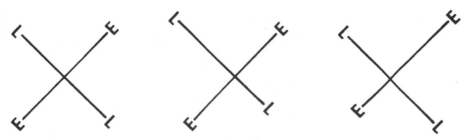

Figure 8.2.
Diagrams of perceived message content: balanced, high logical, and high emotional.

in different events is often stressed (e.g., in ads for Norwegian Cruise Line). Amusement and theme parks and travel agencies are two industries that rely heavily on our desire for adventure.

companionship

3. *Companionship.* A third appeal, **companionship**, arouses in us the desire to be with other people. Have you ever noticed how advertisers seldom associate a product with just one person? Since we are motivated by companionship, motivational researchers have concluded that it would not be wise to associate products with loneliness. For example, Big Red gum ads show how fresh breath derived from chewing the gum enables two people to hold tight and kiss "a little longer." Appeals by organizations, such as Parents without Partners, for membership will frequently stress the benefits of companionship to be found with the organization.

creativity

4. *Creativity.* The appeal to **creativity** may be another motivator. Most of us enjoy expressing ourselves through some creative means such as decorating our homes, designing innovative products, developing a new personal style (such as changing our hairstyle with Topsy Tail), or satisfying our artistic drives. The influence of this motivational force can be demonstrated by the numerous arts and crafts shows and kits as well as the do-it-yourself manuals that are currently so popular.

curiosity

5. *Curiosity.* Another appeal is the appeal to **curiosity**. When our curiosity is aroused, we often respond by seeking answers to the *whys, whens, wheres, whos, whats,* and *hows* that we wish to investigate. Besides capitalizing on our desire to know, the appeal to curiosity frequently operates with our desire for adventure, particularly if we are motivated to travel or explore new territory. For instance, the salesperson who keeps his or her product concealed or service unnamed until near the end of his or her presentation arouses our interest and often motivates us to continue listening. Similarly, the advertiser who uses a sequel of commercials to extend a plot (such as the producer of Taster's Choice coffee does) keeps us viewing so we can discover what occurs in the next commercial episode.

destruction

6. *Destruction.* Some speakers may attempt to use the appeal to destroy. This appeal calls for **destruction** of an existing rule, institution, etc. If the existing factor is made to appear as a real problem, a desire to overthrow it can be aroused. It is a difficult appeal to handle because it can be so destructive. The critical listener should be certain that the speaker has an alternative to replace what is to be destroyed. In the late 1960s, many students—as well as nonstudents—were vehemently calling for the overthrow of the entire institution of higher learning. What was missing in so many of the appeals to destruction, however, was any attempt to offer real alternatives to the existing structure of higher education.

fear

7. *Fear.* The **fear** appeal, presenting a sense of threat to the receiver, attempts to motivate the receiver to act (e.g., to prevent the spread of the HIV virus). Research on the fear appeal indicates that it may be possible for the speaker to overdo a fear appeal so that the listener may be even further

Developing Purposeful Listening Skills

strengthened in opposition to the threat. This strengthening of the opposing view is known as the "boomerang effect" and has been identified in several studies of the appeal. After reviewing research studies of the use of the fear appeal, Colburn recognized that it is difficult to generalize about the effectiveness of the appeal because it will affect each individual receiver differently. He noted, however, that "when fear-arousing appeals are used, speakers and writers will be more likely to gain acceptance of their recommendations if the strength of those appeals is proportionate to the importance of the issue in listeners' minds."[118]

8. Fighting. Closely allied to the appeal to destruction is the appeal to **fighting**. Prior to using the destruction appeal, a speaker often employs the appeal to fighting by arousing the anger of his or her listeners. The fighting appeal probably has more effect if it is used with a group of listeners rather than with one individual in an isolated setting. The speaker who asks, "Are you happy with your tax bills? Do you feel we've had enough?" is tapping the sense of anger in his or her taxpaying listeners. Likewise, this 1994 Republican attack ad appealed to voting listeners' sense of anger: "Are you really fed up with Congress? Well, on November 8, you've got your chance to do something."[119] **fighting**

9. Guilt. A prominent advertising theme today is **guilt**. Working mothers are particularly the target of this type of appeal. Since many mothers must work outside the home and leave their children to the care of others (or to come home after school to an empty house), parents are encouraged to make up for this condition by purchasing expensive toys, clothes, equipment, and so on. Moreover, individuals commonly use the guilt appeal in personal arguments. For example, a custodial parent may attempt to get a noncustodial parent to feel guilty by making a statement such as the following: "You can't imagine how torn up your only child is at your refusal to help him with his car payments." Also, the appeal to guilt, which is quite powerful, can combine with the appeal to sympathy to encourage charitable contributions and volunteer help. **guilt**

10. Imitation. A less hostile appeal is that of **imitation**. This strongly motivates Americans, as indicated by advertising appeals to quench our thirst and satisfy our hunger with products endorsed by television and film stars, such as *Seinfeld*'s Michael Richards drinking Pepsi or Chevy Chase munching Doritos Tortilla Thins. Or, we are told we should purchase shoes worn by great sports figures, such as Shaquille O'Neal's Reebok sneakers or Michael Jordan's Nike sneakers. In our attempts to "be sweet," "be cool," and/or to "keep up with the Joneses," we demonstrate our drive to emulate others. **imitation**

11. Independence. While our desire to emulate others is strong, a conflicting motivation may be our sense of **independence**. Some product advertisers have attempted to use this appeal to associate certain brands of cigarettes, for instance, with the independent cowboy alone on his horse or **independence**

the liberated woman. And automobile companies frequently showcase one of their cars or trucks with a lone driver traveling freely on an open road. Independence lies at the heart of our constitutional democracy; therefore, it is inherent in American value systems. Wartime speakers, too, made considerable use of this appeal to mobilize public support for the war effort.

loyalty

12. Loyalty. Keeping America independent also represents an appeal to **loyalty**. Loyalty to our nation, our friends and family, and our organizations is an important characteristic. Loyalty to the nation, for example, represents patriotic appeals that continue to change. The "America—love it or leave it" movement polarized Americans so that some Americans no longer will respond to flag-waving patriotic appeals. Many others, however, are still highly motivated by patriotic appeals such as those that encourage the buying of products "Made in America," "Made the American way," or "Crafted with Pride in U.S.A." Today, many companies are engaged in "relationship marketing" designed to develop long-term bonds with customers and, thus, loyalty to companies. Such offerings as special services, discounts, newsletters, unique guarantees, special promises, and frequent buyer programs are all examples of "relationship marketing."[120]

personal enjoyment

13. Personal Enjoyment. We are all highly motivated by **personal enjoyment**. Advertisers—recognizing that we long for sensory and psychic pleasures such as comfort, luxury, security, contentment, beauty, recreation, freedom, space, and sensory satisfaction—employ appeals to our experiences of present pleasures, our memories of past pleasures, and our anticipation of future pleasures. These appeals show how we are able to respond on a higher order of Maslow's hierarchy. Thus, if our basic needs are met, we can turn to fulfilling needs of enjoyment and aesthetics by, for instance, doubling our pleasure with Doublemint gum or riding in a Mercedes Benz and never feeling a pot hole.

power and authority

14. Power and Authority. There are times when the speaker may wish to appeal to the listener's sense of **power and authority**. Such a motivator could be appropriate in developing more responsibility in a group of administrators. It is an appeal used in the auto industry to persuade buyers to purchase large engines, an appeal used in education to encourage people to become teachers (e.g., the National Education Association's ad, "Reach for the Power. Teach."), and an appeal used in technology to attract computer novices and computer-shy consumers (e.g., Microsoft commercials touting "empowerment"). The appeal to power is also a strong motivator to mobilize a nation to wage war.[121]

pride

15. Pride. Another powerful emotional incentive is the appeal to our sense of **pride**. Recognizing the motivational force of individual self-esteem, speakers frequently strive to develop a positive self-concept in their listeners. Coaches and managers rely heavily on this appeal in motivating players to "give their all" in sporting events. The Marines use this appeal to recruit individuals: "The few. The proud. The Marines." Moreover, managers in industry rely on an appeal to pride in work well done in order to motivate workers to accomplish rigorous production schedules. Motivational research reveals that job satisfaction frequently stems from factors intrinsic to the job itself.[122]

16. *Reverence.*   Still another appeal is the appeal to **reverence** or worship. This can be seen through manifestations of hero worship—having deep admiration for sports stars, entertainers, or historical figures—or in religious behaviors. In his book *Resurrection*, Senator (and ordained minister) John Danforth describes his use of this appeal before Clarence Thomas first denied Anita Hill's allegations: "I . . . put my hand on Clarence's shoulders and spoke as a minister: 'Go forth in the name of Christ, trusting in the power of the Holy Spirit.'"[123]

reverence

17. *Revulsion.*   A motivator inherent in all of us is **revulsion**. As a specific type of fear, this appeal can be effective. A speaker illustrating the effects of water pollution, for example, may show photographs and cite statistics on the effects of pollution to motivate receivers to support legislation for clean water. Such an appeal, if not overdone, can accomplish an initial arousal to action.

revulsion

18. *Sexual Attraction.*   Found in a great deal of advertising is a more pleasant appeal: **sexual attraction**. This associates the beautiful young woman with Calvin Klein jeans or the handsome young man with a Solo Flex body, or it associates two beautiful young people together with Haagen-Dazs ice cream. A 1994 Clio award-winner for sex appeal was a commercial that showed several female office employees stop working every morning at 11:30 to meet at an office window (overlooking a construction site) and watch a male construction worker remove his shirt and take a Diet Coke break.[124] While sexual attraction is a motivator, it can be overdrawn if the appeal does not relate to the product or the issue under consideration.

sexual attraction

19. *Sympathy.*   A potent appeal is the appeal to **sympathy**. A speaker who depicts homeless children, mistreated elderly, or forgotten veterans can motivate us to give our time, money, and talents. The outpouring of expressions of grief and sorrow for the bereaved family and community of 3-year-old Michael Smith and 14-month-old Alex Smith illustrates how Americans are moved by the appeal to sympathy. The mother of the two boys allegedly drowned them by buckling them in safety seats in her car and then rolling the car into a lake in Union, South Carolina, on 25 October 1994.[125] Political speakers also like to use this appeal to gain support for their causes and for their own elections.

sympathy

Since we are motivated by such appeals, it helps listeners to understand why they are responding as they are if they can identify the specific type of appeal that the speaker is using. At the extreme, the speaker will use only emotional appeals as a persuasive device. Such an attempt may succeed in persuading listeners at the moment. Over time, however, we tend to forget the impact of such appeals and are left with only the core of the argument from the message. If there is no valid logical argument, then the message probably will not have a long-lasting effect.

Dealing Effectively with Emotive Language

In addition to using emotional appeals to arouse the listeners, persuaders frequently employ **emotive language**—often in the forms of name-calling and labeling. Using terms intended to degrade or stereotype a person, party, issue, or event on the basis of limited knowledge are methods speakers use to influence listeners to accept their views. An opponent of a certain candidate, for example, uses name-calling when he or she remarks to a voter, "Don't vote for Menard; she's a radical." Or a person who has seen a long-haired male arrested on television uses labeling when he or she says to a neighbor, "You'd be insane to hire that Colson boy; he's just one of those long-haired freaks who only cause trouble."

"Hate" rhetoric, designed to arouse listeners' emotions, often uses highly emotional language to characterize the racial, ethnic, or religious group that is the target of the speaker. For example, some blacks have labeled Supreme Court Justice Clarence Thomas as an "Uncle Tom" who has forgotten his roots.[126] Moreover, some nonresidents of the Golden State have labeled California as a "haven for nuts."[127] And, many individuals have bashed blonds, lawyers, JAP's (Jewish American Princess), and so on as butts of widely-circulated jokes. Alan Dundes, a folklorist at the University of California—Berkeley, believes "all jokes have elements of hostility in them, and these [blond jokes]—a throwback to the 50s focus on a type of mindlessness that men often liked to see in women, paired with a sex-kittenish availability—he suspects are primarily an aggressive response to feminism."[128] Harvey Saferstein, president of the State Bar of California, fears, too, "there's an undercurrent of hostility towards lawyers that goes beyond a joke."[129] And journalist Myra Patner cites many instances that illustrate that JAP jokes ("jokes about Jewish women, especially purportedly greedy, manipulative, self-centered and shallow Jewish women"[130]) and hostile discriminating behavior continue to persist, especially on college campuses.[131]

As listeners, we tend to react in two ways to language that triggers emotional reactions in us. If the views expressed are congruent with our point of view, we accept—without question—what is said and are ruled by our feelings rather than by our minds. On the other hand, if the views expressed are incongruent with our point of view, we immediately reject what is said and exercise emotional censorship; we become "deaf" to what we do not want to hear and again are ruled by our feelings. Both responses are reactions that the critical listener should avoid.

Critical listeners should attempt to reduce the impact that certain emotionally loaded words have on them. They should first recognize their own biases toward certain emotive words, analyze why these words affect them as they do, and then attempt to perceive the words rationally. With this new awareness, listeners will be better able to deal with such words when they meet them in communicative situations. Dealing with them effectively

Daily, we are flooded with emotional appeals made on the telephone, radio, and TV as well as in person.

consists of recognizing emotive words for what they are, maintaining self-control while listening to the remainder of the speaker's message, examining the speaker's message for evidence to prove or disprove the speaker's claim, asking the speaker to provide evidence to support his or her claim if the evidence has not been presented, and then accepting or rejecting the speaker's view on the basis of having made a rational rather than an emotional decision.

Responsibilities of the Critical Listener

responsibilities of critical listeners

Critical listeners respond to persuasive messages designed to change attitudes and actions voluntarily. Understanding how these messages incorporate speaker credibility, arguments, and emotional appeals can enable listeners to evaluate those messages systematically and soundly and then decide whether to accept or reject the speaker's proposal. According to Charles Larson, the **critical listener has two major responsibilities**:

> First, he must watch himself as he is persuaded or as he is subject to persuasive appeals; second, he must find some way to systematize his awareness by applying carefully considered criteria to the appeals he processes, judging their relevance, their truth, and their applicability to him.[132]

Accepting these responsibilities may make the difference between our being uncritical listeners controlled by others or being critical listeners controlled by ourselves.

Summary

In this chapter, we have examined the need for critical listening—listening to comprehend and *then* evaluate—as it applies primarily to messages that are persuasive in intent. To help the critical listener understand the process of persuasion and establish criteria to be used as a basis for the listener's decision to accept or to reject a persuasive message, we have presented (1) a definition of persuasion, (2) a psychological sequence that the process of influence usually follows, and (3) a detailed explanation of how the three components of persuasion—ethos, logos, and pathos—function in the persuasive effort. We also have provided lists of questions that the critical listener should ask and answer when evaluating various aspects of these three components. Finally, we have discussed the following critical listening skills that the critical listener must develop to more systematically and soundly evaluate persuasive messages: identifying the dimensions of source credibility; recognizing the possible influence that source credibility may have on the listener; analyzing inductive and deductive argument structures to determine their truth and validity; detecting and evaluating reasoning fallacies; judging the clarity, accuracy, and reliability of evidence; recognizing need levels; and identifying psychological appeals and emotive language and recognizing their effects on the listener. The critical listener who develops these skills will have a sound basis upon which to evaluate persuasive messages and hence should have control over his or her decisions.

Suggested Activities

1. Identify at least three radio and television commercials that follow Monroe's motivated sequence. Then, present a detailed description (orally or in writing) of how each commercial uses each of the five basic steps.
2. Rank order from one (most important) to three (least important) what you most often consider when you are evaluating the credibility of a speaker. Describe how you determine whether a speaker possesses each of these dimensions.
3. Create your own examples of inductive arguments and read them to the class; the class will assess the truthfulness of the arguments.
4. Create your own enthymemes, read the enthymemes to the class, and have the class determine the validity and truth of the enthymemes.
5. Identify conjunctions, other than *because*, that imply causal relationships. Examine your own written papers to determine what causal terms you have used and whether your causal reasoning is sound.
6. Bring in examples of logical fallacies found in various forms of communication (speeches, commercials, editorials, etc.). Share the examples with the class.
7. Identify five radio or television commercials that use fallacious testimonies. Then, describe orally each product being endorsed, the person doing the endorsing, and the name, title, or field of a person who would present a credible testimony.
8. Compile a list of special interest groups (religious, racial, political, professional, sexual, economic, etc.). Then, locate three or four statements of fact, opinion, and inference in articles that express the views of special interest groups. Each student will read each of his or her statements, and students will determine what type of statement (fact, opinion, or inference) is being used. When an opinion is stated, students will try to determine why that opinion is held by a particular special interest group.
9. Carefully note several opinions that your other instructors state. Then, privately meet with one instructor and find out why the instructor holds a particular opinion.
10. Find examples of statistics in the various media and share the examples with the class. Students will evaluate critically the soundness of the examples.

11. Identify words or phrases that emotionally upset you. Then, share these words with the class, analyze why these words have such emotional impact, and try to eliminate your conditioned reactions to these words.

12. List examples of emotional appeals and emotive words with which you are confronted over the next few days. Do not rely heavily on commercials. Share these examples with the class at the next class session.

13. Compile a list of biases and stereotypes you possess. Then, consider how and why you have developed them, how they affect your listening behavior, and how you could minimize or eliminate them from your listening and thinking.

14. List all of the examples of bias and stereotyping that you hear in speeches, lectures, conversations, on television, on radio, etc., during a week. Compare your examples with those of other students. What examples are most frequently listed? Why do you think these particular biases and stereotypes exist? How did these examples affect you and your listening behavior when you first heard them? How did they affect other students and their listening behavior?

15. List all of the loaded words and phrases that you hear in speeches, lectures, conversations, and on television and radio during a week. Place each word in one of two columns labeled "positive" and "negative." Compare your list with other students' lists. Which words are most frequently listed? What connotative meanings do the words have? What makes these words "positive" or "negative"?

16. Make a copy of an article or speech that contains highly emotional words. Rewrite the message by replacing the emotional words with neutral words. Examine the revised material to determine the validity of the claim(s) being made.

17. Listen to three radio or television commercials and list the emotive words and propaganda devices used in the commercials.

18. Videotape television commercials that incorporate visual images, music, and verbal messages and determine to what needs and/or feelings each of the three ingredients is intended to appeal. Also, determine what logical appeals are used and evaluate their soundness.

19. Critically analyze the impact that the 1994 child molestation allegations against entertainer Michael Jackson had on Jackson's celebrity endorsement career.

20. Maintain a one-day log of all communication transactions in which you served as a persuasive message sender or as a critical listener.

21. Describe a recent situation in which a speaker attempted to persuade you. List and critically evaluate the speaker's use of skills related to ethos, logos, and pathos. Also, note what your decision was and on what you based your final decision.

Notes

1. M. McConahey, "Memories of Polly Still Vivid," *Santa Rosa Press Democrat*, 25 September 1994, p. B2.
2. M. McConahey, "Polly: Ordinary Girl Touched Many Lives," *Santa Rosa Press Democrat*, 10 December 1993, p. 6.
3. C. Smith, R. Rossman, and J. W. Sweeney, "A Numbing End to 64 Days of Searching," *Santa Rosa Press Democrat*, 5 December 1993, p. A13.
4. Ibid.
5. To compile this information, we drew upon all sources cited in notes 1 through 32 in this chapter and the following sources: E. Nichol, "Eve Nichol's Message to Community," *Santa Rosa Press Democrat*, 7 December 1993, p. A10; J. W. Sweeney and R. Rossman, "Suspect Acted Alone, Picked Polly at Random," *Santa Rosa Press Democrat*, 6 December 1993, p. A10; J. W. Sweeney, "Polly Kidnap Suspect's Mother Reportedly Lives in Petaluma," *Santa Rosa Press Democrat*, 3 December 1993, p. A20; "The Legacy of Polly Klaas," *Santa Rosa Press Democrat*, 10 December 1993, p. 5; R. Digitale, "Poetry from a Police Officer? Not So Unusual," *Santa Rosa Press Democrat*, 11 December 1993, p. A13.
6. McConahey, "Memories of Polly Still Vivid," p. B2.
7. M. Bouchet, "Goodbye, Polly," *Sonoma Index-Tribune*, 14 December 1993, p. A1.
8. B. W. Rose, "Tears, Prayers at Tragic Ending," *Santa Rosa Press Democrat*, 5 December 1993, p. A1.
9. B. W. Rose and E. Klineman, "Remembrances Flow along with Commitments," *Santa Rosa Press Democrat*, 10 December 1993, p. A5.
10. M. Klaas and E. Nichol, "A Message from the Family," *Santa Rosa Press Democrat*, 10 December 1993, p. A5.
11. J. W. Sweeney, "Davis Admits Killing, Says Best Hope Is Life Term," *Santa Rosa Press Democrat*, 3 September 1994, p. A9.
12. R. Murphy, "Events in the Polly Klaas Kidnapping," *Santa Rosa Press Democrat*, 5 December 1993, p. A5.
13. McConahey, "Memories of Polly Still Vivid," p. B2.
14. Ibid.
15. C. Benfell, "Even Tough-Guy FBI Agent Affected by Polly's Tragedy," *Santa Rosa Press Democrat*, 10 December 1993, p. 4.
16. C. Coursey, "Grieving Extends beyond Petaluma," *Santa Rosa Press Democrat*, 6 December 1993, pp. A1, A5.
17. J. W. Sweeney, "Klaas Will Lobby Clinton," *Santa Rosa Press Democrat*, 17 December 1993, p. B1.
18. C. Coursey, "One Child Becomes Symbol of Crimes against All Children," *Santa Rosa Press Democrat*, 10 December 1993, p. 6.
19. Rose, "Tears, Prayers at Tragic Ending," p. A13.
20. Smith, Rossman, and Sweeney, "A Numbing End to 64 Days of Searching," p. A13.
21. Sweeney, "Davis Admits Killing, Says Best Hope Is Life Term," p. A9.
22. Ibid.
23. B. W. Rose, R. Rossman, B. Saludes, and M. Geniella, "Davis Sorry for Killing, Cites Drugs," *Santa Rosa Press Democrat*, 7 December 1993, p. A10.
24. Ibid.
25. J. W. Sweeney and R. Rossman, "Polly Conspiracy Rumors Refuse to Go Away," *Santa Rosa Press Democrat*, 16 December 1993, A1.
26. T. Miller, *California Ballot Pamphlet* (Sacramento, CA: Office of the Secretary of State, 16 August 1994), p. 33.
27. Coursey, "One Child Becomes Symbol of Crimes against All Children," p. 6.
28. B. W. Rose, "Tough Anti-Crime Initiatives Gain New Momentum," *Santa Rosa Press Democrat*, 7 December 1993, p. A8.
29. Ibid.
30. Sweeney, "Davis Admits Killing, Says Best Hope Is Life Term," pp. A1, A9.
31. Ibid., p. A1; Rose, et al., "Davis Sorry for Killing, Cites Drugs," p. A10.
32. Miller, *California Ballot Pamphlet*, pp. 36–37.
33. S. I. Hayakawa, "The Task of the Listener," *ETC* 7 (Autumn 1949): 9–10.

34. It should be recognized, however, that the federal government can and does restrict dishonest speech in particular situations. Truth in advertising laws, for example, provide limitations. Under the Supreme Court's *Garrison v. Louisiana* opinion, government can even restrict dishonest political speech.

35. W. Johnson, "Do We Know How to Listen?" *ETC* 7 (Autumn 1949): 3.

36. J. Daly and Speaking and Listening Skills, Group Three, "Proceedings," in *The National Assessment of College Students Learning: Identification of the Skills to Be Taught, Learned, and Assessed,* ed. A. Greenwood (Washington, DC: U. S. Office of Education, August 1994), p. 277 of the Revised Version of the Work Group Report: Speaking and Listening.

37. M. A. Gunn, "Background Preparation for the Role of Today's Teacher of English" (Paper presented at the National Council of Teachers of English Convention, Chicago, IL, 1960).

38. T. Post, M. Mabry, T. Stanger, L. Kay, and C. S. Lee, "Mystery of the Solar Temple," *Newsweek,* 17 October 1994, pp. 42–44.

39. E. A. Jones and G. Ratcliff, "Critical Thinking Literature Review" (Paper prepared for the National Center for Education Statistics, Washington, DC, May 1993), p. 13.

40. H. Siegel, *Educating Reason: Rationality, Critical Thinking and Education,* (NY: Routledge, 1988), pp. 39–45.

41. R. Manuto, "Critical Thinking Theory and Research: A Movement in Search of Itself" (Paper presented at the Eastern Communication Association Convention, New Haven, CT, 1993), pp. 8–9.

42. Jones and Ratcliff, "Critical Thinking Literature Review," p. 9.

43. P. A. Facione, "A Critique of Richard W. Paul's and Gerald M. Nosich's Proposal for the National Assessment of Higher-Order Thinking at the Community College, College, and University Levels" (Paper submitted to the National Center for Education Statistics, Washington, DC, May 1992).

44. D. F. Halpern, "A National Assessment of Critical Thinking Skills in Adults: Taking Steps toward the Goal" (Paper submitted to the National Center for Education Statistics, Washington, DC, 1992).

45. H. Ruminski, W. Hanks, K. Spicer, "Critical Thinking in Speech Communication: A Survey" (Paper presented at the Eastern Communication Association Convention, Washington, DC, 1994).

46. Ibid., p. 15.

47. Jones and Ratcliff, "Critical Thinking Literature Review," p. 10.

48. R. Paul and G. M. Nosich, "A Proposal for the National Assessment of Higher-order Thinking" (Paper submitted to the National Center for Educational Statistics, Washington, DC, 1991), pp. 4–5.

49. E. M. Glaser, "Critical Thinking: Educating for Responsible Citizenship in a Democracy," *National Forum* 65 (Winter 1985): 25.

50. J. S. McQuillen, "The Development of Listener-Adapted Compliance-Resisting Strategies," *Human Communication Research* 12 (Spring 1986): 359–375.

51. R. Goyer, class notes, Purdue University, 1965.

52. K. Freed and N. Kempster, "Paratroopers on Their Way As Deal Reached," *Santa Rosa Press Democrat,* 19 September 1994, p. A8.

53. B. E. Gronbeck, R. E. McKerrow, D. Ehninger, and Alan H. Monroe, *Principles and Types of Speech Communication,* 11th ed. (Glenview, IL: Scott, Foresman/Little, Brown Higher Education, 1990), pp. 128–141.

54. Aristotle, *The Rhetoric of Aristotle,* trans. Lane Cooper (NY: Appleton-Century-Croft, 1932.)

55. See, for example, S. F. Paulson, "Social Values and Experimental Research in Speech," *Western Speech Communication* 26 (Summer 1962): 133–139.

56. For a discussion of the dimensions of source credibility, see J. C. McCroskey, *An Introduction to Rhetorical Communication* (Englewood Cliffs, NJ: Prentice-Hall, 1972), chapter 4. See also J. C. McCroskey and T. J. Young, "Ethos and Credibility: The Construct and Its Measurement after Three Decades," *Central States Speech Journal* 32 (Spring 1981): 24–34, for McCroskey's critique of the research on the construct of source credibility and his conclusion that source credibility must be considered as part of a broader construct of person perception.

57. K. E. Andersen and T. Clevenger, Jr., "A Summary of Experimental Research in Ethos," *Speech Monographs* 30 (June 1963): 77.

58. D. H. Naftulin, J. E. Ware, Jr., and F. A. Donnelly, "The Doctor Fox Lecture: A Paradigm of Educational Seduction," *Journal of Medical Education* 48 (July 1973): 630–635.

59. L. McAneny and D. W. Moore, "Congress and Media Sink in Public Esteem," *The Gallup Poll News Service*, 1994: 1–2.

60. B. Hohler, "Marion Barry Tries to Reclaim the Office He Lost," *Santa Rosa Press Democrat*, 3 September 1994, p. A11.

61. "Speaking against Drugs," *NEA Today* 8 (November 1989): 12.

62. J. F. Kennedy, "Ich Bin Ein Berliner," *Public Papers of the Presidents: John F. Kennedy, 1963* (Washington, DC: United States Government Printing Office, 1964), p. 525; "Kennedy's Visit Coincides with Anniversary of Airlift," *New York Times*, 27 June 1963, p. 12.

63. W. Schneider, "Clinton Needs to Look Like a Winner," *National Journalism*, 13 August 1994, p. 1950.

64. J. Splaine, *The Critical Viewing of Television* (South Hamilton, MA: Critical Thinking Press, 1987), p. 5.

65. J. McGinniss, *The Selling of the President 1968* (NY: Trident Books, 1969), p. 38.

66. B. Whalen, "He Taught George Bush Telegenics," *Insight* 4 (27 June 1988): 21.

67. Splaine, *The Critical Viewing of Television*, p. 5. See also M. Weisskopf, "The Professionals' Touch," *The Washington Post*, 8 November 1994, pp. A1, A4, for a discussion of the role of political consultants.

68. Splaine, *The Critical Viewing of Television*, p. 27.

69. Research by S. Harp, S. Stretch, and D. Harp cited in M. R. Solomon, "Dress for Effect," *Psychology Today* 20 (April 1986): 22.

70. The reader should note that we are using the term "argument" to refer to reasoned discourse, not the more idiomatic use of argument as verbal battle.

71. S. L. Marcus, "Recall of Logical Argument Lines," *Journal of Verbal Learning and Verbal Behavior* 21 (October 1982): 549.

72. It should be noted that not all communication scholars share the view that the enthymeme is the major inductive format utilized by communicators. See T. M. Conley, "The Enthymeme in Perspective," *Quarterly Journal of Speech* 70 (May 1987): 168–187.

73. From S. Toulmin, *The Uses of Argument* (Cambridge: Cambridge University Press, 1958). It should be noted that Toulmin has developed a more elaborate (but less familiar) model of the process (a *claim* is made, *grounds* support the claim, a *warrant* connects the grounds to the claim, *backing*—foundations for the warrant—is shown, appropriate *modal qualifiers*—such as "some," "many," "most," etc.—temper the claim, and *rebuttals* are considered) in a later book, S. Toulmin et al., *An Introduction to Reasoning*, 2d ed. (NY: Macmillan, 1984).

74. M. Scriven, *Reasoning* (NY: McGraw-Hill, 1976), pp. 39–45.

75. R. E. Crable, *Argumentation as Communication* (Columbus, OH: Merrill, 1976), p. 215.

76. C. Sullivan, "What Drives Mothers to Kill?" *Santa Rosa Press Democrat*, 5 November 1994, p. A17.

77. W. W. Fearnside and W. B. Holther, *Fallacy* (Englewood Cliffs, NJ: Prentice-Hall, 1959), p. 167.

78. P. Baker, "North-Robb Race Nastier," *Santa Rosa Press Democrat*, 14 October 1994, p. A4.

79. S. Farr, "Feinstein Defends Education Vote," *Santa Rosa Press Democrat*, 26 October 1994, p. A4; S. Proffitt, "Down to the Wire with Feinstein, Huffington," *Santa Rosa Press Democrat*, 30 October 1994, p. A4; Feinstein advertisement aired on KPIX-TV, San Francisco, CA, on 4 November 1994; D. Willis, "Prop. 187 Sets Campaign Tone," *Santa Rosa Press Democrat*, 6 November 1994, p. A4.

80. Proffitt, "Down to the Wire with Feinstein, Huffington," p. A4; D. Lesher, "Huffington Employed Illegal Worker," *Santa Rosa Press Democrat*, 27 October 1994, pp. A1, A15; Huffington advertisement aired on KPIX-San Francisco, CA, on 4 November 1994; Willis, "Prop. 187 Sets Campaign Tone," p. A4.

81. "Senate Camps Trade Barbs," *Santa Rosa Press Democrat*, 5 November 1994, pp. A1, A4.

82. P. Taylor, "Armed with Distortions, Candidates Air Attacks," *The Washington Post*, 21 September 1990, pp. A1, A10; P. West, "The Trouble Is, They Work," *Baltimore Sun*, 2 November 1986, p. C1; C. F. Smith, "Positively Negative Campaigns," *Baltimore Sun*, 2 November 1986, p. C3; C. Krauthammer, "Slinging Political Mud," *Santa Rosa Press Democrat*, 30 October 1994, pp. G1, G6; D. Balz, "Campaign 94: The Negatives Add Up," *The Washington Post*, 7 November 1994, pp. A1, A10.

83. D. Brock, "Who Bends Whose Ears This Year?" *Insight* 4 (25 April 1988), p. 8.

84. The real impact of evidence in persuasive discourse may be disputed. After analyzing experimental research studies on the use of evidence, McCroskey drew conclusions that suggest listeners may not be responsive to a speaker's evidence:

1. Including good evidence has little, if any, impact on immediate audience attitude change or source credibility if the source of the message is initially perceived to be high-credible.
2. Including good evidence has little, if any, impact on immediate audience attitude change if the message is delivered poorly.
3. Including good evidence has little, if any, impact on immediate audience attitude change or source credibility if the audience is familiar with the evidence prior to exposure to the source's message.
4. Including good evidence may significantly increase immediate audience attitude change and source credibility when the source is initially perceived to be moderate-to-low credible, when the message is well delivered, and when the audience has little or no prior familiarity with the evidence included or similar evidence.
5. Including good evidence may significantly increase sustained audience attitude change regardless of the source's initial credibility, the quality of the delivery of the message, or the medium by which the message is transmitted.
6. The medium of transmission of a message has little, if any, effect on the functioning of evidence in persuasive communication.

See James C. McCroskey, "A Summary of Experimental Research on the Effects of Evidence in Persuasive Communication," *The Quarterly Journal of Speech* 55 (April 1969): 169–176.

85. R. R. Windes and A. Hastings, *Argumentation and Advocacy* (NY: Random House, 1965), p. 96.
86. Ibid., p. 99.
87. W. V. Haney, *Communication Patterns and Incidents* (Homewood, IL: Irwin, 1960), p. 21.
88. G. Allport and L. Postman, *The Psychology of Rumor* (NY: Holt, Rinehart & Winston, 1947), p. ix.
89. T. Pack, "Businesses Battle Back in War of Strange Rumors," *Santa Rosa Press Democrat*, 24 October 1993, pp. E1, E2; "Winfrey-Claiborne Clash Rumors Killed and Buried," *Santa Rosa Press Democrat*, 11 October 1992, p. D4.
90. J. C. Hughes, "The Devil Made Them Do It," *Working Woman*, November 1985, pp. 88–90; W. Ecenbarger, "Rumors," *Sunday Magazine*, 22 June 1986, p. 18; Pack, "Businesses Battle Back in War of Strange Rumors"; L. Blumenfield, "Procter & Gamble's Devil of a Problem" *The Washington Post*, 14 July 1991, pp. B1, B6.
91. L. Blumenfield, "Procter & Gamble's Devil of a Problem," p. B6.
92. "How to Stop Those Rumors," *Communication Briefings*, May 1994, p. 3.
93. R. L. Rosnow and A. J. Kimmel, "Lives of a Rumor," *Psychology Today* 13 (June 1979): 91.
94. Ibid.
95. Ecenbarger, "Rumors."
96. C. G. Coakley, *Teaching Effective Listening* (Laurel, MD: Carolyn Gwynn Coakley, 1988), p. 359.
97. C. R. Miller, "Detection and Analysis of Propaganda," *Public Opinion Quarterly* 5 (Winter 1941): 662.
98. Ibid.
99. R. P. Newman and D. G. Newman, *Evidence* (Boston: Houghton Mifflin, 1969).
100. Ibid., p. 72.
101. R. Digitale, "Ad Takes Aim at TV News Bias," *Santa Rosa Press Democrat*, 10 February 1993, p. B1.
102. For an interesting case study, see M. Mintz, "The Artful Dodgers," *The Washington Monthly*, October 1986, pp. 9–16.
103. D. Huff, *How to Lie with Statistics* (NY: Norton, 1954).
104. Ibid., pp. 122–142.
105. D. Tannen, *Gender and Discourse* (NY: Oxford University Press, 1994), p. 186. The survey results reported are based on responses from eleven males and fourteen females.
106. Huff, *How to Lie with Statistics*, p. 122.
107. A. Maslow, *Motivation and Personality* (NY: Harper & Row, 1970), pp. 35–38.
108. W. Watts, "The Future Can Fend for Itself," *Psychology Today* 15 (September 1981): 36–48.
109. V. Packard, *The Hidden Persuaders* (NY: David McKay Company, 1957), pp. 72–83.
110. Ibid., p. 83.
111. E. Loftus, *Memory* (Reading, MA: Addison-Wesley Publishing Company, 1980), p. 156.
112. Ibid.
113. Splaine, *The Critical Viewing of Television*, p. 46.
114. Baker, "North-Robb Race Nastier," p. A4.

115. R. Whitney and T. Rubin, *The New Psychology of Persuasion and Motivation in Selling*, cited in R. B. Cialdini, "The Triggers of Influence," *Psychology Today* 18 (February 1984): 45.

116. D. Ehninger, B. E. Gronbeck, and A. H. Monroe, *Principles and Types of Speech Communication*, 8th brief ed. (Glenview, IL: Scott, Foresman and Company, 1980), pp. 104–109.

117. For a scholarly treatment of motivational research and its application in the advertising industry, see J. F. Engel, D. T. Kollat, and R. D. Blackwell, *Consumer Behavior* (NY: Holt, Rinehart & Winston, 1973).

118. C. W. Colburn, "Fear-Arousing Appeals," in *Speech Communication Analysis and Readings*, ed. H. H. Martin and K. E. Andersen (Boston: Allyn and Bacon, 1968), pp. 214–223. See also W. F. Eadie, "Fear Tempers Message Design and Performance," *Spectra*, August 1994, pp. 7, 10.

119. T. B. Rosenstiel, "GOP Readys New Attack Ads," *Santa Rosa Press Democrat*, 28 October 1994, p. A4.

120. A. L. Stern, "New '90s Corporate Credo Let the Buyer Be Wooed," *Santa Rosa Press Democrat*, 17 January 1993, p. E1.

121. For a discussion of this appeal, see D. C. McClelland, "Love and Power: The Psychological Signals of War," *Psychology Today* 8 (January 1975): 44–48.

122. For a review of the research, see T. O. Jacobs, *Leadership and Exchange in Formal Organizations* (Alexandria, VA: Human Resources Research Organization, 1971), pp. 122–154.

123. C. Anderson, "Hearings Reduced Thomas to Tears," *Santa Rosa Press Democrat*, 19 September 1994, p. A5.

124. *The 1994 Clio Awards* aired on KTVU-TV, Oakland, CA, 31 October 1994.

125. G. Henderson, "Saying Goodbye to Slain Brothers," *Santa Rosa Press Democrat*, 7 November 1994, p. A3; "Insanity Defense Possible for Mom in Carjack Case," *Santa Rosa Press Democrat*, 8 November 1994, p. A10.

126. J. Biskupic, "'I Am Not Uncle Tom,' Thomas Tells Blacks," *Santa Rosa Press Democrat*, 28 October 1994, p. A3.

127. S. Stanton, "Californians Who Flee Find Few Welcome Mats, *Santa Rosa Press Democrat*, 10 October 1993, p. B7.

128. R. Flaste, "Funny Girls," *Allure*, December 1991, pp. 48–49.

129. M. Locke, "Hear One about Fuming Lawyer?" *Santa Rosa Press Democrat*, 24 July 1993, p. A2.

130. M. M. Patner, " 'JAP' Jokes: Baiting or Hating?" *The Washington Post*, 4 December 1988, p. L5.

131. Ibid.

132. C. U. Larson, *Persuasion: Reception and Responsibility* (Belmont, CA: Wadsworth, 1973), p. 13.

- *Appreciative listening is listening to obtain sensory stimulation or enjoyment through the works and experiences of others.*

- *Appreciative listening can include listening to such forms as music, oral style, environmental sounds, oral reading of literature, theatre, television, radio, or film.*

- *The effective appreciative listener*
  - *recognizes what he or she appreciates and why*
  - *gains experience in listening appreciatively to a variety of forms*
  - *develops a willingness to listen appreciatively*
  - *concentrates attention*

CHAPTER 9

Appreciative Listening

"We usually know when we are in the appreciative listening role. Someone comes into our office with a smile on her face and says, "Hey, I just heard a good one," and starts to tell the story or joke. We turn on our favorite TV show, put our feet up and relax; we walk into the theatre, concert hall, or auditorium to spend an evening away from usual activities; we take a walk or a jog and enjoy the scenes and sounds around us."[1]

Appreciative listening is the highly individualized process of listening to obtain sensory stimulation or enjoyment through the works and experiences of others. The process is highly individualized—perhaps even more individualized than other purposes of listening—because it incorporates so many of a person's sensitivities to derive impressions and/or pleasure from the stimulus. As such, appreciative listening may represent a basically emotional response. A person may listen appreciatively, for example, to a television movie. If the movie is a romantic comedy, the experience may be pleasurable. As a listener, then, the appreciation may be that of enjoyment. If, however, the television movie is a horror story, the response may not be so pleasurable. The listener certainly will gain images and heightened emotions while feeling considerable tension at the horror depicted on the screen.

appreciative listening: listening for sensory stimulation or enjoyment

The Process of Listening Appreciatively

Since appreciative listening is highly individualized, we cannot draw up a formula for the appreciation of anything that applies to all people. However, an understanding of our and others' views regarding appreciative listening may help you to develop your personal formula.

One view is that of Kaufmann, author of *Sensible Listening*. He suggests that the process of listening appreciatively may consist of (1) attraction—tuning in to the stimulus, (2) contact—using the right brain emotionally to connect with the stimulus and to repeatedly return to it, and (3) critical evaluation—using the left brain to determine if the stimulus is one you value enough to stay with it.[2]

While Kaufmann's three stages may well describe how we approach listening appreciatively, we should recognize that a controversy exists in many of the fine arts fields (art, music, dance, theatre) as to how to develop appreciation. Some scholars in these fields encourage specific training in the

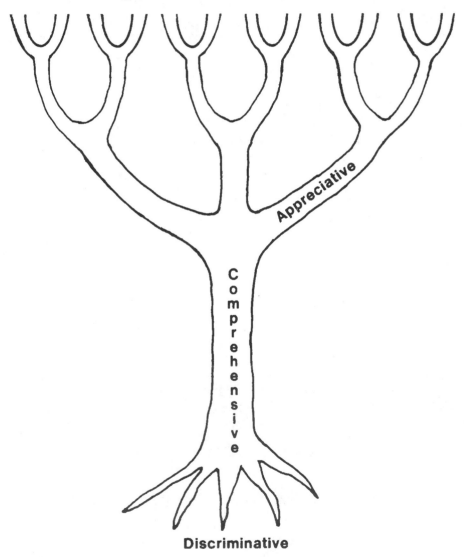

Appreciative branch of the Wolvin-Coakley Listening Taxonomy.

Developing Purposeful Listening Skills

components that make up the artistic expression, for example, the elements of a symphony. The stress here is on understanding the individual parts that make up the whole creative product. Others claim, however, that such specific training can interfere with true appreciation—that such training builds critical facility.

Paul Friedman, writing about training people as appreciative listeners, notes that listeners can recognize "subtle musical nuances that otherwise might go unnoticed" through knowledge of the composition of a musical piece.[3] Friedman recognizes, however, that overemphasis on understanding the intricacies of music may work against the appreciative listener: "If the listener becomes too concerned with the principles of musical form and structure, his or her enjoyment of the pure musical experiences may be diminished."[4]

It is not our purpose here to take sides in the controversy. We have known theatre people, for instance, who could not enjoy a theatre production because they were trained to study every element of the production. Other theatre friends who have had similar backgrounds are able to set aside critical perspectives and truly appreciate a production. It would seem, therefore, that such differences reflect our point: Appreciative listening is an individual process. What some listeners may appreciate, others may not.

The individualized process of appreciative listening involves interpreting spoken, nonverbal, or musical language and relating that language to past experiences. A listener's perception, experience, background, mental set, understanding of the presentation, expectations, motivation, interest, and previous knowledge brought to the appreciative experience combine with the quality of the presentation to determine one's appreciative levels.

Opportunities for Appreciative Listening

Essentially, appreciative listening can include listening to music, the oral style of a speaker, environmental sounds, oral interpretation of literature, theatre, radio, television, and film. It is not so much the source of the appreciative listening act as it is the individual response to it that defines appreciative listening. Clark observes that appreciative listening is the result of deriving pleasure or satisfaction from the form, rhythm, and/or tone of aural stimuli.[5]

The appreciative listener listens for the power and beauty of well-chosen words or music that describes people, places, things, qualities, and abstractions. The color and mood of languages or music and the rhythm of language and music symbols are immeasurable except in an appreciative context. Psychologist Paul Farnsworth suggests that the appreciative listener's interpretation of the mood of a piece depends on the tonal configurations in it as well as the listener's personality structure, the mood of the listener prior to the listening experience, and the prior attitudes held about appreciative listening in general.[6] As the listener listens appreciatively to the reading of literature, a theatre production, a piece of music, a speaker's rhetorical style, or environmental sounds, he or she will be listening to appreciate the works of others, to identify with their experiences, and to establish an emotional bond with them.

Appreciating Music

appreciating music

In order for listeners to develop an emotional bond when listening to music, music educators have stressed that our responses to music should fall in the fluid categories of sensual, emotional, and intellectual. Training in music appreciation is designed to combine these levels so that the listener can derive ultimate appreciation from the sound itself. Machlis has described the role of the appreciative listener in music:

> The enjoyment of music depends upon perceptive listening, and perceptive listening (like perceptive anything) is something that we achieve gradually, with practice and some effort. By acquiring a knowledge of the circumstances out of which a musical work issued, we prepare ourselves for its multiple meanings; we lay ourselves open to that exercise of mind and heart, sensibility and imagination that makes listening to music so unique an experience. But in the building up of our musical perceptions—that is, of our listening enjoyment—let us always remember that the ultimate wisdom resides neither in dates nor in facts. It is to be found in one place only—the sounds themselves.[7]

Another specialist in music appreciation, Charles Hoffer, suggests that there are three interrelated types of listening that can lead to enjoyment of music. One type of listening, sensuous, refers to the physical effect of the music on the listener. A second type of listening involves the feeling or mood evoked by the music itself for the expressive meaning. The third type of music listening requires concentration on what happens in the music in order to appreciate the sounds and their manipulation.[8] At whatever type of listening the music listener may be functioning, it is clear that American listeners enjoy music and listen to several types of music.[9] The late American composer, Aaron Copland, urged the listener to determine what type of listening he or she will do and then become more active as a listener—listening *for* something in the music. "In a sense," wrote Copland, "the ideal listener is both inside and outside the music at the same moment, judging it and enjoying it, wishing it would go one way and watching it go another—almost like the composer at the moment he composes it."[10]

Listening to country music affords an example of how the listener responds appreciatively. Nashville family therapist Esco McBay, observing the appeal of country music to some listeners, describes how the appreciative listener participates in the artistic process: "Obviously, behind every piece of art is a person who expresses that thought or feeling. The music, then the song, becomes a connecting link between that person and the receiver. And so when I respond to that message, when I respond to that song, at some level I'm connecting to that person."[11] Former President George Bush, for example, is a devoted fan of country music. He had a stereo installed in his White House study so that he could listen to his favorites. "When there's good country music playing, it's like a good game of horseshoes," he describes; "I can't help but have fun and loosen up! . . . Country music hits all the right chords—like caring for your family, remembering the good times and keeping faith in God."[12] And it enables the listener to connect. "When you're down and out," says Michael Powell, a Gary Morris fan, "you can listen to the music and say, 'Hey, I'm not alone. There's other people out there. . . . And they're making it. So I can make it too.'"[13]

Appreciating Oral Style

A more complex level of appreciative listening is listening to the oral style of a speaker. It is a difficult form of appreciative listening because, to be truly appreciative, the listener must filter out his or her responses to the speaker's content and concentrate on the speaker's rhetorical style. Jane Blankenship has defined style as an individual's "characteristic way of using the resources of the English language."[14] These resources include the selection of words (word choice) and their combination (syntax) to achieve desired effects.

appreciating oral style

Several other authors have characterized effective speech style. Wilson and Arnold provide us with one such set of characteristics that can be used as listening guidelines:

- Accuracy—the precision by which ideas are expressed
- Clarity—ease of language
- Propriety—the appropriateness of the style to the speaker, the audience, and the occasion
- Economy—conciseness of language
- Force—vigor, power in language
- Striking quality—the vividness of the style
- Liveliness—the energy and movement of the language[15]

These characteristics of style can be applied to appreciate the beauty and the power of the rhetorical language of effective public speakers. Contemporary speakers such as Martin Luther King, Jr., and John F. Kennedy were noted for their speech style. Consider the emotional impact of King's "I Have a Dream" speech presented in Washington, DC, in August 1963, before a huge crowd at the Lincoln Memorial: "With this faith we will be able to work together, to pray together, to struggle together, to go to jail together, to stand up for freedom together, knowing that we will be free one day."[16] And many of us are familiar with the emotional impact of Kennedy's conclusion to his January 1961 inaugural address: "And so, my fellow Americans: Ask not what your country can do for you—ask what you can do for your country. My fellow citizens of the world: Ask not what America will do for you, but what together we can do for the freedom of man."[17] Speechwriter Peggy Noonan captured present-day listeners in her text for Ronald Reagan's televised address to the nation following the Challenger disaster on 28 January 1986. Reagan quoted from the poem "High Flight" to turn the American consciousness away from the replayed videotapes of the disintegration of the shuttle just after lift-off to the heroism of the seven astronauts who had died: "We will never forget them nor the last time we saw them—this morning—as they prepared for their journey and waved goodbye, and slipped the surly bonds of Earth to touch the face of God."[18]

Some observers suggest that Americans are tuning back in to words, due largely to the popularity of rap music. "Ears are being tuned up to listen to words again," observes Bob Holman, who organizes poetry readings at the Nuyorican Poets Cafe in Manhattan.[19] Indeed, poetry has become popular beyond the college campus. Coffee houses and other venues for poetry readings are sprouting up in cities across the country, often near local campuses. College Park, Maryland, for example, boasts Planet X, a "return to the 60s" style coffee house with a regular schedule of poets reading their work. Ithaca, New York, has a similar establishment near the Cornell University and Ithaca College campuses. And consider the popularity of Maya Angelou, the poet who delivered an original poem at President Clinton's inauguration.

Appreciating Environmental Sounds

appreciating environmental sounds

Another unique appreciative listening experience is listening to environmental sounds around us. A walk through a wooded parkland in the spring can provide the listener with a symphony of birds. The wind gently rustling the trees is another appreciative level provided by nature. Novelist-essayist Alice Walker notes that "if you are quiet enough you hear incredible things. . . . You begin to realize that you are everyone and everyone is you."[20] Finding inspiration in nature's sounds as she engages in the creative process of developing her artistic works, she encourages us to go out into the country "to listen to what the earth is saying and hear better our own thoughts."[21] Even the hectic pace of an urban environment can provide us with appreciative listening in the form of people, traffic, and construction crews. And contemporary advocates of meditation reflect on the value of "listening" to silence.

Poet Anne Harper captures the sense of listening to sounds in her short poem, "Listen . . .":

> Listen for a wind, a soft lullaby
> singing
> dreams of boulders,
> snow melting rivers,
> passing stars across treetops,
> Listen.[22]

Illustrating the joys of listening to sounds around us, Olive Ghiselin wrote an extensive description of the sounds of Europe. Some of the vivid sound images she recalls are fascinating to anyone who has traveled to Europe:

> I remembered the splash of fountains in the Alhambra gardens, and the great fall of water at the Fountain of Vaucluse. . . . I recall the booming and

churning of a wild surf at Lequeitio. . . . And the gratified groaning of wooden carts loaded with the grapes of Bordeaux. The pursuing screams of beggar children at Naples. . . . Outside, above the Atlantic, the winds of Normandy wailed. I contrasted this with lusty sizzling in Nice, as a waiter prepared crepes in a silver pan. . . .[23]

Portable audiocassette recorders enable all of us to capture sounds on vacation if we cannot recapture in words and phrases such sounds as vividly as Ghiselin can.

We also create environments through sound. In the 1940s, media specialist Tony Schwartz developed a series of records that are believed to be the first to capture sound that was part of everyday life. Known as the New York 19 project, the recordings enabled the listeners to experience actual sounds. Today, Schwartz (famous for his television "Daisy" commercial for Lyndon Johnson's presidential campaign against Barry Goldwater) argues that we create much of our environment through sounds—electronically mediated and amplified:

> This has radically affected the structure of sound for listeners and created a new relation between sound and space. Sound need no longer be contained within a physical environment that defines boundaries for the sound. Amplification of sound . . . is so overwhelming that it creates its own walls . . . that *contain* a listener.[24]

The world of sound for the appreciative listener does not have to be created electronically. Some of the most enriching auditory experiences are listening to the ocean waves, the majestic "hum" of the Grand Canyon, songbirds in the spring, the squeal of a dog happy to see you, and the soft babble of a mountain brook. Indeed, one of the most valuable listening experiences may well be listening to silence, especially in our noisy world. Gordon Hempton, a self-styled "Sound Tracker," is on a one-man crusade to record and preserve America's quiet spots. His work inspired *USA Weekend* to ask readers to identify their favorite quiet spots. Georgia's Okefenokee Swamp; Arizona's House Rock Bison Refuge; New York's Lake George; Maine's Monhegan Island; Pennsylvania's Poconos; and California's Joshua Tree National Monument were just some of those identified. One reader described listening to silence: "I told everyone to be quiet and listen. One of my friends said, 'I don't hear anything.' I said, 'Exactly.'"[25]

Appreciating Oral Reading of Literature

Listening to the oral interpretation of literature affords a further opportunity for appreciative listening. In reading literature, the reader brings to life the author's material—prose, poetry, and drama—for the listener, providing sufficient interpretation to allow mental pictures to form in the mind of the listener. Oral interpretation can take several forms, from an individual reader presenting a program to the currently popular readers theatre medium.

appreciating reading of literature

A new industry is bringing to the sighted an oral interpretation experience that the blind have known for years: cassette-recorded books.

books on tape

Through listening appreciatively to the reading of oral literature, we can climb mountains, visit lions, touch stars. . . .

Describing the popularity of taped books, Alice Digilio notes that "the habit of listening to books read aloud, an activity replaced a long time ago by the habit of watching television, appears to be making a comeback."[26] And, indeed it is, as customers can now rent or buy tape-recorded books from numerous companies, including Columbia House, which now offers an audiobook club. These companies offer a wide variety of current as well as classic literary selections ranging from J. R. R. Tolkien's *The Hobbit* (read by Tolkien) to Dylan Thomas's poetry (read by Thomas) to *Hamlet* (performed by such recognized actors as Paul Scofield). Found particularly enjoyable by commuters and joggers, this commercially available form of appreciative listening is gaining many avid home listeners. Publishers of these tape cassettes have seen phenomenal growth—with 1993 sales increasing 40 percent over 1992 sales in this 1.3 billion-dollar industry—and have recognized them as a viable part of the publishing market.[27] Flo Gibson, popular tape narrator and president of Audio Book Contractors, notes that a contributing factor to their growth is that 80 percent of all new cars and 80 percent of all American homes now have audiocassette decks.[28]

One avid listener is columnist George F. Will, who has found listening to books on tape to be a satisfying experience:

> The pleasure is not just in the particular books. It is also in learning to listen. I now know that I was not very good at something that I wrongly thought was as natural and easy as breathing.

It is well known that reading is something that can be done with widely varying degrees of efficiency. So is listening. . . .

Listening to a book—not just following the plot but following the syntax of 19th-century sentences rich in semicolons and parenthetical clauses—requires a special kind of concentration, and it exercises segments of my brain that have been unexercised since my father read me the exploits of Horatio Hornblower.[29]

Companies that produce recorded cassettes (and now recorded compact discs, too) have developed strategies to make their audio books listener-friendly. Recorded Books ends each cassette side with an announcement that the reel is about to end and that it is time to flip the tape over, while at the end of the book, the announcer thanks the listener for listening and asks for comments. Books on Tape repeats the last few lines of one side of the reel before beginning the other so that listeners can get back on track with the story.[30]

Flo Gibson believes that the popularity of books on tape can be traced—in addition to the wide availability of cassette decks in cars and homes—to the lack of time people have for reading. While audiotapes may never replace the enjoyment of lingering over the printed word or of family reading, she believes that they serve a valuable function in making literature come alive for people. She recommends that a new listener begin with a familiar story, for instance, Dickens's *The Christmas Carol*; so that if the listener's attention wanders, he or she can readily get back on track.[31]

Books are now available not only on audiotape but also on videotape. Videotapes of popular business books (such as *A Course in Winning*, *Think and Grow Rich*, and *Advanced Selling in Action*) feature their authors as hosts with television and film clips to illustrate principles of the books to the manager/"reader."[32] Numerous libraries and video rental stores stock video books for borrowers.

Americans love to listen to stories. While the popularity of commercial tapes of books illustrates our love affair with **storytelling**, so, too, does the growth of the National Storytelling Festival. For three days, storytellers and listeners come together in Jonesborough, Tennessee, to share stories. Many of the storytellers are professionals, though often the listeners come to swap tales of their own. Among the appreciative listeners are children: "Children sit entranced for long hours. Their parents remember when radio did this to them—or better, when grandmother rocked and told tales."[33] Describing the process, storyteller Jack Torrence says, "We've been living off other people's imaginations for so long. If you can go to the mountain with Jack and ride the unicorn, holding on by a strap, you have forgotten you've got to pay bills."[34] And Jonesborough Mayor Jimmy Neil Smith works to "preserve the intimacy between teller and listener,"[35] even though the attendance at the festival grows every year.

Storytellers also tell tales from their cultures at the Festival of American Folklife held each year on the Mall in Washington, DC. Alan Jabbour, director of the American Folklife Center at the Library of Congress,

storytelling

explains that "storytelling is a way of understanding the past. Our stories reflect our contemporary interests, concerns, anxieties and preoccupations. It's basically human. Other species communicate, but only humans tell stories."[36]

Furthermore, storytelling occurs within the home, where family stories are an important part of our heritage. Bryce J. Christensen, editor of *The Family in America*, stresses the need for parents to tell their children family stories in the home, for family life is "a rich, unfolding story."[37]

Stories have a prominent role in communicating. "A story," writes narrative scholar Paul Friedman, "draws together human actions, highlights their sequence, and attributes to them a role in achieving an ending."[38] Stories are an inherent part of human interaction. Friedman notes that stories are a universal communication form. Children's earliest listening is based on caregivers' stories so we learn to prefer narratives. Also, stories help us to make sense of phenomena that we do not understand.[39] Storytellers who can use narratives effectively are certainly the most memorable and influential communicators. For example, many theologians consider the long-lasting power of Jesus' ministry to stem from his effective use of stories, the parables. Russian storyteller Artiom Soloveychik takes his listeners through Russia by mixing funny and touching personal and imaginary adventures. A critic described Soloveychik's art as "true storytelling, where everything conveyed is meant to catch the listener up in the speaker's words, whisking them off to a new land, a new life."[40]

Authors often testify as to how important it is for them to listen to people's stories as a source for their creative work. Like many writers, novelist Elizabeth Kytle recognizes her dependency on her "attentive ear" for her work: "If people talk to me, I listen."[41] Encouraging storytellers to accommodate to this role of storylisteners, Lane stresses the transactional perspective: "Without the listener's participation in helping to bring the story to life, the singer of tales would be speaking into a languorous void, a night without echoes. Yet the gifts of storylistening are far too often minimized, if not overlooked entirely."[42]

Appreciating Theatre

appreciating theatre

readers theatre

In addition to individual storytellers and readers, readers theatre offers enriching experiences for the appreciative listener. Coger and White, in writing about the **readers theatre** medium, note that audience members can derive substantial benefits from their participation in the activity:

> For them, it provides the opportunity to explore the wide horizons of literature—great novels, memorable short stories, stirring poetry, and distinguished plays seldom produced in the theatre—and it challenges them to participate in the literary experience.[43]

In readers theatre, a group of interpreters presents material to a live audience. It is a popular style of creative performance in schools, churches, and libraries. While readers theatre depends on the interpreters to create the mental pictures, theatre as a medium provides yet another level of appreciative listening. Theatre differs from readers theatre in that it can be more explicit—scenery, lighting, costuming, and makeup combine with the actors to create an illusion for the listener.

Effective theatre calls on the listener to bring to play his or her imagination in creating the illusion. Recent theories of theatre have emphasized the need to involve the audiences as much as possible in the theatrical activity, viewing the listener as 50 percent of the total creative event. Consequently, much of the revolutionary theatre, for instance, is designed to elicit overt responses from the listeners. A popular Broadway production of *Candide* exemplified this involvement: The orchestra and playing spaces were located throughout the audience areas, so the listeners were totally surrounded by the production. The standing-room-only production of *Cats* put the audience into a junkyard scene. The longest-running musical, *The Fantasticks*, asked audience members to imagine the setting, and the current hit musical *The Phantom of the Opera* features a chandelier that crashes over the audience to the stage. Indeed, Dalrymple believes that theatre can serve as a listening "laboratory" in that a theatrical performance "provides the fullest opportunity to practice listening skills."[44]

Appreciating Radio, Television, and Film

On a different level, mass media offers appreciative listening through radio, television, and film. The listener's involvement in the medium has been theorized by Marshall McLuhan and Quentin Fiore. They suggest that the electronic media has shaped our lives, both personally and socially:

> Societies have always been shaped more by the nature of the media by which men communicate than by the content of the communication. The alphabet, for instance, is a technology that is absorbed by the very young child in a completely unconscious manner, by osmosis so to speak. Words and the meaning of words predispose the child to think and act automatically in certain ways. The alphabet and print technology fostered and encouraged a fragmenting process, a process of specialism and of detachment. Electric technology fosters and encourages unification and involvement. It is impossible to understand social and cultural changes without a knowledge of the workings of media.[45]

The popularity of the medium is obvious in this mass media society. While television and film are perennial favorites of the majority of Americans, radio has its devotees, too. Those who enjoy listening to music, talk shows, and nonstop news often prefer the radio medium. Another group of radio followers is baseball fans, who enjoy following along and visualizing as play-by-play announcers describe the action of the game. Phil Jackman, sports writer for the Baltimore *Evening Sun*, suggests a reason for this preference: "Baseball is radio's game, a joy to have as a companion on a warm summer evening, during a long auto trip or most any time. What makes it so is that it gives our often dormant imaginations something to play with."[46] Moreover, radio is becoming a favorite for many listeners as it appears to be making a comeback with a revival of popular radio dramas.

appreciating radio, television, and film

At the University of Wisconsin, for instance, a series of radio plays, "EARPLAY," are produced for the Corporation for Public Broadcasting and distributed to National Public Radio stations. Radio stations in metropolitan centers are rerunning such popular series as "Stella Dallas," "The Great Gildersleeve," and "The Green Hornet." Cassette tape companies are distributing copies of many of the shows from the "Golden Age" of radio for persons who collect these broadcasts. Indeed, the famous Orson Welles's "The Shadow" broadcasts have repopularized the opening question, "Who knows what evil lurks in the hearts of men?"

Radio formats reveal a great deal about our society's listening habits. In Washington, DC, for example, several radio stations have gone to a "golden oldies" format. In fact, one station that was devoted solely to jazz suddenly was switched to a 1950–1960s music station, and jazz fans were outraged. The switch proved to be quite successful, however. Radio listeners listen to the music of their youth, because it can help them to feel young. One observer describes the phenomena: "Most people's musical tastes are formed in their mid-teens and cemented by their early twenties. They rarely add to their personal inventory any music that young people currently enjoy—unless it sounds like the music of their *own* youth."[47] Radio listening works ". . . privately, in our cars, our bathrooms, our headphones, tickling odd nerve endings and boring into old memory pockets, exposing files in our brain marked 'Song: Associations With. . . .'"[48]

In addition to radio listening habits, the film-going habits of Americans create a profile of our society of appreciative listeners. The popularity of romantic, nostalgia films, "Sleepless in Seattle" and "It Could Happen to You," for instance, is reflective of how much we want to escape as listeners in the movie theatre. Recognizing this need to escape, theatre owners are equipping their movie houses with advanced sound technology designed to create a total audio environment. Tomlinson Holman, an audio engineer, developed a system that provides a crystalline layering of sound to create an authentic, life-like auditory experience for the cinema listener. The film "Terminator 2," for example, featured a scene with a hissing lawn sprinkler in one corner of the screen, while John Connor revved up his motorbike and Guns N'Roses music blared out. Meanwhile, the bickering voices of Connor's parents floated from their house into the mix of sound.[49] The result? We, the listeners, are transported into the scene through this highly sophisticated system of manipulating the auditory environment.

Even copywriters for ads encourage us to listen appreciatively. Ads for Sir Walter Raleigh steak and salad restaurants in the Washington, DC, area, for example, encourage people to come to "Listen to the Crackling Fire" of the open grill and of the fireplace in the dining room. Ruth Chris's Steak House urges customers to "Listen to the sizzle of the steak" itself. Another ad, for "Miracle Ear" hearing aids, phrased the appreciative listening experience descriptively: "LISTEN TO LIFE. There is a world of beauty surrounding you . . . the vibrant world of sound . . . the privacy of a whisper, the beautiful sounds of music, the joys of conversation. . . ."[50]

The variety of media for appreciative listening provides the listener with a number of choices of experiences. Despite the type of experience, it may be assumed that exposure to the stimulus, motivation, and attention enable the listener to gain from the experience what will be his or her own individual appreciation. From this appreciation, greater understanding and experience may result, providing the listener with a heightening of his or her appreciative capacities.

How to Improve Appreciative Listening

Although appreciative listening is a highly individualized level of response, some techniques for improving appreciative listening skills have been found to be useful.

Larry Barker offers the listener five suggestions for improving appreciative listening in social or informal situations. He recommends that the listeners determine what they enjoy listening to most and then analyze why they enjoy these listening settings. Listeners are wise, then, to compare their likes and dislikes in listening with those of others and develop a strong sense of curiosity in approaching any appreciative listening setting. Further, Barker observes, it is helpful to read and consult to learn more about the areas in which listeners do find enjoyment.[51]

Charles Hoffer, a specialist in music appreciation, recommends that the listener increase listening ability through engaging in the following seven actions:

1. Improving your memory for music
2. Concentrating on main themes and the important musical ideas
3. Hearing as much detail as possible
4. Encouraging your reactions to music
5. Avoiding the visualization of specific scenes
6. Applying knowledge to your listening
7. Following a listening skills development program[52]

Ultimately, Hoffer suggests, the improvement of appreciative listening rests with the development of a positive attitude for creating increased understanding: "Learning to listen is more accurately a matter of wanting to understand the music than it is of the techniques for understanding music."[53] This understanding, indeed, applies to the appreciation of all the art forms to which we attend as listeners. Through this appreciation we can expand and develop our experiences as human beings.

Describing the influences of the audience on the theatre, Cameron and Gillespie believe that a person should prepare to participate as an audience member by understanding the theatre as an art form and by developing a sympathy for the work to be presented. A good audience participates, they stress, by "making its imagination work when that imagination is stirred by the performance . . . and by remaining open to new ways of being moved, entertained, and excited. . . ."[54]

Thomas R. Lewis and Ralph G. Nichols have identified five steps that listeners can take to enhance the ability to listen appreciatively. These steps include the identification of the things we like most, the verification of why we like these things, and the observation of how these things we like most affect others.[55] Besides dealing with the familiar things we like most, Lewis and Nichols recommend that we broaden our horizons in the search for new aesthetic expression and then study the art form, discuss it with others, and return to it for new insights.[56] "Appreciative listening, then, depends chiefly upon our willingness to learn."[57]

Gaining Experience in Appreciative Listening

gaining experience

The major step in improving our appreciative listening abilities is to **gain experience** as an appreciative listener. The more practice we have in responding to appreciative material, either for pleasure or for impression, the more likely we will be to understand our responses and appreciate them.

It would seem to be helpful to gain experience in many different types of appreciative listening areas. The person who attends just rock music concerts, for instance, is deprived of the opportunity to respond to classical symphony concerts. A live theatre experience enthusiast could try opera or ballet productions. Broadening the range of appreciative listening can lead to understanding your responses and perhaps contrasting those responses with other forms. You may come to realize why you prefer films over stage shows, for instance, and, consequently, establish firmer standards for your appreciative responses. Also, the more frequently you select listening experiences of high quality, the more likely you will be to refine your listening appreciation.

Another way for appreciative listeners to gain experience is by participating in the art forms as a primary source of experience. Arts educator William Waack argues that experience in appreciative listening should involve creating as well as consuming the arts: "Listening to others perform without performing oneself is limiting. We should involve students in creating the art form. In this way they can better understand the conventions of art and become more artistic as listeners and viewers."[58]

Tapping American interest in listening for appreciation, the creator of the game, "Play It By Ear," offers a fascinating opportunity to sharpen appreciative listening skills. One team of players selects one of the twelve categories, reads a question from one of the 297 question cards, and plays the corresponding sound bite on the CD. A correct answer enables the team to advance on the scorecard; an incorrect answer provides the other team with the opportunity to answer. The game features short audio clips of memorable songs, historic speeches, animal noises, sports moments, television memorabilia, short stories, news sound bites, and movie themes. Barry Levine, creator of "Play It By Ear," believes that it provides a wonderful inventory of "the best sounds of the 20th century."[59]

Developing a Willingness to Listen Appreciatively

In addition to gaining experience as an appreciative listener, it is useful to take advantage of appreciative experiences and allow material to elicit an aesthetic response from you as a listener. Friedman suggests that "simply being open to the impact that music can have on us, just allowing it to work its magic on our sensory organs, rather than analyzing its contents or feelings, can be a major part of the listening response."[60] Writer Tom Donnelly makes this suggestion in his "Sounds" column: "Listen to that music which speaks to your secret heart. You don't need someone who's a 'critic' to tell you what touches your secret heart. . . . Take some chances. Music can bring you back to your center. Listen with an open mind, ear and heart, and when you find something that touches you, bind it close and never let it go."[61] As a promotion of its "Symphony" chocolate bar, the Hershey corporation offers a free booklet, "How to Enjoy a Symphony," which offers musical insights from leading maestros on how to enjoy an orchestral symphony. Bandleader Peter Duchin advises: "Sit, clear your mind of extraneous thoughts and visual images so that you are open to the experience of listening to some of the greatest sounds ever created by man."[62] According to Charles Price, the response can be heightened when you are listening to an orchestra if you are willing to not "even listen to the orchestra, strange as it may seem to say. Listen, rather, to the music *through* the orchestra. . . . The musical play's the thing, not the actors. Any orchestra worth listening to should have this transparency about it."[63]

developing a willingness

Comparing bluegrass music to an orchestra, Rhonda Strickland encourages listeners of bluegrass music to listen at several levels:

> Listen to what each instrument is doing and you'll discover bluegrass is as complex as a classical musical orchestra.
> Listen to the voices and the vocal arrangements.
> Listen to the lyrics.
> Be entertained.[64]

Strickland further urges bluegrass listeners to become immersed in the listening experience: "Listening with your heart as well as your mind will open up whole new channels of feelings and new ways of expressing those feelings."[65] Edgar Dale also calls attention to the importance of our being willing to listen appreciatively. Describing film appreciation, he emphasizes that appreciation is "to enjoy with understanding."[66] To understand, he argues, you must have a standard by which to measure the value of the experience: "Growth in appreciation comes through a willingness to try out the standards which others have found effective."[67] Your willingness to listen appreciatively—to let the material have the impact it is designed to have—can enhance your abilities as an appreciative listener.

Concentrating Attention

In addition to gaining experience and developing a willingness to listen appreciatively, you can improve at this level of listening through careful

concentrating attention

attention to the aesthetic stimulus so that you can get the entire emotional impact of it. A person listening to the song of a cardinal or a mockingbird, for example, should concentrate his or her attention to appreciate the subtle nuances in the song. Machlis points out that true aesthetic listening requires more than hearing sounds: "To listen perceptively requires that we fasten our whole attention upon the sounds as they come floating through the air; that we observe the patterns' key form, and respond to the thought and feeling out of which those patterns have emerged."[68]

Dave Kopp, a professional organist, describes how he came to understand the importance of concentrated listening as he listened to other organists—not for the musical whole but for specific musical elements. He offers the following advice to other organists: (1) listen to the entire song, (2) play the song through, (3) listen for the organ registration, (4) listen for single note and harmonic treatment of the melody, (5) listen for the left hand and pedal techniques, (6) listen for introductions and endings in the arrangement, (7) listen for key changes, and (8) imitate techniques. To be an effective organist, the successful artist stresses, the organist must "know how to listen."[69]

Just as the professional must listen appreciatively to function artistically, so, too, can listeners gain a richer experience for listening with appreciation. The State of New Hampshire Travel Office encourages visitors to the state to listen to "The Sounds of New Hampshire":

> If one were to continue thinking on all
> the reasons why New Hampshire
> is so special,
> sounds that tug at the heart strings
> would most certainly come to mind!
> Listen, if you will
> To the soft ripple of water.
> The clear plaintive call of a loon.
> The Sunday ring of steeple bells
> from a pristine white clapboard church.
> The joyful sounds
> of a country festival
> and families having fun.
> Band concerts. The Symphony.
> And seacoast jazz.
> The rolling sound of surf.
> A ten gun naval salute.
> A waterfall.
> An old working mill.
> "Do I hear twenty" at an auction.
> Or the pull of
> steam from an old mountain train.
> Autumn's rustle.
> Winter sleigh bells.
> The sounds of a mountain wind![70]

The broadening of your appreciative listening experiences—as the New Hampshire sounds so vividly illustrate—can increase your enjoyment of life, provide you with a means of relieving daily tensions and releasing pent-up emotions, and offer you the enrichment of expanding your aesthetic horizons and discovering new art forms. At the same time, it can help you discover new dimensions of yourself.

Summary

In this chapter, we have presented some ideas about appreciative listening—the highly individualized process of listening for sensory stimulation or enjoyment. This type of listening encompasses such experiences as listening to music, the oral style of a speaker, environmental sounds, oral interpretation of literature, theatre, television, film, and radio. Some appreciative listeners let the material happen to them; thus, they gain appreciation from the total sensory impact of the experience. Other appreciative listeners gain greater appreciation through information and even technical insight into the material and the presentation techniques. It is recommended that you acquire experience as an appreciative listener, develop a willingness to listen appreciatively, and concentrate your attention to aesthetic stimuli to become more effective appreciative listeners.

Suggested Activities

1. Attend a musical presentation (opera, concert, etc.). Listen attentively to the material. What sensory impressions did you get from the material? Did you enjoy the material? What factors combined to enhance your appreciation of it? Would you want to repeat the experience? What have you learned about your own appreciation of music from this experience?
2. Some early morning, go out into your neighborhood and listen to the environmental sounds around you. Do you hear city traffic sounds or country/woods' sounds? As you listen attentively, can you appreciate what you hear? Do the sounds create any poetic or musical images for you?
3. Attend an oral interpretation reading hour or a readers theatre performance. These presentations are designed to get you, the listener, totally involved through your own creative imagination. Did you visualize the scenes and the characters as you listened to the material? What did the readers do to enhance your involvement in the material?
4. Attend a theatre performance. Listen attentively to the material. What sensory impressions did you get from the material? Did you enjoy the material? What factors combined to enhance your appreciation of it? Would you want to repeat the experience? What have you learned about your own appreciation of theatre from this experience?
5. Some radio stations broadcast reruns of popular old radio drama shows, such as "The Shadow" and "Fibber McGee and Molly," and

many are even available to purchase on audiocassettes. If you can locate such a broadcast in your area, listen carefully to the presentation. What is done to enhance the material to create vivid images in the listeners' minds? Why do you think this type of presentation was so popular during the "Golden Age" of radio?

6. Attend a *new* appreciative listening event (a concert, a ballet, an opera, etc.), something that you have not experienced before. Allow yourself to become involved in the material. After the event, reflect on your appreciation of it. Did you enjoy the experience? Why or why not? Would you like to repeat the experience? Would you like to learn more about this particular art form?

7. What pleasant sounds do you recall from your early childhood? What pleasant sounds do you most enjoy today? Discuss these sounds with the class.

8. Make an audiotape recording of something you listen to appreciatively (music, sounds, reading, etc.) and share your tape with the class. Describe what it is that you particularly appreciate in the material.

9. Each class member takes a turn at telling a family story. Discuss, after each story, how you responded and why. What are some of the factors that make up listening appreciatively to stories?

Notes

1. P. J. Kaufmann, *Sensible Listening* (Dubuque, IA: Kendall/Hunt, 1993), p. 194.
2. Ibid., ch. 10.
3. P. G. Friedman, *Listening Processes: Attention, Understanding, Evaluation* (Washington, DC: National Education Association, 1978), p. 26.
4. Ibid.
5. A. J. Clark, "Appreciative Listening" (Paper presented at the International Listening Association Research Conference, Atlanta, GA, 1989), p. 4.
6. P. R. Farnsworth, *The Social Psychology of Music* (NY: Holt, Rinehart & Winston, 1958).
7. J. Machlis, *The Enjoyment of Music* (NY: Norton, 1957), p. 423.
8. C. R. Hoffer, *A Concise Introduction to Music Listening* (Belmont, CA: Wadsworth, 1974), pp. 10–11.
9. E. L. Fink, J. P. Robinson, and S. Dowden, "The Structure of Music Preference and Attendance," *Communication Research* 12 (July 1985): 301–318.
10. A. Copland, *What to Listen for in Music* (NY: McGraw Hill, 1957), p. 19.
11. L. Choin-Kenney, "Country's Faithful Followers," *The Washington Post*, 24 July 1990, p. E5.
12. G. Bush, "George and the Oval Office Do-Si-Do," *The Washington Post*, 7 October 1990, p. D4.
13. Choin-Kenney, p. E5.
14. J. Blankenship, *A Sense of Style: An Introduction to Style for the Public Speaker* (Belmont, CA: Dickenson Publishing Company, 1968), p. 2.
15. J. F. Wilson and C. C. Arnold, *Public Speaking As a Liberal Art*, 5th ed. (Boston: Allyn and Bacon, 1983), pp. 232–240.
16. M. L. King, "I Have a Dream," reprinted in *Contemporary American Speeches*, eds. W. A. Linkugel, R. R. Allen, and R. L. Johannesen (Dubuque, IA: Kendall/Hunt, 1978), p. 365.
17. J. F. Kennedy, "Inaugural Address," Ibid., p. 369.
18. From a videotape of President Reagan's speech of 28 January 1986. See P. Noonan, *What I Saw at the Revolution* (NY: Random House, 1990), ch. 3.
19. J. C. Simpson, "Hey Let's Do A Few Lines!" *Time*, 16 December 1991, p. 77.

20. E. Foley, "Writer Walker Says We Can Learn by 'Listening' to Trees," *Minneapolis Star and Tribune*, 3 March 1983, p. 1C.
21. Ibid.
22. Anne Harper, "Listen . . . ," *Mountain Echoes* (Winter 1988–1989). Reprinted by permission.
23. O. Ghiselin, "Europe by Ear: Sounds without Score," *Travel and Leisure*, October 1975, p. 11.
24. T. Schwartz, *The Responsive Chord* (NY: Anchor Books, 1974), p. 47.
25. R. Vega, "Where You Can Still Hear Silence," *USA Weekend*, 27–29 November 1992, p. 16.
26. A. Digilio, "The Best Books You've Ever Heard," Book World Section, *The Washington Post*, 20 February 1983, p. 4.
27. J. Tangorra, "Getting the Word Out," *Publishers Weekly* 236 (5 January 1990): 52–53; Audio Publishers Association, "Audio Publishers Association 'Fact' Sheet" (Hermosa Beach, CA: APA, 31 October 1994).
28. Personal interview with Flo Gibson, President, Audio Book Contractors, 27 October 1994.
29. G. F. Will, "Heard Any Good Books Lately?" *The Washington Post*, 12 December 1982, p. C7.
30. W. Thompson, "Books on Tape Have Been Available for Decades," *The Evening Sun*, 22 January 1988, p. B2; see also S. Birkerts, "Close Listening," *Harper's Magazine*, January 1993, pp. 86–90.
31. Personal interview with Flo Gibson.
32. "Seen Any Good Books Lately?" *Time*, 18 November 1985, p. 78; personal observation of business videos on 10 November 1994.
33. M. Childress, "A Time for the Magic of Stories," *Southern Living* 18 (September 1983): 166.
34. Ibid.
35. Ibid.
36. L. Fox, "Telling Tales," *The Washington Post Weekend*, 22 June 1990, p. 6.
37. W. Raspberry, "Family Stories," *The Washington Post*, 29 July 1990, p. C7.
38. P. G. Friedman, "Listening for Narrative," in *Perspectives on Listening*, eds. A.D. Wolvin and C.G. Coakley (Norwood, NJ: Ablex, 1993), p. 202.
39. Ibid.
40. T. A. Dickinson, "Russian Storyteller Spins Tales," *The Eagle*, 21 October 1991, p. B3.
41. M. M. Patner, "Local Woman Listens, Then Writes Books," *Potomac Gazette*, 25 October 1989, p. A15.
42. B. C. Lane, "Gently-Echoed Music: Dynamics of the Storyteller/Storylistener Relationship," *The National Storytelling Journal*, Spring 1986, p. 4.
43. L.I. Coger and M. R. White, *Readers Theatre Handbook* (Glenview, IL: Scott, Foresman, 1967), p. 7.
44. H. R. Dalrymple, "Theatre As a Listening Laboratory," *Communication Education* 36 (July 1987): 243.
45. From *The Medium Is the Massage* by Marshall McLuhan and Quentin Fiore. Coordinated by Jerome Agel. Copyright 1967 by Bantam Books, Inc. Reprinted by permission of the publisher. All rights reserved.
46. P. Jackman, "Oriole Fans Blessed When It's Miller Time on Radio," *The Evening Sun*, 23 June 1983, p. C4.
47. R. Leiby, "Nostalgia Station," *The Washington Post*, 6 January 1994, p. C1.
48. Ibid.
49. E. Pooley, "The Sound and the Movie," *New York*, 9 September 1991, p. 23.
50. Direct mail ad from Miracle-Ear, Minneapolis, Minnesota.
51. L. L. Barker, *Listening Behavior* (Englewood Cliffs, NJ: Prentice-Hall, Inc., 1971), pp. 81–82.
52. Hoffer, *A Concise Introduction to Music Listening*, pp. 11–12.
53. Ibid., p. 10.
54. K. M. Cameron and P. P. Gillespie, *The Enjoyment of the Theatre* (NY: Macmillan, 1980), pp. 42–43.
55. T. R. Lewis and R. G. Nichols, *Speaking and Listening* (Dubuque, IA: Wm. C. Brown Publishers, 1965), p. 192.
56. Ibid.
57. Ibid., p. 193.
58. W. Waack, "Are You Really Listening?" *Teacher Talk* 5 (Winter 1987): 3.
59. D. Oldenburg, "Sounds Like Trivial Pursuit," *The Washington Post*, 13 September 1991, p. C5.

60. Friedman, *Listening Processes: Attention, Understanding, Evaluation*, p. 23.
61. T. Donnelly, "Listening with an Open Mind, Ear and Heart," *Montgomery Journal*, 30 January 1981, p. B2.
62. P. Duchin, quoted in *How to Enjoy a Symphony* (Hershey, PA: Hershey Corporation, 1990), p. 3.
63. C. Price, "Listening to an Orchestra," *Southern World* 2 (December 1980): 36.
64. R. Strickland, "Listening to Bluegrass Requires 'Opening Your Heart,' " *Montgomery Journal*, 10 August 1983, pp. B1, B8.
65. Ibid., p. B1.
66. E. Dale, *How to Appreciate Motion Pictures* (NY: Arno Press, 1970), p. 6.
67. Ibid., p. 7.
68. Machlis, *The Enjoyment of Music*, p. 3.
69. D. Kopp, "Stop, Listen, and Learn!" *Sheet Music Magazine*, August/September 1983, pp. 38–39.
70. "The Sounds of New Hampshire," State of New Hampshire Office of Vacation Travel Supplement.

PART III

Applying Effective Listening Skills

The first part of this book has provided you with an understanding of the complex listening process; the second part has dealt with using this understanding of the listening process to develop specific listening skills according to our taxonomy of listening purposes. The third part of the book places listening behavior in the communication context.

As communicators, we function at different levels of communication: intrapersonal, interpersonal, public, and mass. These different levels of communication affect the way we send and receive messages within the communication context. Consequently, as listeners, we assume different roles, behaviors, and expectations depending on the context in which we find ourselves as communicators.

The communication discipline has, for centuries, focused attention on the effective sending of messages within these communication contexts, but seldom has anyone considered what is involved in the effective *receiving* of messages—listening—at the four levels. What we provide in Part III is a chapter that examines communication from the receiver's point of view. Listeners listen intrapersonally to the self and interpersonally in conversations, interviews, and group discussions of many kinds. At the public communication level, listeners listen to speakers, readers, and actors in various settings. At the mass communication level, listeners also listen to radio, television, and film.

From this analysis of listening at the different communication levels, it should be clear to the reader that as listeners we must adapt our listening behaviors not only to our listening purposes but also to the communication context. Our roles, behaviors, and expectations require us to be flexible and responsible as active listening communicators. Listening can be challenging and rewarding if each listener assumes his or her responsibility as a *partner* in the communication process and applies the listening skills that have been acquired and developed through the systematic study of listening behavior.

PRINCIPLES YOU WILL ENCOUNTER

- *The listener functions with skills appropriate to the different listening purposes at various communication levels: intrapersonal, interpersonal, public, and mass.*

- *At the intrapersonal level, the listener should listen to self.*

- *At the interpersonal level, the listener listens in conversation, in interviews, in small group discussions, and in teleconferences.*

- *At the public level, the listener can listen to speakers, to theatre, or to musical concerts in an audience setting.*

- *At the mass communication level, the listener attends to radio, television, and film—media that have significant impact on listener responses in today's society.*

- *The effective listener*

  - *uses listening skills appropriate to the communication setting in which he or she is involved*

  - *establishes objectives and utilizes his or her listening resources productively*

  - *develops a strong commitment for listening effectively in any communication setting*

CHAPTER 10

The Listener's Communication Roles

During a recent class discussion of this chapter, a student suggested that television talk shows should be called "listen shows" rather than "talk shows" because the majority of the people involved—hosts, guests, studio audience, and television audience—function primarily as listeners rather than as talkers. Intriguing idea!

While a 1993 magazine survey reveals that the hosts of these shows do engage in listening more than they do in talking, the percentage of time ten popular talk show hosts listen and talk on a typical show varies significantly:

Host	Listens	Talks
Montel Williams	*59.5%*	*40.5%*
Oprah Winfrey	*66.8%*	*33.2%*
Vicki Lawrence	*67.2%*	*32.8%*
Jerry Springer	*68.3%*	*31.7%*
Joan Rivers	*70.6%*	*29.4%*
Geraldo Rivera	*73.7%*	*26.3%*
Maury Povich	*76.4%*	*23.6%*
Phil Donahue	*77.8%*	*22.2%*
Sally Jessy Raphael	*80.5%*	*19.5%*[1]

When these television talk show hosts do listen, they perform in different roles as they function at the intrapersonal, interpersonal, public, and mass levels of communication.

Thus far in this book we have analyzed the process of listening as it constitutes an important part of the human communication function. We have looked at listening as communication and have identified it as an equal partner with speaking in the transaction. Further, we have analyzed the listening process, which includes the sequence of receiving, attending to, and assigning meaning to the verbal and nonverbal stimuli. In this process the listener has been perceived as having the responsibility in the communication transaction to respond to the message by providing feedback for the source (and thereby becoming the sender of the feedback message and thus going beyond the technical parameters of listening). This complex interchange operates, then, within specific listening purposes that serve to define what it is that the listener is attempting to gain from the transaction. While not discrete categories, the listening purposes are useful in establishing a taxonomy for the listener's development of skills in discriminative, comprehensive, therapeutic, critical, and appreciative listening.

Completing this analysis of the functions of the effective listener requires that we consider how the listener functions at the various communication levels: intrapersonal, interpersonal, public, and mass. As listeners, we perform in different roles, depending on the setting and situation in which we are placed. We listen *intrapersonally* when we make a conscious effort to listen to ourselves. We listen *interpersonally* in informal conversation, formal interviews, teleconferences, and small group discussions. At the public and mass communication levels, we attend the theatre, listen to speeches, and listen to radio and television. The levels of communication are formal or informal, depending on the structure of the communication context itself.

Intrapersonal Listening

Listening to the Self

intrapersonal
listening

The effective listening communicator is one who, first of all, comes to an understanding of his or her self. "If we are to become more effective listeners in our personal and professional lives," notes Purdy, "we need to first understand the voice within—who we are—and the extent of our personal experience."[2] To understand this voice within, intrapersonal listening "involves shutting out external messages and *listening to ourselves*."[3] A professional counselor described how important it is to listen to herself. She believes she must be honest with herself and listen to herself in order to build interpersonal understanding and trust with her clients.[4]

It is necessary to be able to recognize one's own frame of reference to understand why one is responding in a certain way to a particular verbal or nonverbal message. The beliefs, attitudes, and values a listener holds play a major role in shaping the frame of reference. This frame of reference, in turn, greatly influences how a listener deals with and interprets a communication message to derive some meaning from the information that is presented.

Although self-disclosure represents an important means for understanding the self and why we respond as we do, a good listener needs to make a conscious effort to listen to his or her self. Listening to the self entails

Applying Effective Listening Skills

listening to our inner messages (usually not uttered) through reflection and introspection. Listening researchers Paulin and Canonie have devised a Self Evaluation Listening Form (S.E.L.F.) based on the premise that "there is a definite need to know more about ourselves, to listen to who we are, to accept what we discover, and to act on that information."[5] Listening to the self, then, can be helpful in understanding one's self-concept as it affects communication behaviors.

Listening to the self also is important in that some part of the assignment of meaning may well require a process of "inner speech" in which the listener repeats the verbal message. Lundsteen describes this process as **recoding** in which listeners repeat the words in a message. This process of inner speech results in the recoding of the spoken symbols "by noting changes in sound and in the order in which they occur. As they [listeners] regroup the sounds, they may translate them into images while they rehearse the sounds to themselves."[6] This effort to recode the spoken message may well help the listener to interpret the message as accurately as possible and bring the listener closer to the intended meaning of the speaker.

recoding

If recoding is to function effectively, the listener should make an effort to monitor this process. A good listener must strive to listen to how he or she is recoding the message or, in essence, listen to the inner speech while interpreting the spoken message. This listening requires careful discrimination and comprehension of the recoded message. This monitoring strategy may well lead to greater accuracy in the entire decoding of the communication transaction.[7] Wolff recommends seven strategies for self-monitoring:

self-monitoring

1. Acknowledge the listener self.
2. Access one's store of past joys and traumas.
3. Find supportive friends who will help you explore your self.
4. Bridge the gap between goals and reality.
5. Keep a sense of humor.
6. Recognize and understand the causes that impact the self.
7. Develop one's spiritual self.[8]

Such monitoring requires motivation to attend consciously to one's own inner process, a complicated sequence at best. It requires "taking time-outs to empty our minds of the usual daily chatter and then to listen to our own quiet thoughts."[9] The results can be highly rewarding. Listening to the self enables the listener to become cognizant of his or her own responses as a communicator. "Listening to ourselves," says listening specialist Burley-Allen, "enables us to sift through the many things we experience, so that we can choose those things most valuable to us. Listening effectively to ourselves rests in our attitude that includes being comfortable with ourselves."[10]

Listening to the self, therefore, is a process of intrapersonal communication. The process of listening, being intrapersonal in nature, utilizes the individual's *internal* channels of communication to process the stimuli and to make it more meaningful in the transaction. As Goss notes, "Listening is an intrapersonal process that makes possible all kinds of communication. . . ."[11]

Interpersonal Communication

Conversation

interpersonal listening The person who can listen to his or her own self should be able to function more effectively when listening to others. A solid understanding of the self and why one responds as one does enables the listener better to understand and to regulate responses while communicating with others.

conversation One of the greatest challenges we have in interpersonal communication is that of effective listening in casual **conversation**. In an empirical study of listening behaviors in conversations, Henry demonstrates that "good listeners are lively and stimulating conversational partners" who take an active communication role in the process.[12] Listening in casual conversation necessitates attention, concentration, and—perhaps most important—a willingness to listen. Indeed, in his research on conversational listening, Thomas describes the listener's behaviors as requiring "constant attention and evaluation of the spoken, direct message as well as the more indirect message," which can trigger such questions as "What is the speaker's intent?" and "What does this mean to me?"[13]

Two listening scholars, recognizing that conversational patterns vary from culture to culture, have characterized American conversations. Hirsch observes that "conversational listening is different from the other forms of listening in that it involves two or more people interacting. It does not occur if you only listen without giving any verbal response. Conversational listening requires that there be a constant listen/respond give and take with others."[14] Rhodes also emphasizes this point in his description of "relational listening." Listeners receive and decode messages and, at the same time, encode and send feedback messages to monitor progress toward understanding and to modify the communication if necessary.[15]

Research on conversational listening reveals that the comprehension of informal messages in the interactions is limited and reflects the casual approach that most of us take to these interactions.[16] Communication in conversation is conducted with minimal effort, so the listening is not very systematic. Reviewing the research on listening in conversation, Goss concludes that "unless the situation calls for precise recollection of the utterances, people in everyday conversations comprehend the gist of the conversation more than the exact words spoken."[17]

Although most research on conversation has focused on casual conversation, Mortimer Adler describes four main types of conversation:

1. Social [casual] conversation
2. Personal heart-to-heart talk
3. Impersonal theoretical [informative] talk that is instructive or enlightening
4. Impersonal practical talk that is persuasive

He urges listeners to know the objective of each conversation and "don't listen only to yourself."[18]

Too frequently, conversation patterns for most of us can be characterized as **nonlistening**. Instead of listening, many of us anticipate what the person will say and just eagerly await our turn to chime in with our own tale.

JANET: "And then she said she was sure I had strep throat and that I'd better. . . ."
MARY: "Oh yes, I had strep throat once. I was put on penicillin, and it cleared up very fast. But I certainly was sick until. . . ."
JANET: "Yes, it certainly is miserable. I remember looking at the little white spots in my throat and wondering. . . ."
MARY: "Well, my throat was very red, and all my muscles ached, and I. . . ."
JANET: "I heard that Larry went to Denver yesterday. . . ."

And on it goes. We need to be careful not to fall into this conversation trap of not listening. In an interesting book titled *EgoSpeak,* Addeo and Burger describe this problem of not listening in conversations:

> The reason that no one listens, usually, is that our egos get in the way, in the sense that we're mentally formulating what *we're* going to say when the other person gets through speaking. Instead of digesting the other person's information, we are most often busy thinking only of how best we can *impress* him with our next statement. The result is what we call *EgoSpeak*.[19]

This **interruptive behavior** in conversation does not lead to a very satisfying communication for either person. Steiner suggests that much of this interruption stems from our desire to control the conversation, but the interruption can leave a lasting negative effect on the other person: "Sometimes when I am interrupted in the middle of a sentence, I feel like a bird shot out of the sky. . . . My feelings are a combination of rage and hopelessness."[20] To prevent your communication partner from leaving with rage or hopelessness, you should, as Steiner advocates, listen "to understand how the other person is experiencing the situation. Not necessarily to agree with it, but to become fully aware of how that other person sees whatever it is that she is talking about."[21]

Listening in interpersonal interactions may, like credibility, be a matter of perception. It seems essential that the other communicator in a conversation perceive the listener as an active participant in the transaction. "Actual listening may matter little in the maintenance of most interpersonal interactions," suggests Daly, who goes on to say, "No matter how effective, skilled, or competent an individual is in listening, unless he or she is perceived as listening by the other interactants, little may be accomplished."[22]

Some people who are recognized as great conversationalists may not be as talkative as the image suggests. Indeed, they may be attentive listeners who really say very little in a conversation. Persons in international affairs, for example, often observe the differences between British and American conversation patterns. Britons, who are noted throughout the world as conversationalists, offer verbal responses to their conversation patterns. Americans, on the other hand, tend to rely on "uh huh" and head-nodding responses.

Partners of attentive, responsive listeners tend to leave the conversation feeling good about the experience and grateful for the opportunity to have had someone with whom to converse. People who perceive they are listened to in conversation experience an acceptance and validation of their self-worth and gain considerable satisfaction from interpersonal relationships that are characterized by active, engaged listening.[23]

Interviews

interviews

On a more formal level, we listen in **interviews**. Listening in interviews is critical to the success of any type of interview in which you participate. Just like conversation, a good interview is a give-and-take communication where one must listen carefully and then respond appropriately. Reviewing the effectiveness of popular radio and television interviewers, Bianculli observes that the key to the success of these professional interviewers is their ability to listen.[24] Supporting Bianculli's observation, organization development specialist Serafini stresses, "An effective interview depends on a variety of listening skills."[25] Describing her success as an interviewer, Diane Sawyer of ABC's *Prime Time* agrees that listening is the key: "You listen, ready to move in any direction. You listen without self-consciousness and without self-importance. You listen as a human being first. And as a pursuer of facts second. And as a television personality never."[26]

An interview may be characterized as conversation with purpose. The purpose may be to gather information, to advocate a position, to determine a policy, to solve a problem, or to provide a therapeutic experience. These purposes require listeners, then, to select the appropriate listening purpose and to apply listening skills appropriate for each purpose (e.g., when gathering information, engage in comprehensive listening and, thus, listen for main ideas, significant details, etc.). Professional interviewers recognize the value of careful listening in their work. Individuals who conduct employment interviews for companies must listen to the responses to make decisions about the potential of a particular applicant. Performance appraisal interviewers must be able to listen with considerable empathy to an employee's description of any qualities or circumstances that he or she perceives may affect the job performance under review. Counseling interviewers naturally must listen with empathy to provide the necessary sounding board for the client to begin to understand and deal with his or her own problem. Medical intake interviewers must listen with comprehension to understand the exact nature of the patient's distress before sending the patient to a physician specialist in a clinic.

barriers to listening in interviews

While attention and responsiveness are critical to effective listening in an interview, there are **barriers to listening** effectiveness for which the interview listener should be on guard. Downs, Smeyak, and Martin identify these barriers as *tendencies* to evaluate, to be impulsive, to never respond, to use irritating nonverbal habits (e.g., avoiding eye contact, looking at your watch, doodling), and to allow interruption (either in person or by telephone).[27] Donaghy elaborates further on obstacles to listening in interviews and notes that physical and setting limitations may serve as barriers in an interview. Likewise, he suggests that tension, which arises from stress and

Applying Effective Listening Skills

frustration and improper focusing on the source (and, thus, ignoring what the person is saying) or on the facts (rather than on the ideas) in an interview can be limiting. Urging interviewers and interviewees to be active listeners, Donaghy concludes that "perhaps the biggest obstacle to effective listening is the temptation to take it for granted."[28]

To overcome listening barriers, Stewart and Cash recommend that interviewers and interviewees accept critical **listening responsibilities**. They recommend that the interviewer engage in these eight acts:

listener responsibilities in interviews

1. Listen carefully to the full response of the interviewee.
2. Look at the interviewee while he or she is responding.
3. Keep the evaluative criteria in mind.
4. Avoid making evaluations too quickly.
5. Probe for complete answers.
6. Compare verbal responses with nonverbal behavior and any other evidence.
7. Take detailed notes.
8. Withhold a final evaluation until the interview is completed.[29]

These interviewing experts also characterize six of the interviewee's listening responsibilities:

1. Listen fully to the entire question before responding.
2. Observe the nonverbal cues and behavior that accompany each question.
3. Ask for clarification as necessary.
4. Counter-question if one needs time to think or if one feels trapped.
5. Take sufficient time to ask questions.
6. Obtain details and take notes if possible.[30]

The key to effective listening in interviewing, then, is to listen carefully. Concentrate on what the other person is saying and then adapt your responses accordingly. The interviewer must listen to pursue the train of thought with meaningful questions, and the interviewee must listen to understand the questions and provide the appropriate responses. As is true in more casual conversations, since both persons must adapt to each other, listening becomes the center of communication in an interview.

Small Group Discussions

Many of the principles of effective listening in the interview apply as well to listening in **small group discussions**. People may spend a great deal of time at work in small group discussions at all levels of an organization. Business meetings, seminars, staff sessions, quality circles, and customer meetings all require the application of effective listening skills in small groups. It has been estimated that managers may spend as many as seven hundred hours a year (the equivalent of two out of every five working days) in meetings.[31] The U.S. Travel Data Center estimates that of the 35.3 million business

small group discussions

As participants in group discussions, we must be message receivers when it is appropriate to listen.

travelers in 1991 alone, 48% of those individuals traveled to business meetings.[32] Since so many business people are required to listen in groups, group listening skills are essential. An analysis of listening in groups has led Barker and others to conclude that effective listening in work groups "helps to shorten meetings, create less paperwork, increase group member morale, improve accuracy and raise productivity."[33]

The small group process applies to communication outside of the workplace as well. We engage in small group discussions at the family dinner table, in social and civic organizations to which we belong, and even in more unstructured social settings with friends. Skill in listening when more than one other communicator participates requires special strategies because the communication process becomes so much more complex when other communicators are added to the transaction.

Since a small group discussion typically involves five to seven people, each individual will spend the majority of his or her time engaged in listening. Barker and others estimate that in a three-person group, each member will listen approximately 65 percent of the time; in a ten-person group, 90 percent of the time, and so on.[34] The late S. I. Hayakawa noted the importance of listening in discussions and conferences: "If a conference is to result in the exchange of ideas, we need to pay particular heed to our listening habits."[35] It is a process of careful listening and then adapting remarks to the general thrust of the content of the discussion.

complexities of listening in groups

The process of listening in discussions can be complex, because, as Tuttle notes, there is a group dynamic at work on all of the individuals in a group as they listen to each other.[36] Egan observes just how involved this process can be: "Perhaps listening to the group is even more difficult than listening to individuals because it demands an awareness of subtle interaction patterns."[37] Further, Brack urges that greater attention be placed on listening in the small group process. Poor listening, he says, can be a serious problem in the small group because it (a) disrupts the process and misdirects the flow of thought, (b) weakens one's input because responses are not appropriate, (c) dampens enthusiasm for others to contribute, and (d) undermines the basic assumption of small group communication—that each person contributes.[38] Bormann and Bormann note that effective listening in task-oriented groups requires that the listener be willing to be a message receiver when it is appropriate to listen, to know the basic skills of listening as communication, and to practice and apply effective feedback techniques.[39]

In one of the few works written specifically about listening in group discussions, Kelly argues that we tend to think we should listen critically to messages in group discussion. He suggests that this tendency to critical listening interferes with understanding the message and that we should concentrate on listening empathetically in discussions. To arrive at a level of **empathic listening in groups**, Kelly makes six recommendations for the discussion listener:

empathic listening in groups

1. Remember the characteristics of the poor listener.
2. Make a firm initial commitment to listen.
3. Get physically and mentally ready to listen.
4. Concentrate on the other person as a communicator.
5. Give the person a full hearing.
6. Use analytical skills as supplements to, not instead of, listening.[40]

Barker and colleagues also suggest the value of listening with empathy by identifying three listening strategies to minimize the effects of conflict in group discussions: (1) dampening—hearing out the speaker, (2) diverting—focusing attention on the message content, and (3) digging—communicating empathy and attending to nonverbal messages.[41] "By listening effectively," they argue, "we can consider differing points of view and then apply appropriate problem-solving and decision-making strategies."[42]

Just as individual participants, then, must be careful listeners in a discussion, so too should those individuals who assume leadership roles listen actively. Management specialists such as Peter Drucker and Robert Waterman urge executives to function as listeners when running meetings. Meeting experts provide helpful suggestions for the group leader to listen effectively: "Formulate a replay *after* someone has finished making a statement. Concentrate on what the person is intending to say. Don't get emotionally involved. Keep off tangents. Listen when someone proposes something that's contrary to your beliefs."[43]

listening leaders

It is clear that the accomplishment of the group's objectives requires that each person assume his or her listening role seriously. Most group dynamics experts agree that "mutual understanding among group members depends more on how they listen and respond than on how they speak."[44] The responsibility for the outcome of the group's efforts rests with each and every participant. And listening is the key to the success of that group effort.

Teleconferences

teleconferences

A special type of group discussion that has become a $2.3 billion-a-year business and "the fastest-growing segment of the telecommunications industry"[45] is the **teleconference**: a conference through electronic media (usually the telephone) among persons who are physically separated. Though many of the characteristics of face-to-face group discussions apply to teleconferences, listeners should recognize that the developing technology may lead to special considerations for effective listening in these electronic transactions.

Among the many types of teleconferencing are the following five:

audio

1. **Audio** (transmitting voice via telephone and allowing participants at all sites to interact orally)

audiographic

2. **Audiographic** or audio-plus (transmitting voice and transmitting graphics or any other written materials via facsimile or telecopier through telephone facilities and allowing participants at all sites to interact orally and share the visuals)

captured frame video

3. **Captured frame video**, which is also called slow scan or freeze frame video (transmitting voice and still pictures via television equipment through telephone lines and allowing participants at all sites to interact orally)

computer conferencing

4. **Computer conferencing** (transmitting only written messages by linking computer terminals through telephone lines, permitting only written interaction between/among participants)

full motion video

5. **Full motion video** (transmitting voice and motion pictures from a full motion video conferencing room—in the business establishment itself, a local television station, or other facility with uplink, or transmitting, equipment—via satellite if the distance warrants it or via conventional methods for short distances and allowing participants at all sites to interact orally and visually)[46]

The capabilities of these types of teleconferencing range from one-way audio only to the ultimate two-way audio and two-way video.

Presently, many businesses, organizations, and institutions are offering teleconferencing capabilities and are using the teleconferencing system. Businesses, especially hotels, are providing teleconferencing capabilities by installing permanent dishes (earth stations that furnish access to a variety of satellites) and other necessary equipment and facilities. Many other organizations (such as banks, insurance companies, corporations, associations, universities, and so on) are holding teleconferences in either their own facilities (where they have installed permanent dishes or are utilizing portable dishes) or other facilities equipped for teleconferencing. Among the many ways that teleconferencing is being employed are the following: conferences, seminars, business meetings, strategy sessions, workshops, symposiums, training sessions, employee orientations, project planning sessions, engineering design reviews, policy reviews/decision making, new product introductions, continuing education, sales incentive meetings, and press conferences. Teleconferencing users are discovering that this communication system, in addition to being cost effective, provides many benefits, including increasing the frequency of communication, meeting the needs for communication immediacy, conducting more structured meetings (due primarily to improved preplanning of meetings), providing more people with opportunities to make policy decisions, and obtaining more points of view and opinions from those tied in through the teleconferencing.

benefits of teleconferencing

The role of listening in teleconferences is directly related to one of teleconferencing's major advantages as a communication system: interactivity between/among participants. And, according to the International Teleconferencing Association, 1993 was a year of much interactivity with more than 15,000 two-way interactive videoconferencing rooms in operation and over 2.5 million conference calls held in North America alone.[47]

interactive nature of teleconferencing

The interactive nature of the teleconference process creates some unique communication constraints for listeners. For example, it is necessary for the participants conferring by telephone to identify who they are as they begin to speak so that all parties on the telephone line recognize the speaker. Also, the conversation among the participants tends to be much more structured, and the discussion moderator must play a key role in providing internal summaries throughout the conference. Since telephone time is expensive, it becomes necessary for the discussion to move forward with efficiency; thus, there is little time for handling any interpersonal maintenance functions.

Researchers at Johns Hopkins University have discovered that communicators in teleconferences are much less interruptive and that such communicators present different messages when they do interrupt: "When communicators have the freedom to interrupt, they exchange more messages, messages are shorter, and messages are exchanged faster. . . ."[48] ConferenceExpress executive Ben Park describes the communication that results from videoconferencing formats: "Videoconferencing tends to structure meetings. People are aware that they're paying for their hours and that the meeting isn't open-ended, as so many are. A finite limit forces them to reach a decision. People also tend to keep their remarks short. They know the focus is on them when they're talking, so they get to the point more rapidly."[49]

As teleconferencing continues to gain in popularity as a means of bringing communicators together, the importance of heightened listening skills will be central to the process. We already know that to be successful, teleconference listening requires a high level of discriminative and comprehensive listening and feedback that is timely, direct, and clearly focused. With increased advances in the technology, there will be greater emphasis on understanding the communicators' use of the system through effective listening.

Public Audiences

public listening

Just as active listening is essential in conversations, interviews, group discussions, and teleconferences, it is crucial to effectiveness in **public listening**. As listeners, we participate in all sorts of public audiences. We become part of theatre audiences for live stage productions and/or motion picture screenings. We attend concerts and other types of musical performances. We witness ceremonies and participate in religious services. Also, as listeners, we attend speeches of all types from after-dinner presentations at organizational meetings to political rallies to technical briefings at work to formal lectures sponsored by local historical societies. Participation as a public listener necessitates understanding how we become part of this public audience and applying techniques to derive the most benefits from our public listening experiences.

audience/listener process

social facilitation

The **process of becoming a listener** in a public event is not accidental, but rather it is designed to help you get involved in the event. One element in this carefully constructed process is what is known as **social facilitation**. You are seated next to other people so that their responses (laughter, applause, silence) can affect, or facilitate, how you will respond. You lose some of your self-identity and become part of the audience, perhaps laughing at a speaker's joke that, at home alone with the television set or radio, you would not find funny at all.

polarization

Another dimension of the audience process is known as **polarization**. The lights go down, and all attention is focused on the actors on the stage. You cease your interaction with those next to you (unless you continue to

Supportive listening responses can enhance the public speaker's presentation.

chat during the overture or have to get up for latecomers). This polarizing of attention enhances your willingness to "let go" and to concentrate on the production while you lose some of your own concerns and attitudes in the transformation.

An audience also functions through the process of a **circular response**. The responses you give to speakers, actors, musicians (through your applause, laughter, even coughing and distractions) communicate to them.[50] They, in turn, work to project the ideas, emotions, dialogue, lyrics, or dances to you and adapt as necessary to the response levels of the people in the audience. The response you give to a production ultimately takes you back to your individuality. *Your* standards and values will structure your responses, so your reactions may differ from those of other people in the same audience. The more homogeneous (sharing similar backgrounds, purpose) the audience is, the more likely that the response of the listeners will be similar and predictable.

Kupferberg, writing about the concert audience, notes that audience behavior often offers "perplexities and paradoxes." Concert season subscribers loyally pass down their tickets from generation to generation within a family; yet, they will complain loudly about an orchestra's programs or policies. Leopold Stokowski, the famous conductor, was noted for his scoldings of Friday matinee subscription holders, "especially when they coughed, sneezed or rustled during his performance."[51]

Stokowski's matinee audiences may be all too descriptive of American audiences today. The manager of the Baltimore Symphony Orchestra distributed cough drops to concert goers during the 1979 winter season. A psychologist at the University of Virginia developed a "coughogram" to chart coughing during classroom lectures and discovered that coughing in an audience is indeed contagious: "The closer a cougher is to you, the more likely you will be to pay attention to your own 'cough-related sensations' and hence to cough yourself."[52]

Analyzing the decline of **audience conduct**, Jensen has uncovered research to suggest that poor audience behavior is linked to a general increase in rudeness among Americans. Jensen also hypothesizes that the "Me Generation" of listeners is too likely to judge rather than appreciate a public presentation. This judgmental attitude, coupled with a shortened attention span influenced by video and computer technology, describes the less patient listener in an audience.[53]

Examples of declining audience standards can be found from coast to coast. The *San Diego Union* reports that San Diego Symphony audience members whisper long conversations, watch others, and compete with the music by coughing. While the San Diego Symphony has grown and matured, sighs the writer, "what a pity that the San Diego audience has not done the same."[54] Washington, DC, audiences are described as not being discerning enough and being too willing to applaud and give standing ovations to even the most mediocre: "We will applaud *anything*, no matter how bitterly awful."[55] Inappropriate audience behavior has also been described

circular response

audience conduct

by syndicated columnist Richard Cohen. Writing of the 1984 Republican National Convention in Dallas, Cohen observed that the delegates cheered President Reagan's speech, a speech that was decidedly nonpartisan in conjuring up a dream of America analogous to the Olympic runners passing the torch across the nation. The cheers, suggested Cohen, were inappropriate responses to a poetic speech: "The Great Communicator had communicated—and now no one wanted to listen."[56]

Although American audience standards may be questioned, music critic Vincent Patterson found an audience that *would* listen in Paris. Encouraging American audiences to take a lesson from the Parisians, Patterson suggests that "Parisians know what they're coming to hear. . . . Shoulder to shoulder, the people were not distracting to each other; they chose instead to concentrate on the . . . music."[57]

Despite the problems with the performing arts audience, the live audience is essential to the art form itself. Gillespie describes the audience as being "at the heart of the event we now call theatre. . . ."[58] Theatre critic Eric Bentley describes the role of the audience in the theatre as being "the flow of living feeling that passes from actor to audience and from the audience back again to the actor."[59]

audiences of public speakers

pedestrian, casual audience

passive audience

selected audience

concerted audience

organized audience

listener effects on public speakers

seminar listeners

Just as the performing arts audience is vital to the success of the event, so, too, is the audience a critical factor for the public speaker. In a classic study on the audience, Hollingworth identified five types of audiences that speakers may confront.[60] The **pedestrian, casual audience** reflects the least amount of attention. Shoppers who stop to watch a demonstration of omelet making in a shopping center, for instance, would be a pedestrian audience. A **passive audience**, on the other hand, typically consists of captive listeners, much like those found in a classroom of students required to take a course. A more specific type of audience is the **selected audience** consisting of a group of individuals who have come together for a unified purpose (attending a civic association meeting on neighborhood safety, for example). The **concerted audience** is even more organized in its purpose, as the individuals probably have some direct stake in the outcome. The audience at a political rally, for instance, would be a concerted audience. At the most organized level, then, is the **organized audience** with total orientation to the speaker. A military drill team, for example, would be an organized audience, completely controlled by the speaker.

Listeners can have profound **effects on a public speaker.** Analyzing some of the research about these effects, Glenn concludes that the behavior of listeners can be a significant factor in the anxiety level of speakers; listeners should provide supportive, encouraging, reassuring, positive feedback.[61] Such responsiveness requires listener skill and involvement in the communication.

One informative exposition of the listener's public performance is offered by management specialist John E. Baird, Jr. He advises participants who attend management seminars to develop listening skills to benefit from the presentations by speakers in the seminars. Baird encourages seminar

Applying Effective Listening Skills

participants—the listeners—to begin by establishing objectives for attending the seminar, establishing one's overall goal and subgoals to focus subsequent listening. Then, the seminar listener should take stock of what he or she already knows about the topic of the seminar and, equally important, what attitudes and beliefs he or she holds about the subject. Such self-analysis can lead to developing priorities for acquiring knowledge or for modifying behaviors relevant to the seminar topic. Further, the participants—while in the seminar—should use listening strategies (focusing on the content, maintaining objectivity, capitalizing on "thought speed," taking notes, asking questions) to derive the most from the seminar itself. "Efficient listening," concludes Baird, "means identifying things to listen for so that it becomes easier to note what is important and to sort out those ideas from others that are of secondary concern."[62]

Echoing Baird's advice for listening in management seminars, Andrews recommends that the "public listener" incorporate seven tactics for active public listening. "Since a piece of communication is designed to get a response from you," says Andrews, "you ought to ask yourself what it is doing to and for you as you listen."[63] The seven tactics that Andrews recommends are good suggestions for listeners in any public communication:

1. Think about your own identity.
2. Listen with a purpose.
3. Understand the setting.
4. Try to understand to whom the speaker is talking.
5. Examine your assessment of and knowledge about the speaker.
6. Consider the speaker's purpose.
7. Listen defensively.[64]

In other words, the defensive public listener understands his or her own response to the public communication and seeks actively to adapt that response to the appropriate objective of the communication. Thus, the individual who joins an audience to listen to a public speech should be able to concentrate all of his or her time, energy, and attention on the speech itself. Much of Ralph Nichols's research on listening comprehension deals with listening to lectures and speeches, so his advice to concentrate is especially useful. The principles of listening comprehension are pertinent if the speech is informative or inspirational. If the speaker is attempting to persuade the audience, then critical listening techniques will also be necessary. These techniques have been detailed in previous chapters. The theatre or concert listener, on the other hand, usually is listening for appreciation. Consequently, our suggestions for gaining greater appreciation from a listening experience may be helpful.

Whether one is a public listener to a speech or at a theatrical or musical event, it is helpful to recognize that we become part of an audience through a systematic process. This process plays a significant role in shaping our responses as listeners and in developing the public communication transaction.

Mass Communication

media listening

In addition to listening in the theatre and to live public speakers, we listen to the public communication **media.** The popularity of mass media today means that we spend a great deal of our waking time as listeners—attending to radio and television broadcasts. In their infancy, both radio and television were much more oriented to larger audiences. Because only a few people could afford receivers, entire extended families or even communities would come together in the home of the fortunate radio or television set owner for an evening of listening. Indeed, in some less-developed countries, these gatherings are still common. Preparing television commercials for South American television, for instance, requires a broader approach, aimed at larger audiences in homes.

In the United States, however, we usually are isolated listeners, so that radio and television have become intimate media. Going to and from work, we listen to our car radios on the expressway. Frequently, we have more than one television set in a home, so we are the sole viewers. Thus, to create more of a sense of public communication, producers will tape shows before a live studio audience or incorporate a laugh track to help cue the listener at home to respond as if he or she were in a larger audience.

Radio

radio listening

Radio, of course, relies solely on sound to project images. Consequently, we let **radio listening** happen to us through our auditory channels. In its heyday of popularity, radio became a very creative instrument for American culture and entertainment. The power of radio was demonstrated when Orson Welles stunned the nation by his 1938 Halloween eve broadcast of "The War of the Worlds," a script that "reported" an invasion of Martians in New Jersey. Other popular shows such as "The Shadow" and "Fibber McGee and Molly" reflected the effort by broadcasters to spark the imagination of the listener. Through vocal inflections and sound effects, the listener was involved in the experience and, with concentration, could become a true participant in the event. This involvement has been vividly described by recorded book critic Vic Sussman:

> One of life's great pleasures when I was a boy growing up in the '40s was listening to the radio. Like most kids, I was an avid listener, sitting absorbed in front of an old white Emerson table radio, its four-inch speaker my passageway into a magical world. I laughed at Red Skelton, flew high above Metropolis alongside Superman, kicked in doors with Sam Spade, and held my breath whenever I heard the Shadow's weirdly filtered voice asking, "Who knows what evil lurks in the hearts of men?"[65]

Tapping the listener's imagination today, radio offers such personalities as Garrison Keillor who told about his mythical Minnesota town of Lake Woebegon on the popular "Prairie Home Companion."

While using imagery, radio today also provides listeners with opportunities to become more active participants *on the air*. Listeners participate not only in call-in contests (in which they can win prizes and money) but also in call-in **talk shows** hosted by such nationally-known personalities as Larry King and Rush Limbaugh. Many local radio stations feature talk shows with controversial hosts who invite listeners to talk with them via telephone. In some cities, the host generates a strong "drive time" following in a highly competitive audience market. The trend in talk radio is away from the abusive "in your face" approach of a few years ago to a more rational discussion of issues—a "town meeting" of the airwaves.[66] In addition to town meetings, many talk radio shows offer a strong therapeutic base, allowing individuals to explore their problems with the host or even with another caller. The popular television show, *Frasier*, features a psychiatrist who hosts such a radio program. Indeed, the talk radio audience reflects the need many people have to establish relationships in a fragmented, urban society: "Callers are no longer lonely night owls. They're as diverse as America and looking for shared values."[67]

talk radio shows

Contemporary radio reflects some effort to return to its creative roots. Certain stations are willing to do more than broadcast the "Top 40" records and commercials with perhaps 5 minutes of news every hour. Radio drama has been revived, and even commercials have become more creative. For instance, commercials for Motel 6 (where we will find the lights on) feature clever "invites" by Tom Bodett. **Radio advertising** is especially suited for adaptation to the demographics of an audience in a particular locality. In recent years, spending for radio advertising has increased markedly to 9.457 million dollars in 1993.[68]

radio advertising

Radio commercials represent a unique problem to advertising specialists and illustrate the complexity of a medium aimed at the listening ear. Since visual images are not possible in radio commercials, the audio images must be highly compelling. This need becomes even more significant when one realizes that most radio serves as background accompaniment to what individuals are doing: driving, doing household chores, typing, completing homework, etc. Consequently, radio "listening is almost always accompanied by simultaneous activity that places widely varying demands on the individual's attention process."[69] One result is what some researchers have called the "NOLAD level"—the non-listening attention demand.[70] Interestingly, little is known in the industry about how best to solve some of these problems inherent in radio advertising in order to reach potential listeners who are relying solely on the auditory channel for communication.

Not all radio is aimed at the commercial market. The National Public Radio is designed to provide a meaningful alternative to the "Top 40" and "All News" stations so readily available. National Public Radio features public affairs interviews and panels and a wide variety of creative formats from classical music to "radio art" productions. Other noncommercial uses extend to special populations. In Baltimore, for example, the Baltimore Radio Reading Service has more than 125 volunteers who read news, local information, and literature to the elderly and visually handicapped within the listening range.[71]

noncommercial radio

The power of radio in listeners' lives is described by James Earl Jones, whose resonant voice is heard on many radio and television commercials. In a commercial for the National Association of Broadcasters, Jones states in dramatic fashion: "The radio is more than news, it's more than music, it's more than sports. It's a melody of celebration, a voice of hope, the sound track of our lives."[72]

Television

television listening

Television, on the other hand, is designed to be more of a visual medium. We look at the screen and watch the action. Tony Schwartz, the famous media specialist, argues, however, that television is more auditory than we think. He recommends an experiment—turn out the picture and listen to the sound. He suggests that we would be impressed with how much, like radio, the television audio portion does involve us as listeners.[73] An experiment designed to determine the relative power of visual, audio, and audiovisual experiments revealed that audio alone is just as effective as a combined audio and visual presentation for conveying information in a news story.[74]

Most of us have regular access to television sets. Some 93 million (98%) American households owned at least one set as of 1993,[75] and the medium grows increasingly more dominant in these households. Moreover, viewing of cable programming has expanded so much that 61 percent of Americans were cable subscribers in 1993.[76] During the same year, 77 percent of all American homes had at least one videocassette recorder,[77] and Americans rented per night an average of 7 million prerecorded videocassettes for home viewing.[78] Americans are turning to the VCR for viewing films rather than attending film productions in movie theaters.

influence of television

The history of the television medium reflects the profound influence that it has had on shaping American society. Television has heightened the Army-McCarthy hearings that brought down McCarthy's witchhunt for American communists, mourned the loss of the popular American president John F. Kennedy, taken us to the moon with the Apollo astronauts, invigo-rated the imaginations of an entire generation of children through "Sesame Street," (see fig. 10.1.), forced the exposure of the dangers of communism, explored the seas with Jacques Cousteau, demonstrated the extremity of Iraq's Saddam Hussein, and shown us devastating starvation and suffering in Rwanda. It is not surprising that, according to Roper's annual survey question asking Americans where they "usually get most of . . . [their] news about what's going on in the world today," respondents have stated—since 1963—that television is their major source of news information. Respondents in the 1993 Roper survey revealed that 69 percent turned to television, 43 percent cited newspapers, 16 percent used the radio, 6 percent learned from other people, and 4 percent noted magazines as their major news source.[79]

televised violence and sex

Despite the societal benefits that television as a medium has brought to the world, concern about **television violence and sex** as well as distorted images and editorial bias remains widespread. Concern regarding the

Figure 10.1.
Reprinted with permission of Jim Henson Productions, Inc.

impact of televised violence has prompted the television industry to fund a two-year study of all programming (news, sports, and entertainment) at the University of California—Los Angeles Center for Communications Policy.[80] The study was prompted by findings of other studies including one funded by the Harry Frank Guggenheim Foundation and another by the American Psychological Association (APA).

The 1994 Guggenheim Foundation study of media violence revealed that violence on broadcast and cable television had increased 41 percent since the 1992 *TV Guide* major survey on the same subject. Among the 1994 findings are the following four:

1. Life-threatening violence on television (such as assaults with a deadly weapon) rose 67 percent in those 24 months.
2. Violence in promotional announcements for series and made-for-TV movies almost doubled.

3. The steepest rise of all came in news programs, both network and local, with a 244 percent increase.
4. The average rate of violent incidents increased from 10 to almost 15 per channel per hour.[81]

The 1994 findings showed an increase of 759 violent scenes—or a total of 2,605—over the 1,846 found during the same 18-hour period in 1992.[82]

In its 1992 report of a 5-year study of television's influence on society, the APA researchers—after having reviewed a wide body of research on the effects of television—concluded that "accumulated research clearly demonstrates a correlation between viewing violence and aggressive behavior—that is, heavy viewers behave more aggressively than light viewers."[83] Furthermore, the APA reported that "portrayals of sexual activity on television can increase physiological arousal in both adults and adolescents" and that "repeated exposure to such arousing content can lead to desensitization."[84] Addressing both television violence and sex, communication specialist George Gerbner testified that the violent, sexy, and sexist world of television reinforces prevailing inequalities in American culture.[85]

television's image
distortions

Distorted images are also prevalent on television. The APA researchers determined that children, the elderly, minorities, women, and gays/lesbians are often underrepresented or portrayed in stereotyped, narrow roles through television.[86] For example, in the majority of popular rock videos, women—through their dress—project the role of sex object.[87] Moreover, the AMA researchers warn us about distortions in television's portrayals of family relationships:

> Family relationships can also suffer when real folks compare themselves to their television counterparts. Children and parents alike may use television as a source for norms for family interaction. Families may feel inadequate when comparing themselves to the competent, affluent and successful families that predominate in prime-time programs.[88]

Critic Ben Stein argues that the televised view of society depicted in adventure shows and on sitcoms—from the Los Angeles orientation of television writers and producers—is perhaps not representative of the other geographical regions of the United States.[89] Two other prominent distortions are seen in the depictions of law enforcement officers who are often unrealistic and fallible in their identification and apprehension of criminals[90] and "workers" who seldom if ever are shown doing real work.[91] Even the television depiction of parents has come under fire: "Parents are one of the few remaining groups that are regularly ridiculed, caricatured and marginalized on television. Ask a typical viewer to describe how parents are portrayed on most shows and the answer usually is: stupid."[92]

Television advertising has also led critics to voice concern about the distorted perceptions that viewers can receive. For example, Mothers Against Drunk Driving and other organizations have made efforts to link ads for alcoholic beverages to increased consumption, but the results are not very conclusive.[93] Another group, the Action for Children's Television, has lobbied for stricter regulation of children's advertising. They argue that children lack the critical powers to distinguish the cartoon program (for example, *Mighty Max*, *Transformers*, *Batman*, and *Ninja Turtles*) from the commercials for the toys. Despite the concerns about television advertising, there is increasing evidence in market research that as the number of these commercials increases, their effectiveness decreases: "Television viewers are apparently less and less able to distinguish one commercial from another, one brand from another, one advertising message from another."[94]

Like the 15-second commercials, the 15-second sound bites are very much the norm in television news broadcasts. With Americans turning to television as their main news source, it should be recognized that television news has inherent **editorial bias** much like that found in newspaper organizations. Consequently, editing decisions very much affect what becomes part of the news broadcast. Because the news broadcast must operate in a very short time frame, what is presented to the viewer is greatly compressed and limited. Recent court cases concerning unfair treatment by such shows as CBS's *Sixty Minutes* and ABC's *20/20* reflect the recognition that what is edited in and edited out of a news piece may present an unfair perception. Journalism professor James Carey reminds us that television news is journalism: "All journalism, including objective reporting, is a creative and imaginative work, a symbolic strategy; journalism sizes up situations, names their elements, structure, and outstanding ingredients, and names them in a way that contains an attitude toward them."[95]

television's editorial bias

Even though we Americans rely heavily on television for news and for entertainment, how efficient are we as television listeners? In a study conducted by Jacob Jacoby, a consumer psychologist, 2,700 viewers in twelve geographic areas were asked questions about televised segments that they were shown. It is significant to note that the vast majority of the viewers in this study—more than 90 percent—misunderstood some part of what they saw. The range of misunderstanding was between one-fourth and one-third of any type of broadcast, though viewers were less likely to misunderstand commercials than entertainment or news programs. Jacoby argues, however, that the television listener brings to each viewing his or her past experiences and mental frame of reference as a means of interpreting and misinterpreting the messages: "Given that it is not possible to eradicate either the influence of past experience or the individual's current mental set, it may well be impossible to eradicate miscomprehension."[96] We might add that miscomprehension may also result from passivity; according to the American Psychological Association researchers, television "does not inherently encourage passivity, intellectual or physical. People can watch television actively or passively."[97]

listener comprehension of television

Miscomprehension of television messages may well be the result of how people listen or, more typically, *not* listen to the broadcast. Reviewing the research on viewer behaviors, Shatzer concludes that television viewing is "a complex set of behaviors which occur at varying levels of attention to the television screen. Listening is a very important part of the 'viewing' process. Monitoring television allows the viewer to look away from the screen, and enables the viewer to be involved in secondary and tertiary activities. In fact, viewing actually occurs in short periods of visual attention to the screen with continuity being maintained by auditory monitoring."[98] The auditory mode, suggest researchers Anderson and Lorch, plays an important role for the television listener by "maintaining continuity in the processing of content information and directing visual searches for additional information."[99]

effects of exposure to television

What effect does this extensive **exposure to television** have on listeners? A Canadian study on the impact of television on children and adults alike documented that people exposed to television suffered a 20 percent decrease in creativity. The researchers also discovered reduced persistence at problem solving, a stronger tendency for sex-role stereotyping, and a significant increase in verbal and physical aggressive behavior in both sexes.[100] Some experts are concerned that this loss of creativity upsets the visual imagery that people need to solve math and science problems. Other education experts decry the time spent in front of a television set as time taken away from reading; the United States now rates 24th worldwide in per-capita book readership.[101]

The power of television has led federal researchers, examining the influences of television on North Americans of all ages, to conclude: ". . . television will no doubt continue to be pervasive and ubiquitous in American life. Information about its role and its effects will be needed by all those who will help to shape television's future and to make decisions about it."[102]

receivership skills

Anderson urges that television listeners develop **"receivership skills,"** which include the literate decoding of the medium along with a critical understanding of how they relate to the medium within the communication system in the society. Anderson's concept of receivership skills encourages children (as well as *all* listeners) to become decisive, active television viewers with the ability to monitor their own viewing and evaluate their own reasons for their viewing preferences.[103]

In recognition of the profound effects that television does have on American viewers, many television researchers consider that teaching about television to create a more critical viewing public is an important priority. Educators who have studied the effects of television on listening behavior draw some depressing conclusions. Arnold, for example, suggests that television leads students to have shorter attention spans, to tune out more easily, and to be more prone to talk while others are talking.[104] Emphasizing that "people do things *with* television; television does not do things *to* people," Anderson calls for educators to teach "receivership skills" so that a more educated radio and television audience will be able to understand just how and why he or she is reacting to any particular programming. Anderson defines these skills in three parts: "As a knowledgeable consumer the individual has need of common skills of analysis . . . medium specific skills of reception and interpretation . . . and content specific skills of understanding."[105] Additionally, media critic Neil Postman, who has authored a book titled *How To Watch TV News*[106] calls for introducing in the curriculum what he calls "media ecology"—study to help students "understand how media control the form, distribution, and direction of information, and how such control affects people's cognitive habits, political beliefs, and social relations."[107]

One specific curriculum designed to develop "receivership skills," as well as some of the "media ecology" content advocated by Postman, and, thus, more critical television viewers identifies six objectives:

1. Ability to describe own television-viewing habits
2. Ability to describe why a program is selected
3. Ability to identify the role of television in personal life amid the activities it competes with
4. Ability to describe the consequences of viewing and the other activities with which television competes
5. Ability to identify program-content characteristics
6. Ability to identify uses of different programs[108]

Understanding how television works to shape perceptions, then, can be an important step for becoming discerning, effective media listeners.

The Listening Grid

It is apparent, then, that listeners function in a variety of listening roles in intrapersonal, interpersonal, public, and mass communication. We listen for different purposes, purposes that have been categorized as discriminative, comprehensive, therapeutic, critical, and appreciative. As effective listeners, we also may need to establish distinct listening objectives for different listening situations, overlaying our objectives on the listening roles that we have selected. This concept can be illustrated by a **listener's grid**. (See fig. 10.2.) **listener's grid**

This grid illustrates the interactive nature of our purposes and roles as listeners. It should be recognized that these are by no means discrete categories; for example, an individual may select a discriminative purpose but also find him- or herself listening therapeutically once the communication transaction gets underway. The listener's grid can further illustrate the concept by adding key variables to it. (See fig. 10.3.)

As this grid emphasizes, it is apparent that attention and concentration represent keys to effective listening in all of these listening modes. Depending upon the role that he or she is to assume and the purpose that the listener and the other communicator wishes to achieve, the good listener will establish objectives and use his or her listening resources.

Listening Commitment

The way we listen and the responses we give, thus, become major tasks for the listener who wishes to be an effective communicator. The listener who

	Self	Conversation	Interview	Small Group	Tele-conference	Public Speech	Theatre/Concert	Radio/Television
Discriminative								
Comprehensive								
Therapeutic								
Critical								
Appreciative								

Figure 10.2.
The Listener's Grid.

Wolvin-Coakley Listening Grid

	Self	Conversation	Interview	Small Group	Teleconference	Public Speech	Theatre/ Concert	Radio/ Television
Discriminative	Attention Concentration Sensory Acuity	Attention Concentration Sensory Acuity	Attention Concentration Sensory Acuity	Attention Concentration Sensory Acuity	Attention Concentration Sensory Acuity	Attention Concentration Sensory Acuity	Attention Concentration Sensory Acuity	Attention Concentration Sensory Acuity
Comprehensive	Attention Concentration Understanding	Attention Concentration Understanding	Attention Concentration Understanding	Attention Concentration Understanding	Attention Concentration Understanding	Attention Concentration Understanding	Attention Concentration Understanding	Attention Concentration Understanding
Therapeutic	Attention Concentration Understanding Empathy	Attention Concentration Understanding Empathy	Attention Concentration Understanding Empathy	Attention Concentration Understanding Empathy	Attention Concentration Understanding Empathy	Attention Concentration Understanding Empathy	Attention Concentration Understanding Empathy	Attention Concentration Understanding Empathy
Critical	Attention Concentration Understanding Evaluation	Attention Concentration Understanding Evaluation	Attention Concentration Understanding Evaluation	Attention Concentration Understanding Evaluation	Attention Concentration Understanding Evaluation	Attention Concentration Understanding Evaluation	Attention Concentration Understanding Evaluation	Attention Concentration Understanding Evaluation
Appreciative	Attention Concentration Sensitivity	Attention Concentration Sensitivity	Attention Concentration Sensitivity	Attention Concentration Sensitivity	Attention Concentration Sensitivity	Attention Concentration Sensitivity	Attention Concentration Sensitivity	Attention Concentration Sensitivity

Figure 10.3.
Wolvin-Coakley Listening Grid.

By accepting the responsibility of genuinely caring about how our listening affects us as well as others, we become enriched and enriching listeners.

listening commitment

assumes responsibility for the communication transaction cannot be a passive, noninvolved participant in the process. Rather, effective **listening requires commitment** and the acceptance of our obligation to give the speaker a fair hearing. Ross describes the importance of this commitment to a fair hearing: "We should show *tolerance* and work at understanding intent. Fair hearing replaces force in a free society."[109] Maintaining a free society, therefore, requires that we develop the necessary listening skills and attitudes to offer a fair hearing in all of our communication transactions.

Johannesen, a scholar of communication ethics, has described the need for listening commitment as an ethical responsibility. He suggests that the two major responsibilities of listeners are to approach messages with "reasoned skepticism" (judging the soundness and worth of arguments) and to approach speakers with appropriate feedback (communicating the level of comprehension and acceptance of the message).[110] Indeed, as we develop more concern for the ethical responsibilities of communicators in today's society, that concern must extend to listeners as well.

Each semester, as a project in our listening course, we ask our students to interview a person whose livelihood depends to a great extent on effective listening. Students interview a variety of professionals—psychiatrists, counselors, physicians, attorneys, customer service representatives, ministers, diplomats, and account clerks. The interviews yield interesting information about how these listeners do listen and what techniques and training they feel are important. Much of the information parallels what we have covered in this book, but there is a further dimension to effective listening that professional listeners almost always cite—**caring**. They stress that all the techniques and theory prove to be meaningless unless listeners assume responsibility for the process by genuinely caring about how their listening behavior will affect them as well as the others in the communication.

caring

Taking the time and the trouble to listen well is rewarding. If you care about yourself as a listener and if you care about the other person as a human being, you both will feel enriched for the experience. And that intangible reward may be the greatest payoff we have in human relationships at home, at work, and in the world at large. Indeed, Steffen suggests that we may well need a "theology of listening, for a willingness to listen ultimately expresses an attitude of love."[111]

Summary

In this chapter, we have examined the roles that a listener assumes. We function intrapersonally when we listen to ourselves. In addition, we assume interpersonal listening roles when we participate in conversations, interviews, group discussions, and teleconferences. And, we play different roles as members of public and mass media audiences (speeches, theatre, radio-television).

The objectives we set for our listening behavior within these roles will depend, to a great extent, on what we want to derive from the listening experience and on what the source of the message wants us to derive from it. Consequently, attention and concentration are keys to effective listening in all situations, but other factors may vary, depending on our listening goals and the particular demands of the role we must assume.

Suggested Activities

1. Consciously attempt to listen to yourself. Concentrate on this when you are alone, processing your own thoughts, and concentrate on this when you are in communication with someone else. Listen to your self as you speak with this other person; monitor what you are saying and why you are saying it. What are you discovering about your self as a communicator?
2. Arrange to interview a specialist in your major field of study. Ask this person about the role that listening plays in your field. What is the importance of listening in your field? What different types of listening are required at various levels within the field? Ask the specialist to suggest any articles in your field that discuss the role of listening. Compose a short paper summarizing the role of listening in your field.
3. Arrange to conduct an interview as the interviewer; draw up a schedule to give you some general guidelines as you ask the questions.

Do not take notes, but arrange to close with a summary of the information you have gained. After the interview, analyze your listening behavior. Were you able to comprehend the interviewee's responses and to adapt your questions to these responses? What were your listening objectives? Did you achieve them? Do you feel that you were an effective listener? Do you feel that the interviewee perceived you as an effective listener? Why or why not?

4. Arrange to participate in a group discussion. In addition to offering meaningful comments, strive to be an attentive, comprehensive listener throughout the discussion. As you listen, try to adapt your responses to meet task or maintenance needs of the group as the needs arise. At the end of the discussion, summarize for the group what has been accomplished. After the discussion, analyze your listening behavior. Did you accomplish your objectives as a listener? Were you effective as a listener in the group discussion? Why or why not?

5. Attend a live public speech and endeavor to be a comprehensive listener. Observe the other listeners around you. After the speech, try to participate in the question-answer session to clarify any points you may have had difficulty following. Summarize the content of the speech by identifying the central point and the main points of the speech. Was the speech clearly organized? Was it effectively developed and presented? What efforts were made to develop and maintain the group as an audience? Did you note efforts at social facilitation? Polarization? Speaker adaptation to audience feedback? Were you an effective public listener?

6. Attend a live theatre production and observe the audience. What efforts were made to develop social facilitation? Polarization? Do you feel that the actors were responsive to the audience? Was there supportive feedback at the curtain call?

7. Contact the customer service division of your local telephone company and arrange to talk with an individual who has responsibility for setting up teleconferences for customers. What insights can this individual give you about the unique features of participating in a teleconference? What facilities are available in your area for setting up teleconferences?

8. Listen attentively to a radio broadcast of a radio drama. What efforts are made to communicate the characters and the setting? What efforts were made to create tone and mood? Note vocal work by actors and the sound effects.

9. Watch a television broadcast of a situation comedy taped before a live studio audience. What effect does the audience response have on your responses at home? Do you feel that the presence of audience laughter, applause, and so on, causes you to respond at home to situations that you might not find funny if you did not hear the audience response?

10. Reflect on the descriptors in each segment of the listening grid on page 409. Are there other skills you would add to this chart? What are they?

Notes

1. "Mouthing Off," *Santa Rosa Press Democrat*, 5 June 1993, p. A9.
2. M. Purdy, "Intrapersonal and Interpersonal Listening," in *Listening in Everyday Life*, eds. D. Borisoff and M. Purdy (Lanham, MD: University Press of America, 1991), p. 23.
3. P. J. Kaufmann, *Sensible Listening* (Dubuque, IA: Kendall/Hunt, 1993).
4. K. Rao, "How Do Counsellors Listen?" Unpublished paper, College Park, MD: University of Maryland, 1994.
5. K. Paulin and P. J. Canonie, "It's Time to Listen to Ourselves," *Effective Listening Quarterly* 3 (December 1983): 1.
6. S. W. Lundsteen, *Listening: Its Impact on Reading and the Other Language Arts* (Urbana, IL: ERIC Clearinghouse on Reading and Communication Skills, 1979), p. 391.
7. The variables in this decoding process are described in S. C. Rhodes, "Listening and Intrapersonal Communication," in *Intrapersonal Communication Processes*, eds. C. V. Roberts and K. W. Watson (New Orleans: Spectra, 1989), pp. 547–569.
8. F. Wolff, "The Listener 'Self': Impact on the Listening Process" (Paper presented at the International Listening Association Convention, Seattle, WA, 1992).
9. R. S. Ivker, "Life Lessons," *Men's Fitness* 8 (December 1992) p. 64.
10. M. Burley-Allen, *Listening: The Forgotten Skill* (NY: Wiley, 1982), p. 83.
11. B. Goss, "A Cognitive Look at Intrapersonal Communication" (Paper presented at the Speech Communication Association Convention, Washington, DC, 1983), p. 15.
12. D. M. Henry, "Listening Skills and Relational Messages: Analyzing the Flexibility and Dynamism Inherent in Relational Message Responses of Good Listeners" (Paper presented at the International Listening Association Convention, Atlanta, GA, 1989), p. 26.
13. L.T. Thomas, "Interactive Listening: An Examination of Listening Ability and Gender Differences in an Interactive Conversational Context" (Paper presented at the International Listening Association Convention, Seattle, WA, 1992), p. 9.
14. R. O. Hirsch, *Listening: A Way to Process Information Aurally* (Dubuque, IA: Gorsuch Scarisbrick, 1979), p. 33.
15. S. C. Rhodes, "Listening: A Relational Process," in *Perspectives on Listening*, eds. A. D. Wolvin and C. G. Coakley, (Norwood, NJ: Ablex, 1993), p. 225.
16. For an interesting research study of conversational listening, see V. Emmert, "Listening in Interpersonal Relationships" (Paper presented at the International Listening Association Convention, San Diego, CA, 1986).
17. Goss, "A Cognitive Look at Intrapersonal Communication," p. 15.
18. M. J. Adler, *How to Speak How to Listen* (NY: Macmillan, 1983), pp. 131, 142, 144.
19. E. G. Addeo and R. E. Burger, *EgoSpeak* (Radnor, PA: Chilton Book Company, 1973), p. xii.
20. C. M. Steiner, *The Other Side of Power* (NY: Grove Press, 1981), p. 182.
21. Ibid., p. 183.
22. J. Daly, "Listening and Interpersonal Evaluations" (Paper presented at the Central States Speech Convention, Kansas City, MO, 1975), pp. 1–2.
23. M. Fitch Hauser and M. A. Hughes, "The Conceptualization and Measurement of Listening," *Journal of the International Listening Association* 6 (1992): 6–22.
24. D. Bianculli, "Nice Guys Can Interview, But 'Naturals' Get Results," *The Baltimore Sun*, 19 May 1984, p. E3.
25. C. R. Serafini, "Interviewer Listening," *Personnel Journal*, July 1975, p. 398.
26. "People Etc.," *The Baltimore Sun*, 26 April 1987, p. 5G.
27. C. W. Downs, P. Smeyak, and E. Martin, *Professional Interviewing* (NY: Harper & Row, 1980), pp. 79–80.
28. W. C. Donaghy, *The Interview: Skills and Applications* (Glenview, IL: Scott, Foresman, 1984), p. 154.
29. C. J. Stewart and W. B. Cash, *Interviewing*, 4th ed. (Dubuque, IA: Wm. C. Brown Publishers, 1985), p. 46.
30. Ibid.
31. S. L. Tubbs, *A Systems Approach to Small Group Communication* (NY: Random House, 1988), p. 8.
32. "1991 Survey of Business Travelers," Washington, DC.: U.S. Travel Data Center, 1991.
33. L. L. Barker et al., *Groups in Process* (Englewood Cliffs, NJ: Prentice-Hall, 1991), p. 81.
34. Ibid., p. 74.

35. S. I. Hayakawa, "How to Attend a Conference," *ETC* 3 (Autumn 1955): 5.
36. G. E. Tuttle, "Listening Strategies and Behavior for Participants in Small Group Processes: A Need Based Prescription" (Paper presented at the International Listening Association Convention, Seattle, WA, 1992).
37. G. Egan, *Encounter: Group Processes for Interpersonal Growth* (Belmont, CA: Wadsworth, 1970), p. 248.
38. H. A. Brack, "Listening—A New Priority in Small Group Process" (Urbana, IL: ERIC Clearinghouse on Reading and Communication Skills), p. 4.
39. E. B. Bormann and N. C. Bormann, *Effective Small Group Communication* (Minneapolis: Burgess Publishing Company, 1976), pp. 27–28.
40. C. Kelly, "Empathic Listening," in *Small Group Communication: A Reader*, eds. R. S. Cathcart and L. S. Samovar (Dubuque, IA: Wm. C. Brown Publishers, 1970), pp. 257–258.
41. L. L. Barker, P. M. Johnson, and K. W. Watson, "The Role of Listening in Managing Interpersonal and Group Conflict," in *Listening in Everyday Life*, eds. D. Borisoff and M. Purdy (Lanham, MD: University Press of America, 1991), pp. 144–151.
42. Barker, et al., *Groups in Process*, p. 93.
43. J. Conlin, "Who's Running This Show Anyway?" *Successful Meetings*, November 1987, p. 46.
44. J. K. Brilhart and G. J. Galanese, *Effective Group Discussion* (Dubuque, IA: Wm. C. Brown Publishers, 1989), p. 101.
45. R. Zemke, "The Rediscovery of Video Teleconferencing," *Training*, September 1986, p. 28.
46. "The ABC's of Audio-Video Teleconferencing: Coming to Terms with 'Satellite Speak,' " *Meeting News*, December 1982, pp. 44, 45, 61. The cost of videoconferencing continues to make it inaccessible to many; see L. Ginsberg, "Videoconferences: Wave of the Present?" *Meeting News* 14 (March 1991), p. 54.
47. Press Release. International Teleconferencing Association, McLean, VA, 19 June 1994, pp. 1–2.
48. A. Chapanis and C. M. Overbey, "Studies in Interactive Communication: III. Effects of Similar and Dissimilar Communication Channels and Two Interchange Options on Team Problem Solving," *Perceptual and Motor Skills* (Monograph Supplement 2–V38, 1974), p. 373.
49. C. Elias, "Strides in Videoconferencing Keep Executives in the Office," *Insight* 4 (29 February 1988): 45.
50. Dervin urges audience researchers to listen to their audiences in conducting public campaigns: B. Dervin, "Audience as Listener and Learner, Teacher and Confidante: The Sense-Making Approach," in *Public Communication Campaigns*, eds. R. E. Rice and C. K. Atkin, (Newbury Park, CA: Sage, 1989).
51. H. Kupferberg, "The Audience," *Stagebill*, July 1980, p. 20.
52. "Social Coughs," *Psychology Today* 14 (August 1980): 25.
53. M. D. Jensen, "The Decline of the Audience" (Paper presented at the International Listening Association Convention, Orlando, FL, 1985).
54. C. Fulbright, "Poor Listeners," *San Diego Union*, 19 March 1986, p. B7.
55. B. McClain, "Please Hold Applause (Until It's Deserving)," *Montgomery Journal*, 12 July 1985, p. B5.
56. R. Cohen, "The Audience That Wouldn't Listen," *Washington Post*, 26 August 1984, p. C8.
57. V. Patterson, "Parisians Know How to Listen," *Montgomery Journal*, 13 September 1985, p. E4.
58. P. P. Gillespie, "The Performing Audience," *Southern Speech Communication Journal* 46 (Winter 1981): 137.
59. E. Bentley, *What Is Theatre?* (Boston: Beacon Press, 1956), p. 224.
60. H. L. Hollingworth, *The Psychology of the Audience* (NY: American Book Company, 1935), pp. 19–35.
61. E. Glenn, "Speech Apprehension and the Perception of Audience Listening Behavior" (Paper presented at the International Listening Association Convention, Indianapolis, IN, 1990).
62. J. E. Baird, Jr., "Getting the Most Out of Seminars: Listening by Objectives," *IEEE Transactions on Professional Communication*, PC-24 (December 1981): 190.
63. J. R. Andrews, *Essentials of Public Communication* (NY: Wiley, 1979), p. 34.
64. Ibid., pp. 34–36.
65. V. Sussman, "Whispering in the Dark," *The Washington Post Book World*, 26 October 1986, p. 10.
66. S. M. Barbieri, "Talk Radio May Set New Tone for the '90s," *Omaha World Herald*, 8 June 1990, p. 42.

67. M. Barone and J. M. Schrof, "The Changing Voice of Talk Radio," *U.S. News & World Report* 108 (15 January 1990): 51. Also popular, talk television, which is less interactive, probably offers as much of a therapeutic experience for the guests as for the viewers. See P. J. Priest and J. R. Dominick, "Pulp Pulpits: Self-Disclosure on 'Donahue,'" *Journal of Communication* 44 (Autumn 1994): 74–97.

68. Radio Advertising Bureau, *Media Facts: The Complete Guide to Maximizing Your Advertising* (NY: Radio Advertising Bureau, 1994), p. 4.

69. R. C. Gross, W. H. Wallace, and W. G. Robertshaw, "The 'NOLAD' Concept," *Journal of Advertising Research* 23 (February/March 1983): 47.

70. Ibid.

71. D. I. Greene, "Radio Readers Enhance Lives," *The Evening Sun*, 14 June 1984, p. D1.

72. S. McKerrow, "Radio Promotes Itself," *The Evening Sun*, 26 May 1989, p. B11.

73. T. Schwartz, "Listen," *TV Guide*, 24 February 1979, pp. 5–7.

74. A. N. Crigler, M. Just, and W. R. Neuman, "Interpreting Visual Versus Audio Messages in Television News," *Journal of Communication* 44 (Autumn 1994): 123–149.

75. Nielsen Media Research, *1992–1993 Report on Television* (NY: Nielsen Media Research, 1993), p. 5.

76. Ibid.

77. Ibid.

78. B. Story, "$3 Billion in '93," *Video Store Magazine*, December 1993, p. 4.

79. Network Television Association, National Association of Broadcasters, and the Roper Organization, *America's Watching: Public Attitudes toward Television, 1993* (NY: NTA, NAB, and the Roper Organization, 1993). Robinson and Davis conducted surveys of television viewers to discover that while people receive most of their information from TV news, their comprehension of this information may be short-lived. See J. P. Robinson and D. K. Davis, "Television News and the Informed Public: An Information-Processing Approach," *Journal of Communication* 40 (Summer 1990): 106–119.

80. J. Leeds, "Harder Look At Violence on TV," *Santa Rosa Press Democrat*, 30 June 1994, p. A6.

81. N. Hickey, "New Violence Survey Released," *TV Guide*, 13 August 1994, p. 37.

82. Ibid.

83. D. Dart, "Down the Tube," *Santa Rosa Press Democrat*, 26 February 1992, p. A1.

84. Ibid.

85. "TV Sex and Violence Reinforces Society's Ills, Professor Says," *The Washington Post*, 6 October 1984, p. C6.

86. A. C. Huston, E. Donnerstein, H. Fairchild, N. D. Feshbach, P. A. Katz, J. P. Murray, E. A. Rubinstein, B. L. Wilcox, and D. Zuckerman, *Big World, Small Screen* (Lincoln: University of Nebraska Press, 1992), p. 140.

87. S. McKerrow, "The Savvy Approach to Rock Video," *The Evening Sun*, 4 June 1985, pp. C1, C7.

88. Dart, "Down the Tube," p. A1.

89. B. Stein, *The View from Sunset Boulevard* (NY: Basic Books, 1979).

90. L. S. Lichter and S. R. Lichter, *Prime Time Crime* (Washington, DC: The Media Institute, 1983), p. 60.

91. E. Cornish, "Do We Need a Department of Play?" (Speech presented at the World Future Society Conference on Working Now and in the Future, July 1983), reprinted in *Vital Speeches of the Day* 49 (15 September 1983): 725.

92. M. Rosenfeld, "Father Knows Squat," *The Washington Post*, 13 November 1994, p. G1.

93. "What Happens When Beer and Wine and Television Mix?" *New York Times*, 26 May 1985, p. E16.

94. J. A. Trachtenberg, "Viewer Fatigue?" *Forbes* 142 (26 December 1988): 120.

95. J. W. Carey, "The Communications Revolution and the Professional Communicator," in *The Sociology of Mass Media Communicators, The Sociological Review Monograph*, no. 13, ed. P. Halmos (University of Keele, January 1969), p. 32.

96. "The Miscomprehension of Televised Communications" (Report by the Educational Foundation of the American Association of Advertising Agencies, NY, May 1980), p. 7. See, too, B. Gunter, *Poor Reception* (Hillsdale, NJ: Lawrence Erlbaum, 1987).

97. Huston, et al., *Big World, Small Screen*, p. 140.

98. M. J. Shatzer, "Listening and the Mass Media," in *Listening Behavior: Measurement and Application*, ed. R. N. Bostrom (NY: The Guilford Press, 1990), p. 191. Kubey and Csikszentmihalyi have found that television viewers divide their attention between viewing television and engaging in some other activity 64 percent of the time; see

R. Kubey and M. Csikszentmihalyi, *Television and the Quality of Life: How Viewing Shapes Everyday Experience* (Hillsdale, NJ: Lawrence Erlbaum Associates, 1990).

99. D. R. Anderson and E. P. Lorch, "Looking at Television: Action or Reaction?" in *Children's Understanding of Television*, eds. J. Bryant and D. R. Anderson (NY: Academic Press, 1983), p. 8.

100. F. Casey, "Minds At Risk," *The Washington Post*, 29 July 1991, p. C5.

101. Ibid.

102. "Television and Behavior" (Washington, DC: National Institute of Mental Health, 1982), vol. 1, p. 87.

103. M. Ploghoft and J. A. Anderson, eds. *Education for the Television Age* (Athens, OH: The Cooperative Center for Social Science Education, Ohio University, 1980), pp. 19–27.

104. J. Arnold, "Who Listens?" *The Independent School Bulletin* 33 (December 1973): 36–38.

105. J. A. Anderson, "Receivership Skills: An Educational Response," in *Education for the Television Age*, eds. M. Ploghoft and J. A. Anderson, pp. 22–23.

106. N. Postman and S. Powers, *How to Watch TV News* (NY: Penguin Books, 1992).

107. N. Postman, "Critical Thinking in the Electronic Era," *National Forum* 55 (Winter 1985): 8.

108. J. A. Anderson and M. E. Ploghoft, *The Way We See It: A Handbook for Teacher Instruction in Critical Receivership* (Salt Lake City: Media Research Center, 1978).

109. R. S. Ross, *Speech Communication Fundamentals and Practice*, 6th ed. (Englewood Cliffs, NJ: Prentice-Hall, 1983), p. 22.

110. R. L. Johannesen, *Ethics in Human Communication* (Prospect Heights, IL: Waveland Press, 1983), p. 125.

111. L. Steffen, "The Listening Point," *The Christian Century*, 107 (21–28 November 1990), p. 1088.

At the outset of this book, we expressed our concern that the United States is a nation of nonlisteners. This book attempts to resolve what we perceive to be some of the problems that result from so little emphasis on listening skills in our communication transactions. Our purpose has been to provide the listener with a solid understanding of how he or she functions in the listening process. We have identified the major purposes of listening and the key factors that influence the way we listen. Furthermore, we have offered the listener a perspective on how we function in a variety of communication roles. Throughout our discussion, we have stressed that the listener must understand what he or she is doing in the process and that the listener must make intelligent decisions as to which listening strategies will facilitate effective listening at any given time within the communication transaction.

It should be evident at this point, then, that listening—like all of human communication—is a highly complex process, a process that requires a lifetime commitment to improving skills, attitudes, and behaviors on the part of the listening communicator. One unit on listening in a communication course, or even one complete semester in a listening course, cannot begin to provide the listener with all that is needed to be truly effective in the process. Rather, we hope to provide a solid foundation for the serious listener to develop an understanding of the process and a thorough awareness of how he or she does function as a listener. This understanding and awareness, combined with a sincere motivation to improve, should be a strong basis for making plans for continuing improvement.

But how does the listener know that he or she is charting the right course for listening improvement? We have provided you with extensive strategies for increasing your skill as a listener, and your listening instructor will have given you ample opportunity to practice these skills. In addition, standardized tests are available for follow-up assessment. Our students also find it useful to maintain journals in which they record listening experiences and chart their listening growth and development. Such a journal can be an effective vehicle for a comprehensive self-assessment of one's own listening growth at the end of formal listening instruction.

In a summary essay, one of our students concluded her journal by assessing her own strengths as a listener, identifying areas that she felt she still needed to improve, and highlighting what she still intended to do to build that improvement. This essay is illustrative of what you, as a listener, can do to formulate your own self-assessment.

One of the real benefits from this course for me has been the opportunity to examine and analyze my listening behaviors, which has added a dimension to my personal awareness. The knowledge that I have been utilizing some listening skills appropriately has been gratifying, while on the other hand, I see challenges ahead as I continue to learn and improve upon others. The opportunities for me to practice and apply these skills are endless—not only can I pursue them in my personal life, but also I foresee the personal benefits of this pursuit in my working relationships.

My immediate plans are to concentrate on my weakest listening behaviors, integrating the necessary skills/attitudes/habits into my daily interactions, so that I can become more accomplished.

Learning to ask clarifying questions is one particular area that I plan to improve upon. This is going to require a real effort on my part because I've always had a tendency to withhold questions for fear of appearing incompetent. However, since I've recently changed to a new career field, I find myself constantly in situations where I need to ask clarifying questions regarding my work. I see an opportunity here to begin work immediately on changing my old image of myself as incompetent to one of a sensible person utilizing questions to take care of my communication needs of the moment.

Putting a real effort into listening to the speaker rather than using my time to formulate my response is another specific area I am working on. Reaching the point of becoming more accepting of myself, I find the need to "impress" people has lessened for me somewhat, and I feel more free to let go of this behavior. My plans are to remain on guard for any recurrence of this and to keep my focus and mind on the speaker/speaker's message. I have an excellent opportunity to practice what I'm preaching in my work situation with my supervisor. Since I've received my promotion, I'm feeling a little less confident about my abilities to handle my new job, and I constantly find myself needing to impress my boss with all the right answers, worded in just the right way. Therefore, in my daily contacts with him, I plan to spend my thinking time reviewing his ideas and thoughts rather than planning my response to him—I have a feeling that he'll appreciate it also!

Seeking out opportunities to gain experience in appreciative listening is another area which I plan to pursue. My excuse has always been that I never have the time, but now I want to make the time to enrich my life. I've observed the benefits derived from appreciative listening and have become more willing to let myself relax and enjoy. My plans for the future are to spend more time taking nature walks and listening to the sounds around me, attending concerts, continuing to sing in my church choir, and taking advantage of any new opportunities that will widen my listening experiences.

Finally, I've made a conscious decision to be on guard against falling back into some of my old inconsiderate listening behaviors at all listening levels—the discriminative, comprehensive, therapeutic, critical, and appreciative levels. I believe my consideration for others will always be the basis for my effectiveness as a listener. Along this same line, I plan to try and communicate to others the impact effective listening attitudes, skills, and behaviors has upon personal relationships. I may not be able to prevent any wars, but perhaps I can help mend a broken relationship or two![1]

Such self-assessment should characterize our listening behavior as communicators not only at the end of formal listening instruction but also throughout our lifetimes as listeners. As we continue to function as listeners, we should continue to grow and increase effectiveness in our communication transactions. The key to this development is our word *continue*. Although we have introduced you, the listener, to the complexities of listening and to skills and behaviors to improve listening, listening—like all the communication functions—is not something you can fix quickly and permanently. Communication development requires continuous modification and fine tuning throughout one's lifetime as a communicator. Just as effective writers and speakers are constantly perfecting their craft and as readers are monitoring and altering their reading behaviors, so, too, must the listener constantly work at understanding, changing, and refining his or her listening abilities. This realization of our abilities as total communicators can help us to overcome our failure to listen and, hopefully, enable us to begin to achieve greater social priority for effective listening. Perhaps then we can be a world of listening role models.

Notes

1. Jeanne L. Rector, "Plans for Future Listening Improvement." Unpublished paper, College Park, Maryland: University of Maryland, 1981. Used by permission.

BIBLIOGRAPHY

Adler, Mortimer J. *How to Speak How to Listen*. New York: Macmillan, 1983.

Anastasi, Thomas E., Jr. *Listen! Techniques for Improving Communication Skills*. Boston, MA: CBI Publishing Company, 1982.

Anastasi, Thomas E., Jr., and Dimond, Sidney A. *Listening on the Job*. Reading, MA: Addison-Wesley Publishing Company, 1972.

Banville, Thomas. *How to Listen, How to Be Heard*. Chicago: Nelson-Hall, 1978.

Barbara, Dominick. *The Art of Listening*. Springfield, IL: Charles C. Thomas, 1968.

———. *How to Make People Listen to You*. Springfield, IL: Charles C. Thomas, 1971.

Barker, Larry. *Listening Behavior*. Englewood Cliffs, NJ: Prentice-Hall, 1971.

Borisoff, Deborah, and Purdy, Michael, eds. *Listening in Everyday Life: A Personal and Professional Approach*. Lanham, MD: University Press of America, 1991.

Bostrom, Robert N. *Listening Behavior: Measurement and Application*. New York: The Guilford Press, 1990.

Brammer, Lawrence M. *The Helping Relationship*. 2d rev. ed. Englewood Cliffs, NJ: Prentice-Hall, 1979.

Brownell, Judi. *Building Active Listening Skills*. Englewood Cliffs, NJ: Prentice-Hall, 1986.

Coakley, Carolyn Gwynn. *Teaching Effective Listening*. New Orleans: Spectra, 1993.

Coakley, Carolyn Gwynn, and Andrew D. Wolvin, eds. *Experiential Listening: Tools for Teachers and Trainers*. New Orleans: Spectra, 1989.

Colburn, C. William, and Sanford B. Weinberg. *An Orientation to Listening and Audience Analysis*. Chicago: Science Research Associates, 1981.

Crable, Richard E. *Argumentation As Communication: Reasoning with Receivers*. Columbus, OH: Merrill, 1976.

Duker, Sam. *Listening: Readings*. New York: The Scarecrow Press, 1966.

————. *Listening Bibliography*. Metuchen, NJ: The Scarecrow Press, 1968.

————. *Listening: Readings II*. Metuchen, NJ: The Scarecrow Press, 1971.

————. *Time-Compressed Speech: An Anthology and Bibliography in Three Volumes*. Metuchen, NJ: The Scarecrow Press, 1974.

Erway, Ella. *Listening: A Programmed Approach*. New York: McGraw-Hill, 1978.

Faber, Carl A. *On Listening*. Pacific Palisades, CA: Perseus Press, 1978.

Fiumara, Gemma C. *The Other Side of Language A Philosophy of Listening*. London: Routledge, 1990.

Floyd, James J. *Listening A Practical Approach*. Glenview, IL: Scott, Foresman, 1985.

Friedman, Paul G. *Listening Processes: Attention, Understanding, Evaluation*. 2d rev. ed. Washington, DC: National Education Association, 1983.

Gigous, Goldie M. *Improving Listening Skills*. Dansville, NY: Owen Publishing Corporation, 1967.

Girzaitis, Loretta. *Listening a Response Ability*. Winona, MN: St. Mary's College Press, 1972.

Glatthorn, Allan A., and Adams, Herbert R. *Listening Your Way to Management Success*. Glenview, IL: Scott, Foresman, 1983.

Goss, Blaine. *Processing Communication*. Belmont, CA: Wadsworth, 1982.

Handel, Stephen. *Listening*. Cambridge, MA: MIT Press, 1989.

Hirsch, Robert O. *Listening: A Way to Process Information Aurally*. Dubuque, IA: Gorsuch Scarisbrick Publishers, 1979.

Howell, William S. *The Empathic Communicator*. Belmont, CA: Wadsworth, 1982.

Jamieson, Kathleen Hall, and Campbell, Karlyn Kohrs. *The Interplay of Influence*. Belmont, CA: Wadsworth, 1983.

Johnson, Wendell. *Your Most Enchanted Listener*. New York: Harper & Row, 1956.

Kaufmann, Paul J. *Sensible Listening: The Key to Responsive Interaction*. 2d ed. Dubuque, IA: Kendall/Hunt, 1993.

Kerman, Joseph. *Listen*. 3d rev. ed. New York: Worth Publishing Company, 1980.

Koile, Earl. *Listening As a Way of Becoming*. Waco, TX: Calibre Books, 1977.

Larson, Charles U. *Persuasion: Reception and Responsibility*. Belmont, CA: Wadsworth, 1983.

Levin, David M. *The Listening Self*. London: Routledge, 1989.

Loftus, Elizabeth. *Memory*. Reading, MA: Addison-Wesley, 1980.

Long, Lynette. *Listening/Responding*. Monterey, CA: Brooks/Cole, 1978.

Lorayne, Harry, and Lucas, Jerry. *The Memory Book*. New York: Ballantine, 1974.

Lundsteen, Sara W. *Listening: Its Impact on Reading and the Other Language Arts*. Urbana, IL: ERIC Clearinghouse on the Teaching of English, 1979.

Maidment, Robert. *Tuning In*. Gretna, LA: Pelican Publishing Company, 1984.

Merker, Hannah. *Listening*. New York: Harper Collins, 1994.

Mills, Ernest Parker. *Listening: Key to Communication*. New York: Petrocelli Books, 1974.

Montgomery, Robert L. *Listening Made Easy*. New York: AMACOM, 1981.

Moray, Neville. *Attention and Listening*. Baltimore: Penguin Books, 1969.

Morris, Jud. *The Art of Listening*. New York: Industrial Education Institute, 1968.

Newman, Robert P., and Newman, Dale R. *Evidence*. Boston: Houghton Mifflin, 1969.

Nichols, Ralph G., and Stevens, Leonard A. *Are You Listening?* New York: McGraw-Hill, 1957.

Reik, Theodor. *Listening with the Third Ear*. New York: Pyramid Books, 1948.

Rosenblum, Daniel. *A Time to Hear; A Time to Help*. New York: The Free Press, 1993.

Sayre, Joan M. *How to Listen*. Danville, IL: The Interstate Printers and Publishers, 1987.

Schwartz, Tony. *The Responsive Chord*. New York: Anchor Books, 1974.

———. *Media: The Second God*. New York: Random Books, 1981.

Spearritt, Donald. *Listening Comprehension—A Factorial Analysis*. Melbourne, Australia: Australian Council for Educational Research, 1962.

Steil, Lyman; Barker, Larry L., and Watson, Kittie W. *Effective Listening Key to Your Success*. Reading, MA: Addison-Wesley, 1983.

Steil, Lyman, deMare, George, and Summerfield, Joanne. *Listening . . . It Can Change Your Life*. New York: Wiley, 1983.

Taylor, Stanford E. *Listening: What Research Says to the Teacher*. Washington, DC: National Education Association, 1973.

Weaver, Carl H. *Human Listening*. Indianapolis, IN: Bobbs-Merrill, 1972.

Wolff, Florence I., and Marsnik, Nadine C. *Perceptive Listening*. 2d ed. New York: Holt, Rinehart & Winston, 1992.

Wolvin, Andrew D., and Coakley, Carolyn Gwynn. *Listening Instruction*. Urbana, IL: ERIC Clearinghouse on Reading and Communication Skills, 1979.

Wolvin, Andrew D., and Coakley, Carolyn Gwynn, eds. *Perspectives on Listening*. Norwood, NJ: Ablex, 1993 .

Figure 1.1.
Reprinted by permission of Dean Witter Discover and Company.
Figures 2.1., 2.3., and 3.1.
Drawings by Ted Metzger.
Figure 2.2.
Reprinted by permission of Hitachi America, Ltd.
Figures 3.2. and 3.3.
Drawings by Neal Ashby.
Figure 3.4.
Reprinted by permission of the National Committee for Prevention of Child Abuse.
Figures 4.1. and 4.2.
Reprinted by permission of Joseph Luft, *Group Process: An Introduction to Group Dynamics* 3d ed (Mountain View, CA: Mayfield Publications, 1984).
Figure 4.3.
Reprinted by permission of SAAB-SCANIA of America Company.
Figures 5.1. and 5.2.
Reprinted by permission of British Airways.
Figure 10.1.
Reprinted with permission of Jim Henson Productions, Inc.

Photos on pages 58, 61, 78, 119, 174, 180, 249, 353, 370 by Tom Noonan and the Sonoma *Index-Tribune*.
Photo on page 6 by Glenn Moll.
Photo on page 300 by Andrew D. Wolvin.
Photos on pages 392, 396, and 410 by Robert Tocha.

NAME INDEX

Abelson, Robert P., 104, 256
Ackerson, G., 256
Adams, Herbert R., 422
Addeo, Edmond B., 389, 413
Addington, D.W., 202
Adler, Mortimer J., 26, 29, 44, 45, 259, 388, 413, 421
Adler, R. B., 104, 305
Adler, S., 304
Aiello, J.R., 203, 206
Ailes, Roger, 31, 45, 211, 256, 325
Algier, A.S., 46
Algier, K.W., 46
Allen, J.L., 146
Allen, R.R., 380
Allison, C., 257
Allman, J., 147
Alloway, T., 205
Allport, Gordon, 338, 360
Ames, W., 256
Amidon, M., 207
Anastasi, Thomas E., 138, 148, 421
Andersen, Janis F., 147, 208
Andersen, Kenneth E., 322, 358, 361
Andersen, Peter A., 147, 204, 208
Anderson, C., 361
Anderson, D.R., 406, 416
Anderson, Harold A., 36, 46, 47
Anderson, J.A., 406, 416
Anderson, R.C., 87, 103
Anderson, R.J., 202
Andrews, James R., 399, 414
Angelou, M., 368
Apple, W., 259
Applegate, J., 145
Argyle, Michael, 185, 188–89, 203, 205, 206, 207, 208, 304
Aristotle, 321, 328

Arredondo, Daisy E., 260
Arnold, Carroll C., 367, 380
Arnold, John, 406, 416
Arnold, W.E., 145
Association of American Colleges, 33, 45
Atkin, Charles, 414
Atkinson, R.C., 83, 102
Atwater, Carol, 202
Audio Publishers Association, 43, 381
Austin, Bruce, 34, 46
Austin, George A., 88, 103
Austin, Nancy, 204, 206
Austin, R.A., 47
Ausubel, David P., 215, 256
Averbach, Emmanuel, 101

Babbitt, F.C., 306
Baddeley, A.D., 102
Badzinski, D.M., 168, 202
Baird, John E., 398–99, 414
Bakan, Paul, 102
Baker, P., 359, 360
Baldauf, Robert J., 258
Balkany, T., 101
Balz, D., 359
Banville, Thomas, 421
Barbara, Dominick A., 421
Barbieri, Susan, 414
Barbour, John, 41
Barefoot, J., 204, 205
Barker, Deborah A., 148
Barker, Karlyn, 304
Barker, Larry L., 14, 42, 43, 63, 88, 102, 103, 121–22, 141, 143, 145, 146, 149, 259, 375, 381, 392, 393, 413, 414, 421, 423

Barker, R.T., 11, 42
Barnlund, Dean, 139, 144, 148
Baron, Ken, 257
Barone, Michael, 415
Barrientos, T., 64
Barry, Marion, 323
Bartlett, Sir Frederic C., 82, 102
Basil, M.D., 102
Bassett, Ronald E., 258
Bayes, Marjorie S., 200, 204, 208
Beatty, Michael J., 104, 139, 144, 148
Becker, F.D., 208
Becker, Hal, 86
Bednar, A.S., 35, 46
Beebe, S.A., 205
Beery, Althea, 258
Behnke, Ralph R., 144, 148
Beier, Ernest G., 267, 304
Bem, Daryl J., 43
Benderly, Beryl Liefe, 256
Benfell, C., 357
Benjamin, B. J., 128, 147
Bentley, Eric, 398, 414
Benton, Chris, 44
Berg, Paul, 42
Bering-Jensen, Helle, 102
Berko, Roy M., 45, 64, 171, 204, 205, 206, 207, 259
Berlo, David, 63
Better Vision Institute, 101
Bhowmik, Dilip K., 108, 143
Bianculli, David, 390, 413
Bird, Donald E., 14, 42
Birdwhistell, Ray L., 71, 100, 170, 203, 307
Birkerts, S., 381
Bishop, S., 207
Bishop, Walton B., 144

427

Selbert, Joy Hart, 35, 46
Sellers, Daniel F., 131, 147
Serafini, Claudio R., 390, 413
Sewell, Edward H., 71, 101
Shadden, B.B., 147
Shales, Tom, 258
Shane, Scott, 101
Sharkey, B., 259
Shatzer, Milton J., 405–06, 415
Shedletsky, Leonard J., 146, 147
Sher, Barbara, 288
Shiffrin, R.M., 82, 83, 102
Shimanoff, Susan B., 294, 306
Shoaf, Frank, 234
Shockley-Zalabak, Pamela, 34, 46
Short, Sarah, 233
Siegel, B., 205
Siegel, H., 317, 358
Simon, Cheryl, 257
Simonson, Maria, 148
Simpson, J.C., 380
Simpson, O.J., 20–21, 266, 326
Skotko, V.P., 206
Skrzychi, C., 43
Sloane, R. Bruce, 306
Smeltzer, Larry R., 47, 223, 257
Smeyak, Paul, 390, 413
Smith, Anderson D., 221
Smith, C., 357
Smith, C. Frazer, 359
Smith, Dennis, 59–60, 64
Smith, E.W. L., 145
Smith, Harold T., 34
Smith, Jane A., 101
Smith, J.H., 36, 46
Smith, Jimmy Neil, 371
Smith, Larry, 169
Smith, Mary John, 104
Smith, Susan, 332, 351
Smith, T.W., 68, 100, 258
Snyder, M., 202
Snyder, Mark, 115, 144
Solomon, Michael R., 359
Soloveychik, A., 372
Sommer, R., 206
Sonnenfeld, J., 147, 148
Sonstegard, Manford, 267
Sorenson, Theodore, 324
Sorrell, B.D., 268, 304
Spearritt, Donald, 47, 68, 100, 423
Speech Communication Association
    (SCA), 34, 46
Spence, Janet T., 102, 103
Spence, Kenneth W., 102, 103
Sperling, George, 102
Sperry, Roger, 130, 147

Spicer, C., 258
Spicer, K., 318, 358
Spielberger, Charles D., 148
Spiro, Rand J., 104
Splaine, J., 19, 43, 324–25, 325–26, 359,
    360
Stacks, Don W., 131, 147
Stafford, F.P., 41
Staley, Constance C., 34, 46
Stammer, John, 8, 41
Standing, L.G., 102
Stanger, T., 358
Stanton, S., 361
Staples, Fred R., 306
Stark, Joel, 258
Steffen, L., 416
Steil, Lyman K., 11, 38, 42, 47, 423
Stein, Ben, 404, 415
Steiner, Claude M., 389, 413
Stephens, Ronald D., 35, 46
Stern, A.L., 361
Stern, Barbara, 306
Stevens, Leonard A., 26, 27, 42, 44,
    148, 423
Stewart, Charles J., 391, 413
Stewart, John, 60, 64, 208, 306, 307
Sticht, T.G., 44
Stokes, John Paul, 145, 304, 305
Stokowski, Leopold, 397
Story, B., 43, 415
Storytelling, 371–72
Streeter, L., 259
Stretch, Shirley, 359
Strickland, Rhonda, 377, 382
Strongman, K.T., 205
Strupp, Hans D., 304
Sullivan, C., 359
Sully, John, 314
Summerfield, Joanne, 423
Sundstrom, E., 306
Suplee, C., 256, 257
Sussman, Lyle, 34, 45, 47
Sussman, Vic, 400, 414
Swanda, John R., 14, 15, 40, 42, 47
Swanson, Charles H., 47
Sweeney, J.W., 314, 357
Swezey, Lawrence W., 144
Sypher, Beverly Davenport, 35, 46

Tangorra, Joanne, 381
Tannen, Deborah, 125, 126, 127, 145,
    146, 344, 360
Tannenbaum, J., 252, 260
Task Force on Education, 33
Taylor, A., 101

Taylor, Paul, 359
Taylor, Sandford E., 14, 42, 423
Tepper, D.T., 145, 203, 204, 205, 304
Thayer, S., 206, 207
Thiederman, Sondra, 203
Thomas, Clarence, 351, 352
Thomas, L.T., 102, 145, 388, 413
Thomlison, T. Dean, 125, 145
Thompson, T., 146
Thompson, William, 381
Tomkins, S.S., 204
Torrence, Jack, 371
Toulmin, Stephen, 329–30, 359
Towne, N., 104 , 305
Trachtenberg, Jeffrey A., 415
Treisman, Anne M., 80, 81, 101, 102
Treisman, Michel, 101
Trout, Jack, 114, 143
Tubbs, Stewart L., 120, 140, 144, 145,
    148, 413
Tucker, W., 68, 100
Tulving, Endel, 88, 103, 257
Turer, Stephen, 315
Turner, P.H., 36, 46
Turvey, M.T., 102
Tutolo, Daniel, 202
Tuttle, George F., 257, 392, 414

Ubell, Lori, 257
United States Department of Labor, 15,
    43
Unruh, J., 203

Valens, Evans G., 267, 304
Van Rheenen, Dwayne D., 47
Vega, R., 381
Veitch, Russell, 192, 201, 207, 208
Venema, Joe, 252
Ventura, Paul G., 34, 46
Vernon, Magdalen, 102
Verny, Thomas, 42
Villaume, William A., 128–29, 146, 147
Vinson, Larry, 117, 144
Voist, Judith, 306

Waack, William, 376, 381
Waldhart, Enid S., 83, 84, 103, 257
Walker, Alice, 368
Wallace, Wallace H., 415
Wallen, John L., 306
Wardlaw, D., 17
Ware, John E., 358
Wasylik, James E., 34, 45, 47
Waterman, R.H., 137, 148, 393

SUBJECT INDEX

Accentual differences, 168–69
Action-reaction principle, 273
Advance organizers, 215
Affiliative conflict theory of intimacy, 185
Appearance, 183
Appreciative listening, 154, 362–82, 407–09
  as a highly individualized process, 363–65
  improvement of, 375–79
  opportunities for, 365–75
  process of, 363–65
  purposes of, 363
Artifacts, 183–84
Assigning meaning, 87–95
  incorrect assignment of meaning, 90–95
  theories of, 87–90
    categorical system, 88, 90–95
    information-processing model, 88
    schema theory, 88–90, 90–95
      scripts/schemata, 88–90, 213
Attending, 79–87
  energetic attention, 82–84
  fluctuation of attention, 85–87
  selective attention, 79–82
  models of attention, 79–82
Attending behaviors, 122–24, 196, 270–72
  back-channel behaviors, 196
  bodily positioning, 122–23, 271
  comforting acts, 271
  eye contact, 122, 196, 270–71
  facial expressions, 123, 196, 271
  head nodding, 123, 196, 271
  silence, 272

touching, 271–72
  verbal expressiveness, 123, 196, 271
  voice tone, 123, 271
Attention, focusing of, 270–71
Attention deficit hyperactivity disorder, 85
Attitudes toward listening, 114, 135–38, 225
  equal, 137
  interested, 135
  openminded, 137–38
  other-oriented, 136
  patient, 136
  responsible, 135–36
Auding, 68–69
Audiocassette tapes, 15–16, 369–71
Auditory and visual discrimination, 192–97
  deception cues, 192–93
  regulatory cues, 193–97
    leave-taking, 196–97
    turn-denying, 196
    turn-maintaining, 195
    turn-requesting, 195–96
    turn-yielding, 194–95
  skills of, 192–97
Auditory discrimination, 158–70
  importance of, 160–62
  skills, 162–170
    accentual differences, 168–69
    dialectal differences, 168
    environmental sounds, 169–70
    phonology, 164–65
    vocal cues, 165–68
      influence of, 166–68
      sensitivity to, 168
      types of, 165

Weaver and Rutherford's hierarchy, 162–64
  uses of, 158–60
Auditory stimulation, 164

Back-channel behaviors, 196
Biases of chief information sources, 336, 342–43
Bodily actions and posture, 122–23, 176–79, 271
Brown-Carlsen Listening Comprehension Test, 26, 220

Caring, 410–11
Coercion, 320
Communication
  apprehension, 52
  as a simultaneous process, 59–61
  components of, 50
    channel, 50
    environment, 50
    feedback, 50
    message, 50
    noise, 50
      external, 50
      internal, 50
    receiver, 50
    source, 50
  flow of information, 20–21
  levels, 111–16, 383, 386–407, 407–09
    group, 383, 391–94, 407–09
    interpersonal, 383, 386, 388–95, 407–09
    intrapersonal, 111–16, 383, 386–87, 407–09
    mass, 383, 407, 407–09
    public, 383, 396–99, 407–09

Listening
        for accuracy, 250–53, 293–302
        active, 28–29, 118–19
        and agreement, 30–31
        basic competency, 37
        basic language skill, 13
        behaviors, 1, 383
        and commitment, 410–11
        as a distinct behavior, 67–68
        expectations, 383
        frequency of, 13–15
        importance of, 11, 13–21
        improvement of, 151–382, 417–19
        influencing factors, 124–41
        and intelligence, 26–27
        and obedience, 30–31
        perceived, 31–32, 121, 389
        process of, 68–96
        purposes of, 151–382, 407–09
        and reading, 27–28
        and responsible decision-making,
                108–11
        in seminars, 398–99
        and sharing, 108
        and social conditioning, 114, 117–18
        with understanding, 250–53,
                279–84, 293–302
Logical arguments, 326–44. See also
        Logos
        argument structure, 326
        deductive arguments, 327–29
                conditional, 328
                disjunctive, 328
                enthymemes, 328
                syllogisms, 327–28
                truth of, 328
                validity of, 328
        inductive arguments, 326–27
                evaluation of, 327
                explanation of, 326–27
        reasoning fallacies, 331–35
                arguing in a circle, 334
                faulty analogical reasoning,
                        332–33
                faulty causal reasoning, 331–32
                hasty generalizations, 331
                ignoring the issue, 334–35
                        ad hominem, 334
                        ad ignoratiam, 335
                        ad populum, 335
                non sequitur, 333
        Toulmin's model of reasoning,
                329–30
Logos, 326–44. See also Logical
        arguments

Long-term memory, 82–84, 95–96, 214,
        215, 220

Main ideas, 235–37
Maslow's need levels, 344–45
Mass media, 17–21, 383, 400–07,
        407–09
        impact of, 19–21
        radio listening time, 18
        television viewing time, 18
Memory, 82–84, 213–22
        memory aids, 216–22
                categorical clustering, 220
                chunking, 220–21
                link system, 216
                loci system, 216
                mnemonic devices, 219–20
                peg-word system, 218–19
                phonetic system, 217–18
                rhyming, 218
        memory system, 82–84
        reasons for forgetting, 213–14
        remembering names, 221–22
        schema theory, 213
        theories of forgetting, 213–14
Misconceptions about listening, 25–32
Motivated sequence, 320–21
Motivation, 116–18, 225

Nationwide Insurance, 22, 44
Noise pollution, 76–77
NOLAD Level, 401
Nonlistening, 389
Nonverbal communication. See Visual
        discrimination
Note-taking, 239–45
        types of, 240–45
                Cornell system, 240
                fact versus principle system,
                        243, 244
                mapping, 243, 245, 246
                outlining method, 241, 242
                precis writing, 241, 243
        values of, 239

Opinions, 336–37
Organizational patterns, 236–37, 242
        deductive, 242
        inductive, 242
        one-point, 236
        partitioning, 236–37
        unfolding, 236

Paraphrasing, 250–53, 298–301

Pathos, 344–54. See also Emotional
        appeals
Perceived listening, 31–32, 121, 389
Perception-checking, 293–302
Perceptual filter, 53, 91–95
Persuasion, 319–21
Phonology, 164–65
Propaganda, 340–42
Propaganda techniques, 341–42
Proxemics, 184–87
Public audiences, 383, 386, 396–99, 407–09
        conduct of, 397–98
        dimensions of the audience, 396–97
                circular response, 397
                polarization, 396–97
                social facilitation, 396
        listening tactics, 398–99
        types of, 398
                concerted, 398
                organized, 398
                passive, 398
                pedestrian, 398
                selected, 398
Purposes of listening, 151–382, 407–09
        appreciative, 154, 362–82, 407–09
        comprehensive, 152, 210–60, 407–09
        critical, 154, 308–61, 407–09
        discriminative, 152, 156–208,
                407–09
        therapeutic, 153–54, 262–307,
                407–09

Questioning, 247–50, 292–93

Radio, 18, 400–02, 407–09
Reasoning fallacies, 331–35
Receivership skills, 406–07
Receiving, 72–79
        hearing process, 73–79
                malfunctions of, 74–79
                organs involved in, 73–74
                restoration of auditory acuity,
                        75–76
        seeing process, 72–73
                care of, 73
                disorders of, 73
Recoding, 387
Regulatory cues, 193–97
Rehearsal, 82–84, 220–21
Remembering, 82–84, 95–96, 213–22
Responding, 50, 69–70, 73–74, 95–96,
        119–24, 196, 247–53, 273–79, 284–89,
        291–302. See also Feedback
        covert response, 69–71